australia

FODOR'S TRAVEL PUBLICATIONS
NEW YORK • TORONTO • LONDON • SYDNEY • AUCKLAND

WWW.FODORS.COM

Contents

KEY TO SYMBOLS

- Map reference
- Address
- Telephone number
- Opening times
- Admission prices
- Underground station
- Bus number
- Train station
- Ferry/boat
- Other information
- Airport
- Tours
- Restaurant
- Café
- Shop
- Number of rooms
- No smoking
- Swimming pool
- Gym
- Air Conditioning
- Driving directions

UNDERSTANDING AUSTRALIA

It will take you more than a few days to grasp the depth and breadth of Australia; it can't be done just by spending a few days in Sydney or Melbourne. These are cosmopolitan cities where global culture has applied a universal veneer that takes some peeling back. The solid Victorian buildings and modern architecture remind you of many world cities, and the TV programs are familiar to American and British audiences—with the best and worst on offer. Some city icons—the Sydney Opera House and the Melbourne Cricket Ground—distil something of the national character, but a real understanding of this country only comes through contact with the Australian people.

Left to right: Aboriginal art in Melbourne Museum; Kimberley tour guide Sam Lovell; 26 January—Australia Day; Ladies Day at Flemington Racecourse, Melbourne; Outback accommodation in New South Wales

AUSTRALIANS

In 2003 the Australian population was about 20 million, including Australians temporarily overseas. Population density is only 2.5 persons per square kilometre (1 person per square mile); the United Kingdom has 10 times that level. Compared with other Western countries, Australia's population is increasing at quite a rate, mostly through immigration. Throughout the 20th century, waves of immigrants came from Europe, and more recently from Asia. Only 71.0 per cent of the population were born in Australia, and that includes Aboriginal Australians (2 per cent). Moreover, Australia's people are young compared to Europe: Around 36 per cent of the population are aged below 25 and only 12 per cent are over 65.

When it comes to religion, 77.4 per cent of the population profess Christianity, though the other major religions—Buddhism, Islam, Hinduism and Judaism—are represented in significant numbers.

A LUCKY COUNTRY?

Australians are not immune to the malaises of modern society: poverty, unequal distribution of wealth, and pressures on rural and city environments. But there is a peculiar optimism that pervades this multicultural society and a pride that many things have been done well. There is a feeling that things are generally OK. As far as visitors are concerned, friendly people can easily be found in the cities, but it is the regional cities and towns and rural villages that seem to offer that quintessential Aussie experience—whether from a friendly nod or help with directions or by their relaxed air. It is not unknown for complete strangers to take you in their care and give you a tour of the local sights.

THE ECONOMY

Australia's Western-style capitalist economy is based on a wealth of natural resources and agricultural products, service industries such as tourism, and a small manufacturing sector. The main exports are coal, gold, iron ore, alumina, petroleum products, meats, cereals, wool, wine and cotton. The agriculture and mining industries are competitive worldwide and manufacturing industries like car production have developed export markets. Japan is Australia's largest trading partner by a factor of two over the next largest, the United States.

Australia is the world's fourth-largest wine exporter, supplying about 7 per cent of the global market; the UK is their top market, taking 40 per cent of exports, while the US accounts for 33 per cent. Total wine exports by volume in 2002 were 471 million litres (104 million gallons).

POLITICS

The federal government is based on both the British and American democratic systems. A multiparty, elected parliament, led by the prime minister, is responsible for matters of national importance such as defence, foreign affairs, trade, treasury, social services and immigration. A governor general, appointed by the British monarch on the advice of the prime minister, must give assent to all laws passed. Each of Australia's six states and two territories has its own parliament.

A CONTINENT
It's easy to underestimate the scale of Australia. The island continent has a land mass of 7.6 million sq km (3 million sq miles) and occupies 5 per cent of the earth's land area; it is the sixth largest country in the world. If you travel between cities, particularly the six-hour flight between Sydney and Perth, you start to appreciate the size. Beyond the mainland, Australia is surrounded by many thousands of small fringing islands and numerous larger ones, the largest being the southern island state of Tasmania.

Almost two-thirds of the continent belongs to the Western Plateau, covering the western and much of the central and northern regions of the country. Mostly flat and low, it is interrupted by spectacular individual features like Uluru (Ayers Rock), rocky strongholds like the Kimberley and Arnhem Land, and by rugged ridges like those of the MacDonnell and Flinders ranges.

The Great Dividing Range runs down the eastern coastline from Cape York in the far north to the hills of Victoria in the south; mountainous Tasmania is an extension of the range across Bass Strait. Although the mountains are not particularly high—Mount Kosciuszko in New South Wales is the highest at 2,230m (7,310ft)—they have a huge effect on climate, resulting in this area housing the bulk of the population.

Between the Western Plateau and the Great Dividing Range lies the Central Eastern Lowlands, running north to south. River basins succeed one another, including the country's greatest river system, the Murray-Darling-Murrumbidgee.

CLIMATE
In view of its size—Australia spans nearly 35 degrees of latitude—the earth's driest continent after Antarctica has a surprisingly small range of climates. The highest rainfall is in the tropical north, where temperatures stay high all year round, averaging 29°C (84°F) in summer and 24°C (75°F) in winter. The wettest recorded place is the summit of Mount Bellenden Ker in north Queensland, at a height of 1,555m (5,100ft): Average annual rainfall here is about 8,000mm (315in), but in 2000 an Australian record was set at 12,461mm (490in). Such rainfall occurs when warm, moist sea air rises over coastal ranges, cooling as it rises and then losing the moisture as rain.

Unlike the north, where the rain falls during the summer, temperate southern Australia experiences slightly higher rainfall in winter and spring, and there is more variation in average temperatures, between 24°C (75°F) in summer and 10°C (50°F) in winter, when snow falls on the highest peaks. Much of the interior is arid, with little rain, and the mostly dry Lake Eyre records an annual average of just 125mm (4.9in).

Inland temperatures soar to scorching heights—an unimaginable 53°C (127.4°F) was recorded at Cloncurry in Queensland in 1889—although nights can be cold. The lowest recorded temperature, -23°C (-9.4°F), was in 1994 in the Australian Alps at Charlotte Pass, New South Wales.

MAKE THE MOST OF YOUR STAY
Most visitors opt for the flying triangle holiday—Sydney, Red Centre, Cairns—and miss the other bits. But many of the places off the beaten path are worth the extra effort or constitute a holiday in themselves—including World Heritage attractions such as Fraser Island, Shark Bay and the Tasmanian wilderness. Elsewhere, long coastlines, with uncrowded beaches and mountain ranges, interspersed with towns and cities, provide scenery, outdoor dining and cultural options away from the noise of well-known cities. Or retreat to the hinterland communities among the hills of

Sunset from Mount Ainslie, just northeast of central Canberra

the Great Dividing Range, and the small Outback towns beyond the mountains.

A QUICK TOUR
Australia is divided into six states and two territories. New South Wales's tourist regions famously include Sydney and surrounds, where urban icons such as the Opera House and the Harbour Bridge are within striking distance of the Blue Mountains and the Hunter Valley vineyards. Farther north, Queensland has Cairns, the focus of activity for Great Barrier Reef tours, tropical rainforests and Outback adventures, but also the Gold and Sunshine coasts, with world-class beaches. Island-hopping and yacht cruising are a good way to see the Whitsundays.

Remote Darwin and the tropical Top End have their own major attractions. Kakadu National Park is a World Heritage Site, while Uluru-Kata Tjuta National Park (Ayers Rock and the Olgas) and the MacDonnell Ranges epitomize the arid Red Centre. Just as remote are Broome and the Kimberleys in the north of Western Australia: discover the romance of pearling days and rugged mountain scenery. Busier is Perth, the commercial heart of the southeast of Western Australia.

Adelaide and the Barossa Valley vineyards have a European charm, though South Australia's wines are distinctly Australian. Melbourne is cosmopolitan and the rest of Victoria has mountains, desert and fertile coast. Few international visitors see Tasmania, but its scenery is on a grand scale.

AUSTRALIAN CITIES AT A GLANCE

Sydney, flashy and brash, has arrived as an international city, the harbour city's multicultural vibrancy underlining a pressure-cooker pace of life.

Canberra, the national capital, planned to within an inch, is fast losing its tag as a collection of suburbs in search of a city.

Melbourne, four seasons in a day, perhaps, but a city solid and orderly, its grid of city streets carrying purposeful shoppers on a mission.

Brisbane, clamouring for a place on the Pacific Rim, retains an air of informality and subtropical charm along the banks of the Brisbane River.

Darwin, survivor of air raids and tropical cyclones, is Australia's Asian gateway and its most informal city.

Adelaide wears a civilized air—well-planned streets, a meandering river, a belt of green parklands and a reputation as a city of culture.

Perth, one of the world's most remote cities, serenely overlooks the Swan River as Kings Park brings the bushland almost into the city.

Hobart, to the eternal joy of its citizens, stays solid and familiar from year to year, guarded by the brooding mist-covered Mount Wellington.

Left to right: Great Australian ports—Hobart, Sydney and Melbourne

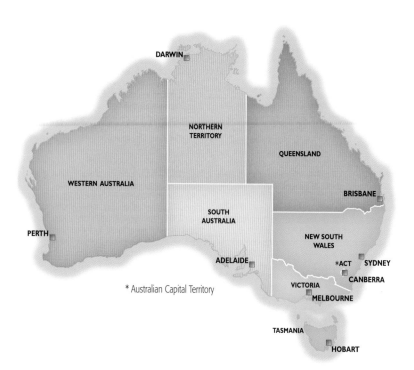

DARWIN

NORTHERN TERRITORY

QUEENSLAND

WESTERN AUSTRALIA

BRISBANE

SOUTH AUSTRALIA

PERTH

NEW SOUTH WALES

ADELAIDE

*ACT   SYDNEY

CANBERRA

* Australian Capital Territory

VICTORIA

MELBOURNE

TASMANIA

HOBART

THE BEST OF AUSTRALIA

BEST OF NEW SOUTH WALES

Sydney Harbour (see pages 66–70) Get the sea-level view on a ferry ride from Circular Quay

Sydney Opera House (see page 68) Book as early as you can for performances

Blue Mountains (see pages 74–77) Great landscapes, activities and fresh air are just a couple of hours away from Sydney

Hunter Valley (see page 79) Explore the verdant slopes of a leading wine area

Outback NSW (see page 81) Rugged and remote, but dotted with names like Broken Hill

Above: Sydney's Opera House and the Harbour Bridge

Right: Parliament House, Canberra

BEST OF AUSTRALIAN CAPITAL TERRITORY

Parliament House (see page 73) Canberra's billion-dollar government home is not just a fine modern building, it is also a showcase for Australian art, or go and see parliament at Question Time

Above: Luna Park at St. Kilda, Melbourne

Right: Melbourne Cricket Ground

BEST OF VICTORIA

Melbourne Cricket Ground (see page 85) For an enthusiastic crowd experience, try an Aussie Rules game at the MCG during the winter months

Federation Square (see pages 86–87) Melbourne's new and shiny focus, completed in 2002

St. Kilda (see page 90) See the best of Melbourne's vibrant street culture

Ballarat (see page 92) The creek running through the reconstructed Sovereign Hill gold-mining town is seeded with gold—try your hand at gold panning

Great Ocean Road (see pages 96–99) This classic route weaves around breathtaking cliffs, quiet bays and wild surf beaches

BEST OF QUEENSLAND

Cairns and the Tropical North (see pages 106–107) Queensland's northern capital, tropical rainforest and a fabulous scenic drive to Cape Tribulation

Great Barrier Reef (see pages 110–114) More than 1,200km (744 miles) long, this is the world's largest coral reef system

Gold Coast (see page 115) Theme parks galore—Warner Bros. Movie World, Wet'n'Wild Water World, Dreamworld and more

Lamington National Park (see page 116) Hiking heaven through rainforest accompanied by parrots and other tropical birdlife

Port Douglas (see page 117) A fashionable but still relaxed tourist enclave, just north of Cairns

Noosa Heads (see page 118) The resort for a relaxed lifestyle and safe year-round swimming on the Sunshine Coast

Rockhampton (see page 120) You're spoiled for choice—the Botanic Gardens, cruises to Great Keppel Island or mines at Mount Morgan

Whitsunday Islands (see page 123) Keen sailors can navigate an archipelago of 74 forested peaks with sandy beaches for world-class food and luxury relaxation

Above: Surfers Paradise on the Gold Coast, Queensland

Below: Great Barrier Reef, Queensland

UNDERSTANDING AUSTRALIA 7

BEST OF NORTHERN TERRITORY

Alice Springs (see page 126) The famous town, and a good base for the Larapinta and Namatjira drives through Watarrka National Park and the MacDonnell Ranges, through spectacular gorge scenery

Kakadu National Park (see pages 128–129) Ubirr and Nourlangie Rock are among the best accessible Aboriginal rock art sites

Uluru (Ayers Rock) (see pages 132–135) Vast and dramatic, this is justifiably one of Australia's greatest and most mysterious attractions

BEST OF SOUTH AUSTRALIA

Adelaide Festival Centre (see page 137) Every even-numbered year sees performances of opera, dance, drama and music

Adelaide Hills (see page 141) Beautiful scenery, natural bushland and pretty gardens surrounding Adelaide

Barossa Valley (see page 142) The home of many of Australia's best-known and award-winning wines

Above: Kakadu National Park— Nourlangie rock art; a frill neck lizard

BEST OF WESTERN AUSTRALIA

Rottnest Island (see page 152) On a cool day, explore the Indian Ocean coastline on a bicycle

Broome (see page 155) Book ahead for a camel ride along the beach at this remote resort

Margaret River (see pages 158–159) You may be interested in award-winning wines or excellent surfing, but also consider visiting the caves, the forests and the beaches

Shark Bay (see page 160) Not as menacing as it sounds: Meet and feed dolphins at Monkey Mia

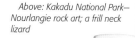

Margaret River: a river, a town and a great wine region

Memories are made of this—sunset on Cable Beach, Broome

BEST OF TASMANIA

Cradle Mountain-Lake St. Clair National Park (see page 163) Keep an eye open for wallabies, wombats, possums— or possibly an elusive platypus

Strahan and West Coast (see page 167) Strahan's waterfront sports complement one of the world's last great wilderness areas

Port Arthur (see page 166) For a taste of convict life

BEST DOING/SHOPPING

The Rocks (see page 64) The place in Sydney for quality Australiana—Akubra hats, Driza-Bone coats and opals—and a lively weekend market

David Jones (see page 191) The department store branch on Bourke Street, Melbourne, has most major Australian brands and an excellent food hall

Eumundi Markets (see page 118) This Saturday morning Queensland market gets crowded, so arrive early

Creative Native (see page 210) This Perth gallery is possibly the largest outlet for Aboriginal crafts in Western Australia

Salamanca Market (see page 214) For Tasmanian gifts and bargains, head for Hobart's harbour on a Saturday

Street entertainment at The Rocks, Sydney

BEST EATING

Guillaume At Bennelong (see page 255) Among Sydney's finest restaurants, the Bennelong Point location overlooks the harbour

Rockpool (see pages 255–256) Not just Sydney's but one of Australia's best restaurants—but go with a friend who's paying

Shimbashi Soba On The Sea (see page 256) A rare chance to enjoy Japanese *soba* (noodle) cuisine

The Summit (see page 256) At 47 storeys above George Street, Sydney, the food matches the view

Sydney Fish Market (see page 256) Buy from the market or try one of many seafood eateries, at prices for all budgets

Ottoman Cuisine (see page 257) For the best Turkish dishes, come to Canberra

Buy or try at Sydney Fish Market

Zuppa (see page 259) This Katoomba café in the Blue Mountains is a great, inexpensive place to be refreshed and to relax

Bedi's (see page 260) Delve into the suburb of South Melbourne for one of the city's best Indian restaurants

Jimmy Watson's Wine Bar and Restaurants (see page 261) Here, in a north Melbourne suburb, it's more a case of what food to have with the fine wines

Doyle's On The Beach, Watsons Bay, Sydney

Doyle's On The Beach (see page 254) Relish the superb view from Watsons Bay across Port Jackson to Sydney Harbour with fine seafood and great wines

Below: Dove Lake in Cradle Mountain-Lake St. Clair National Park, Tasmania

The Stokehouse (see page 262) Dine on superb seafood in a Melbourne suburb with the backdrop of Port Phillip

Windsor (see page 285) Afternoon tea at Melbourne's grand 19th-century hotel is an occasion of genteel dignity

e'cco Bistro (see page 266) Simple, stylish food in a glamorous Brisbane setting

Red Ochre Grill (see page 267) Bush tucker at its best in Cairns

Mermaids Café and Bar (see page 267) Good, informal meals beside a Gold Coast surfing beach in Burleigh Heads

Ky Chow (see page 271) This Cantonese Adelaide restaurant is crowded because it's good—and inexpensive

Sounds of Silence (see page 270) Top-notch Outback barbecues in view of Ayers Rock—at a price

Indiana Tea House (see page 274) Enjoy a Moreton Bay bug salad overlooking Perth's Cottesloe Beach

Sail and Anchor (see page 275) An Aussie pub with views over Fremantle that brews its own beer

Black Rock Café (see page 276) After visiting Kalbarri National Park, take a rest here and look out over the Indian Ocean

Jackman McRoss (see page 276) A Hobart bakery serving great savouries and coffee

Fee and Me (see page 278) Tasmania's best formal dining, at Launceston, in the north

BEST STAYING

The Russell (see page 282) Victorian-style accommodation in The Rocks, Sydney

Hyatt Hotel (see page 283) Art-deco luxury in Canberra parkland

The Crown and Anchor Inn (see page 283 and right) A tranquil 19th-century inn gazing across the South Pacific Ocean

Peppers Guest House (see page 284) The luxury and the Hunter Valley scenery in New South Wales are hard to beat

Robinsons in the City (see page 285) Melbourne's only central guest house provides a friendly option to the large hotels

Mount Buffalo Chalet (see page 286) The clincher here is the location, in Victoria's Mount Buffalo National Park

Cape Trib Beach House (see page 288) Basic accommodation—no phones or TV—where the Queensland rainforest creeps down to the beach

THE BEST OF AUSTRALIA

The Workman's Cottage (see page 290) A cottage in the Barossa wine region—make sure you book early

Gagadju Crocodile Inn (see page 289) A good rest stop for tourers in the immense Kakadu National Park, Northern Territory

Lemonthyme Lodge (see page 292) A Tasmanian wilderness experience iwithout the suffering—luxurious wood cabins north of Cradle Mountain

Up and away in South Australia

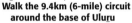
BEST EXPERIENCES

Enjoy a glass of Australian wine while looking across the vineyard, or take a winery tour to understand the production process

If you don't have the opportunity—or the courage—to meet Australia's wildlife in its natural setting, a visit to an Australian wildlife sanctuary or zoo is the next best thing

Savour the fusion of European and Asian cooking styles in any of the state capitals

View the deep canyons, valleys and sheer cliffs, and take in the aroma of eucalypts from a lookout in the Blue Mountains

If you cannot stomach witchetty grubs, then try the nuts and fruits on an Aboriginal-led forage for bush tucker in the outback

For those who don't want to get their feet wet there are a number of dry options to see the Great Barrier Reef, from semi-submersibles and glass-bottomed boats to scenic flights in a helicopter

Walk the 9.4km (6-mile) circuit around the base of Uluru (Ayers Rock) to appreciate its overwhelming magnificence

Book a guided tour to explore tropical rainforest if you want to see (or avoid) crocodiles, fruit bats, pythons, birdwing butterflies and spiders

It is surprisingly easy to see kangaroos in rural areas if you're around at dawn or dusk—ask a local for directions

At night the stars in the outback are so big and bright it's almost as if you could touch them

Tackle the spectacular mountains and forests of the Tasmanian wilderness via a range of trails, from the five-day Overland Track to one-hour strolls on paths suitable for wheelchairs and buggies (strollers)

Hot-air balloons offer a unique view of the Australian landscape, and each state has a variety of options

Several historic prisons are now tourist attractions—a visit gives a good idea of the harsh reality of the lives of the first European settlers

Climb to the top of Kings Canyon in Watarrka National Park for a spectacular view of the desert

You may not think of Australia as a major cheese-making nation, but boutique cheese manufacturers produce several world-class varieties

Above: Look for dolphins in Western Australia

Above: A rainforest boardwalk at Cape Tribulation, Queensland

Right: Mother and joey in South Australia

Above: The Blue Mountains, near Katoomba, New South Wales; Ripe pickings from Australia's vineyards

Living
Australia

Left: Melbourne's Chinatown, in Little Bourke Street, celebrates the Chinese New Year

Right: A traditional Australian verandah house in Charters Towers, Queensland

Right: A car country—the Sydney rush hour

Urban and Rural
Australia

Living sustainably

Per capita each Australian creates more than 1.4 tonnes of rubbish a year. Up until the 1950s relatively little waste was produced. There wasn't much packaging, most containers were reused or refilled, and food scraps were used as garden compost. Nowadays consumer products come in more and more packaging and disposable containers are the norm. Plus it's nearly always cheaper to buy a new product than fix a broken one. Local councils are training residents to separate their waste products so that they can be disposed of in a sustainable manner. The next goal is to reduce consumption generally, but ultimately, sustainablility means a return to the ways of the past.

Although one of the world's most urbanized nations, Australia still gets plenty of mileage out of trading on the myths of its rural past. However, the nation has changed from the days when it supposedly 'rode on the sheep's back'. Over three-quarters of Australia's population is concentrated on the coastal strip from north Queensland to Adelaide, and 85 per cent of the population live in state or territory capitals or in cities of more than 100,000 people. Continued migration has only intensified this trend, as almost all new arrivals settle in the cities. Rural Australia is alive and kicking, though, despite poor commodity prices, successive droughts, the trials of access to education and the general tyranny of distance. No doubt country people have generations of tenacity built into them. And they are the most friendly folk you're likely to encounter—perhaps it is because they are isolated, but more likely it's because as members of smaller communities, they have had to work together to get by. Everyone pitches in when there's a bushfire, and if your tractor breaks down, a neighbour is likely to help out. So don't be afraid to get to know the people in the country— you never know when you'll need some help!

Right: The three-storey Big Merino relief in Goulburn, New South Wales— this is sheep country

Left: Sheep-shearing in the city—a display in the Argyle Centre, The Rocks, Sydney

Below: A cattle muster on an outback station

A road stop in South Australia

Left: Camel travel in the Rainbow Valley Conservation Reserve, south of Alice Springs, Northern Territory

Landcare

During the past 15 years a green revolution has occurred in rural Australia. Communities have banded together to form Landcare groups and taken on the task of repairing an environment that has suffered degradation through over-clearing, bad farming practices, the damming of rivers and excessive irrigation. The loss of topsoil to wind and water erosion, and increased salinity caused by rising water tables, has the potential to devastate huge areas; about 70–80 per cent of irrigated land in New South Wales is affected by salinity problems. Salinity is also a threat to the health and productivity of many river catchments, and can be economically ruinous to the rural and urban communities that live in them. Now government agencies are funding Landcare and the future looks brighter.

Urban renewal

For the past 50 years, most Australian city dwellers have been realising their dream to own a plot of suburban land. A brick-veneer home with a big backyard for gardening and recreation completes the picture. So suburb after suburb of 1,000sq m (3,280sq ft) house blocks have been created and they stretch out to the mountainous limits of cities like Sydney and Melbourne. Today, with rising prices, shortages of available land, lower birthrates and the move towards single-person households, the trend is to build medium- and high-density housing in areas well served by public transport. New housing in the inner city and suburbs is now predominantly multi-level apartments. And as suburbs of old terrace (row) houses become gentrified in inner-city Sydney and Melbourne, an urban vibrancy is born.

Car mania

Since the end of World War II, increased affluence has led to the rise and rise of the motor vehicle. Today, Australia has the second highest level of car ownership in the world—one car for every 2.2 people. Cars are destroying the ambience of major cities, especially Brisbane and Sydney where geography works against efficient transport routes. Despite talking public transport, governments are building super roads to handle the traffic. As fast as these roads are built, they become congested—car culture shapes the cities and the nation. Australia has the third highest rate of fuel consumption per capita in the world. So until the Aussie's love affair with the car subsides, a brown pall of pollution will often hang over major cities.

The Outback

'Where is the Outback?' This is the first question many visitors to Australia ask. Unfortunately, there's no one place to point to and, apart from Victoria and Tasmania, each state has its outback regions. Of course the Red Centre is in the Outback, but how far inland from Australia's huge coastline does the Outback begin? Some people define this somewhat mythical place as where you get a wave from a driver coming in the opposite direction, while others simply say it's 'back of beyond'. Others assume they have arrived when they see lots of 'Eat Beef, You Bastards!' stickers on the back of dusty vehicles! However, since the Outback implies remoteness and a sparse population, you'll certainly know when you've arrived!

An expression of ethnicity: traditional face-painting of a Tiwi Aboriginal

Wooden fish sculpture by Aboriginal artist Craig Koomeeta, from the Cape York peninsula, Queensland

Pacific culture in the Melbourne Museum

Aboriginal rock art in Mutawintji National Park near Broken Hill, New South Wales

Aboriginal Australia

Aboriginal languages

Languages are inextricably linked to cultural and spiritual identity and are connected to creation stories, cultural laws and traditional practices. Prior to colonization, there may have been as many as 250 Aboriginal languages and about 700 dialects. Fewer than half remain today; many are known to a handful of the elderly, and only about 30 are spoken regularly. While their communities are reviving some languages, many are threatened. In remote areas, relative isolation from western influences has resulted in the continued use of local dialects, while indigenous languages are taught to many school children. With Aboriginal bands like Yothu Yindi performing many songs in their own languages, the future for some surviving languages looks brighter.

Aboriginal Australia has a complexity that defies stereotypes. Its people are living in the 21st century with traditions that go back more than 40,000 years and they are coping more or less well depending on how they have adapted to the changes. The major push from traditional Aboriginal people has been to return to their homelands—the places from which they either voluntarily left or were forcibly removed. For urban Aboriginal people of mixed descent, the continual re-appraisal of their heritage has meant coming to terms with fragments of their past while keeping a foot in the realities of present-day Australia. As a visitor to the country there is a dilemma that, in wanting to experience the culture of the original inhabitants, you may demean their traditions through tourism. This is not the case. Aboriginal people have had to make compromises in order to face the reality of modern times. Many of them maintain cultural practices such as dance or art by forging new ways that synthesize the past with the present. The energy of this raw artistic renaissance is a cultural phenomenon which has both enlivened Australian culture and given back pride to a people who for too long have suffered the patronage of a white society determined to forget the injustices of the past.

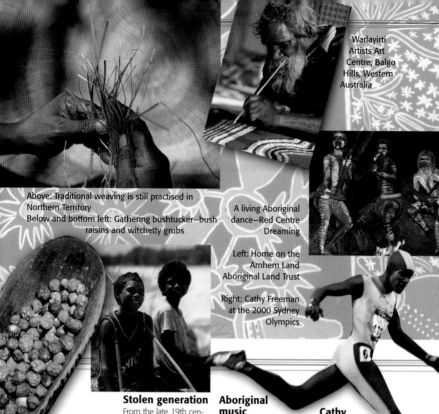

Warlayirti Artists Art Centre, Balgo Hills, Western Australia

Above: Traditional weaving is still practised in Northern Territory
Below and bottom left: Gathering bushtucker—bush raisins and witchetty grubs

A living Aboriginal dance—Red Centre Dreaming

Left: Home on the Arnhem Land Aboriginal Land Trust

Right: Cathy Freeman at the 2000 Sydney Olympics

Aboriginal bush tucker

While the use of bush ingredients is fashionable in many city restaurants, to many Aboriginal people they are a means of sustenance and, on occasions, survival. From the rainforests of north Queensland, with its myriad fruiting plants, to dry deserts where plants are scarce, local people have a vast store of knowledge of what to collect or hunt and where to find it. Children accompany their older family members to gain an intimate knowledge of the land, the seasons, plants and animals, and the collection skills necessary to exist in often harsh terrain. While some foods can be eaten straight from the plant, many poisonous fruits require leaching for days in streams before preparation can begin.

Stolen generation

From the late 19th century to the 1960s, Australian governments had a policy of removing part-Aboriginal children from their homes in order that they could be raised as part of white society. Exact numbers were uncertain, but tens of thousands of babies and children were removed, often by force. As these young people grew up, their sense of grief was a personal burden, and political pressure forced a federal inquiry in 1995. The report, *Bringing Them Home,* published two years later, branded the policies as genocide and called for an official apology, compensation for those affected, and the establishment of a national Sorry Day. While the conservative federal government couldn't summon up the word 'sorry' in a parliamentary debate, in May 2000 some 250,000 people marched across Sydney Harbour Bridge to show support for reconciliation.

Aboriginal music

Yothu Yindi put the reconciliation of Aboriginal people in the limelight with their 1991 hit song 'Treaty'. Combining sounds of western rock with songs and performances that go back in time, the band have adapted the ancient song cycles of Arnhem Land, mixing instruments such as didgeridoos and clapsticks with electric guitars. Their shows feature adaptations of traditional mythology, but songs that include Dreamtime or sacred content are first approved by clan leaders. Yothu Yindi has been described as 'the most beautiful blend of indigenous and modern music to emerge from the world's music scene'. As band leader, the charismatic Mandawuy Yunupingu, 1992 Australian of the Year, and a school principal, says: 'It is not colour of skin that defines our identity but the culture into which we were born.'

Cathy Freeman

Born in Mackay, north Queensland, in 1973, Cathy Freeman became the first Aboriginal track and field athlete to represent Australia. Named Young Australian of the Year in 1991, she has created new Australian and Commonwealth records in the 400m and 200m sprints. She won gold medals in the 1990 and 1994 Commonwealth Games, and silver in the 1996 Atlanta Olympic Games, and continued her good form to win back-to-back 400m World Championships in 1997 and 1999. Her career came to a splendid peak when she took the gold medal in the 400m event at the 2000 Sydney Olympic Games before an adoring local crowd. Since then, sports injuries dogged her, and in July 2003 she announced her retirement.

ABORIGINAL AUSTRALIA 15

Left: The Australia Youth Olympics, at Olympic Park, Sydney

Right: Surfing off the Yorke Peninsula, South Australia

Right: Outback golf at Tennant Creek, NT

Below: The annual Henley-on-Todd regatta, Alice Springs

Aussie Rules—the Adelaide Crows (red and yellow)

Sporting Australia

Without a doubt, most Aussies are obsessed with sport. The Sydney 2000 Olympics, where many Australians appeared on the winner's podium, presented a sports-loving people to the world. Where else, for example, does a nation come to a standstill for a horse race? Even if the annual Melbourne Cup is the only day most Australians take an interest in racing, are there any cities besides Melbourne and Adelaide which proclaim a race day as a public holiday? The prestigious race, run over 3,200 metres (2 miles), is held on the first Tuesday in November.

But Australians participate in sports as well as watch them, and on any weekend in the appropriate season you'll find plenty of junior and amateur cricket, football, basketball, netball, hockey, tennis and golf competitions going on. Suburban bowls grounds attract any number of retired older folk, while the bays and harbours are packed with sailing crafts of all kinds competing in club events. And Aussies on holiday are always likely to start up a friendly family game of cricket or touch football on the beach. Generally, all comers are welcome, so feel free to join in!

High ideals at the Australian Institute of Sport

Aussie Rules

The home-grown football game is Australian (Aussie) Rules. The game originated in Victoria in the 1850s and has been described as a cross between rugby, soccer and Gaelic football. Melbourne is the home of Aussie Rules, although Hobart, Perth and Adelaide are also strongholds. Teams from Brisbane, Sydney, Adelaide and Western Australia compete with Victorian teams in a national competition. The top eight compete to play in the grand final at the end of the season in September, when Melbourne is infected with an extra dose of footy fever. Over 80,000 spectators pack the Melbourne Cricket Ground, and it's a special experience to watch this tactical and athletic sport, while sitting among cheering fans.

Above: Surfing on sand: Dune hill at Kangaroo Island, South Australia

Above: By a neck—the Alice Springs Camel Cup

Right: Thredbo, in the Snowy Mountains

Below: Ian Thorpe at the Sydney 2000 Olympics

The 2003 Australian Open at the National Tennis Centre, Melbourne Park

Cricket

No cricket contest is as keenly followed as an Ashes series between Australia and England. The prized 'Ashes' refer to a tiny urn believed to contain the charred remains of a stump bail. This harks back to 1882, when Australia beat England for the first time on their home soil, and a sports newspaper ran a mock obituary for English cricket which had 'died' and stated that: 'The body will be cremated and the ashes taken to Australia'. After England won in Australia the following year, the mythical Ashes became reality when the urn was presented to the victorious captain. Despite Australia's overwhelming supremacy in recent years—they have won every series since 1989 —the revered Ashes are kept at cricket's spiritual home, the Marylebone Cricket Club (MCC) at Lord's in London.

The Thorpedo

As a young swimmer, Ian Thorpe was allergic to chlorine! Now, barely out of his teens, he is one of the greatest and most respected swimmers of all time. Having broken 22 world records, he is currently the world record holder for the 200m, 400m and 800m freestyle. Before a proud nation, at his home-town Olympics in Sydney in 2000, Thorpe won three gold and two silver medals and carried the Australian flag at the closing ceremony. In addition to his achievements, honours and celebrity status, Thorpe has founded a charity to support children who are challenged by illness. As he says: 'Sometimes we question things that we have done in our lives, but how many times do we question what we haven't done in someone else's?'

Australian Institute of Sport

When Australia's sporting stars returned disappointing results at the Montreal Olympics in 1976, the federal government decided to set up a sports institute. Based in Canberra and opened in 1981, the AIS provides athletes with world-class training facilities, specialist coaching, state-of-the-art training equipment, and access to sports medicine and sport science. It conducts 35 sport programs in 26 sports in locations around Australia. With accommodation for 350 residents on site, the Canberra facility supports archery, artistic gymnastics, basketball (men and women), boxing, netball, rowing, soccer (men), swimming, athletics (including athletes with disabilities), volleyball (men and women) and water polo (men). Of the record 58 medals that were won at the Sydney Olympics, 32 came from current or former institute athletes.

Tennis

Tennis has long been a favourite Aussie sport, for players and spectators alike. Although recent greats have included Pat Cash and Pat Rafter, there was a feeling that the sport was in decline after the 1950s and 60s when the likes of Rod Laver, Ken Rosewall and John Newcombe dominated world men's tennis, and the sixties and seventies when Margaret Court and Evonne Goolagong Cawley dominated the women's game. Now Lleyton Hewitt, recognized by his trademark backwards hat and regular fist pumps, has reached the top. His success shouldn't be a surprise since, at the age of four, he could consistently hit balls back over the net. And for motivation, he has watched the movie *Rocky* over 100 times!

Left: Paul Jennings' children's novel, *Tongue-Tied!*

Right: Mural in Smith Street, Collingwood, northeast Melbourne

Above: Peter Carey's Booker Prize winner, *True History of the Kelly Gang*

Right: Sydney Dance Company in Graeme Murphy's *Ellipse*

Cultural Australia

Australia's cultural achievements are often overshadowed by its success in the sporting arena. Until recent years, Australian writers, musicians, actors, artists and dancers who aspired to international recognition were forced to travel overseas—this was especially so during the sixties and seventies. Today, world-class actors such as Russell Crowe are able to work in the US or Europe and still make Australia their home. And the 'cultural cringe', which once caused Australians to defer to artistic and intellectual achievements in Europe and the US, has mostly disappeared. Australia has made a solid contribution to the world popular music scene with bands such as Australian Crawl, INXS, AC/DC and Midnight Oil, and there have been enduring solo performers such as Kylie Minogue and Nick Cave who have a solid international reputation. Modern Aboriginal art has become very popular, and the influential Papunya Tula artists, who took body decoration and sand designs based on Dreamtime stories and applied them in a series of dots and lines on canvas, are responsible for starting one of the twentieth century's great art movements. Author Peter Carey, whose acclaimed novel *True History of the Kelly Gang* (2000) won the 2001 Booker Prize, is today the exception rather than the rule, in that he makes New York his home.

TV wild man Steve Irwin

Literature

Children's writer Paul Jennings has managed to work his way into the hearts of millions of children worldwide. Born in England in 1943, and arriving with his family in Australia as a boy of six, Jennings trained as a teacher before studying speech pathology and lecturing in special education. His first book, *Unreal*, published in 1985, was an instant success. Since then he has written 20 collections of quirky and humorous short stories including *Unseen* and *Unbelievable*, and has co-authored *Wicked*. His empathy with children—a frequently asked question is 'How do you know what it's like to be me?'—arises out of his varied teaching experiences, plus the fact that he is a father of six children.

The pattern of nature and people in Aboriginal art—at the Cherbourg Emu Farm, Queensland

Below: Drag line—still from *Priscilla Queen of the Desert*

Street furniture at Fitzroy Nursery on stylish Brunswick Street, Melbourne

Pop princess, Kylie Minogue

Nicole Kidman

Music

Pop diva Kylie Minogue has come a long way since her days as Charlene in early episodes of the TV soapie *Neighbours*. Her two 1987 pop hits, 'Locomotion' and 'I Should Be So Lucky', followed in the next year by 'Got To Be Certain', set her on the path to success. In the nineties, Kylie moved from pop to club music and reinvented herself for a whole new audience. She recorded with various artists including Pet Shop Boys, and in 1995, with punk legend Nick Cave, performed the beautiful ballad 'Where the Wild Roses Grow' which went to number 2 in Australia. In 2000 she wowed audiences worldwide at the closing ceremony of the Sydney Olympic Games. She now lives in London.

Australian films

There are not many more successful movie stars than Nicole Kidman. After *Dead Calm* (1989), Kidman co-starred with Tom Cruise in *Days of Thunder* the following year. After starring roles in high-profile movies such as *To Die For* and *Batman Returns,* Kidman took to the London stage in 1998 in David Hare's *The Blue Room,* a role that included a highly publicized nude scene. In 2001, Kidman and her partner Tom Cruise separated after 11 years of marriage, and she starred in the film musical *Moulin Rouge*. Even as she attains new heights in her career, Kidman eschews the affluent affectations often associated with the profession—which is pretty amazing, considering that she can earn up to $15 million for a film.

Aboriginal art

As custodians of Dreamtime stories, Michael Nelson Jagamara and Billy Stockman Japaltjarri keep their culture alive by passing the stories on through their art. Jagamara, born at Pikilyi in Central Australia in about 1947, is Australia's most prominent Aboriginal artist. He created a mosaic for the forecourt at Parliament House in Canberra, and his 8-metre (26ft) painting adorns the foyer of the Sydney Opera House. Before becoming a painter, he was a buffalo shooter, truck driver and drover. Japaltjarri, born in 1925, was one of the founders of the Papunya Tula art movement. Jagamara and Japaltjarri visited the USA in 1988, are both widely collected and have had many international exhibitions. Their art has engendered a sense of pride and renewed cultural identity among Aboriginal people.

Dance

Since his appointment as artistic director of the Sydney Dance Company in 1976, Graeme Murphy has led the company on more than 20 international tours to Asia, Europe and the US, including five New York seasons. Among his credits are an arrangement of Benjamin Britten's *Death in Venice,* the direction of Richard Strauss's *Salome,* and his choreography of Michael Askill's *Free Radicals.* Murphy has a discerning interest in music from a variety of 20th-century composers, and his innovative production of Maurice Ravel's *Daphnis and Chloë* attracted rave reviews. He also collaborated with Nederlands Dans Theater *(Song of the Night)* and produced a solo work for Mikhail Baryshnikov *(Embodied).* Murphy's dramatic choreography for the skaters Torvill and Dean demonstrated the versatility of his talent.

A termite mound on the plains of Old Mornington, in the Kimberley

Left: Take extra care for koalas crossing roads

Right: The family way— emu walking with a chick

Queensland's tropical rainforests are among the oldest in the world

Natural Australia

From the coral formations of the Great Barrier Reef to the gorges, rocky outcrops, and sandy plains of the dry outback, Australia has a wealth of natural wonders. Unique plants and animals have evolved on this ancient continent and its surrounding islands since they were isolated by sea from the mega-continent of Gondwana over 50 million years ago.

Today's distinctive flora and fauna, including the eucalypts, have developed over the millennia on a continent once completely covered in rainforest.

Fortunately for the traveller, many of Australia's best parks and reserves are easily accessible. Within the boundaries of major towns and cities are many parks, gardens and bushland reserves that give the short-term visitor a good over-all picture of Australia's plants and animals. Less than an hour drive from state capitals are superb scenery and diverse ecosystems ranging from coastal heathlands and riverine estuaries to mountain forests. Even many World Heritage-listed places, such as Fraser Island, are not far off the beaten path. A variety of animals can be seen in the wild and there are any number of quality wildlife parks and zoos with koalas, kangaroos, dingoes, wombats, emus, crocodiles (and more) on view.

A New Holland Honey Eater feeds on a Bird of Paradise flower, Centennial Park, Sydney

Eucalypts and fire

Eucalypts, known as gum trees, are the most common trees in Australia. Comprising more than 500 different species, they evolved from rainforests and developed a resistance to fire through aeons of natural and man-made conflagrations. When managed fires lit by the Aboriginals ceased, the land was settled and the remaining forests were protected as timber reserves and national parks. Fire was generally excluded and fuel levels often built to intolerable levels. While regular controlled burning has reduced the chances of devastating wildfires, each year there are hundreds of major bushfire outbreaks caused by lightning strikes or, more often, careless humans. Even Australia's capital cities may be ringed by fires, and water-bombing aircraft have to be enlisted to save life and property.

LIVING AUSTRALIA

Left: Wild budgerigars in South Australia

Below: Coastal scenery of Fraser Island, Queensland

DANGER
WILDLIFE ON ROAD

No hopping on the greens of Anglesea Golf Club, Victoria

Above: A freshwater crocodile
Left: Not man's best friend: Keep clear of dingoes

Fraser Island

Mass tourism is not without its problems. When Fraser Island, the world's largest sand island, was added to the World Heritage register in 1992, unique rainforests and half the world's perched freshwater lakes received permanent protection. Also preserved were cliffs of coloured sands, mangroves and coastal heathlands, as well as eastern Australia's purest population of dingoes. For the dingoes, increased visitor numbers meant more food to scavenge, and the visitors were only too keen to feed 'tame' dingoes. All this came to a head when a nine-year-old boy was killed by dingoes in 2001; since then, dozens of dingoes have been shot by rangers. The goal now is to achieve some balance between the rights of people who visit the island and the rights of these protected animals.

Cane toads

These amphibians, with a dry warty skin and poison glands, were introduced from Hawaii to Australia in 1935 to control scarab beetles that were infesting sugar cane fields. Cane toads have now spread from far northern New South Wales, across coastal and savanna Queensland, to Kakadu National Park. Although they have poisoned some native animals that have tried to eat them, there is evidence that animals are adapting to their presence, and their menace status is somewhat over-rated. The toads average 10–15cm (4–6in) in length, with a record female measuring 24cm (9.5in), and their habitats range from sand dunes and coastal heath to rainforest and mangrove margins. However, they are most abundant in open clearings in urban areas where artificial lighting attracts plenty of insects.

Crocodile attacks

Crocodiles have been a protected species in Australia since 1971, and numbers have increased dramatically in recent years. So who would ignore prominent signs warning against swimming in crocodile infested waters? And who would swim at night? Kakadu National Park tour leaders, apparently. When a 24-year-old German tourist, swimming in a water-hole with her tour group, was killed by a crocodile in 2002, she was a victim of complacency. Witnesses heard her scream and she vanished beneath the water. Next day, rangers found the offending 4m (13ft) croc about 2km (1 mile) up river and harpooned it. Despite this attack, deaths from crocodiles in Australia are very rare and there have only been 14 recorded fatalities.

A bearded dragon, Queensland

Tasmanian tigers

Naturalists have concluded that when the last known thylacine, or Tasmanian tiger, died in a Hobart zoo in 1936, it was the end of the line for a unique family of carnivorous marsupials that had lived in Australia for millions of years. The 1.5m (5ft) thylacine was native to Tasmania, but existed on the mainland before becoming extinct there thousands of years ago. Common even around the beginning of the 20th century, thylacines were hunted to extinction in Tasmania because they were a threat to sheep. Or are they extinct? The most recent reliable sighting was in 1995, when a Parks and Wildlife Service officer thought he saw one in the east of the state, but there are about a dozen unconfirmed sightings each year. So watch this space.

NATURAL AUSTRALIA

Left: Rainbow Lorikeets on Kangaroo Island, South Australia

Right: Sturt's desert rose, the plant symbol of the Northern Territory

Right: One of Australia's largest birds, the southern cassowary

Above: Whales cruising off the Eyre Peninsula, South Australia
Below: The Great Barrier Reef, Queensland

Monkey Mia

Shark Bay, 850km (530 miles) north of Perth, is one of only a handful of regions in the world to meet all four criteria for World Heritage listing. In the shallow waters of the Shark Bay Marine Park, with its abundant marine life and vast seagrass meadows, where dugong graze and manta rays, turtles and whales come in to feed, are the dolphins of Monkey Mia, which visit the beach each morning to interact with visitors. They are fed freshly caught local fish under the strict supervision of national park rangers. Since these are wild animals that must support themselves, no more than one-third of each dolphin's daily food requirement is provided, but visitors are surprised when they sometimes get offered fish that the dolphins themselves have caught!

The endangered cassowary

Perhaps fewer than 1,200 of the southern cassowary remain in the wild. An adult bird can be up to 1.5m (5ft) tall and has a coarse, black plumage that contrasts with the distinctive red and blue neck. Cassowaries range from Paluma, north of Townsville, to north of Cairns. The heavier, taller female bird is the dominant sex, and the male incubates the eggs and rears the chicks for between 9 to 12 months. While they have a measure of protection under World Heritage listing, attacks by domestic dogs, hits by speeding motor vehicles and the clearing of adjacent habitats are pushing this flightless bird towards extinction. As the gene pool shrinks, so does their chance of survival in the wild.

Birdwatching in the city

There are many large parks in urban Australia where you can watch birds. Birds congregate in logical places, so look for them around water areas on a hot day, flowering trees and shrubs, and even places where humans are likely to feed them, such as at the seaside. Willie wagtails are very common, and can be seen chasing other birds away from their nests. Flowering eucalypts soon attract screeching rainbow lorikeets, and the shrill cry of the sulphur-crested cockatoo is commonly heard in urban areas. Perhaps the most common sound in the early morning, the loud laughing call of the kookaburra, signals the start of the day for these scavenging birds. Watch out, though—they're liable to steal food from your picnic!

World Heritage Australia

Australia's natural heritage is recognized by 15 UNESCO World Heritage listings—more natural areas than any other country. Queensland's Great Barrier Reef, Wet Tropics rainforests, Riversleigh fossil fields and Fraser Island are all listed. The the subtropical rainforests of the Lamington Plateau, in southern Queensland, are part of the Central Eastern Rainforest Reserves that extend into New South Wales. West of Sydney is the Greater Blue Mountains Area, and in southwest New South Wales is the Willandra Lakes Region Aboriginal cultural site. The Tasmanian Wilderness has rugged mountain scenery. Seagrass beds mark Shark Bay in Western Australia, and Purnululu National Park in the same state contains the Bungle Bungle Range. Kakadu National Park and the iconic Uluru (Ayers Rock) are in the Northern Territory.

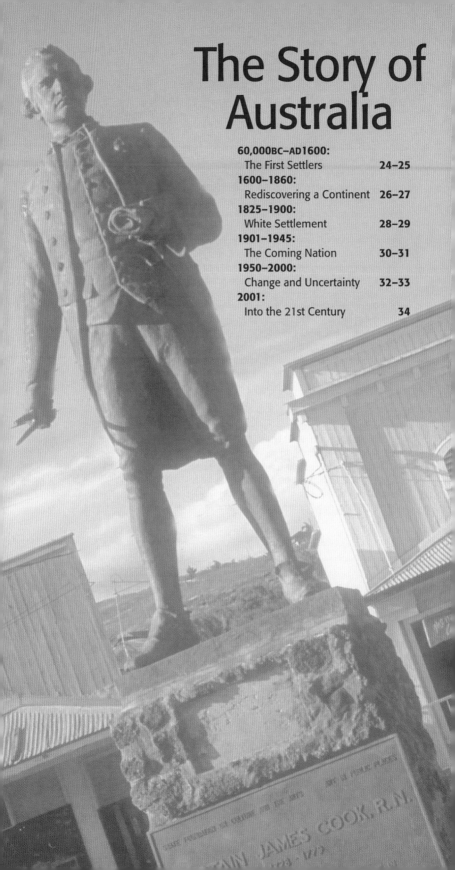

The Story of Australia

The First Settlers

At the time of white settlement, the Aboriginals of Australia were not a single group of primitive people, as has been reported for nearly two centuries. Rather, they lived across a series of distinct, complex societies, which incorporated at least 600 language groups and employed a variety of technologies and cultural practices. The first Australians crossed over to the northern part of the continent from Indonesia around 70,000 years ago, an estimation confirmed by the 60,000-year-old remains found at the World Heritage-listed Mungo site in outback New South Wales. As the population increased, small family groups began to scatter in search of new hunting grounds, settling most of the continent within 2,000 or 3,000 years, leaving the harsh desert lands of the interior until last. Most groups lived a semi-nomadic, hunter-gatherer lifestyle, but each employed distinct survival techniques in response to the environmental and climatic conditions of the area they occupied. Spiritual belief and tribal law were, likewise, directly influenced by the specifics of the landscape, which led to great cultural diversity. Trade, inter-marriage and a complex web of family relationships maintained contact between different groups. Around 5,000 years ago, various groups began refining their food-gathering techniques to include, among other things, the building of fish traps, the use of harvesting techniques and the processing of some foods to remove toxins.

Dreamtime

The Dreamtime refers to the creation period of Aboriginal spiritual belief. Stories of the Dreamtime vary greatly, but the notion of an Ancestral Spirit is a common thread. For the tribes of the southeast corner of the continent, this figure was known as Bunjil—also Baiami, Nurelli and Nurrundere depending on the region. During the Dreamtime, Bunjil, with the aid of other spirits, created the landscape, its vegetation and animals, as well as the people, their laws and religion. He then ascended to the heavens, where he lives as a star. In a rock shelter in the Grampians in central Victoria, there is a painted image of Bunjil: It shows a human-like figure with two dingoes and is said to be an impression left by the spirit when he squatted down to rest.

60,000 years ago

Above and right: Rock art at Old Mornington in the Kimberley, Western Australia

Lifestyles in Victoria

The Gunditjmara people of Lake Condah, Victoria, enjoyed a fairly stable existence. They had a large supply of fresh fish, which they caught by building traps and engineering canals. Because they did not have to move often to find food, they built stone houses and lived in permanent settlements. By contrast, the Jaitmathang, who lived in the Victorian Alps, moved in accordance with the seasonal availability of food resources. They built small huts made of stringybark that could be erected quickly to provide some protection from the cold. Bogong moths—large, fleshy creatures—were an important food source and bogong-feasting ceremonies, which involved hundreds of people from a number of clans, were held regularly.

Relationship with the land

Aboriginal people were—and still are—linked to their land by powerful stories. These serve to mark out territory, advise on the availability of resources, chart routes through deserts, and preach caution and conservation. From the Adnyamathanha people of the Flinders Ranges in South Australia comes a tale about the creation of the region's spiky grass trees around the chasms of Weetooltla Creek. A greedy woman was climbing high on the rocks looking for arta, the edible substance at the core of the plant. She fell and was dashed to pieces on the rocks. These pieces became the spiky flares of these distinctive grass trees—and a permanent reminder of the need to take care while negotiating a dangerous landscape.

Art

At the Ubirr Art Site in Kakadu National Park, the largest repository of rock art in Australia—if not the world—is a representation of the wily Namarrgarn Sisters. They are depicted pulling apart taut pieces of string, which, according to the Gundjeihmi people of the region, they used as a means of sending down sickness into people's bodies. There is a tale told about them that is used to warn children against the dangers of crocodiles. One sister turned herself into a crocodile as a joke. The other tried it as well, and soon they both decided to become crocodiles permanently so that they could eat anyone at any time. The palms that are found around the springs in the area grew from the teeth the 'crocodile' sisters pulled from their mouths.

The Palawa

Tasmania's Aboriginal people, descendants of mainland Aboriginals, are known as Palawa. They migrated to the island some 35,000 years ago. At the time of European settlement it had a population of more than 4,000. In the early 1830s George Augustus Robinson gathered together the last 130 tribal Aboriginals and sent them to the bleak shores of Flinders Island in the Bass Strait for their own 'protection'. In 1847 the 47 survivors were relocated to Oyster Cove near Hobart. The last full-blood Aboriginal, Truganini, died in 1876, but many mixed-race descendants of Aboriginals and white seal hunters from the Bass Strait islands lived on. In recent years, they have asserted their heritage and, controversially, the right to make claims on land in Tasmania.

Closer to Indonesia —a Torres Strait Islander

One of the last 19th-century native Tasmanians

Above: Pukumani, poles marking graves on the Tiwi Islands, Northern Territory

1600

Above: Camping in the ancient landscape of Flinders Ranges National Park Right: Traditional subsistence— kangaroo hunting

Rediscovering a Continent

Australia existed as a place in the imagination for many centuries before it was discovered. The ancient Greeks referred to an unknown continent called Utopia of the South, and Chinese classics described a mythical south land with black pygmies. Before the earth was known to be round, cartographers based their knowledge about the existence of a great southern mass on the fact that the disk-like earth would surely tip over if there were not something there to balance the great bulky continents of the north. Dutch colonization of the East Indies opened the way to discovery by accident more than design: Ships blown off course on the voyage to Java sighted land, and some were wrecked on the coast of Nova Holland. Between 1642 and 1644 Dutchman Abel Tasman charted large parts of what had become known as New Holland. In the late 17th century, the Englishman William Dampier explored and partially mapped the northwest coast of the continent. In the late 18th century British strategists made the discovery of the south land a priority, convinced as they were that they would find a continent larger than Asia supporting a population of 50 million, and that subsequent colonization of such a place would give them trade advantages over other European nations.

The coming of Cook

In 1768, the British Government gave Lieutenant James Cook command of the *Endeavour*. His goals were to chart the transit of Venus and establish the eastern extent of the great southern land, which was still the subject of speculation. Despite the scientific nature of the mission, political and strategic interests were at work. Cook, on finding the coast, made contact with the Aboriginal inhabitants, described plants and animals, named prominent features and laid down charts. Then, at a flag-raising ceremony at Botany Bay in April 1770, he claimed the entire east coast on behalf of King George III and the British Empire.

Right: Matthew Flinders circumnavigated the continent in 1801–03

1600

The 1819 Hyde Park Barracks, Sydney, originally housed convicts

Above: Captain Cook's cottage in Fitzroy Gardens, Melbourne
Right: Statue of Captain Cook in Fitzroy Gardens, Melbourne

Transportation to a penal colony

In the 18th century, poverty, harsh laws and the imposition of long prison sentences created a chronic shortage of space in the prisons of Britain. In May 1787, under the command of Admiral Arthur Phillip, the First Fleet, comprising 11 ships carrying 1,487 people—759 of them convicts—set sail. They set up camp on the shores of what would come to be known as Sydney Harbour which, according to Phillip, was 'one of the finest harbours in the world'. Despite Phillip's upbeat assessment, the landscape was thought universally appalling by all who landed there, with one officer moved to comment: 'In the whole world there is not a worse country than what we have seen of this.' The alien nature of the landscape was to prove a deterrent to escape, and no jails were built for many years.

Claiming the continent

Fear that the French and Dutch would come and claim a piece of the vast Antipodean continent forced the British into some pre-emptive colonial action, which included the establishment of a penal settlement in Van Diemen's Land, later Tasmania, in 1803. Over the next 50 years, nearly 60,000 convicts—more than a third of Australia's entire convict consignment—were sent to this impossibly remote and chilly place, which soon gained a reputation for violence and lawlessness. Many prisoners worked on buildings and infrastructure, examples of which have survived. From 1830, re-offending prisoners from other prison colonies were housed in the dreaded confines at Port Arthur, the sandstone ruins of which stand today in eerie splendour overlooking the Tasman Sea.

Civilizing the colony

Governor Lachlan Macquarie ruled the colony from 1808 to 1821. Along with his wife Elizabeth, he made an unprecedented attempt to transform a rough and ready prison colony into an ordered, elegant and benevolent society. He opened up new lands, established villages, set aside land for parks and commissioned fine public buildings in the belief that quality architecture would raise the moral tone of the community. In his belief that men were basically good, he treated the convicts with fairness and compassion. But this attitude annoyed the wealthy settlers whose prosperity depended upon a compliant convict workforce. They lobbied England and Macquarie was eventually recalled after an unfavourable inquiry into his administration.

Exploring the interior

The colonists, driven by curiosity and a greed for grazing land, set out to explore and claim the vast interior. Despite successes, the explorers who failed have had the strongest hold on the popular imagination, and not any more so than Burke and Wills. These two, along with a large party and too much equipment of the wrong kind, set out in 1860 to cross the continent from south to north. They came within several kilometres of the north coast, but turned back thinking that it was much farther away than it was. They made the 1,600km (1,000-mile) journey back to base camp only to find the party, after many patient months, had packed up and departed that morning. They eventually perished, but not before rejecting offers of help from Aboriginals.

Doomed explorers Robert O'Hara Burke (left) and William John Wills

Right: An early map of Botany Bay

1860

Right: A certificate of freedom granted to a convict by the governor of New South Wales
Left: The replica of the *The Bounty* in Campbell's Cove, Sydney, represents a late 18th-century sailing ship

White Settlement

When Captain Cook's botanist, Sir Joseph Banks, proposed the east coast of Australia as an ideal place for a penal colony, he felt confident enough about his recommendation to say 'if the people formed among themselves a Civil Government, they would necessarily increase', going on to add that such a place would serve well as a market for British products. Banks's hope that something good could emerge from what must have been one of the most unpromising beginnings of any nation, bore fruit. The British government played its part, not just by sending more prisoners and some fairly eccentric characters to govern them, but with its program of assisted immigration. From 1832 money raised from the sale of colonial land paid the passages of emigrants from the British Isles. Preference was given to skilled workers, farm workers and single women. The colonies obtained much-needed labour and the mother country was relieved of some 'surplus' population. The other factors at work were a mix of design and good luck. The success of various agricultural pursuits, particularly sheep farming, the phenomenon of the gold rush, and the development of an identifiable national character—pioneering, hardy and humorous—all helped to ensure that, by the 1860s, Australia—then consisting of six colonies—was not only functioning economically, but flourishing socially and politically as well.

Convict legacy

The 160,000 or so convicts transported to Australia formed a mixed bag. Some were career criminals of the lower orders; some considered themselves political prisoners; and others were skilled professionals. In the last category was Francis Greenway, an architect whose legacy is the Georgian colonial buildings that survive in and around Sydney. He was convicted of forgery in 1814 and transported to Australia for a 14-year term. He designed some 40 buildings, including St. James Church and the Hyde Park Barracks in central Sydney. Governor Macquarie pardoned him in 1819. His image has appeared on one of the notes of the national currency, which may make him the only convicted forger in history to have enjoyed such an honour.

Panning for gold at Sovereign Hill, Ballarat

A 19th-century travel guide

1825

Grave in the Memorial Cemetery, Alice Springs, of prospector Harold Lasseter, who died in 1931 looking for gold in the desert

The fate of the Aboriginals

The losers in the Australian story of this period were the Aboriginal peoples. Many died as a result of exposure to disease and alcohol. And some were killed by whites in isolated instances and a series of massacres. The most infamous massacre took place in June 1838 at Myall Creek in western New South Wales, when 12 men killed 28 Aboriginals. Unusually, the perpetrators were rounded up and charged. The trial generated great public interest and opinion was sharply divided. Many agreed with the official line of the defence—that the killing of Aboriginals did not constitute a crime. Others were outraged at the barbarity of the massacre—the victims included women and very young children. Seven of the men were convicted and hanged.

A citizen of the colony

William Charles Wentworth personified the ideals and opportunities of early Australian society. Born in 1790, two years after the first settlement, he was the son of a convict mother and surgeon father. In 1813, he was one of a team of three to cross the Blue Mountains, opening up valuable grazing land beyond. He married Sarah Cox, also of convict stock, with whom he already had a number of children. He became wealthy and set his large family up on an estate at Vaucluse (now open to the public). Despite his assets, Wentworth and his wife had a tenuous relation with Sydney society, which tended to cling to propriety and the prejudices of class. He was a passionate advocate for the independence of the colonies, long before it was a fashionable cause.

Golden age

The discovery of gold in 1851 transformed the colonies. Thousands came from around the world, and the population exploded. In Melbourne and central Victoria, ornate public buildings and lush parklands started to grace what had previously been fairly functional streetscapes. An armed insurrection occurred on the goldfields when, in 1854, miners led by Peter Lalor rose up against the inequities of laws governing mining fees—34 miners and 6 soldiers were killed. The ringleaders were brought to trial for high treason, but public opinion and the press were on their side and they were acquitted. Shortly after the licensing system was reformed. The events marked the beginning of the end of colonial rule and the birth of the myth of the Australian sense of 'a fair go'.

Resettled Aboriginals at Oyster Cove, Tasmania, 1866

Bushrangers

Bushrangers were both feared and admired in the 19th century. Some, like Mad Dan Morgan, were vicious criminals; others, like Ned Kelly, were maverick youths with social ideals. Of the more benign variety was Martin Cash. Known as the 'Gentleman Bushranger', he came from Ireland as a convict in 1827. Sentenced for property crimes in Australia, he was sent to the escape-proof Port Arthur, from which he escaped with two colleagues. Charged with murdering a policeman, he was sentenced to hang. Escape this time came in the form of a reprieve, just an hour before his date with death; rumour has it that the good matrons of the colony lobbied hard on behalf of this notorious ladies' man. Sentenced to the grim penal colony of Norfolk Island, he became a reformed character and, on his release, wrote a bestseller dealing with his adventures on the wrong side of the law.

1900

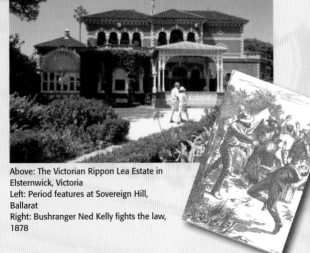

Above: The Victorian Rippon Lea Estate in Elsternwick, Victoria
Left: Period features at Sovereign Hill, Ballarat
Right: Bushranger Ned Kelly fights the law, 1878

The Coming Nation

Australia is one of the few nations to choose democracy and then to implement it in an orderly, measured and non-violent way. In 1856 all the Australian colonies—except Western Australia, which waited until 1893—received bicameral legislatures. Legislative Assemblies (the lower houses) were elected by universal male suffrage. Legislative Councils (upper houses), seen as a bulwark against democratic excesses, were elected on a high property franchise in Tasmania, South Australia and Victoria; in New South Wales and later Queensland the governor appointed members for life. The British government retained the right to veto legislation. The need for uniform immigration and tariff legislation, concerns about threats from Germany and Japan to the north, and a desire on the part of many to be free from the British and self-determining as a nation, were the driving forces behind the federation movement. The foundation of the Australian Labor Party in 1891, and the rise of the coalition parties of the right to defend the propertied classes against threats of socialism, established the present two-party system. Newly federated in 1901, Australia had the capacity and fortitude to take on the challenges of the first half of the 20th century: the Depression, two world wars, enormous social change and nation building.

Federation

Visionaries began advocating a union of the Australian colonies in the 1840s. In 1889 the New South Wales premier, Henry Parkes, made a strong case for federation, saying that 'what the Americans had done by war, the Australians could bring about in peace without breaking the ties that held them to the mother country'. Voters accepted federation at a referendum held in 1899. In January 1901 the Governor General proclaimed the Commonwealth of Australia in Centennial Park in Sydney. As fireworks exploded, crowds gathered to celebrate the newest nation on earth.

1901

Left: Memorial in Alice Springs to the builders of the 1929 Adelaide–Alice Springs railway, the Ghan

Above: Colonies to country—politicians gather in 1890 for the Australasian Federation Conference in Melbourne
Right: Building bridges, a nut on the Sydney Harbour Bridge

The other half

The much-vaunted egalitarianism of the Australian bush and the gold fields did not apply to women. Admiration for women was conditional on them remaining uncomplaining as they bore large numbers of children in extraordinarily isolated circumstances. But when a feminist voice emerged, it was loud and effective. South Australia gave women the vote in 1894—only the second province in the world to do so. Prominent feminists emerged into the public sphere, including the indomitable Vida Goldstein, who rose to national prominence as a campaigner for women's rights and better working conditions (in 1894, New South Wales's 90,000 female breadwinners earned half what their male counterparts did). Women voted for the first time federally in 1903, but it was not until 1921 that the first woman, Edith Cowan, was elected to an Australian parliament.

The Anzac tradition

The Allied landings at Gallipoli on 25 April 1915 have come to be regarded as the symbolic beginning of Australian nationhood. Stories about the Australian and New Zealand Army Corp (Anzac) have a greater hold on the collective imagination than do the events of settlement or federation. Under British command, 2,000 of the 16,000 men who landed on that first day were killed—a devastating number given the countries' small populations. Among the heroes of the campaign was John Simpson Kirkpatrick, a former cane cutter and miner. Using a donkey, he rescued hundreds of injured soldiers until he too was shot and killed. In total, 60,000 Australian men and women died in World War I.

Depression relief

The construction of the Sydney Harbour Bridge, one of the symbols of modern Australia, provided some relief from the economic depression of the early 1930s. It was designed by John Bradfield and employed 1,400 workers. Its massive 503m (1,650ft) steel arch earned it the nickname 'coathanger'. The project, although popular, was also controversial: 800 homes in the workingclass Rocks district were destroyed to make way for the structure; 16 workers died in accidents; and country people complained that the bridge was a symbol of the 'vampire city … sucking the life-blood out of the country'. The 1932 opening ceremony was disrupted when a disgruntled right-wing royalist rode in on horseback and cut the ribbon ahead of the left-wing premier Jack Lang.

Invasion

Australia joined the European war in 1939, but resources were soon redeployed closer to home in response to Japanese aggression. In 1942, Australia came close to being invaded. The country's most remote and northerly city, Darwin, had become a strategic naval, air and supply base. On 19 February 1942, 200 Japanese planes flew towards the city. A priest on Bathurst Island saw the planes and made frantic radio calls to the airforce, but these were ignored. In that first attack, 240 people were killed, ships were sunk and almost every Allied plane was destroyed. Some 60 more raids took place, by which time much of the civilian population had decamped to the bush or southern cities.

The Japanese attacked Fenton airbase, south of Darwin, in 1943

1945

Above: Anzacs dug in at Gallipoli, 1915
Left: Australia's war dead are honoured at the Cenotaph in Martin Place, Sydney
Insets: The Shrine of Remberance in Kings Domain, Melbourne; Women begin to stand out in Victorian society

WE WILL REMEMBER THEM

Change and Uncertainty

During the 1930s, immigration had virtually ceased and the birthrate had fallen to the lowest level in Australia's history. But war in the Pacific brought home the threat of invasion, and by the war's end, everyone from Halls Creek to Hobart knew that Australia, with its population of 7.5 million, had no hope of defending an area the size of Europe and bordered by a coastline of nearly 60,000km (37,200 miles). Under the guidance of former engine driver Joseph Chifley, prime minister from 1945 to 1949, the catchcry was 'populate or perish' and a massive immigration program was put in place. The economy expanded as governments initiated large national projects to keep pace with the growing population. Of these, none was bigger than the Snowy Mountains Hydro-Electric Scheme, which diverted water inland to power generating stations and employed large numbers of newly arrived migrants. Despite the almost visionary economic and political developments that were taking place, mainstream society for the first 30 years after the war was deeply conservative: Governments banned unsuitable books, the Communist Party was very nearly voted out of existence, women left their jobs when they married, black people were barred from rural swimming pools. When change came, which it did in 1972 with the election of Gough Whitlam, it was radical, wide-ranging and, for many Australians, a bit too much all at once.

Right: Italian immigrants arrive in Sydney, 1956

White Australia

An official 'White Australia Policy' was introduced in 1901. The government could exclude non-white or undesirable immigrants by using a dictation test in an unfamiliar European language. In 1934, a left-wing Czech writer took the government to the High Court when he was set a test in Scottish Gaelic. After World War II Australia had no choice but to relax its 'standards'. In 1947 it signed an agreement to take displaced persons from European camps, and by 1968 more than 800,000 non-English-speaking Europeans were living a version of the Australian dream. At first non-whites were not among them but the notion of 'White Australia' was gradually abandoned, and by the early 1970s the country was ready to receive refugees from war-torn southeast Asia.

1950

Above: Australian soldiers bound for Korea in 1950
Right: Protest for Aboriginal land rights in the 1990s

Communism at home and abroad

Australia was gripped by anti-communist fever in the 1950s and 1960s, but not always to a point that defied reason. In 1951, the conservative Prime Minister, Robert Menzies, attempted to ban the Communist Party. A referendum was held and the 'no' vote won by a narrow 53 per cent. A disgruntled Menzies claimed the people had been 'misled by a wicked and unscrupulous "No" campaign'. Anti-communism helped convince Australians to join America in Vietnam, but its power to motivate public opinion wore thin. The realities of conscription—64,000 young men were conscripted and 15,000 were actually deployed—the seeming futility, if not abject failure, of the Vietnam campaign, and the growing divisions on the domestic front, convinced Australians that communist aggressors in foreign places were a low priority.

'It's Time'

In 1972 Australia voted in Gough Whitlam and his Labor government, thereby ending 23 years of conservative rule. Whitlam's tenure was brief but spectacular. He granted recognition to China, abolished conscription, ended Australia's involvement in Vietnam, ran inquiries into Aboriginal Land Rights, legislated for equal pay for the sexes and pensions for single mothers, created a universal health-care system and introduced free tertiary education. His radical programme was thwarted by a hostile Senate and undermined by incompetence in his government. When the Senate blocked essential legislation in 1975, the governor-general John Kerr sacked Whitlam and appointed the opposition leader to head an interim government. Despite the unpopularity of the move, and the subsequent demonizing of Kerr, Whitlam was defeated at the polls one month later.

Indigenous affairs

In a referendum in 1967, 90 per cent of white Australia voted to count Aboriginal people—Australia's first inhabitants—as Australian citizens, a right that had previously been denied them. Despite the benevolence of the result, the fact that such a referendum was necessary speaks of the sorry history of white-black relations. Since the 1970s, land rights for Aboriginal people has been seen as a positive way forward, and court decisions of the 1990s opened the way for vast tracts of Crown land to be transferred to traditional owners. But it remains to be seen whether native title will enable remote Aboriginal communities to find salvation in closer economic and spiritual ties with traditional lands, and thus overcome two centuries of discrimination and dispossession.

New power—the Murray 1 hydroelectric power station in the Snowy Mountains, New South Wales

Environmentalism

Since 1788, a common attitude towards the environment has been 'if it moves, shoot it, if it doesn't, cut it down'—a not untypical pioneer sentiment. The battle for the Franklin River marked a shift in the nation's green consciousness. In the late 1970s the Tasmanian government decided to dam the mighty Franklin to generate electricity. Conservationists swung into action: They targeted government seats, ran a non-violent blockade, and argued that there was no economic need for the project. Hearing the publicity, Australians who had rarely taken a walk in the bush now began discussing the ecological value of old-growth forests. The issue was resolved in the High Court and the area is now protected as a World Heritage Site.

The Parkes Observatory, New South Wales, tracked Apollo 11 in 1968 (scene from *The Dish*, 2000)

2000

Above and left: Aboriginals celebrating the 10th anniversary of the 1992 Mabo decision

Into the 21st Century

Australia's population grew from 7.6 million in 1947 to 19.7 million in 2001, mainly through immigration. Those born overseas account for 23 per cent of the population and are drawn from 110 countries; they have contributed greatly to the cultural diversity of the nation. Australia has grown up on myths of the bush and outback, but it is the coastline that dominates the contemporary consciousness. With the exception of Canberra, all Australian cities are located on the coast; Australians holiday on the coast, retire there and engage in 'seachange' fantasies about dropping out of mainstream society and leading a simple life in Byron, Broulee or Barwon Heads. At the beginning of the 21st century, Australians are starting to look beyond life in the suburbs to discover the delights of the long-neglected inner city. In Sydney and Melbourne particularly, the brick veneer on the quarter-acre block is forsaken for an apartment in a high-rise in the middle of town or reclaimed dockland precinct replete with cafés and shops. A great trading nation, Australia had a painful period of adjustment to economic rationalism and deregulation during the early 1990s. More recently, a low dollar and an increasingly skilled workforce have enabled the nation to capture new markets, with minerals, wine and food products high on the list of exported items.

Domestic politics and world events

In 1996 John Howard was elected prime minister. He is conservative, a self-confessed traditionalist and an ardent advocate for the family. At the time of his election he said he wanted Australians to 'feel comfortable and relaxed'. As they enter the 21st century, many Australians are anything but. International events— September 11, Afghanistan, Iraq and, closer to home, the Bali bombings—have created an edginess that is felt the world over.

Cultured export

One of Australia's best-known characters is Barry Humphries. An actor and comedian of exceptional talent, he has long conquered British audiences and, more recently, persuaded a hitherto mystified American public to love his alter-ego character, Melbourne housewife and mega-star Dame Edna Everage.

John Howard, prime minister since 1996

2001

Above: A modern lifestyle—Australians look to the sea
Right: The nation's flags fly at half mast after the Bali bombing on 15 October 2002
Below: Metropolis—the monorail glides over Sydney

On the Move

ARRIVING

Flying to Australia

Australia's main airline is Qantas. Many other international airlines fly to the state capitals, including British Airways (which shares schedules with Qantas), Singapore Airlines, Malaysia Airlines and Cathay Pacific. Qantas and Virgin Blue provide domestic flights.

STOPOVERS

You can plan your trip independently with the help of travel brochures and the Internet, or online travel specialists such as Travelbag in the UK (www.travelbag.co.uk) can provide an itinerary and arrange stopovers.

A stopover on a long-haul flight can be a good idea: the additional cost is usually not great, and the break helps you to get used to the new time zone. Popular choices for travellers to Australia are Bangkok, Singapore and Hong Kong.

If you know of a hotel you want to stay at, you can arrange your stopover direct by phone or via the web, or you can ask your travel supplier to arrange it (you are not restricted to the hotels in a company's brochure).

Remember to check passport, visa and health requirements in the stopover country.

AIRPORT FACILITIES

All Australian airports offer the same general facilities to arrivals, though larger airports may provide a wider range. Expect the following services in the arrivals area:
● Accommodation information desk
● Automatic teller machines (ATMs)
● Currency exchange
● Duty-free and tax-free shopping
● Lost and found desk
● Luggage trolleys (usually free but sometimes a small charge of around A$3—coins needed)
● Pharmacy
● Porterage services
● Post office or mailbox
● Rental car agencies
● Shopping and refreshment facilities

USEFUL WEBSITES

Qantas
www.qantas.co.uk

British Airways
www.britishairways.com

Singapore Airlines
www.singaporeair.com

Malaysia Airlines
www.malaysiaairlines.com

Cathay Pacific
www.cathaypacific.com

● Taxi ranks
● Telephones
● Toilets and showers
● Tourist information
● Wheelchairs and assistance for disabled travellers—call the airport administration offices or your airline staff in advance if you have special requirements.

AIRPORTS

Sydney

Terminal and transportation information is online at www.sydneyairport.com.au.

Transfers

● The international and domestic terminals are 1.6km (1 mile) apart—a shuttle bus operates between them.
● A train station at the airport provides a fast, easy way of getting to the city. Staff are on hand to advise on tickets for your destination. There can be few more agreeable ways to arrive in Sydney than on one of the fast, frequent, double-decker trains.
● A single-journey ticket takes you to Central Station (15 minutes), where you can change trains if you are staying in the suburbs. Tickets for multiple journeys are also available. Tickets can be used on other forms of transport, including the Manly ferry (see page 54).

ARRIVAL AIRPORTS		
AIRPORT	**LOCATION**	**TRAIN**
Sydney	9km (5.5 miles) S of city centre	Airport to Central Station (15 min); every 15 min Mon–Thu 5am–12pm, Fri–Sun 5am–1am
Melbourne	25km (15.5 miles) NW of city centre	None
Brisbane	13km (8 miles) NE of city centre	Airport to Brisbane City Station (Airtrain; 22 min); adult one-way A$9. AirtrainConnect to the Gold Coast; every 30 min (72-min journey)
Cairns	8km (5 miles) N of city centre	None
Perth	12km (7.5 miles) NE of city centre	None

● Leaving the airport by car is simple; it is a straight run into the city and the entire route is clearly marked from the car park exit

Melbourne
The airport's efficient website (www.melair.com.au) has an interactive map of the airport.
Transfers
● Airport shuttle buses: for information or to arrange a hotel pick-up, tel 03 9670 7992.
● Taxis are metered and, while negotiation is uncommon, drivers may be happy about agreeing a fare beforehand. Fares to the city are publicized as being A$40, but this can rise to A$50 with GST and a 10 per cent surcharge for paying by credit card. Automatic tolls are in operation along the City Link and these are reflected in the taxi fare. Pre-booking a taxi incurs a A$1.10 booking fee, and departing passengers must pay a A$2 taxi parking fee.
● Maps are available at the

BUS/COACH	TAXI	CAR
Express Bus (131 500) to city centre and Kings Cross; daily 5am–11pm. A$12 return, A$7 one-way; approx 25 min. Airporter (02 9666 9988) to hotels in Darling Harbour, Kings Cross, city centre	About A$25 to city centre; passengers pay road toll charges	South Dowling Street from airport to city centre
Skybus (03 9670 7992) to Spencer Street Station; every 30 min 6am–12am, hourly 12am–6am. Adult one-way A$13.	About A$45 to city centre; 30 min	Tullamarine Freeway from airport to city centre
Airport to city centre (07 3236 4700); every 15 min 5am–7.30pm, every 30 min 7.30pm–10.45pm. Adult one-way A$9. Airport to the Gold Coast; daily every hour A$35. Airport to the Sunshine Coast; daily every 2 hours 6.10am–6.35pm A$38	About A$21 to city centre. About A$175 to Gold Coast. About A$280 to Noosa	Kingsford Smith Street from airport to city centre
Australia Coach to city centre and hotels. Adult one-way A$12. Coral Coaches to Port Douglas. Adult one-way A$30	About A$20 to city centre; 15 min. About 1 hour to Port Douglas: A$125	Sheridan Street from airport to city centre
Airport City Shuttle to city centre. Adult one-way A$13/A$11. Fremantle Airport Shuttle to hotels (08 9383 4115). Adult one-way A$20	About A$28 to the city centre; 30 min. About A$44 to Fremantle	Great Eastern Hwy/Tonkin Hwy from airport to city centre

GOODS AND SERVICES TAX (GST)

Visitors to Australia can claim back Goods and Services Tax (GST) paid on items above A$300. A purchase must be made within 30 days of the date you are due to leave Australia.

- At Sydney Airport you can claim back GST on the spot in a designated refund booth (you will be given cash or a cheque which you can convert at one of the currency exchange facilities, or you can request a credit payment). The items in question must be available for inspection, so keep them in your hand luggage.
- Melbourne Airport has a GST Free Zone for internationally departing passengers, located after Customs. The GST-free prices are at point of purchase—no paperwork, no minimum spend requirement.
- There are 2,000 shops in Australia operating a 'sealed bag' system where goods are sent to the airport. More than 60 shops in The Rocks area in Sydney operate this system. This allows you to spend more or less than the A$300 minimum, and removes the necessity of obtaining a GST refund before departing.

airport to help drivers travelling to Melbourne city centre. The best route from the airport to the city is the City Link freeway. Follow signs from the airport to City Link, then after the Bolte Bridge take the left-hand lane and then one of the exits to the city (e.g. City Road exit). After leaving City Link follow the signs to the city centre. City Link is a toll road and a City Link pass must be purchased before or after travelling. A City Link pass can be purchased before or up to midnight three days after travel; tel 13 26 29 for credit card purchases (A$9.20 for one day of unlimited travel). City Link passes can also be purchased from a post office or fuel station. Failure to obtain a pass will incur a fine.

Brisbane

Brisbane has fast links to the Sunshine Coast in the north and the Gold Coast and northern NSW to the south, via the Gateway Arterial Highway. brisbaneairport.com.au is useful for checking arrivals and departures and internal flight planning.

Transfers

- The shuttle connecting the domestic and international terminals runs about every 15 minutes. It's free for airline ticket holders in transit, A$2.70 for non-travellers.
- For general information on coach services call Coachtrans: tel 07 3236 1000.
- AirtrainConnect is a door-to-door rail service to

accommodation on the to Gold Coast. About every half hour: adult A$25, child A$15.

- Passengers departing by taxi must pay an additional A$1 on top of the charge.

Cairns

All flights and terminal information can be found at www.cairnsport.com.au.

Transfers

- A five-minute walk along a covered walkway takes you from the international to the domestic terminal. Alternatively, a shuttle bus (Australia Coach) connects the two: cost A$2.
- Shuttles leave for Brisbane from immediately in front of the arrivals area at both terminals.
- Most major hotels in Cairns provide a courtesy coach service to and from the airport—check with your hotel in advance.

Perth

The official website contains all the airport information: www1.perthairport.net.au.

Transfers

- In addition to the airport shuttle buses, Transperth routes 37 and 39 operate between the domestic terminal and Perth city centre: every half hour during the day, hourly after 6pm and all day Sunday. Journey time about 35 minutes.
- If you drive to the city centre, all routes are well signed from the airport and traffic generally is light.

	TAXI RANK	CAR RENTAL		
		AVIS	BUDGET	HERTZ
Sydney	South end of International Terminal	13 63 33	1300 362 848	13 30 39
Melbourne (Tullamarine)	Arrivals ground floor level	13 63 33	1300 362 848	23 30 39
Brisbane	Domestic Terminal and Arrival Level 2 International Terminal	13 63 33	13 362 848	13 30 39
Cairns	Arrivals hall; free taxi phones in Arrivals hall	13 63 33	07 4035 9500	13 30 39
Perth	Outside Arrivals hall	13 63 33	13 27 27	13 30 39
		www.avis.com	www.budget.com	www.hertz.com

Cruises

If you dislike flying, or wish to avoid jet-lag, you may consider visiting Australia as part of a world cruise.

Visitors arriving in Australia by air can still take advantage of the many cruises that call at the major cities, all of which are located on the coast. Trips range from the height of luxury on one of the largest liners, to a 'small ship' cruise. The choice is greatest around the Queensland coast and the Great Barrier Reef.

Cruises to Australia depart from many ports around the world, including Southampton, New York and Los Angeles; ports of call in Australia are frequently combined with Asian destinations. Cruise ships also ply the Tasman Sea between Australia and New Zealand. The website at www.cruisecritic.com provides useful background about many of the cruise lines, their ships and tips on life at sea.

The Queen Elizabeth II *in Sydney Harbour*

P&O
Tel UK 0845 3555 333
USA +1 415 382 8900/+1 206 727 3199
Germany +49 6102 811002
www.pocruises.com
For up-to-date information on P&O's Australian cruises, go to www.pocruises.com.au.

Example cruises:
Sydney–Auckland via Melbourne, Hobart, Milford Sound, Dunedin, Christchurch and Wellington (7 nights)
Sydney–Bangkok via Cairns, Darwin, Indonesia, Malaysia, Singapore and Vietnam (18 nights)

Cruise options and the following information are on the P&O websites:
Accommodation; Activities; Booking; Dining; Dress code; Embarkation; Entertainment; Facilities for children; Health and fitness; Luggage; Money matters; Prices; Tours and hotels for shore visits; Travel documents

CUNARD
Tel Australia 02 9250 6666, 1800 728 6273
UK 0800 052 3840
Germany +00 800 180 84 180
USA and Canada +1 800 728 6273
www.cunard.com

Example cruises:
QE2 World Cruise
Southampton–Southampton 122 nights
Sea cruising and ports of call around Australia:
Tasman Sea; Auckland; Bay of Islands; Melbourne; Sydney; Brisbane; Cairns and Great Barrier Reef; Torres Strait; Arafura Sea; Darwin; Timor Sea.
Includes an overland excursion to Uluṟu (Ayers Rock)
QE2 Polynesian Cruise
Los Angeles–Sydney 27 nights
Honolulu, Hawaii; Pacific Ocean; Papeete, Tahiti; Moorea, French Polynesia; Auckland; Bay of Islands; Melbourne; Tasman Sea; Sydney
QE2 Australian/Asian Cruise
Sydney–Hong Kong 27 nights
Sydney; Brisbane; Great Barrier Reef; Cairns; Torres Strait; Arafura Sea; Darwin; Timor Sea; Flores Sea; Makassar Strait; Kota Kinabalu, Malaysia; South China Sea; Manila, Philippines; East China Sea; Nagasaki, Japan; Kobe, Japan; Taipei, Taiwan; Formosa Strait; Hong Kong

SMALL SHIP CRUISES

Captain Cook Cruises
Tel Australia 02 9206 1122
www.captaincook.com.au
The family-owned company runs cruises around Australia and the Fiji Islands, including:
Great Barrier Reef
Three, four, or seven nights
Sydney Harbour
Daily, and two-night Weekend Explore cruise
Murray River
Five nights or weekend cruise (on 120-passenger paddlewheeler)
Fiji Islands
Three, four or seven nights
Fiji Sailing Safari
Three or four days, on a tall ship

Sunlover Cruises
Tel Australia 07 4050 1333, 1800 810 512
www.sunlover.com.au
Sunlover's reef and island cruises are centred around Cairns:
One-day Reef cruises
Two-day Reef and Rainforest cruise
Three-day Tropical Tour
Sunlover Cruises has links to Sunlover Helicopters, who offer one-day Fly and Cruise tours
Tel 07 4035 9669
www.sunloverheli.com.au

GETTING AROUND

Interstate Air Travel

Most of Australia's tourist destinations are located in or near the coastal regions, among the large states, or are a great distance inland. Air travel between states or inland is often the best form of transport to make the best use of your available time.

Qantas and Virgin Blue operate a range of domestic flights to popular but remote destinations such as Alice Springs, Uluru, the far north and the Kimberley. There is also a wide choice of flights available up and down the length of the east coast, connecting the popular tourist attractions of Sydney, the Gold Coast and the Great Barrier Reef.

QANTAS

Head Office and Customer Relations:
Qantas Centre
203 Coward Street
Mascot, NSW 2020
Tel 02 9691 3636
Information and reservations within Australia: tel 13 13 13
Holiday packages: tel 13 14 15
www.qantas.com
www.jetstar.com.au

Qantas operates domestic flights throughout Australia—some under the Qantas banner, others under the company's cheaper, no-frills brand, JetStar.

Holders of a Qantas international flight ticket can take advantage of the discounted Boomerang Pass for internal flights within Australia and New Zealand. (The pass is also available when travelling with other airlines—check with your travel agent when booking.)

● Must be purchased before you depart.
● You must book a minimum of two or a maximum of 10 flights.
● Reductions apply for children.
● The Australian continent is divided into four zones for

booking—a single fare entitles you to travel within one zone only; a multi-zone fare allows travel in further zones.
Airpasses may save money off full fares, but cheaper, discounted local fares are often available.

Sample fares
When booked in the UK:
Single fare zone £105 per flight
Multi-fare zone £125 per flight

VIRGIN BLUE
Head Office
(administration only):
PO Box 1034
Spring Hill
Brisbane, QLD 4000
www.virginblue.com.au
Information and reservations:
tel 13 67 89
www.reservations@virginblue.com.au
Group bookings (10 or more):
tel 13 67 00

Virgin Blue operates no-frills flights throughout Australia.
The emphasis is on booking by phone or online. The interactive

Qantas is the national carrier

map on the company's website enables you to click on a destination and receive advice on how to get there from various major cities.

● To find airlines that fly to your chosen destination, check the following table.

STATE	LOCATION	
NSW	Albury	
	Armidale	
	Canberra ACT	
	Coffs Harbour	
	Sydney	
	Tamworth	
VIC	Melbourne	
	Mildura	
QLD	Brisbane	
	Cairns	
	Gold Coast	
	Longreach	
	Mackay	
	Mount Isa	
	Rockhampton	
	Roma	
	Townsville	
WA	Broome	
	Kalgoorlie	
	Perth	
	Port Hedland	
NT	Alice Springs	
	Uluru (Ayers Rock)	
	Darwin	
SA	Adelaide	
TAS	Hobart	
	Launceston	

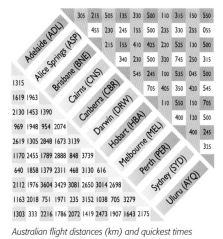

Australian flight distances (km) and quickest times

Information stand at Sydney airport

SYDNEY	MELBOURNE	BRISBANE	CAIRNS	PERTH	ADELAIDE
QS					
QS		QS	QS		
QS, VB	QS, VB	QS, VB		VB	QS, VB
QS, VB	VB	QS, VB			VB
	QS	QS	QS	QS	
QS					
QS		QS	QS	QS	QS
	QS				
QS	QS		QS	QS	QS
QS, VB	QS, VB	QS, VB		VB	VB
QS, VB	QS, VB	QS, VB		VB	VB
		QS			
QS, VB	QS, VB	QS, VB	QS	QS, VB	VB
		QS			
VB	VB	QS, VB			VB
		QS			
QS, VB	VB	QS, VB		VB	VB
VB	VB			QS	VB
				QS	QS
QS	QS	QS			QS
				QS	
QS, VB	QS, VB	VB	QS	QS	QS, VB
QS			QS	QS	
QS, VB	QS, VB	QS, VB	QS	QS	QS
QS	QS	QS		QS	
QS, VB	QS, VB			VB	VB
QS, VB	QS, VB			VB	VB

QS: QANTAS   VB: VIRGIN BLUE

Interstate Rail Travel

For a more leisurely and comfortable alternative to flying between the states, Australia's long-distance trains offer first and economy-class compartments, sleeping berths and reclining seats.

Reservations are advisable: bookings can be made up to nine months in advance, or when you arrive in Australia. The rail map at www.railaustralia.com.au highlights the route and extent of the main lines. (Note: There are no passenger trains in Tasmania.)

RAIL AUSTRALIA

PO Box 445
Marleston Business Centre
Marleston, SA 5033
Tel 08 8213 4592
UK 0870 751 5000
Germany +31 35 69 55 111
USA +1 310 643 0044 ext. 420

RAIL PASSES

An **Austrail** pass (best purchased outside Australia—contact your travel agent) gives unlimited economy class travel for rail networks and some coaches. Prices range from A$660 for 14 days to A$1,035 for 30 days. If purchased in Australia, a pass costs A$600 for 8 days, or A$862 for 15 days.
www.railaustralia.com.au

A **Great Southern Railway Pass** allows six months of unlimited travel on the Indian Pacific, the Ghan and the Overland. Prices start from A$590, with reductions for students and backpackers.
Great Southern Railway
Tel 1800 888 480, 13 21 47
www.gsr.com.au

The **East Coast Discovery Pass** from CountryLink provides economy travel between Melbourne and Cairns. Significant reductions are available on many routes when you book at least 15 days in advance.

CountryLink Reservations
PO Box K349
Haymarket, NSW 1238
Tel 13 22 32
Germany +31 35 69 55 155
UK 08701 210 606
USA +1 310 643 0044 ext 420
www.countrylink.nsw.gov.au

NEW SOUTH WALES

CountryLink (see above) is the long-distance passenger rail and coach operator for regional NSW, serving Canberra, Melbourne and

Brisbane. Trains run from Sydney to Melbourne and Brisbane.

For information on routes, timetable and fares call at the CountryLink Travel Centre in the town where you are staying. Many are dedicated CountryLink offices; others are agencies within travel agents' offices.

VICTORIA

The Ghan covers 2,979km (1,847 miles) from Adelaide to Darwin, following the opening of the route north from Alice Springs in February 2004.

This 47-hour trip is truly one of the great train journeys of the world. You can stop off at Alice Springs, which is 18 hours from Adelaide.
Tel 13 21 47
www.gsr.com.au

SOUTH AUSTRALIA

The Overland runs four times each week from Melbourne to Adelaide (11 hours), including a daytime service from Adelaide to Melbourne. Regional and interstate connections depart from the Keswick terminal in Adelaide.
Tel 13 21 47
www.trainways.com.au;
www.transadelaide.sa.gov.au

WESTERN AUSTRALIA

The ocean to ocean 4,352km (2,698-mile) **Indian Pacific** route runs between Sydney and Perth via Adelaide, twice each week in each direction.

At 70 hours, this is one of the

world's longest train journeys—a holiday in itself.
Tel 08 8213 4592, 13 21 47
www.gsr.com.au

QUEENSLAND

The **Queenslander** follows a tropical, coastal route between Brisbane and Cairns (32 hours). Unlike any other journey in Australia, this is the one to choose if you want a mix of rainforests, coastal ranges and Pacific reef scenery.

Complete your journey to the north of Queensland with a trip on Queensland Rail's **Kuranda Scenic Railway** (see page 107), with its station adorned with tropical palms.
www.railaustralia.com.au

The **Spirit of the Outback** combines part of the lush Queenslander coast route from Brisbane to Rockhampton with a journey through the harsh outback to Longreach—the best of both worlds (24 hours).
Queensland Rail
Tel 07 3235 1122, 13 22 32
www.traveltrain.qr.com.au

The modern **Tilt Train** runs between Brisbane and Cairns (25 hours) with three trains each week, through the tropical scenery of north Queensland. The 1,681km (1,042-mile) route has stops at all the major coastal cities, including Rockhampton, Mackay and Townsville.
Bookings: tel 13 22 32
www.traveltrain.qr.com.au

AUSTRALIAN CAPITAL TERRITORY

Canberra's train station (for interstate services only) is located to the south of the Parliament area, in Kingston. There are direct trains to Sydney, but to travel to Melbourne you must first drive to Yass.

Vehicle Rental

Australia has an enormous number of rental hire firms offering new or used models. Daily rates are not high but many agreements are restricted to driving within a limited area; you may not be allowed to take the vehicle on unsealed roads or beyond a particular town.

Rates may increase at peak holiday periods and you must expect to pay more for unlimited mileage. Also you may have an unpleasant surprise when you collect a 4WD vehicle or campervan—there will probably be a 'bond' to pay of several hundred dollars, which may not have been explained at the outset, plus 'government duty'.

RENTING

To rent a vehicle you must hold a current driving licence and, preferably, an International Driving Permit. These must be carried with you when you drive.

If you are a young or inexperienced driver, check the minimum requirements for age and driving experience before you travel; generally drivers must be 21 or over and must have held a licence for at least three years.

If you have any problems with a rental vehicle you must contact the rental company to arrange any breakdown assistance (see page 38 and 44).

It is possible to collect a rental vehicle in one state and return it in another. This can be expensive, however, because the vehicle has to be driven back to its state of origin (clearly known by the distinctive state number plates).

Sample rates for rentals
Small car: A$50–A$70 per day
Large car: A$70–A$90 per day
4WD: A$100–A$125 per day

Most car rental companies have deals with various associations whereby discounted rates are available for their affiliates. Travellers should investigate possible links to such associations.

RENTING A CAMPERVAN OR MOTORHOME (RV)

If you decide to 'go bush' during your holiday, a campervan or 4WD may be more appropriate to cope with country roads and the immense distances in greater comfort.

Campervans and motorhomes are available for rent in all the states. All are equipped with cutlery and crockery, cooking utensils, sleeping bags, pillows and towels, plus optional awnings. Some deluxe vehicles have showers and toilets.

Minimum rental period is usually seven days; savings are offered on rentals of three weeks or longer. There are restrictions concerning travel on unsealed roads and the contract may not cover unlimited mileage—important if you plan to cover a large distance.

Sample mid-season rates
Campervan 2/3 berth:
A$620–A$990 per week
Motorhome 4 berth:
A$1,180–A$1,500 per week
Motorhome 6 berth:
A$1,250–A$1,800 per week

Britz Australia specializes in tourist rental—their white, orange-banded vehicles often stand out in remote areas. Britz has depots in Sydney (NSW), Melbourne (Vic), Brisbane, Cairns (Qld), Alice Springs, Darwin (NT) Adelaide (SA), Broome, Perth (WA) and Hobart Airport (Tas). Tel 1800 331 454; 03 8379 8890, **www**.britz.com.au

The freedom of a motorhome

NQ Rentals in north Queensland offers last-minute rates: **www**.nqrentals.com.au.

RENTING A MOTORCYCLE

Rental rates for motorcycles are between A$150–A$300 per day or A$600–A$1,600 per week, depending on engine size. A refundable credit card deposit of about A$2,000 is required.

You must have an International Motorcycle Licence. A helmet is compulsory; you can rent a helmet, gloves and wet/cold-weather gear.

GREY NOMADS

If you are touring in the north of Australia in 'winter', you may encounter 'grey nomads' or 'geriatric gypsies'—retired people from the cooler states who follow the sun throughout the year, gravitating north in winter. Campsite society is generally very congenial.

Driving

ROAD ROUTINE

People routinely drive great distances in Australia: It's not unusual to drive for an hour and a half just for a lunch engagement.

Most visitors adjust to the scale of the country and make the epic journeys part of their holiday.

Vehicles, private or rental, are geared to the road conditions. The majority are automatic and have air conditioning, which makes driving much more comfortable and allows you to keep windows closed when driving through dusty areas.

The main highways are straight sealed (metalled) roads and you can cover long distances reasonably quickly. Coastal and mountain roads can be winding. Roadhouses provide welcome comfort stops, and are usually sited about every 100km (62 miles). They supply most necessities for travellers, as well as fuel.

BREAKDOWN ASSISTANCE

The Australian Automobile Association (AAA) represents the seven state motoring organizations that provide roadside assistance. AAA is also a member of the Alliance Internationale de Tourisme (AIT), through which national motoring organizations assist each other's members. Check with your organization before travelling that they are a member of AIT.

Whichever Australian state you are travelling in, call 13 11 11 for assistance. Remember to carry your organization's membership or road service card.
AAA
Tel 02 6247 731
www.aaa.asn.au.

DRIVING IN TASMANIA

Fuel is expensive relative to the cost in the mainland Australian cities (typically 10–20c per litre more). Remote places like Strahan can be 10c per litre more expensive again.

TIPS

● Before setting out on a long journey, ensure your vehicle is in top condition.
● Make sure you have a good, up-to-date map—a scale of at least 1:200,00 in built-up areas, and at least 1:1,000,000 for country driving.
● Plan your journey in advance, building in stops to counteract the effects of tiredness.
● Beware of the risks of boredom and loss of concentration—some drivers find listening to the radio or to music keeps them alert.
● Freeways in Australia may have exits to the right as well as the left.
● Take great care when overtaking road trains—make sure you can see for at least 1km (0.6 mile) ahead of the road train before pulling out, and signal your manoeuvre in good time. When you are overtaken by a road train, your vehicle may be buffeted by the slipstream as they passes; if it is safe, pull over to the left of the highway and let them pass.
● Avoid driving at night in the outback.
● Look out for kangaroos, especially at dawn and dusk.
● Do not be tempted to drive off-road unless you have an appropriate vehicle, expertise and access to local knowledge.

● Roads in the Outback may be closed at certain times of year; for example, in the Northern Territory during the Wet from November to April, or in New South Wales and Victoria during May to August, when roads in the high country may be snowbound. Check with the local tourist office or parks office before starting your journey; important traffic information is usually found on prominent display boards. Flash floods are another hazard; avoid camping in or too close to riverbeds.
● Always carry plenty of water in case of breakdown in remote areas. Hardware stores and supermarkets stock insulated water carriers of all sizes. If you are going to camp in an area with no facilities, you will need a large water container, available from camping shops.
● Carry ample fuel when driving in the outback, as petrol stations are few. Ensure your tank is full before setting out. Many 4WD vehicles have a supplementary fuel tank—fill this too.
● Heavily laden vehicles are at risk of 'bogging' in soft ground—take care where you stop or park.
● If your car breaks down in the Outback, build a shelter that provides some shade, and stay with your vehicle and summon assistance.

WILDLIFE CROSSING

Right: Use the map on page 47 and the table opposite to find the distance in kilometres (green) and duration in hours and minutes (blue) of a car journey

ROAD SIGNS

Take care at country rail crossings that lack gates

Emergency phones are found beside highways

Cyclists sometimes share paths with pedestrians

Yellow signs warn of potential danger

On toll roads, signs give drivers advance notice of charges

Work out the freeway exit you need well in advance

All speed limits are given in kilometres per hour

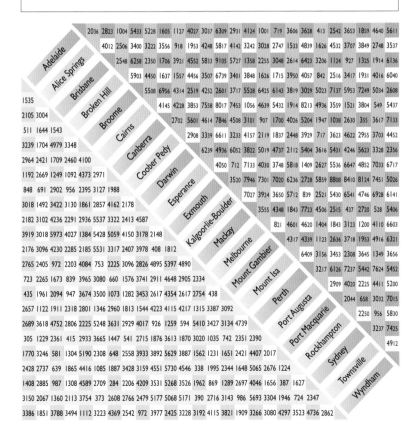

Driving Regulations

Broome
Port Headland
Exmouth
Carnarvon
85
WESTE
Kalgoorlie
Boulder
PERTH
94
Fremantle
Esperance
Albany

STARTING OFF

In Australia you drive on the left. In order to drive you must hold a current licence and, preferably, an International Driving Permit. You may drive in Australia for a limited period such as a holiday on your own licence.

UK drivers who don't have the new Photocard licence may want to consider obtaining one, as photo-licences are the norm in Australia. For this reason an International Driving Permit (IDP), although not required by law, is recommended. You must carry your national licence, with the IDP if taken, when driving.

Front and back seat belts must be worn and small children must be seated in an approved child seat or restraint appropriate to their size and height. These can be hired from car rental companies, as they must meet the strict Australian standards.

The use of hand-held mobile (cell) phones is forbidden, whether on the move or stationary in traffic.

Many drivers in Australia habitually 'undertake' (overtake on the left on a freeway); there has been a campaign to persuade drivers to overtake only on the right.

Roundabouts are still a novelty in some areas, so do not assume

TIP
● UK visitors can obtain an International Driving Permit (IDP) by calling the AA on 08705 500600 or at **www.theAA.com**. Click on Travel & Leisure and then International Driving Permit.

that all drivers will give way to the right.

You must come to a complete stop at a STOP sign.

SPEED LIMITS

Rules of the Road and speed limits vary from state to state.

Make sure you know those that apply to the state you are in, as traffic police are exceedingly zealous and will pursue and prosecute offenders.

Speed limits are generally signed alongside roads, including freeways.

SPEED LIMITS	
ROAD	**LIMIT**
Cities and suburbs unless otherwise signed	50kph (31mph); 60kph (37mph) on major arterial roads
Near schools	40kph (23mph)
Suburban roads	up to 80kph (49mph)
Freeways	100kph (62mph) or 110kph (68mph); 80kph (49mph) on busier sections and near signals
Highways within built-up areas	up to 100kph (62mph)
Country roads	100kph (62mph)

Melville Island

Weipa

DARWIN

Groote
Eylandt

Wyndham

Port Douglas
Cairns

Normanton

Townsville

NORTHERN TERRITORY

Mount Isa

Mackay

Rockhampton

Longreach

Fraser Island

QUEENSLAND

Alice Springs

Charleville

Toowoomba

BRISBANE

Grafton

Coober Pedy

SOUTH AUSTRALIA

Broken
Hill

Port
Macquarie

Port
Augusta

**NEW SOUTH
WALES**

Newcastle

ADELAIDE

Wagga
Wagga

SYDNEY

Kangaroo
Island

CANBERRA

ACT

VICTORIA

Geelong

MELBOURNE

Mount Gambier

Warrnambool

Kings Island

Flinders Island

Launceston

Strahan

TASMANIA

HOBART

JSTRALIA

TIPS

- The speed limit for open roads is 110kph (68mph) in some states.
- In the Northern Territory there is no prescribed upper limit on open roads.
- New South Wales has different speed limits for Learner, Provisional and Unrestricted licence holders; in the Australian Capital Territory the speed limit is the same for all.
- Speed limits are lower for cars towing trailers and some other vehicles. Check with the motoring organisation in the state(s) you intend to visit.
- Roadside cameras are in use, and police frequently set up roadside 'speed traps'.

ALCOHOL LIMIT

The level of alcohol in the blood limit is 0.05, which means 50 milligrams per litre. The limit is enforced rigorously—especially in Victoria—with random breath tests at any time. On-the-spot fines are issued, payable within 28 days, or you may be required to make a court appearance.

For learners, provisional licence holders—P plates are compulsory for newly qualified drivers—and drivers under 25 who have held a licence for less than three years, the limit is zero: No alcohol at all may be consumed before driving.

ROAD ACCIDENTS

All road accidents involving injury or vehicle towing must be reported to the police at once, or within 24 hours. Your rental contract provides the procedures to follow after an accident.

In Western Australia all accidents must be reported if damage exceeds A$1,000, if drugs or alcohol are involved, or if there is any dispute.

DRIVING INTERSTATE

Regulations may change when you cross state boundaries. While road signs indicate an 'honour system', do not be surprised to find your vehicle being checked thoroughly for any fruit or vegetables, flowers and seeds, as these are not allowed to be taken from one state to another.

Information on how road rules differ from state to state is available from the National Road Transport Commission, **www.nrtc.gov.au**.

DRIVING WITH TRAMS

Special regulations apply in Melbourne when driving in streets where trams operate.
● No vehicle may overtake a stationary tram at a recognized tram stop, unless there are barriers between the tram and the road. You must stop level with the rear of the tram and wait for people to get on and off.
● Give way to trams moving into or across a roundabout.
● Do not pass on the right of a tram (unless tram tracks are at or near the far left side of the road).
● Buses travelling along the tram tracks must be treated as trams.
● Continuous yellow lines on the road give priority to trams at all times. You may cross a broken yellow line and drive on the tram tracks, but you must not pull out in front of or delay a tram.

PARKING

Signs indicate when and where parking is permitted. You must park pointing in the same direction as the flow of traffic. 'No Standing' means 'No Waiting'.

ABORIGINAL LAND

Apart from public roads, you need to obtain a transit permit to travel on other roads through Aboriginal land. You must not use tracks off the road for sightseeing. Aboriginal land, which is privately owned, is marked on road atlases. Further conditions about access are explained on application or are noted on the Land Council websites. A permit is also required to visit an Aboriginal community.

Central Region (area south of Tennant Creek)
Permits Officer
Central Land Council
31–33 Stuart Highway
PO Box 3321
Alice Springs, NT 0871
☎ 08 8951 6320
www.clc.org.au
🕐 Mon–Fri 8–noon, 2–4; closed public holidays

Northern NT Region
Permits Officer
Northern Land Council
9 Rowlings Street
PO Box 42921 Casuarina
Darwin NT 0811
☎ 08 8920 5178
www.nlc.org.au

Western Australia
Aboriginal Affairs Department
1st Floor Capita Centre

197 St. Georges Terrace
PO Box 7770
Perth WA 6850
☎ 08 9235 8000
www.aad.wa.gov.au

South Australia
Anangu Pitjantjatjaraku Yankunytjatjara Land Council
PMB Umuwa
via Alice Springs NT 0872
☎ 08 8950 1511

MAKING IT EASY—THE HOOK TURN

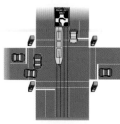
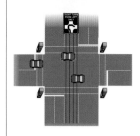

In Melbourne and Canberra, regulations stipulate when to make a hook turn at an intersection. In Melbourne, hook turn signs are found at some intersections: the signs may be at the side of the road or hung from wires. A driver turning right at an intersection with traffic lights and a hook turn sign must do as shown here:

1 Approach the intersection in the left lane
2 With a green light, move straight ahead to the far left corner of the intersection box and wait until traffic clears, and traffic lights change to green on the road you are entering
3 Complete the right turn and continue straight ahead.

In Melbourne a cyclist can make a hook turn at any intersection—not just at signed hook turn intersections. When turning right at an intersection in Canberra, cyclists have the option of making a hook turn, rather than a normal right turn. This may be safer on roads where there is heavy traffic.

www.path.unimelb.edu.au/~bernardk/victoria/melb/hook_turn.html

LOCAL/URBAN TRAVEL

Buses

A State Transit bus, Sydney

NEW SOUTH WALES

Sydney

Sydney Buses are run by State Transit, which also runs CityRail and Sydney Ferries (see pages 52, 54).

Tickets are available from ticket agents and from the Sydney Buses Ticket and Information Offices at Circular Quay and Wynyard. Pick up a bus information leaflet to check which 'sections' (zones) you need to travel, or see the zone maps displayed in bus and train stations.
Tel 13 15 00
www.131500.com.au

● You validate the magnetic stripe ticket when you board the bus, by dipping it in the green machine on board.
● When travelling with a companion, you can 'dip' your ticket the correct number of times to pay for that person.
● If you travel only occasionally on Sydney Buses, purchase a single fare from the driver.

Multiple Journeys

For multiple trips, there is a range of discount ticket options. Prices depend on sections travelled—each section is based on a nominal length of 1.6km (1 mile).

TravelPasses

TravelPasses are colour-coded according to price, with red covering the central section, and pink and purple the outer zones:

TravelPass	Weekly	Quarterly
Red	A$30	A$330
Pink	A$45	A$495
Purple	A$52	A$572

TravelPasses can be used on buses and trains too.

Sydney DayTripper

The DayTripper allows all-day travel on 'Blue and White' Sydney Buses, CityRail trains within the suburban area, and Sydney Ferries. You can buy tickets on the buses or at CityRail ticket offices or Sydney Ferries ticket outlets.
Tel 13 15 00
Fare: Adult A$13.00, child A$6.50

TravelTen

Available only from agents (usually newsagents/newsstand) displaying Sydney Buses Ticket Kiosk flag: tickets cover 10 journeys.

VICTORIA

The VicTrip website provides the latest information about Victoria's buses, trains and trams:
www.victrip.com.au.

MetCards not only save you time queuing to buy public transport tickets, but also money, depending on the number of zones to be travelled (1–3) and period of use (hourly to monthly): www.victrip.com.au/metcard.

Melbourne

Melbourne's integrated transport allows you to use tickets interchangeably on trains, trams or buses. Tickets are available at the outlets mentioned below. The exception is single fares or 'short journeys'.

Single Fares

A 'short trip' consists of up to two sections (several stops) on trams and buses within Zone 1. You purchase tickets from the driver; cost about A$1.70.

Multiple Journeys

The wide choice of Metcard ticket options must be pre-purchased from various outlets, including newsagents, chemists and coffee-bars—look for the blue Metcard Sales flag. Tickets can also be purchased at railway stations, including Spencer Street and Flinders Street. The vending machines at stations take notes, coins and debit cards. In addition, you can buy tickets at the Met Shop at Melbourne Town Hall, on the corner of Little Collins and Swanston streets.

You can also buy a Metcard over the phone by credit card: Tel 1800 652 313
🕐 Mon–Thu 8.30–6, Fri 8.30–9, Sat 9–1.

ON THE MOVE

TIPS

There are several ways to save money with a Metcard: a 10 x 2-hour Metcard gives ten trips for less than the price of nine.

Melbourne's free City Circle tram

Metcard unlimited travel within Zone 1

Daily Metcard	A$5.20
Weekly Metcard	A$22.90
Monthly Metcard	A$85.90

Melbourne Trams

The famous Melbourne trams are a symbol of the city, but it can be daunting to board one immediately upon arrival without knowing how the system works.

Don't bother watching the locals as most of them have Metcard tickets (see above) and may not be familiar with the onboard ticket machines.

● Trams warn of their approach by ringing a bell. They run down the centre of the road and you have to walk out to board them at the signed tram stops.

● They operate Mon–Sat 5am–midnight, Sun 8am–11pm, about every 10 minutes; more frequently on busy routes, less on quieter routes.

● It is important to know which tram route you need to take, and where you want to get off. Tram guides are displayed on the tram stops, or a map of the popular routes is available from the Met Shop at Melbourne Town Hall. If in doubt, ask the driver to let you know when you reach your destination.

● For short journeys, buy a ticket on board: Get on and then move to the centre of the tram and select the 'Short Trip' buttons on the machine (don't try to select the Zone as well). Cost for a short journey is about A$1.80. These tickets are automatically validated for that trip—other tickets, which can be purchased in advance, must be validated on board. The machines take coins only.

● If you are going to use the trams frequently, it is more economical to buy a Metcard. For information on Metcards, see Buses above. Tickets can be ordered by phone on 1800 652 313, as for buses.

City Circle Trams

Several old maroon-and-cream trams have been renovated to provide the free—yes, there is no charge—City Circle tram service that tours the perimeter of the city-centre grid. An excellent way to see the city on a rainy or a too-hot day.

Park and Tram

For vehicle drivers, park at either of the secure car parks at the Telstra Dome or Melbourne Museum, buy a Park and Ride ticket from the car park

---

TIP

● If you have mobility difficulties, there is a tall step up to board the old City Circle trams. The newer types on the other routes are more easily accessible.

attendant, then catch a tram. You can use as many trams as you like within the day (validating your ticket each time you board). There are 600 parking spaces.
Tel 13 16 38
www.yarratrams.com.au
🅿 Parking Mon–Fri 7–7
Fare: A$8.50

AUSTRALIAN CAPITAL TERRITORY

The Action Bus is the key to travelling around Canberra, whether for work or sightseeing. Routes range around the four bus interchanges: City, Woden, Tuggeranong and Belconnen. Catch a bus from any other stop on the routes by signalling the driver.

Timetables are available from the bus interchanges, newsagents, 'Canberra Connect' Shopfronts, the Canberra Visitor Centre, or the website. Tickets can be purchased from the driver or from the above locations.
Tel 13 17 10
www.action.act.gov.au

GRAY LINE
Explorer
1300 85 86 87

Tour
Melbourne
City Sightseeing
Melbourne's Tourist Bus Service
STOP No.
Phone: (03)9376 6900

TIP

● A 'shopper's off-peak daily' ticket represents good value at A$3.50. Use Mon–Fri 9–4.30 and after 6, Sat–Sun and public holidays all day. For senior citizens the price falls to only A$1.30.

Single journey (purchase from driver)	A$2.40
Multiple journeys (pre-purchased tickets)	
Daily	A$6.00
Faresaver 10	A$21.00
Weekly	A$23.50
Monthly	A$80.50

WESTERN AUSTRALIA

Perth

Perth's buses are operated by Transperth. The city's integrated transport system means that tickets can be used on trains, buses and ferries. Two types of ticket are available: cash tickets and Multiriders. Buses run Mon–Fri 6am–11.30pm; reduced services Sat–Sun and public holidays.
Tel 13 62 13
public.transperth.wa.gov.au

Cash Tickets

Buy a cash ticket from the bus driver when you start your journey.

Multirider Tickets

These must be bought in advance, from newsagents or from the Transperth InfoCentres at: Perth City Busport, Mounts Bay Road; Plaza Arcade, between Murray and Hay streets; Wellington Street Bus Station; Perth Railway Station, 376 Wellington Street.

For sample fares, see 'Trains', page 53

CAT

Transperth's Central Area Transit (CAT) system operates frequent free buses around Perth and Fremantle.

A local Sunshine Coast bus, Queensland

● Look out for the Black Cat logo.
● There are Blue, Red and Yellow CAT routes for Perth, and Orange for Fremantle.
● Colour-coded bus stops tell you which CAT to board, and lighted displays tell you when the next bus is due.
● The CAT system is accessible for wheelchair users.

SOUTH AUSTRALIA

Adelaide

Adelaide's bus and tram services are provided by Transadelaide, which also run the trains (see page 53). Transadelaide tickets are of three types: Singletrip, Multitrip and Daytrip.
Tel 08 8218 1000
www.transadelaide.com.au

Singletrip

A Singletrip ticket pays for one journey. A Zone Singletrip ticket allows you to travel anywhere on the transport system within a 2-hour period. Buy these on board the tram.

Multitrip

A Multitrip ticket must be bought in advance; the ticket gives you 10 trips for about the price of seven. Tickets can be bought at a range of outlets including newsagents and convenience stores displaying the Metroticket sign; selected post offices and

post office agencies; Adelaide Railway Station; the Passenger Transport Information centre, corner King William and Corrie streets.

Daytrip

Daytrip tickets can be bought either in advance or on board the trams. As the name suggests, the ticket allows you to travel throughout the city for a whole day. At weekends and public holidays you can take two children under 15 free on your adult ticket.

Sample fares

Single trip (short journey)	A$1.80
Multitrip (short journey)	A$8.60
Daytrip	A$6.00

Free Bus Service

The free Bee Line bus service (No. 99b) runs in a loop from Victoria Square via King William Street and North Terrace.
● Frequent service from 8am (starts later Sat–Sun)
● Board at any stop on the route—look for the bee symbol.

QUEENSLAND

Brisbane

Brisbane's integrated transport system of buses, trains and ferries incorporates the services of some private operators who match their fares to those of Brisbane Transport.
Tel 13 12 30
www.transinfo.qld.gov.au

● Tickets are obtainable from bus and ferry drivers and from agents ('ticket resellers')—the majority of agents are provided by newsagents.
● The TransInfo website Journey Planner works out routes, fares and timetables. Transport route maps are also available on the website, including one showing Brisbane's five fare zones.

Sample fares (for one zone)

Single	A$1.80
10 Trip Saver	A$13.80
Day Rover	A$8.40

ON THE MOVE

Brisbane Loop

This two-way circular downtown route stops either way beside the Brisbane River at Wharf Street, Riverside. Eagle Street Pier and Stamford Plaza.

The clockwise service then goes from Stamford Plaza via Alice Street (Botanic Gardens), George Street (Government Precinct, Queen Street Mall) and Adelaide Street (City Hall, Central Station).

The counter-clockwise goes from Wharf Street via Ann Street (Central Station, City Hall), William Street (Queen Street Mall, Government Precinct), and Margaret Street (Botanic Gardens).

● An excellent map is at www.transinfo.qld.gov.au/TransInfoMaps

TASMANIA

Bus services In Burnie, Hobart and Launceston are run by Metro.

The main bus mall for Hobart is in Franklin Square, right by the main post office. Buses run every 15–30 minutes on major routes, and maps and timetables are on the website.
Tel 13 22 01
www.metrotas.com.au

● Buy single trip and daily off-peak tickets from the bus driver.
● Discounted Ten Trip or Ten Day tickets are bought from most newsagents, some convenience stores, or the post office at Macquarie Street, Hobart. Passengers validate their ticket each time they board the bus at the validating machine next to the driver; the machine will return your ticket with the travel details and a display shows how many trips or days are left on the ticket. The driver can help with any difficulties.
Tel 1800 654 184

● Wheelchair-accessible buses on some routes.

Urban Trains

Sydney

Metropolitan trains are operated by CityRail, which also runs day trips to tourist destinations such as the Blue Mountains and Newcastle. Trains from the airport arrive at Central Station.
Tel 13 15 00
www.131500.com.au

● There are eight stations in the city centre: Central, Town Hall, Wynyard, Circular Quay, St. James, Museum, Martin Place and Kings Cross. If you ask for a ticket to the city, your ticket allows you to get off at any one of them. You can also return from any station in the city with a return ticket.
● Trains run every 2–3 minutes in both directions on the City Circle line to Central, Town Hall, Wynyard, Circular Quay and Museum stations. Trains to the suburbs and the airport station run every 10 minutes at peak times and every 15 at other times. Single, return and off-peak return tickets are available.
● The 131500.com.au website includes all timetables, a full list of facilities at each station, and a fare calculator showing all fares and concessions for all destinations on the network.

Sample fares for short journey
Single
Adult A$2.80   Child A$1.40
Return
Adult A$5.60   Child A$2.80
Off-peak return
Adult A$3.40   Child A$2.30

Sydney Monorail

The monorail follows a loop route through the city to Darling Harbour, Powerhouse Museum, and back.
Tel 02 8584 5288

● Runs every few minutes Mon–Thu 7am–10pm, Fri–Sat 7am–midnight; Sun 8am–10pm.
● One fare for all journeys–A$4.
● City stop on the corner of Pitt and Market streets.

A timetable for Sydney's tram

● The widely available free Visitor Guide includes a route map.

Light Rail

A tram runs from Central Station to Darling Harbour, calling at several stops including the Casino, the Convention Centre and the Fish Market.
Tel 02 8584 5288

● The circuit takes about 15 minutes.
● Prices vary according to zones: a full fare return is A$5.

Melbourne

The main stations in Melbourne

TIPS
- Perth's DayRider ticket gives unlimited all-day travel on all Transperth services Mon–Fri after 9am, Sat–Sun and public holidays all day.
- If you are sightseeing only in Perth city centre, travel on any Transperth service is free at all times within the Free Transit Zone in the Perth Central Business District (CBD).

are Flinders Street, serving local metropolitan lines, and Spencer Street, for country and interstate travel.

The metropolitan lines are operated by M-Train and Connex. VicTrip timetable info:

Sign for a Melbourne city station

tel 131 638 (daily 6am–10pm)
Connex customer line: tel 1800 800 705 (daily 6am–10pm)

M-Train:
www.movingmelbourne.com.au
Connex:
www.connexmelbourne.com.au

- Fares are divided into zones, as for trams (see page 50), and tickets may be bought at the same outlets.
- Route maps are in the widely available free Visitors' Guide.

A Sydney tram at Central Station

Sample Metcard fares
2-hour Zone 1
Adult A$2.70   Child A$1.50
2-hour Zone 2/3
Adult A$3.80   Child A$2.00
2-hour all zones
Adult A$6.30   Child A$3.20

V/Line
V/Line trains go from Melbourne to Geelong, Ballarat, Bendigo, Echuca, Seymour, Wodonga, Traralgon and Sale. In the metro area V/Line trains connect with some of the outer stations of Zone 2. A train network map is on the V/Line website.
Tel 13 61 96
www.vlinepassenger.com.au

Perth
Transperth trains run from the main station on Wellington Street to Fremantle—a 30-minute journey including stops. Other lines run north to Joondalup, east to Guildford and Midland, and south to Armadale.
Tel 13 62 13
www.transperth.wa.gov.au

- Buy tickets on the platform from machines (coins—change given). The cost depends on zones travelled. Tickets are valid for 1.5 hours (2 hours from zones 5–8) and can also be used on Transperth buses and ferries. Route maps are in the

widely available free Visitors' Guide.
- A MultiRider 10 ticket gives you 10 trips at a saving of 15 per cent on the cash fare. A MultiRider 40 ticket gives 40 trips, saving 25 per cent on the cash fare. Available from Transperth Infocentres at the main bus and train stations in Wellington Street and at Plaza Arcade, and most newsagents.

Sample adult fares

	1 zone	2 zones
Cash	A$2.00	A$3.00
MultiRider 10	A$17.00	A$25.50
MultiRider 40	A$60.00	A$90.00
DayRider	A$7.50	N/A

Adelaide
Trains and trams in the metro area are operated by TransAdelaide.
Tel 08 8218 2362
www.transadelaide.sa.gov.au

Brisbane
Train services in the city are operated by Queensland Rail Citytrain.
Tel 13 12 30
www.qr.com.au

Canberra
There are no local train services in Canberra; visitors use the buses (see page 50) or rent a vehicle.

Ferries

Sydney
Ferries depart from the wharves at Circular Quay, where signs and notice boards indicate services to Manly Beach, Darling Harbour, Watsons Bay, Rose Bay, Double Bay, the North Shore and Balmain.

Tickets are obtained from the Sydney Ferries booking offices on wharves 2, 3, 4 and 5, from information offices, and from local newsagents. Tickets can also be used on buses and trains.

TIP
● The SydneyPass inclusive sightseeing ticket allows unlimited travel on: All regular bus, ferry and train services Harboursights cruises Sydney and Bondi Explorer buses It is available from ferry ticket offices, and visitor information centres.

Sydney Ferries
Tel 131 500
www.sydneyferries.nsw.gov.au

Matilda Cruises Rocket Harbour Express
Aquarium Wharf
Pier 26, Darling Harbour
Tel 02 9264 7377
www.matilda.com.au

● Darling Harbour (Aquarium)–Circular Quay–Opera House–Watsons Bay–Taronga Zoo–Darling Harbour (Harbourside)
● Mon–Sun 8.30–7.30
● Buy tickets on board

Melbourne
Ferries run half-hourly from St. Kilda to Williamstown, and from Southgate to Williamstown featuring a cruise along the Yarra. Buy tickets on board.
Tel 03 9506 4144
Ferries run on the hour between Queenscliff Harbour

and Sorrento Pier, daily 7–6.
Tel 03 5258 3244
www.searoad.com.au

Adelaide
Ferries to Kangaroo Island are run by Kangaroo Island SeaLink. The ferry departs from Cape Jervis daily at 9am and 6pm; also at noon, 3pm and 9pm when there is sufficient demand.
SeaLink office
440 King William Street
Adelaide
Tel 08 8202 8666 or 13 13 01
www.sealink.com.au
Sample fares
Adult one way	A$32
Adult return	A$64
Passenger vehicle return	A$138
Journey time 45 minutes.

Brisbane
Brisbane Transport operates the ferries that ply across and along the Brisbane River.

The Inner City Ferry Service and the Cross River Ferry Service cross the central section of the river between North Quay and Mowbray Park.

CityCats operate between the University of Queensland (St. Lucia) and Bretts Wharf (Hamilton).

For timetables, routes and fares: tel 13 20 30; 07 3403 8888
www.transinfo.qld.gov.au

Perth
Transperth ferries operate between Barrack Street jetty (near Swan River Bell Tower) and Mends Street jetty in South Perth

(near Perth Zoo); daily 6.45am–7.15pm (also Fri–Sat 7.15–9.15pm in summer)
Tel 13 62 13
public.transperth.wa.gov.au

Rottnest Ferry
Ferries operate to Rottest Island from Perth (Barrack Street jetty), Hillarys Boat Harbour north of the city, or Fremantle.

Ferries from Hillarys daily 8.30, 10.30 and 3 (also Friday 6pm).
Hillarys Fast Ferries
Tel 08 9246 1039
www.hillarysfastferries.com.au
Sample return fares
From Perth, Adult	A$55
From Fremantle, Adult	A$30

Tasmania
Apart from air travel, the major link to Tasmania is the Bass Strait Ferry Service. Two large roll-on-roll-off vehicle ships operate between Melbourne and the East Devonport terminal, across the river from the town centre.

Accommodation options range from family cabins down to a lounge seat. Fares are from A$115 (one way, seat, no cabin). Crossings are every night at 9pm (journey time 10 hours), and days (9am) from 20 Dec–18 Jan, and on weekends until 25 Apr. Cars are carried free in the summer peak period.
Reservations: tel 1800 634 906.
www.spiritoftasmania.com.au
Ferries also run from Sydney to Devonport; fares from A$230.

Daintree River ferry, Queensland

Cycling in Australia

Road traffic is generally light in many parts of Australia, which makes cycling an ideal way to go sightseeing. Most cities have dedicated cycleways, and there are routes in the surrounding countryside and the national parks—families are frequently seen out cycling together. However, there are always risks from other traffic and you must observe all safety regulations that apply to the state you are visiting.

Beyond the cities there is much fine touring country, but only the very experienced should venture into the dry centre by bicycle, and all safety and survival precautions must be taken, together with extensive forward planning.

BICYCLE HELMETS

Bicycle helmets are compulsory for both children and adults; they must conform to approved designs and fit correctly. Bicycle dealers and hire companies can give advice. Local bicycle dealers can be found in the Yellow Pages: www.yellowpages.com.au.

CYCLE WEBSITES

www.bicycles.net.au
Lists of all bicycle shops, clubs and organizations, plus a calendar of events. There are links to tour operators in Australia who cater for cyclists.
www.bikesa.asn.au
Good list of South Australian and national links.
www.pedalpower.org.au
Represents Pedal Power ACT Inc, an Australian Capital Territory cycling organization, but there are links to tours throughout all the states.

NEW SOUTH WALES
Sydney

There are cycling maps of Sydney at www.rta.nsw.gov.au. The ongoing Bikeplan 2010 project is creating a series of bicycle routes across New South Wales.

AUSTRALIAN CAPITAL TERRITORY
Canberra

Except in the rush hour, Canberra's roads are not too busy and cycling is a good way to cover the distance between the city and the attractions around Lake Burley Griffin.
● Cyclists are permitted to ride two abreast—a third may overtake two abreast.

● When turning right at an intersection a hook turn (see page 48) may be safer on roads where there is heavy traffic.
● A leaflet, *Enjoy Safe Cycling in the ACT,* is available from the Government Shop Front and other outlets: tel 13 22 81, **www**.canberraconnect.act.gov.au.

VICTORIA
Melbourne

Where to ride information and bicycle maps are available at www.vicroads.vic.gov.au. Look for the Rail Trails link: Nearly 300km (186 miles) of disused railway lines across Victoria have been turned into recreational routes.

QUEENSLAND
Brisbane

Brisbane City Council promotes cycling as a means of transport and exercise: there are 500km (310 miles) of city 'bikeways', with 1,200km (744 miles) more in development. Download maps of the bikeway network from www.ourbrisbane.com, under the website's Transport tab.

NORTHERN TERRITORY
Alice Springs

Alice Springs has some 25km (15.5 miles) of paved bicycle track. A map of the bicycle network is available from the Town Council offices or www.alicesprings.nt.gov.au.

SOUTH AUSTRALIA
Adelaide

The city's wide roads and flat terrain make it ideal for cycling. There are also the popular parklands encircling the city. Torrens Linear Park has bicycle trails linking the city to the sea and the Adelaide Hills; Linear Park Bike Hire, Elder Park (adjacent to Torrens Lake).

A set of eight BikeDirect maps covers the Adelaide area from Gawlor in the north to Willunga in the south, showing bicycle routes and lanes. These are available free from good bicycle shops, or tel 08 8343 2911, or download from www.bisa.asn.au.

WESTERN AUSTRALIA
Perth

Bicycle tracks run alongside most city and suburban roads, and also throughout King's Park (see page 149) and all along the Swan River frontage. Bicycles can be hired at points along the river, in King's Park, and most importantly on Rottnest (see page 152), where vehicles are banned. Maps of Perth's bicycle network are available from the Bicycle Transportation Alliance: tel 08 9420 7210, www.multiline.com.au/~bta
● The 42km (26-mile) cycleway that runs along both sides of the river from Perth to Fremantle is the longest in Australia. www.dp.wa.gov.au

TASMANIA
Hobart

Tasmania is a rewarding place to cycle although most towns are quite hilly. Traffic is light and cyclists are permitted to ride two abreast on roads. Bicycle hire is hard to find outside of organized tours; enquire at bicycle shops.

Hobart has a bicycle track from the Cenotaph by the Domain to Glenorchy (city to northern suburbs). In Devonport a track goes along the Mersey River, past the Bluff to the Don River.

ON THE MOVE WITH A DISABILITY

Access for people with disabilities in Australia has improved significantly in recent years and remains a priority. Hotels, airlines, tourist attractions and transport carriers usually provide access facilities. Always check in advance whether your particular need can be met at the site you plan to visit.

ACROD

The head office of the National Industry Association for Disability Services (ACROD) is in Canberra, but each state has an individual office. All state offices are listed on www.acrod.org.au.

HELPFUL WEBSITES

www.youreable.com
The Travel tab has good checklists for travellers.
www.accessibledownunder.co.uk
The UK travel agency specializes in accessible holidays.
www.nican.com.au
The Australian federal-funded website has a database of links with information on recreation, tourism, sport and the arts, and transport and public services.

DRIVING
Car Rental

There are few suitable vehicles available for rent for people with disabilities, so drivers should bring their own hand-held controls and have them adjusted for a standard vehicle on arrival. State paraplegic and quadriplegic groups can assist with the fitting of controls, or can direct you to an approved service. Contact vehicle rental firms in advance to explain your requirements.
● Disability Hire Vehicles specializes in vehicle hire for the independent disabled traveller:
49 Hession Road, Oakville, Sydney, NSW 2765
Tel 02 4573 6788, 02 4572 7424
www.disabilityhire.com.au

Parking

Reciprocal disabled parking rights exist for overseas visitors for up to three months. For information, contact ACROD (above).

SYDNEY

● www.cityofsydney.nsw.gov.au includes an access guide to public toilets, ATMs, buses, train stations, taxi ranks and parking.
● All taxi firms have vehicles that can accommodate wheelchairs.
Tel 02 8332 0200
● Ferries, trains and some buses have lifts and ramps.
Tel 13 15 00
● The Australian Quadriplegic Association (AQA) produces a guide, Access Sydney.
Tel 02 9661 8855

MELBOURNE

● TADAS provides equipment and facilities, and computers for visitors to access information: Travellers Aid Disability Access Service, Level 2, 169 Swanston Street, Melbourne, VIC 3000 (lifts via alcove two shops south of Bourke Street Mall)
Tel 03 9654 7690; 03 9654 5412 (telephone typewriter)
www.vicnet.net.au/~tadas
● The Victorian Government is working to make all trains, trams and buses fully accessible for all users. A first step is the Tram 109 project, creating 'Superstops' with raised platforms to fill the gap between the door and platform.

CANBERRA

● Information for visitors with mobility, visual and hearing impairments is available from: Canberra Visitor Centre 330 Northbourne Avenue, Dickson, ACT 2601
Tel 1300 554 114
www.visitcanberra.com.au

PERTH

● All buses on CAT routes and Circle routes in the city are accessible, as are buses displaying a blue wheelchair symbol. A special taxi service for wheelchair users is available daily 24 hours. Book 24 hours in advance: tel 08 9333 337.
● To hire a wheelchair, or an electric scooter, contact the Australian Red Cross on 08 9325 1463, or the Independent Living Centre on 08 9382 2011.

BRISBANE

● The Access Brisbane website has a searchable database of accessible facilities in the city: www.brisbanestories.powerup.com.au
● www.accessiblequeensland.com is a general directory of accessible sites in Queensland.

ADELAIDE

● Adelaide claims its has the nation's highest percentage of accessible buses and taxis within each fleet. The yellow free buses, the Bee Line (see page 51), have special ramps and low floors. Bus and taxi details are described at www.service.sa.gov.au.
● Access Cabs
Tel 1300 551 156
● Units at bus interchanges, stations and major stops provide timetable and route information featuring Braille, engraved signs and push-button recorded details.

TASMANIA

● Information is available from: Department of Health and Human Services, GPO Box 125B, Hobart, TAS 7001
Tel 1800 067 415, 03 6233 3185
www.dhhs.tas.gov.au/disability/services/index.html
● Taxi companies in each city have disabled access vehicles: Hobart and Southern Maxi Taxis
Tel 03 6227 9577
Taxi Combined (Devonport)
Tel 03 6424 1431
Maxi Taxi (Launceston)
Tel 03 6344 4205

This chapter is divided into the seven states of Australia. Places of interest in each capital city are listed alphabetically, followed by the remaining sights within each state. Major sights are listed at the front of each section. For maps showing all the sights turn to the atlas on pages 315–331.

The Sights

NEW SOUTH WALES AND ACT

Although New South Wales covers only one tenth of the country, it's Australia's most populous state. The capital, Sydney, is known for its sparkling harbour and iconic structures. Australian Capital Territory and the nation's capital city, Canberra, lie on the hills of the Great Divide 248km (155 miles) to the southwest of Sydney.

KEY SIGHTS

Sculpture in the grounds of the Art Gallery of New South Wales

The lightship Carpentaria outside the National Maritime Museum

Enjoying the weekend sun at Bondi Beach

SYDNEY

ART GALLERY OF NEW SOUTH WALES

➕ 61 C3 • Art Gallery Road, The Domain ☎ 02 9225 1744 (enquiries); 02 9225 1790 ('What's-on Line') 🕐 Daily 10–5 (also Wed 5–9pm) 💲 Free; charge for exhibitions 🚌 441 from Queen Victoria Building; Sydney Explorer bus (stop 6) 🍴 🛍 ♿ www.artgallery.nsw.gov.au

The state's premier art gallery is one of Australia's very best. There is an excellent collection of Australian, Aboriginal, Asian, American and European paintings, sculptures, photographs, prints, drawings and other works of art. Some of the best examples of 19th- and 20th-century Australian art are here, including works by Tom Roberts, Arthur Streeton, Hans Heysen, Elioth Gruner, Rupert Bunny, Norman Lindsay, Sidney Nolan, John Olsen and Brett Whiteley. If you're short of time, join the free guided tour to avoid missing the highlights.
Don't miss The Yiribana Gallery has a good collection of Aboriginal and Torres Strait Islander art. Also Aboriginal song or dance or didgeridoo performances Tuesday through to Saturday at noon.

AUSTRALIAN MUSEUM

➕ 61 C4 • 6 College Street ☎ 02 9320 6000 🕐 Daily 9.30–5 💲 Adult A$8, child (5–15) A$3, under 5s free 🚇 Museum (City Circle Line) 🚌 Sydney Explorer bus (stop 7) 🍴 🛍 ♿ www.amonline.net.au

Don't be put off by the Victorian classical façade and the old-fashioned glass-case displays in some of the galleries: This is an excellent museum of humankind and natural history. It's a particularly good place to discover Aboriginal culture, as well as Australia's ecology, and unique plant and animal life. Hands-on displays and insect costumes for dressing up in are among the attractions for children. A self-guided 1-hour tour points out the best features.
Don't miss The Chapman Mineral Collection has more than 850 mineral specimens—one of the best collections in the world.

AUSTRALIAN NATIONAL MARITIME MUSEUM

➕ 60 A3 • 2 Murray Street, Darling Harbour ☎ 02 9298 3777 🕐 Daily 9.30–5 (also 5–6pm in Jan) 💲 Adult A$10 (+ A$4; Big Ticket A$20); child (5–15) A$6 (+ A$1; Big Ticket A$10). Prices in brackets are for admission to HMAS Vampire or the James Craig tall ship. The Big Ticket includes admission to the Vampire, James Craig and Onslow, as well as an audio guide 🚌 443 from the city 🚝 Metro Monorail to Harbourside 🚢 From Circular Quay to Aquarium Wharf 🛍 ♿ www.anmm.gov.au

The ANMM is one of Australia's best museums—a must. There are ships and boats moored at the museum's wharves, including the restored 1874 tall ship, James Craig. Themed galleries focus on indigenous people and the ocean, migration by sea, the Navy, and the discovery of Australia by the great navigators such as James Cook (1728–79). The USA Gallery illustrates the shared maritime heritage of Australia and the US.
Don't miss Touring HMAS Onslow, a retired submarine.

Steady, steady—a surfing lesson at Bondi

BONDI BEACH

➕ 331 W14 ℹ️ Leaflets available at the Bondi Pavilion, beachfront; Sydney Visitor Centre, 106 George Street, The Rocks, tel 02 9240 8788 🚇 Bondi Junction 2km (1.2 miles); frequent bus services to the beach www.sydneyvisitorcentre.com.au; www.waverley.nsw.gov.au

'Bondi' is believed to derive from an Aboriginal word meaning 'the sound of tumbling waters'. Visitors to Australia's most famous beach—a 1km (0.6-mile) curved strip of golden sand between two rocky headlands—are keen to walk along its promenade, take a dip or even try surfing. But popularity makes the beach very crowded in summer, and beach- and cliffside walks in winter may be preferable.

The area has a large selection of cafés, restaurants, pubs and bars. Bondi is also the venue for many festivals and sporting events, including surf carnivals, iron-man/woman contests, a lively South American festival and Sculpture by the Sea.
Don't miss The Bondi to Bronte Walk is a scenic 3.5km (2-mile) cliffside track; the beach at Bronte is popular with families.

ELIZABETH BAY HOUSE

➕ 61 D3 • 7 Onslow Avenue, Elizabeth Bay, NSW 2011 ☎ 02 9356 3022 🕐 Tue–Sun 10–4.30; closed Mon (except public holidays) 💲 Adult A$7, child A$3, under 5s free 🚇 Kings Cross (Eastern

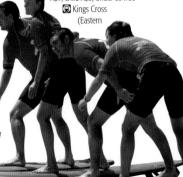

This splendid staircase is at Elizabeth Bay House

Hyde Park Barracks was designed by Francis Greenway

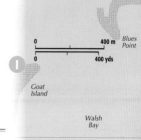

Suburbs line) 🚌 311 from Circular Quay, the city, or Kings Cross ❓ Historic Houses Trust Ticket Through Time gives admission to the Trust's 11 museums/historic houses; adult A$23, child A$10 www.hht.nsw.gov.au

In its heyday this sandstone Greek-revival style villa was known as the finest house in the colony, its grounds originally stretching down to the harbour, and it remains one of Sydney's best examples of colonial architecture. It was built in 1835–39 for Alexander Macleay, the Colonial Secretary of New South Wales, and his family, after their arrival from England in 1826.

A video in the cellar explains the history of the building. Six rooms are open on the ground floor and an upper level includes bedrooms and a morning room, all furnished in period style. **Don't miss** There are excellent views of the harbour from McElhone Park in front of the house, a survivor of the former grounds.

HYDE PARK BARRACKS MUSEUM & HYDE PARK

➕ 61 C3/C4 • Hyde Park Barracks Museum, Queens Square, Macquarie Street ☎ 02 9223 8922 🕐 Museum: daily 9.30–5; park: daily 24 hours 💲 Museum: adult A$7, child A$3, under 5s free; park: free 🚇 St. James (City Circle line) 🚌 Sydney Explorer bus (stop 4) 🅿 Museum and park 🏛 www.hht.nsw.gov.au

The attractive three-storey Barracks is one of Sydney's oldest buildings, built by convicts in 1817–19. It was designed by the ex-convict Francis Greenway, the architect of many of Sydney's most attractive Georgian buildings. The former prison now contains a museum of convict and early

settler history. The galleries feature archaeological objects found on the site and stories of the former inhabitants. The Greenway Gallery hosts changing exhibitions on Australia's convict and penal colony history.

Just south of the museum, Hyde Park is the city's largest green area, with its formal gardens, tree-shaded seating, fountains and statues. The area was declared public land as early as 1792 and it has been an official park since 1810. **Don't miss** Walk to the moving art-deco Anzac War Memorial at the southern end of the park.

KOALA PARK SANCTUARY

➕ 331 W14 • 84 Castle Hill Road, West Pennant Hills, NSW 2125 ☎ 02 9484 3141 🕐 Daily 9–5 💲 Adult A$17, child (4–14) A$8, under 4s free 🚉 Pennant Hills, then private bus service (Glenorie Buses) to the park 🅿 🏛 🚌 25km (15.5 miles) northeast of the city via the Hills Motorway (Metroad 2) www.koalapark.com

The sanctuary, 4.1ha (10 acres) of rainforest, eucalypt forest and gardens, is not just for koala fans. Other native animals include kangaroos, wallabies, wombats, dingoes, emus, echidnas, possums, cockatoos and kookaburras. You can feed kangaroos, pat dingoes and cuddle koalas. There are also shows involving koalas (*daily 10.20, 11.45, 2*), wombats (*daily 2*), and sheep shearing (*Thu–Mon 10.30, 2.30*).

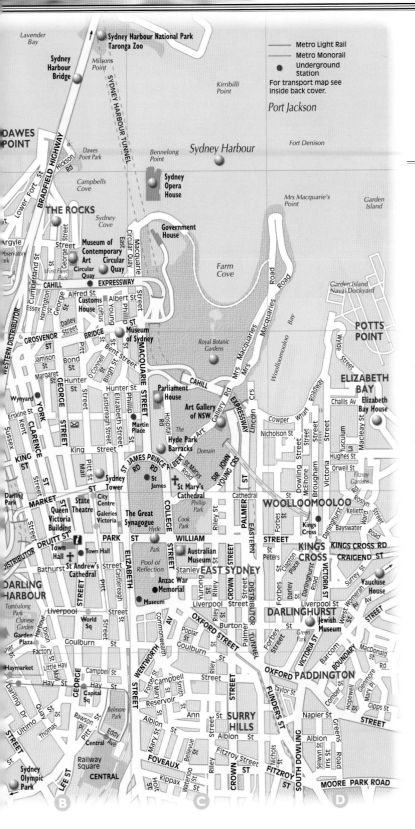

Lavender
Bay

Sydney Harbour National Park
Taronga Zoo

Sydney
Harbour
Bridge

Milsons
Point

Kirribilli
Point

Metro Light Rail
Metro Monorail
Underground
Station
For transport map see
inside back cover.

Port Jackson

DAWES
POINT

Dawes
Point Park

Campbells
Cove

Bennelong
Point

Sydney Harbour

Fort Denison

Sydney
Opera
House

THE ROCKS

Sydney
Cove

Government
House

Mrs Macquarie's
Point

Garden
Island

Museum of
Contemporary
Art
Circular
Quay

Circular Quay

Circular
Quay

Farm
Cove

Macquarie

CAHILL   EXPRESSWAY

Alfred St
Customs
House

Albert Street

Macquaries

Road

Road

Garden Island
Naval Dockyard

Museum
of Sydney

Royal Botanic
Gardens

Woolloomooloo
Bay

POTTS
POINT

GROSVENOR
ST

Jamison
St

Margaret
St

Hunter St

Bond
St

Hunter St

Phillip
ST

St Julia

Bent St

Bridge

O'Connell St

MACQUARIE STREET

Elizabeth Street

Castlereagh Street

Phillip Street

Parliament
House

CAHILL

Mrs

Mrs

Macquaries

Macquaries

Rd

Crs

EXPRESSWAY

Lincoln

ELIZABETH
BAY

Challis Av   Elizabeth
Bay House

Wynyard

YORK

CLARENCE

Erskine St

Kent

Art Gallery
of NSW

Gallery

Cowper

Nicholson St

Wharf

Rd

Tusculum

Maclean St

Martin
Place

King
Street

Hospital

The
Hyde Park
Barracks

Domain

Art

Street

Dowling

McElhone

Broughm

Victoria

St

Hughes St

Orwell St

Fitzroy
Gardens

KING
ST

Sussex

ST

Pitt St
Mall

King
Street

ST JAMES

PRINCE
RD

ALBERT St

St Mary's
Road

Cathedral

PALMER

SIR JOHN
YOUNG CRS

EASTERN

Lincoln

Cathedral

Street

Street

WOOLLOOMOOLOO

Roslyn

St

Cowper

Nicholson St

Darling
Park

Sydney
Tower

City
Centre
Galeries
Victoria

RD

St
James

St Mary's
Cathedral

Phillip
Park

Cook
Park

Kellett

Forbes

Kings
Cross

Darlinghurst

Bayswater

MARKET

State
Theatre

The Great
Synagogue

Hyde

PARK   ST

WILLIAM

Riley

St

St
Peters

COLLEGE

KINGS
CROSS

KINGS CROSS RD

Queen
Victoria
Building

DRUITT ST

Town
Hall

Park
Pool of
Reflection

Australian
Museum

Stanley

EAST SYDNEY

Clapton
Place

Darlinghurst

Road

Victoria

St

CRAIGEND ST

DARLING
HARBOUR

St Andrew's
Cathedral

Bathurst

Street

Castlereagh

ELIZABETH

Anzac War
Memorial

Museum

Yurong

Riley

Crown

Liverpool

Street

Street

Forbes

Darley

Liverpool St

Darlinghurst

West Womerah

Av

Surrey

St

Vaucluse
House

STREET

Tumbalong
Park

Chinese
Garden

Liverpool

World
Sq

Street

Goulburn

Poplar
St

Goulburn

Burton

Palmer

DISTRIBUTOR

TUNNEL

DARLINGHURST

Jewish
Museum

Green
Park

Victoria St

Barcom

STREET

Garden
Plaza

Factory

Campbell St

Commonwealth

Wentworth

Foster

Campbell

Smith

Riley

Street

OXFORD STREET

OXFORD

PADDINGTON

MacDonald
St

Rd

Hopewell

Glenmore

Mary Pl

Gipps St

Haymarket

Little Hay

Hay   St

GEORGE

Hay

Capital
Sq

Reservoir

Mary

Ann

St

St

SURRY
HILLS

Flinders

St

Taylor St

Comber St

Boundary

Paddington

STREET

Ultimo

Darling Dr

Quay

Thomas

Rawson
Pl

Pitt

Belmore
Park

Albion

St

Bellevue

St

Eddy
Ave

Albion   St

Fitzroy Street

Nichols

St

Crown

ST

Albion

St

Selwyn St

Iris St

Road

Haymarket

STREET

LEE ST

Railway
Square

Central

FOVEAUX

Kippax

Waterloo

Holt

St

FITZROY
ST

SOUTH DOWLING

MOORE PARK ROAD

Sydney
Olympic
Park

CENTRAL

B   C   D

The Chinese Garden of Friendship has a dramatic cityscape backdrop

RATINGS	
Good for kids	● ● ● ○
Shopping	● ● ● ○
Walkability	● ● ● ○

TIP
If you are planning to see most of Darling Harbour, start early in the day as there is lots to see and do.

BASICS
✚ 61 B4
ℹ Sydney Visitor Centre • Darling Harbour, tel 02 9281 0788; Darling Harbour Infoline (information on events and festivals) 1902 260 568, www.sydneyvisitorcentre.com.au
Ⓜ Town Hall (City Circle line) www.darlingharbour.com • Easy access to attractions, dining and shopping pages–or just getting around.

DARLING HARBOUR

Sydney's most popular entertainment precinct is the scene of major festivals and events, with restaurants, cafés, bars, nightclubs and shops galore.

Opened in 1988 for Australia's bicentenary, this former port and industrial area around the inlets of Cockle Bay and Darling Harbour is Sydney's premier purpose-built entertainment district, home to the Sydney Convention Centre and the massive Sydney Exhibition Centre. Lawns, gardens, palm tree groves, fountains, waterways and marinas soften the bold architectural outline. The southern end is beginning to look rather tacky, but despite this the area is a magnet for tourists and locals alike. The New Year's Eve celebrations and many of the Sydney Festival events are held here.

HIGHLIGHTS

Major attractions include the Australian National Maritime Museum (see page 59), Sydney Aquarium, IMAX Theatre and Chinese Garden. For access, the Metro Monorail runs from the city to Darling Harbour, Chinatown and return, while the Metro Light Rail operates from Central Station to Darling Harbour, the Sydney Fish Market, Glebe and other inner west suburbs. The **Harbourside** is the main shopping and dining complex, with over 100 shops and 35 or so cafés, bars and restaurants. One of the best shops is the Gavala Aboriginal Art Centre. Australia's Northern Territory & Outback Centre on Darling Walk specializes in Aboriginal arts and crafts, with Aboriginal musical and dance shows several times daily.

Cruises operate from the Aquarium Wharf, and fast jet boat rides and water taxis depart from in front of Harbourside. Heritage sights include Pyrmont Bridge, a 1902 steel and timber structure, the world's oldest surviving electrically operated span bridge; and the *South Steyne*, a 1938 steam ferry that now houses a floating restaurant.

Sydney Aquarium (*daily 9.30am–10pm*) on Aquarium Pier is Australia's largest. There are some 650 species of aquatic creatures in themed displays, including fish, turtles, eels, saltwater crocodiles, seals, fairy penguins, platypus and sharks.

Don't miss The Chinese Garden of Friendship (*Mon–Fri 9.30–5.30, winter until 5, Sat–Sun 9.30–6, winter until 5.30; admission charge*) is a traditional Chinese walled garden, complete with lakes, bridges, pagodas, pavilions, mini-forests, willows, water lilies, statues and courtyards. Designed by Chinese landscape architects in Guangdong Province to celebrate Australia's bicentenary, it's a remarkably tranquil space amid the bustle of Darling Harbour.

Take a ferry north from Circular Quay to Manly Beach

Find out about the origins of the city in the Museum of Sydney

The Powerhouse Museum is a short walk from Darling Harbour

MANLY AND THE NORTHERN BEACH SUBURBS

✚ 331 W14 ℹ Manly Visitor Centre, Manly Wharf, NSW 2095, tel 02 9977 1088 🚢 Ferry or fast JetCat from Circular Quay to Manly. There are then bus services to the other beachside suburbs
www.manlytourism.com

Manly has been a popular seaside resort since the late 1840s, when the first paddle-steamer ferry service to the city began. The present scenic ferry ride across Sydney Harbour is a major attraction in itself. Stretching from Manly to Palm Beach are 21 golden sandy surf beaches, headlands, lagoons and lakes, and beachside suburbs.

Manly offers surfing, the Oceanworld aquarium (*daily 10–5.30*), North Fort and the Royal Australian Artillery Museum (*Wed and Sat–Sun 11–4*), Manly Art Gallery and Museum (*Tue–Sun 10–5*), Manly Waterworks fun pool and waterslide complex (*Sat–Sun 10–5*), plus walks and great harbour views from North Head (part of Sydney Harbour National Park).
Don't miss Palm Beach for its long surf beach, boating and ferry rides on neighbouring Pittwater and out into Broken Bay, cafés, restaurants and upscale shops, and a walk to the lighthouse in Ku-ring-gai Chase National Park.

MUSEUM OF CONTEMPORARY ART

✚ 61 B2 • 140 George Street, The Rocks (main entrance on Circular Quay West) ☎ 02 9252 4033 (general enquiries); 02 9241 5892 (recorded information) 🕐 Daily 10–5 💲 Free; charge for special exhibitions 🚉 Circular Quay (City Circle line) 🚌 Any Circular Quay bound bus 🚻 ♿
www.mca.com.au

The MCA may not be a Sydney highlight, but admirers of contemporary art will appreciate the avant garde and often controversial displays and exhibits. The museum is in part of the former Maritime Services Board building beside Sydney Cove, built in 1947–52 in art-deco style.

Although it has a permanent collection of around 4,500 works of art, little of this is on display, concentrating instead on changing exhibitions. The museum also hosts regular special artistic events: talks by artists and curators, art workshops, discussions and musical performances.

MUSEUM OF SYDNEY

✚ 61 B3 • Bridge Street ☎ 02 9251 5988 🕐 Daily 9.30–5 💲 Adult A$7, child (under 5s free) A$3 🚉 Circular Quay (City Circle line) 🚌 Any Circular Quay bound bus 🚻 ♿
www.hht.nsw.gov.au

Opened in 1995, the MOS aims to explore the diverse stories of Sydney and its people—from early Aboriginal times to the present day. The stone and glass structure stands on the site of Sydney's first Government House, the foundations of which can be seen through a glass panel in the floor.

Three levels of themed galleries focus on Sydney's indigenous and other people, history and environment. The displays are more imaginative and unusual than those of more traditional museums; some, perhaps, are rather avant garde and unsatisfying.
Don't miss The Edge of the Trees sculpture in the forecourt 'speaks' through Aboriginal voices.

PARLIAMENT OF NEW SOUTH WALES

✚ 61 C3 • Macquarie Street ☎ 02 9230 2047 (general enquiries); 02 9230 3444 (tour information and reservations) 🕐 Mon–Fri 9.30–4; closed public holidays 💲 Free. Tours (on non-sitting days only—call in advance) 9.30, 11, 12.30, 2, 3 🚉 Martin Place (Eastern Suburbs line) or St. James (City Circle line) 🚌 Sydney Explorer bus (stop 4)
www.parliament.nsw.gov.au

This has been the home of the New South Wales State Parliament—the Legislative Assembly (Lower House) and Legislative Council (Upper House)—since 1829. The original building was the northern wing of the Rum Hospital, built by convict labour in 1812–16 on the profits of the lucrative rum importation trade. You enter through the simple but very attractive verandah of this original building. The present Parliamentary chambers date from the mid-19th century. You can watch the proceedings from the public galleries on sitting days.
Don't miss The 1-hour guided tour is the best way to see the public rooms.

POWERHOUSE MUSEUM

✚ 60 A5 • 500 Harris Street, Ultimo, NSW 2007 ☎ 02 9217 0111 (enquiries); 02 9217 0444 (Infoline) 🕐 Daily 10–5 💲 Adult A$10, child (5–15) A$3; free after 4; additional charge for exhibitions 🚉 Metro Light Rail (from Central Station) or Metro Monorail to Haymarket 🚻 ♿
www.phm.gov.au

This is one of Australia's most popular and worthwhile museums, housing thousands of items from the vast Museum of Applied Arts and Sciences collection. The museum, to the south of Darling Harbour, is in a former power station that powered the city's tram system.

The exhibits and galleries are on four levels; imaginative displays cover social history, decorative arts, music, technology, design, industry, transport and space exploration. There are more than

Above: The view of Circular Quay from the Harbour Bridge Inset: Cadmans Cottage in the Rocks

RATINGS	
Good for kids	●●●○
Historic interest	●●●●
Shopping	●●●○
Walkability	●●●●

TIP
● Walking is the best way to explore the area—try a self-guide walk (a A$1 map/guide is available from the Sydney Visitor Centre).

BASICS
✚ 61 B2
🅘 Sydney Visitor Centre • 106 George Street, tel 02 9240 8788; 1902 222 222 (The Rocks Infoline), open daily 9–6 www.sydneyvisitorcentre.com.au www.therocks.com • The website can be slow but the main menu provides simple access to dining, drinking, accommodation, stores, activities, galleries and what's happening.

HIGHLIGHTS
● Museum of Contemporary Art (see page 63)
● Sydney Observatory (*daily 10–5*)
● Susannah Place Museum (*Sat–Sun 10–5*), 19th-century houses; Clyde Bank (*Wed–Sat 10–6*), colonial art and furniture

THE ROCKS AND CIRCULAR QUAY

The Rocks is Australia's oldest 'village', where the convicts of the First Fleet set up their tents in January 1788.

Both The Rocks and the Circular Quay area are set around Sydney Cove, about 1km (0.6 mile) north of the central area. It's very easy to walk round, and there are plenty of colonial buildings, narrow streets, cobbled lanes such as Nurses Walk and Suez Canal, museums and galleries, shops, cafés and restaurants, and great views of the harbour, Sydney Harbour Bridge and the Opera House.

THE ROCKS
The Rocks, at various times, has been the domain of convicts and soldiers, lawless sealers and whalers, brothels, rough inns and gangs of thugs, and the gentry. The area was also the site of Australia's first fort, hospital, windmill and wharves. Despite much demolition in 1900 and again in the 1960s, the area has retained historic streetscapes and lanes, and many buildings dating from the 1820s to the 1840s.

The built heritage includes Cadmans Cottage (1816) which is now an information point for Sydney Harbour National Park, Campbells Storehouses (1839–90), the Argyle Stores (1828), Sydney Observatory (1858), and the Garrison Church (from 1840) at Argyle Place. Among the atmospheric pubs are the Lord Nelson Hotel (1834) and the Hero of Waterloo (1844) at Millers Point, and The Fortune of War (1922), Orient Hotel (1844) and Mercantile Hotel (1915) along George Street.

The area is packed with arcades, art galleries and souvenir and gift shops. The Rocks Market takes over the upper end of George Street at weekends, and there are free musical performances, street theatre and live bands in the pubs. The Sydney Visitor Centre has a free History of The Rocks display. The Puppet Cottage with puppet shows (*Sat–Sun 11, 12.30, 2*) and Toy Museum (*daily 10–5.30*) in Kendall Lane entertain the children.

CIRCULAR QUAY
Fronting Sydney Cove, this was the area in which the British flag was first raised by Governor Phillip in 1788. It has since become the city's ferry and cruise boat hub, much frequented by tourists. The Overseas Passenger Terminal at West Circular Quay has fashionable restaurants and bars, while a late 1990s development at East Circular Quay has waterfront shops, restaurants, bars, cafés, a hotel and a cinema. The Sydney Opera House (see page 68), Museum of Contemporary Art (see page 63) and the Justice and Police Museum are in this area.

The pyramid tropical glasshouses of the Royal Botanic Gardens

Try to see a game of cricket or Aussie Rules at the SCG

The stadium at Olympic Park still attracts the crowds

200 fun interactive exhibits for children (and adults). Exhibitions are a regular feature and free 45-minute guided highlight tours are usually available (11.30, 1.30).

ROYAL BOTANIC GARDENS

✚ 61 C3 • Mrs Macquaries Road, The Domain ☎ 02 9231 8111/8125 ⚫ Gardens: daily 7–8; Sydney Tropical Centre: daily 10–4 ⚫ Free. Sydney Tropical Centre: adults A$2.20, child A$1.10 ⚫ Circular Quay (City Circle line) 🚌 441 from the Queen Victoria Building (York Street bus interchange) to the Art Gallery of NSW 🍴 ⚫ ♿ www.rbgsyd.nsw.gov.au

This is a tranquil place to walk and relax within the heart of the city. Founded by Governor Lachlan Macquarie in 1816, the gardens incorporate the land used for Australia's first farm, established by members of the First Fleet in 1788. Covering 30ha (74 acres) on the shores of Sydney Harbour, they contain one of Australia's best collections of native and introduced plants.

Among the themed areas are the Rose, Herb, Oriental and Succulent gardens, and also the Sydney Fernery and the Palm Grove. A free guided tour (daily 10.30, also Mon–Fri 1) picks out the highlights and explains more about the area's history. Beyond the eastern and southern boundaries are the Domain parklands. **Don't miss** Sydney Tropical Centre—two large modern glasshouses contain palms, orchids and other tropical plants.

SYDNEY CRICKET GROUND

✉ Driver Avenue, Moore Park, NSW 1363, 3.5km (2 miles) southeast of the city ☎ Match information 1900 963 132; Ticketek (tickets to sporting events) 9266 4800; Coca-Cola Sportspace Tours 02 9380 0383 ⚫ Mon–Fri tours 10 and 1 (excluding public holidays and major

event days); Sat–Sun generally (various times) for sporting events ⚫ Admission to sporting events varies. Sportspace Tours: adult A$19.50, child A$13 🚌 372–377, 390 or 391 from Circular Quay and central Sydney 🚶 20-minute walk or buses 372, 393 or 395 from Central Station ⚫ ♿ www.scgt.nsw.gov.au

Known to locals as the 'SCG', the Sydney Cricket Ground is one of Australia's most famous sporting venues, with a history of sporting events going back to the 1860s. In summer this 43,562-seater stadium is a venue for state and Test cricket; at other times the SCG is used primarily for exciting Aussie Rules Football games (see page 16)—it is the home ground of the Sydney Swans team.
Don't miss The Coca-Cola Sportspace Tour goes behind the scenes to visit dressing rooms, the players' tunnel, the SCG Members' Pavilion, the Walk of Honour area and SCG Museum.

SYDNEY JEWISH MUSEUM

✚ 61 D4 • 148 Darlinghurst Road, Darlinghurst, NSW 2010 ☎ 02 9360 7999 ⚫ Mon–Thu, Sun 10–4, Fri 10–2; closed Sat and Jewish holidays ⚫ Adult A$10, child (4–16) A$6 ⚫ Kings Cross (Eastern Suburbs line) 🚌 324 or 325 from Circular Quay to Kings Cross ♿ www.sydneyjewishmuseum.com.au

This small museum tells the moving story of Jewish people in Australia from the first days of European settlement—there were 16 Jews on the First Fleet in 1788. In a wider context it explains Jewish culture and traditions, documents the Holocaust and its aftermath, and serves as a memorial to the Jews who perished in World War II.
Don't miss The Children's Memorial and 'Reflection and Remembrance'—the stories of Australian Holocaust survivors.

SYDNEY OLYMPIC PARK

✚ 61 B5 ℹ Sydney Olympic Park Visitor Centre, 1 Herb Elliott Avenue, Sydney Olympic Park, NSW 2127, tel 02 9714 7545 (enquiries); 02 9714 7888 (recorded information); 1300 889 388 (What's On infoline) ⚫ Park: daily 24 hours; venues vary 🚉 Olympic Park www.sydneyolympicpark.nsw.gov.au

Olympic Park was the focus of Sydney's highly successful Olympic and Paralympic Games in 2000 and is now a world-class sporting and leisure venue. The site takes in five parks and 15 sporting and other venues, and many festivals and special events are held here. Bicentennial Park and The Parklands adjoin the site—a large area of grass, trees and open space. Bicentennial Park consists of 100ha (247 acres) of wetlands, mangroves, parkland, fountains, playgrounds, cycle paths and walkways.

Although Sydney Olympic Park can be reached by train, the best way to arrive is by RiverCat ferry along the Parramatta River from Circular Quay. Once at the site, an Olympic Explorer Bus tour is the easiest way to cover the area and see all the sights. This daily hop-on hop-off tourist service takes in 10 stops around Olympic Park and its surrounds and operates about every 30 minutes. Look out for the State Sports Centre, home of the New South Wales Hall of Champions, a museum dedicated to the state's champion athletes; Sydney Showground, used mainly for the Royal Easter Show, a mainly agricultural festival; the Sydney SuperDome, a major musical, concert and sports venue; and the Sydney International Tennis Centre, open to anyone keen for a game.
Don't miss Jump in at the Sydney Aquatic Centre. In addition to two Olympic-size pools, there is a waterslide and other fun aquatic areas, a gym and café.

Sydney Harbour

Sydney's harbour, bridge and opera house are known the world over. The Sydney Opera House is not only Sydney's most distinctive landmark, it is the city's—and perhaps Australia's—most important venue for the performing arts. A walk beside the shoreline is a must for visitors to the city.

Sydney's Opera House and Bridge are Australian icons

Fireworks light up Sydney Harbour Bridge at New Year

SEEING SYDNEY HARBOUR

From the South Pacific Ocean, a 240km (149-mile) shoreline extends inland around the harbour, beneath Sydney Harbour Bridge and west along the Parramatta River. The harbour is surrounded by tall offices, port facilities, cruise ship terminals, beaches, bays, headlands and, of course, the suburbs of Sydney residents. Yet most unusual for a major city is the survival of extensive areas of bushland, which are preserved in the Sydney Harbour National Park. The best place to start exploring the harbour is the water itself—take one of the ferries from Circular Quay to view the many coves and beaches and get close to the spectacular waterfront houses and seemingly remote bushland. After viewing the Bridge and visiting the Opera House don't miss out on exploring the Royal Botanic Gardens (see page 65) and parts of the Sydney Harbour National Park.

HIGHLIGHTS

SYDNEY HARBOUR BRIDGE

✚ 61 B1 • Pylon Lookout, Cumberland Street, The Rocks ☎ 02 9240 1100, **www.pylonlookout.com.au** 🕐 Daily 10–5 💵 Adult A$8.50, child (8–12) A$3
❓ BridgeClimb booking: 02 8274 7777, **www.bridgeclimb.com** 💵 Adult A$145/175, child (12–16 accompanied by adult) A$100/125
This distinctive steel arched structure, with its pairs of stone pylons at each end, is a Sydney icon. The rounded shape has led to its nickname of the 'Coathanger'. Construction began in 1923 and it was opened in March 1932. It remains the world's longest bridge span of its width. The main span is 502.9m (1,650ft) long and 48.8m (160ft) wide and carries two railway tracks, a walkway, cycleway and eight road lanes. The top of the arch is 134m (440ft) above sea level. The bridge is still a vital link between the north and south sides of the harbour, but due to increasing traffic it has been supplemented by the Sydney Harbour Tunnel, constructed in the early 1990s.

There are several ways to experience the bridge. To view it from below, walk from Campbells Cove in The Rocks to Dawes Point, or take a ferry across the harbour to Milsons Point. The bridge walkway

RATINGS				
Good for kids	●	●	●	
Historic interest	●	●	●	
Photo stops	●	●	●	●	●
Walkability	●	●	●	

TIPS

● Allow time for more than one harbour cruise or ferry ride—the experience and views are addictive. Also try to take an evening dinner cruise: The city and suburbs look superb when lit up at night.
● Opera House tours can be cancelled at short notice—they are subject to the availability of theatres, which may be booked for performances, rehearsals and other activities. You cannot book a tour in advance, so get to the Opera House early for a better chance of getting on a tour.

Opposite: Don't forget to book ahead if you want to climb the bridge

from the Rocks to the Pylon Lookout allows you to see the structure close up, and gives good city and harbour views. The exhibition in the Pylon Lookout describes the history and construction of the bridge, and there is a great view from the top (200 steps).

The most exciting way to see the bridge is on a day or night BridgeClimb tour (3.5 hours; tours every 10 minutes from early morning to evening; night climbs by demand), which takes you along catwalks and ladders to the very top of the structure. The climb might be expensive, but it is well worth the price—book in advance.

Below: Ferries from Circular Quay stream past the Opera House

The Concert Hall (left) is the largest performance space in the Opera House

Above: A close-up of the Opera House's sails

MAKE A DAY OF IT
- The Rocks and Circular Quay; 500m (545 yards) to the south and west (see page 64)
- Museum of Contemporary Art; 500m (545 yards) to the west (see page 63)
- Customs House; 250m (273 yards) to the south
- Justice & Police Museum; 250m (273 yards) to the south
- Royal Botanic Gardens; immediately to the south (see page 65)
- Sydney Harbour and Bridge (see page 67); the harbour is reached from Circular Quay (see page 64); access to the bridge is 600m (654 yards) to the west

The following locations are all on the harbour or Parramatta River and can be reached by ferry from Circular Quay:
- Cremorne Point
- Taronga Zoo (see page 71)
- Manly (see page 63)
- Eastern Suburbs (Darling Point, Double Bay, Rose Bay, Watsons Bay)
- Parramatta

SYDNEY OPERA HOUSE
🔁 61 C2 • Bennelong Point, NSW 2000 ☎ 02 9250 7777 (general enquiries and box office, open Mon–Sat 9–8.30); 02 9250 7250 (tours) 🕐 Performances mostly evenings; tours daily 8.30–5 🚻 Front of House Tour (1 hour; every 45 min): adult A$16.20, child A$11.10. Backstage Pass Tour (75 min; infrequently and generally Sun): A$26.50 (over 12). Bennelong Walk (1 hour; generally Sat afternoon): adult A$16.20, child A$11.10
www.soh.nsw.gov.au

The Opera House contains five performance spaces, and the outside forecourt is also used for entertainment. Its arching 'shell' or 'sail' roofs, covered with over a million Swedish-made ceramic tiles, and dramatic stepped terraces are recognized the world over. The NSW Government launched an international competition for an opera house in 1955. It was won by Danish architect Joern Utzon, with the extraordinary design. Work started in 1958 and the Opera House was completed 14 years later in 1973. The project was fraught with problems, disputes and controversy (mainly regarding the cost), and Utzon resigned in 1966, long before the building was completed; a team of Australian architects then took over. Utzon has never returned to see his masterpiece, but he was a consultant to the building's refurbishment in 2002.

The Opera House is now an essential stop on a visit to Sydney. You can join a tour of the interior, attend a performance or just admire the architecture. The location, too, is spectacular: Bennelong Point juts out into Sydney Harbour with views across Sydney Cove to the Harbour Bridge. For the historical and architectural background, try the 1-hour Bennelong Walk tour around Bennelong Point and the exterior of the Opera House. The most popular tour, the Front of House, takes you into the various theatres and theatre foyers. These are the Concert Hall (seating 2,679 people) and Opera Theatre (seating 1,547), both under the main roof, and three smaller spaces (The Studio, Playhouse and Drama Theatre) on the lower level. The less frequent Backstage Pass Tour takes visitors into technical areas, rehearsal rooms and other behind-the-scenes spaces.

The Opera House does not have its own resident company, but is used by various companies that perform opera, ballet, symphonies, theatre, modern dance and other art forms. These companies include some of Australia's best, such as Opera Australia, the Australian Ballet,

SYDNEY

Sydney Symphony Orchestra, Bell Shakespeare Company, Sydney Dance Company and Sydney Theatre Company. Jazz and contemporary music concerts are also held in the building.

SYDNEY HARBOUR NATIONAL PARK

⊞ 61 B1 • Sydney Harbour National Park Information Centre, Cadmans Cottage, 110 George Street, The Rocks, NSW 2000 ☎ 02 9247 5033 ⊘ Cadmans Cottage (tel 02 9247 8861): daily 9–4.30; most of the national park is open 24 hours daily ✋ Most sections free; fees vary for tours to Goat Island, Fort Denison and the Quarantine Station at North Head; landing fees for Shark Island, Clark Island and Rodd Island: A$3 per person (under 5s free)
www.npws.nsw.gov.au

Scattered around Sydney Harbour to the east of the bridge, the national park takes in islands, headlands, beaches, bushland, bays and historic Aboriginal and colonial sites. These relatively unspoiled areas are a remarkable feature for any metropolis, but their close proximity to the city makes them particularly unusual.

Try to sample at least one area of the national park. The easiest access is by taking a ferry from The Rocks to either Manly (see page 63) or Watsons Bay, both of which are located on peninsulas between ocean and harbour. The Manly Scenic Walkway is a spectacular 10km (6-mile) coastal walk from Manly to the Spit Bridge at Middle Harbour (it takes 3–4 hours to do the entire route, but the walk can be shortened). South Head, with great views of the harbour,

Above: The evening sun bounces off the water of Sydney Harbour Inset: The QEII *visiting Sydney*

BASICS

Sydney Visitor Centre
⊞ 61 C1 • 106 George Street, The Rocks, Sydney, NSW 2000 ☎ 02 9240 8788 ⊘ Daily 9–6 ❓ Sydney Ferries: 13 1500. Sydney Harbour National Park: 02 9247 5033

🚉 Circular Quay (City Circle line). From here ferries depart for destinations all around the harbour and along the Parramatta River. For the Harbour Bridge walkway, Circular Quay or Milsons Point (station on the northern side)
www.sydneyvisitorcentre.com.au

The view of Sydney's darkening skyline from Milsons Point

MAKE A DAY OF IT

There are many different ways to see the harbour:

- Sydney Ferries—either take one of the regular ferry services or a special cruise
- Cruise companies—a variety of private companies offer harbour cruises. These range from a short (75-min) 'Harbour Highlights' trip to lunch and dinner cruises and even a two-night excursion. Vessels include large cruise ships, a paddle wheeler, tall ships and sailing yachts
- Harbour adventures—from sea kayaking and sailing to jet boating and parasailing
- Seaplanes and helicopters—view the harbour from above
- Sydney Harbour National Park—visit one of the islands or foreshore areas

ocean and North Head, is a 1.5km (1-mile) walk from Watsons Bay, and it can be combined with a visit to the beach at Camp Cove. Closer to the city, the north side Chowder Head/Bradleys Head section is south of Mosman near Taronga Zoo (see page 71). Perhaps the best way to enjoy the park is just to take a short walk, laze on a beach or picnic area, and enjoy the views.

Don't miss Fort Denison, an island north of The Domain and Royal Botanic Gardens, was formerly a place of convict punishment and then a military fort in the 19th century. Access to Fort Denison is via the National Parks and Wildlife Service tours only.

BACKGROUND

Sydney Harbour (the official name is Port Jackson) was bypassed by Captain Cook on his 1770 exploration of Australia's east coast, but in 1788 the ships, crew and convicts of the First Fleet, disappointed by the barren surrounds further south at Botany Bay, entered the waterway and set up their tents in the area now known as The Rocks. Since those times, the harbour has been vital for communication and transport and it is now also a great attraction. Bennelong Point is named after an Aboriginal man who lived there in the late 18th century. In 1955 this site, then a tram depot, was chosen as the setting for the Opera House.

Sydney Tower dominates the city skyline

Taronga Zoo is a ferry ride from the central business district

The drawing room at Vaucluse House

SYDNEY TOWER

61 B3 • Podium Level, 100 Market Street ☎ 02 9223 0933 ⏰ Daily 9am–10.30pm (also Sat 10.30–11.30) 💷 Adult A$22, child (5–16) A$13.20, under 5s free (admission to both Skytour and the Observation Deck) 🚉 St. James or Town Hall (City Circle line) 🚌 Sydney Explorer bus (stop 14) 🍴 📷 ♿
www.sydneyskytour.com.au

The views from the Observation Deck of Sydney's tallest building, 250m (820ft) above street level, are fantastic—as far as the Blue Mountains, about 90km (56 miles) away. It's also a good way to orientate yourself to the city. Skytour, a 'virtual tour' complete with headphones and a commentary in English and several Asian languages, provides an introduction to Australia's culture, history and geography, but it's only a sideshow to the main experience. **Don't miss** Go later for the view at sunset.

TARONGA ZOO

61 B1 • Bradleys Head Road, Mosman, NSW 2088 ☎ 02 9969 2777 (general enquiries); 1900 920 218 (recorded information) ⏰ Daily 9–5 💷 Adult A$25, child (4–15) A$13.50, under 4s free. ZooPass: adult A$30.30, child A$15.10 🚌 247 from the city centre, Wynyard Station ⛴ Ferry from Circular Quay 📷 ♿
www.zoo.nsw.gov.au

Taronga is Australia's premier zoo, set in 28ha (69 acres) of

landscaped gardens, native bushland and foreshore on the northern side of Sydney Harbour. There are buses from the city to Taronga Zoo. The best way to arrive is by ferry from Circular Quay; if you take this option, then purchase an economical ZooPass, which includes the return ferry fare, entrance to the zoo, the bus trip to or from the main entrance, and a ride on the Sky Safari cable car.

There are around 380 species of marsupials, mammals, birds, fish and reptiles here, representing a total of more than 2,200 individual animals. From Australia itself there are koalas, dingoes, kangaroos, wallabies, echidnas, platypuses, wombats, Tasmanian devils, crocodiles and snakes, and bird species such as pelicans, emus, fairy penguins and parrots. Exotic animals include snakes, reptiles, elephants, snow leopards, orangutans, lions, tigers, red pandas, Kodiak bears and sun bears. At the Backyard to Bush exhibition, children can meet domestic and farm animals, as well as baby animals born at the zoo.

VAUCLUSE HOUSE

61 D4 • Wentworth Road, Vaucluse, NSW 2030 ☎ 02 9388 7922 ⏰ Tue–Sun 10–4.30; closed Mon except public holidays 💷 Adult A$7, child A$3, under 5s free 🚌 325 from Circular Quay, central Sydney and Kings Cross; Bondi Explorer bus (stop 9) 📷 ♿
www.hht.nsw.gov.au

Dating from 1827, this Gothic-revival mansion was originally the home of William Charles Wentworth. It is one of only a few large historic houses in and around Sydney. Wentworth was a famous Australian explorer and barrister, the founder of the University of Sydney (Australia's first), and the 'Father of the

Australian Constitution'. The three-storey house is furnished in mid-19th-century period style and visitors can see the cellars, kitchen and scullery, dining and drawing rooms, and the bedrooms. It is surrounded by 11ha (27 acres) of grounds and gardens, only a fraction of the estate's original 200ha (494 acres). The Vaucluse House Tearooms, in the grounds, are also worth a visit.
Don't miss Walk around the grounds.

WONDERLAND SYDNEY

330 W14 • Wallgrove Road, Eastern Creek. NSW 2766 ☎ 02 9830 9100; 02 9830 9106 (recorded information) ⏰ Wonderland Sydney: daily 10–5; Australian Wildlife Park: daily 9–5 💷 Adult A$48.40, child (4–13) A$31.90; Wildlife Park only: adult A$17.60, child A$11 🚉 Rooty Hill, then Busways bus link to Wonderland 🚗 42km (26 miles) east of Sydney via Western Highway (Metroad 4) 🍴 📷 ♿
www.wonderland.com.au

Wonderland is the largest theme park in the southern hemisphere, a fun day of rides and displays. The 200ha (494-acre) site also includes the Australian Wildlife Park, a popular attraction in its own right, where visitors can meet more than 500 species of Australian animals and birds, including koalas, kangaroos and wombats.

Rides and displays include Goldrush and Old Botany Bay, based on Australia's settlement and pioneer history; The Beach, complete with pool, beach and water slides (closed winter); and Transylvania, with the southern hemisphere's biggest and fastest rollercoaster. Children can also meet a range of Marvel characters.
Don't miss The Outback Woolshed has sheep-shearing displays.

Canberra
(Australian Capital Territory)

Australia's meticulously planned capital city is unlike any other in the country, and is the home of several national galleries and museums.

The National Museum of Australia stands beside Lake Burley Griffin

RATINGS	
Good for kids	● ● ●
Photo stops	● ● ● ●
Shopping	● ● ●
Walkability	● ● ● ●

TIP

● The City Sightseeing hop-on-hop-off tourist bus service takes in most of the city's major attractions.

BASICS

➕ 330 V15

🅸 Canberra Visitor Centre • 330 Northbourne Avenue, Dickson, ACT 2602, tel 02 6205 0044 (calls from within the ACT and NSW); 1300 554 114 (calls from other parts of Australia); open Mon–Fri 9–5.30, Sat–Sun 9–4 🚉 Canberra, 4.5km (3 miles) southeast of the city. The journey from Sydney takes 4 hours 10 minutes; from Melbourne (no direct rail link) about 8 hours www.canberratourism.com.au • Packed homepage somewhere between a newspaper and a directory, but most of Canberra lies within

Built over the last 90 years, Canberra's straight avenues and circular streets have been planted with more than 10 million trees and shrubs to produce an attractive and elegant city. The main sights are clustered near Parliament House to the south of Lake Burley Griffin, while the commercial area is to the north.

HIGHLIGHTS

AUSTRALIAN WAR MEMORIAL
✉ Treloar Crescent, Campbell, ACT 2612 ☎ 02 6243 4211 (enquiries); 02 6243 4518 (to arrange a special tour); 02 6243 4598 (special events information) 🕐 Daily 10–5
The domed building at the end of Anzac Parade is one of the world's best war museums. The site includes The Hall of Memory, Tomb of the Unknown Australian Soldier, the Roll of Honour (naming over 100,000 service men and women who have died during war) and a courtyard with the Eternal Flame and Pool of Reflection. There is a Discovery Room for children with hands-on exhibits, and sound-and-light shows in the Object Theatre in Anzac Hall.

NATIONAL GALLERY OF AUSTRALIA
✉ Parkes Place, Parkes, ACT 2600 ☎ 02 6240 6502 (enquiries); 02 6240 6501 (recorded information); 02 6240 6588 (tours) 🕐 Daily 10–5
This is Australia's premier art gallery, with a permanent collection of more than 109,000 Australian, Aboriginal, European, American, Asian and other works. Of particular note is the Aboriginal and Torres Strait Islander collection, and the Asian art collection.

NATIONAL LIBRARY OF AUSTRALIA
✉ Parkes Place, Parkes, ACT 2600 ☎ 02 6262 1111 (enquiries); 02 6262 1271 (tours); 02 6262 1699 (recorded information) 🕐 Exhibition Gallery: daily 9–5; Main Reading Room: Mon–Thu 9–9, Fri–Sat 9–5, Sun 1.30–5
Australia's largest collection of library material, the archive includes

books, maps, journals, letters, sheet music, magazines, newspapers, ephemera, films, videos, oral history media, over 500,000 photographs and around 40,000 works of art.

NATIONAL MUSEUM OF AUSTRALIA

✉ Lawson Crescent, Acton Peninsula, ACT 2600 ☎ 02 6208 5000 or 1800 026 132 🕐 Daily 9–5

Opened in 2001, the nation's social history museum has galleries relating to the land, the nation and the people. Exhibits range from Aboriginal bark paintings to a convict jacket.

OLD PARLIAMENT HOUSE AND THE NATIONAL PORTRAIT GALLERY

✉ King George Terrace, Parkes, ACT 2600 ☎ Old Parliament House 02 6270 8222; National Portrait Gallery 02 6270 8236 🕐 Daily 9–5

Completed in 1927, Old Parliament House was the home of Australia's Federal Parliament until 1988. The building now contains the National Portrait Gallery, with portraits ranging from Captain James Cook to satirist Barry Humphries and singer Kylie Minogue.

PARLIAMENT HOUSE

✉ Capital Hill, ACT 2600 ☎ 02 6277 5399 (enquiries); 02 6277 2727 (recorded information); 02 6277 4889 (Question Time tickets) 🕐 Daily 9–5

Parliament House is one of Canberra's most popular attractions. The Australian Federal Parliament moved to this modern building from the nearby Old Parliament House in 1988. Free tickets for the public galleries are available for Question Time when Parliament is in session. The building also contains paintings, sculptures and other artworks.

QUESTACON–THE NATIONAL SCIENCE AND TECHNOLOGY CENTRE

✉ King Edward Terrace, Parkes, ACT 2600 ☎ 02 6270 2800; 1800 020 603 (recorded information) 🕐 Daily 9–5

Australia's leading interactive science and technology centre turns education into great fun for all ages. Most of the exhibits are hands-on and irresistible for both adults and children.

SCREENSOUND AUSTRALIA

✉ McCoy Circuit, Acton, ACT 2601 ☎ 02 6248 2000 🕐 Mon–Fri 9–5, Sat–Sun 10–5

Subtitled the National Screen and Sound Archive, the museum is in an impressive art-deco building and concentrates on Australia's moving image (television and film) and recorded sound (radio and music) heritage. A film theatre presents screenings.

BACKGROUND

After the federation of the Australian colonies in 1901 there was fierce rivalry between Sydney and Melbourne for the status of capital city. As a compromise, Canberra was chosen in 1908 as the site for the capital, in a 'neutral' farming region some 300km (190 miles) from Sydney and 600km (370 miles) from Melbourne. In 1911 an international design competition for the cityscape was won by American architect Walter Burley Griffin. Construction began in 1913 and the Parliament moved to Canberra in 1927.

Left: Balloons float past Old Parliament House
Centre: The giant globe of the Captain Cook Memorial
Above: The National Carillon on Lake Burley Griffin

ATTRACTIONS

AUSTRALIAN INSTITUTE OF SPORT

✉ Nestle Sports Visitors Centre, Leverrier Crescent, Bruce, ACT 2617 ☎ Tours: 02 6214 1444/1010 🕐 Mon–Fri 8.30–5, Sat–Sun and public holidays 10–4

The national training centre includes an interactive sports exhibit gallery.

CANBERRA SPACE DOME

✉ Hawdon Place, Dickson, ACT 2602 ☎ 02 6248 5333 🕐 Planetarium sessions 7–8.30pm

The night sky is re-created in a domed theatre.

NATIONAL ZOO & AQUARIUM

✉ Scrivener Dam, Yarralumla ☎ 02 6287 8400 🕐 Daily 9–5

Australia's largest private zoo is good for big cats.

TELSTRA TOWER

✉ Black Mountain Drive, Acton, ACT 2601 ☎ 02 6219 6111 🕐 Daily 9–10

View ACT from this communications tower on Black Mountain.

Blue Mountains

A superb wilderness area with truly magnificent scenery and within easy reach of Sydney.

Above: The Three Sisters and the Skyway cable car (inset) are both near Katoomba
Above centre: Parrots such as this rosella are common in the Blue Mountains

RATINGS	
Good for kids	●●●
Photo stops	●●●●●
Outdoor pursuits	●●●●●
Shopping	●●●

SEEING THE BLUE MOUNTAINS

The Blue Mountains region begins around 75km (45 miles) west of Sydney and extends west to Mount Victoria, 140km (90 miles) from the city. These are not really mountains, rather a high plateau that has been weathered over many thousands of years. The area is visited primarily for its superb sandstone cliff, canyon and valley scenery, much of it encompassed by Blue Mountains National Park. This wilderness can be enjoyed from many spectacular lookouts, or more actively by bushwalking or adventure sports such as abseiling, canyoning, horse riding, rock climbing and 4WD tours. There are several day trips available from Sydney (your hotel or tourist office can supply details), but most visitors rent a car and explore at will.

HIGHLIGHTS

LOWER BLUE MOUNTAINS
✚ 330 W14 • Great Western Highway, 68km (42 miles) west of Sydney
Glenbrook marks the eastern approach to the national park, with a visitor centre, short bushwalks, and Aboriginal rock art in Red Hands Cave about 5km (3 miles) to the southwest. The Norman Lindsay

Above: The Hanging Rock overlooks the hazy Jamison Valley (above right)

Gallery and Museum, former home of artist and author Norman Lindsay (1879–1969) is at Faulconbridge, 16km (10 miles) farther west along the Great Western Highway (*daily 10–4*). Continuing along the highway, Wentworth Falls has the Victorian mansion of Yester Grange (*tel 02 4757 1110*), Wentworth Falls Lake just north of the town, and of course the falls themselves to the south.

UPPER BLUE MOUNTAINS
LEURA
✚ 330 W14 • Great Western Highway, 108km (67 miles) west of Sydney, 3km (2 miles) east of Katoomba

Leura is perhaps the most picturesque of all the Blue Mountains villages. The delightfully old-fashioned main street is lined with cafés, art and craft shops, clothing boutiques, delicatessens and bakeries. In addition to a golf course and some short, relatively easy bushwalks, the main attractions are large gardens and superb views of the Blue Mountains National Park.

The Everglades Gardens (*daily 10–5*) were designed by the Danish-born master gardener Paul Sorensen in the 1930s. The Leuralla Gardens Toy and Railway Museum (*daily 10–5*) is based around an Edwardian mansion, the former home of Dr H. V. Evatt, an Australian politician who became president of the United Nations in 1948. As the name suggests, there are attractive gardens, and a large collection of toys, dolls, trains and NSW Railways memorabilia. South of Leura, Sublime Point lookout has wonderful views of the Jamison Valley and surrounds—arguably better than those at the more famous, and much more crowded, Echo Point at Katoomba.

KATOOMBA
✚ 330 W14 • Great Western Highway, 111km (69 miles) west of Sydney

Katoomba is the region's largest town, a good base for bushwalking, rock climbing and abseiling in the Blue Mountains National Park. Bushwalks range from an hour or so along the clifftop to the long (3-day) and arduous Six Foot Track walk to Jenolan Caves. For gentle browsers there are galleries, craft shops, cafés and restaurants, including the Paragon, an ornate café established in 1916 but renovated in

TIPS
● Visit during the week as at weekends it becomes crowded (mostly with Sydneysiders looking for an escape), and accommodation is more expensive.
● For a serious bushwalk, ensure you have maps, water, food and suitable clothing. Contact the National Parks and Wildlife Service at Blackheath for advice: 02 4787 8877.

The Zig Zag Railway is near Lithgow

1925 in art-deco style. The Edge Cinema (see page 184) has a six-storey high screen that shows a spectacular film on the Blue Mountains and its scenery. The long steep main street leads south 1km (0.6 mile) to Echo Point, the region's most famous lookout, with celebrated views of the deep forested Jamison Valley, cliffs, ridges and the Three Sisters rock formation. Nearby Scenic World (*daily 9–5*) incorporates the Skyway cable car (equally great views), Sceniscender and Scenic Railway (which both descend to the valley floor). The forest boardwalk at the base of the Scenic Railway is ideal for those who wish to see the lush valley, but who lack the equipment for a serious bushwalk.

The Hydro Majestic Hotel at Medlow Bath, 7km (4 miles) northwest, is not just a hotel but a tourist attraction in itself. Built in 1904, it stands on an escarpment overlooking the Megalong Valley.

BLACKHEATH
🚹 330 W14 • Great Western Highway, 12km (7.5 miles) northwest of Katoomba

The small town of Blackheath is not particularly attractive in itself but it is the main access point for the spectacular Grose Valley and the northern section of the Blue Mountains National Park. The town has a golf course, a good selection of cafés, craft and antiques shops, and a famous sourdough bakery. The Blue Mountains Heritage Centre—a National Parks and Wildlife Information Centre—is a couple of kilometres away from the main street on Govetts Leap Road, just within the national park boundary (*daily 9–4.30*). It's a good start for tourist information and walking tracks, and there is a shop and displays on the culture and natural history of the national park. Nearby Govetts Leap Lookout has awe-inspiring views of Bridal Veil Falls and the deep forested Grose Valley with its dramatic sandstone cliffs. There are equally good views from Evans Lookout, about 3km (2 miles) southeast of the heritage centre; the landscape is quite different to the Katoomba-Leura region.

To the south of Blackheath, the agricultural Megalong Valley has a number of horse-riding establishments. Reached along Megalong Road after 10km (6 miles), the Megalong Australian Heritage Centre presents horse riding, farm animals and sheep shearing, and Clydesdale horse demonstrations. Retracing your steps back to Blackheath and going about 1km (0.6 mile) north brings you to Bacchante Gardens (*daily 9–4*), a woodland garden that specializes in rhododendrons, azaleas, ferns, conifers and deciduous trees; it's particularly good in autumn. Mount Victoria, along the Great Western Highway, is a small village with a few antiques shops and spectacular views from the lookouts at nearby Mount York and Mount Piddington.

JENOLAN CAVES
🚹 330 W14 • Jenolan Caves, NSW 2790 ☎ 02 6359 3311 🕐 Tours daily 10–5. There are evening tours on Saturdays at 7.30 or 8pm and in school holidays when the caves may open later—phone to check ♿ Prices vary according to the number of caves visited: adult A$15–40, child A$10–26.50; 2-hour night tours A$27.50 per person

First discovered by Europeans in the 1830s, Jenolan Caves is an world of limestone caverns and underground rivers, and stalagmites and stalactites. Even today the location is still remote, some 60km (37 miles) south of Lithgow, and there is no public transport to the area: you have to drive or join a coach tour. The guided tours explore up to nine spectacular caves, lasting from one to two hours. Lucas Cave is the most popular, with the widest and highest chambers. The Orient Cave is richly decorated with delicate crystalline formations. In all, the Jenolan karst cave system has as many as 300 caverns. Four are used for adventure

Abseiling is popular in the Blue Mountains

caving. Above ground, the scenery is equally impressive, a mixture of bushland, rock formations, eucalypt forests, pools, rivers and waterfalls at the edge of the Kanangra-Boyd National Park. Rugged attractions include adventure caving and abseiling. Otherwise the Jenolan Karst Conservation Reserve has walking tracks, scenic lookouts and native flora and fauna. To experience this isolated area properly it is best to overnight at Jenolan Caves House (a restored 1920s hotel) or one of the less expensive accommodation options.

MOUNT TOMAH BOTANIC GARDEN
✚ 330 W14 • Bells Line of Road, Mount Tomah, NSW 2758 ☎ 02 4567 2154
🕐 Daily 10–4, Apr–Sep; 10–5, Oct–Mar 🚻 Adult A$4.40, child (4–16) A$2.20
Lithgow is an unattractive coal-mining town at the western foot of the Blue Mountains. From here the Bells Line of Road meanders east through the northern section of the national park via Mount Tomah,

and makes an alternative scenic route to and from Sydney. The only way to reach Mount Tomah is by driving or joining a coach tour.

About 15km (9 miles) east from Lithgow at Clarence is the Zig Zag Railway (*daily train rides at 11, 1 and 3; tel 02 6353 1795*). You can ride a steam or vintage rail motor along the steep zig-zagging 1860s rail line, a masterpiece of engineering in its day.

Occupying a 1,000m (3,280ft) ridge overlooking the northern Blue Mountains region, 38km (23.5 miles) east from Lithgow, Mount Tomah is the cool climate garden of Sydney's Royal Botanic Gardens (see page 65). It is one of the Blue Mountains' highlights. The 28ha (69-acre) gardens include lawns, woods, a formal garden, a rock garden and pond. In particular there are native and exotic collections of rhododendrons, conifers, heathland plants, roses, herbs, alpine plants, ferns, tree ferns and the rare Wollemi pine. The shady Gondwana Forest Walk passes some of Australia's unique plants and trees.

The on-site Mount Tomah Restaurant serves modern Australian cuisine and is an attraction in its own right. (Many people come here primarily for lunch rather than to visit the gardens.) If you have time, a sealed road west of Mount Tomah branches north to the small village of Mount Wilson and the Cathedral of Ferns, where there is a short walk through shady woodland.

Left: The Jenolan Caves provide adventure caving as well as guided tours
Centre: Wentworth Falls are south of the town named after them
Above: Katoomba has galleries and gift shops, and there is good bushwalking nearby

BACKGROUND

Although Aboriginal people lived in the area for tens of thousands of years, the Blue Mountains proved impenetrable to the earliest Europeans. The explorers Wentworth, Blaxland and Lawson only found a route through the mountains in 1813. After the arrival of the railway from Sydney in the 1860s the region became a retreat for Sydneysiders, particularly during the summer. The Blue Mountains National Park was established in 1959 and is significant for its outstanding biodiversity of plant and animal communities—there are some 90 species of eucalypts. The Wollemi pine, one of the world's rarest plants, was discovered north of the Blue Mountains in 1994. The entire region—the Greater Blue Mountains World Heritage Area—was designated a World Heritage Area by UNESCO in November 2000. This wilderness is conserved in seven national parks (Blue Mountains, Kanangra-Boyd, Wollemi, Gardens of Stone, Nattai, Yengo and Thirlmere lakes) and the Jenolan Caves Karst Conservation Reserve.

BASICS
✚ 330 W14
Blue Mountains Visitor Information Offices
🛈 Great Western Highway, Glenbrook, NSW 2773
🛈 Echo Point, Katoomba, NSW 2780
☎ 02 4782 9865, Freecall 1300 653 408 🕐 Daily 9–5 🚩 Glenbrook, Springwood, Wentworth Falls, Leura, Katoomba, Blackheath, Mount Victoria, Lithgow
www.bluemountainstourism.org.au

The Australian Reptile Park is on the Central Coast

Near Dorrigo you'll find the Dangar Falls

Whale-watching cruises are available on the South Coast

NEW SOUTH WALES

CENTRAL COAST

✚ 331 W14 ℹ Central Coast Tourism Information Centre, Terrigal Rotary Park, Terrigal Drive, Terrigal, NSW 2260, tel 02 4385 4430; (local call rate) 1300 659 285 ⊠ Gosford; Woy Woy (southern region); Tuggerah and Wyong (northern region and the lakes) www.cctourism.com.au

The Central Coast has been an escape for Sydneysiders since the railway arrived in the late 1880s. Apart from Gosford, there are just peaceful coastal or rural towns and villages, with beautiful coastal and bushland scenery.

Attractive seafront towns include Ettalong, Terrigal and The Entrance, and there are sandy beaches and surf at Umina, Avoca, MacMasters and Toowoon Bay. Of the seven national parks in the area, Brisbane Water, Bouddi and Wyrrabalong have coastal walkways and wildlife. Inland there are lakes and waterways at Brisbane Water, Tuggerah Lake, Budgewoi Lake and Lake Munmorah. Among the wildlife sanctuaries, the Australian Reptile Park has native and imported animals (*daily 9–5*).

COFFS HARBOUR AND DORRIGO NATIONAL PARK

✚ 327 X13 ℹ Coffs Coast Visitor Information Centre, cnr Elizabeth and Maclean streets, Coffs Harbour, NSW 2450, tel 02 6652 1522; (local call rate) 1300 369 070, open daily 5am–10pm ⊠ Coffs Harbour www.coffstourism.com.au

Fairly unattractive in itself, and crowded during the Christmas holidays, the fishing harbour of Coffs is graced by golden sandy beaches. Attractions include water sports, cruises, a marine park, oceanarium, zoo, botanic garden, art gallery, and white-water rafting on the nearby Nymboida River.

Inland, near the picturesque farming town of Dorrigo, is the 11,732ha (28,980-acre) Dorrigo National Park within the Central Eastern Rainforest Reserves World Heritage Area. There are trails, picnic areas, waterfalls and the Dorrigo Rainforest Centre, but the highlight is the rainforest itself, best seen from the Skywalk boardwalk above the canopy.

EDEN AND THE FAR SOUTH COAST

✚ 330 W16 ℹ Eden Gateway Centre, Princes Highway, Eden, NSW 2551, tel 02 6496 1953; Bega office, Freecall 1800 633 012 www.sapphirecoast.com.au

This beautiful, unspoiled region is a long way from Sydney, 465km (290 miles), but a visit could be combined with a tour to Melbourne or the Snowy Mountains. The 'Sapphire Coast' has some of the state's most attractive beaches, where water sports, fishing, whale-watching cruises, river cruises and coastal walks are popular.

Eden, the southernmost town of New South Wales, has had a long whaling history. To the north and south of the town, Ben Boyd National Park is a beautiful environment of beaches, visible geology and some historic buildings. Farther north the seaside towns of Bermagui, Tathra and Merimbula, and Pambula Beach, all have secluded beaches.

HAWKESBURY REGION

✚ 331 W14 ℹ Hawkesbury Visitor Information Centre, Bicentenary Park, Windsor Street, Clarendon, NSW 2756, tel 02 4588 5895 ⊠ Windsor, Clarendon or Richmond www.hawkesburyvalley.com

This low-lying region outside Sydney was settled in the early 1790s by farmers drawn by the fertile land. The area's most important feature is the Upper Hawkesbury River, which winds from the Great Dividing Range to the ocean north of Palm Beach.

Other than Richmond, the area's main commercial town, most of the historic towns and villages are picturesque. Windsor was laid out in 1810; its old buildings include the Macquarie Arms hotel, St. Matthew's Church, Courthouse and the Observatory. The Macquarie Towns refer to Pitt Town, Wilberforce and Castlereagh, founded by Governor Macquarie in 1810: They are still small farming towns.

JERVIS BAY AND THE SHOALHAVEN REGION

✚ 330–331 W15 ℹ Shoalhaven Visitors Centre, Princes Highway, Nowra, NSW 2541, tel 02 4421 0778; (local call rate) 1300 662 808 ⊠ Bomaderry www.jervisbaytourism.com.au

Like the Eden and the Kiama areas, Shoalhaven is another unspoiled South Coast beach-resort region. It includes the large town of Nowra, Jervis Bay and the coastline south to Ulladulla. The best is Jervis Bay, a large inlet famous for its dazzling white sand, blue waters and wildlife such as migrating whales and resident dolphins. Other attractions include national parks, bushwalking, Aboriginal history and culture at Wreck Bay, and more than 90km (55 miles) of surf.

Nowra dates from the 1850s and is the region's largest town and commercial focus. Stop for Australia's Museum of Flight (*daily 10–4*), cruises on the Shoalhaven River, wineries and notable historic houses. North of Nowra, the picturesque historic village of Berry is renowned for its art and craft shops, antiques outlets and cafés.

The Blowhole and lighthouse at Kiama

HUNTER VALLEY

Take the opportunity to sample some fine wines in one of Australia's premier winegrowing regions.

⊞ 327 W14

Hunter Valley Wine Country Visitor Information Centre • Main Road, Pokolbin, NSW 2325, tel 02 4990 4477; open Mon–Fri 9–5, Sat 9.30–5, Sun and public holidays 9.30–3.30

🚉 Maitland, 27km (17 miles) from Cessnock

www.winecountry.com.au

RATINGS	
Good for kids	◑ ◑
Historic interest	◑ ◑ ◑
Photo stops	◑ ◑ ◑ ◑
Specialist shopping	◑ ◑ ◑ ◑ ◑

TIP
● The valley is extremely popular at weekends. Visit during the week when the area is quieter and accommodation is generally cheaper.

The Hunter Valley is Australia's oldest winegrowing region. Vines were first planted here in the 1820s and the broad valley is now one of the nation's major wine areas. There are more than 100 wineries and cellar doors, most located around the hamlets of Pokolbin, Lovedale, Broke and Rothbury, with some closer to Cessnock and the village of Wollombi in the south. Cessnock is the region's largest town, founded on coal mining. Maitland, Morpeth and Wollombi are notable among the early colonial settlements, the historic village of Wollombi having changed little since the 19th century.

WEEKEND ESCAPE

The valley is a popular weekend escape for Sydneysiders and people from the Central Coast and the Newcastle regions. Numerous restaurants offer fine modern Australian cuisine, while a variety of musical events (jazz, blues and opera, for example) are held at wineries throughout the year. Art, craft and antiques shops are found all around the valley. Among the activities are golf, tennis, hot-air ballooning, tandem skydiving, horse riding, carriage rides around the wineries, cycling and 4WD vehicle tours.

WINERIES

There are too many to mention in detail, but suggestions are:
Brokenwood Wines—excellent shiraz.
Ivanhoe Wines—a small boutique winery.
Lakes Folly Vineyard—some of the area's best reds.
Lindemans—reliable for all wine varieties.
Tulloch Wines—particularly good for sparkling wines.
Tyrrell's Vineyards—a long-established family-owned winery.
Wyndham Estate—established in 1828, producing quality wines.
 Northwest of the main Hunter Valley region, around the village of Denman, the Upper Hunter Valley is another winery area; best wineries are Arrowfield Wines and Rosemount Estate.

KIAMA AND THE JAMBEROO VALLEY

⊞ 331 W15 🛈 Kiama Visitors Centre, Blowhole Point, Kiama, NSW 2533, tel 02 4232 3322, (local call rate) 1300 654 262 🚉 Kiama
www.kiama.com.au

'Discovered' by maritime explorer George Bass in 1797, Kiama has long been a fishing port. Within easy reach of Sydney, this small town has excellent sandy surf and swimming beaches, and many historic buildings. Its most famous attractions are the 1887 Kiama Lighthouse and the Blowhole, through which the sea spurts when the conditions are right. To the south, Gerringong and Gerroa have further beautiful beaches, including the Seven Mile Beach, ideal for surfing.

KOSCIUSZKO NATIONAL PARK

⊞ 330 V16 🛈 Snowy Region Visitor Centre, Kosciuszko Road, Jindabyne, NSW 2627, tel 02 6450 5600; daily 8–5.30 🚗 Park A$15 per vehicle per day 🚌 Coaches from Sydney and Canberra call at Cooma, Jindabyne and Thredbo (and Skitube railway in winter); bus from Cooma airport 🚉 🚲
www.npws.nsw.gov.au

At almost 675,000ha (1.66 million acres), Kosciuszko is the largest national park in New South Wales. It also contains Australia's highest mountain, Mount Kosciuszko at 2,228m (7,308ft). This highland wilderness, part of the Great Dividing Range and within the Snowy Mountains, is known for its winter skiing and summer bushwalking. The largest ski resorts in the region are Perisher Blue and Thredbo, with smaller facilities at Charlottes Pass, Jindabyne and Mount Selwyn. Always check weather warnings before bushwalking or cross-country skiing.

The MV Loyalty *paddles the Murray near Wentworth*

THE SIGHTS

MURRAY RIVER

➕ 329 T15 ℹ️ Echuca-Moama Visitor Information Centre, 2 Heygarth Street, Echuca, VIC 3564, tel 03 5480 7555, Freecall 1800 804 446
www.echucamoama.com

The Murray River flows for 2,700km (1,678 miles) from the Great Dividing Range of New South Wales to the ocean in South Australia—it is Australia's longest and most important waterway, and one of the world's longest navigable rivers. The slow stretch along the Victoria border from the old river ports of Echuca-Moama and Barham to Swan Hill takes in forests, lakes and farming scenery, Aboriginal and European history, paddle-steamer cruises, houseboat holidays and fine local foods, including cheeses and yabbies (freshwater crayfish).
Don't miss The Barmah State Forest and the Barmah State Park are north and east of Echuca-Moama.

MYALL LAKES NATIONAL PARK

➕ 327 X14 • NSW National Parks and Wildlife Service, The Lakes Way, Pacific Palms, NSW 2428 ☎ 02 6591 0300 🕐 Daily 24 hours 💲 A$6 per vehicle per day
www.npws.nsw.gov.au

This popular national park consists of tranquil lakes, forests and 40km (25 miles) of sandy surf beaches. The lakes cover 10,000ha (24,700 acres) and form the largest natural fresh or brackish water system on the state coast. The landscape includes rainforest, paperbark swamps, heath and dry eucalypt forests—home to goannas, possums, kangaroos, swamp wallabies and many birds. It's an ideal place for canoeing, boating, most water sports, walking—or relaxing.

NEW ENGLAND

A superb upland rural and wilderness area with several national parks, spectacular scenic drives and historic towns and cities.

➕ 327 X12
Armidale Visitor Information Centre • 82 Marsh Street, Armidale, NSW 2350, tel 02 6772 4655, Freecall 1800 627 736; Mon–Fri 9–5, Sat 9–4, Sun 10–4 🚏 Armidale, Tamworth and Glen Innes
www.new-england.org/armidale

RATINGS			
Good for kids	●	●	●
Historic interest	●	●	● ●
Photo stops	●	●	● ●
Activities	●	●	● ●

TIP
● Be prepared for chilly nights in winter—though log fires and a welcoming atmosphere make up for any discomfort.

The New England area of northern New South Wales is primarily a farming area high on the Great Dividing Range. It is known for its cool climate and distinct seasons. The region was first settled by farmers in the early 1830s, and the main towns are Armidale, Glen Innes, Inverell and Tamworth. Apart from farming, New England's prosperity is based on minerals and tourism.

TOWNS
Armidale is home to the University of New England and is renowned for its gardens, historic buildings (including two cathedrals) and genteel atmosphere. Among the museums and galleries, the New England Regional Art Museum (*Tue–Sun 10.30–5*) has an excellent collection of Australian art. The Saumarez Homestead is a magnificent 1860s National Trust property (*Mon–Fri 10–4, Sat–Sun 10–5, Sep to mid-Jun*).

Inverell is a small town long associated with farming and mining—the area still produces around 80 per cent of the world's sapphires. Attractions include Copeton Waters State Park (a large lake and its surrounds) and a fossicking reserve, where visitors can search for gemstones.

The main claim to fame of the large agricultural town of Tamworth is its annual Country Music Festival, which draws thousands of people each January. The Australian Country Music Foundation Museum (*Mon–Sat 10–2*) may explain why.

NATIONAL PARKS
Oxley Wild Rivers NP and New England NP are part of the large Central Eastern Rainforest Reserves of Australia World Heritage Area. Oxley Wild Rivers features rivers, waterfalls, gorges and Australia's largest area of dry rainforest, and New England is renowned for its wet and dry rainforest, caves and cliffs.

Guy Fawkes River NP is northeast of Armidale, a rugged and remote wilderness, with rivers and some challenging walks.

Cathedral Rock NP lies east of Armidale. It is known for its sub-alpine heath, huge granite boulders and eucalypt forests.

This road is typical of the New South Wales outback

Flynns Beach is one of the sandy beaches near Port Macquarie

The White Horse Inn at Berrima was founded in 1832

THE SIGHTS

OUTBACK NEW SOUTH WALES–BROKEN HILL

⊞ 320 R13 🛈 Broken Hill Visitor Information Centre, cnr Blende and Bromide streets, Broken Hill, NSW 2880, tel 08 8087 6077 🚉 Menindee or Broken Hill www.murrayoutback.org.au

Broken Hill is about 1,160km (720 miles) northwest of Sydney and 510km (320 miles) northeast of Adelaide. It's certainly a long way from the state capital—a three-day drive along Route 32—but a visit to any of the state's outback towns is recommended for a different perspective on Australian life. A train or plane to Broken Hill is quicker.

This is rugged country—mostly dry and very hot in summer, exceptionally flat with long straight roads and scattered settlements. The only contrast in scenery is provided by low hills, and rivers such as the Darling and Lachlan.

Broken Hill (population 25,000), known as the 'Silver City', developed after the discovery of silver in 1883. Mining is still the major industry and there are above-ground and underground mine tours. The town also has museums, galleries, an Afghan mosque (1891), Aboriginal art and craft outlets, and the Living Desert Reserve, with trails, lookouts and sculptures. Broken Hill is on Central Standard Time, 30 minutes behind the rest of NSW.

Menindee is a small town 110km (68 miles) southeast of Broken Hill, beside the Darling River and the Menindee Lakes system, with fishing and boating. Nearby Kinchega National Park is a 44,000ha (108,680-acre) reserve with lakes, Aboriginal sites, the historic Kinchega woolshed and waterbirds.

The remote, arid Mungo National Park, about 350km (220 miles) southeast of Broken Hill, has provided evidence of at least 60,000 years of Aboriginal occupation. Its famous feature is the Walls of China, a long crescent dune that has been spectacularly eroded over thousands of years.

PORT MACQUARIE

⊞ 327 X13 🛈 Port Macquarie Visitor Information Centre, cnr Clarence and Hay streets, Port Macquarie, NSW 2444, tel 02 6581 8000, (local call rate) 1300 303 155 www.portmacquarieinfo.com.au

Port Macquarie is one of the best North Coast holiday towns and is definitely worth a visit. The small city traces its origins to a penal settlement founded here in 1821. St. Thomas's Church is one of Australia's oldest churches, built by convict labour in 1824–28. Other attractions include sandy beaches, surfing, fishing, cruises on the Hastings River (dolphin-spotting trips), beach camel rides, golf, skydiving, parasailing and wineries.

PORT STEPHENS AND NELSON BAY

⊞ 327 X14 🛈 Port Stephens Visitor Information Centre, Victoria Parade, Nelson Bay, NSW 2315, tel 02 4981 1579, Freecall 1800 808 900 www.portstephens.org.au

With over 20 sandy beaches and the vast Port Stephens bay, this area likes to describe itself as a 'Blue Water Paradise'. The sheltered bay is flanked by small settlements, including the main town of Nelson Bay. The appeal of the area is of an old-fashioned holiday resort. The surrounds consist of heath, forest and rocky headlands.

Port Stephens has a large resident population of bottlenose dolphins, and the area is on the seasonal (May–July) whale migration route—cruises to see these creatures are very popular. The 30km (18.5-mile) Stockton Beach is remarkable for its massive sand dunes.

Don't miss Walk to the headland of Tomaree National Park for great views of the coast.

SOUTHERN HIGHLANDS

⊞ 330 W15 🛈 Tourism Southern Highlands, 62–70 Main Street, Mittagong, NSW 2575, tel 02 4871 2888, (local call rate) 1300 657 559 🚉 Mittagong, Bowral, Moss Vale, Exeter and Bundanoon www.southern-highlands.com.au

The Southern Highlands is an attractive upland farming region to the southwest of Sydney. There are old towns and villages, large country houses, antiques shops, art galleries, craft shops, private and public gardens, historic pubs, good-quality restaurants, and cafés and tea rooms.

Unlike Sydney, the Highlands experience four distinct seasons, and winter snow is not unknown. In the late 19th century wealthy Sydneysiders built country houses here to escape the hot summers. Berrima is one of Australia's best-preserved Georgian villages, founded in 1829 and retaining many historic buildings; the Courthouse (1838) serves as a museum and information office. Apart from its parks and gardens, and antiques and craft shops, the commercial town of Bowral is known for the Bradman Museum (daily 10–5), in honour of the cricketer Sir Donald Bradman, who spent his boyhood here and played for the local club.

Morton National Park is ideal for bushwalkers; particularly good is the view of the waterfall and valley from Fitzroy Falls.

Don't miss Several of the Wombeyan Caves are open to the public and guided tours are available (daily 9–5).

SYDNEY

See pages 59–71.

VICTORIA

Victoria is the smallest mainland state but still has a mountainous northeast, deserts in the northwest and fertile coastal areas. Regional towns recall past gold-rush days, while the state capital of Melbourne has a skyline that combines the greenery of abundant parks and gardens, impressive 19th-century buildings and glittering office towers.

KEY SIGHTS

THE SIGHTS

The stark outline of ACCA stands next to the Playbox Theatre

Brunswick Street comes alive during the Melbourne Fringe Festival parade in late September

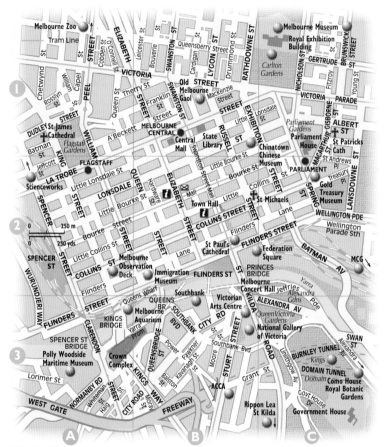

MELBOURNE

AUSTRALIAN CENTRE FOR CONTEMPORARY ART (ACCA)

✚ 83 B3 • 111 Sturt Street, Southbank, VIC 3006 ☎ 03 9697 9999 ◷ Tue–Sun 11–6 🎟 Free; exhibits change every six weeks 🚋 Trams 1, 3, 5, 8, 16, 64, 67, 72 🚉 Flinders Street ▣
www.australiancentreforcontemporary-art.com.au

There is no permanent collection here: instead the modern (2002) building's four cavernous spaces are devoted to short exhibitions.

Whether sculptures, videos, 'space' or multimedia, not every show will be to everyone's taste, but each is challenging and thought-provoking. The window-less, steel shell is an architectural attempt to symbolize the majesty and mystery of Uluru (Ayers Rock), albeit in a busy city streetscape.

BRUNSWICK STREET, FITZROY

✚ 83 C1 🚋 Tram 96

Melbourne's nightlife is found in the five or six bustling inner-city

street-scenes or urban villages that ring the central area, and which all have their own flavour and style. Brunswick Street, in the suburb of Fitzroy, about 2km (1.2 miles) northeast from the city, is perhaps the most varied of them all—neither the hippest nor the most cool, but it certainly has the greatest variety and mix of ethnic food, pub life, cafés, bookshops and inexpensive restaurants. The busiest part lies between Johnston Street and Alexandra Parade. Many of the events of the annual Melbourne Fringe Festival take place in Fitzroy.

The Dai Loong processional dragon is the world's largest

The Old Treasury Building was built in 1858 to store bullion

A replica immigrant ship at the Immigration Museum

CHINATOWN, CHINESE MUSEUM

🔲 83 B1 • Chinese Museum, 22 Cohen Place, Chinatown, VIC 3000; information desk for Chinatown inside the Chinese Museum ☎ 03 9662 2888 🕐 Daily 10–5 💷 Adult A$6.50, child A$4.50 🚊 Tram 86 or 96 to Exhibition Street 🚇 Parliament Station

During the 1850s more than 40,000 Chinese left Guandong province to the north of Hong Kong for Victoria and the lure of the goldfields. Melbourne's Chinatown dates from the early 1850s and is the longest continuous Chinese settlement in the Western world. It's a bustling precinct near the eastern end of Little Bourke Street, an area dominated by restaurants, cafés and Asian grocery stores. Authentic Chinese food is readily available, and Chinatown really starts to buzz after 7pm.

The Chinese Museum has items and photographs from the gold-rush days, portraying both the struggle and the contribution made by these early immigrants. The precinct explodes with fireworks and dancing dragons during the Chinese New Year Festival (February) and the Autumn Moon Lantern Festival (September).

COMO HISTORIC HOUSE AND GARDEN

🔲 Off 83 C3 • Cnr Williams Road and Lechlade Avenue, South Yarra, VIC 3141 ☎ 03 9827 2500 🕐 Daily 10–5 💷 Adult A$10, child A$6, family A$30 🚊 Tram 8 (stop 35) 🚇 South Yarra then tram 8 east 🔲 🖶 www.nattrust.com.au

Como was built on Toorak Hill overlooking the Yarra River in 1847, 4km (2.5 miles) from the young city. It was Melbourne's first colonial mansion, an unusual mix of Regency and Italianate styles surrounded by gracious gardens running down to the river. From 1865 to 1959 it was lived in by the Armytage family who owned a string of grazing properties in western Victoria and Queensland. Como gives an insight into the lifestyle of the wealthy during the mid- to late 1800s, when the city's population ballooned from 77,000 to more than 600,000. The grounds were designed by the master of 19th-century garden design, William Sangster, and part of them still survives.

GOLD TREASURY MUSEUM

🔲 83 C2 • Old Treasury Building, Spring Street, Melbourne, VIC 3000 ☎ 03 9651 2233 🕐 Mon–Fri 9–5, Sat–Sun 10–4 💷 Adult A$7, child A$3.50 🚊 Trams 11, 12, 42, 109, City Circle 🚇 Parliament 🖶 www.oldtreasurymuseum.org.au

The Old Treasury Building was built as gold wealth turned Melbourne into a rich and substantial city. Located as close as possible to the adjacent Parliament House (1855–56), the Treasury was built to house the offices of the colony's leaders, and to store the bullion pouring in from the colony's goldfields of Ballarat and Bendigo. The Renaissance style building faces down the city's most elegant thoroughfare, Collins Street. Three permanent exhibitions and temporary exhibitions recall the city's history, gold-rush days, architecture and 19th-century life.

HEIDE MUSEUM OF MODERN ART

✉ 7 Templestowe Road, Bulleen, Victoria, VIC 3105, 10km (7 miles) northeast of Melbourne ☎ 03 9850 1500 🕐 Tue–Sun 10–5 💷 Georges Mora Gallery: adult A$8, under 12s free. Heide: adult A$8, under 12s free. All areas: adult A$12. Park: free 🚇 Heidelberg then connecting bus to Heide Park 🔲 🖶 www.heide.com.au

Australian art underwent a revolution in the 1940s and 50s when controversial works emerged from a small artist community on the banks of the Yarra River, attracted by the home of wealthy art benefactors John and Sunday Reed, in the unlikely bush suburb of Bulleen. The art of Arthur Boyd, Joy Hester, Sidney Nolan, John Perceval and Albert Tucker is now renowned, and the Reeds' Victorian farmhouse, modernistic home and the Georges Mora Gallery house an outstanding collection of modern art—a cultural destination of national significance. Don't miss The walk through the 5ha (12-acre) grounds, with native gum trees and bush, leads down to the Yarra River.

IMMIGRATION MUSEUM

🔲 83 B2 • Old Customs House, cnr William and Flinders streets, Melbourne, VIC 3000 ☎ 03 9927 2700 🕐 Daily 10–5 💷 Free to ground floor (Immigration Discovery Centre). Exhibitions: adult A$6, under 15s free 🚊 Tram 55, City Circle Tram, any tram along Flinders Street 🚇 Flinders Street 🔲 🖶 www.immigration.museum.vic.gov.au

Over the past 200 years people have journeyed to Australia from all over the world, seeking a better life, a new start or to escape conflict in their homeland. The Immigration Museum, housed in the 1876 Customs House on the northern bank of the Yarra River, relives their stories through images, interactive screens, voices, memories and belongings. Visitors can use the museum's resources to research their family's origins in Australia, to look up the passenger shipping lists, or even discover if their relatives were convicts, unwillingly shipped out to Australia in the First Fleet.

The neo-Grecian Shrine of Remembrance

View the fish of the Melbourne Aquarium from below

Crowds of more than 90,000 gather at the MCG

KINGS DOMAIN AND THE SHRINE OF REMEMBRANCE

➕ 83 C3 • St. Kilda Road, Melbourne, VIC 3000 ☎ 03 9658 9658; Shrine of Remembrance 03 9658 9975; Sidney Myer Music Bowl 03 9281 8000 🕐 Daily 24 hours; Shrine of Remembrance: daily 10–5 🎟 Free 🚋 Any tram from Flinders Street Station down St. Kilda Road 🚉 Flinders Street 🍴 🚻 ♿
www.shrine.org.au

The parklands of the Kings Domain have been beloved by Melburnians for more than 130 years: gravel paths meander through lawns, tree-lined avenues and well-tended gardens. Adjoining the Domain are the Royal Botanic Gardens (see page 89).

The Shrine of Remembrance stands on a slight rise, about 1.5km (1 mile) south of the city. Completed in 1934, it commemorates the 114,000 Victorians who volunteered, and the 19,000 who died, in World War I. Other memorials have been added for World War II, Korea, Vietnam and the Gulf. A new A$7.5 million Visitor and Education Centre features exhibitions including 40m (130ft) of war medals.

MELBOURNE AQUARIUM

➕ 83 A3 • Cnr Flinders and King streets, Melbourne, VIC 3000 ☎ 03 9923 5999 🕐 Daily 9.30–9, Jan; 9.30–6, Feb–Dec 🎟 Adult: A$22, child A$12 🚋 City Circle Tram; trams 109, 112, 96 from Spencer Street; any tram from Flinders Street 🚉 Spencer Street, Flinders Street 🍴 🚻 ♿
www.melbourneaquarium.com.au

Melbourne Aquarium overhangs the Yarra River beside Kings Bridge. Within are thousands of creatures from the cold and wild Great Southern Ocean, where 85 per cent of marine species are found nowhere else in the world. This is the place to see sea dragons, cuttlefish, moray eels, giant crabs and sharks, as well as reef and school fish. There are also fish from southern Australia's freshwater rivers and billabongs, and marine life from the rock pools, tidal shelves and sandy coves of Port Phillip and the Bass Strait.
Don't miss The aquarium's simulated underwater rides are great fun—choose between the Dolphin ride and the Subsonic rollercoaster ride.

MELBOURNE CRICKET GROUND (MCG)

➕ Off 83 C2 • Gate 1, Jolimont Terrace, Jolimont, VIC 3002 ☎ 03 9657 8879 🕐 Daily tours (on non-event days) every half-hour 10–3 🎟 Matches at MCG: adult A$16–45, child A$3.50–A$10. Tours at MCG: adult A$16 🚋 Trams 48, 75 🚉 Jolimont 🚻 ♿
www.mcg.org.au

Established as a cricket oval in 1853, the MCG is one of the world's great sport stadiums, seating more than 90,000 people. The 'People's Ground' is famous as the birthplace of Australian Rules Football in 1858, the main venue of the 1956 Melbourne Olympic Games, and the scene of international Test cricket matches. Watching a game of Aussie Rules Football on a Friday night, Saturday afternoon or Sunday afternoon (*Apr–Sep*) will give a glimpse into the role sport plays in the Australian psyche. The MCG is currently undergoing a major redevelopment: A new gallery of sport, a museum titled MCG City and a new stand will open in 2005, in time for the 2006 Commonwealth Games.
Don't miss A traditional outing in Melbourne on December 26 is going to the first day of the annual cricket Test match at the MCG between Australia and the international touring side.

MELBOURNE MUSEUM

➕ 83 C1 • Carlton Gardens, Carlton, Victoria, VIC 3053 ☎ 13 11 02 or 03 8341 7777 🕐 Daily 10–5 🎟 Adult A$6, child free 🚋 Trams 86, 96; City Circle 🚉 Parliament 🍴 🚻 ♿
www.museum.vic.gov.au

Melbourne Museum, in Carlton Gardens, uses the latest technology to give visitors an insight into Australia's flora, fauna, culture and way of life. Touch a fossil in the Evolution Gallery (DNA, dinosaurs and Darwin); sense the look, sounds and smells of a mountain ash forest in the Forest Gallery; or see the Robinsons' kitchen in Ramsay Street (a set from the TV show *Neighbours*) and discover Charlene's 1987 wedding cake still in the fridge. The Children's Museum thrives in the bright Big Box Gallery, and Australia's only interactive cinema game, ICE (Immersion Cinema Experience), is a hit with teenagers.

MELBOURNE OBSERVATION DECK

➕ 83 A2 • Level 55, Rialto Towers, 525 Collins Street, Melbourne, VIC 3000 ☎ 03 9629 8222 🕐 Sun–Thu 10–9, Fri–Sat 10am–11pm 🎟 Adult A$11.80, child A$6.80, family A$33.80 🚋 Trams 11, 12, 42, 109, City Circle 🚉 Spencer Street 🍴 🚻 ♿
www.melbournedeck.com.au

The high-speed lift takes just 38 seconds to reach Level 55 of the blue-glass Rialto skyscraper, the tallest office building in the southern hemisphere. Once there, the Melbourne Observation Deck gives a spectacular 360-degree panorama of Melbourne and the surrounding area—on a clear day the view extends up to 60km (37 miles). This is a stunning way to start off a visit to Melbourne, both for the views and the excellent 20-minute Melbourne orientation film shown in the ground-floor theatre.

THE SIGHTS

MELBOURNE

Federation Square

The size of a city block, Melbourne's vibrant new hub is both the city's piazza and cultural focus. It's also the place to start your visit to Melbourne: information, sights and plenty of wonderful places to sit and watch the world go by.

Federation Square has given the city a new focus

RATINGS	
Good for kids	●●●○
Shopping	●●●○
Value for money	●●●○
Walkability	●●●●●

TIPS

● The Visitor Centre can get really hectic—get there close to 9am to be sure of finding a staff volunteer for advice, especially if you want to use the booking desk.
● Some of the restaurants can be expensive; consider crossing the river to Southgate for better value dining.

Federation Square is such a popular and essential addition to Melbourne, both for visitors and locals, that it is hard to imagine how the city lived without it. It's a great place to begin any trip to the state capital. The Square is built atop the commuter railyards, between the slow-flowing Yarra River and the main retail and business parts of the CBD. Opened in November 2002, the Square commemorates the centenary of the founding of the Commonwealth of Australia. Make up your own mind about the merits of its jigsaw architecture of jagged zinc, steel and glass; Melburnians either love it (the majority), or hate it (a vocal few).

HIGHLIGHTS

MELBOURNE VISITOR CENTRE

At the northwest corner, close to Flinders Street Station and St. Paul's Anglican Cathedral, the subterranean Visitor Centre is an essential stop for anyone wanting information and advice on things to do and places to go in the city, its near surrounds or in rural Victoria. Stock up with free travel and tour brochures, and regional guides. A shop sells guidebooks, maps and souvenirs.

THE SQUARE

At the core is the open space of the Square itself, paved in pink and ochre sandstone cobbles from the remote Kimberley region of Western Australia. Sections of the paving form a giant artwork, with stories and events that have taken place on or near this site through the centuries, chiselled into the stone. From here there are views over the Yarra River to Southgate and the Victorian Arts Centre (see page 91). Capable of hosting 10,000 people, the Square is the focus for much of Melbourne's busy calendar of festivals, events and promotions, while its tiered steps have become the new meeting place for Melburnians, as well as a great space to watch sports matches on the giant digital screen; key tennis matches are relayed direct from the Australian Open in January. Restaurants, cafés and bars, and the showcase Victorian Wine Precinct, embellish the atmosphere. Coffee is better than expected from the small trolleys on the piazza steps. If you are in Melbourne for New Year's Eve, the Square is the hub of celebrations and live music.

AUSTRALIAN CENTRE FOR THE MOVING IMAGE
☎ 03 8663 2258 ◷ Mon–Fri 10–5, Sat–Sun 10–6; cinema screenings 6.30–9pm 🎟 Free. Cinemas: adult A$11–12, prices vary to screenings
On the north, city-side of the Square, the Australian Centre for the Moving Image projects visions from early cinema to the latest digital media. Containing displays relating to the Australian screen industry, including interactive hands-on features, the ACMI also has two multi-format cinemas screening unusual and historic films and documentaries.

ATRIUM
Next to the ACMI, the glass-shell Atrium acts as both a forecourt to the National Gallery of Victoria Australia and as a public festival and event space. It leads down to the riverside BMW Edge, an indoor amphitheatre designed for small music, cabaret and corporate events, which has stunning views across the Yarra River through its glass walls.

NATIONAL GALLERY OF VICTORIA AUSTRALIA
☎ 03 8662 1555 ◷ Mon–Thu 10–5, Fri 10–9, Sat–Sun 10–6. Free guided tours Mon–Fri 11, 12, 2, 3; Sat–Sun 11, 2 🎟 Free. Charge for exhibitions
Housed within the Square's main buildings, the Ian Potter Centre, the gallery presents the most extensive collection of Australian art in the nation: traditional and contemporary indigenous art, and art from the colonial period through to the present. International art is held at the National Gallery of Victoria International on St. Kilda Road, a 10-minute walk away (see page 88). The idea of an Australian-art only gallery has proved an enormous hit, and should not be missed, while its architecture is an absolute triumph of daring. The 20 sub-galleries flow chronologically: Australian indigenous art, traditional and contemporary, is on the ground level. Famous works include paintings by Wurundjeri elder William Barak, painted around 1890–1900; the early works by contemporary Limmen River artist, the late Ginger Riley Munduwalawala; and the much-loved *Big Yam Dreaming* by Emily Kame Kngwarraye of the Central Desert. On the second level are paintings from Australia's late 19th-century Impressionist movement (Tom Roberts, Fred McCubbin, E. Phillips Fox and Arthur Streeton) and art from the mid- to late 20th century (Fred Williams, Russell Drysdale, Sidney Nolan and John Brack). The four-panel 1964 work by Sidney Nolan, *Landscape (Salt Lake)* is exhibited here for the first time. The third level is used for temporary Australian exhibitions.

BIRRARUNG MARR
☎ Federation Bells ringing, information hotline 03 9658 9658, Mon–Fri 6.30am–7pm ◷ Daily 24 hours 🎟 Free
Birrarung Marr is the first new park to be added to Melbourne's inner city parks and gardens for more than a century. It stretches from the river's edge of Federation Square down between Batman Avenue and the Yarra River to reach the Melbourne Park complex. Birrarung is the Aboriginal name the local Wurundjeri people gave to the river, meaning 'river of mist', while Marr means 'side of the river'. The 8ha (20-acre) riverside park is designed more for strolling and quiet sitting than for its floral displays. Federation Bells in the park consist of 39 bells ranging in size from a handbell to one weighing a tonne. The bells are computer controlled and ring once daily. From Federation Square, you can follow the Yarra River beside Birrarung Marr to Melbourne Park and the Melbourne Cricket Ground (see page 85).

The Federation Bells are in Birrarung Marr

MAKE A DAY OF IT
● St. Paul's Cathedral (opposite Federation Square), see page 89.
● Melbourne Observation Deck (Rialto Towers) 1km (0.6 mile) west, see page 85.
● Gold Treasury Museum 0.75km (0.5 mile) northeast, see page 84.

BASICS
✚ 83 B2
Melbourne Visitor Centre • Cnr Flinders Street and St. Kilda Road, Federation Square, Melbourne, VIC 3000 ☎ 03 9658 9658 www.visitmelbourne.com; www.melbourne.vic.gov.au ◷ Daily 9–6 🚋 City Circle Tram; Flinders Street Station stop 🚉 Flinders Street 🚢 Williamstown ferry stops at Southgate, just across Princes Bridge from Federation Square. Melbourne River Cruises boats or river water taxis ply upstream or downstream on the Yarra moor alongside Federation Square at Princes Wharf
❓ Multilingual facilities, interpretative multimedia, Internet access, accommodation and tour booking service
🚉 Flinders Street
www.fedsq.com • An over-designed and poorly working website.

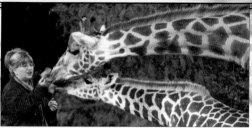

When you arrive at Melbourne Zoo, check out the animal feeding times which are generally between 9 and 1

The three-masted Polly Woodside now sits in dry dock

MELBOURNE ZOO

⊞ 83 A1 • Elliott Avenue, Parkville Victoria, VIC 3052 ☎ 03 9285 9300 🕐 Daily 9–5 🎫 Adult A$17.50, child A$8.50, under 4s free 🚋 Trams 55, 68 🚉 Royal Park from Flinders Street 🍴 🛋 ♿
www.zoo.org.au

The 22ha (54-acre) zoo in Royal Park, Parkville, is known for its authentic re-creations of animal habitats. More than 350 species of rare animals and birds from around the world are on display, many of them endangered. The large animal enclosures represent different climatic habitats (rainforest, bush and savannah), including the Lion Park, the Arboreal Primate Enclosure, the Great Flight Aviary and the beautiful Butterfly House, and the popular Trail of the Elephants. To see Australian animals in the best surroundings you should go to Healesville Sanctuary in the Yarra Valley (see page 94).

NATIONAL GALLERY OF VICTORIA INTERNATIONAL

⊞ 83 B3 • 100 St. Kilda Road, Melbourne, VIC 3004 ☎ 03 8662 1555 🕐 Mon–Fri 10–5 (also Fri 5–9pm), Sat–Sun 10–6 🎫 Free. Charge for exhibitions 🚋 Trams 3, 5, 6, 8, 16, 25, 64, 67, 72 🚉 Flinders Street 🍴 🛋 ♿
www.ngv.vic.gov.au

The revamped 1968 gallery houses the state's international collection of European paintings, Asian art, decorative arts, textiles, photographs and sculptures. Australian art is now on show at the Federation Square gallery (see page 87), a 10-minute walk away. Inside the St. Kilda Street gallery

you first meet a water wall, where water cascades down glass sheets. Artworks include Egyptian, pre-Columbian, Greek and Roman antiquities. There are Asian art galleries, and European paintings and sculpture from the 14th to the 17th centuries. Late 20th-century art, including new media and photography, is also featured.

Don't miss Leonard French's 1967 stained-glass ceiling in the Great Hall is the largest in the world.

OLD MELBOURNE GAOL

⊞ 83 B1 • Russell Street, Melbourne, VIC 3000 ☎ 03 9663 7228 🕐 Daily 9–5. Night tours Wed, Fri–Sun from 8.30 (7.30 in winter); bookings, Ticketek 132 849 🎫 Adult A$12.50, child A$7.50, family A$33.50; UK National Trust members free. Night tours: adult A$20, child A$13 🚋 Trams 23, 24, 30, 34; City Circle 🚉 Melbourne Central 🛋 Opening 2005 ♿
www.nattrust.com.au

Built in 1841, Victoria's oldest surviving prison housed hardened murderers and criminals. Its most infamous resident was bushranger Ned Kelly, who was imprisoned here and hanged on 11 November 1880. This dehumanising place, where the prisoners were kept in solitary confinement, was the scene of 136 hangings until the prison closed in 1929. The prisoners' grim stories are retold using contemporary newspapers, photos, letters, audio recordings and death masks—including Kelly's.

Don't miss The candle-lit night tour is not for the faint-hearted. Tests for 'paranormal activity' in mid-2003 supposedly detected the faint sounds of a woman's voice.

POLLY WOODSIDE MELBOURNE MARITIME MUSEUM

⊞ 83 A3 • Lorimer Street East, Southbank, VIC 3006 ☎ 03 9699 9760/1 🕐 Daily 10–4 🎫 Adult A$9, child A$6; UK National Trust members free 🚋 Trams 96, 109; City Circle 🚉 Spencer Street 🛋 ♿
www.nattrust.com.au

From 1835 until about 1970 almost all of Melbourne's immigrants arrived by sea. The city remains the biggest port in Australia, and many of the city's inhabitants live around Port Phillip. This maritime heritage is preserved in one of the warehouse sheds that once lined the Yarra River, where old clipper boats and steam ships tied up after perilous voyages from England and Europe. Historic photographs, models and film capture the early sailing days. The key exhibit is the three-masted iron barque, the *Polly Woodside*. Built in 1885, the vessel made 16 voyages around Cape Horn before sailing for 20 years around the Pacific.

RAAF MUSEUM

✉ RAAF Williams Base, Point Cook Road, Point Cook, VIC 3027, 20km (14 miles) southeast of Melbourne ☎ 03 9256 1300 🕐 Tue–Fri 10–3, Sat–Sun 10–5 🎫 Free 🚋 Werribee Park Shuttle from Flinders Street station ♿
www.raafmuseum.com.au

In 1913 the Australian Flying Corps (later the Royal Australian Air Force) was formed at Point Cook. The first Australian pilots trained three years later in a Maurice Farman bi-plane and this same plane is in the museum, along with more than 20 other aircraft from little Tiger Moths to Phantom fighter jets. There is also an excellent collection of RAAF memorabilia, film footage and photographs from the two world wars, Korea and Vietnam.

Rippon Lea is about 8km (5 miles) south of the city

On a hot day try to find some shade in the Botanic Gardens

The Royal Exhibition Building dates from 1880

RIPPON LEA ESTATE

✠ Off 83 C3 • 192 Hotham Street, Elsternwick, VIC 3185 ☎ 03 9523 6095 ⊙ Daily 10–5 🖐 House and garden: · adult A$10, child A$5. Garden: adult A$6, child A$3. UK National Trust members free 🚊 Tram 67; buses 216, 219 🚻 Ripponlea ▣ ⊞ www.nattrust.com.au

Rippon Lea is one of Australia's great 19th-century estates to survive largely intact, and is the largest mansion of its period open to the public. It was built and enlarged between 1868 and 1903 by one of Melbourne's leading businessmen and politicians, Frederick Thomas Sargood. Along with the garden, the atmosphere is more like Victorian England than the young colony, and the house is remarkable for its polychrome brickwork, oak and mahogany parquetry floors, stained-glass windows, rich European wallpapers and gilt decorations. This was the backdrop for family gatherings and huge society parties. In 1938 the then owner, Louisa Jones, modernized the house, and much of the furniture of this glamorous period is retained in the mansion today. **Don't miss** During summer, plays are often performed outdoors in the garden and grounds.

ROYAL BOTANIC GARDENS

✠ Off 83 C3 • Birdwood Avenue, South Yarra, VIC 3141 ☎ 03 9252 2300 ⊙ Daily 7.30am–8.30pm, Nov–Mar; 7.30–5.30 rest of year 🖐 Free 🚊 Trams 3, 5, 8, 16, 64, 67 to interchange of St. Kilda and Domain roads ▣ ⊞ www.rbg.vic.gov.au

Established in 1846, the Royal Botanic Gardens are the pride of Melburnians and renowned as one of the finest examples of 19th-century garden landscaping in the world. The rolling 36ha (89 acres) are both a botanic garden and a public park, with broad sweeps of grass, lakes, tall riverside eucalypts, acacias and native hoop pines, rainforest, palms, cacti and woodland. There are more than 12,000 species of native and exotic plants. The RBG also hold the national camellia collection, planted in a mass bed near the equally stunning rhododendron and magnolia gardens. **Don't miss** The Children's Garden (near the Observatory Gate) has touching and feeling plants, as well as its story-telling tree.

ROYAL EXHIBITION BUILDING AND CARLTON GARDENS

✠ 83 C1 • Nicholson Street, Carlton, VIC 3053 ☎ 03 3341 7777 ⊙ REB by tour only (1 hour): daily 2pm from Melbourne Museum foyer. Carlton Gardens: daily 24 hours 🖐 Tour: adult A$7.50, child A$2. Gardens: free 🚊 Trams 86, 96 www.museum.vic.gov.au/reb

The Royal Exhibition Building is one of Australia's most important 19th-century buildings. It was completed in 1880 as the central attraction of the Melbourne International Exhibition, which ran for eight months and attracted 1.3 million visitors. Apart from the Eiffel Tower, it is the only structure to remain from the series of grand international exhibitions held around the world from 1850 to 1890. The classical basilica was designed by the Melbourne architect Joseph Reed, and the dome's shape reflects Florence Cathedral (Duomo); within the dome allegorical figures depict Peace, War, Federation, Government and the four seasons.

The first Commonwealth Parliament of Australia was opened here on 9 May 1901. Since then it has been a hospital during the Spanish influenza outbreak of 1919, a concert hall, a venue for the 1956 Melbourne Olympic Games, and now back as an exhibition space. The surrounding Carlton Gardens contain a grand Victorian marble fountain, an ornamental lake and formal avenues of shady elms.

In 2002 the Australian government nominated the building and Carlton Gardens as a World Heritage Site.

ST. PAUL'S CATHEDRAL

✠ 83 B2 • Cnr Flinders and Swanston streets, Melbourne, VIC 3000 ☎ 03 9650 3791 ⊙ Sun–Fri 8 until after Evensong (about 6), Sat 8–5 (6 in summer) 🖐 Free 🚊 City Circle Tram; any tram along Swanston or Flinders streets, or St. Kilda Road 🚻 Flinders Street ⊞ www.stpaulscathedral.org.au

The Anglican cathedral is one of Melbourne's most visited landmarks. St. Paul's stands on the site where the first public Christian services in Melbourne were led by Dr. Alexander Thomson in 1836. St. Paul's Parish Church was built here in 1848–52 and demolished in 1885 to make way for the present cathedral. The neo-Gothic style of the cathedral was designed by the British architect William Butterfield, who steadfastly refused to visit Melbourne. He resigned from the project in 1884 and the building was completed by Joseph Reed, who designed many of Melbourne's public buildings.

The cathedral was consecrated on 22 January 1891, but the spires were not begun until 1926, and then to the design of John Barr of Sydney rather than Butterfield's plan. The building's interior is remarkable for its polychrome stonework, marbles, rich mosaics and stained glass. However, it is the church's

St. Paul's is a quiet haven compared to the bustle outside

musical contribution to Melbourne that is unsurpassed: The choir, organ and bells repay any visit. The peal of 13 bells can be enjoyed from a café on Federation Square or Southgate, between 6.30pm and 9pm. **Don't miss** Try to attend Evensong at either 5 (winter) or 6 (summer).

SCIENCEWORKS MUSEUM

Off 83 A2 • 2 Booker Street, Spotswood, VIC 3015 ☎ 03 9392 4800/131102 Daily 10–4.30 Scienceworks and the Planetarium: adult A$12, child A$4 Ferries from Southbank to Williamstown stop at Scienceworks (40-min trip); tel 03 9506 4144 www.scienceworks.museum.vic.gov.au

This museum tries to answer the question: What is science? In the Sports Works section, there are fun activities that test your fitness and athletic skills: Race against the Olympic 200 metres sprinting champion, Cathy Freeman; see how well your heart and lungs are working; or throw balls, ride bicycles and pump iron. In the Stayin' Alive section, you can see how your body will handle extremes of heat and cold, Antarctic conditions or even outer space. These and similar hands-on displays engage children of all ages in the fascination of science, while quietly educating adults into the bargain.

The award-winning Scienceworks Museum is based around the 1880s Spotswood Pumping Station, which has enormous working steam pumps that once rid Melbourne of its sewage. **Don't miss** Melbourne Planetarium re-creates the night sky on a domed ceiling, and allows a simulated three-dimensional journey to the moon, stars, galaxies and beyond.

ST. KILDA AND LUNA PARK

The bayside suburb of St. Kilda pulsates with activity 24 hours a day.

83 C3 Port Phillip Council 03 9209 6777 Trams 16, 96 www.portphillip.vic.gov.au

St. Kilda is so full of tourist destinations that it is sometimes easy to forget how beautiful and special it is. The elegant pier, the Moorish palace-style baths and the fine restaurants balance the old-fashioned rides at Luna Park, live music at the famous Esperance (Espy) Hotel and the ubiquitous backpacker joints. On weekends, Melburnians walk, cycle and skate along the palm-lined foreshore or sit in an outdoor café, enjoying the panorama of Port Phillip. Many of the suburb's 19th-century mansions have been converted into smart apartments.

RATINGS			
Good for kids	●	●	● ○
Photo stops	●	●	● ○
Shopping	●	●	● ○
Activities	●	●	● ●

TIP

● This is probably one area of Melbourne where walking alone after dark, away from Fitzroy and Acland streets, is not advisable.

HIGHLIGHTS

A walk along the 1857 pier is a must, with its views of the bay and the city skyline, and the historic fish and chips kiosk perched at the end. Next to the pier is the St. Kilda Sea Baths, originally opened in 1850 and still Melbourne's only indoor heated sea-water pool (*Mon–Fri 6am–10pm, Sat–Sun 7am–9pm*).

Farther along the beach, the much-loved Luna Park is an institution. First opened in 1912, it was modelled on New York's Coney Island; the smiling face entrance and the timber and iron Scenic Railway are both classified historic monuments. The park received a A$10 million upgrade in 2001.

Away from the foreshore, much of the activity is concentrated on the two main action strips of Fitzroy and Acland streets. Fitzroy Street is renowned for its cafés, pubs, restaurants and bars, and is one of the city's most interesting eating and drinking streets. Acland Street is more eclectic, a mix of restaurants, Continental cake shops, book and record shops, and retro clothing boutiques. The oldest and the best café is Monarch (No. 103); enjoy one of the many treats from a window seat. On Sundays there is a popular open-air art and crafts market along the Upper Esplanade. **Don't miss** Rent roller blades (or a bicycle) from near the beach end of Fitzroy Street and head up the special beachside path around the bay towards Port Melbourne.

Southbank is at its best on sunny weekends

Check out visiting exhibitions at the Victorian Arts Centre

Williamstown is an easy ferry ride from central Melbourne

SOUTHBANK

✚ 83 B3 • Crown Entertainment Complex, Whiteman Street, Southbank, VIC 3006 ☎ Southgate customer information: 03 9699 4311. Crown: 03 9292 8888 🚋 Trams 109, 112, 96, City Circle 🚉 Spencer Street
www.southgate-melbourne.com.au
www.crowncasino.com.au

The 15-minute walk along the south promenade of the Yarra River from Princes Bridge to Spencer Street Bridge takes in the two arts and leisure precincts of Southbank. Unless you are interested in gambling, the main reason to visit either Southgate or the Crown Complex is for a meal or coffee, and the lovely views across the Yarra River to central Melbourne. The Southgate complex, just 100m (330ft) from Princes Bridge and Federation Square (see pages 86–87), has shops, wine bars, art galleries and gourmet food and wine shops; opened in 1992, it was quickly embraced by Melburnians as the city's hottest restaurant location. On weekends there is live music in the forecourt, and on Sundays a craft market winds down to the river. Ferries and cruises depart up- or downstream. The more nondescript Crown Complex is not only a casino, but also contains restaurants, cafés, cinemas, late night dance and club venues, and exclusive brand stores such as Armani, Versace, La Perla, DKNY and Gucci. Brash and flash, it's more a night destination, especially for keen gamblers, though some of Melbourne's best Asian restaurants are here. The Crown's 14 cinemas include the world's first four Gold Class cinemas, complete with reclining chairs and table service.

Don't miss Once it gets dark, don't miss the giant fireballs that shoot skywards every hour in the evenings from the flame towers lining the Crown Complex.

VICTORIAN ARTS CENTRE

✚ 83 B3 • 100 St. Kilda Road, Melbourne, VIC 3004 ☎ 03 9281 8000 ⓒ Concert Hall building closed until performance times. Theatre complex Mon–Fri 8am–midnight, Sat 9am–midnight, Sun 9–5 💷 Public spaces free. Front of House tours (1 hour, A$10): Mon–Sat 12, 2.30. Back of House tour (80 min, A$13.50): Sunday 12.15; not appropriate for children under 12 🚋 Any tram along Swanston Street 🚉 Flinders Street 🍴 🛒 🏛
www.artscentre.net.au

Unlike its Sydney counterpart, the Opera House, the Victorian Arts Centre has most of its performance spaces and art treasures concealed underground. It was built in 1973–84 by architect Sir Roy Grounds and interior designer John Truscott. The landmark 162m (531ft) tubular white spire is lit at night by blue neon tubing and laser lights.

The Centre's theatres and halls host the Melbourne Theatre Company, Opera Australia, the Australian Ballet, and the Melbourne Symphony Orchestra, and is a popular venue for choirs, small chamber orchestras and international performing artists. The plush, four-tiered State Theatre, effectively Melbourne's Opera House, has the world's second-largest stage.

The Centre also exhibits Australian art, with works by Sir Sidney Nolan, Arthur Boyd, John Olson and Jeffrey Smart, and massive Aboriginal artworks from the Western Desert. The Performing Arts Museum (Mon–Fri 11–5, Sat–Sun 12–5) celebrates the magic of the stage. Half-price tickets are available on the performance day from the HalfTix box at the Town Hall (corner of Swanston and Collins streets).

The three-week Melbourne Festival in October brings the Arts Centre alive.

Don't miss Visit the Sunday market (10–5) of 150 art and craft stalls in the undercroft of the Melbourne Concert Hall.

WILLIAMSTOWN

ℹ Williamstown Tourist Information Centre, cnr Nelson Place and Syme Street, Williamstown, VIC 3016, 9km (6 miles) southeast of Melbourne ☎ 03 9397 3791 🚉 Williamstown; from Flinders Street change at Footscray 🚢 Ferries leave Melbourne Southgate quay every half hour to Williamstown (50-minute river trip)
www.williamstowninfo.com.au

The pretty seaport lies on a peninsula between the mouth of the Yarra River and the beaches of Port Phillip. Port Gellibrand or Williamstown began life in 1835 as a suitable place to unload cargo from Tasmania for the fledgling Melbourne settlement. Within five years the sheltered harbour had 100 buildings and was Melbourne's main port. Seafaring traditions continue in the yacht clubs, shipyards, port, naval dockyards and sea and river cruises. The suburb is now a heritage area, preserving its beautiful churches, pubs and timber cottages. Modern life fills the cafés, bars and seafood restaurants clustered around the maritime precinct of Nelson Place.

Every third Sunday of the month a craft market is held in Commonwealth Reserve on Nelson Place; the Message Tree here was used to pin messages for those disembarking from sailing ships. The 1876 Customs House is now an art gallery, and ferries still dock at Gem Pier, built by convicts in 1839. The relaxing river ferry to Williamstown stops at Scienceworks (see page 90).

Don't miss The World War II minesweeper, HMAS Castlemaine, moored at Gem Pier, has a maritime museum on board (Sat–Sun 12–5).

THE SIGHTS

MELBOURNE

Gold-mining relics at Bendigo

The re-created gold town of Sovereign Hill

THE SIGHTS

VICTORIA

BEECHWORTH

✚ 329 U16 ℹ Beechworth Visitor Information Centre, Ford Street, Beechworth, VIC 3747, tel 03 5728 3233 www.indigoshire.vic.gov.au

The small town of Beechworth nestles in the foothills of the Victorian Alps in the northeast of the state. Beechworth is one of Victoria's best-preserved gold-rush towns, close to the Rutherglen, Milawa and Beechworth wine regions. Gold was discovered in the area in 1852. Many early buildings are preserved, while the nearby hamlets of Yackandandah and Chiltern are little changed since the 19th century.

The impressive Beechworth Court in the Beechworth Historic and Cultural Precinct (*daily 9–5*) is complete with its original furniture and fittings; Ned Kelly stood trial here before his execution at Old Melbourne Gaol in 1880.

BENDIGO

✚ 329 T16 ℹ Bendigo Visitor Information Centre, 51–67 Pall Mall, Bendigo, VIC 3550, tel 03 5444 4445 🚆 Bendigo www.bendigotourism.com

Gold was found in Bendigo in 1851, and from 1870 to 1880 the area was considered the richest goldfield in the world. The 19th-century boom-town architecture includes the magnificent former post office, now the visitor office. The Chinese prospectors that flocked to the Bendigo goldfield are celebrated in the Golden Dragon Museum and Classical Chinese Gardens (*daily 9–5*).

Mining heritage continues at the Central Deborah Gold Mine on Violet Street, with tours below the city. Many of Bendigo's attractions are linked by vintage trams, which give a recorded commentary. Stop off at View Street for the Bendigo Art Gallery (*daily 9–5*).

BALLARAT

Gold is still extracted from the site of the world's biggest gold rush in 1851.

✚ 328 S16 ℹ Ballarat Visitors Information Centre • 39 Sturt Street, Ballarat, VIC 3350, tel 03 5320 5741, open daily 9–5 🚆 Ballarat www.ballarat.com

RATINGS	
Good for kids	●●●●●
Historic interest	●●●●
Photo stops	●●●●●
Walkability	●●●●

TIP
● The Ballarat Welcome Pass gives entry to Sovereign Hill, the Gold Museum, the Ballarat Fine Art Gallery and the Eureka Centre; adult A$33.50.

On 21 August 1851 gold was discovered near Sovereign Hill. Fortune hunters flocked to Ballarat from across the world, carving out a rough and ready and defiantly independent community. The wealth from Ballarat resulted in the rapid growth and prosperity of Melbourne and the colony of Victoria, and also a miners' rebellion against British rule, the Eureka Stockade.

SOVEREIGN HILL

The goldfields are realistically re-created at Sovereign Hill, 2km (1.2 miles) south of the town (*daily 10–5.30, Sep–Mar; 10–5, rest of year*). The 25ha (62-acre) outdoor museum has more than 60 working period buildings, including banks, post offices, furniture shops, bakeries, saloons, steam-driven battery houses and even an undertaker. Costumed actors and local volunteers provide a living reflection of the times, with street theatre staged all day. Modern fortune seekers can pan for gold in creeks and there is a tour of underground mines. After sunset a sound-and-light show, Blood on the Southern Cross, re-enacts the Eureka Stockade rebellion. Entrance to Sovereign Hill includes the Gold Museum, next door.

About 1km (0.6 mile) from Sovereign Hill in East Ballarat, is the Eureka Centre (*daily 9–4.30*), on the site of the 1854 rebellion: Ballarat's miners took up arms against the unjust goldfields administration by the British colonial government. The overnight battle, when miners built their own stockade and many died during the fight, is regarded as a struggle against injustice and oppression.

Nearer the middle of town is the grand 1884 Ballarat Fine Art Gallery (*daily 10.30–5*). The gallery has superb Australian prints and drawings, and its collection of colonial and Heidelberg School paintings is also particularly good.

Puffing Billy climbs into the Dandenongs several times a day

THE DANDENONGS

The Dandenongs have been a cool summer retreat for Melburnians for more than 150 years.

The bush-covered Dandenong Ranges stretch north for 30km (19 miles) from Ferntree Gully in Melbourne's east, through the hill village of Olinda in the heart of the Ranges to Lilydale and the start of the Yarra Valley wine-growing plains. Tall mountain ash forests blend with some of Australia's most beautiful gardens, where exotic flowers and trees meld with native species. Visit in late winter and early spring when the hills are full of daffodils, camellias, rhododendrons and azaleas.

HIGHLIGHTS

At the southern end of the Dandenongs near Belgrave is Puffing Billy, Australia's oldest preserved steam railway and one of Melbourne's best-loved icons (*departures daily 10.30, 12; additional trains in summer and at weekends*). The 25km (15-mile) journey goes east through thick forests and fern-filled gullies to Emerald Lake Park and Gembrook. Break the journey at the Steam Museum at Menzies Creek station.

The region, however, is best explored by car and on foot. The Mount Dandenong Tourist Road zigzags north from Ferntree Gully to Montrose; the landscape is heavily forested, with few village communities. Much of the region is protected within the 3,200ha (7,900-acre) Dandenong Ranges National Park, which has picnic grounds and walking tracks, and plays an important role in protecting its population of lyrebirds, notable for their distinctive long tail feathers. The 30-minute walk to Sherbrooke Falls, near Olinda, is popular. For a longer walk of some 7 hours, the 17km (10-mile) Dandenong Ranges Tourist Track runs southeast from the hill village of Sassafras along the cool Sassafras and Menzies creeks, across mountain ridges to Clematis. Maps are available from the Parks Victoria website (www.parkweb.vic.gov.au) and from the Dandenongs Visitor Information Centre.

In contrast to the wild landscape of the Dandenongs are its gardens. The 40ha (100-acre) National Rhododendron Gardens cascade down a hillside near Olinda (*daily 10–5*). An astounding display of 250,000 daffodils, 3,000 camellias, 12,000 azaleas and 15,000 rhododendrons bloom from June through to December. **Don't miss** The William Ricketts Sanctuary in Mount Dandenong is more unusual (*daily 10–4.30*). Set among rocks and fern gardens are kiln-fired clay sculptures of Aboriginal figures.

RATINGS	
Good for kids	●●●●●
Historic interest	●●
Photo stops	●●●●●
Activities	●●●●

TIPS

● Take advantage of the picnic, barbecue and swimming facilities at Emerald Lake Park on the Puffing Billy railway line.
● Avoid the rash of kitsch cafés and restaurants housed in mock Tudor ugliness.

BASICS

⊞ 329 T16 ⓘ Dandenongs Visitor Information Centre • 1211 Burwood Highway, Upper Ferntree Gully, VIC 3156, tel 03 9758 7522, open daily 9–5 🚆 Ferntree Gully, Belgrave www.visitvictoria.com

William Ricketts' sculptures were inspired by his time living in Central Australia

The Daylesford Hotel offers spa treatments

There are more than 50 marked trails traversing the ranges and peaceful bush valleys of the Grampians National Park

THE SIGHTS

BRIGHT AND MOUNT BUFFALO NATIONAL PARK

🖪 329 U16 🛈 Bright Visitor Information Centre • 119 Gavan Street, Bright, VIC 3741, tel 03 5755 2275 **www.visitvictoria.com**

Bright is a peaceful town in the Ovens Valley below Mount Buffalo and the Victorian Alps. The resort attracts trout fishermen, cyclists and walkers in spring and summer, skiers in winter, and anybody for its autumn foliage. The many deciduous trees in the town are a legacy of the pioneers who planted avenues of elms, chestnuts, poplars and scarlet oaks.

West of Bright, the 31,000ha (76,570-acre) Mount Buffalo National Park has cliffs, granite tors, waterfalls and ski fields. Park visitors walk and rock climb in summer, and ski from late June to September. The terrain is also good for caving and hang-gliding.

THE DANDENONGS

See page 93.

DAYLESFORD AND HEPBURN SPRINGS

🖪 329 I 16 🛈 Daylesford Visitor Information Centre • Vincent Street, Daylesford, VIC 3460, tel 03 5348 1339 🚆 Ballarat then regular bus services to Daylesford **www.visitdaylesford.com**

These neighbouring towns arose during the 1850s gold rush, and became spa resorts in the late 19th century, drawing visitors to the area's mineral springs. Water from each of the 70 springs has its own distinctive taste—no visit is complete without trying some. Bathing in the springs is also popular, and various spa resorts provide a range of treatments.

Day visits should also include the weekend markets, antiques shops, galleries, cafés and lakeside restaurants.

GEELONG

🖪 329 T17 🛈 Geelong Visitor Information Centre • Stead Park, Princes Highway, Corio, VIC 3214, tel 03 5275 5797 🚆 Geelong **www.greatoceanrd.org.au**

Victoria's second-largest city was built on wool: Within four years of the first sheep being grazed on Victorian pastures in 1836, wool was being exported from Geelong to British mills. See and hear the story (great 'yarns') at the National Wool Museum, housed in an 1872 stone wool store near the seafront on Moorabool Street (*daily 9.30–5*). The beautiful waterfront of Corio Bay is ideal for strolling. At Steampacket Quay is an 1892 steam carousel, with 36 carved wooden horses and two chariots. If it's hot, try the art-deco sea baths at Eastern Beach. On the headland above, Eastern Park contains the Botanic Gardens. West of the beaches and the city's central area, the wide tree-lined Pakington Street is Geelong's answer to Melbourne's café society and love of ethnic food. Don't miss Along the foreshore are 104 bollards standing 2m (6.5ft) high, painted by local artist Jan Mitchell; each shows a character from Geelong's history.

THE GRAMPIANS

🖪 328 S16 🛈 Halls Gap Visitor Information Centre • Centenary Hall, Grampians Road, Halls Gap, VIC 3381, tel 03 5356 4616, 1800 065 599 **www.thegrampians.com.au**

The Grampians are the western foothills—still over 1,000m (3,280ft) high—of the Great Dividing Range, which stretches down the east coast of Australia. Halls Gap is the main tourist focus of the region, at the base of the spectacular Pinnacle Lookout. Ararat, on the east side of the region, is the only town in Australia founded by Chinese immigrants, following their discovery of the Gum San (Hill of Gold) goldfield in 1857. The Gum San Chinese Heritage Centre highlights the contribution of Chinese culture to the development of Australia (*daily 10–4.30*).

Bunjil's Shelter east of Pomonal is the most important of the area's many Aboriginal rock art sites, stunningly depicting Bunjil, the traditional creator of Gariwerd (the Grampians). The Brambuk Living Cultural Centre, 2km (1.2 miles) south of Halls Gap, brings the history of the local Aboriginal people up to date (*daily 10–5*). Close by, the Grampians National Park Visitor Centre (*daily 9–5*) is perhaps the best introduction for newcomers to the park.

GREAT OCEAN ROAD

See pages 96–99.

HEALESVILLE SANCTUARY

🖪 329 T16 • Badger Creek Road, Healesville, VIC 3777 ☎ 03 5957 2800 🕐 Daily 9–5 💵 Adult A$17.50, child A$8.50, under 4s free 🚌 Coach tours from Melbourne daily ▯ ▯ **www.zoo.org.au**

Go to Healesville Sanctuary for native animals and authentic bush sights and smells. Expect close encounters with dingoes, kangaroos, wombats and duck-billed platypus, as well as brightly feathered native birds, all in a natural bush setting within the Yarra Valley (see page 100). There are 200 species of birds, mammals and reptiles, some of which—kangaroos, emus and wallabies—roam freely. You can also see echidnas and wombats at play—or asleep—and glimpse possums, flying foxes and tiny sugar gliders. There is a beautiful koala area, and a reptile house for viewing Australian snakes and lizards.

Get close up to a wombat at Healesville Sanctuary

The Penguin Parade at Phillip Island is Victoria's most popular tourist attraction for foreign visitors

Don't miss Watch the Birds of Prey presentation—a wedgetail eagle (pictured below) soars low over the crowd.

MELBOURNE

See pages 83–91.

MORNINGTON PENINSULA

🚻 329 T17 ℹ️ Mornington Peninsula Visitor Information Centre • Point Nepean Road, Dromana, VIC 3936, tel 03 5987 3078 🚆 Frankston then twice-daily bus connection to Portsea www.melbournesbays.org

Melburnians come to Mornington Peninsula to laze on the beach, fish in Port Phillip, walk along the ocean cliffs and relax. The southern 'back' beaches facing the Bass Strait are prone to dangerous tides and rough seas, though there is good rock fishing, diving in calm weather and surfing. The 'front' beaches facing the bay are calm, gently sloping and sandy, without any dangerous tides—ideal for swimming, sailing and windsurfing. Mornington Peninsula National Park extends along the ocean coast from the 1859 Cape Schanck Lighthouse (*daily for tours 10–5*) to Point Nepean, where Fort Nepean was a vital part of Victoria's defences from the 1880s. Sorrento is probably the heart of the peninsula, a village with elegant eateries, boutiques, galleries and specialist shops. The ferry leaves here for Queenscliff across The Rip seaway (*daily 7–6*). Near Dromana on the front shore, the 314m (1,030ft) mound

known as Arthurs Seat looks over the bay and peninsula. For children, go to the gardens at Ashcombe Maze near Shoreham (*daily 10–5*).

MOUNT MACEDON

🚻 329 T16 ℹ️ Woodend Visitor Information Centre • High Street, Woodend, VIC 3442, tel 03 5427 2033 🚆 Woodend then bus or taxi to Mount Macedon and Hanging Rock www.visitvictoria.com

Many of Melbourne's wealthy families built summer retreats in the Mount Macedon range in the late 1800s, creating magnificent gardens within the bush. Some of these English-style woodland gardens are open all year. Mount Macedon itself is over 1,000m (3,280ft)–drive up to the summit for spectacular views and walks.

To the north across the volcanic plains is Hanging Rock (*daily 8–6*), a small steep volcanic plug rising 105m (345ft) from the surrounding bush. The rock was made famous as the setting for Joan Lindsay's novel, *Picnic at Hanging Rock*, and a subsequent film, about the strange disappearance of three schoolgirls in 1900.

PHILLIP ISLAND

🚻 329 T17 ℹ️ Phillip Island Visitor Centre • Phillip Island Tourist Road, Newhaven, VIC 3925, tel 03 5956 7447 www.visitvictoria.com

Reached by bridge, low-lying Phillip Island is just 26km (16 miles) long and 9km (5.5 miles) wide. The island faces Western Port bay to the north and the Bass Strait to the south. Cowes, on the bay side, is the largest town. From here, weather permitting, boat trips go to Seal Rocks, where Australia's largest

colony of fur seals lives. A clifftop walk also gives views of the seals, and a path leads down to the spectacular Blowhole. The three main tourist attractions—Penguin Parade, Churchill Island and the Koala Conservation Centre—are managed by the Phillip Island Nature Park, and a combined entry ticket is available. Each night at dusk (*around 8 in summer, 5–6 other times*) dozens of groups of Little Penguins return to Summerland Beach to rest and to feed their young—the breeding season is from August to March—after fishing in the waters off Phillip Island. Pre-book and bring warm clothing. At the Koala Conservation Centre (*daily 10–5*), a thick section of bush is home to 900 koalas; raised boardwalks provide a treetop aspect of them. For walkers, the route to Cape Woolamai is the best of 15 tracks around the island.

RUTHERGLEN

🚻 329 U15 ℹ️ Rutherglen Visitor Information Centre • 13/27 Drummond Street, Rutherglen, VIC 3685, tel 02 6032 9166 🚆 Glenrowan, Wangaratta; connecting bus service to Rutherglen www.wangaratta.vic.gov.au

Winemakers have taken advantage of the fertile land and mild climate around Glenrowan, Rutherglen and Wahgunyah since the early 19th century. Wineries abound and there are cellar-door tastings. The main street of Rutherglen is lined with historic buildings, antiques shops and restaurants. South of Rutherglen, the main town of Wangaratta is famous for its annual jazz festival.

Little Glenrowan is the site of the siege where the bushranger Ned Kelly and his gang made their last stand on 27 June 1880, dressed in their distinctive hand-forged armour. Kellyland is a cinematic and theatrical portrayal of the siege (*daily 9.30–4.30*).

Great Ocean Road

Victoria's famous tourist drive snakes and weaves around 250km (155 miles) of spectacular cliffs, scenic lookouts, beaches and rainforests, and through hair-raising bends, clifftop tunnels and steep forest-clad hills.

SEEING THE GREAT OCEAN ROAD

The Great Ocean Road (or less poetically, the B100) follows a sprawling stretch of coastline in Victoria's southwest, with spectacular lookouts and vistas. It runs between Torquay on the Surf Coast and the town of Warrnambool on the west coast, taking in the highlights of Lorne, Apollo Bay, the Loch Ard Gorge, the Twelve Apostles and Port Campbell, a distance of more than 250km (155 miles). Torquay is 100km (62 miles) southwest of Melbourne via Geelong. Apart from striking views across the Bass Strait and the Southern Ocean, the Great Ocean Road region has laidback coastal towns and maritime villages, and there are plenty of opportunities for bushwalking, swimming, surfing, fishing and whale-watching. One of the most visited stretches is the Port Campbell National Park, home to the stunning Twelve Apostles rock stacks, chilling Loch Ard Gorge and the windswept Bay of Islands near Warrnambool.

HIGHLIGHTS

SURF COAST

329 T17 • Surf Coast Information Office, Beach Road, Surf City Plaza, Torquay, VIC 3228, tel 03 5261 4219; open daily 9–5

The first 12km (7-mile) stretch of the Great Ocean Road between Torquay and Anglesea is Victoria's famous Surf Coast. The beach town of Torquay is widely regarded as Australia's surfing capital. The fun Surfworld Museum (*daily 9–5*) on Beach Road focuses on surfing history and culture, while alongside are two temples of surfing wear, the RipCurl and Quiksilver factories. Nearby Bells Beach is one of the world's greatest surf beaches, hosting the Rip Curl Pro and Sunsmart Classic, which attracts many of the world's best boardriders each Easter. Sit on your board—they can be rented in town—out on the break and watch surfgear millionaires mix with drop-out surfies. Nearby Jan Juc is another world-famous surf beach.

Beyond the Surf Coast proper, Anglesea, Fairhaven and Aireys Inlet are popular holiday towns, all with their own surf beaches and lifesaving teams. Lorne is a thriving area of cafés, restaurants, boutiques and stylish accommodation, ringed by the cool gullies, rainforest and waterfalls of surrounding Angahook-Lorne State Park. A walk in the state park inland from Lorne takes you to the lovely

RATINGS				
Historic interest	●	●	●	
Photo stops	●	●	●	●
Shopping	●	●		
Activities	●	●	●	

TIPS

● It might appear that the Great Ocean Road, starting 100km (62 miles) from Melbourne and stretching for over 250km (155 miles), can be easily driven in a day. Be warned: The route—following clifftops and hills—is slow and winding, and there are many distracting views and things to see.

● Day bus tours from Melbourne are often the only way many visitors get to see the beauty of the Great Ocean Road. Do it if you must, but seriously consider renting a car to explore and enjoy this magnificent route at your own pace and time, preferably over at least two days.

Left and above left: The Twelve Apostles have been formed over the last 20 million years
Middle: Loch Arch Gorge was named after the wreck of the iron-hulled clipper
Above right: Horse-riders on the beach at Cape Otway

cascading Erskine Falls. From Lorne, the Great Ocean Road twists and turns, marked by stunning lookouts, constant sea views and descents into the little beach holiday hamlets of Wye River, Kennett River and Skenes Creek, before the relaxing and picturesque haven of Apollo Bay is reached.

APOLLO BAY

✚ 328 S17 • Apollo Bay Visitor Information Centre, Great Ocean Road, Apollo Bay, VIC 3233, tel 03 5237 6529, open daily 9–5

Spread around a sweeping beach, bay and harbour, with the lush Otway Ranges rising behind, Apollo Bay is a popular and peaceful overnight or weekend stop along the Great Ocean Road. Its popularity revolves around its main beach, right in front of the town, its Saturday morning art and local produce market, its local fishing fleet, which keeps the town well supplied with lobsters and fish, and

its cultural bent—there are resident artists, sculptors and the Apollo Bay music festival in March. Part of the pleasure of Apollo Bay is to eat crays and fish straight from the boats on the jetty and the fishermen's co-op. From Apollo Bay, the Great Ocean Road turns into a magnificent inland drive through the thick, cool rainforest and mountain ash bush of the Otway National Park. Stop at signposted Maits Rest for an unforgettable 30-minute walk through giant, ancient rainforest trees and fern gardens, complete with boardwalks, bridges and viewing platforms.

Above: Approaching Apollo Bay from inland
Middle: An aerial view of Bells Beach
Right: Cape Otway lighthouse guards the Shipwreck Coast

CAPE OTWAY

✚ 328 S17 • Cape Otway Lighthouse, Cape Otway Lighthouse Road, Cape Otway, VIC 3233 ☎ 03 5237 9240, www.lightstation.com ◷ Daily 8.30–6 💰 Adult A$8, child A$6

About 20km (12 miles) west of Apollo Bay is the turnoff to one of Australia's most rugged points, Cape Otway. Not surprisingly, this is the location of Australia's oldest surviving lighthouse, founded in 1848. After climbing the heights of Lavers Hill, in the heart of the Otways, the Great Ocean Road descends back through farmland to beaches and clifftops on the entirely different southwest coastline. After the hamlet of Princetown the green volcanic plains collide with tall limestone cliffs and the wild Southern Ocean.

SHIPWRECK COAST

✚ 328 S17 • Port Campbell Information Centre, 26 Morris Street, Port Campbell, VIC 3269, tel 03 5598 6053, open daily 9–5 www.parks.vic.gov.au

More than 700 ships are thought to have sunk along Victoria's Shipwreck Coast—the coastline between Princetown in the east and Port Fairy in the west—mainly in the late 19th century, victims of wild weather, human error and the rocky coast. Hundreds of people lost their lives. While much wreck evidence is at the bottom of the sea, some relics are displayed at museums and on the foreshore at many towns along the Great Ocean Road, including Port Campbell, which also has a lovely surf beach. A Discovery Walk heads west from the town.

THE TWELVE APOSTLES

✚ 328 S17 • 12 Apostles Interpretative Centre, near Port Campbell, VIC 3233, tel 131963 www.12apostlesnatpark.org; open daily 9–5 ◷ Free

Port Campbell National Park protects much of the southwest coastline alongside the road, which over 20 million years has been battered to form a series of striking natural features. The main stop is the unforgettable Twelve Apostles, the isolated rock stacks marooned off the coast, sculpted by surging seas and the wild storms that howl in from the frigid waters above Antarctica. There are not actually 12 stacks, which are in a continual state of erosion and change as the ocean wears away the soft limestone. But no matter what their number, the Apostles are among the true natural icons of Australia and remain captivating no matter how often you see them. At dawn, the towering stacks glow golden against a blue-grey sky. Visit in the late afternoon and the sunlight filters through the sea haze, dramatically silhouetting the Apostles against the fading light. The 12 Apostles Interpretative Centre was designed to blend into the environment. It contains information about the area's history and Port Campbell National Park, and explains how nature has shaped the coastline. There are extensive boardwalks and lookouts on the clifftop overlooking the Apostles, with display boards describing features of the unique coastal landscape and its flora. Other eroded limestone arches, caves and island stacks worth looking at in the national park include Pudding Basin Rock, Island Arch, the Razorback, Muttonbird Island, Thunder Cave, the Blowhole, Bakers Oven, London Bridge and the Grotto.

LOCH ARD GORGE

 328 S17 • Loch Ard Gorge, near Port Campbell, VIC 3233 🏛 Free

About 5km (3 miles) on from the Twelve Apostles are the plunging, eerie depths of the Loch Ard Gorge. This is the haunting, tragic scene of the *Loch Ard* shipwreck. The vessel foundered on Mutton Bird Island reefs in 1878, and only two people survived: Tom Pearce, a cabin boy, and Eva Carmichael, 18, who was sailing to Australia from Ireland with her well-to-do family. At Loch Ard Gorge you can see where the disaster unfolded, walk the beach where Tom and Eva struggled ashore, and see the monument to the Carmichael family in the clifftop cemetery where the few bodies recovered from the shipwreck are buried. Nearby Glenample Homestead (*Fri–Mon 10.30–5*), where Tom and Eva recuperated from their shipwreck trauma, has displays telling the story of the *Loch Ard* tragedy and the history of its survivors.

WARRNAMBOOL

 328 S17 • Shipwreck Coast/Warrnambool Information Office, 600 Raglan Parade, Warrnambool, Victoria 3280, tel 03 5564 7837, 1800 637 725 www.warrnamboolinfo.com.au; daily 9–5

The spectacular part of the Great Ocean Road, and the Port Campbell National Park, end at Peterborough. Just west of the town is the Bay of Islands Coastal Park, a 32km (20-mile) coastal strip that stretches almost to Warrnambool. Its spectacular ocean views and offshore stacks are equal in beauty and majesty to their more famous 12 cousins up the coast, and the park is much quieter and more deserted too. The Great Ocean Road arrives at the major city of Warrnambool through farmland. Overlooking Lady Bay, Warrnambool was a busy port in the 19th century, its history recalled at the lively Flagstaff Hill Maritime Museum with its re-created maritime village (*daily 9–5*). Warrnambool's other draws are the giant southern right whales that calve every year off Logans Beach from late May to September, and the majestic Tower Hill Game Reserve (*daily dawn–dusk*), 15km (9 miles) west of Warrnambool, where the bowl of an extinct volcano is a beautiful haven for kangaroos, koalas, emus, waterbirds and bushwalkers. Port Fairy, 28km (17 miles) west of Warrnambool, is a fishing village, complete with river wharves, offshore seals, a strong Irish heritage, old pubs, and beautifully preserved colonial buildings and whalers' cottages. Although Port Fairy is not exactly undiscovered, many overseas visitors don't call in at the village after their tour of the Great Ocean Road. Consider making it an overnight stay, as it is a real gem, nestled beside the Moyne River.

BACKGROUND

The Great Ocean Road is an epic in both scope and history. The main eastern section linking Anglesea and Apollo Bay was constructed in 1918–32. Key mover was Geelong businessman and mayor Howard Hitchcock, who saw it as a way of employing soldiers returning from World War I; the road would create a lasting monument to those who died and also provide a tourist route. The high cliffs, bad weather and rocky terrain made it backbreaking toil, using picks and shovels—and the occasional explosive—and horses and drays. On 26 November 1932 the route was officially opened by a cavalcade of official vehicles, with bands and waving schoolchildren lining parts of the route. People using the road initially paid a hefty toll between Aireys Inlet and Lorne, but the levy was abolished in 1936.

Triplet Falls is one of the many cascades in the Otway Ranges

BASICS

Great Ocean Road Visitor Information Centre (Geelong)

 329 T17 • Stead Park, Princes Highway, Corio, VIC 3214 ☎ 1800 620 888 🚋 Daily 9–5

🚂 Geelong, then regular bus services down the Great Ocean Road; Warrnambool

www.greatoceanroad.org

GREAT OCEAN ROAD BY BUS

Return bus services operate along the Great Ocean Road between Geelong and Apollo Bay. V/Line and McHarry's Buslines provides regular services between Geelong, Lorne, Apollo Bay, Port Campbell and Warrnambool. However, these bus services are not daily, so check with V/Line to plan schedules. There is always a public bus from Geelong Station down the Great Ocean Road every Friday; departing the station about 9.30am, it arrives in Lorne at 11.20am, Apollo Bay at 12.30pm, 12 Apostles at 3.15pm and Warrnambool at 5pm.

Safari buses take visitors to the animals at the Open Range Zoo

The tasting room at Domaine Chandon winery near Healesville has views over the Yarra Valley and the Great Dividing Range beyond

THE SIGHTS

WERRIBEE PARK

✚ 329 T16 • K Road, Werribee, VIC 3030 ☎ Mansion: 03 9741 2444 or 131963. Zoo: 03 9731 9600
🕐 Mansion: Mon–Sun 10–4.45, Nov–Mar; Mon–Fri 10–3.45, Sat–Sun 10–4.45, rest of year. Zoo: daily 9–5
💰 Mansion: adult A$11, child A$5.50. Zoo: adult A$17.50, child A$8.50. Combined Heritage and Wildlife Pass: adult A$25.70, child A$12.65, family A$64.85 🚌 Shuttle from Flinders Street station daily 9.30 🚆 Werribee then bus 439 🔲 🏛
www.visitvictoria.com/mansion
www.zoo.org.au

The mansion and magnificent formal garden at Werribee Park testify to the success of the early Australian pastoralists. The Victorian Italianate house was built by the brothers Thomas and Andrew Chirnside between 1874 and 1877 from the profits of their sheep, and based on the plan of an English country estate. The main bedrooms, billiard room, reception rooms and servants' quarters are open. The adjacent State Rose Garden has 4,500 rose varieties, which are at their best during November to March. In the north of the park, the 200ha (494-acre) Open Range Zoo is formed around the picturesque Werribee River. An hour-long bus safari tours the fields where grassland animals from Africa, Asia, North America and Australia roam free.

Endangered species include the Mongolian wild horse and the white rhinoceros. Some species, such as the zebra, giraffe and rhino, co-exist in the same area as they would on the African plains. Try to visit in the morning when the animals are more active.

WILSONS PROMONTORY NATIONAL PARK

✚ 329 U17 • Wilsons Prom National Park Office, Tidal River, VIC 3960 ☎ 03 5680 9555 or 1800 350 552 🕐 Park: daily 24 hours. Office: daily 8–5 💰 Free; charges for camping and overnight hikes (book well in advance) 🔲 🏛

The 'Prom', the southernmost point of the Australian mainland, is the most loved national park in Victoria. It has great spiritual significance to local Aboriginal people, who know the area as Yiruk or Wamoom. The granite promontory, with a 130km (80-mile) coastline, is the survivor of a former land bridge to Tasmania, until the sea level rose 15,000 years ago. In 1859 a lighthouse was built on South East Point to mark the Prom's position in the turbulent waters of Bass Strait.

The small settlement of Tidal River, 30km (18.5 miles) inside the park boundary, is the focus for tourism and recreation. The camping ground here fronts Norman Bay, a safe, popular swimming spot, while the white 'squeaky' sands of Squeaky Beach are only a half-hour walk away. The Lilly Pilly Gully nature trail circuit is an easy walk (2–3 hours) through banksias, casuarinas and gum trees, where koalas live, down into a cool rainforest gully and back to Tidal River. The views from Mount Oberon, south of Tidal River, are spectacular. Bird-watching is magnificent, with more than half of all Victorian bird species found in the park; tame crimson rosellas flock around Tidal River. Wombats, echidnas and koalas are all commonly seen too.

YARRA VALLEY

✚ 329 T16 🛈 Healesville Visitor Information Centre, Harker Street, Healesville, VIC 3777, tel 03 5962 2600; open daily 9–5 🚆 Lilydale then bus to Healesville
www.visitvictoria.com

The Yarra Valley, within the area of Dixons Creek, Yarra Glen, Coldstream and Healesville, is the historical home of the Victorian wine industry. The state's first vineyard was planted here in 1837, at what is now Yering Station. There are more than 40 wineries in the valley, growing a range of grape varieties, though it is the Chardonnay and Pinot Noir grapes that receive the highest accolades. Almost all of the major wineries are open daily (*usually 10–4*) when guests can sample varieties from the current vintage in special tasting rooms, as well as tour the wineries. Harvest in the Yarra Valley is from March to May. Wineries offering both tastings and restaurants include De Bortoli's at Dixons Creek (*daily 10–5*) and De Bortoli's restaurant (*daily 12–2*), Yering Station, south of Yarra Glen (*Mon–Fri 9–5, Sat–Sun 10–6*), and Domaine Chandon on the Maroondah Highway (*daily 10.30–4.30*).

The broad farming valley is now as famous for its food as for its wine, and you can find good local produce at the farmers' market at Yering Station winery (*third Sunday of every month*) or at the Yarra Valley Pasta Shop in Healesville. This former forest town is better known for the nearby Healesville Sanctuary, the best place in Australia to view native animals in the bush (see page 94). Just 2km (1.2 miles) east of Healesville Sanctuary is Badger Weir Park, within the Yarra Ranges National Park. Short walks loop amid tree ferns and towering mountain ash forests, or alongside babbling creeks. In spring you can often see and hear lyrebirds, which are great 'mimics', scrabbling under the ferns.

Don't miss Mont de Lancey (*Wed–Sun 10–5*) is a late 19th-century homestead in the south of the Yarra Valley at Wandin North (Wellington Road).

QUEENSLAND

Straddling the Tropic of Capricorn, Queensland is known as the Sunshine State. Stunning beaches complement dense rainforest, remote desert areas lie to the west, and the Great Barrier Reef protects a long and fertile coastline. Brisbane, the state's capital, lies to the south, and its buildings are a combination of 19th-century charm and stylish modernity.

KEY SIGHTS

The Tropical Dome at Mount Coot-tha

Part of the 20ha (50-acre) City Botanic Gardens

The copper dome of the Customs House in Queen Street

BRISBANE

BRISBANE BOTANIC GARDENS—MOUNT COOT-THA

⊞ Off 102 A1 • Western Freeway Route 5, Toowong, QLD 4066 ☎ 07 3403 2531 (Mon–Fri 4–4.30) ⏰ Gardens: daily 8–5.30 (5 Apr–Aug). Tropical Dome: daily 9.30–4. Bonsai House: Mon–Fri 10–12, 1–3, Sat–Sun 10–3. Planetarium: daily 9–5 💷 Free 🚌 471 from Adelaide Street 🍴 ♿
www.anbg.gov.au

At the foot of Mount Coot-tha, 8km (5 miles) west of the city,

this subtropical botanic garden, covers 52ha (128 acres) and is home to 25,000 plants. Themed sections include a scented garden and an arid zone, while cascades and waterfalls weave through rainforest terraces. Check out the Tropical Dome, a geodesic-domed greenhouse, for its range of tropical plants, the Japanese Garden and the excellent Bonsai House. **Don't miss** Also within the gardens is the Cosmic Skydome and Planetarium, where images of the southern hemisphere's night sky are projected on to a large domed ceiling.

CITY BOTANIC GARDENS

⊞ 102 C2 • Alice Street, Brisbane, QLD 4000 ☎ 07 3403 0666 ⏰ Daily 24 hours 💷 Free 🚌 CitySight bus, alight at QUT stop ♿
www.brisbane.qld.gov.au

One of Brisbane's top free attractions, the City Botanic Gardens are among the city's loveliest parks. The area was first cleared by convict workers in 1828 to grow crops for the infant town of Brisbane. The first of the present gardens was created in 1855 for experimental plantings used to develop colonial agriculture.

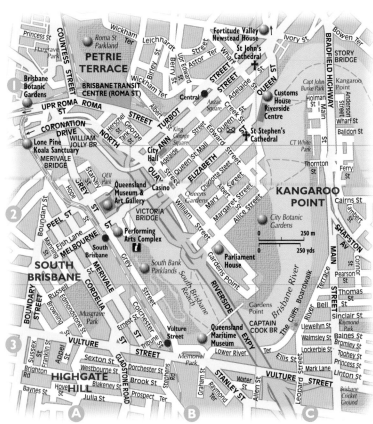

Chinatown in Fortitude Valley has the city's best Asian cuisine

The gardens of Newstead House make an excellent picnic spot

A view of the harbour of North Stradbroke Island

CUSTOMS HOUSE

➕ 102 C1 • 399 Queen Street, Brisbane, QLD 4000 ☎ 07 3365 8999 🕐 Daily 10–5; free guided tours Sun 10–4 👤 Free 🚌 CitySight bus, alight Telstra House 🚢 CityCat stop at the Riverside Centre 🍴 ♿
www.customshouse.com.au

The Customs House is the home of the Stuartholme Behan Collection of Australian Art. Dr. Norman Behan's collection was assembled over 40 years and comprises more than 100 works dating back to 1788. Prominent Australian artists represented include Impressionists Tom Roberts, George Lambert, Frederick McCubbin, Rupert Bunny and Arthur Streeton.

The domed Victorian building was opened in 1889 in what was a bustling waterfront area. It served as the city's Customs House for almost a century before the port moved closer to the mouth of the Brisbane River.

FORTITUDE VALLEY

➕ Off 102 C1 🚇 Queen Street Mall, tel 07 3236 2020 🚇 Brunswick Street
www.brisbanetourism.com.au

Known locally as 'The Valley', this is Brisbane's liveliest and most multicultural suburb. Some of Brisbane's best nightspots and pubs are here, and at night the Valley comes alive as a place for live entertainment and ethnic dining. Brunswick Street is the Valley's main thorough-fare, a 10-minute walk north of the Queen Street Mall. It is lined with bars, cafés, restaurants, cinemas and galleries. The McWhirters Building, a graceful old emporium, continues as an indoor market.

Nearby Chinatown Mall is home to some of the city's best Asian cuisine. The park has playgrounds, flowerbeds, and a theatre and performance space, the Powerhouse.

LONE PINE KOALA SANCTUARY

➕ Off 102 A2 • Jesmond Road, Fig Tree Pocket, QLD 4069 ☎ 07 3378 1366 🕐 Daily 8.30–5 👤 Adult A$15, child A$10, family A$38 🚌 445; 430 🚢 Mirimar boat cruise departs North Quay; tel 07 3221 0300 👤 ♿
www.koala.net

If you want to hold a koala, feed kangaroos, emus and lorikeets, and learn about reptiles and other native fauna, this is the place. Opened in 1927, the koala sanctuary also shelters wombats in their hollow log homes, Tasmanian devils, the flightless cassowary, and many other bird species. Enjoy the 20ha (50 acres) of natural setting and have a picnic beside the Brisbane River.

MORETON ISLAND

➕ 327 X11 🚇 Moreton Island Recreation Area, Tangalooma, QLD 4025, tel 07 3408 2710 🚢 From Scarborough: Combie Trader Ferry 07 3203 6399. From Holt St. Wharf, Brisbane: Tangalooma Wild Dolphin Resort 07 3840 7555
www.epa.qld.gov.au
www.tangalooma.com

Popular with day trippers from Brisbane, Moreton Island is a coastal wilderness experience within easy reach of the city. The 19,000ha (46,930-acre) island is virtually all national park. Flora include eucalypts, banksias and heathland, while freshwater lakes and wetlands support more than 180 bird species. Whales migrate along the coast between July and October. The scenery is stunning and there are long, empty beaches. Access is by a 75-minute ferry trip. The only means of travel on the island is by all-terrain vehicle. Permits for island access and camping are available from ferry operators and national park officers.

On the sheltered western side of the island, the Tangalooma Wild Dolphin Resort caters for holiday visitors. The dolphins that visit the shallows near the resort can be hand-fed. Various other accommodations are available.

NEWSTEAD HOUSE

➕ Off 102 C1 • Newstead Park, Breakfast Creek Road, QLD 4010 ☎ 07 3216 1846 🕐 Mon–Fri 10–4, Sun 2–5 👤 Adult A$4.40, child A$2.20 🚌 300
www.brisbanelivingheritage.com

Newstead House is situated on the banks of Breakfast Creek and the Brisbane River. It was built by the Scotsman Patrick Leslie in 1846 in the colonial Georgian style and is now the city's oldest surviving domestic dwelling. The two-storey house-museum has been fitted out with fine late-Victorian fittings and period furniture. There are regular Sunday concerts and traditional cream teas and theme days.

NORTH STRADBROKE ISLAND

➕ 327 X11 🚇 Stradbroke Island Visitor Centre, Junner Street, Dunwich, tel 07 3409 9555 🚢 Cleveland to Dunwich daily every hour 5.30am–8.30pm. Booking essential: Stradbroke Ferries 07 3286 2666
www.stradbroke-island.com.au

'Straddie', as the locals call it, is on Moreton Bay to the east of Brisbane. The island is a one-hour ferry ride from suburban

Elegant Parliament House was designed by Charles Tiffin

Brisbane has several lovely green spaces; the Roma Street Parklands is north of the central business district

Cleveland—the effort is rewarded by stunning coastal and bushland scenery. Activities include surfing, fishing and horse riding, or you can take the one-hour Goompi Trail from Dunwich with a local Aboriginal guide to learn about the local flora and fauna.

Accommodation is mostly based around Point Lookout. The settlement of Dunwich was a convict out-station, Catholic mission, quarantine station and benevolent institution during the 19th century. **Don't miss** Take the North Gorge trail around the headland and past the Blowhole for near-guaranteed sightings of dolphins and manta rays in the waters below, especially in summer.

PARLIAMENT HOUSE

102 B2 • William Street, Brisbane, QLD 4000 ☎ 07 3406 7562 ⚙ Guided tours Mon–Fri 9–5, Sun 10–2 ⚗ Adult A$5.50, child A$2.80 🚌 CitySight bus, alight at QUT stop 🍴 ♿
www.parliament.qld.gov.au

Completed in 1868, when Queensland was a fledgling colony, Parliament House is an elegant Victorian Renaissance-style building—a fine example of colonial architecture. There are free tours on weekdays unless Parliament is sitting, when visitors can watch proceedings from the public gallery. Many of the materials in the interior, including stained glass and ornamental fittings, were imported from England.

QUEENSLAND ART GALLERY

102 A2 • Melbourne Street (south end of the Victoria Bridge), South Brisbane, QLD 4000 ☎ 07 3840 7303 ⚙ Mon–Fri 10–5, Sat–Sun 9–5 ⚗ Free. Charge for exhibitions 🚌 The Cultural Centre Busway is outside the gallery, with regular buses from central Brisbane 🚉 South Brisbane ♿ ⚗
www.qag.qld.gov.au

The Queensland Art Gallery is part of the Queensland Cultural Precinct, just south of Victoria Bridge. The excellent collection covers Australian art from colonial times to the present, and includes painting, sculpture, prints, drawings, photographs, decorative arts and crafts, and Aboriginal art of the last 30 years. **Don't miss** The small collection of European and Asian artworks includes Picasso's *La Belle Hollandaise.*

QUEENSLAND MARITIME MUSEUM

102 B3 • Sidon Street, South Brisbane, QLD 4000 ☎ 07 3844 5361 ⚙ Daily 9.30–4.30 ⚗ Adult A$6, child A$3 🚌 The Cultural Centre Busway is 500m (1,640ft) northwest, outside the Queensland Art Gallery 🚉 South Bank, 250m (820ft) west ♿
www.qmma.ecn.net.au

The museum, at the southern end of South Bank Parklands, recalls Queensland's maritime history using models and displays of sailing, merchant and early cargo ships, modern vessels and marine memorabilia. The site also features dry docks dating from 1881. Among the historic boats is *Happy II,* a small sailing boat that in the 1980s voyaged from the United States, through the Panama Canal and across the Pacific to the north coast of New South Wales. The coal-fired tug SS *Forceful,* built in 1925, cruises the Brisbane River and Moreton Bay. **Don't miss** HMAS *Diamantina* is a World War II frigate with cabins featuring wartime objects.

QUEENSLAND MUSEUM

102 A2 • Melbourne Street (south end of Victoria Bridge), South Brisbane, QLD 4000 ☎ 07 3840 7555 ⚙ Daily 9.30–5 ⚗ Free. Charge for special exhibitions 🚌 The Cultural Centre Busway is outside the nearby

Queensland Art Gallery ♿ South Brisbane ⚙ ⚗
www.qmuseum.qld.gov.au

As the name suggests, the museum is an introduction to Queensland's natural and cultural history. Spread over four levels, the range of exhibits takes in a Dinosaur Garden, Aboriginal objects as art, pioneer women in the outback, endangered species, and the story of the local whales, including the complete skeleton of a humpback whale. No cliché—there is something for everybody. The museum is next to the Queensland Art Gallery.

ROMA STREET PARKLAND

102 A1 • 1 Parkland Boulevard, Brisbane, QLD 4000 ☎ 07 3006 4545 ⚙ Daily 24 hours. Spectacle Garden 6.30am–7pm ⚗ Free 🚉 Roma Street 🍴 Café Tomoko ♿ Activity Centre
www.romastreetparkland.com

Roma Street Parkland opened in 2001 on the former site of the Brisbane Markets, here from 1884 to 1964. The 16ha (40-acre) Parkland is the world's largest subtropical garden in a central city area, with more than 100,000 shrubs, 1,200 mature trees and 350 palms. The Forest Walk features rainforests, palm groves and open forests via a pathway system and boardwalk over cascading waterways and rocky outcrops.

A lookout gives views towards the city skyline. Free guided walks depart from The Hub in the middle of the Parkland (*Thu–Sun; bookings 07 3006 4531/4545*). There are also playgrounds for children. **Don't miss** Spectacle Garden consists of several themed gardens including the Topiary Maze Garden, Lilly Pilly Garden and a wall of epiphytes.

SOUTH BANK PARKLANDS AND QUEENSLAND PERFORMING ARTS COMPLEX

A great family destination, 17ha (42 acres) of parklands, riverside walks, museums, shops, cinemas, theatre, a beach, restaurants, markets and picnic spots.

South Bank opened in 1992 and is now the city's major recreation precinct. Street entertainers, pubs and a varied events schedule ensure that the area is a popular place for Brisbanites. There is a Lantern Village Market on Friday evenings (5–10) and a Craft Village Market on Saturday (11–5) and Sunday (9–5). The nearby Brisbane Convention and Exhibition Centre hosts special events and exhibitions. South Bank Beach is a man-made shore overlooking the Brisbane River and the central city area, comprising a crystal-clear lagoon with clean, white sand beaches, palm trees, rocky creeks and shady shallows with subtropical vegetation. The beach is patrolled seven days a week by lifeguards. South Bank is easily reached from Queen Street Mall via the Victoria Bridge (300m; 990ft) or from the City Botanic Gardens (500m; 1,640ft) via the Goodwill Bridge, a pedestrian and bicycle bridge.

Fireworks bursting over the South Bank Parklands

QUEENSLAND PERFORMING ARTS COMPLEX

The complex (QPAC; tel 13 6246) is home to Brisbane's key cultural institutions including the Queensland Theatre Company, Queensland Opera and the Queensland Symphony Orchestra. Opera, concert and theatre lovers should check the local papers or website for details of current performances at the Optus Playhouse (850 seats), Lyric Theatre (2,000 seats), Concert Hall (1,800 seats) and Cremorne Theatre (312 seats). The Queensland Performing Arts Museum at the QPAC presents small exhibitions of theatre memorabilia and theatre design in the Tony Gould Gallery, near the Cremorne Theatre entrance.

ENERGEX BRISBANE ARBOUR

A stunning arbour winds for over a kilometre (0.5 mile) through the parklands, connecting all the main sights. It is made of 403 curving steel posts threaded with parallel wires covered with magenta bougainvillea.

SUNCORP PIAZZA

This large covered piazza, at the heart of the South Bank, is a venue for a range of entertainments, including concerts and sporting events.

CINEMA

Movies are shown on a massive screen at the IMAX Theatre at 167 Grey Street (*daily 10–9*). Greater Union Hoyts (*daily 10–9.45*) also has new-release movies in the Queen Street Mall and the Myer Centre Cinemas, Level 3, at corner of Albert and Elizabeth streets.

MARKETS

Little Stanley Street is busy with art and craft markets every Friday, Saturday and Sunday, and is a great place to browse for a craft souvenir. Street performers add to the fun, and the street itself is a Brisbane eating spot. If you're lucky to be in town on the first or third Saturday of the month then the morning farmers' and seafood markets have fresh local produce; at the Cultural Forecourt near the QPAC.

RATINGS			
Good for kids	●	●	●
Shopping	●	●	● ●
Walkability	●	●	● ●
Activities	●	●	● ●

TIP

● Brisbane's major attraction is deservedly popular—there may be few quiet corners.

BASICS

➕ 102 A2/B2

Visitor Information Centre, Stanley Street Plaza, South Bank, tel 07 3867 2051; open Sat–Thu 9–6, Fri 9–9

❓ The Visitor Centre can book tickets for concerts, theatre and events, and provides wheelchair hire.

🚌 Busway stations in Melbourne Street (Cultural Centre Station) and cnr Colchester and Tribune streets (South Bank Busway Station). Brisbane City buses stop at several locations around South Bank 🚉 Vulture Street and South Brisbane 🚢 CityCat terminal outside the riverside restaurants on the Clem Jones Promenade.

www.south-bank.net.au • A simple menu leads you easily to the South Bank's arts, cultural and lifestyle facilities. Useful What's On calendar.

Cairns and the Tropical North

Queensland's tropical capital is a stepping stone to the Wet Tropics of Queensland and Great Barrier Reef World Heritage areas.

Lizard Island lies to the north of Cooktown

RATINGS				
Historic interest	●	●	●	
Photo stops	●	●	●	●	●
Shopping	●	●	●	●
Activities	●	●	●	●	●

TIPS

● The tourist high season is the cooler and drier winter months, from April to October.
● It may be a good idea to avoid the tropical north's wet season, which runs from December to March. Heavy rain and flooding make access to some areas chancy; destructive cyclones may also occur at this time. Temperatures can be in the mid-30s°C (mid-80s°F) and the humidity approaches 100 per cent.

BASICS

✚ 322 T6
Tourism Tropical North Queensland Visitor Information Centre • 51 The Esplanade, Cairns, QLD 4870, tel 07 4051 3588; open daily 9–5 🚻 Cairns; timetables 13 22 35
www.great-barrier-reef.com • Some good tips for tours, attractions and general visitor information, but it is mainly a site for trendy accommodation.

SEEING CAIRNS AND THE TROPICAL NORTH

Cairns is Queensland's most cosmopolitan city north of Brisbane. The area around the city is best explored with a rental car but there are hundreds of day tours to choose from: boat trips to the reef and coach tours up the coast and into the hinterland.

HIGHLIGHTS

CAIRNS

An initial walk along the Esplanade, where there's all manner of shopping, entertainment and dining options, will get you in the holiday mood. The stunning swimming lagoon in front of Fogarty Park is the best place for a year-round dip. Cairns central shopping mall, in McLeod Street, has more than 100 specialty shops, food courts and a six-screen cinema complex. Other Cairns attractions include a casino, the Pier Marketplace and a busy nightlife. The city also has a splendid botanical garden and a historical museum. The Cairns Regional Art Gallery is on the corner of Shields and Abbott streets (*Mon–Sat 10–5, Sun 1–5*).

Sea and rainforest at Cape Tribulation

For many visitors the city is a fun starter for journeys along the coast, inland or farther north. There are easy tours of the Great Barrier Reef and a sedate view of the rainforests from Skyrail. Also nearby are adventure activities such as bungee jumping, white-water rafting, scuba diving, ballooning and parasailing. Those who find the summer humidity of the coast too stifling head for the Atherton Tableland (see page 108) where temperatures can be several degrees cooler.

GREAT BARRIER REEF MARINE PARK

Away from dry land, the Great Barrier Reef Marine Park is renowned as the world's largest system of coral reefs (see pages 110–114). It extends over 2,000km (1,240 miles) from the Torres Strait north of the Cape York Peninsula to just south of the Tropic of Capricorn, and is made up of about 2,800 individual reefs, coral cays and atolls, and hundreds of continental islands. A huge variety of soft and hard corals growing in warm, shallow waters form a thin, living veneer.

Hundreds of coral cays and continental islands lie off the North Queensland coast and many of these can be visited. Lizard Island, 80km (50 miles) north of Cooktown, best accessed by air, is a base for deep-sea game fishing and scuba diving. Fitzroy Island, 26km (16 miles) east of Cairns, with a rainforest and a clam and pearl oyster hatchery, has a resort with varied accommodations. Forty-five minutes by boat offshore from Cairns, Green Island is a 15ha (37-acre) national park coral cay with a superb underwater observatory and aquarium.

RAINFORESTS

The Wet Tropics World Heritage Area encompasses nearly all of the tropical rainforest in Australia and is regarded as one of the world's most significant ecosystems. Tropical rainforests have a diverse array of flora and fauna. The Wet Tropics stretch from Black Mountain, south of

Cooktown, to just south of Townsville, with Cairns roughly central. The mountain ranges have fast-flowing streams and waterfalls; in places, the tropical rainforest runs down to the sea.

Cairns is the gateway to the Queensland tropics

NORTH TO CAPE TRIBULATION

The drive from Cairns to Cape Tribulation is one of the world's great scenic drives, with rainforests, waving fields of sugar cane and long sandy beaches. Just 11km (7 miles) north of Cairns, at Smithfield, is the lowland terminus of Skyrail, the aerial cableway that runs over the rainforest canopy via a series of pylons to the mountain village of Kuranda and back. There are two stations along the way: Red Peak, which has a forest walkway, and Barron Falls with an interpretative unit and a lookout. An alternative is to take the popular 34km (21-mile) scenic Cairns–Kuranda rail journey on one of the legs of your trip. The indigenous experience at the Tjapukai Aboriginal Cultural Park at Smithfield includes didgeridoo performances, fire-making demonstrations, bush food displays and boomerang throwing.

Farther north is a series of beaches; the best is at Palm Cove, a 20-minute drive north of Cairns. A 1-hour drive north of Cairns is the stylish coastal resort town of Port Douglas (see page 117). The sugar milling town of Mossman, 75km (46 miles) north of Cairns, is set amid fields of sugar cane. Nearby is picturesque Mossman Gorge, which has picnic facilities. After crossing the Daintree River by car ferry, on the way to Cape Tribulation, there are a number of walks giving spectacular views over the rainforest out to sea. Although Cape Tribulation is accessible by ordinary vehicles in most weather conditions, the road past this point to Bloomfield is for 4WD vehicles only.

The bird life in these areas is prolific and over half of Australia's bird species are found here; these include the rare cassowary.

BACKGROUND

In the 19th century Cairns was a swampy backwater, renowned for its wild frontier style. Port Douglas to the north was then the region's main town, serving the Palmerston goldfields in the 1870s. In the 1880s tin was discovered on the Atherton Tableland and Cairns became the railhead and administrative hub. Sugar and timber dominated the local economy during the 20th century, until tourism boosted the city from the 1970s.

BASICS

DAINTREE RAINFOREST ENVIRONMENT CENTRE
✉ Cnr Cape Tribulation and Tulip Oak roads, Cow Bay, QLD 4873 ☎ 07 4098 9171 🕐 Daily 8.30–5

KURANDA SCENIC RAILWAY
✉ Cairns Railway Station, Cairns, QLD 4870 ☎ 07 4036 9249 🕐 Departs daily 8.30 and 9.15am (also Wed–Fri and Sun 10). Returns daily 2 and 3.30pm (also Wed–Fri and Sun 2.30) 🎫 Adult A$34 one way, A$48 return; child A$17 one way, A$24 return

SKYRAIL
✉ Smithfield, QLD 4878. ☎ 07 4038 1555 🕐 Daily 9–5 🎫 Adult A$34 one way, A$49 return; child A$17 one way, A$24.50 return

TJAPUKAI ABORIGINAL CULTURAL PARK
✉ Smithfield, QLD 4878 ☎ 07 4042 9999 🕐 Daily 9–5 🎫 Adult A$28, child A$14 🚗 13km (8 miles) north from Cairns on the Captain Cook Highway

Millaa Millaa Falls are in the Atherton Tableland

Hahn River Crossing in Cape York's Lakefield National Park

Carnarvon National Park is within the Great Divide Range

THE SIGHTS

QUEENSLAND

ATHERTON TABLELAND

322 T6 ⓘ Kuranda EnviroCare Information Centre, Kennedy Highway, Kuranda, QLD 4872, tel 07 4093 8834 ⓘ Malanda Falls Visitor Centre, Atherton Road, Malanda, QLD 4885, tel 07 4096 6957 🚂 Cairns. Kuranda Scenic Railway departs Cairns daily, tel 07 4036 9249. Skyrail cableway from Smithfield to Kuranda, tel 07 4038 1555 www.athertontableland.com

A refreshing change from busy Cairns, this upland region, situated between the Bellenden Ker Range and the Great Dividing Range, is several degrees cooler and much less humid than the coast. Atherton is the main town. The fertile soils are the result of volcanic activity, which also gave the Tableland its wealth of natural attractions, including the crater lakes Eacham and Barrine near Yungaburra, Mount Hypipamee Crater, hundreds of waterfalls, and the rainforests of the Wet Tropics World Heritage Area.

In the north, Kuranda bustles with a large daily market (9–5). Barron Gorge National Park adjoins the town; the Barron River is impressive after wet-season rain. The information office at Malanda explains the region's volcanic past. Stop in the township for crafts and a drink at the classic old wooden pub. Malanda also has Australia's only tropical dairy, the Dairy Heritage Centre (daily 9–4.30; tel 07 4095 1234). The Malanda Falls trail is a short rainforest walk, and the Millaa Millaa waterfall circuit from Malanda takes you past three waterfalls in rainforests. The historic village of

Yungaburra has a monthly market (fourth Saturday of the month 7–1), restaurants and craft shops. Don't miss The Curtain Fig tree, near Yungaburra, has an enormous 'curtain' of aerial roots.

BUNYA MOUNTAINS NATIONAL PARK

327 W11 • Bunya Mountains National Park Information Centre, Bunya Road, Bunya, QLD 4055, tel 07 4668 3127; open daily 9–5 ⓒ Park open daily 24 hours 🅿 Free 🍴 ⬛ 🏛 www.qld.gov.au

This remote park protects the world's last remaining major stand of bunya pines. All routes to the Bunya Mountains are steep; caravans and trailers are not recommended. The mountains were formed over 30 million years ago by volcanic activity, and the eroded basaltic red-brown and black soils support many different types of rainforest, the densest dominated by bunya pines. There are 40km (25 miles) of trails; a good starting point is the Danabah picnic ground. The most popular route is the Scenic circuit track, which features a huge strangler fig, the Festoon and Tim Shea Falls, and the Pine Gorge Lookout.

CAIRNS

See page 106.

CAPE YORK PENINSULA

319 S4 ⓘ Cooktown Visitor Information Centre, Botanic Gardens, Cooktown, QLD 4871, tel 07 4069 6004; open daily 9–5, including café www.cooktown.com

The huge expanse of wilderness that occupies the northern point of Australia requires plenty of time to see. But a day's drive (via the inland route) from Cairns to Cooktown will take you through the southern part, an adventure

in itself. Much of the journey to Cooktown is through sparse woodlands with termite mounds and dry creeks. In some places, towards the coast, this changes to rainforest and coastal wetlands. A self-drive 4WD vehicle tour starts from Cairns or Mareeba and proceeds via Mount Molloy, Lakeland and Black Mountain to Cooktown. Take a side trip from Lakeland to Laura to visit the Split Rock Gallery with its Aboriginal rock art. Farther on, the Lakefield National Park has broad flood plains where water-holes attract prolific bird life and allow great barramundi fishing.

Cooktown retains many of its late 19th-century buildings, when it was the coastal port for the Palmerston gold fields. The James Cook Historical Museum has relics from Cook's Endeavour, which was beached near here in 1770 (daily 9.30–4). Chillagoe, inland from Cairns, is renowned for the nearby limestone outcrops and the extensive cave systems protected within Chillagoe-Mungana Caves National Park.

CARNARVON NATIONAL PARK

324 V10 • Visitor Centre, Carnarvon National Park, Carnarvon Gorge, tel 07 4984 4505; open daily 8–5 ⓒ Park daily 24 hours 🅿 Free ⬛ 🏛 www.carnarvongorge.com

Carnarvon Gorge is one of a series of mostly inaccessible gorges that make up the spectacular Carnarvon National Park. Because of its isolation, the place is not often crowded and it's best to visit during the cooler months from April to October. Among the impressive features of the sandstone gorge are the Moss Garden, a hollow filled with tree ferns, and the Amphitheatre, where two fault lines have formed a giant cavern. Don't miss The Art Gallery has one of Queensland's finest displays of Aboriginal rock art.

The Gold Discovery Monument at Charters Towers

CHARTERS TOWERS

✚ 322 U7 ℹ Charters Towers Tourism Information, 74 Mosman Street, Charters Towers, QLD 4820, tel 07 4752 0314 🔲

www.charterstowers.qld.gov.au

This former gold-mining town, once the financial hub of north Queensland, with its own stock exchange, has some of the grandest historic buildings in rural Queensland. A possible day trip from Townsville, Charters Towers is a classic example of an outback town. It was built during the gold boom of the late 19th century By the end of 1872 some 3,000 people inhabited the new gold field. The alluvial miners left soon after for the Palmer River discoveries to the north, but the hard rock miners remained, seeking the gold in the deep veins underground. By 1899 gold production was at its peak and the city had developed streets. The wealthy built fine homes, impressive public buildings were erected, and no fewer than 65 hotels quenched the thirst of the miners. Sport, music and the arts flourished and the cosmopolitan city was affectionately known as 'The World'.

After 1945, mining declined, but modern methods are bringing new life to the old mines. For a walking tour, start at the 19th-century Stock Exchange Arcade in Mosman Street, next to the tourist office. The Assay Room and Mining Museum (*daily 9–3*) is at the end of the arcade. The Zara Clark Museum (*daily 10–3; tel 07 4787 4161*) has a collection of old farming gear, domestic wares and period clothing. Ay Ot Lookout, on the corner of Hodgkinson and High streets, is a mining magnate's mansion (*Mon–Fri 8–3*).
Don't miss The Venus Gold Battery, 5km (3 miles) east of town, is a restored gold ore processing site (*daily 9–3*).

Top: Fraser Island's beach is its main thoroughfare
Inset: Take a refreshing dip in the freshwater Lake MacKenzie

FRASER ISLAND AND HERVEY BAY

Tall rainforest, huge sand dunes and crystal-clear lakes are all on Fraser Island, the world's largest sand island.

✚ 325 X10
Fraser Island National Park Office • Eurong, Fraser Island, QLD 4581, tel 07 4127 9128, open Mon–Fri 9–5, Sat 9.30–12.30

ℹ Fraser Experience Tours 1800 063 933; Fraser Island Adventure Tours 07 4125 2343; Kingfisher Ranger Guided Tours 07 4125 5511. Safari 4WD Hire, Hervey Bay 07 4124 4244 🚢 Inskip Point to Hook Point 07 4125 2343; Mary River Heads to Kingfisher Bay 07 4125 2343; Urangan to Moon Point 07 4125 2343
www.dkd.net/fraser • The homepage has links in the text; it's better to navigate by the comprehensive menu at the bottom of the page.

RATINGS					
Historic interest	●	●			
Photo stops	●	●	●	●	●
Shopping	●				
Activities	●	●	●		

TIPS
● Self-drive 4WD vehicles can be rented from Hervey Bay or Rainbow Beach. Only use this option if you are a very experienced off-road driver.
● Only travel along the beach within 2 hours of low tide and watch for washouts caused by the freshwater streams.

Hervey Bay is the main departure point to the Fraser Island World Heritage Area, and one of the world's best places to observe humpback whales. From August to October, groups of them rest in the calm, relatively shallow waters off the coast. Barges also leave from Inskip Point, near Rainbow Beach, to the south. The island stretches 123km (76 miles) from north to south, has an average width of 14km (8.7 miles) and was inhabited by Aboriginal people for thousands of years. In more recent times, timber cutters, sand miners and fishermen had the island to themselves, but after protests the logging and sand mining were halted.

Fraser Island is a popular beach-fishing destination, and camping is permitted on the fore dunes. Plan to spend at least two days here. A typical island tour would include a drive through the heaths and rainforests, and along the eastern beaches. The remarkable lakes lie well above sea level—their waters often stained by the tannins of the lakeside plants.
Don't miss The lakes are more popular as swimming spots than the dangerous eastern surf beaches. Inland there is a cool walk among the giant Hoop pines of the Yidney Scrub, the last of the island's virgin rainforests.

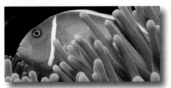

The Great Barrier Reef

The world's largest coral reef system is made up of some 2,800 individual reefs, coral cays and atolls, and hundreds of continental islands, stretching over 2,000km (1,240 miles) from Torres Strait, north of Cape York, down to Lady Elliot Island, just south of the Tropic of Capricorn.

SEEING THE GREAT BARRIER REEF

Nothing prepares you for the profusion of marine life encountered on a snorkel or dive in the protected waters of the Great Barrier Reef Marine Park, the largest marine reserve in the world. This finely balanced environment includes hundreds of species of corals, thousands of different molluscs, sponges, worms, crustaceans and echinoderms, and more than a thousand species of fish. Reef invertebrates and fish have adapted to make the most of their environment, such as the parrot fish that uses its beak-like teeth to scrape algal food from the hard underlying calcareous layer beneath the reef. The reef is also home to green and loggerhead turtles, sharks, manta rays and one of the largest dugong (sea cow) populations in the world. In winter (July–September) humpback whales gather in the warm waters around the Whitsunday Islands (see page 123) on their annual migration to and from Antarctica.

Numerous tour operators run cruises to the continental islands, reefs and cays from coastal locations, including Bundaberg, Gladstone, Rockhampton, Airlie Beach, Townsville, Mission Beach, Cairns and Port Douglas. And many of the continental islands, such as those in the Whitsundays, have fringing reefs that are easily accessible. As part of a trip to the reef, you are likely to be offered a glass-bottomed boat tour, a ride in a semi-submersible or a snorkel above the coral. Most people who visit the Great Barrier Reef on a boat tour have a go at snorkelling.

RATINGS	
Good for kids	● ● ●
Photo stops	● ● ● ● ●
Value for money	● ● ● ●
Activities	● ● ● ● ●

BASICS
✚ 323 U7
Great Barrier Reef Marine Park Aquarium, Reef HQ, 2–68 Flinders Street, PO Box 1379, Townsville, QLD 4810 ☎ 07 4750 0800 www.reefhq. org.au; www.gbrmpa.gov.au
⊙ Daily 9.30–5 🎟 Adult A$19.50, child A$9.50, family A$49

Opposite: The reef appears brighter when diving with lights at night

WHAT IS CORAL?

Coral is the stony skeleton produced by various polyps—small colonial marine animals—which builds up to form reefs. The complex food chain begins with the free-floating plankton, the small, mostly microscopic plants and animals that inhabit the sunlit layer of the ocean. These are devoured by small fish and reef invertebrates, which are in turn eaten by larger predators. In late spring or early summer there is a spectacular display of coral spawning, when coral eggs and sperm are simultaneously released and the waters are brightly speckled by a mass of reproductive cells.

HIGHLIGHTS

BUNDABERG

✚ 325 X10

Some of the best shore diving in Queensland is in Bundaberg's Woongarra Marine Park, with soft and hard corals, urchins, rays, sea snakes, and more than 50 fish species. Salty's Dive Centre rents dive gear and runs learn-to-dive courses (*tel 07 4151 6422*). A vegetated coral cay, Lady Elliot Island, is the southernmost Great Barrier Reef island and offers reef walks, snorkelling, and diving. From November to January loggerhead turtles come ashore to lay their eggs. Air transport from Bundaberg or Hervey Bay is the best way to arrive, since the island has a small airstrip. The Lady Elliot Island Resort provides

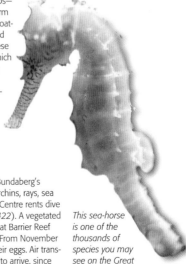

This sea-horse is one of the thousands of species you may see on the Great Barrier Reef

several standards of accommodation and conducts diving certificate courses (tel 07 4156 4444). The uninhabited Lady Musgrave Island is a tiny coral cay covered in rare pisonia forest, about 100km (62 miles) northeast of Bundaberg. Camping is permitted in several locations, otherwise day-trip cruises leave from both Bundaberg and The Town of 1770. The island's 1,200ha (3,000-acre) navigable lagoon is a good calm spot for beginner divers and snorkellers. For those averse to getting wet, semi-submersible and glass-bottomed boats take visitors over coral reefs. Lady Musgrave Barrier Reef Cruises is based at Bundaberg Port Marina (tel 07 4159 4519).

HERON ISLAND
✚ 325 X9

Two hours by fast boat from the city of Gladstone, Heron Island (see page 116) is a 16ha (40-acre) vegetated coral cay, part of the Capricorn-Bunker Group. From November to January, sea turtles come ashore to lay their eggs. Island activities include some of Australia's best snorkelling, scuba diving and reef walks. Offshore, Heron Bommie is renowned for its rays and eels, and also Spanish dancers—a very pretty shell-less marine mollusc that floats in the water and looks like a Spanish dancer. P&O runs the island resort (tel 13 2469).

GREAT KEPPEL ISLAND
✚ 325 W9

Great Keppel Island (see page 120) is surrounded by the clear Coral Sea. About 18km (11 miles) of beautiful sandy beaches surround the island, and snorkelling and diving can be enjoyed on the fringing reefs off Monkey Beach. The island is just 30 minutes by fast cruise boats from Rosslyn Bay Harbour near Rockhampton.

AIRLIE BEACH AND THE WHITSUNDAYS
✚ 323 V7

This coastal town is usually crowded with visitors, particularly backpackers, from all around the world. Boats leave from the busy marina and neighbouring Shute Harbour to the Great Barrier Reef, the Whitsunday Islands and other popular destinations. There are countless dive sites, both among the islands and on the outer Great Barrier Reef, 90 minutes away, including Bait Reef, known for its cascading drop-offs. Snorkellers will find plenty of coral and marine life around many island shores. There are several ways to explore the 74 Whitsunday Islands (see page 123). Airlie Beach and some of the larger islands such as Hamilton Island make a good base for sailing and reef trips. You can get to the islands on your own by ferry, or join one of the many organized day trips. Bareboat rental would suit those who want a full-on sailing experience, while crewed charters are fun for those prepared to bunk down with a crowd. Fanta Sea Cruises runs a day trip to Ball Hai, where you can snorkel and view the coral from a large semi-submersible; day trip costs: adult A$89, child A$49; tel 07 4946 6900.

TOWNSVILLE
✚ 323 U7

Reef HQ on Flinders Street East, Townsville, is the best place in Australia to learn about marine life on the Great Barrier Reef (daily 9.30–5). There are interactive exhibits, and the main tank includes a replica of one of the world's top wrecks, the SS Yongala, which forms a backdrop to sharks, rays and reef fish. The SS Yongala itself, sunk by a cyclone in 1911, lies in the Coral Sea off Townsville. Large schools of trevally, kingfish and barracuda circle the wreck, while giant Queensland grouper live under the bow, turtles graze on the hull, and hard and soft corals have settled on the wreck. Oceanpro runs a day trip (tel 07 4750 0800) to the Yongala. Orpheus Island is a 1,300ha (3,211-acre) continental island 70km (43 miles) northwest of Townsville. Bordered by sheltered bays and deserted sandy beaches, the island is covered in coastal forests and is rich in bird life. Snorkellers and divers can explore the fringing coral reefs. Orpheus Island Resort, closed to day-trippers, nestles in a protected bay on the west

Diving allows you to get close up to the reef's residents

TIPS

• Day trips out to islands or the reef usually depart early— often from 8am—so check timetables in advance.

• Experienced divers with a scuba diving ticket can dive to depths where marine creatures dwell in gullies and caves. Otherwise for an extra charge some operators offer an introductory dive, which is a diving experience for those without diving qualifications.

• Most boat tours travel to the outer reef, the platform and ribbon reefs that lie an average of 65km (40 miles) off the coast. These trips take from 60 to 90 minutes by fast catamaran and travel conditions are dependent on the weather. If you suffer from seasickness, remember to take appropriate medication before a voyage. For those not keen on a long boat trip, explore one of the fringing reefs around the continental islands that lie closer to the mainland.

• An important factor is water clarity—wait until you arrive at your destination and see what the weather and water is like before booking a tour.

side of the island and caters for a maximum of 42 guests; access to the resort is by seaplane from Townsville (*tel 07 4777 7377*).

DUNK ISLAND

✚ 322 U6

The resort on rainforested Dunk Island, a 40-minute ferry ride from Mission Beach (see page 117), provides many water- and land-based activities. Dunk Island Ferry & Cruises runs round-trip cruises daily from Clump Point Jetty, including use of snorkelling gear. The cost is adult A$29, child A$14.50; tel 07 4068 7211.

CAIRNS

✚ 322 T6

Cairns is an embarkation point (see page 106) for cruises to many parts of the Great Barrier Reef, whether for day trips or longer vacations. Sunlover Cruises runs an outer reef day trip in a catamaran, departing Trinity Wharf, which stops at Fitzroy Island National Park for a 1-hour guided rainforest walk before arriving at Moore Reef. A guided snorkel safari is included. The cost for a day is A$179, child A$92; Sunlover Cruises, tel 07 4050 1333. Great Adventures also runs a catamaran from Trinity Wharf, to a three-level pontoon on the outer reef. The pontoon has a children's swimming area, a semi-submersible and an underwater observatory. The cost for a day is A$157, child A$81.50; Great Adventures, tel 07 4044 9944. Fitzroy Island National Park, 26km (16 miles) east of Cairns, has a well-established rainforest, and a clam and pearl oyster hatchery. Fitzroy Island Resort has accommodation (*tel 07 4051 9588*). Farther

Top and above right: Snorkelling tours are popular with those who don't want to dive
Main: Combine a trip out to the reef with a helicopter ride over Heart Reef near Airlie Beach

north but the same distance from Cairns, Green Island National Park is a 15ha (37-acre) coral cay with a superb underwater observatory. The exclusive Green Island Resort, limited to 90 guests, has been designed for low impact on its ecologically sensitive surroundings. At this popular day-trip destination, you can snorkel off the island's beach and ride in a glass-bottomed boat. A walk around the island takes about 20 minutes. Green Island Resort (tel 07 4052 7855). Lizard Island National Park, 245km (152 miles) north of Cairns, is Australia's northernmost island resort. The island is a base for deep-sea game fishing and scuba diving; snorkel above 150-year-old giant clams or, at the famous Cod Hole, dive to hand-feed a school of giant potato cod. Lizard Island P&O Resort is a one-hour flight north from Cairns (tel 1800 737 678). Great Adventures, Quicksilver (below) and Sunlover all offer helicopter flights over the reef from pontoons.

PORT DOUGLAS
✠ 322 T5
Port Douglas, 60km (37 miles) north of Cairns, is the main access point to the northern section of the reef. Quicksilver's air-conditioned catamarans carry over 300 passengers daily on the 90-minute trip to Agincourt Reef, an outer ribbon reef 72km (45 miles) from Port Douglas. A two-storey pontoon is moored on the reef, where you spend over three hours; introductory dives cost extra. Boats depart from Marina Mirage daily. The cost for a day is A$174, child A$90; Quicksilver, tel 07 4099 5500. Boats also depart from Marlin Marina in Cairns. The journey time is accordingly longer, 120 minutes, and the cost for a day is A$184, child A$95; Quicksilver, tel 07 4031 4299. The Low Isles, just 15km (9 miles) northeast of Port Douglas, are tiny coral cays covered with lush vegetation surrounded by white sand and fringing coral reef. Although the coral is not quite as abundant as that on the outer reef, the fish life is prolific and the proximity to the mainland means you'll have more time to snorkel the reef and explore the island—and the tour costs less; introductory dives are extra. A Quicksilver boat departs from Marlin Marina in Cairns and Palm Cove Jetty on the northern beaches to connect with Wavedancer departures from Port Douglas. The cost is A$120, child A$63; Quicksilver, tel 07 4087 2100. Wavelength also offers trips to the Low Isles with transfers from your hotel. Specialist half-day snorkelling trips include a guided beach walk and a snorkelling tour with a marine biologist. Trips depart Wednesday and Saturday from the Wavelength jetty in Wharf Street. The cost for a half day is A$130, child A$90; Wavelength, tel 07 4099 5031.

Aerial view of Lady Elliot Island, accessible by air from Bundaberg

You'll be amazed by the sheer quantity of life on the reef

BACKGROUND
The origin of these reefs goes back millions of years. Changing sea levels alternately flooded and exposed the coastal reefs, the coral dying as the sea became either too deep or too shallow, leaving the reefs drowned or exposed. After the end of the last ice age, about 10,000 years ago, when the ice caps melted and rising sea levels reclaimed the coastal lowlands, the corals grew once again on the eroded reef platforms of past ages. Living coral polyps settled on past coral skeletons and their exquisite structures were once more home to marine life.

The Great Barrier Reef is now under pressure from rising ocean temperatures due to global warming, agricultural pollution, crown-of-thorns starfish (a destructive predator of corals), and commercial fishing. Tourism is managed by the Great Barrier Reef Marine Park Authority, and a range of conditions ensure that the reef is not 'loved to death'. A reef management fee, levied on reef visitors, helps to fund reef research.

GOLD COAST

Australia's premier holiday destination is a string of seafront towns with a fine, mild climate, enjoying an average of 300 days of sunshine each year.

The Gold Coast spreads from Coolangatta, near the New South Wales border, 70km (43 miles) north to Beenleigh. Visitors from around the world soak up the sun, visit theme parks, party at nightspots, shop at malls and specialty shops, and dine at some of the state's best eateries.

SURFERS PARADISE
Surfers Paradise developed from a series of old beachside houses into Australia's high-rise holiday resort. A one-hour drive south of Brisbane, 'Surfers' has surf beaches, excellent shopping and dining, and plenty of evening fun. The action is focused around the area bounded by Cavill Avenue, the Esplanade and the Gold Coast Highway.

BURLEIGH HEADS
About 10km (6 miles) south of Surfers, Burleigh Heads is one of Australia's top surfing locations, known for its fast and deep barrel rides. A walking trail runs around the rocky headland and a small reserve that is part of the tiny Burleigh Heads National Park.

COOLANGATTA
The laid-back holiday town of Coolangatta, on the New South Wales border, combines old-fashioned charm with modern amenities. Its broad, long beaches are uncrowded and surfers mingle with holidaying families. Good diving can be found at Nine Mile Reef, Cook Island.

CURRUMBIN WILDLIFE SANCTUARY
Northwest of Coolangatta the 27ha (67-acre) Sanctuary has the world's largest collection of Australian animals (*daily 8–5*). You can feed the wild lorikeets and get close to koalas, kangaroos, emus and other wildlife. Aboriginal dancers perform daily.

THEME PARKS
Sea World (*daily 9.30–5*) has entertaining rides and attractions. A dolphin show, the Water Ski Spectacular, the Corkscrew Rollercoaster, Cartoon World, a 3-D pirate movie and an aquarium will fill the day. Head for Dreamworld (*daily 10–5*), if you enjoy scary rides—the Giant Drop and the Tower of Terror speak for themselves. Go behind the scenes to learn all about movie-making at Warner Bros Movie World (*daily 9.30–5.30*). And there's a rollercoaster ride for good measure. Wet'n'Wild Water World (*daily 10–5*) is a water-themed fun park with some of Australia's best water slides.

Inset: Surfers Paradise high-rise skyline with the Conrad Jupiters casino at Broadbeach

RATINGS				
Good for kids	●	●	●	●
Photo stops	●	●	●	
Shopping	●	●	●	
Value for money	●	●	●	

TIP
● Avoid mid-November to mid-December when school groups invade the place for 'Schoolies Week'.

BASICS
✚ 327 X11
Gold Coast Tourism Bureau • Cavill Avenue, Surfers Paradise QLD 4217, tel 07 5538 4419; open Mon–Fri 8.30–5.30, Sat 9–5.30, Sun 9–3.30
www.goldcoasttourism.com
🚌 Services from Brisbane (timetables: tel 13 12 30)

Turtles nest on the beach at Heron Island

HERON ISLAND

✚ 325 X9 🏠 P&O Australian Resorts, GPO Box 478, Sydney NSW 2001, tel 02 9277 5050; email: reservations @pore-sorts.com 🚌 Gladstone www.gladstoneholidays.info

Heron Island is a tiny, 16ha (40-acre) vegetated coral cay, part of the Capricorn-Bunker group of reefs. The corals and marine life are among the best in the world. The island is also home to a variety of bird life, including black noddies, mutton birds and reef herons during the nesting season. From November to January, sea turtles come ashore to lay their eggs in the warm sand. Island activities include diving, snorkelling, reef and island walks, and birdwatching.

HINCHINBROOK ISLAND

✚ 322 U6 🏠 Hinchinbrook Island Wilderness Lodge and Resort, Cape Richards, Hinchinbrook Island, QLD 4849, tel 07 4066 8585 🚌 Cardwell 🚢 Hinchinbrook Island Ferries, tel 07 4066 8270 www.hinchinbrookferries.com.au

Australia's largest island national park, 393sq km (153sq miles), is a truly stunning wilderness experience, with mangrove wetlands, eucalypts, long white beaches and rainforests. The granite outcrop of Mount Bowen rises 1,121m (3,677ft) in the middle. Visitors come for the bushwalking, fishing, snorkelling, swimming and birdwatching. Insect repellent, sunscreen, water and a good hat are essential. Keen hikers undertake the 32km (20-mile), four-day trek along the Thorsborne Trail, one of the world's great wilderness treks.

The only accommodation is the Hinchinbrook Island Wilderness Lodge and Resort. Boats leave Cardwell daily. Camping is by permit only; contact the Queensland National Parks and Wildlife Service (tel 07 4066 8601).

LAMINGTON NATIONAL PARK

Spectacular rainforests blend with classic mountain scenery, steep valleys, sheer gorges, tumbling waterfalls and rocky creeks.

✚ 327 X11 Gold Coast Tourism Bureau • Cavill Avenue, Surfers Paradise QLD 4217; tel 07 5538 4419, www.goldcoasttourism.com.au; open Mon–Fri 8.30–5.30, Sat 9–5.30, Sun 9–5.30 🏠 O'Reilly's Rainforest Guesthouse, Lamington National Park Road, via Canungra, QLD 4275; tel 07 5544 0644, www.oreillys.com.au 🚌 Services from Brisbane to the Gold Coast

RATINGS				
Good for kids	●	●	●	
Photo stops	●	●	●	●
Walkability	●	●	●	
Activities	●	●	●	

TIP

● Temperatures are generally 4–5°C (7–9°F) cooler than Brisbane and the Gold Coast. Take a rain jacket or umbrella, since rain showers can occur without notice, and be prepared to rug up in winter.

A great natural destination within easy reach of Brisbane and the Gold Coast, Lamington National Park has over 160km (100 miles) of trails, both long and short, to suit all hikers. Serious hikers should pack appropriate gear and try some of the longer trails.

HIGHLIGHTS

A well-known trek involves a visit to the site of the famous Stinson airplane wreck and rescue in 1937. Alternatively, well-formed and gently graded trails lead to the majority of the park's features, from palm-filled valleys with waterfalls and streams, to misty mountain tops (1,100m; 3,608ft) in cool temperate rainforests, dominated by Antarctic beech trees.

The bird life includes the satin and regent bowerbirds, which build distinctive ground bowers for courting and nesting. Lorikeets, crimson rosellas and other parrots will feed from your hand in the cleared areas around visitor offices, while tame pademelons—a variety of small wallaby—feed on grass along the edge of the forest in the evenings. There is an excellent treetop canopy walk at the O'Reilly's accommodation. In the evenings, visitors can gather around a log fire after a hearty dinner, take a guided walk to see the glow worms, spotlit pademelons, possums and gliders, and view a rainforest audio-visual presentation of the district's flora and fauna.

Climb to this treetop lookout point for spectacular views over the McPherson Ranges

A decorative wooden butterfly on display in Mackay

A model of a cassowary at Mission Beach

The resort of Port Douglas has excellent restaurants and shops

MACKAY AND EUNGELLA NATIONAL PARK

✚ 324 V8 ℹ Visitor Information Centre, 320 Nebo Road, Mackay QLD 4741, tel 1300 130 001; open Mon–Fri 8.30–5, Sat–Sun 9–4 🚆 Mackay www.mackayregion.com

The port and solid regional city of Mackay is a good base for excursions to the Great Barrier Reef, the Eungella Range National Park to the north, and the stunning coastal Cape Hillsborough National Park, where the rainforest comes down to the sea. Or you can just relax on one of the many local beaches. Mackay sits at the junction of the Pioneer River and the Coral Sea. This thriving sugar-growing district produces one-third of the nation's crop. From June to November you can watch the sugar-making process on a sugar mill tour. A self-guided Heritage Walk goes past many of the city's late Victorian buildings.

Finch Hatton Gorge, the valley entrance to Eungella National Park, 66km (41 miles) west of Mackay, has a series of walks that wind their way up from the rocky creeks to superb vantage points over tumbling waterfalls. Farther up the valley you come to the rainforest-draped upper reaches of the park. Various trails, many with identified plant species, make exploration of the rainforests easy. Just 47km (29 miles) north of Mackay, Cape Hillsborough National Park also offers a rainforest walk, with explanations of the Aboriginal uses of plants. Some 150 or so bird species are found here. Look for the tropical butterflies, wallabies,

brush turkeys and possums, which congregate around the picnic and resort grounds. Kangaroos can be seen on the beach. **Don't miss** The Broken River picnic ground in Eungella National Park has a viewing platform where platypus come to the surface in the early mornings and evenings.

MISSION BEACH AND DUNK ISLAND

✚ 322 U6 ℹ Mission Beach Information Centre, Porters Promenade, Mission Beach, QLD 4852, tel 07 4068 7099; open daily 10–5 🚆 Tully www.missionbch.com www.poresorts.com.au/dunk

Some of Australia's prettiest coastal scenery is around Mission Beach, 140km (87 miles) south of Cairns. The coastal villages of Clump Point and Bingal Bay to the north, Wongaling Beach, South Mission Beach and Mission Beach itself offer white, sandy beaches, coastal wetlands and rainforests that reach down to the sea. This is one of the few places in Australia where you can see the elusive flightless cassowary. The lookout on Bicton Hill offers views over outlying islands, while the Ulysses Link Walk, named for the brilliant blue butterflies, winds along the Mission Beach foreshore.

Dunk Island is a 15-minute ferry ride from Mission Beach; the largest of the Family Islands, it was popularized by the author and naturalist Edmund J. Banfield, an island resident from 1897 until his death in 1923. Much of the island fits the popular image of a tropical island: swaying palms, great beaches, and grassy knolls offering fine vantage points. Camping on Dunk Island is possible and the resort (tel 13 24 69) has excellent accommodation with the option of many activities. **Don't miss** There are superb coastal views from the summit of

Mount Kootaloo (271m; 888ft) on Dunk Island.

PORT DOUGLAS

✚ 322 T5 ℹ Port Douglas Daintree Tourism, 23 Macrossan Street, Port Douglas, QLD 4871, tel 07 4099 4588; open Mon–Fri 9–5 🚆 Port Douglas www.pddt.com.au

The road from Cairns, 70km (43 miles) north to Port Douglas, and on to Cape Tribulation, is a great scenic drive, with coastal ranges, verdant sugar cane fields and impressive panoramas (see Cairns, page 106–107). Port Douglas is a laid-back seafront town with a tropical ambience, though for the more adventurous there is diving, paragliding, horse riding and bicycle tours.

Port Douglas was the gateway to the Hodgkinson River gold-fields in the 19th century, a role later usurped by Cairns. In recent years, the town has become a trendy resort, yet it retains much of its charm. There are excellent restaurants and a range of accommodation. Reef tours depart from the town wharf, and Ben Cropp's Shipwreck Museum is a good place to retreat to on a rainy day (daily 10–5; tel 07 4099 5858). The lookout on Flagstaff Hill overlooks Four Mile Beach and the Low Isles. The town's main street has good shopping and trendy eateries. Marina Mirage is an exclusive shopping complex. There may be more chance of a bargain at the famed Sunday Markets, where crafts, clothing and tropical produce are sold. **Don't miss** The nearby Rainforest Habitat on Port Douglas Road (tel 07 4099 3235) is a re-created natural environment housing over 180 species of tropical birds and animals such as koalas, kangaroos and crocodiles (daily 8–5.30; adult A$25, child A$12.50).

THE SIGHTS

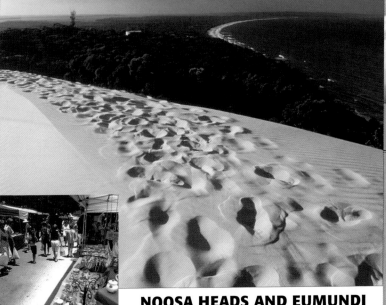

Above: Dunes at Noosa Heads National Park
Inset: The Saturday morning market stalls at Eumundi have excellent gifts

RATINGS	
Good for kids	●●●
Photo stops	●●●●●
Shopping	●●●●●
Walkability	●●●●●

TIP

● Noosa's main beach is not always flush with sand—nearby Sunshine Beach is good for swimming and surfing, as are the southern beaches of Sunrise, Marcus and Peregian.

BASICS

✚ 325 X11
Visitor Information Centre • Hastings Street, Noosa Heads, QLD 4567, tel 07 5447 4988,
www.tourismnoosa.com.au; open daily 9–5 🚄 Cooroy
www.noosa.com.au • Visit the simpler, official tourist website above first

NOOSA HEADS AND EUMUNDI

Noosa Heads, at the northern end of the Sunshine Coast, has great beaches, beautiful national parks, top restaurants and trendy shops. Nearby Eumundi is renowned for its markets.

The Lifestyle Capital of Australia? Noosa's Hastings Street stores have all the best brands while the quality of the Noosa district restaurants rivals that of eateries in Sydney and Melbourne. But in recent years Noosa has become a victim of its own popularity and, like other parts of the Sunshine Coast (see page 121), the town can be crowded during the holiday seasons of Easter and Christmas. There are three main beaches: Noosa Main Beach (a sheltered bay), Alexandria Bay (a clothes-optional surf beach) and Sunshine Beach (one of the Sunshine Coast's best surfing beaches).

HIGHLIGHTS

A mixture of coastal heath, eucalypt forests and rainforest, Noosa National Park is only a leisurely 10-minute walk from Hastings Street. A good interpretative unit at the entrance to the park has information on the trails. The excellent coastal trail passes beautiful beaches before arriving at the promontory of Noosa Head, which has sweeping views out to sea and over pristine Alexandria Bay.

Only minutes from Noosa Heads, the seaside village of Sunshine Beach lies on the southern edge of Noosa Heads National Park. Head for Duke Street, near the beach, for restaurants with ocean views.

Noosa Heads is on the Noosa River, one of Queensland's cleanest waterways. There are over 40km (25 miles) of navigable water. Rent a boat or take a day cruise through Lake Cooroibah and Lake Cootharaba to the Everglades, an undeveloped stretch of the river lined by mangroves and featuring bird life.

Along the Noosa River, between Tewantin and Noosa Heads, is the suburb of Noosaville. Gympie Terrace has a long park on its riverside, while the other side is lined with a host of shops, cafés and restaurants. The Noosa Regional Gallery, in the service town of Tewantin, exhibits local, national and international art, and local crafts.

Eumundi, a 20-minute drive southwest of Noosa, has been revitalized as the home of one of Australia's best art and crafts markets. The town comes alive on Saturday mornings (7–1) when over 400 stalls fill out Main Street and the side streets around with art, crafts, clothing and produce; also music and street theatre. There is a market on Wednesday (8–1) with about 250 stalls. Eumundi is worth a visit outside market days for its many art and craft shops and its range of cafés and food outlets.

OUTBACK QUEENSLAND

The vast Queensland outback is a holiday region with a difference—make the diversion from the seaside paradise.

Queensland's enormous outback is bisected by the Landsborough (or Matilda) Highway running from Karumba on the Gulf of Carpentaria in the north almost to the New South Wales border. When planning a trip, air travel may be necessary if your time is limited. Much of the outback is arid, with broad areas used only for grazing.

THE NORTH

In the far northwest, Lawn Hill National Park has permanent spring waters, and the moisture allows rainforest species and bird life to flourish along the gorge. Two Aboriginal rock art sites are accessible on part of the 20km (12 miles) of trails.

Set among the ochre-red Selwyn Ranges, the city of Mount Isa is dominated by the world's largest silver, lead and zinc mine. The world of mining is the key experience at the Outback @ Isa Explorers' Park (*daily 9–5*), and there is a Fossil Centre in the city's visitor office.

About 118km (73 miles) east of Mount Isa, Cloncurry has a reputation as a lively frontier mining town. It holds the record as Australia's hottest town, with the temperature recorded at 53°C (127.4°F) in 1887. The John Flynn Place Museum and Art Gallery (*Mon–Fri 8–4.30, Sat–Sun 9–3*) is a tribute to the founders of the Flying Doctor Service.

AROUND THE TROPIC OF CAPRICORN

Walk the streets of Winton and check out the old pubs and the open-air Royal Theatre. The Waltzing Matilda Centre (*daily 8.30–5*) explores Australia's national song and has a collection of pioneering memorabilia. Lark Quarry Conservation Park (*tours daily 9, 11 and 2*), 115km (71 miles) southwest, protects dinosaur footprints preserved in rock.

Longreach, Queensland's most prosperous central western town, sits beside the Thomson River. There is a wide, tree-lined main street, and the Australian Stockman's Hall of Fame and Outback Heritage Centre (*daily 9–5*) is a major outback attraction.

FARTHER SOUTH

Charleville lies at the heart of a rich pastoral and opal mining district, while Roma has many grand historic buildings and several of the streets are lined with bottle trees—one planted for each local serviceman killed in World War I. Birdsville is a tiny settlement in the state's far south, on the edge of the Simpson Desert. Travelling the 500km-long (310-mile) Birdsville Track, from here to central South Australia, is one of the great Australian motoring adventures, best attempted in the cooler months.

Top: Dry landscape near Mount Isa
Inset: The Stockman's Hall of Fame at Longreach

RATINGS				
Historic interest	●	●	●	●
Photo stops	●	●	●	● ●
Outdoor pursuits	●	●	●	
Activities	●	●	●	

TIPS

● Avoid driving between dusk and dawn; watch for animals.
● Slow down and move off the road for on-coming road trains.
● Leave all gates as you find them; watch your fuel levels; keep your vehicle well maintained; and carry plenty of spare water and a first aid kit.
● If your vehicle breaks down, stay with it until help arrives.

BASICS

🚫 318 R8
ℹ️ Birdsville, Information Centre, Billabong Blvd, Birdsville, QLD 4482, tel 07 4656 3300; open Mon–Fri 8.30–6, Sat–Sun 9.30–5.30, Apr–Oct; Mon–Fri 8.30–4.30, Nov–Mar
ℹ️ Longreach Visitor Information Centre, Eagle Street, Longreach, QLD 4730, tel 07 4658 1776; open daily 9–5
🚉 Longreach (from Brisbane via Rockhampton)
ℹ️ Mount Isa Visitor Centre, Centenary Park, Mount Isa, QLD 4825, tel 07 4749 1555; daily 9–5 🚉 Mount Isa (from Townsville)
www.outbackholidays.info

Top: Artesian wells are common in the Capricorn Region
Main: Leeke's Beach on Great Keppel Island is the focus for water sports
Inset: Many houses in Rockhampton still have their Victorian ironwork

RATINGS	
Good for kids	●●●○
Historic interest	●●●○
Photo stops	●●●●○
Activities	●●●●●

TIP

● Check with lifeguards before swimming in case of 'stingers'—box jellyfish—which can be deadly.

BASICS

✚ 319 W9
Capricorn Tourism • Capricorn Spire, Gladstone Road, Rockhampton, QLD 4700, tel 07 4927 2055, www.capricorn-coast.com.au, daily 9–5
🚉 Rockhampton 🚢 Freedom fast Cats, Keppel Bay Marina, Rosslyn Bay, QLD 4703, tel 07 4933 6244.
www.keppelbaymarina.com.au

ROCKHAMPTON AND CAPRICORN REGION

Central Queensland's Capricorn Region contrasts popular coastal attractions—resorts, Great Keppel Island, a historic gold-mining town and gem fields—with a more peaceful rural life inland.

HIGHLIGHTS

ROCKHAMPTON

Billed as the beef capital of Australia because of the surrounding cattle grazing, Rockhampton stretches out along the banks of the Fitzroy River, 40km (25 miles) from the sea. A walk around central Rockhampton will pass many buildings dating back to the late 19th century. Include the city's art gallery (Tue–Fri 10–4, Sat–Sun 11–4) as part of a tour. On the south side of the river, the Botanic Gardens are fine tropical gardens; there is a lagoon, a large collection of palms, an orchid and fern house and a Japanese garden. Mount Archer Environmental Park (daily 24 hours) has a lookout over the city and surrounding areas, and has picnic and hiking options. The Dreamtime Aboriginal Cultural Centre (Mon–Fri 10–3.30), in 12ha (30 acres) of natural bushland, is 6km (4 miles) north of the city on the Bruce Highway. There is a traditional dance performance, didgeridoo music, a Native Plant Tour and a boomerang display, after which you can test your own skill.

GREAT KEPPEL ISLAND

Northeast of Rockhampton, the resort of Yeppoon has beautiful beaches washed by the warm, clear waters of the Coral Sea. Rosslyn Bay Harbour, 6km (4 miles) from Yeppoon, is the departure point for the 30-minute ferry to Great Keppel Island, a continental island in the Great Barrier Reef Marine Park. Glass-bottom cruises also depart from Rosslyn Bay Harbour (daily 9.15) for views of the coral reef that sur-rounds Great Keppel Island. The island itself, covering 14sq km (5.5sq miles), has accommodation ranging from budget to a smart resort. Attractions include 17 beautiful white sand beaches, snorkelling and diving, and plenty of hiking options across the bushland interior.

MOUNT MORGAN

A 30-minute drive southwest of Rockhampton will bring you to the former gold- and copper-mining town of Mount Morgan, which once serviced one of Australia's richest mines. Huge mounds of mine tailings, a mining museum (tours daily 9.30am and 1.30pm) and a railway station provide a reminder of a past way of life.

Caloundra lies at the southern end of the Sunshine Coast

SUNSHINE COAST

The coast's 60km (37 miles) of beaches, an hour's drive north of Brisbane and set against the backdrop of the Blackall Range, are among Australia's best.

The Sunshine Coast stretches from just north of Brisbane to the resort of Noosa Heads (see page 118). With average winter temperatures around 25°C (77°F), and little of the summer humidity prevalent in the tropical north of the state, the Sunshine Coast has close to perfect weather. The region attracts artisans who sell their crafts in shops and the weekend markets. Eumundi Markets (see page 118) are the best, but Maleny also has a highly regarded craft market. The dominant feature of the Sunshine Coast is the Glass House Mountains, 30km (18 miles) southwest of Caloundra, a dramatic group of 13 volcanic plugs.

THE COAST
Caloundra has excellent surf beaches, top fishing spots and great windsurfing locations. The town is quieter and less developed than Noosa Heads, and this adds to its appeal. Just north of the Caloundra turnoff on the northern expressway, Aussie World (*daily 9–5*) is a fun outing for families. There are theme rides, an Aboriginal Cultural Centre, camel rides and craft outlets. Inland from Caloundra, 4km (2.5 miles) south of Landsborough, the 20ha (50-acre) Australia Zoo houses more than 550 animals, including reptiles, fishes, birds, otters and the world's oldest captive giant tortoise (*daily 8.30–4*). The biggest attraction is the crocodile show, which sometimes features wildlife TV and film star and zoo owner Steve Irwin. Maroochydore and Alexandra Headland lie at the heart of the Sunshine Coast: They have great surf beaches, and the parkland along the Maroochy River is ideal for picnics. The calm river is good for boating, fishing and other aquatic pastimes. The Wharf, a boardwalk village on the Mooloolah River, is a shopping and eating complex that includes the Underwater World aquarium (*daily 9–6*).

THE HINTERLAND
For a change from the beach culture, the mountain towns of Maleny, Montville, Mapleton and Flaxton, high in the Blackall Range, are popular. The former dairying town of Maleny, 84km (52 miles) south of Noosa, is known for its cafés and restaurants, art and craft galleries. Nearby Mary Cairncross Park has rainforest walks and magnificent views of the Glass House Mountains. Mapleton, on the most northerly point of the Blackall Range, has great views of the surrounding country. Nearby Flaxton has more galleries and craft shops, and is close to Kondalilla National Park. Montville is popular with weekend visitors who enjoy the mountain scenery and potteries, galleries and cafés. The Big Pineapple (*daily 9.30–5*), 7km (4 miles) south of Nambour, is a pineapple plantation with train rides, a macadamia orchard, a boat ride and shops. The Ginger Factory in Yandina has a large ginger processing plant (*daily 9–5*).

The Big Pineapple near Nambour

RATINGS	
Good for kids	● ● ● ●
Photo stops	● ● ● ● ●
Specialist shopping	● ● ● ●
Activities	● ● ● ●

TIPS
● Public transportation is limited—a rented car is the best option.
● Parts around Maroochydore are over-developed—Noosa Heads (see page 118) in the north is the most scenic.
● During school holidays accommodation on the Sunshine Coast is stretched to the limit, so book ahead.

✚ 325 X11
Caloundra Tourist Information Centre • 7 Caloundra Road, Caloundra, QLD 4551 ☎ 07 5491 0102 www.sunshinecoast.com ⓘ Mon–Sat 9–5
Maroochydore Tourist Information Centre • Cnr Sixth Avenue and Aerodrome Road, Maroochydore, QLD 4558 ☎ 07 5479 1566 ⓘ Mon–Fri 9–5, Sat 9–4
🚂 Nambour

Enjoy the crocodile show at Australia Zoo

A view of Townsville from Castle Hill lookout

TOWNSVILLE AND MAGNETIC ISLAND

🗺 323 U7 🏛 Bruce Highway, Townsville, QLD 4810, 07 4778 3555 ℹ Flinders Mall, Townsville, QLD 4810, tel 07 4721 3660 🚂 Townsville 🚢 Magnetic Island: Sunferries 07 4771 3855
www.townsvilleonline.com.au

The tropical city of Townsville is a good base for exploring the Great Barrier Reef, the outback, national parks and rainforests, and nearby Magnetic Island. Set around the craggy lookout of Castle Hill, the university city is north Queensland's largest regional complex, where many grand historic buildings hold their place among more recent additions. The Strand is a popular waterfront precinct with a protected swimming enclosure. On Sundays the Flinders Mall hosts an art and crafts market. Overlooking Ross Creek, the Museum of Tropical Queensland on Flinders Street East includes finds from the wreck of HMS *Pandora,* the ship sent to capture the mutineers of HMAV *Bounty* in 1790–91 (*daily 9.30–5*). Next door, the Reef HQ, allied to the Great Barrier Reef Marine Park, presents the world's largest coral reef aquarium (*daily 9–5*).

Magnetic Island is 20 minutes by catamaran ferry from Townsville, or 60 minutes by car ferry. Land- and water-based activity trips are popular on the island in almost year-round sunshine. With a good bus service and rental 'Mokes' as transport, it's easy to reach the many bays with their sandy beaches bounded by granite headlands and distinctive hoop pines. Walks are best in the cool of the morning or evening when it is often possible to see koalas in the wild in the island's large national park. Tours to the Great Barrier Reef depart from the island daily.

TOOWOOMBA AND THE DARLING DOWNS

The land west of the Great Dividing Range on the rolling plains of the Darling Downs is a great introduction to rural Australia.

🗺 327 W11/X11
Toowoomba Visitor Information Centre • cnr James and Kitchener streets, Toowoomba, QLD 4352, tel 07 4639 3797 www.toowoomba-tourism.com.au; open daily 9–5

RATINGS			
Historic interest	●	●	● ●
Photo stops	●	●	●
Shopping	●	●	●
Activities	●	●	●

TIP

● Roads are mostly all sealed, but take care on narrow country roads.

TOOWOOMBA

The fertile Darling Downs were first settled in the 1840s, and the black volcanic soils now produce 90 per cent of the state's wheat and half of its maize (corn). The region is also a major producer of sheep, cattle and dairy products. The garden city of Toowoomba is known for its 19th-century buildings and Botanic Gardens, and is the perfect base for exploring the Downs. There is a craft market on the third Sunday of each month, while tree-lined Margaret Street has restaurants, cafés and antiques shops. The Cobb & Co. Museum on Lindsay Street (*daily 10–4*) has Australia's largest collection of horse-drawn vehicles.

JONDARYAN WOOLSHED

Near the eastern Downs town of Oakey, 55km (34 miles) west of Toowoomba, the Jondaryan Woolshed is a working museum of 19th-century rural life (*daily 9–4*). The Flypast Museum of Australian Army Flying at Oakey has a top collection of military aircraft and memorabilia (*Wed–Sun 10–4*).

GRANITE BELT

The Granite Belt, around the town of Stanthorpe in the south, is the heart of Queensland's expanding wine industry. At 924m (3,030ft) this is Queensland's coldest district; the cool sunny days of spring, when the trees are in blossom, are a good time to visit. Fruit and wine are the region's principal industries. Most vineyards open on weekends for tastings, and there are plenty of roadside stalls where you can buy fresh fruit and vegetables in season. The Stanthorpe Historical Museum (*Wed–Fri 10–4, Sat 1–4, Sun 9–1*) has local memorabilia as well as the town's old timber jail, of 1876. The Girraween National Park, 26km (16 miles) south of Stanthorpe, is renowned for its spring wildflowers, huge granite boulders, scenic trails, grey kangaroos and excellent campground (*Mon–Sat 8–4; free*).

Keep a lookout for wildlife in the Undara Volcanic National Park

UNDARA VOLCANIC NATIONAL PARK

✚ 322 T6 ⓘ Undara Experience, Lava Lodge, Mount Surprise, QLD 4871, tel 07 4097 1411 🚌 Cairns
www.undara-experience.com.au
www.savannah-guides.com.au

The remote national park is a temperate and unusual outback destination, set on the eastern edge of the rugged Gulf Savannah, part of a tropical landscape of grass and scattered trees that stretches across northern Australia. With minimal humidity, the pleasant climate has warm days and cool evenings. But the park's big attraction is its unique tubular caves, remnants of a shield volcano that erupted 190,000 years ago. Over time, sections of the caves have collapsed, and indigenous rainforest animals and plants have evolved in these fallen cavities. All tours are run from the Undara Experience camp, where the Undara Lava Lodge can provide accommodation in tents or restored railway carriages, or a place to camp if you bring your own gear. The various lava tube tours visit different sections of the tubes and last from two hours to a full day. Openings allow easy access for visitors who can see the unusual rock formations and how the lava flow dramatically changed course. There is also a separate Aboriginal Culture tour. Lunch is included on some tours, and all outings feature morning or afternoon tea. At night, campfire activities are organized with attractions such as bush poetry, singalongs and night walks. Be sure to rise early for the hearty camp kitchen bush breakfasts, which make for a great start to the day's activities. During the hot, summer months, Undara operates on reduced staff, so it is best to phone in advance for details.

WHITSUNDAY ISLANDS

Whatever your nautical skills, rent a yacht, join a crew, or just board an excursion to discover the sheltered turquoise waters and reefs of the Whitsunday Islands.

✚ 323 V7
Airlie Beach Tourist Information Centre, 277 Shute Harbour Road, Airlie Beach, QLD 4802, tel 07 4946 6665 www.thewhitsundays.com
🚢 From Shute Harbour

RATINGS				
Good for kids	●	●	●	
Outdoor pursuits	●	●	●	
Photo stops	●	●	●	●
Walkability	●	●		

TIP
● The best way to see the islands is from the deck of a sailing vessel.

The Whitsundays consist of 74 continental islands—many fringed by reefs. Cruises and ferries depart from Airlie Beach and neighbouring Shute Harbour; you can also charter yachts—with or without crew—at these ports. Southeast of Airlie Beach, mangrove bays along the coastline of the Conway National Park shelter amazing fish life, while estuaries are home to crocodiles. Inland, rainforests shroud the ranges and valleys. The islands themselves attract snorkellers and divers, who can swim with manta rays, dolphins, green turtles and hundreds of species of tropical fish. Migrating humpback whales pass nearby from July to September.

HIGHLIGHTS

Only 5km (3 miles) from Shute Harbour, Daydream Island is popular with day visitors. A 20-minute hike over the steep, rocky middle of the island brings you to the beach.

The most developed island of the group, Hamilton Island has an airport, shops, bank, school, marina and a hotel resort.

Hayman Island is the northernmost, 25km (15.5 miles) from Shute Harbour and is closest to the Great Barrier Reef. This 400ha (988-acre) island, its tallest peak at 250m (820ft), is covered in eucalypt and hoop pine vegetation and has prolific bird life. Its luxury resort provides dive courses, and there are regular trips to the reef on the resort's own vessel, the *Reef Goddess*.

Only basic, budget accommodation is available on Hook Island, 20km (12.5 miles) northeast of Shute Harbour, but there are the usual diving, snorkelling and reef trips.

Mostly national park, Lindeman Island is one of the most southerly, with over 20km (12.5 miles) of trails, and many secluded bays and beaches.

At 109sq km (42.5sq miles), Whitsunday Island is the largest of the group. Many tour vessels stop at Whitehaven Beach for walks on the stunning 6km (3.4-mile) stretch of sand, while snorkellers explore the coral off the southern end of the beach.

NORTHERN TERRITORY

The Northern Territory divides neatly into two regions. The Red Centre is a land of craters, boulders and empty watercourses, where animals and birds seek the refuge of waterholes fed by rare rainstorms. In dramatic contrast the tropical monsoon rainfall of the Top End feeds gorges and wetlands that teem with wildlife. The tropical capital of Darwin is relaxed and modern.

KEY SIGHTS

Parliament House, in State Square, was opened in 1994

DARWIN

Darwin's distance from other cities and its frontier history have given it a distinct character—part Asian, part Australian.

Largely destroyed by Japanese bombing in 1942 and Cyclone Tracy in 1974, Darwin today is a prosperous city with a mostly young population. There is a large Aboriginal community, as well as a strong Asian presence from its pearling and goldmining days.

HIGHLIGHTS

DARWIN BOTANIC GARDENS
✉ Gardens Road, The Gardens, NT 0820 🕐 Daily 7–7 💲 Free
The 42ha (104-acre) gardens are a tropical world of palms, orchids, rainforest species, bottle trees and mangroves. Themes include a rainforest gully, a wetland and a mangrove boardwalk.

EAST POINT MILITARY MUSEUM AND RESERVE
✉ East Point Road, East Point, NT 0820 ☎ 08 8981 9702 🕐 Daily 9.30–5
💲 Adult A$10, child A$5
The museum displays war memorabilia and objects, photographs and a video showing the bombing of Darwin. The 4ha (10-acre) tropical grounds are home to wallabies and a remnant monsoon rainforest.

FANNIE BAY GAOL MUSEUM
✉ East Point Road, Fannie Bay, NT 0820 ☎ 08 8999 8201 🕐 Daily 10–5 💲 Free
Darwin's notorious penal institution operated from 1883 to 1979. The starkness of prison life and the old gallows are still evident.

INDO-PACIFIC MARINE EXHIBITION
✉ Stokes Hills Wharf, Darwin, NT 0820 ☎ 08 8981 1294 🕐 Daily 10–5, Apr–Oct; 9–1, rest of year 💲 Adult A$16.40, child A$6
Here, live coral, fish and tanks containing complete ecosystems are on display. The sealife includes box jellyfish, sea horses and stonefish.

MUSEUM AND ART GALLERY OF THE NORTHERN TERRITORY
✉ Conacher Street, Fannie Bay, NT 0820 ☎ 08 8999 8201 🕐 Mon–Fri 9–5, Sat–Sun 10–5 💲 Free
The Northern Territory's premier cultural institution covers art and crafts, natural history, Aboriginal culture, maritime archaeology and history. The Cyclone Tracy Gallery recalls Christmas Day in 1974, when the cyclone devastated the city.

TIP
● November to April's wet season can cause flooding on the roads. Temperatures can be in the mid-30s°C (mid-80s°F) with humidity approaching 100 per cent. For road conditions, tel 1800 650 881.

BASICS
✚ 318 L3
ℹ Tourism Top End Visitor Information, Knuckey and Mitchell streets, Darwin, NT 0800; tel 08 8936 2499
🕐 Daily 9–5
www.tourismtopend.com.au

*Above: The Museum and Art Gallery of the Northern Territory
Below: A Darwin market*

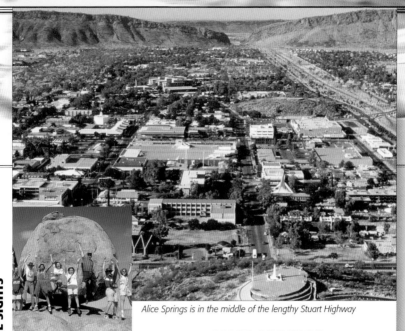

Alice Springs is in the middle of the lengthy Stuart Highway

Visitors have fun at the Devils Marbles near Tennant Creek

RATINGS	
Good for kids	●●●●
Photo stops	●●●●
Shopping	●●●
Activities	●●●●

TIP

● Reserve your accommodation ahead as the Alice is very popular.

BASICS

➕ 318 M9
ℹ️ Central Australian Tourism Industry Association, Gregory Terrace, Alice Springs NT 0870; tel 08 8952 5800
🕐 Mon–Fri 8.30–5.30, Sat–Sun 9–4
🚆 Ghan train from Sydney, Melbourne, Adelaide or Darwin; vehicles can be transported
www.alicesprings.nt.gov.au
The tourism and travel menu is upfront on this sometimes slow community website. There are some useful links.

ALICE SPRINGS

The main base for a tour of Australia's Red Centre—truly hot, but there's much to see and do.

Set between the East and West MacDonnell Ranges, the Alice Springs area is the home of the Arrernte Aboriginal people. The town was named after a waterhole that enabled European expansion and control of central Australia in the late 19th century. Following the footsteps of explorer John McDouall Stuart, the construction of the telegraph line from Adelaide to Darwin was completed in 1872, which made it viable for pastoralists to take up leases in the area. Discovery of gold 100km (62 miles) east of the Alice in 1887 led to a population boom. The settlement was first known as Stuart and the telegraph station was Alice Springs. The latter became a reference for the town in 1933 to avoid confusion.

ALICE SPRINGS

On the Todd River (usually dry), the Alice lies almost in the geographical middle of the continent, 1,500km (930 miles) from the nearest state capital. But remote as it is, the town offers enough facilities to qualify as a holiday spot. I love dinner, take in a show and perhaps wander into Lasseters Casino, next to the top hotel, the Rydges Plaza. There's a good choice of quality restaurants. Outdoor pursuits include rock climbing, bush walking, horse riding and off-road driving.

More than 100 domestic flights arrive each week with visitors who take tours to Uluru-Kata Tjuta National Park (see pages 132–135) and Watarrka National Park and Kings Canyon (see page 131).

ALICE SPRINGS DESERT PARK

✉️ Larapinta Drive, PO Box 1046, Alice Springs NT 0871 ☎ 08 8951 8788 🕐 Daily 7.30–6 🎫 Adult A$18, child A$9
At this parcel of Australia's arid zone just west of the Alice, a 1.5km (1-mile) trail leads through three re-created desert habitats—Sand Country, Woodland and Desert Rivers—with native animals and plants.

TENNANT CREEK

The classic outback town of Tennant Creek is 530km (330 miles) north of Alice Springs on the Stuart Highway (*Information Centre, tel 08 8962 3388*). This former gold-mining town is best known for the Devils Marbles Conservation Reserve, a landscape of precariously balanced boulders 90km (56 miles) south on the Stuart Highway.

Body-painting is part of the Tiwi people's way of life

Hungry crocodiles arrive on cue for their lunch at Crocodylus Park

Canoe through Nitmiluk (Katherine Gorge) National Park

ADELAIDE RIVER QUEEN

318 L4 • Adelaide River Bridge, Arnhem Highway, via Humpty Doo; 64km (40 miles) southeast of Darwin 08 8988 8144 Cruises: daily 9am, 11am, 1pm, 3pm, May–Aug; 9am, 11am, 2.30pm, rest of year Adult A$36, child A$20 Twice daily shuttle from Darwin (bookings 08 8988 8144): departs 9.15, returns 1.15; departs 1.15, returns 5.15
www.jumpingcrocodilecruises.com.au

During the 90-minute cruise on the *Adelaide River Queen,* you'll be entertained by saltwater crocodiles that jump out of the murky river for a meal. The river birdlife is less voracious and includes magpie geese, brolgas, dollar birds and hawks.

Kingfishers and corellas gather in large flocks on the floodplains and it is not uncommon to see wild pigs and buffalo through the tall grasses along the riverbanks.

AYERS ROCK

See Uluṟu, pages 132–135.

BATHURST AND MELVILLE ISLANDS

318 L3 Visitors to the islands must obtain permits from the Tiwi Island Land Council 08 8981 4891 Tiwi Tours run 1- or 2-day tours (meals and camping accommodation included) 1800 811 633 (or local travel agents)
www.nlc.org.au
www.aboriginalartonline.com/regions/tiwi.html

Also known as the Tiwi Islands, Bathurst and Melville are popular one- or two-day trips 80km (50 miles) north from Darwin across the Beagle Gulf.

Both islands are thickly forested with eucalyptus, woolly-butt and paperbark, and there are open marshlands and wetlands. Among the wildlife are wallabies, possums, reptiles and many

kinds of birds. The sandy beaches accommodate nesting turtles, while the waters allow for stingrays, sharks, manta rays and saltwater crocodiles. Mangroves provide a habitat for mud crabs and many fish varieties.

The Tiwi people have traditionally painted their bodies in preparation for ceremonies. The same patterns have also been used on graveposts and bark baskets. Dancing is a part of everyday life on the islands, again particularly for ceremonial events.

CROCODYLUS PARK

815 McMillans Road, Berrimah, NT 0828, 10km (6 miles) east from Darwin on National Highway 1 08 8922 4500 Daily 9–5. Feeding times 10am, noon, 2pm Adult A$25, child A$12.50, family A$65 5 from Darwin
www.wmi.com.au/crocpark

The wildlife park, a 15-minute drive east of Darwin, cares for lions and tigers, iguanas, cassowaries, dingoes and wallabies—as well as hundreds of saltwater crocodiles, the largest living relics of the dinosaur age.

Bellair's Lagoon is home to more than 70 crocodiles. Twenty pens house breeding pairs of crocodiles, which can be seen from an overhead walkway.

KATHERINE

317 M4 Katherine Visitor Information Centre, cnr Lindsay Street and Katherine Terrace, Katherine, NT 0852 08 8972 2650
www.ntholidays.com

Katherine is a popular town about 300km (190 miles) from Darwin and 640km (400 miles) from Alice Springs.

The Jawoyn people once lived along the Katherine River, on which they depended for food and water. The town developed after a telegraph station was

established in the 1870s and subsequently Katherine became the focus of a grazing economy.

The photographs and objects at the Katherine Museum on Gorge Road relate to the history of the region (*Mon–Fri 10–4, Sat 10–1, Sun 2–5, Mar–Oct; Mon–Sat 10–1, Sun 2–5, rest of year*). Katherine Hot Springs are 3km (2 miles) southwest along the Victoria Highway, near the Katherine River. The therapeutic benefits of these springs, kept at a constant 32°C (90°F), are said to be better during the cooler months. Trails, a picnic area and a camping ground are nearby.

Springvale Homestead, 8km (5 miles) southwest of Katherine on Shadforth Road, dates from 1878 and is the oldest surviving homestead in the Northern Territory (*daily 9–5; free tour at 3*). The Cutta Cutta Caves are 27km (17 miles) south of Katherine off the Stuart Highway (*daily guided tours in the dry season at 9am, 10am, 11am, 1pm, 2pm and 3pm; adult A$12, child A$6*). These spectacular limestone caves are a habitat for the rare orange horseshoe bat and the ghost bat.
Don't miss Nitmiluk (Katherine Gorge) National Park, 30km (18 miles) north of Katherine, is worth a stopover in its own right (*daily 7–6*). A good way to see the park is by a boat tour of one of the five accessible gorges. If you don't have time to do this, though, the 3,000sq km (1,170sq mile) park has more than 100km (62 miles) of trails, with walks from one hour to five days. You can see ancient Aboriginal rock art, and among the wildlife are freshwater crocodiles, rare crimson and double-barred finches, bats and wallabies.

Entry to the park is free but fees apply for powered and unpowered camping grounds.

Kakadu National Park

Wetlands teaming with wildlife, sheer rock cliffs, monsoon forests and ancient Aboriginal rock art put Kadadu firmly in the league of Australia's finest national parks.

Inset: Nourlangie rock art shows Barriginj, the wife of Lightning Man

RATINGS	
Good for kids	●●
Historic Interest	●●●●
Photo Stops	●●●●●
Walkability	●●●

SEEING KAKADU

Although the park is most accessible in the dry season (May–Sep), it is actually at its most impressive in the wet season (Nov–Apr), when evening storms create huge floodplains teaming with tens of thousands of waterbirds. At Jim Jim, Gunlom and Twin Falls, water tumbles from the 200m (660ft) sandstone escarpments. The dry season is the best time to get around and the humidity is lower. There is accommodation at Jabiru, Cooinda (near Yellow Water) and South Alligator, and plenty of camping grounds.

HIGHLIGHTS

SOUTH ALLIGATOR AREA

The Arnhem Highway crosses the South Alligator River 40km (25 miles) past the northern park entrance. From Kakadu Resort, just before the river, the 3.5km (2-mile) Gungarre walk goes through monsoon forest and woodlands along the edge of Nggardabal Billabong. The Mamukala Wetlands, 7km (4.5 miles) east of the South Alligator River bridge, are accessed by a 3km (2-mile) walk.

JABIRU AREA

Jabiru, the service town for the Ranger Uranium Mine, is at the northeast edge of the park.. Book tours of the park at the travel office. The Bowali Visitor Centre, 5km (3 miles) west of Jabiru, has exhibits and videos giving a useful overview of the region. The Marrawuddi Gallery sells Aboriginal arts and crafts and there is a café. A 2km (1.2-mile) woodland trail leads to the Gagudju Crocodile Hotel.

EAST ALLIGATOR AREA

The rock art sites of Ubirr are the main attraction in this area. Near the end of the Arnhem Highway, a sealed road branches 34km (21 miles) north to Border Store/Manbiyarra and the Ubirr Rock Art Site (*daily 8.30–sunset, Apr–Nov; 2–sunset, rest of year*). A 1km (0.5-mile) trail (mostly accessible by wheelchair) leads past several galleries, and the 250m (820ft) climb to the lookout is rewarded with panoramas over the Narbab floodplain and rocky terrain. Around Border Store are walks through rainforest, riverside vegetation and sandstone country.

NOURLANGIE AREA

The Kakadu Highway leads southwest from Jabiru. A sealed road to Nourlangie Rock branches off 21km (13 miles) from the Bowali Visitor Centre. The rock is best viewed from the Gunwarddehardde Lookout. A 1.5km (1-mile) walk passes an Aboriginal shelter and rock art sites. The 3.5km (2-mile) Bubba Trail runs from the Muirella Park camping ground and passes through wetland waterbird habitats.

Below from left: the waters and rockfaces of the Graveside Gorge; a jabiru wading in the wetlands; hundreds of waterfalls flow off the Arnhem Land escarpment in the wet season

JIM JIM AND TWIN FALLS

About 39km (24 miles) from the Bowali Visitor Centre, a vehicle track leads south to the Jim Jim Falls—a 60km (37-mile), two-hour drive. The falls are at their spectacular best after the wet season. The rock pool, with its white sandy beach, can be accessed by 4WD only from June to November. Surrounded by dense forest, nearby Twin Falls, with its sandy beaches, is open from May to November.

YELLOW WATER AREA

The Warradjan Aboriginal Cultural Centre (*daily 9–5*), 55km (34 miles) southwest of the Bowali Visitor Centre, provides an introduction to Aboriginal life in Kakadu. The art and craft shop has an excellent range of products. A boat tour on South Alligator floodplain, with its prolific birdlife and dramatic wetland scenery, is a must. Crocodile sightings are common. Scenic flights operate from Cooinda airstrip.

MARY RIVER AREA

About 45km (30 miles) southwest along the Kakadu Highway from Yellow Water a 4WD track reaches the Maguk Plunge Pool after 12km (7 miles). This is a popular destination in summer. A 2km (1.2-mile) partly raised boardwalk follows a creek bed to the natural rock pool fed by a waterfall. This southern section of the park has a number of walks and two camping grounds.

BACKGROUND

A 19,000sq km (7,410sq mile) World Heritage Site, Kakadu has been home to Aboriginal people for more than 50,000 years. Cave paintings, rock carvings and archaeological sites tell the story of their beliefs, skills and culture. More than 5,000 sites have been catalogued, including the remarkable rock art galleries at Ubirr and Nourlangie Rock. Many paintings depict everyday scenes, with images of fish, birds and animals. They include Aboriginal Dreamtime creation legends such as Namarrgon the Lightning Man and Ngalyod the Rainbow Serpent.

The landscape is a rare complex of interlinked ecosystems—tidal flats, floodplains, lowlands and plateaux—habitats for rare or endemic plants and animals. There are 1,600 varieties of plant, 275 bird species, 75 types of reptile and 25 types of frog. Mammals include species of kangaroo, wallaby and flying foxes.

TIPS

● Detailed maps and brochures are available from Bowali Visitor Centre, near Jabiru, and the entrance stations on the Arnhem and Kakadu highways.
● You can see much of the park in a conventional vehicle, but some areas are accessible only to 4WD vehicles. Whatever you are driving, make sure the vehicle is roadworthy and you have adequate supplies of fuel.
● The wet season is November to April and roads can flood. Some park roads are closed from the start of the wet season for six months. For road conditions, tel 1800 650 881.

BASICS

✚ 318 M4
🏠 Bowali Visitor Centre, Jabiru, NT 0886; tel 08 8938 1120 🕐 Daily 8–5
🏠 Tourism Top End Visitor Information Centre, corner Knuckey and Mitchell streets, Darwin, NT 0800 ☎ 08 8936 2499 🕐 Daily 9–5 🎫 National Park entry pass A$16.25 per person, valid for 14 days. Children under 16 free 🚌 AAT Kings 08 8941 3844 📷 🌐 www.ea.gov.au/parks/kakadu
Excellent pages about the park's sights, plant and animal life, geology, Aboriginal culture and modern history.

LITCHFIELD NATIONAL PARK

Waterfalls, rainforest and dramatic sandstone formations makes this national park popular with locals.

🗺 318 L4 🛈 Tourism Top End Visitor Information Centre, cnr Knuckey and Mitchell streets, Darwin, NT 0800 ☎ 08 8936 2499 ℹ Odyssey Safaris (08 8948 0091) run a 2-day Hidden Secrets Safari www.nt.gov.au

TIP

● Most 4WD tracks are closed during the wet season. Some swimming areas, such as Wangi Falls, are closed for swimming after heavy rain.

Litchfield, 100km (62 miles) south of Darwin, is a popular place at weekends for picnics and swimming. The famous waterfalls cascade off the Tabletop Range plateau; the larger ones are fed by springs that flow all year round, but all are particularly impressive during the wet season.

FLORENCE FALLS AND BULEY ROCKHOLE
The double Florence Falls waterfall cascades into a swimming hole surrounded by monsoon forest. There are panoramic views from the escarpment, a short walk from the parking area, and a steep trail with stairs leads to the swimming pool. You can also swim in nearby Buley Rockhole, a series of waterfalls and rockholes.

LOST CITY
A 4WD track leads to an area known as the Lost City, where strange sandstone formations resemble buildings, people and animals.

TOLMER FALLS
One of the most dramatic, this long, narrow waterfall has viewing platforms and good walking tracks. Caves at the base of the falls house colonies of rare ghost bats and orange horseshoe bats.

WANGI FALLS
Wangi Falls waterfalls and swimming hole are the most popular attractions. A 3km (2-mile) trail goes through monsoon rainforest to the top of the falls. There is a large picnic area and kiosk.

Tjaynera Falls (May–Nov) is only accessible by 4WD and a trail

Standley Chasm is part of the Termite Ancestress Dreaming

MACDONNELL RANGES AND STANDLEY CHASM

🗺 318–319 M9 🛈 Central Australian Tourism Industry Association, 60 Gregory Terrace, Alice Springs, NT 0870 ☎ 08 8952 5800 www.centralaustraliantourism.com

The magnificent gorges and rocky ridges of the MacDonnell Ranges have inspired artists for decades. The scenery has a dynamic character that changes with the rising and setting of the sun. Simpsons Gap, with a rare, permanent waterhole, is a good introduction to the landscape, only 18km (11 miles) from Alice Springs (*daily 8–8*). The walk to Cassia Hill gives commanding views of the MacDonnell Ranges. A good time to visit is late afternoon or early morning, when the black-footed rock wallabies are more active.

Farther west, Standley Chasm is a spectacular narrow gap in the MacDonnell Ranges, 50km (31 miles) from Alice Springs (*daily 8–6, last entry 5; adult A$6, child A$5*). At noon the sun hits the chasm floor and ignites its sheer quartzite walls, which for a few brief moments light up fiery orange. The rest of the day it is cool and shady but still impressive, surrounded by cycads, ferns and river gums. The pretty 1km (0.5-mile) trail from the parking area and kiosk to the chasm follows Angkerle Creek. A café, built into the side of the hill, provides cold drinks and refreshments.

To the west along the Namatjira Drive, the picturesque waterholes at Ellery Creek Big Hole—89km (55 miles) from Alice Springs—Ormiston Gorge and Glen Helen Gorge are perfect for a dip. Also in this area are the Ochre Pits, which the Aboriginal people once quarried. Ochre was traditionally a valuable material used for cave paintings and ceremonial body decorations.

THE SIGHTS

The Territory Wildlife Park is set in natural bushland

TERRITORY WILDLIFE PARK

⊞ 318 L3 • Cox Peninsula Road, Berry Springs, NT 0837 ☎ 08 8988 6000
🕐 Daily 8.30–4.30 💲 Adult A$18, child A$9, family A$40 🚌 Daily service to and from the outer Darwin region; bookings essential, tel 08 8948 4248
▢ ⊞
www.territorywildlifepark.com.au

The park, set in 400ha (988 acres), is an excellent introduction to the wildlife of the Northern Territory. More than 6km (3.5 miles) of trails weave through managed habitats, past a huge aviary, a lagoon teeming with waterbirds, and open fields of kangaroos and wallabies. An entire Top End river system has been re-created in an aquarium and the nocturnal house has rare native species. A free shuttle train links major exhibits.

TJUWALIYN (DOUGLAS) HOT SPRINGS PARK

⊞ 317 L4 • Off Oolloo Road from Stuart Highway ☎ 08 8976 0282
🖐 Free. Camping: adult A$6.60, child A$3.30 🚌 200km (124 miles) south of Darwin
www.nt.gov.au

An easy day trip from Darwin, the park encloses a section of the Douglas River where thermal pools create an oasis in the dry woodland. The waters attract wildlife such as bandicoots, frill-necked lizards (below) and flying foxes. The most comfortable time to visit is in the dry season; heavy rains in the wet season can cut off roads. Swimming is banned in the main hot springs—make for the cooler pools up and downstream.

Inset: The Garden of Eden is a cool oasis within the park

WATARRKA NATIONAL PARK

The spectacular sandstone walls of Kings Canyon are among the biggest attractions in the Red Centre.

⊞ 317 L9 🛈 Central Australian Tourism Industry Association, 60 Gregory Terrace, Alice Springs, NT 0870 ☎ 08 8952 5800 🚌 Tours to Kings Canyon and Uluṟu 🚗 Kings Canyon 🏨 Kings Canyon
www.nt.gov.au

RATINGS				
Good for kids	●	●	●	
Photo stops	●	●	●	●	●
Walkability	●	●	●	●	
Activities	●	●			

TIP
● The climate can be very hot and dry—visitors should follow park safety regulations and carry enough water, wear a hat, and use sunscreen and insect repellent.

Watarrka National Park is 330km (205 miles) south-west of Alice Springs. Two routes lead from the Stuart Highway. At Henbury, 133km (82 miles) south of the Alice, the unsealed Ernest Giles Road branches west for 107km (66 miles) to join the sealed Luritja Road that leads to Watarrka. This route passes the Henbury Meteorites Conservation Reserve, where 12 craters were formed 4,700 years ago when fragments of a meteor hit the surface.

Overall, Kings Canyon is part of the rugged George Gill Range, where moist gorges provide a refuge for plants and animals within the surrounding desert. Although the park is accessible year round, April to September are the coolest months. Accommodation and camping facilities are available at the Kings Canyon Resort (*tel 08 8956 7442*), near to Kings Canyon, or at Kings Creek Station at the southern entrance (*tel 08 8956 7474*).

CANYON WALK
This 6km (3.5-mile) walk goes from the parking area to and around the rim of Kings Canyon and back by Kestral Falls (4 hours). Blue trail markers show the way, which has steps and boardwalks. Cool off in the palm-fringed pools of the Garden of Eden waterholes—very welcome from September to May. Walkers at any time should be fit and healthy. In case of difficulties there are four emergency radio call boxes along the way and a first-aid box at the top.

KINGS CREEK WALK
This is a less strenuous walk than the Canyon; a 2.5km (1.5-mile) circuit at the southeast entrance to the park (1 hour). About half of the walk is wheelchair accessible, otherwise strong footwear is required. Orange trail markers show the way.

Uluru-Kata Tjuṯa National Park

●

**There are some world wonders that are simply breathtaking—
Uluṟu (Ayers Rock) is one of them.**

SEEING ULURU-KATA TJUṮA NATIONAL PARK

Uluṟu and Kata Tjuṯa are the local Aboriginal names for Ayers Rock and The Olgas, and although these are strictly correct, they are referred to by either the old or new names. Uluṟu is one of the world's greatest natural attractions, a giant red monolith rising from the semi-arid plains in the middle of Australia's outback. Kata Tjuṯa is equally remarkable, 36 enormous domes about 50km (30 miles) west of Uluṟu. Both outcrops are sedimentary rocks. At sunset, Uluṟu and Kata Tjuṯa change from bright red to orange to lilac in a matter of minutes; sunrise is equally dramatic. Both landforms have great spiritual and cultural significance to the Aṉangu (Traditional Owners).

The Uluṟu-Kata Tjuṯa National Park is a Unesco World Heritage Site, covering 1,325sq km (515sq miles). The park is listed for both its natural and cultural significance. Uluṟu measures 9.4km (6 miles) around the base and is 340m (1,115ft) high. The domes of Kata Tjuṯa rise up to 546m (1,791ft). Away from the main sights, the park offers the silence and beauty of the Australian outback. There are excellent and varied accommodations at Ayers Rock Resort, from campgrounds to five-star hotels, and also souvenir shops, a post office, a bank and a supermarket.

RATINGS	
Good for kids	● ● ● ○
Historic interest	● ● ● ○
Photo stops	● ● ● ● ●
Walkability	● ● ● ○

TIPS

● Try to stay for at least two nights.
● If you are walking independently, do so early in the morning as temperatures soar later on.

TOURS

There are a number of great ways to see the Uluru-Kata Tjuta National Park. Harley Davidson tours, fixed-wing and helicopter flights are all enjoyable, but the best way to appreciate it is by foot. Paths are marked and several walks can be taken independently; a self-guided walks brochure is available from the Cultural Centre close to Uluru. Other walks are enhanced by having an Anangu guide, who will help you to appreciate the Aboriginal influence on the landscape.

SELF-GUIDED WALKS

Uluru: Base *9.4km (6 miles) 3–4 hours*
The longest defined walk goes around the circumference of Uluru. You can start at either the Mutitjulu or Mala parking areas. This walk soaks up the atmosphere of the cave paintings and various rock features. Be aware that there are a number of sacred Aboriginal sites that cannot be entered or photographed, but these are clearly marked.

Uluru: Mala *2km (1.2 miles) 1.5 hours*
This track begins at the base of the Uluru Climb parking area and is wheelchair accessible. A Ranger at the Mala Walk sign explains the local Aboriginal perceptions of Uluru and how the Anangu and the rangers look after the park together.

Uluru: Mutitjulu *1km (0.5 miles) 45 minutes*
The walk follows the track from the Mutitjulu parking area to a special waterhole that is home to Wanampi, an ancestral watersnake.

Kata Tjuta: Valley of the Winds *7.5km (4.5 miles) 3 hours*
This is a magnificent, reasonably flat walk and is highly recommended. Two lookout points provide excellent views of the spectacular landscape.

Kata Tjuta: Walpa Gorge *2.5km (1.5 miles) 1 hour*
The walk takes you to the end of the gorge and, as the track rises gently, there are great views of the surrounding countryside.

GUIDED TOURS
Anangu Tours
☎ 08 8956 2123 www.anangutours.com.au
Anangu Tours was established by the Aboriginal owners of Uluru and Kata Tjuta to provide tours with an Aboriginal guide. Bookings can be made at the Anangu Tours desk within the Touring Information Centre

Top: Uluru (Ayers Rock) at sunrise is awesome at any time of year
Above: Helicopter tours give the best overview

Harsh sunlight and shadow on the desert sands

Some of the peaks of Kata Tjuṯa, which means 'many heads' to the local Aboriginal people

at Ayers Rock Resort, at hotel receptions throughout the Ayers Rock Resort, or through a travel agent. Tours do not include park entry fees unless specified.

Aboriginal Uluṟu Tour *2km (1.2 miles) 5 hours*
This morning tour takes in sunrise at Uluṟu and a short walk along its base. To complete a morning you can join the Liru Walk afterwards (*adult A$108, child A$74*).

Liru Walk *2km (1.2 miles) 2 hours*
An excellent morning walk from the Cultural Centre through mulga scrub to the base of Uluṟu. Learn about the area's plants, wildlife and indigenous bush tucker (food) (*adult A$52, child A$27*).

Kuniya Walk *1.5km (1 mile) 2 hours*
From the Cultural Centre a guide takes you on an afternoon walk to the Muṯitjulu Waterhole on the east side of Uluṟu; on the way you learn about Aboriginal creation stories associated with Uluṟu and how to prepare bush tucker (*adult A$52, child A$27*).

Kuniya Sunset Tour *1.5km (1 mile) 4.5 hours*
This tour is based on the Kuniya Walk and ends with sunset at Uluṟu. It includes collection from your accommodation (*adult A$84, child A$58*).

Uluṟu-Kata Tjuṯa Pass
To experience sunrise and sunset, join the Aboriginal Uluṟu Tour in the morning and visit Kata Tjuṯa in the afternoon. Includes national park entry fee (*adult A$168, child A$110*).

Aṉangu Culture Pass
Do both the Aboriginal Uluṟu Tour at sunrise and the Kuniya Sunset Tour and get a 10 per cent discount (*adult A$172, child A$118*).

Kuniya and Morning Olgas Pass
This Pass includes a morning tour of the Valley of the Winds in Kata Tjuṯa and the Kuniya Sunset Tour (*adult A$154, child A$92*).

BACKGROUND

The region is culturally significant to the local Pitjantjatjara and Yankuntjatjara Aboriginal people, collectively known as the Aṉangu. The Aṉangu believe their ancestors have lived here since time began; archaeological evidence suggests the area has been occupied for 10,000 years.

Tjukurpa, the Aboriginal law, was laid down at the creation and it still defines and guides the daily lives of the Anangu people. For them it clarifies the nature of the earth's creation and the relationship between people, plants, animals and landscapes. It also explains rules for social structure, living together and caring for each other and the land. There's a story to be told in the many nooks and crannies in the rock surfaces, as well as in the ancient rock paintings.

Tjukurpa also determines sacred places, which are often associated with important Aboriginal ancestors. The creation story of the Kuniya Python Woman explains the scars on Uluru and the ripples in the nearby Mutitjulu Waterhole. It is the religious duty of the Anangu, as traditional custodians of Uluru and Kata Tjuta, to protect certain sites in the area and preserve their traditions. In the national park sacred sites are further protected by law.

From left: Doing the Mala Walk at Uluru; the Uluru-Kata Tjuta Cultural Centre; Kata Tjuta

Visitors are encouraged to join the many walks and tours led by the Anangu, who have a wide knowledge of the environment, plantlife and wildlife, and survival in the landscape. They prefer visitors to refrain from climbing the rock, though it is permitted.

The area has been known to white immigrants only since 1872, when Ernest Giles came across Kata Tjuta. He named it Mount Ferdinand after the botanist Baron von Mueller, who in turn renamed it Mount Olga after Queen Olga of Württemburg. In 1873 William Gosse led a party that discovered and named Mount Connor, a 863m (2,830ft) tabletop mountain, which is often mistaken for Uluru by those driving west along the Lasseter Highway. Farther west Gosse spotted a hill and accordingly stated: 'The hill, as I drew closer, presented a most unusual appearance with the upper portion being covered with holes or caves. When I got clear of the sandhills and was only two miles distant, and the hill for the first time coming fairly into view, what was my astonishment to find was one immense rock rising abruptly from the plain. I have named this Ayers Rock after Sir Henry Ayers, the premier of South Australia.' (The Aboriginal name for the rock, Uluru, has no English translation.)

With the increasing number of European visitors and settlers, conflict arose between the foreign and native cultures. In the early 1900s grazing stock and drought impinged on the Anangus' food and hunting. The government set aside land (reserves) for the Anangu, who regarded these areas as temporary refuges. Government officials hoped that in time the Anangu would 'fit in' to white society; instead they continued their traditional lifestyle.

Tourism developed in the 1950s with the construction of motels and an airstrip. During the early 1970s Yulara Resort (now Ayers Rock Resort) tourist village was built just outside the national park about 20km (12 miles) from Uluru and 50km (30 miles) from Kata Tjuta. This replaced the earlier accommodation that had been built too close to Uluru and had impacted negatively on the environment. By 1973 the Aboriginal people had become involved in managing the park and in 1979 the federal government finally recognized their traditional ownership.

In October 1985 the Anangu were granted freehold title to the national park, which was then leased back to the government's Parks Australia for 99 years. It is now one of Australia's most popular national parks.

BASICS

🔳 317 L10

🛈 Uluru-Kata Tjuta Cultural Centre, National Park Headquarters, Yulara, NT 0872; 1km (0.6 mile) from Uluru on the road from Ayers Rock Resort ☎ 08 8956 3138 🕙 Daily 7–6, Nov–Mar; daily 7–5.30, rest of year 🎟 Free www.deh.gov.au/parks/uluru

Uluru-Kata Tjuta National Park

☎ 08 8956 2299 🕙 1 hour before dawn to 1 hour after dusk (5–6.30am and 7.30–9pm) 🎟 3-day visit or part thereof: adult A$16.25, under 16s free 🛈 The Visitors Centre, Yulara Drive, Yulara, NT 872 ☎ 08 8957 7377, 08 8952 5800 🕙 Daily 8.30–7.30 www.centralaustraliantourism.com

SOUNDS OF SILENCE

Another unforgettable experience is the Sounds of Silence dinner in the desert. Watch the sun set over both Kata Tjuta and Uluru while sipping champagne. A didgeridoo plays in the background, a gourmet buffet of Australian delicacies is served and an astronomer explains the stars (see page 270).

SOUTH AUSTRALIA

South Australia is the driest of the Australian states. Virtually all the rain falls on the undulating grasslands in the south, whose wine regions are still able to produce world-class vintages. Yet it is in Adelaide that over three-quarters of the state's population live, an elegant, well-planned city, with squares and parkland shaping its heart.

KEY SIGHTS

The Palm House at Adelaide's splendid Botanic Garden

The Adelaide Festival Centre stages musicals, theatre and an annual cabaret festival, and is home to the Adelaide Symphony Orchestra

ADELAIDE

ADELAIDE BOTANIC GARDEN

✚ 137 C2 • North Terrace (east end), Adelaide, SA 5000 ☎ 08 8222 9311 ⏰ Daily 9–4, Apr–Oct; 9–5, rest of year 💲 Free. Conservatory: adult A$3.40, child A$1.70 🚌 Free 99B and 99C City Loop buses 🚊 Adelaide, 1km (0.6 mile) west from North Terrace entrance 🍴 🛍 ♿
www.botanicgardens.sa.gov.au

The botanic garden, just north-east of the city, is remarkable for its huge Moreton Bay fig trees.

The conservatory, with the largest single span in the southern hemisphere, houses tropical rainforest plants. Trails lead from here to the Palm House, Museum of Economic Botany and a lakeside restaurant. October is the best month for the Italianate Garden, the Wisteria Arbours and the Rose Garden.

ADELAIDE FESTIVAL CENTRE

✚ 137 B2 • King William Road, Adelaide, SA 5000 ☎ 08 8216 8600 ⏰ Varies according to performances 💲 Bookings via BASS: www.bass.net.au; local call 13 1246 (Mon–Sat 9–8); 24-hour infoline1900 933 303. Current performances are listed in the Adelaide Advertiser 🚌 Many bus routes stop outside the Centre or nearby on North Terrace 🚊 Adelaide 🛍 ♿
www.afct.org.au

Surrounded by Elder Park, on the south bank of the Torrens River, the Centre provides a world-class theatre and concert hall for top international and local performers. It is the venue for the Adelaide Festival, held from February to March during even-numbered

THE SIGHTS

ADELAIDE

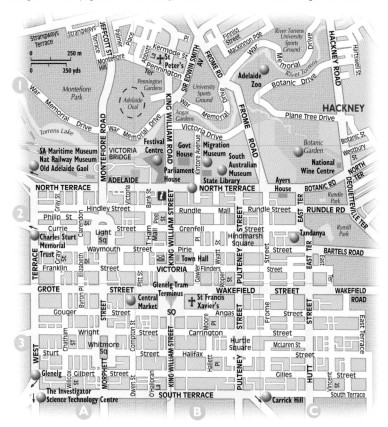

Carrick Hill is an unexpected haven in suburban Adelaide

ADELAIDE CITY

As the food and wine capital of Australia, Adelaide is not only sophisticated but lively and fun.

⊞ 137 B2 ℹ️ South Australian Visitor and Travel Centre, Ground Floor, 18 King William Street, Adelaide, SA 5000, tel 1300 655 276 🕐 Mon–Fri 8.30–5, Sat–Sun 9–2 ❓ www.adelaidemetro.com.au for all city transport options 🚉 Adelaide (the departure point for all suburban trains) www.southaustralia.com

TIPS

● The free Bee Line bus 99B or City Loop make numerous stops around the city, allowing passengers to hop on and off.
● Day and multipass transport tickets are available from the Passenger Transport Information Centre on the corner of Currie and King William streets.

In 1836, Colonel William Light, whose statue is on Montifiore Hill, planned a workable city with wide streets, attractive terraces and spacious parks. The simple grid layout is still admired and there is a British feel to its buildings and social accents. The population is just over a million, and there are more wining and dining options per head than any other state capital city. The central area is a compact, walkable square mile, and most of the city's attractions are gathered here. Often referred to as the city of churches, Adelaide's 'sleepy' reputation is far from accurate.

HIGHLIGHTS

On North Terrace (see page 140) is the South Australian Museum (see page 141) and a row of magnificent colonial buildings. Continue for 1km (0.6 mile) to the Botanic Garden (see page 137) also on North Terrace, and a little farther to the National Wine Centre of Australia (*Mon–Fri 10–6, Sat–Sun 10–5.30*), with wines from more than 50 regions, some of which you can taste.

The Adelaide Festival Centre (see page 137) is on King William Road, and across the river are the neo-Gothic St. Peter's Cathedral (1904), and the Adelaide Oval, venue for interstate and Test cricket.

Rundle Mall has fragrant flower stalls, department stores, arcades and cafés, with some of the best eating in the city on Rundle Street.

The National Wine Centre presents 10,000 Australian wines

years and now the second-most popular festival of arts in the world after Edinburgh in Scotland. WOMADelaide (World of Music and Dance), an outdoor world music festival, is held in March during odd-numbered years at nearby Botanic Park.

ADELAIDE ZOO

⊞ 137 C1 • Frome Road, Adelaide, SA 5000 ☎ 08 8267 3255 🕐 Daily 9.30–5 💷 Adult A$15, child A$9 🚌 272, 273. The Adelaide Explorer, departing King William Street outside the SA Tourism Commission, stops at the zoo 🚉 Adelaide, 1km (0.6 mile) southwest on North Terrace 🛒 One of the best Australian souvenir shops in Adelaide www.adelaide-zoo.com.au

You know you are close to the zoo when you hear the hoots of siamang gibbons. The usual way in is from Frome Road, but another way to arrive is via the Popeye ferry from Lake Torrens along the river. Although the zoo is small, it has more than 1,400 mammals, reptiles and fish, as well as one of the world's largest collections of birds. It also cares for many endangered species, such as the yellow-footed rock wallaby, so rare in the Flinders Ranges that few Australians have seen it. Other natives include koalas, Tasmanian devils, hairy-nosed wombats and the world's most venomous snake, the inland taipan.

Don't miss There are Sun bears and the endangered Malayan tapir in the South-East Asian Rainforest area, while the Australian rainforest aviary is home to 60 parrot species.

CARRICK HILL

⊞ Off 137 C3 • 46 Carrick Hill Drive, Springfield, SA 5062 ☎ 08 8379 3886 🕐 Wed–Sun 10–5 (house closes 4.30); tours 11.30, 2.30 💷 Adult A$9, child A$6.50, under 5s free 🚌 171C from

THE SIGHTS

ADELAIDE

Get fresh fruit and vegetables from the Central Market

Education through fun at the Science and Technology Centre

Glenelg's sandy beach is a great escape from the city

King William Street, Sun; 171 stops outside Mercedes College, Springfield, then long walk via Carrick Hill Drive 🚌 🏧 www.carrickhill.sa.gov.au

This Elizabethan-style mansion is set in 40ha (100 acres) 6.5km (4 miles) south of Adelaide. It was built in the 1930s for Sir Edward Hayward, a descendant of a wealthy Adelaide merchant family, and is one of the few residences of this period with interior and grounds unchanged. Edward and Ursula filled their home with European paintings, sculptures, drawings, antiques and furniture, and added Australian paintings by Russell Drysdale and William Dobell, among others.
Don't miss The magnificent gardens combine the best of English flora and native Australian bushland.

CENTRAL MARKET

➕ 137 A3 🛈 Central Market Precinct, Grote and Gouger streets, off Victoria Square, Adelaide, SA 5000, tel 08 8203 7494 🕐 Tue 7–5.30, Thu 9–5.30, Fri 7–9, Sat 7–3 💷 Free 🚌 Free Bee Line bus to Victoria Square from train station 🚌
www.southaustralia.com

The famous Adelaide Central Market is a bustling, multicultural food market in the heart of the city. The covered market is a blend of more than 40 ethnic cultures, where you can buy delicious fresh produce and gourmet foods. It seems that everyone in Adelaide shops at the market, which is an enduring culinary inspiration. Lucia's Pizza & Spaghetti Bar is a popular meeting place, with good coffee and food.

Gouger Street, on the south side, is a dining precinct popular for its seafood restaurants; some may look a bit basic, but they serve Australia's best whiting and crayfish (lobster).

CHARLES STURT MEMORIAL TRUST

➕ Off 137 A2 • Jetty Street, Grange, SA 5022 ☎ 08 8356 8185 🕐 Fri–Sun 1–5; times liable to change, phone first 💷 Adult A$4, child A$1.50 🚌 112 from Grenfell Street, Adelaide, then walk east along Jetty Street 🚉 East Grange, then walk south along the paved footpath 🏧

Born in India and educated in London, Captain Charles Sturt, a professional soldier who guarded convicts dispatched to New South Wales, was one of Australia's most courageous explorers. He discovered the course of the Macquarie, Murrumbidgee and Darling rivers, and made forays into South Australia's interior in search of an inland sea (but found the outback Cooper Creek instead). His large brick villa, built in 1840, stands 10km (6 miles) west of Adelaide in a splendid garden with views to Mount Lofty and contains period family furniture.

GLENELG

➕ Off 137 A3 🛈 Glenelg Visitor Information Centre, Foreshore, Glenelg, SA 5045, tel 08 8294 5833 🚋 Tram (City to Bay; journey time 25 minutes) leaves about every 15 minutes from Victoria Square, Adelaide, to Moseley Square, Glenelg
www.holdfast.sa.gov.au

Only 10km (6 miles) southwest of Adelaide on Gulf St. Vincent, Glenelg is the most popular of the long sandy beaches near the city. The vintage City to Bay tram stops directly opposite the beach and is a good excuse to leave your vehicle behind. The attractions here include alfresco dining, outdoor festivals and entertainment, beachfront lawns and, of course, the warm, clear blue water.

The Victorian Town Hall dominates Moseley Square and from here the main street, Jetty Road,

is packed with cinemas, shops and cafés, alongside the neo-Gothic St. Andrew's Church and fine Victorian mansions.

In 1836, Glenelg became the site of the first mainland settlement in South Australia. Captain John Hindmarsh, the first governor, landed on the beach on 28 December and proclaimed South Australia a province. Thus Proclamation Day is celebrated as a public holiday in South Australia only, and every year at the Old Gum Tree in McFarlane Street, the site of the proclamation, a full costume re-enactment is held. At the mouth of the Patawalonga Haven is a splendid replica of HMS *Buffalo,* one of the ships that carried the early settlers from England. It is now a popular seafood restaurant.
Don't miss The Bay Discovery Centre in the Town Hall tracks the history of Holdfast Bay. The Holdfast Shores Marina complex is worth a visit for its shops and fine restaurants.

THE INVESTIGATOR SCIENCE AND TECHNOLOGY CENTRE

➕ Off 137 A3 • Rose Terrace, Wayville, SA 5034 ☎ 08 8410 4123 🕐 Daily 10–5 💷 Adult A$8.75, child A$5.75 🚌 296, 297, 210, 214 and T21 stop on Goodwood Road 🚉 Goodwood, then a short walk 🚌 🏧
www.investigator.org.au

This informative science complex, 2km (1.2 miles) southeast of the city, next to the Royal Adelaide Showground, aims to create an awareness and understanding of science and technology in children. It grabs their interest through fun hands-on activities, interactive exhibitions and themed shows. Good for adults too, then. Some displays require basic physical competencies, such as climbing, and so may not be suitable for all ages.

The Migration Museum takes you back to early settlers' days

The war memorial at Government House on North Terrace

The strict rules of routine at Old Adelaide Gaol

MIGRATION MUSEUM

137 B2 • 82 Kintore Avenue, Adelaide, SA 5000 ☎ 08 8207 7580 Mon–Fri 10–5, Sat–Sun 1–5 Free (donations welcome). Guided tours: adult A$8, child A$4 Free 99C City Loop and many other routes Adelaide www.history.sa.gov.au/migra/migra.htm

The first of its type in Australia, the Migration Museum chronicles the hopes, origins and destinies of millions of immigrants. The building was once the Destitute Asylum where many unfortunates found themselves, in particular women who had given birth to unwanted, illegitimate children of miners in Victoria's gold rush days.

The museum has a constantly changing accent on the various traditions brought here by people of 100 different nationalities. Don't miss The commemorative tiles in Settlement Square outside the museum record peoples around the world who fled persecution. The Aboriginal Kaurna people are also remembered.

Chinese clothing on display

NATIONAL RAILWAY MUSEUM

Off 137 A2 • Lipson Street, Port Adelaide, SA 5015 ☎ 08 8341 1690 Daily 10–5 Adult A$10, child A$4.50 118, 118N stop at Commercial Road; Lipson Street is a block to the east Port Adelaide

Station, from Adelaide Station www.natrailmuseum.org.au

Although this is one of several museums in Port Adelaide, a serious train buff could easily spend a day here. It has one of the most comprehensive undercover collections of heritage locomotives, passenger carriages, freight vehicles and rail memorabilia in Australia. Younger enthusiasts can enjoy the Friends of Thomas the Tank Engine event over nine days in July, when a scale version of the children's book character is the star.

NORTH TERRACE

137 B2 18 King William Street, Adelaide, SA 5000, tel 08 8463 4500 Free 99C City Loop stops along North Terrace Adelaide www.tourism.sa.gov.au

When designing Adelaide's grid plan in 1836, Colonel William Light chose North Terrace as the area of state government, culture, commerce, education, medicine and the arts, a role it continues to fulfil. At the west end, by the university campus, the Lions Art Centre houses the Mercury arthouse cinema and behind it is the Jam Factory, with contemporary crafts and design. Beyond the central railway station, the Sky City Casino occupies the original historic railway building. Next door is Parliament House. Across the King William Street intersection are the gates of Government House, bordered by Prince Henry Gardens, with a Boer War memorial in front. The State Library, on the corner of North Terrace and Kintore Avenue, contains the Bradman Collection, an assembly of memorabilia about the great cricketer, Sir Donald Bradman (Mon–Fri 10–5, Sat–Sun 12–5).

Farther east are the South Australian Museum (see page 141) and the State Art Gallery.

The gallery (daily 10–5) has a comprehensive collection, with the emphasis on paintings by colonial and contemporary Australian artists. There is also the second-largest collection of Rodin sculptures in the world.

On the south side, beyond the Frome Road intersection, is Ayers House, the (exterior only), the Regency mansion of former state premier Henry Ayers, after whom Ayers Rock was named.

OLD ADELAIDE GAOL

Off 137 A2 • 18 Gaol Road, Thebarton, SA 5031 ☎ 08 8231 4062 Mon–Fri 11–4. Tours Sun, first tour 11, last tour 3.30 Adult A$6.50, child A$4 151–155 stop on intersection of Port Road and Gaol Road

In 1873, Elizabeth Woolcock was the only woman to be executed for murder in South Australia, and she was one of a total of 49 people hanged within the walls of Adelaide Gaol. Dating from 1841, it is one of the oldest surviving colonial public buildings in Adelaide, still functioning as a prison until 1988.

SOUTH AUSTRALIAN MARITIME MUSEUM

Off 137 A2 • 126 Lipson Street, Port Adelaide, SA 5015; 14km (9 miles) northwest of city ☎ 08 8207 6255 Daily 10–5 Adult A$8.50, child A$3.50, under 5s free 118, 118N from North Terrace terminate at Commercial Road Port Adelaide from Adelaide Station www.history.sa.gov.au/samm/samm.htm

The Maritime Museum, close to the lighthouse, is a berth for some of the world's greatest maritime stories. The main gallery occupies the former 1850 bond stores and contains a replica of a sailing ketch. Displays illustrate the conditions under which European migrants sailed to South Australia. There is also a

Wooden ship figureheads on display at the Maritime Museum

floating collection that includes the 1949 *Yelta,* the state's last working steam tug, and the 1942 military launch *Archie Badenoch.* **Don't miss** There is a magnificent view of the Adelaide plains and the Mount Lofty Ranges from the top of the lighthouse.

SOUTH AUSTRALIAN MUSEUM

➕ 137 B2 • North Terrace, Adelaide, SA 5000 ☎ 08 8207 7500 🕐 Daily 10–5 💲 Free 🚌 Free 99C City Loop and many other routes 🚉 Adelaide Railway Station 🛒 ♿
www.samuseum.sa.gov.au

This grand 19th-century building has four floors of exhibits. The Australian Aboriginal Cultures Gallery is the largest of its kind, exploring the indigenous people through hands-on displays and more than 3,000 items. Other galleries describe mammals from around the world, marine wildlife, fossils and minerals.
Don't miss A gallery is devoted to the Antarctic explorer Sir Douglas Mawson (1882–1958), exhibiting his sled, an ice wall and Antarctic rock.

TANDANYA–NATIONAL ABORIGINAL CULTURAL INSTITUTE

➕ 137 C2 • 253 Grenfell Street, Adelaide, SA 5000 ☎ 08 8224 3200 🕐 Daily 10–5 💲 Adult A$4, child A$3 🚌 Free 99C City Loop 🚉 Adelaide 🛒 ♿
www.tandanya.on.net

Paint a boomerang, learn how to play a didgeridoo or do the Kangaroo Dance—these are just some of the fun ways to discover indigenous culture. Forming the first major Australian Aboriginal cultural facility, the galleries here feature art, crafts and music, and a glimpse of the hunter-gatherer lifestyles and traditions of more than 85 communities.

The National Motor Museum in the Torrens Valley

ADELAIDE HILLS

The Mount Lofty Ranges and Adelaide Hills form a crescent of pretty towns, natural bushland, vineyards and gardens around the city.

➕ 320 Q15 ℹ️ Hahndorf Visitor Centre, 64 Main Street, Hahndorf, SA 5245, tel 08 8388 1319 🕐 Mon–Fri 9–5, Sat–Sun 10–4 ℹ️ Mount Lofty Summit Information Centre, Mount Lofty Summit Road, Crafers, SA 5152, tel 08 8370 1054 🕐 Daily 9–5
www.adelaidehillsinfo.asn.au

RATINGS			
Historic interest	●	●	●
Photo stops	●	●	●
Specialist shopping	●	●	
Activities	●	●	●

TIP
● When driving, be extra careful on the windy, hilly roads.

The Adelaide Hills is one of few regions in Australia with four distinct seasons. Temperatures are about 2–4ºC (3.5–7ºF) cooler than Adelaide city, so it's popular in summer. The Hills are 10km (6 miles) southeast of Adelaide, and much of their early colonization was by Prussians and Silesians fleeing religious persecution in the 19th century. This history and heritage is evident in the buildings and vineyards.

MOUNT LOFTY
Mount Lofty is a physical and spiritual gateway to the Hills. Close to the summit is Cleland Conservation Park and Wildlife Park (*daily 9–5*), full of friendly marsupials. Farther north, Norton Summit lies amid fruit orchards, rocky gullies and vineyards.

TORRENS VALLEY
Quiet country roads and native wildlife in traditional bushland characterize the Torrens Valley. The winding drive from Adelaide along the gorge is spectacular. At dawn and dusk, kangaroos and emus graze near Chain of Ponds, with breathtaking backdrops of giant reservoirs and towering pine trees. The National Motor Museum at Birdwood is a must for vintage car enthusiasts (*daily 9–5*), but you should also visit some wineries.

ONKAPARINGA VALLEY
The town of Hahndorf, in the Onkaparinga Valley southeast of Adelaide, was settled in 1839 by German immigrants and is the former home of landscape artist Sir Hans Heysen (1877–1968); the academy, Cedars, is dedicated to his work (*Sun–Fri 10–4*). Lenswood, in the heart of the valley, has some of the Hills' most beautiful vineyards, orchards and farmland.

THE SIGHTS

The Miamba Vineyard is part of the Grant Burge Wine Group; Jacobs Creek is world famous

RATINGS

Good for kids	● ● ●
Historic interest	● ● ● ●
Photo stops	● ● ● ●
Specialist shopping	● ● ● ●

TIPS

● Because the Barossa towns, villages and wineries are spread through an area measuring 25 by 10km (15 by 6 miles), a car is the best way to visit. Otherwise join a tour or rent a bicycle and ride through the backroads.

● Check major festival dates when accommodation can be difficult to find unless reserved well in advance.

BASICS

✚ 320 Q15

ℹ Barossa Wine and Visitor Centre, 66–68 Murray Street, Tanunda, SA 5352, tel 08 8563 0600, 1300 852 982
🕐 Mon–Fri 9–5, Sat–Sun 10–4
www.barossa-region.org

BAROSSA VALLEY

The Barossa Valley makes an excellent one- or two-day trip from Adelaide for food and wine lovers.

Australia's best-known wine region is only a 1-hour drive, 68km (42 miles) north of Adelaide. There are more than 50 cellar door wineries, plus fine restaurants and accommodation in cottages, farmhouses and stately homes. Add heritage towns and villages spread among the undulating hills and valleys, and it's a classic area for touring.

South Australia was a free settlement, only proclaimed in 1836, and in 1840 the English settled in Angaston and Lyndoch. Dissidents from Germany made their way to the Barossa Valley soon after, and the region retains an Anglo-European accent reflected in the architecture and the traditional skills of smoking meats, preserving fruits and making cheeses. The English gentry were responsible for the development of a commercial wine industry, which grew rapidly from the 1880s. Today, more than 6 million litres (1.3 million gallons) of quality wine is exported each year.

Food Barossa is now a regional food brand and there is a Farmers' Market in Angaston on Saturday morning (7.30–11.30). Music also plays a role in the area's charm and atmosphere, with brass band and jazz festivals. The Barossa International Festival of Music is held each October and the Jazz Weekend every August.

The wineries vary dramatically in size and attractiveness, but many have kept their original buildings, like the Rockford Winery in Tanunda and the Saltram Wine Estate in Angaston. Chateau Tanunda has been restored to its former glory with a croquet lawn and attractive gardens. The Jacobs Creek Visitor Centre offers historical information, tastings of Orlando wines and a good restaurant in a superb setting on Jacobs Creek. Peter Lehmann Wines, Wolf Blass and Penfolds are also well known outside Australia and so attract visitors. But don't forget the smaller wineries, directions to which are available at the Barossa Wine and Visitor Centre in Tanunda.

You can walk off the after-effects of too much good food and wine along many walking trails. There are marked walks in the Barossa Goldfields and six trails in the Para Wirra, around Mengler Hill and the Sculpture Park. Maps are available from the visitor office in Tanunda.
Don't miss The Barossa Reservoir, west of Lyndoch, is noted for its Whispering Wall, a dam begun in 1899. Then the highest dam in Australia, its innovative curving wall proved an influential design. It's equally famous for its acoustic properties as ordinary speech travels across the parabolic surface.

Original railcarts outside the Old Timers Mine at Coober Pedy

Don't miss the ride on the Steam Rangers Cockle Train along the coast between Goolwa and Victor Harbor on the Fleurieu Peninsula

SOUTH AUSTRALIA

ADELAIDE

See pages 137–141.

ADELAIDE HILLS

See page 141.

COOBER PEDY

320 N12 ✚ Coober Pedy Visitor Centre, Hutchison Street, Coober Pedy, SA 5721, tel 1800 637 076 ◉ Mon–Fri 8.30–5 ✖ Coober Pedy; daily flights from Adelaide
www.opalcapitaloftheworld.com.au

Coober Pedy is the world's opal capital, disgorging about 95 per cent of this fiery semiprecious stone. Craters, shafts and waste heaps mark the frontier landscape, where homes are gouged from bare hillsides, originally by pioneer miners escaping the searing summer heat and cold nights (March to November is the best time to visit). You can stay at the world's only international-standard underground hotel or a subterranean bed-and-breakfast; there are even underground churches.
The Umoona Opal Mine and Museum (daily 9–7, tours at 10, 2 and 4) explores the local geology and Aboriginal Dreamtime. Some 4WD tours include a 70km (43-mile) round trip along part of the Dog Fence—5,500km (3,410 miles) of barbed wire that protects sheep from dingoes.
Don't miss Martin's night stargazing tour goes into the desert (tel 08 8672 5223).

COONAWARRA

320 R16 ✚ Penola Coonawarra Visitor Centre, 27 Arthur Street, Penola SA 5277, tel 08 8737 2855
www.thelimestonecoast.com

Coonawarra, inland from the Limestone Coast, is best known for the excellence of its wines, particularly the reds.

The first winery was established in 1890, and later became Wynns Coonawarra Estate. The John Riddoch Interpretative Centre (Mon–Fri 9–5, Sat–Sun 1–4) is where to learn about the region's agricultural history.
Penola, south of Coonawarra, is the home of Mother Mary Mackillop, founder of the Order of St. Joseph and the first Australian to be beatified.

COORONG NATIONAL PARK

320 Q16 • National Parks and Wildlife SA, Coorong District Office, 34 Princes Highway, Meningie, SA 5264
☎ 08 8575 1200 ◉ Office times vary according to rangers' activities (call first). Camping permits are available from this office, or roadhouses and information units in the region
◉ Camping permits (per night) A$6 per vehicle or boat, A$3.50 per hiker or bike rider ◻ Premier Stateliner daily service from Adelaide to Meningie, Kingston and Mount Gambier
www.environment.sa.gov.au/parks/coorong/visit.html

Visitors flock to this 50,000ha (123,500-acre) south coast park to observe the 238 bird species, which have migrated from as far as Siberia, and to enjoy 130km (80 miles) of wetlands, lagoons and dunes facing the Southern Ocean. By walking for a day, into the boat-accessible parts of the Coorong, a genuine wilderness experience is possible, although accommodation and caravan parks are within striking distance for those needing civilization. There is surf fishing on the beach or by boat or jetty at Long Point and Jacks Point; and fishing at Lake Albert, Meningie.

EYRE PENINSULA

320 N15 ✚ Port Lincoln Visitor Information Centre, 3 Adelaide Place, SA 5606, tel 08 8683 3544
◉ Daily 9–5

www.visitportlincoln.net
www.epta.com.au

From the eastern steelworks city of Whyalla on Spencer Gulf to Ceduna on the Great Australian Bight, 1,000km (620 miles) of peninsula coastline produces more than 60 per cent of the nation's seafood. Port Lincoln, at the southern point, is the world's tuna capital, with Tunarama (January: Australia Day weekend) the only festival dedicated to the big fish. The world's largest oysters are farmed along the coast between Coffin Bay and Ceduna; the molluscs are celebrated at Ceduna's October Oysterfest. There is a maritime museum and theatre at Whyalla, while Port Lincoln has many museums. Coffin Bay National Park is great for fishing, water sports, walking and wildlife.

FLEURIEU PENINSULA

320 Q15 ✚ Fleurieu Peninsula Tourism, 10 Dawson Street, Goolwa, SA 5214, tel 08 8555 5554
www.fleurieupeninsula.com.au

The Fleurieu Peninsula is a holiday playground of craft markets and country music, art and jazz festivals. There are 60 wineries for tasting and dining. Victor Harbor is the main resort town, where you can whale-watch from June to September or take a horse-drawn tram to Granite Island and see nesting penguins. Strathalbyn, inland, is good for browsing antiques and craft stores.
The peninsula is fringed with beaches, while the interior has several national and conservation parks; ideal for bird- and wildlife-spotting, water sports or walking. Cape Jervis is the ferry point for Kangaroo Island (see page 144).
Don't miss The Cockle Train steams between Goolwa and Victor Harbor at Easter, Sundays and school holidays.

Wilpena Pound: venerated for 15,000 years by Aboriginals

The Remarkable Rocks are a huge natural sculpture

FLINDERS RANGES

➕ 320 Q13 ℹ️ Flinders Ranges Tourist Information Centre, 3 Seventh Street, Quorn, SA 5433, tel 08 8648 6419 www.flindersrangescouncil.sa.gov.au

Moody, awesome, spiritual home of the Adnyamathanha people, the Flinders Ranges extend from Peterborough to the untamed Gammon Ranges. The ranges take in five national and four conservation parks, and offer challenging walking trails, including the 1,500km (930-mile) Heysen Trail from Cape Jervis on the Fleurieu Peninsula to Parachilna. Sir Hans Heysen (see page 141) depicted the ranges in his landscapes of huge red river gums and creeks and gorges.

The Ranges' landmark is Wilpena Pound, a serpentine train of mountain peaks and waterfalls. Non-adventurers may opt for a flight over the area. Farther north, the settlement of Blinman, once the region's largest copper-mining complex, now has art and craft galleries.

The Ranges' capital is Quorn, a 3-hour drive from Adelaide. Its Pichi Richi tourist railway to Port Augusta (Mar–Nov) attracts rail enthusiasts, as do Peterborough's return Steamtown weekend winter journeys to Eurelia or Ororoo.

Outside the towns this is a wild, often forbidding country, much of it accessible only by 4WD vehicles; various operators conduct tours. Northeast of Quorn, the central part of the Ranges largely lies within the 92,746ha (229,000-acre) Flinders Ranges National Park. Besides its rich natural and cultural heritage, the park is a challenge for lovers of outdoor activities (*entry and camping fees apply; tel 08 8648 4244*). **Don't miss** Arkaroola Wilderness Sanctuary's Ridgetop 4WD tour and stargazing at its astronomical observatory (*tel 08 8648 4848*).

KANGAROO ISLAND

Visitors travel from around the world to experience the natural heritage of Kangaroo Island, Australia's third-largest island.

➕ 320 P15 ℹ️ Gateway Visitor Information Centre, Howard Drive, Penneshaw (near Sealink ferry terminal), tel 08 8553 1185
🕐 Mon–Fri 9–5, Sat–Sun 10–4
🚢 Sealink ferries make several crossings daily from Cape Jervis to Penneshaw, more in peak seasons, tel 08 8553 1122; www.sealink.com.au
❓ Sealink organizes coach travel from Adelaide to Cape Jervis www.ki.com.au

RATINGS					
Good for kids	●	●	●	●	●
Historic interest	●	●	●	○	○
Photo stops	●	●	●	●	○
Activities	●	●	●	●	○

TIP
● Distances are very long and visitors in self-contained accommodation away from the main settlements should ensure they have adequate water, food and fuel.

A 15km (9-mile) ferry ride across the Backstairs Passage separates Kangaroo Island from Cape Jervis on the Fleurieu Peninsula (see page 143). At 155km (96 miles) long and up to 60km (37 miles) wide, with 450km (279 miles) of spectacular cliff coastline and gentle beaches, the island is too big to circumnavigate in a day. The coastline includes wonders such as Remarkable Rocks, Admiral's Arch and Kelly Caves. There are 19 national and conservation parks, interspersed with pastoral land and thick scrub.

Discovered by the explorer Matthew Flinders in 1802, Kangaroo Island was settled at American River by renegade American sealers in 1803, later to become South Australia's first capital at Reeves Point, near Kingscote. Lack of water meant re-establishment of the capital to Adelaide in 1836.

Some 850 native plant species thrive here and wildlife includes a colony of sea lions on pristine Seal Bay. There are kangaroos (of course), Tammar wallabies, emus, Cape Barren geese, platypuses and koalas at Flinders Chase, the largest of the conservation parks. Fairy penguins parade at dusk at northern Penneshaw and at Kingscote.

Other ways to spend time include visiting museums, fishing, diving around 50 shipwrecks, sailing, surfing, bushwalking, cycling, or watching for rare glossy black cockatoos and the 256 other bird species. Make sure you try the Ligurian-style honey, cheeses, corn-fed chicken, crayfish (lobster) and local wine. **Don't miss** Pelican feeding (*daily 5pm*) and penguin walks are at Kingscote Marine Centre (*tel 08 8553 3112*).

Sea lions gather at Seal Bay

The Kapunda Chimney was built in 1852 to ventilate the mines

An aerial view of Mount Gambier and its extinct volcano

One of many restored paddle-steamers on the Murray River

KAPUNDA

320 Q15 Kapunda Tourist Information Centre, 76 Main Street, Kapunda, SA 5373, tel 08 8566 2902 www.clarevalley.com.au

Kapunda, and South Australia's fledgling 19th-century economy, were built on the wealth of the copper mines, producing the highest grade in the world. The southern approach is dominated by Map Kernow (son of Cornwall), an 8m (26-ft) bronze statue that commemorates the Cornish miners who worked the early mines. The copper seams had become exhausted or were flooded by the end of the 19th century and the township subsequently became the base for cattle ranching.

The 10km (6-mile) Kapunda Heritage Trail passes old mine areas, tunnels, open cuts and cottages; the landmark Kapunda Chimney is here. Many Victorian buildings in the south end of town are adorned with magnificent metal openwork. Kapunda Museum (daily 1–4, Sep–May; Sat–Sun 1–4, rest of year; adult A$4, child A$2) contains historical town objects.

MOUNT GAMBIER

320 R16 Lady Nelson Visitor and Discovery Centre, Jubilee Highway East, Mount Gambier, SA 5290, tel 08 8724 9750 www.mountgambier.sa.gov.au

The town of Mount Gambier, in the southeast corner of the state on the Limestone Coast, lies on the slopes of an extinct volcano. The water-filled crater, known as the Blue Lake, is normally crystal clear with the water that has filtered through limestone beneath the city. But each November the lake changes from a subdued winter blue to brilliant turquoise, and then back again in March.

The lake provides water for Mount Gambier's residential, commercial and industrial needs. A 3.5km (2-mile) trail follows the rim of the Blue Lake. In the town itself, its strong café society imbued with country charm, historic buildings, antiques stores, shopping malls, museums, galleries, cinemas and heritage pubs provides the entertainment. **Don't miss** The limestone caves tour under the town's streets.

MURRAY BRIDGE

320 Q15 Murray Bridge Visitor Information and Tourist Centre, 3 South Terrace, Murray Bridge, SA 5253, tel 08 8539 1142 www.murray-river.net

The mighty Murray is one of the world's great rivers. The South Australian course is divided into two regions, the lower Murraylands and the upper Riverland, where Waikerie is Australia's gliding capital. Carving through sandstone cliffs dotted with red gum trees, the river is a sanctuary for wildlife, as well as offering houseboat cruises, fishing and water-skiing. Where paddle-steamers once carried wool, tea and gold bullion to towns from Tailem Bend to Echuca in central Victoria, they now carry holiday-makers. The giant *Murray Princess* paddle-wheeler runs overnight cabin cruises from Mannum, upstream from Murray Bridge, and Tailem Bend, while the *Proud Mary* runs from Murray Bridge. **Don't miss** There is a scenic drive around Monarto Zoo on the way to Murray Bridge; Ruston's rose garden at Renmark.

ROBE

320 Q16 Robe Visitor Information Centre, Mundy Terrace, Robe, SA 5276, tel 08 8768 2465 www.robe.sa.gov.au October to April is really the best time to visit Robe, when the crayfish (lobster) are in full season.

This popular, pretty seafront holiday spot on Guichen Bay is known for its seafood, best accompanied by a wine from Coonawarra or a local winery. Robe was once the third-largest port in South Australia and was where miners disembarked in the mid-1800s on their way to the Victorian goldfields. A heritage walk through the town takes in Victorian buildings and the ruins of the 1861 Old Gaol.

The bay is suitable for sailing and swimming, and there are plenty of opportunities for fishing and diving along the coast. **Don't miss** There are panoramic views at Beacon Hill Lookout.

YORKE PENINSULA

320 P15 National Dry-Land Farming Centre, 50 Moonta Road, Kadina, SA 5554, tel 08 8821 2333 www.yorkepeninsula.com.au

You are never more than 25km (15.5 miles) from the sea on the Yorke Peninsula. Inland the peninsula is the granary of South Australia, while along the coast it is a fishing paradise. Many of the small seafront towns have jetties for those without boats.

Among the coastal towns, Ardrossan is known for its soaring cliffs, local history museum and the shipwreck of the *Zanoni*—one of Australia's best diving challenges. Little Cornwall comprises the 'copper triangle' towns of Moonta, Wallaroo and inland Kadina. This was once a rich copper-mining region that attracted Cornish miners in the 19th century. Biennially these towns host the world's largest Cornish festival, Kernewek Lowender, in May during odd-numbered years.

Innes National Park, at the foot of the peninsula, is a haven for bushwalking, camping, diving and surfing.

The Breakaways, near Coober Pedy, provide a typical outback scene

RATINGS	
Good for kids	● ●
Historic interest	● ● ● ●
Photo stops	● ● ● ● ●
Activities	● ● ●

TIPS

● Unless you're on an organized tour, inform friends of your travel plans. If you deviate from a major town or road, inform police of your schedule and destination.

● Carry good maps (many roads are not signposted) and extra water, food, fuel and a spare fan belt.

● If you break down, do not leave your vehicle. Lie under it for shade until you are found.

● Always check road conditions ahead—it's easy to get stuck in rain and mud.

BASICS

✚ 320 P12

ℹ Wadlata Outback Centre (includes tourist information), 41 Flinders Terrace, Port Augusta, SA 5700, tel 08 8642 4511
www.portaugusta.sa.gov.au
www.rangelands.sa.gov.au
🕐 Mon–Fri 9–5, Sat–Sun 10–4
www.hawkermotors.com.au
For organized 4WD or coach tours to isolated communities, contact the Port Augusta or Flinders Ranges tourist offices.

OUTBACK SOUTH AUSTRALIA

Go to the outback to agree with explorer Charles Sturt, who said in 1845 of its harsh, brilliant, unyielding splendour that it had 'no parallel on earth's surface'.

The South Australian outback is a vast backyard in the driest state in the second-driest continent, and remains one of the world's great adventure challenges. It was first explored in 1839, and later by the ill-fated Burke and Wills (see page 27), who perished by Cooper Creek. Memorials to them both are near Innamincka. The main north–south road is the 3,245km (2,010-mile) sealed Stuart Highway, which can be left for forays into the eastern outback. Locals will helpfully direct people from point A to B, but be aware of the distances and dangers.

South Australia's outback is a landscape of stony red desert and boulder-strewn plains, pockets of saltbush and scrub, blinding-white salt lakes, rocky eruptions and endless star-filled night skies.

Heading northwest to the Great Victoria Desert, key towns along the Stuart Highway are Port Augusta, Woomera, Glendambo, Coober Pedy (see page 143) and Marla. From Marla, if you don't want to continue to Alice Springs, turn southeast to Oodnadatta, William Creek, Lyndhurst and Leigh Creek back to Port Augusta.

WOOMERA
Woomera has the southern hemisphere's only rocket-launching range. To the north, modern Roxby Downs serves Olympic Dam, the world's biggest copper-uranium complex, with mine tours. Andamooka is another mineral town, little changed since opals were discovered here in 1930. It has yielded the world's biggest opal.

WILLIAM CREEK
This town lies within the world's largest cattle station, Anna Creek. It's a gateway to Lake Eyre North (4WD only), which has filled only four times since its discovery (last time in 2000, attracting prolific birdlife).

MARREE
The road southeast to Marree follows the Oodnadatta Track and passes Lake Eyre South. Marree itself has a mosque, founded by Afghan cameleers who took supplies to remote settlements and returned with wool. The Birdsville Track heads north to Birdsville through the Stony Desert. Farther south, you can tour the coal mines at Leigh Creek.

WESTERN AUSTRALIA

Western Australia is larger than the combined area of Alaska and Texas. The long western coast runs from the temperate forests of the south, where karri trees grow to 100m (328ft), to the sandstone ranges of the Kimberley in the tropics. Perth, on the Swan River, is just inland from the historic port of Fremantle. Farther inland still, farmland gradually yields to an immense landscape of scrub and desert.

Kununurra
Timber Creek
Broome
Port Hedland
Tennant Creek
Newman
Alice Springs
Carnarvon
95
Meekatharra
Geraldton
Kalgoorlie-Boulder
PERTH
94
Eucla
Fremantle
Margaret River
Esperance
Albany

KEY SIGHTS

The sea turtle is just one of the underwater creatures at the Aquarium of Western Australia

A black swan and cygnets in Kings Park

PERTH

AQUARIUM OF WESTERN AUSTRALIA

✚ Off 148 A2 • Southside Drive, Hillarys Boat Harbour, Hillarys, WA 6024 ☎ 08 9447 7500 ⏰ Daily 10–5 (Wed 5–9pm, Dec–Apr) 💰 Adult A\$20, child (4–17) A\$12.50 🚌 Warwick then bus 423 🚻 📶 www.aqwa.com.au

This is a great place to see live corals and marine life from Western Australia's 12,000km (7,440 miles) of coastline. Sharks, stingrays, turtles and fish circle a walk-through tunnel.

ART GALLERY OF WESTERN AUSTRALIA

✚ 148 B2 • Perth Cultural Centre, Perth; entry from the city station or Barrack Street via the James Street Mall or William Street ☎ 08 9492 6600 ⏰ Daily 10–5 🎟 Free 🚌 Bus station adjacent 🚉 Perth City 🚻 📶 www.artgallery.wa.gov.au

The gallery shows Australian and international paintings, sculpture, prints, craft items and decorative arts. The collection of Aboriginal art is one of the finest in Australia, comprising some 2,400 artworks.

CAVERSHAM WILDLIFE PARK

✚ Whiteman Park, Lord Street, Whiteman, WA 6068, 15km (9 miles) northeast from city ☎ 08 9248 1984 ⏰ Daily 8.30–5.30 💰 Adult A\$12.50, child (2–14) A\$5.50 🚌 From Perth to Whiteman 🚉 Whiteman 🚻 📶 www.cavershamwildlife.com.au

Caversham Wildlife Park, in the Swan Valley (see page 154), has more than 2,000 animals representing around 200 species. Most are native so this is a good opportunity to see Australian animals close up.

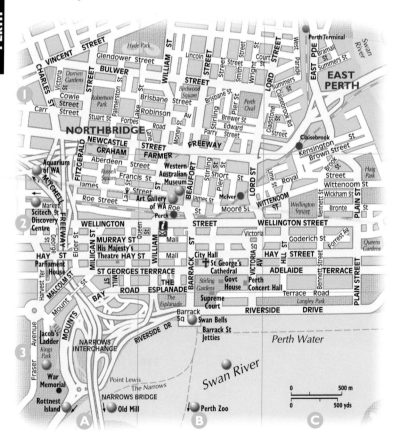

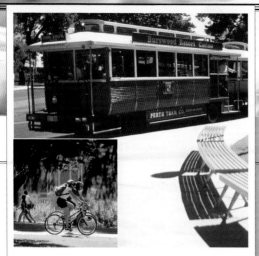

The natural monoliths of the Pinnacles Desert

KINGS PARK AND BOTANIC GARDEN

Sweeping parklands, gardens, wildflowers and native bushland only a few minutes from the middle of Perth.

🔲 148 A3 • Kings Park, Fraser Avenue, West Perth, WA 6005 ☎ 08 9480 3600 🕐 Daily 24 hours 🎫 Free 🚌 32 and 33 from central Perth. The Perth Tram links Kings Park with the city 🚃 The Kings Park Volunteer Guides lead free tours through the bushland and gardens daily at 10am and 2pm, 1.5 hours 🍴 🛍 📷 www.kpbg.wa.gov.au • More pictures than detailed information but the park map is useful.

RATINGS	
Good for kids	●●●○
Photo stops	●●●○
Value for money	●●●●●
Walkability	●●●●●

TIPS

● Self-guide pamphlets are available at the information office in the Fraser Avenue precinct.
● The park is very popular with locals on the weekend—midweek is usually quieter.
● One of the best ways to experience the park is to rent a bicycle or explore one of the walking tracks.

Kings Park has always been a popular playground for the people of Perth, whether for a walk or to enjoy a picnic. It was first reserved in 1872 and originally called Perth Park. The name was changed to Kings Park in 1901 to mark the accession of King Edward VII and the visit to Perth of his son the Duke of Cornwall and Princess Mary (later King George V and Queen Mary).

The park occupies some 400ha (988 acres) of Mount Eliza overlooking the Swan River and the city of Perth, 1.5km (1 mile) to the east. It is mainly natural bushland and partly developed parkland. Of the 470 species of plants recorded in the bushland, almost 300 are native to Kings Park; the remainder are native to other parts of Australia. Spring is a good time to visit when wildflowers are in bloom. The **Western Australian Botanic Garden** within the park covers 17ha (42 acres) and has some 1,700 native species.

The main entrance in Fraser Avenue leads to two honour or memorial avenues, May Drive and Lovekin Drive, flanked by towering lemon-scented gums. Near the main entrance are the park's shops, bicycle rental outlets, Kings Park Tram (one-hour tours), restaurants and galleries including the Aboriginal Art and Craft Gallery. The State War Memorial is also close by.

Roads, bicycle tracks and trails criss-cross the park and there are picnic areas and playgrounds for families. The Pioneer Women's Memorial Fountain is a great place to relax. During summer the park is a venue for outdoor theatre, concerts and movies.

NAMBUNG NATIONAL PARK

🔲 316 C13 • Cnr Aragon and Seville streets, Cervantes, WA 6511 ☎ 08 952 7041 💰 Day: vehicle (up to 8 people) A$9, motorcycle A$3, tour or bus passenger A$3.40. Camping fees extra www.naturebase.net

The 17,491ha (43,203-acre) Nambung National Park protects the Pinnacles Desert, a 400ha (988-acre) area where thousands of limestone pillars rise from shifting yellow sand. The pillars come in all shapes and sizes: Some are jagged, sharp-edged columns rising to a point, while others resemble tombstones; many are only ankle high and pencil thin. The largest pillar is nearly 4m (13ft) high and 2m (6.5ft) wide. The park is also renowned for its beaches, coastal dunes, shady groves of tuart trees and low heathland rich in flowering plants. Kangaroo Point has great ocean views and picnic spots, and the sandy beach at Hangover Bay is good for surfing and swimming. Nambung can be seen in a day from Perth—it's a 245km (152-mile), 3-hour drive north— but it's worth staying for a couple of days.

THE OLD MILL

🔲 Off 148 A3 • Mill Point Road, off Kwinana Freeway, South Perth, WA 6151 ☎ 08 9474 0777 🕐 Subject to change www.ntwa.com.au

Standing on the Mill Point headland across the Swan River from the city, the Old Mill is one of Perth's oldest buildings. The foundation stone was laid by the first governor, James Stirling, in 1835 for the owner William Kernot Shenton (it is also known as Shenton's Mill). The mill, adjacent miller's cottage and grounds are furnished with relics of the colonial period. Flour milling continued here until 1859.

Fremantle

A thriving cosmopolitan maritime community dominated by restaurants, great historical buildings, markets and galleries.

The Fremantle-based replica of the Dutch vessel Duyfken, which reached Australia in 1606

RATINGS	
Good for kids	◕ ◕ ◕ ◕
Historic interest	◕ ◕ ◕ ◕
Specialist shopping	◕ ◕ ◕
Walkability	◕ ◕ ◕

TIPS

● The Fremantle Tram provides a range of great tours round Fremantle.
● The Fremantle CAT bus is a free, quick and easy way to get about.
● The city gets very crowded at weekends when there is the most action.

Fremantle is an enjoyable place to spend the day for its mixture of historical buildings and shops. It is 19km (12 miles) southwest of Perth on the mouth of the Swan River, which leads into Fremantle Harbour and the Indian Ocean. A number of attractions are along the harbour and the ocean. On the harbour side is the overseas passenger terminal and the Maritime Museum. On the ocean side is Fishing Boat Harbour, which shelters Fremantle's 500-strong fishing fleet and is a great venue for a seafood or fish-and-chip lunch or dinner. Fremantle is also renowned for its alfresco cafés, many of which are on the cappuccino strip of South Terrace and are popular with locals and visitors alike.

VICTORIAN PAST

The main streets of Fremantle retain numerous restored Victorian buildings, many of which are classified by the National Trust. Most popular among the heritage sights is Fremantle Prison on The Terrace (*daily 10–5; adult A$14.30, child A$7.15*). It was built by convicts between 1850 and 1855 from limestone quarried on the site. After the end of transportation in 1868 the convict population declined and in 1886 it became a state prison, for men and women. Since then military prisoners, enemy aliens and prisoners of war have been held here. The prison closed in 1991.

The Round House on Arthur Head is Western Australia's oldest building, constructed in 1830 as a gaol. Despite the name the simple Georgian structure is 12-sided and the cells are arranged around a central courtyard (*daily 10.30–3.30*).

Fremantle History Museum, on the corner of Ord and Finnerty streets, is another heritage landmark (*Sun–Fri 10.30–4.30, Sat 1–5*). It was constructed by convicts in the early 1860s as the colony's first asylum, in a confusion of Georgian and neo-Gothic styles. The museum focuses on the history of the city and Western Australia, and there are changing exhibitions. For city life in late 19th-century Fremantle, try the Samson House Museum on Ellen Street (*Sun 1–5*). This was the home of the prominent Samson family and many period features survive.

For a lighter take on Victorian Fremantle, visit the 1897 Fremantle Markets on the corner of Henderson Street and South Terrace

(*Fri 9–9, Sat 9–5, Sun–Mon 10–5*). Over 170 stalls sell fresh and cooked food, art, crafts, clothing, antiques and—just about anything. Worth a visit for the ethnic colour and street performers alone.

WESTERN AUSTRALIA MARITIME MUSEUM

✉ Victoria Quay, WA 6160 ☎ 08 9335 8921, **www**.mm.wa.gov.au 🕐 Daily 9.30–5
🎫 Adult A$10, child (5–15) A$3

The Maritime Museum, on the edge of Fremantle Harbour, is part of a historical maritime precinct that includes the convict-built Shipwreck Galleries on Cliff Street and the 1969 submarine HMAS *Ovens* (*both daily 9.30–5*). The Shipwreck Galleries contain Australia's earliest Dutch shipwrecks, the remains and objects of the 1629 Dutch East India Company ship *Batavia* (Australia's second-oldest surviving wreck), and tales of travel, trade, mutiny and murder.

HMAS *Ovens* is on a World War II slipway next to the Maritime Museum and depicts the arduous and cramped conditions of submariner life in the late 20th century (*adult A$8, child A$3*).

Opened in 2002, the Maritime Museum also shelters the America's Cup-winning yacht *Australia II* and the yacht Jon Sanders used for his record-setting triple solo circumnavigation of the world in the 1980s. Boats range from the historical to the latest in sailing technology. Themed exhibits, some interactive, cover the maritime developments of the Swan River and Fremantle, naval defence, trade, fishing and the movements of people and goods and cultures throughout the Indian Ocean region. The museum also highlights the maritime traditions and cultures of Aboriginal people.

Left: The Western Australia Maritime Museum
Middle: The Round House
Right and above: The architecture of Fremantle Prison

BACKGROUND

Aboriginals were the first inhabitants of the Fremantle area. On 1 June 1829, 68 settlers established the Swan River Colony, the first European settlement in Australia to consist entirely of freemen. They eventually decided to accept convicts in order to provide cheap labour for the colony. From the 1850s a number of substantial buildings began to appear, most notably the convict prison. Fremantle was declared a city in 1929, but it was still regarded as a sleepy port. Then in 1983, after the yacht *Australia II* won the America's Cup, it underwent a major facelift. Although the cup was lost in 1987 when the races were held off Fremantle, the party atmosphere and restored Victorian buildings remain.

BASICS

✚ 316 C14

Fremantle Tourist Bureau • Town Hall, Kings Square, Fremantle, WA 6160, tel 08 9431 7878, **www**.holiday-wa.net/freotour.htm 🕐 Mon–Fri 9–5, Sat 10–3.00 🚆 Fremantle www.countrywide.com.au • More Perth than Fremantle, and you have to search hard for specific information.

Cooling off in the Asian Rainforest of Perth Zoo

PERTH HILLS

⊞ 316 C13 ⊞ Mundaring Tourism Information Centre, The Old School, 7225 Great Eastern Highway, Mundaring, WA 6073, tel 08 9295 0202 ⊞ Visitor centres are available in the other towns
www.mundaringtourism.com.au

The area known as Perth Hills or Darling Range, about 30km (18.5 miles) east of Perth, encompasses the shires of Mundaring and Kalamunda and is known for its wineries, bushland, orchards, semi-rural villages, galleries, gardens and national parks. Mundaring covers 644sq km (251sq miles), a third of which is state-owned forest—Mundaring was once a major logging centre. The John Forest and Kalamunda national parks contain trails, waterfalls and picnic areas as well as a huge diversity of native wildflowers; John Forest is noted for its jarrah and marri trees. The 1903 Mundaring Weir reservoir supplies water by pipeline to the Kalgoorlie region.

PERTH ZOO

⊞ Off 148 B3 • 20 Labouchere Road, South Perth, WA 6151 ☎ 08 9474 3551 ⊙ Daily 9–5 ⊞ Adult A$15, child (4–15) A$7.50 ⊞ 35 from the City Bus Port ⊞ Regular services from Barrack Street Jetty to South Perth Esplanade, then a short walk to the zoo ⊞ ⊞
www.perthzoo.wa.gov.au

Perth Zoo is home to more than 1,800 animals, representing 230 indigenous and exotic species. The 19ha (47-acre) zoo has three thematic habitats: the Australian Walkabout (reptiles, an aviary, a penguin area, crocodiles and an Australian bush walk); the African Savannah (lions, rhinos, giraffes, meerkats, hyenas, cheetahs and zebras); and the Asian Rainforest (elephants, orangutans, otters, gibbons, bears and Sumatran tigers).

ROTTNEST ISLAND

Great beaches and bays, a colourful past and historic buildings, and native marsupials known as quokkas.

⊞ Off 148 A3
Rottnest Island Visitor and Information Centre • Thomson Bay, Rottnest Island, WA 6161, tel 08 9372 9752 ⊙ Daily 8.15–5.30 ⊞ Bus service operates around the island ⊞ Ferries from Perth and Fremantle
www.rottnest.wa.gov.au • A rare, straightforward website whose simple menu takes you straight to the facts.

RATINGS					
Good for kids	●	●	●	●	●
Historic interest	●	●	●		
Photo stops	●	●	●	●	
Activities	●	●	●	●	●

TIPS

● Many visitors just come for the day—stay longer if you want to appreciate the beauty of the island.
● While the island's quokkas are extremely appealing, you are not allowed to feed them.

About 19km (12 miles) west from Fremantle in the Indian Ocean, Rottnest Island is 11km (7 miles) long and 4.5km (2.8 miles) at its widest point. Before changes in the sea level around 7,000 years ago Rottnest was attached to the mainland. The Aboriginal people originally referred to the island as Wadjemup: It was named Rottnest in 1696 by Dutch explorers after they mistook quokkas for large rats.

The warm Leeuwin current flows around Rottnest Island, attracting more than 97 species of tropical fish. The sheltered beaches and bays are ideal for swimming, surfing, snorkelling and scuba diving, especially the Basin, Longreach Bay, Little Parakeet Bay and Mary Cove. Cars are not allowed and some of the best beaches are some distance from the ferry—transport is either the Bayseeker Bus or bicycle rental. Most accommodation, shops and historical attractions are near the main jetty.

The sea wall was constructed from 1846 to 1849 by men of the Aboriginal penal settlement, which lasted from 1838 to 1903. Other buildings from the prison period include the Governor's Summer Residence (1840), the Administrator's Cottage (late 1840s), the Moral Agent's Residence of 1847, the Quod (prison) built in 1864, and the Rottnest Island Chapel built in 1858 as a school house and chapel. The Boys' Reformatory was built in 1881 for the children of European settlers.

The island's museum displays relics of the convict days and shipwrecks. The Oliver Hill Guns and Tunnels, Kingstown Barracks and Bickley Battery belong to coastal defence during World War II. Rottnest was an internment camp during both world wars.

Left: An island quokka
Below: Pinky's Beach

You are the pilot—a helisub in the Scitech Discovery Centre

Sunset Coast—the end of a day's surfing

Cruising upstream along the Swan River

ROCKINGHAM

⊞ 316 C14 ⓘ Rockingham Tourist Centre, 43 Kent Street, Rockingham, WA 6168, tel 08 9592 3464 ⓡ From Perth to Fremantle then a bus to Rockingham www.westernaustralia.net

Sea lions, penguins, dolphins and a wealth of bird and marine life abound along Rockingham's coast and nearby islands. The town lies on the bay of Cockburn Sound, a 55km (34-mile) drive south from Perth. Dolphins are regular visitors to the waters of the Sound and Shoalwater Bay—boat tours are available from September to May, with trips from June to August, subject to conditions. A boat leads to Penguin Island with its colony of fairy penguins—a viewing facility allows close-ups without disturbing their natural environment.

SCITECH DISCOVERY CENTRE

⊞ Off 148 A2 • 1st Floor, City West Railway Parade, West Perth; PO Box 1155, West Perth, WA 6872 ☎ 08 9481 5789 ⓞ Mon–Sun 10–5 ⓦ Adult A$12, child (3–15) A$8 ⓡ Free train from Perth City to City West on the Fremantle line ▤ www.scitech.org.au

Scitech occupies a modern building about 2km (1.2 miles) north-west of the city centre. More than 160 hands-on exhibits allow you to discover and enjoy science and modern technology. Interactive adventures, exhibitions and theatre shows add to the upbeat educational fun, which appeals to both parents and children.

SUNSET COAST

⊞ 316 C13 ⓘ Tourist Information Office, Sunset Rent a Car, 206 West Coast Highway, Scarborough, WA 6019, tel 08 9245 3279 ⓡ Currambine from Perth City www.sunsetcoast.com.au

The Sunset Coast contains some 66km (41 miles) of beaches, national parks, golf courses, shopping and nightlife venues. The Coast itself roughly comprises the coastline from Cottesloe, 10km (6 miles) west of the Perth CBD, in the south to Two Rocks in the north, and the immediate hinterland.

The white sandy beaches are ideal for swimming, surfing, windsurfing, sailing and fishing. The southern section of the coastal strip is a mix of native bushland and beachside suburbs with restaurants, cafés and bars. The northern coast is more rural and includes Yanchep National Park (see page 154).
Don't miss Hillarys Boat Harbour near Sorrento has good restaurants, shops, the Aquarium of Western Australia (see page 148), ferries for Rottnest Island, and whale-watching cruises from September to November.

SWAN BELLS

⊞ 148 B3 • Barrack Street, Riverside Drive, Perth, WA 6000 ☎ 08 9218 8183 ⓞ 10–5, last entry 4.45. Bells ring daily 11.30–12.30 ⓦ Adult A$6, child (4–15) A$3 ⓡ Free blue CAT bus stops in Barrack Square ▤ www.swanbells.com.au

The Swan Bells is one of the world's largest musical instruments, consisting of 18 change-ringing bells. The bells are housed in a modern concrete, glass and steel tower, opened in 2000, which has seven levels and an 82.2m (270ft) spire. The observation deck on level six has great views over Perth. The ringing chamber is on level

two, while level four houses the bells which you can see in action from behind double-glazed panels. Twelve of the bells originally hung at St. Martin's-in-the-Fields Church, London, where they rang to mark the homecoming of Captain James Cook in 1771. The church presented the bells to Perth in 1988.

SWAN RIVER

⊞ 148 B3 ⛴ Captain Cook Cruises, Pier 3, Barrack Square, Perth, WA 6000 ☎ Perth 08 9325 3341, Fremantle 08 9336 3311 www.captaincookcruises.com.au

The Swan River gives Perth much of its appeal, separating the downtown area from the southern suburbs. Locals cycle, fish and walk along the banks, while the river provides habitats for many plants and animals.

The 240km (149-mile) river runs from the foothills of the Darling Range east of Perth, to Fremantle and out into the Indian Ocean. Upriver, the Avon River changes to the Swan at Wooroloo Brook. Moving downstream through Walyunga National Park, the Upper Swan Valley is the state's traditional wine-growing area. The river passes Guildford, Perth's oldest inland suburb, where the riverbanks are dotted with colonial homes.

Near Perth the banks fan out into a wide expanse. Before the Swan flows into the Indian Ocean, the river narrows at the port of Fremantle.
Don't miss Take a river cruise from Perth either upstream to the wineries of the Swan Valley or downstream to Fremantle.

SWAN VALLEY

Western Australia's oldest wine-growing region is renowned for its restaurants, galleries and heritage.

✈ 316 C13
Swan Valley Visitors Centre. • Cnr Meadow and Swan streets, Guildford, WA 6055, tel 08 9379 9400 🕐 Daily 9–4 🚂 Guildford from Perth City
www.swanvalley.info

TIPS

● The Valley gets very crowded on weekends; mid-week is a better time to visit.
● The best way to explore the Valley is via signed route 203, which loops up one side of the river and down the other.

A LIVING RIVER

The Swan Valley is just an 18km (11-mile) drive north-east from the heart of Perth and follows the Swan River to the foot of the Darling Range. Aboriginal people have inhabited the Swan Valley region for 40,000 years.

Along the river course are small towns and settlements, Guildford (established in 1830) being one of the oldest; the town retains many fine houses, buildings and shops from its colonial past. For landscape and native animals, there is the nearby Caversham Wildlife Park (see page 148). The region hosts a number of special events, including Spring in the Valley held in October and A Taste of the Valley held in April, many of which are focused on the local food and wine.

VINTAGE REGION

There are more than 30 wineries in the region, ranging from third-generation family vineyards to multinational wine producers. As well as cellar door sales, many of the wineries also have restaurants and cafés. The fertile alluvial flats along the Swan River attracted a British expedition in 1827 and the Swan River Colony was founded in 1829. The earliest vineyard, Olive Farm, was established at Guildford at this time and still operates as a winery and café. By 1862 the first commercial wine vintage in Western Australia was made at Houghton Wines. The Houghton Homestead, built in 1863, is a survivor from this period.

GOOD TASTE

Sandalford Wines on the Caversham Estate is one of the Valley's most popular vineyards (*daily 10–5*). Some cruises up the Swan River (see page 153) include a visit to wineries. The Swan Valley Cheese Company produces gourmet cheeses, the Merrich Estate has olive oil products to taste and buy, while the Margaret River Chocolate Company in West Swan lives up to its name.

Vines growing in the fertile soil of the Swan Valley

The Western Australia Museum in central Perth

WESTERN AUSTRALIA MUSEUM

✈ 148 B2 • Francis Street, Perth, WA 6000 ☎ 08 9427 2700 🕐 Daily 9.30–5 💷 Free 🚌 Wellington Street bus terminal 5-minute walk 🚂 Perth City 🍴 🏛
www.museum.wa.gov.au

Set in the heart of Perth's cultural precinct, the museum focuses on the natural history and people of Western Australia. The main collections are Western Land and People, Marine Gallery, Bird Gallery, Diamonds to Dinosaurs and a Mammal Gallery. Head to the Discovery Centre for answers to questions about Australian culture and nature. More recent history is preserved in the 1856 Old Gaol. Keep an eye open for the micro fossils found in the Pilbara, which represent the earliest evidence of life on Earth.

YANCHEP NATIONAL PARK

✈ 316 C13 ☎ 08 9561 1004 💷 A$9 per car, A$3 per car for seniors or A$3.40 per bus or coach passenger 🚌 Yanchep National Park has day and overnight tours that include pick-up and drop-off from Perth 🚂 Joondalup, then Transperth bus 490 to Yanchep; buses can be irregular 🚗 50km (31 miles) north of Perth off State Route 60; McNess House Visitor Centre is in the main recreation complex 🍴 🏛
www.naturebase.net/yanchep

This 3,000ha (7,410-acre) park is a popular escape for Perth people. It has a large koala colony and is renowned for its native flora and fauna, heritage sites, wetlands and limestone caves. Tuart and banksia woodlands are endemic and wildflower gardens have a collection of the state's native plants. Crystal Cave on the east side of the park is noted for stalactites. Nyoongar Aboriginal culture is presented at the *Wangi Mia* (talking place).

THE SIGHTS

PERTH

Two People's Bay, the rocky ocean coastline east of Albany

BROOME

The climate and wonderful beach form an oasis among the Indian Ocean, the Great Sandy Desert and the Kimberley, one of Australia's great wilderness areas.

➕ 316 F6
Broome Visitor Centre • Cnr Northern Highway and Bagot Street, PO Box 352, Broome, WA 6725, tel 08 9192 2222; Mon–Fri 8–5, Jan–Dec; Sat–Sun 9–4; Apr–Oct, 9–1, Nov–Mar 🚌 Service between Broome and Cable Beach
www.ebroome.com

RATINGS			
Good for kids	● ●		
Photo stops	● ● ● ●		
Shopping	● ● ●		
Activities	● ● ● ●		

TIP
● Box jellyfish can be a problem off Cable Beach from November to May—don't swim at this time.
● Broome's major attractions are Cable Beach and its hot weather—the few museums, historic buildings and restaurants do not justify a visit.

PEARLS
Pearlers first arrived in the 1870s and by 1910 Broome had become the pearl capital of the world, producing around 80 per cent of the world's pearl shell. The first divers were Aboriginal people, followed by divers from Asia and the Pacific. The Japanese Cemetery in Port Drive has the graves of more than 900 Japanese divers who died in Broome. Restored pearl luggers in the heart of Broome show how divers worked in the 19th and 20th centuries. After a downturn in demand during the 20th century, the pearl industry is back in full swing, except that now the pearls are farmed. Willie Creek Pearl Farm, 38km (24 miles) north of Broome, demonstrates how pearls are produced (*tour bookings 08 9193 6000*).

BETWEEN BAY AND BEACH
The small town of Broome lies at the northern end of the mangrove-filled shores of Roebuck Bay. Shopping areas include the historic Chinatown and several pearl outlets. Chinatown was originally a collection of eateries and pearl sheds, but it now ranges from small traditional wooden buildings to modern shopping complexes. The 1916 Sun Pictures movie theatre is believed to be the world's oldest open-air cinema; watch the latest movies under the stars. Broome is perhaps best known for Cable Beach, 22km (14 miles) of white sand north of the town. A beach sunset is a must, whether on a camel ride or idling on the sands.

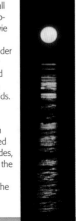

STAIRCASE TO THE MOON
The Staircase to the Moon is a phenomenon caused by a full moon rising over the exposed mudflats of Roebuck Bay at extremely low tides, creating an illusion of a staircase reaching to the moon. It occurs from March to October for three nights every month. Town Beach and the Mangrove Hotel are good viewpoints.

WESTERN AUSTRALIA

ALBANY

➕ 316 D15 ℹ️ Old Railway Station, Proudlove Parade, Albany, WA 6330, tel 08 9841 1088, Freecall 1800 644 088
www.albanygateway.com.au

Established in 1826, Albany is WA's oldest colonial town, built around the picturesque harbour between the viewpoints of Mount Melville and Mount Clarence. Heritage sights include the 1851 Old Gaol (*daily 10–4.15*); the WA Museum, a former convict store dating back to the 1850s (*daily 10–5*); and the 1893 Princess Royal Fortress (*daily 9–5*). Try a wine from the nearby Mount Barker region with your lunch. The coastal scenery is some of the most spectacular in Australia, and there are whale-watching tours from July to October. The Torndirrup National Park peninsula is pounded by the Southern Ocean.

AUGUSTA

➕ 316 C15 ℹ️ Augusta Visitor Centre, 70 Blackwood Avenue, Augusta, WA 6290, tel 08 9758 0166
www.margaretriverwa.com

Augusta is sheltered by Cape Leeuwin, the point where the Indian and Southern oceans meet. The small seafront resort is known for its water activities and attractive coastline, but accommodation is limited; many people visit on a day trip. From June to December whales can be seen from the viewpoint of the 1896 Cape Leeuwin Lighthouse (*daily 8.45–5*). From the cape the Leeuwin-Naturaliste National Park extends 120km (74 miles) north along the coast; Jewel Cave, in the park 10km (6 miles) northwest of the town, is massive, with amazing stalactites (*daily, tours 9.30–3.30*).

THE SIGHTS

All yours—the West Beach at Esperance

Saline levels and mangroves on Exmouth Gulf

THE SIGHTS

BUNBURY

➕ 316 C14 ℹ️ Bunbury Visitor Information Centre, Old Railway Station, Carmody Place, Bunbury, WA 6230, tel 08 9721 7922 🚉 Bunbury www.bunburybreaks.com.au

Western Australia's second largest city after Perth is the gateway to the southwest of the state. Occupying a peninsula, Bunbury has great, often deserted, beaches. Victoria Street is a cappuccino strip, a refreshment stop after a visit to the large regional art gallery or the historic churches. Out of town there are more than 70 species of water birds at the Big Swamp Reserve and Boardwalk, 1.5km (1 mile) south.
Don't miss Swim with the dolphins or join a dolphin boat tour in Koombana Bay via the Dolphin Discovery Centre *(daily 8–5, Sep–May; 9–3, Jun–Aug).*

DENMARK

➕ 316 D15 ℹ️ Denmark Visitor Centre, 60 Strickland Street, Denmark, WA 6333, tel 08 9848 2055 www.denmarkvisitorcentre.com.au

Denmark's natural beauty and the warm climate are good reasons to break a tour along WA's south coast. The town spreads along the western bank of the lower Denmark River and Wilsons Inlet and is popular with artists and city folk seeking a less stressful lifestyle. Since being settled in 1895 as a timber town, Denmark has supported fishing, potato and fruit growing, dairy farming, and now wineries and tourism.
Don't miss The Treetop Walk in the Valley of the Giants is a 600m (1,968ft) walkway, 40m (131ft) above ground in the tree canopy, with fantastic views. The Valley is 45km (28 miles) west from Denmark near Walpole.

ESPERANCE

➕ 316 F14 ℹ️ Esperance Visitor Centre, Historical Museum Village, Dempster Street, Esperance, WA 6450, tel 08 9071 2330 www.visitesperance.com

Esperance, on Esperance Bay, is a small town mainly popular for its coastal scenery, wildlife and pristine, quiet beaches. Remote from the main tourist routes, the place is a relaxing stop, even during the summer months. The coastal scenery ranges from massive granite outcrops to small bays, and there are four national parks in the region.
Don't miss Join a cruise round the Recherche Archipelago of over 100 offshore islands, for close views of the wildlife.

EXMOUTH

➕ 316 B8 ℹ️ Exmouth Visitors Centre, Murat Road, Exmouth, WA 6707, tel 08 99491176 🚌 Buses from Exmouth to Turquoise Bay daily during high season www.exmouth-australia.com

Exmouth was established only in 1967 and is fairly small. If not worth a visit in its own right—it was much rebuilt after a cyclone in 1999—Exmouth is the best base for exploring Cape Range National Park, Ningaloo Reef and the surrounding region. Cape Range National Park is 40km (25 miles) from Exmouth going north round the North West Cape to Yardie Road. The 50,581ha (124,935-acre) park has limestone ranges, deep canyons and 50km (31 miles) of beaches. Yardie Creek Gorge is particularly impressive, with deep blue waters and coloured rock strata.
The same access route leads to Ningaloo Reef, the backbone of Ningaloo Marine Park, which stretches for 260km (161 miles) from Bundegi Reef in the Exmouth Gulf around the North West Cape to Coral Bay. The reef

extends about 18.5km (11.5 miles) into the Indian Ocean and is home to 520 species of fish, 250 species of coral and an abundance of turtles and whales. It is only about 100m (330ft) offshore at its nearest point and less than 7km (4.5 miles) at its farthest. From mid-March to June the reef is visited by the world's biggest species of fish, the whale shark. Boat tours leave from Coral Bay and Exmouth.

FREMANTLE

See pages 150–151.

KALBARRI NATIONAL PARK

➕ 316 B11 • National Park Office, Kalbarri/Ajana Road, PO Box 37, Kalbarri, WA 6536 ☎ 08 9937 1140 🚗 Day passes: A$9 per vehicle, A$3 per motorcycle, A$3.40 per bus passenger. No camping in the park 🚉 Kalbarri ℹ️ Kalbarri Visitors Centre, Grey Road Kalbarri, tel 08 9937 1104 www.kalbarriwa.info

Kalbarri National Park covers 183,004ha (452,020 acres) and has two distinct features: the river gorges inland, and the coastal cliffs together with the rolling sandplains. The cliffs are near Kalbarri, on the park's southwest boundary, and rise more than 100m (330ft) above the Indian Ocean.
The red and white banded gorges are around 40km (25 miles) from the town and were formed by the Murchison River; there are great views from the Loop and the Z Bend. The park has about 1,000 species of wildflowers—in spring (after July) the heathlands are spectacular.

KALGOORLIE-BOULDER

➕ 316 F13 ℹ️ Kalgoorlie-Boulder Tourist Centre, 250 Hannan Street, Kalgoorlie, WA 6430, tel 08 9021 1966 🚉 Kalgoorlie; Prospector train daily from Perth and return. Indian Pacific

Natures Window above a gorge in Kalbarri National Park

The remote Bungle Bungles in the Kimberley region—an amazing cone karst landscape cut through by seasonal waterfalls and pools

stops at Kalgoorlie four times a week
www.kalgoorlieandwagoldfields.com.au

Kalgoorlie-Boulder has been a goldfield town for over a century. The operating Super Pit open-cut gold mine in Boulder is 290m (950ft) deep, 1.5km (1 mile) wide and 4km (2.5 miles) long. Since gold was first discovered in 1893, Kalgoorlie ore deposits have produced over 35 million ounces of gold. Lying 5km (3 miles) apart, Kalgoorlie and Boulder operated as separate towns until the 1980s when they amalgamated. The wide streets survive from the early days when the Afghan camel drivers needed large areas to turn their mounts around. The town's museums have a general appeal but some are of specialist interest only. **Don't miss** The Australian Prospectors and Miners Hall of Fame highlights Australia's mining industry. Try gold panning or join an underground tour (daily 9.30–4.30).

KARIJINI NATIONAL PARK

316 D9 • Visitor Centre, Banyjima Drive, Karijini National Park 08 9189 8121 Visitor Centre daily 9–4 Day passes: A\$9 per vehicle, A\$3 per motorcycle, A\$3.40 per bus passenger. Camping fees: adult A\$5 per night, child (5–16) A\$2 per night www.naturebase.net

Karijini is a truly spectacular park, well worth the long journey. The 627,442ha (1.5million-acre) national park protects some of Australia's most impressive gorge scenery, and many of the finest sights are easily accessible. Set just north of the Tropic of Capricorn, the Pilbara region climate is tropical semi-desert. Late autumn, winter and early spring are best; winter days are warm and clear, but nights are cold and sometimes frosty. In the cooler

months the land is covered with yellow-flowering cassias and wattles, northern bluebells and purple mulla-mullas. After rain, many plants bloom profusely. Walking tracks take in the gorges and fern-filled pools and waterfalls.

THE KIMBERLEY

317 J6 Derby Visitor Centre, 1 Clarendon Street, PO Box 48, Derby, WA 6728, tel 08 9191 1426 Kununurra Visitor Centre, East Kimberley Tourism House, Coolibah Drive, PO Box 446, Kununurra, WA 6743, tel 08 9168 1177 There are tourist offices also at Broome, Fitzroy Crossing, Halls Creek and Wyndham www.kimberleytourism.com

The remote Kimberley region covers the far northern part of Western Australia, bordered by Northern Territory, the Great Sandy Desert, the Indian Ocean and the Timor Sea. This is true outback: rugged ranges, gorges, arid desert and vast open plains. Heading east from Broome (see page 155), two routes lead to the inland town of Kununurra near the Northern Territory border. The longer, easier route is along the Great Northern Highway. At Fitzroy Crossing, boat tours venture up the large gorge of Geikie Gorge National Park, where the Fitzroy River cuts through the Geikie Range.

Northeast of Halls Creek, the Bungle Bungles in the Purnululu National Park—a World Heritage Site—are among the world's most unusual geological formations. Thousands of beehive-shaped sandstone hills rise up out of the plain, striped in red, orange and black bands. Access to the park from the highway is by a 55km (34-mile) 4WD track.

The Gibb River Road from Derby is a dirt track best suited to a 4WD, but which passes stunning scenery. At

Windjana Gorge National Park the gorge itself encompasses a section of the Lennard River; the area is rich in birds and freshwater crocodiles.

Seasonal rains from December to April can close sealed roads for hours or even days; unsealed roads are likely to be closed for the duration of the wet season.

MILLSTREAM-CHICHESTER NATIONAL PARK

316 D8 • Millstream Homestead Visitor Centre 08 9184 5144 Day passes: A\$9 per vehicle, A\$3 per motorcycle, A\$3.40 per bus passenger. Camping fees: adult A\$5 per night, child (5–16) A\$2 per night 75km (46.5 miles) from Roebourne; access by 50km (31-mile) unsealed road from the North West Coastal Highway www.naturebase.net

The 200,000ha (494,000-acre) park is a green oasis in the heart of dusty and spinifex-covered desert hills in the Pilbara region. Some freshwater pools support water lilies and paperbark, and palm trees surround the deep Chinderwarriner Pool on the Fortescue River; there is also an expansive wetland area. The Millstream Homestead Visitor Centre is dedicated to the Yinjibarndi people, early settlers and the natural environment. **Don't miss** Python Pool is a permanent freshwater plunge pool at the base of the Chichester Range escarpment.

Huge mining trucks rumble through the mining areas of Kalgoorlie-Boulder

Margaret River

Western Australia's prime wine region lies close to the spectacular coastline of the Leeuwin-Naturaliste National Park.

Top: Canoes at the mouth of the Margaret River
Above left: Luminous Lake Cave
Middle: An easy choice at the Vasse Felix winery restaurant
Above right: Local grass trees

RATINGS	
Good for kids	● ● ● ○
Historic interest	● ●
Photo stops	● ● ● ●
Activities	● ● ● ● ●

TIPS

● To get the best out of the Margaret River region you need a car—many of the attractions are some distance from the main towns.
● Margaret River gets very busy on weekends during the high season and public holidays; midweek is the best time to visit, otherwise ensure you reserve accommodation.
● If you are planning to drive and try wine, then designate a non-drinking driver—the police are strict about drink-driving.

The small town of Margaret River is midway between Cape Naturaliste in the north and Cape Leeuwin to the south. The Margaret River flows through the town, 10km (6 miles) east from the estuary to the Indian Ocean; walking and cycling tracks are marked along the banks of the river and through the town. The river, combined with parkland, art and craft galleries and a number of excellent restaurants, many of which are attached to wineries, add to the town's relaxed appeal. The Margaret River region has more than 70 wineries, mainly concentrated between the Bussell Highway and the more scenic Caves Road, which runs from Dunsborough on Geographe Bay in the north to Karridale in the south (see tour, pages 242–243). Apart from wine, a number of local producers cater for gourmet tastes. These include Berry Farm, specializing in fruits, the Fonti Farm and Margaret River Dairy Company, which makes fine cheeses and yoghurt (including ricotta and the flagship brie), and the Margaret River Chocolate Company.

WINE STOP

Wine enthusiasts should start a visit at the Margaret River Wine Tourism Showroom in the Margaret River Visitor Centre. Find out about all the wineries in the region and decide which to visit; several offer wine appreciation classes, which are great fun.

LEEUWIN-NATURALISTE NATIONAL PARK

Windswept granite headlands and weathered sea cliffs, such as Canal Rocks and Sugarloaf Rock, characterize the coastal national park, which stretches 120km (74 miles) from Bunker Bay and Cape Naturaliste in the north to Augusta in the south. Walking trails, caving, camping and water sports are among the ways to enjoy the park. Most access roads in the area are sealed; gravel roads are usually suitable for two-wheel drive vehicles. From June to December whales are visible off the coast. The hilly Boranup Forest, between Margaret River and Augusta, is home to the impressive karri tree, the farthest point west that it grows; the karris stand up to 60m (196ft) high. Boranup Lookout, off the Caves Road, looks across the forest to Hamelin Bay.

WAVES

Surfers from around the world flock to the Margaret River coastline, and the Caves Road connects the popular beaches. For surfing (or

The Margaret River meanders to the Indian Ocean

watching) try Yallingup, 43km (27 miles) north of Margaret River; Ellensbrook, 14km (8.5 miles) northwest; or Redgate, 15km (9.5 miles) southwest. Safe swimming beaches include Cowaramup Bay, 19km (12 miles) northwest of Margaret River; Gnarabup, 12km (7.5 miles) west; and Hamelin Bay, 42km (26 miles) south.

CAVES

Some of Western Australia's best-known caves lie between Margaret River and Augusta (see page 155), 45km (28 miles) to the south. They occur within the Leeuwin-Naturaliste Ridge, which is composed of granite, limestone and dunes; the caves are formed in the softer, more soluble limestone strata. Several caves are open to the public. Calgardup Cave and Giants Cave are a short distance south of Margaret River: Calgardup's shallow mirror lake multiplies the stalactites above (*daily 9–4.15*); the Giants Cave, going down 86m (282ft), is one of the deepest (*daily 9.30–3.30 in school holidays and public holidays*). Farther south are Mammoth Cave, with fossils (*daily 9–5, last entry 4*); Lake Cave (*daily 9.30–3.30*); and Jewel Cave, with one of the longest stalactites found in any tourist cave (see Augusta, page 155). On its own to the north at Yallingup, Ngilgi Cave, with stalactite and stalagmite formations (*daily 9.30–4.30, also to 5 or 6 in school holidays*), is associated with the Aboriginal legend of Ngilgi (a good spirit) and Wolgine (evil spirit). While torches and helmets are often provided, you should wear strong shoes or boots.

CHANGING LANDSCAPE

Settlement in the area dates from the 1850s and there was timber felling from the 1870s. The town largely developed from the Group Settlement Scheme in the early 1920s, an attempt to expand agricultural land in the southwest of the state. The scheme attracted migrants from Britain where there was high unemployment after World War I, but was hindered by poor planning. The wine industry dates only to the 1960s when the area was found suited to viticulture. There were experimental plantings of grapes in 1966, and in the following year the first winery, Vasse Felix, was established.

BASICS

316 C14
Margaret River Visitor Centre, 100 Bussell Highway, Margaret River, WA 6285, tel 08 9757 2911; daily 9–5 www.margaret-river-online.com.au • Straightforward menus and useful everyday information on this community website.

Cheese selection at Margaret River Dairy Company, Cowaramup

Limber up for a tree climb near Pemberton

Dolphins line up to be fed at Monkey Mia's beach

The fantastic granite wall of Wave Rock

NEW NORCIA

➕ 316 C13 ℹ️ New Norcia Tourist Information Centre, New Norcia Museum and Art Gallery, New Norcia, WA 6509, tel 08 9654 8056 www.newnorcia.wa.edu.au

Australia's only monastic town was founded in 1846 by Benedictine monks as a mission for the Aboriginal people of the Victorian Plains district. The missionary ideal of civilizing and evangelizing turned to a progressive education role for the indigenous children of the state. In the early 20th century the monastic community focused on the care of Western Australia's rural population. Despite gradual decline through the second half of the century the monastery has flourished in recent years, as a place of peace and reflection for citizens, students and tourists. A heritage trail takes in many of the historic buildings. The Museum and Art Gallery houses the monks' art collections, including Spanish and Italian old masters.

PEMBERTON

➕ 316 C15 ℹ️ Pemberton Visitor Centre, Brockman Street, Pemberton, WA 6260, tel 08 9776 1133 www.pembertontourist.com.au

Pemberton, together with Manjimup to the north and Walpole 140km (87 miles) away on the coast, is part of the Southern Forests Region. The attractive small town was built in 1913 for timber workers, and despite art and craft studios and wineries it still has the feel of a timber town. Some of the world's tallest and oldest trees are protected in the national parks around the town. Tall karri trees dominate, though there are also plenty of jarrah and marri trees. The trees in Warren National Park to the southwest stand up to 89m (292ft) high. Gloucester

National Park, just east of the town, contains the Gloucester Tree, the highest fire lookout tree in the world at 60m (197ft). Beedelup National Park to the west is renowned for waterfalls and its karri forest.

For a change of scenery, D'Entrecasteaux National Park on the Southern Ocean has coastal wetlands, dunes and white beaches, and granite outcrops.

One of WA's best-known walking tracks, the 1,000km (620-mile) Bibbulmun Track, passes through Pemberton on its route from Kalamunda outside Perth to Albany on the south coast.

PERTH

See pages 148–154.

SHARK BAY

➕ 316 B10 ℹ️ Shark Bay Tourist Bureau, 71 Knight Terrace, Denham, WA 6537, tel 08 9948 1253 www.outbackcoast.com

Shark Bay is a World Heritage Site because of its unique, rare and superlative natural beauty. The bay is formed by two peninsulas and 1,500km (930 miles) of coastline on the westernmost point of Australia, and covers about 8,000sq km (3,120sq miles). The bay is home to numerous threatened reptile species, rare birds, dugongs and loggerhead turtles. Around the coast the contrast of vast seagrass beds, dunes and blue water is stunning; look for the stromatolites, algae that form dome-shaped fossil-like deposits.

The only town in Shark Bay is Denham, which is the centre of the bay's tourism and fishing industry. At Monkey Mia, 26km (16 miles) northeast of Denham, bottlenose dolphins visit the beach: You can feed them under the supervision of park rangers. Boat excursions and 4WD tours are based at Monkey Mia.

STIRLING RANGE NATIONAL PARK

➕ 316 D15 • Albany Visitors Centre, Old Railway Station, Proudlove Parade Albany, tel 08 9841 1088 🅿️ A$9 per vehicle, A$3 for motorcycles www.albanygateway.com.au

Encompassed by the 116,000ha (286,520-acre) national park, the peaks of the Stirling Range stretch 65km (40 miles) from east to west. The park is renowned for the mountain landscape, and its wildflowers and bird life. At least 1,500 species of plants have been recorded and around 140 bird species have been identified. Spring is the prime time to visit when many plants are in flower.

Don't miss Bluff Knoll, at 1,095m (3,592ft), is the highest peak in the southwest of Western Australia. It takes four hours to complete the 6km (4-mile) return climb.

WAVE ROCK

➕ 316 E14 ℹ️ Hyden Tourist Information Centre, Wave Rock Wildflower Shop, Wave Rock, Hyden, WA 6359, tel 08 9880 5666 www.waverock.com.au

Why travel 350km (217 miles) from Perth or elsewhere to see a giant rock formation? Because the 15m (49ft) high, 110m (360ft) long, granite cliff really does look like a huge wave about to break. According to geologists Wave Rock was originally vertical but has been sculpted and coloured by the weather for more than 60 million years. The vertical rusty red, ochre and sandy grey bands have been caused by run-off waters charged with carbonates and iron hydroxide from the rock. There are other granite outcrops nearby, while Mulka's Cave, 21km (13 miles) north from Hyden, preserves Aboriginal hand paintings.

THE SIGHTS

TASMANIA

Australia's island state is its smallest—equivalent to the size of Ireland or West Virginia. There are quiet historic villages and undulating farmland to explore, and challenging mountains are reflected in clear lakes. Much of the remote southwest has been declared a World Heritage Area. The state capital of Hobart lies at the foot of Mount Wellington and has a wealth of colonial buildings.

KEY SIGHTS

HOBART

The small but spectacular harbour city is a dynamic mix of colonial heritage and vibrant contemporary culture. Historic Battery Point is arguably the prettiest urban village in Australia.

Burnie, on Tasmania's northwest coast, is a thriving port

✠ 331 U19
Tasmanian Travel and Information Centre • Cnr Davey and Elizabeth streets, Hobart, TAS 7000, tel 03 6230 8233; Mon–Fri 8.30–5.30, Sat–Sun 9–5
www.tasvisinfo.com.au

RATINGS	
Good for kids	◕ ◕ ◕
Historic interest	◕ ◕ ◕ ◕
Photo stops	◕ ◕ ◕
Shopping	◕ ◕ ◕

TIP
● The city requires 2–3 days but try to be in Hobart on a Saturday when the weekly Salamanca market is a distillation of all things Tasmanian.

Founded in 1804 (16 years after Sydney), Hobart is the second-oldest Australian city and the most southerly. It sits below Mount Wellington, which rises to 1,270m (4,166ft). The majority of interest and nightlife is close to the docks and waterfront warehouses, constructed on land reclaimed by the back-breaking work of the earliest convicts. A great number of colonial buildings survive, especially the warehouses in Salamanca Place and along Sullivans Cove. The state Parliament is close to Sullivans Cove, among many of the busiest pubs, restaurants and galleries. Victoria Dock is packed with the local fishing fleet. At the end of December a food and wine festival around the dock peaks with the finish of the Sydney to Hobart Yacht Race.

A lively dining precinct lies north of the city on Elizabeth Street. The Republic Bar is home to music, poetry and a radical spirit that gave birth to the world's first green political party.

The city's strong seafaring character is portrayed at the Maritime Museum of Tasmania (*daily 10–5*), one block up from the waterfront. The Tasmanian Museum and Art Gallery (*daily 10–5*) around the corner has important colonial paintings.

Set on a hill, Battery Point is the old seamen's quarter, with great cafés and restaurants and the Narryna Folk Museum (*Mon–Fri 10.30–5, Sat–Sun 2–5*) on Hampden Road.

South of the city, via Davey Street, is the historic Cascade Brewery, a tall sandstone building set against a backdrop of bush and Mount Wellington (*tours Mon–Fri 9.30, 1*).

Don't miss The Royal Tasmanian Botanical Gardens at Queens Domain, 2km (1.2 miles) northeast from the city, were established in 1818 (*daily from 8am*).

BICHENO

✠ 331 V19 🛈 Bicheno Penguin Tours, Tasman Highway, Bicheno, TAS 7215, tel 03 6375 1333

This small fishing port nestles among white sandy beaches on the island's beautiful east coast, sheltered by high granite boulders liberally splashed with bright orange, yellow and green lichens. Eucalyptus forests inland and the Douglas Apsley National Park to the north are great for walking. The port has a history of sealing and whaling; today it's a base for cray boats and abalone divers.

Crayfish and sea horses feature in the Sea Life Centre (*daily 9–5*), while Bicheno Penguin Tours offer trips to watch the native fairy variety. Redbill Beach is the pick of the beaches—lines of swell pour in past pretty Diamond Island.

BURNIE

✠ 331 T18 🛈 Tas Travel and Information Centre, Little Alexander Street, Burnie, TAS 7320, tel 03 6434 6111 www.burnie.net

Once an industrial paper-making town, Burnie is transforming itself into one of the best stops in the northwest. Tourism, cottage industries and a developing café culture are injecting new life into this deepwater port set between a green escarpment and a string of sandy Bass Strait beaches.

The Emu Valley Rhododendron Gardens (*daily 9–5*) on Breffny Road are impressive from August to February, and try the Lactos Cheese Tasting Centre (*daily 9–5*) on Old Surrey Road. Guide Falls, just to the south, is an accessible waterfall and wet forest walk.

Don't miss Creative Paper Mills combines a contemporary gallery and working hand-made paper mill (*daily 9–5*).

CRADLE MOUNTAIN–LAKE ST. CLAIR NATIONAL PARK

Tasmania's best-known wilderness attraction has the island's highest peaks and the deepest lake. Cradle Mountain at 1,545m (5,068ft) overlooks the northern end of the 85km (53-mile) Overland Track.

Cradle Mountain is a wilderness icon, a dolerite that was squeezed up through other earth layers 174 million years ago. Its distinctive cradle shape was caused largely by glacial action 500,000 years ago. The highest peak in the park, at 1,617m (5,304ft), is Mount Ossa, which can be reached along the Overland Track to or from Lake St. Clair. The lake, at the southern edge of the park, is surrounded by other impressive peaks, including mounts Olympus, Gould and Ida. The weather across this highland region can change very quickly and heavy dumps of snow can occur, sometimes even in summer.

For shorter visits Cynthia Bay on Lake St. Clair is easily accessed off the Lyell Highway and, at the northern end of the park, Cradle Mountain is linked to the Cradle Link Road by a reasonable 7km (4-mile) gravel drive. At both ends of the park, fantastic rainforest waterfalls and ridgeline lookouts can be reached by as little as a 30-minute walk. The native wildlife includes wallabies, wombats, echidnas and sometimes Tasmanian devils. Park rangers, restaurants and accommodation are available at either end. The Lake St. Clair Park Centre (*daily 8–5*) has displays on the geology, natural history and colonization of the highland area. A ferry plies between Cynthia Bay and Narcissus River at the lake's northern end (*tel 03 6289 1137*). **Don't miss** The sensational Wilderness Gallery at Doherty's Resort on the road into Cradle Mountain is packed with Tasmanian crafts.

BACKGROUND

It's believed that Tasmanian Aboriginals used the general route of what is now the Overland Track as a migration path in summer. An Austrian, Gustav Weindorfer, made the sublime beauty of Cradle Mountain known to the world when he campaigned for it to be reserved 'for the people of the world, for all time' in the 1920s. Weindorfer and his partner Kate had come from Melbourne to farm but fell in love with the remote high country. Waldheim Chalet, where Weindorfer lived for much of his life, fell into disrepair in the 1970s but has since been rebuilt. The national park was listed as part of the Tasmanian Wilderness World Heritage Area in 1982.

Above: Cradle Mountain
Inset: A park mountain shelter

RATINGS				
Good for kids	●	●		
Historic interest	●	●	●	
Photo stops	●	●	●	●	●
Walkability	●	●	●	●	●

TIPS

● Avoid December to February for a purer experience—even the Overland Track can host a crowd.

● Even if only doing one of the short walks, be prepared for changes in weather conditions. Take warm back-up clothes, even if the sun is hot and the sky clear.

● Time a trip to the park in late April, when the magnificent autumn reddy-golds of the native beech dominate the landscape.

BASICS

✚ 331 T19 • Cradle Mountain Visitor Centre, park entrance, off route C132, ☎ 03 6492 1133 🕐 Daily 8–5 💷 Tasmanian National Parks entry fees: daily (24 hours), vehicle A\$10, person A\$3.50 🏪 Park shop in the Visitor Centre: postcards, books, film and clothing. Some groceries available from the campsite shop, Cradle Mountain Lodge Store and Cradle View Restaurant ♿ At the Visitor Centre, Waldheim and Lake Dove; all are wheelchair accessible www.dpiwe.tas.gov.au • The Tasmanian government website includes a Parks & Wildlife page with a wealth of details.

Coles Bay with Freycinet National Park beyond

The overnight Melbourne ferry arrives in Devonport

Ready, steady—penny-farthings at the Evandale February fair

THE SIGHTS

COLES BAY AND FREYCINET NATIONAL PARK

⊞ 331 V19 • Park via Coles Bay; park rangers based at Freycinet National Park Office ☎ 03 6256 7000
🔲 See Cradle Mountain, page 163
www.dpiwe.tas.gov.au

Coles Bay, at the entrance to the Freycinet Peninsula and within the national park, is the jewel of the east coast with the island's most idyllic coastal scenery. Peaceful beach walks, good food (local oysters) and summer swimming in perfect blue water are all found at the resort.

Tasmanian Aboriginals spent summers diving for shellfish and collecting duck eggs from nearby Moulting Lagoon. The remains of their diet are recalled by the middens (shell-refuse mounds) on the coast. French navigator Nicholas Baudin named Freycinet in 1802.

Granite cliffs stretch along the peninsula to the north and south with a soft fringe of she-oaks (casuarina) on most shorelines. The energetic can enjoy the national park's mountain and coast walks, the rock-climbing and sea-kayaking.
Don't miss Wineglass Bay, on the east, ocean side is one spectacular beach, often ranked among the world's best. It's a moderate climb (1.5 hours return) from Coles Bay for the view, longer (2.5 hours return) to the beach.

DELORAINE

⊞ 331 U18 ⓘ Deloraine Visitor Centre, 98 Emu Bay Road, Deloraine, TAS 7304, tel 03 6362 3471
www.meandervalley.com

The 'hippest' town in the north relies less on attractions and more on atmosphere and lifestyle. This rural river-bank settlement has a distinctly English feel allied to a strong creative community. Since the 1970s the beauty of the nearby Western Tiers mountain range and bush has attracted and inspired artists and alternative lifestylers. So hip meets the homespun in galleries and cafés, and in Australia's biggest art and craft fair every October and November.
Don't miss Liffey Falls, a 35km (22-mile) drive south, is the best of many good bush getaways beneath the Western Tiers.

DEVONPORT

⊞ 331 U18 ⓘ Devonport Visitor Centre, 92 Formby Street, Devonport, TAS 7310, tel 03 6424 8176
www.dcc.tas.gov.au

The Bass Strait ferries from Melbourne arrive at this port on the Mersey River, a rural town within reach of wilderness areas like Cradle Mountain and Walls of Jerusalem. Mersey Bluff is the local highlight, with a sheltered beach, surf club and playground. Walk round Bluff Head to the lighthouse or the Tiagarra Aboriginal Cultural Centre and Museum, close to rock carvings.
Don't miss The Don River Railway operates steam or diesel weekend rail trips in town.

EVANDALE

⊞ 331 U19 ⓘ Evandale Tourism and History Centre, 18 High Street, Evandale, TAS 7212, tel 03 6391 8128
www.tasvisinfo.com.au

The hub of this historic village is a 19th-century streetscape. In February, the Evandale Village Fair brings the streets to life, including the National Penny-Farthing Championships. Antiques stores add to the character. A drink at the central Clarendon Arms (1847) is recommended for local stories. Also refreshing is the Ingleside Bakery for its sweet treats in an original colonial period bakery. Evandale Village Market each Sunday sells antiques and home-made fare. Clarendon House, about 10km (6 miles) south of Evandale, was built in 1838 and is considered Australia's finest grand Georgian mansion (daily 10–5). The colonial painters John Glover and Tom Roberts, and Melbourne founder John Batman, lived in this flat area of grazing country.

FRANKLIN-GORDON WILD RIVERS NATIONAL PARK

⊞ 331 T19 • North via Lyell Highway (A10) or south via Gordon River Road (B61) ☎ 03 6471 2511 🔲 See Cradle Mountain, page 163
www.dpiwe.tas.gov.au

This is a spectacular wilderness, protected by its own very rugged nature and tempestuous climate. Most of it is difficult to access, unless you're really serious about bushwalking or rafting. The Franklin and Gordon rivers achieved world fame in 1983 when they were saved from a hydroelectric dam project by a massive environmental protest.

Visitors to the area need not be put off by the layers of mountains above 1,200m (3,936ft) and dense temperate rainforest. There are easy walks to waterfalls and vantage points, including one by the banks of the Franklin River. Less sedate are the guided white-water rafting tours through Franklin's dramatic gorges.
Don't miss Nelson Falls is a flat, 20-minute return walk through stunning rainforest to a high waterfall; Donaghy's Hill Lookout walk is a moderate 40-minute return climb for views of Frenchmans Cap, the most dramatic peak in the park, as well as the upper Franklin River.

HOBART

See page 162.

The Painted Cliffs of Maria Island National Park

Beware of the Tasmanian devils in Mole Creek's wildlife park

The Russell Falls in Mount Field National Park

LAUNCESTON

✚ 331 U18 **ℹ** Tasmanian Travel and Information Centre, 12–16 St. John Street, Launceston, TAS 7250, tel 03 6336 3133
www.gatewaytas.com.au

This small city—Tasmania's second largest—is loaded with charm. Built around the head of the broad Tamar River, many of the central streets are lined with Victorian houses and cottages and graced by the pretty City Park and Princes Square.

Established in 1805, a year after Hobart, Launceston has historically vied with the southern city for capital status. For much of the 20th century, it was a thriving industrial town, with textile factories, the Boags Brewery and mining interests. Tourism is now a mainstay.

All roads lead to the waterfront and a busy yacht basin. You can walk along the banks of the Tamar and the two Esk rivers, which meet in the heart of the city. Quadrant Mall, a historic, cobbled walkway, curves from Brisbane Street to St. John Street, where the clock tower of the post office is a prominent landmark. The Albert Hall is another commanding Victorian building, on the east side of the central district by the entrance to the beautiful City Park. The park has rotundas, a botanical pavilion and a popular macaque monkey enclosure.

On the west side of the city is the remarkable Cataract Gorge, a rocky chasm through which runs the South Esk, a sometimes thundering wild river. A magnificent walkway takes you through the cliffs to parkland, a restaurant and a chairlift.
Don't miss The innovative Queen Victoria Museum and Art Gallery at Inveresk (*daily 10–5*), in the city's former railway yards, houses a good art collection and colonial treasures.

MARIA ISLAND NATIONAL PARK/ORFORD

✚ 331 U19–V19 • Via ferry (near Triabunna Visitor Centre) ☎ Ferry booking 0427 100 104, 03 6257 1589 **◉** Ferry departs Triabunna Mon–Sun 9.30, also Sat–Sun 1.30 **◉** Ferry return: adult A$25, child (under 15) A$12. Park fees: see Cradle Mountain, page 163
ℹ Triabunna Visitor Centre, cnr Charles Street and Esplanade, Triabunna, TAS 7190, tel 03 6257 4772
www.dpiwe.tas.gov.au
◉ See Cradle Mountain, page 163

No cars, no shops—sometimes no people. Be prepared to walk or take a bicycle to fully enjoy the 11,550ha (28,528-acre) island, which can be explored in two days. Ferries leave from Triabunna, just north of Orford, for the 25-minute crossing.

Mount Maria at 709m (2,326ft) dominates a coastline of sandstone cliffs, quartzite folds, fossils and sheltered bays. Remains of a penal settlement and a late 19th-century entrepreneurial dream of wine, silk, tourism and cement works survive as ruined buildings, mostly at the former port town of Darlington. Orford, on the mainland, is also rich in history, pretty beaches and fishing spots.
Don't miss Visit the eroded sandstone Painted Cliffs (2-hour return walk).

MOLE CREEK

✚ 331 U19 **ℹ** Deloraine Visitor Centre, 98 Emu Bay Road, Deloraine, TAS 7304, tel 03 6362 3471
www.meandervalley.com

The one-street settlement of Mole Creek is central to some of the best attractions in the northern region. Mole Creek Hotel is a good Aussie pub with Tasmanian tiger 'memorabilia'—if the marsupial mystery interests you, this is a good place to ask the locals.

Otherwise track down the Trowunna Wildlife Park (*daily 9–5*). Wombats and wallabies roam the bushy park and keepers show why you should respect the Tasmanian devil's jaws. For a souvenir, try the local Tasmanian leatherwood honey.
Don't miss There are two limestone caverns nearby, about 16km (10 miles) west of Mole Creek; Marakoopa Cave has a glow worm display while King Solomons Cave is rich with great stalactites and stalagmites.

MOUNT FIELD NATIONAL PARK

✚ 331 U19 • Via the Gordon River Road (B62/B61) to National Park and park entrance at Mount Field, TAS 7140
☎ 03 6288 1149 **◉** See Cradle Mountain, page 163
www.dpiwe.tas.gov.au

Mount Field has a range of wild experiences, from a picnic just off the track to a 16km (10-mile) drive into the high country; you may need snow chains in winter. Some of the most spectacular features are within easy walking distance of the park entrance.

Originally home to the Big River tribe of Tasmanian Aboriginals, the area attracted European trappers in the early 19th century. In 1885 Russell Falls was declared Tasmania's first nature reserve, and in 1916 Mount Field became its first national park.

The lower part of the park has a mix of eucalypt and sub-alpine forests, small rivers and often spectacular waterfalls. The upper part of the park is largely rocky alpine moorland, dotted with tarns (small glacial lakes) and the ski-field. A wheelchair-friendly path leads to Russell Falls, an emblem of Tasmania's temperate rainforest environments, and one of the most photographed waterfalls in Australia.

THE SIGHTS

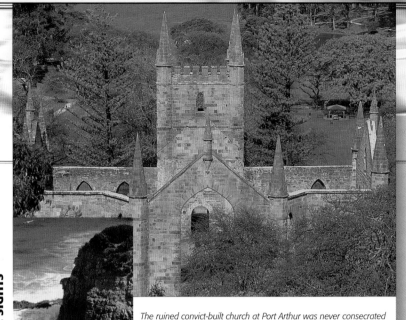

The ruined convict-built church at Port Arthur was never consecrated

PORT ARTHUR AND THE TASMAN PENINSULA

The Tasman Peninsula cliffs are Australia's highest, up to 300m

Serenely beautiful today, Port Arthur is a memorial to a grim past when the prison was a hell on earth for convicts transported from Britain.

RATINGS	
Good for kids	● ● ● ●
Historic interest	● ● ● ● ●
Photo stops	● ● ● ● ●
Walkability	● ● ● ●

TIP

● If you're cooking for yourself, be sure to shop in normal trading hours because there are no large supermarkets here and the towns are quiet.

BASICS

⊞ 331 U19 • Port Arthur, TAS 7182
☎ 1800 659 101 ⊙ Port Arthur Historic Site information office and grounds daily 8:30–9:30 (dusk); restored buildings 9–5 🖐 Adult A$22, child (4–17) A$10
❓ Convict Cemetery Tour (daily except Aug; 30-minute tour), adult A$7.50, child A$5.50; Historic Ghost Tour (summer 9pm, 9:30pm, winter 6:30pm, 8:30pm; 90-minute tour, booking advised), adult A$14, child A$8.60 ☐ The Port Café (in information office) for meals, snacks, beverages; Museum Coffee Shop (in Asylum building) for light meals, snacks, beverages
🍽 Felons (in information office, open evenings), à la carte restaurant based on Tasmanian ingredients 🏛 Port Arthur Gift Shop: souvenirs, Tasmanian crafts, books (daily 9–6)
www.portarthur.org.au • An excellent guide to the prison site.

The dramatic Tasman Peninsula first comes into view as you descend to Eaglehawk Neck, overlooking the spectacular Pirates Bay. The isthmus was once guarded against convicts escaping from Port Arthur. White pointer sharks along this coast were also a deterrent to would-be escapees; the surfers don't seem to care, but you may. The long beach at Eaglehawk Neck is perfect for walking, surfing and fishing.

Tall eucalypt forests are thick across the peninsula right up to the fore-shore, and the highest sea cliffs in Australia run along its eastern flank. Port Arthur Historic Site, 20km (12 miles) south of Eaglehawk Neck, occupies one of the more peaceful and low-lying bays. Some 40ha (100 acres) of parkland are dotted with over 30 prison ruins, including a roofless convict-built church (1837), the four-storey penitentiary, and a stone cottage once occupied by the Irish revolutionary, William Smith O'Brien. Across the water is the Isle of the Dead, where convicts were buried. An impressive visitor information office enlivens the ruins.
Don't miss The aptly named Tesselated Pavement, below the Lufra Hotel at Eaglehawk Neck, is actually formed by erosion of the shoreline rocks; the Historic Ghost Tour at Port Arthur leads through a genuine heritage of supernatural happenings—scary. Remarkable Cave, amid a dramatic cliff coastline, is a 10-minute drive south of Port Arthur, past Palmers Lookout.

BACKGROUND

About 12,000 sentences were served at Port Arthur from 1833 to1877. It was an experimental prison, where from 1849 reform was sought through extreme sensory deprivation in solitary cells. This regime of rehabilitation by isolation was actually worse than the floggings of the early years and drove some prisoners insane. Other inmates were put to mining coal or felling timber either for the colony of Van Diemen's Land or the penal settlement itself, which was almost self-sufficient in producing ships, clothing, bricks, furniture and food. Decline in numbers started in the mid-19th century with the end of transportation. The rugged coast surrounding the settlement is typical of Tasmania.

Take a rapid ride on the Derwent River at New Norfolk

STRAHAN AND WEST COAST

Try sea-kayaking along the weather-beaten west coast or venture inland to the wilderness of rainforests, mountains and waterfalls.

🔲 331 T19
ℹ️ Strahan Visitor Centre, The Esplanade, Strahan, TAS 7468, tel 03 6471 7622; daily 11–6 (may vary) www.destinationstrahan.com.au/ tasvisinfo.com.au

RATINGS					
Good for kids	●	●	●	●	
Historic interest	●	●	●		
Photo stops	●	●	●	●	●
Walkability	●	●	●	●	

TIP

● Study local weather forecasts before every move. The west is dramatic in any weather but heavy rain can make walking unpleasant.

The West Coast Wilderness Railway steams to Strahan

Tasmania's west coast was one of Australia's most isolated regions until the mid-20th century. Strahan was established only in 1883 as a port on the huge Macquarie Harbour for the mining prospects in the mountains around Queenstown, Zeehan, Rosebery and Tullah. The Sarah Island penal settlement in Macquarie Harbour (boat from Strahan) pre-dates the port by half a century. This was the most brutal prison in the British Empire—10,000 lashes were felt in the first three years. The convicts felled the durable, ship-building timber, Huon pine, unique to western Tasmania. This industry and a lumberjack-style bush culture flourished until the 1960s.

The small settlement of Strahan sprawls around the shores of Long Bay. Rainforest and buttongrass plains border the town and in places come close to the heart of town. Mount Sorell is a distant backdrop. Railway and steamboat relics dot the shallows of the harbour, and wooden wrecks evoke pioneering times. Morrison's Huon Pine Mill (*daily 9–5*), the Strahan Visitor Centre and the West Coast Wilderness Railway station are all by the harbour. The railway's steam trains run through stunning scenery to and from Queenstown (*daily 10, 3; bookings 03 6471 1700*). River cruises, seaplanes, charter-fishing tours and jet-boats leave from the port, or you can try sea-kayaking under your own steam.

Driving a loop through Strahan, Queenstown and Zeehan is a rewarding day trip. Zeehan has the best museum, Queenstown dramatic coloured mountains mid-afternoon, but Strahan has comfort, coffee and food. Farther inland, a dense temperate rainforest full of unique species gives way to mountains, waterfalls and the Franklin-Gordon Wild Rivers National Park (see page 164).

Don't miss Zeehan verges on ghost town. The museum (*daily 8.30–6, 5 Apr–Sep*) sits in a row of surviving grand buildings from the boom times—a fascinating capsule of 'wild west' history. A 5km (3-mile) gravel road from Strahan leads to Ocean Beach, Tasmania's longest; 34km (21 miles) of sand, breakers, huge dunes and the chance of a wild sunset.

NEW NORFOLK

🔲 331 U19 ℹ️ Derwent Valley Information Centre, Circle Street, New Norfolk, TAS 7140, tel 03 6261 3700

Just 33km (20 miles) west of Hobart, this classified historic town in the picturesque Derwent Valley is a good stop before the long drive to the west coast. Oast houses (tall drying sheds) in the landscape recall a tradition of hop growing. Local hops continue to enhance the highly regarded Tasmanian beers.

The Bush Inn (1815), overlooking the Derwent River, claims to be the oldest continually licensed hotel in Australia. The river is good for peaceful fishing or a thrilling jet-boat ride over rapids.

Don't miss The Oast House Hop Museum (*daily 9–5*) on the east (Hobart) side of town is a working museum.

RICHMOND

🔲 331 U19 ℹ️ Old Hobart Town (brochures only, not a booking office), TAS 7025, tel 03 6260 2502

Richmond is one of Australia's earliest and best-preserved historic villages. It is now the hub of a wine region and this is reflected in the town's café culture.

The rural river valley was originally explored by English settlers as early as 1803. It is now a pleasant short stop on the way to Port Arthur. Coal was the initial lure and also wallaby meat; the gaol and military barracks soon followed. Richmond Bridge, built 1823–25, is one of the best examples of convict architecture. **Don't miss** Richmond Gaol (*Bathurst Street; daily 9–5*), built in 1825, is Australia's oldest intact prison, and once accommodated the real-life rogue who inspired Charles Dickens' Fagan, from *Oliver Twist*.

A tarn and pines in the Walls of Jerusalem National Park, which lies to the south of Deloraine

Table Cape and Wynard Coastline

THE SIGHTS

ROSS

🚹 331 U19 🚹 Tasmanian Wool Centre, 50 Church Street, Ross, TAS 7209, tel 03 6381 5466
www.taswoolcentre.com.au

Ross, between Hobart and Launceston, was one of the earliest sites selected for a town in Tasmania and named by Governor Macquarie in 1821. It remains a hub for one of the island's finest wool-growing areas and the history of this industry is told at the Tasmanian Wool Centre (daily 9–5).

After Richmond (see page 167), Tasmania's other great convict-built bridge (1836) is here, with 186 carvings by convict stonemason Daniel Herbert. The Man O'Ross Hotel (1835), just past the bridge, is a classic pub, with old 'cockies' (sheep farmers) lining the bar.

SHEFFIELD

🚹 331 U18 🚹 Sheffield Visitor Information Centre, 5 Pioneer Crescent, Sheffield, TAS 7306, tel 03 6491 1036
www.tasvisinfo.com.au

A rural one-street supply town, Sheffield wound down in the 1980s until locals hit on the idea of painting the town—in fact much of the district—with large murals (below). Today it thrives as a lunch stop on the way to Cradle Mountain and a place to absorb the Tasmanian lifestyle. The murals tell of pioneering bushmen, farmers and wildlife but there is little to do after viewing them.

STRAHAN AND WEST COAST

See page 167.

TAMAR VALLEY

🚹 331 U18 🚹 Tamar Visitor Information Centre, Main Road, Exeter, TAS 7275, tel 03 6382 1700
www.tasvisinfo.com.au

A meander through the little towns along the broad Tamar River, from Launceston (see page 165) to the Bass Strait, makes an excellent day or overnight trip. Apples and pears were once the principal produce of the valley but the region is now better known for its vineyards. Some of the best are around Rosevears, and there is a wine route for discerning tasters. The orchards, vineyards and roadside fruit and jams have been joined by a growing number of craftspeople and artists, seeking inspiration and a ready market. Batman Bridge is the only link between the east and west banks, crossing near the towns of Deviot and Rowella.

One of Tasmania's earliest settlements was founded in 1804 near Beaconsfield, on the West Tamar. Beaconsfield itself was built around a gold rush in 1869, and one of the mines was reopened in the 1990s; some of the original buildings house the Grubb Shaft Gold and Heritage Museum (daily 10–4).

Seahorse World at Beauty Point is the world's only commercial seahorse farm with literally thousands on show (daily 9.30–4.30).

Farther north near the western side of the Tamar mouth, two beaches dominate uncrowded Narawntapu National Park. **Don't miss** Low Head Lighthouse (1888), at the mouth of the East Tamar, stands on a headland with dramatic views.

WALLS OF JERUSALEM NATIONAL PARK

🚹 331 U19 • Via the B12 west from Deloraine then Mersey Forest Road to Lake Rowallan ☎ 03 6363 5182 🚹 See Cradle Mountain, page 163
www.dpiwe.tas.gov.au

A spectacular plateau at 1,250m (4,100ft), the park provides a full-day walk. The Walls themselves are the dramatic but easily climbed dolerite peaks ringing the area—climb two in a day if you're camping (summer only). Note: You must be well equipped.

From Launceston or Devonport, drive to Mole Creek then on to Lake Rowallan. A steep 1-hour climb through dry forest reaches the plateau. Beneath the peaks are groves of gnarled pencil pines up to 1,000 years old. From the West Wall you can see Cradle Mountain.

WYNARD

🚹 331 T18 🚹 Wynard Visitor Centre, corner of Goldie and Hogg streets, Wynard, TAS 7325, tel 03 6442 4143
www.tasvisinfo.com.au

Wynard—a small fishing port and rural supply town on the estuary of the Inglis River—is a good place to just retreat. Quiet beaches are overlooked by the Table Cape at the northern edge of town. From 28 September to 18 October a large tulip farm on top of the cape is in full bloom (open 10–4).

Farther west, Boat Harbour Beach is a special spot in summer. Inland, the red volcanic soil produces rich greenery.

This chapter gives information on things to do in Australia other than sightseeing. Australia's best shops, arts venues, nightlife, sports, activities and events are listed state by state.

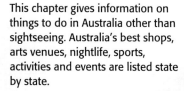

What to Do

SHOPPING

Shopping is big business in Australia. There is competition among all the states as to which of them is the best for shopaholics, but most agree that Sydney and Melbourne are the shopping capitals of Australia. And while many Sydney people are willing to admit Melbourne is the best, few Melbournians pay Sydney a similar compliment.

Airlines once ran shopping tours to the Victorian capital from all around Australia, so if you plan to shop in Melbourne you can't go far wrong.

The best selection of shops are found in the central business districts (CBDs) of all the capital cities. Here the major department stores, boutiques and speciality shops line the main streets or shelter in arcades.

Shop in style—the Queen Victoria Building, Sydney

SHOPPING PRECINCTS
Many locals shop at large sub-urban shopping malls and spe-cialist shopping streets. Melbourne has many such streets, including Greville Street, and Prahran and Chapel streets, South Yarra, where Australia's young and upcoming designers show their work. Brunswick Street, Fitzroy, is similar to New York's Greenwich Village, with bohemian boutiques, cafés, bookshops and gift shops.

In Sydney, the Paddington end of Oxford Street has some of the best Australian fashion and food on show. Other pop-ular shopping spots in the city include the Strand Arcade and

Queen Victoria Building (both beautiful Victorian edifices), Pitt Street Mall and Darling Harbour.

In Darwin the locals go to the Smith Street Mall, the Casuarina Shopping Centre, Parap Shopping Village and the Fannie Bay Shopping Centre.

Most Brisbane shoppers browse the Queen Street Mall, Wintergarden, Roma and Brisbane arcades, the South Bank and Paddington Circle.

In Cairns there's Broadbeach Mall, Orchid Plaza and The Conservatory Shopping Village.

Adelaide has the Rundle Mall, Southern Cross and Adelaide Arcade and Glenelg.

In Hobart try the Elizabeth Street Mall, the Cat and Fiddle Arcade and Gasworks Village.

Perth's shopping includes the Hay Street and Murray Street malls, the Forrest Chase complex, London Court, the Carillon Centre and Piccadilly Arcade.

BARGAIN TIME
Like shoppers all over the world, Australians like to take advantage of the great sales offered by stores at the end of each season. Discount retail parks, which are big in many parts of the world, are not well established in Australia—though more are appearing—so bargains are found mostly during the sales.

However, Melbourne and Sydney excel in factory outlets selling seconds, out-of-season and discontinued lines. In Melbourne, these outlets are in Bridge Road and Swan Street, Richmond.

In Sydney the clothing trade is based mainly in the cosmo-politan, inner-city suburb of

Surry Hills. Scores of small, intersecting streets house factory outlets and wholesalers selling men's and women's clothing and accessories. The area around Regent and Redfern streets, a few minutes south of Sydney's central business district, is another mine for bargains.

MARKETS
The many markets held all around Australia have opportu-nities for the devout bargain hunter. Some open weekdays but most are run on weekends.

In Sydney, Paddy's Market, which is more than 150 years old, is a compendium of about

The Weekend Market at Fox Studios in eastern Sydney

800 stalls, selling everything from clothes to potatoes.

Queen Victoria Market, in Melbourne, offers an equally, if not more, impressive range. St. Kilda Market, along the beachfront Esplanade on Sundays, is known for art and crafts, while the Sunday Victorian Arts Centre Market at 100 St. Kilda Road sells tradi-tional and contemporary ceramics, handmade picture frames and jewellery.

Open-air shopping at Brisbane's weekend markets is a summer delight. Riverside Markets, along Eagle Street, features art, jewellery, fabric painting and wood-carving.

South Bank Craft Markets has more than 100 stalls.

In Cairns, the weekend Mud Markets at the Pier and Rusty's Bazaar Markets, on Fridays and Saturdays, deal in a complete range of art and crafts.

Adelaide's Central Market in Grote Street runs on Tuesdays and Thursdays to Saturdays and has scores of stalls selling fruit, craftwork and jewellery.

Hobart's Salamanca Market, held on Saturdays, is a treasure trove of craftwork made from native woods, pottery and glass.

SHOPPING—LOCAL GOODS

Clothing, opal jewellery and Aboriginal items are often high on the list of unique presents or souvenirs. Of course, you will

The Akubra hat, classic Australian outback kit

also have no problem finding souvenirs ranging from tea towels to fridge magnets, but as most are not made in Australia, always check the labels first for an authentic item.

WEARING OUT

It doesn't cost a lot to pick up a genuine Australian souvenir. Surfing gear, wool and sheepskin products, Drizabone oilskin raincoats, Akubra hats (widebrimmed and usually made of felt) and bushwear (including boots and moleskin trousers) are all unmistakeably Australian. You can find them in all the major cities and in most larger country towns, both in

tourist shops and local clothing outlets. They really are worn by those working in the bush.

Australia has a distinct style of clothing, from colourful and challenging to simple and classic. Good names include Trent Nathan, Country Road, Covers, Perri Cutten, Scanlan & Theodore and Collette Dinnigan.

Also distinctively Australian is wearable art in the form of swimwear, fashion garments, fabrics and souvenirs from Ken Done (the artist and designer), Desert Designs, Weiss Art and Balarinji Designs. Weiss Art is known for its black-and-white symbolic graphics on bags, mugs and childrenswear.

Knitwear, from vivid children's clothing to Jumbuk- brand greasy wool sweaters is in major shopping areas. Australia is renowned for its sheep farming—the fine fleece of the merino breed is ideal for spinning.

CULTURED GIFTS

Australia's multicultural population makes it a great shopping spot for art and crafts. Markets are full of tubular wind chimes, intricate stained-glass panels, bowls carved from native timber, natural crystal, jewellery dripping with local gemstones, original T-shirt designs and framed pen-and-wash sketches of city or Outback scenes. Most craft galleries show locally made pottery, jewellery and other handmade goods.

Aboriginal art is becoming more popular. All the major cities have galleries and stores devoted exclusively to the products of Aboriginal Australians—dot paintings, boomerangs and didgeridoos. There is a good selection of stores in areas where Aboriginal culture is especially promoted, such as Broome, Darwin, Alice Springs, Ayers Rock and Cairns. Many Aboriginal-based attractions

also sell traditional items, and in some cases the items have been made on the premises.

If you want to buy a major piece of Aboriginal art, try to ensure that it is the real thing. To prevent the sale of fake Aboriginal art, Australia's indigenous people have developed the Label of Authenticity, a symbol that helps guarantee Aboriginal and Torres Strait Islander art and other cultural products as authentic. Each label has a serial number that can be traced to the maker of the artwork or craft.

NATURAL FINDS

Australia is a natural source for diamonds, sapphires, gold and other precious stones, as well

Opals from the outback around Coober Pedy, South Australia

as around 95 per cent of the world's opal.

White opals are mined from the fields of Andamooka and Coober Pedy in South Australia. Boulder opals come from Queensland, and black opals from Lightning Ridge and White Cliffs. Stores selling opal jewellery abound in all Australian cities, including duty-free shops.

Australia also possesses an abundance of pearls. Pearls produced in the waters off Broome, Western Australia are known by the trade name South Sea. Numerous shops in Broome sell them, but don't expect too many bargains—pearls are always expensive.

Chain stores

Australia has two main department stores, Myer (operating as Grace Bros in New South Wales and the ACT) and David Jones, and three large discount stores: Big W, Target and K Mart.

There are also two major supermarket chains, Coles and Safeway/Woolworth.

Smaller chain stores specialize in everything from clothing to jewellery. The range of goods found in these stores depends on their location. One of the best times to shop is at the end of December and the end of June when they all have end of season sales.

The largest branches of Myer/Grace Bros and David Jones are in Sydney and Melbourne; the other branches in suburban and regional shopping malls offer similar products but lack

WHAT TO DO

NAME	Clothing	Fashion accessories	Souvenirs and gifts	Books and music	Outdoor and sport	Shoes	Pharmacy and toiletries	Stationery	Food and drink	Jewellery	PHONE NUMBER
Amcal Chemist			✔				✔				03 9542 9400
Angus & Robertson				✔							03 8623 1111
Australian Geographic	✔		✔	✔	✔						02 9473 6700
Aussie Disposals					✔						03 9702 9699
Big W	✔	✔	✔	✔	✔	✔	✔	✔			1800 251 311
Coles	✔	✔		✔	✔	✔	✔	✔	✔		1800 061 562
Country Road	✔										1800 801 911
Darrell Lea Chocolate									✔		02 9529 3366
David Jones	✔	✔	✔	✔		✔	✔	✔	✔	✔	1300 300 110
Dymocks				✔							02 9224 0411
Esprit Pty Ltd	✔	✔									02 9267 0255
Fletcher Jones	✔	✔									02 9659 8022
Goldmark										✔	03 9654 1122
Guardian Pharmacy		✔					✔				1300 888 666
Harris Scarfe Australia	✔	✔	✔	✔	✔	✔	✔	✔			08 8150 5888
Jay Jays Trademark	✔	✔									02 9283 1611
Jeans West	✔	✔									02 9223 3842
Just Jeans Pty Ltd	✔	✔									1800 630 122
K Mart	✔	✔	✔	✔	✔	✔	✔				1800 811 611
Kathmandu					✔						1800 333 484
Katies/Millers	✔	✔									02 9231 2848
Kenny's Cardiology			✔	✔				✔			07 5501 8888
Kingsize Menswear	✔										1800 810 702
Mathers						✔					1300 135 180
Myer	✔	✔	✔	✔	✔	✔	✔	✔	✔	✔	1800 811 611
Paddy Pallin					✔						1800 805 398
Portmans	✔	✔									02 9223 1726
Rebel Sport					✔						02 9795 6500
Rivers						✔					03 5335 1234
Sanity				✔							02 9399 5552
Shoo Biz						✔					02 9232 3315
Sportsgirl	✔	✔									02 4365 4896
Target	✔	✔	✔	✔	✔	✔	✔	✔			03 5246 2000
Toy Kingdom			✔								03 9768 3771
Witchery	✔	✔									02 9231 1233

the range. K Mart and Target are part of the Myer group and have a good spread of shops in Australia, although K Mart are generally in suburban and regional towns whereas Target are usually in central business districts (except Sydney) and suburbs and regions.

If you're searching for name brands, the department and specialist stores are better, but if price is a main factor then discount stores provide an extensive range of goods.

The range and size of goods on offer in supermarkets also varies with location. Although at one time there were no supermarkets in the central areas of most state capital cities, the increasing move to inner city living has resulted in a need for more supermarkets in town. Even though they are not as big as the stores found in suburban shopping areas, these supermarkets still have a wide selection of food. In regional areas, supermarkets often have more general merchandise than their city counterparts. Supermarkets that serve large regional areas can have a range of general and sometimes 'tourist' items.

Many locals do their shopping at the large shopping malls

in suburban and rural areas because of the array of shops available—many national boutiques and larger stores are found in these centres—and because it is easier to park.

NUMBER OF SHOPS	DESCRIPTION	SHOP WEBSITE
500	National pharmacy chain with own brand products	www.amcal.com.au
170	National chain of booksellers	www.angusrobertson.com.au
46	National chain selling nature-based gifts	www.australiangeographic.com.au
35	Inexpensive camping and outdoor gear with outlets in NSW, SA and Vic	www.aussiedisposals.com.au
250	National discount department store	www.bigw.com.au
260	Supermarket chain with outlets all round the country	www.colesmyer.com
43	Classic casual men's and women's clothing and homeware in all states	www.countryroad.com.au
400	Manufacturer and retailer of chocolates and other confectionary Australia-wide	www.dlea.com.au
38	Smart department store with outlets in NSW, Qld, SA, Vic and WA	www.davidjones.com.au
74	National bookselling chain	www.dymocks.com.au
120	Women's mid-price fashion retailer with stores in all states	www.esprit.com
46	High quality men's and women's clothing in all states	www.fletcherjones.com.au
107	National chain of mid-price jewellery retailers	www.anguscoote.com.au
200	National pharmacy chain	www.guardianpharmacies.com.au
24	Discount fashion and homewares with shops in SA, Vic and Tas	www.harrisscarfe.com.au
146	Casual gear for young adults	www.jayjays.com.au
200	National chain selling jeans and casual wear	www.jeanswest.com.au
300	Casual clothing for men and women	www.justjeans.com.au
162	National discount department store	www.kmart.com.au
18	Quality outdoor equipment and clothing with stores in NSW, SA, Tas and Vic	www.kathmandu.com.au
578	Mid-price women's apparel with stores countrywide	www.millersretail.com.au
50	Greeting card and gift retailer with branches nationally	www.kennyscardiology.com.au
8	Retailer selling menswear in larger sizes in NSW, Qld, Vic and WA	www.kingsize.com.au
76	Retailer selling shoes for all the family in NSW, Qld, SA and Vic	www.mathers.com.au
67	Good department store selling fashion and homewares with outlets nationally	www.colesmyer.com
15	Adventure sports clothing and equipment in NSW, Qld, SA, Tas, Vic and WA	www.paddypallin.com.au
220	Mid-price women's apparel with stores in NSW, Qld, SA, Tas, Vic and WA	www.portmans.com.au
50	Sports equipment and clothing stores in all states except Tas	www.rebelsport.com.au
84	Casual wear for all the family available in NSW, Qld, SA, Tas, Vic and WA	www.rivers.com.au
250	National music retailer	www.sanity.com.au
47	Shoe retailer with stores nationally except SA and NT	www.shoobiz.com.au
103	National chain of retailers selling women's fashion	www.sportsgirl.com.au
250	Discount department store selling fashion and homewares nationally	www.target.com.au
90	National chain of toy shops	www.toykingdom.com.au
87	Women's fashion with stores in all states	–

PERFORMANCE ARTS

Culture addicts will not be deprived in Australia. Or at least, not in the main cities and towns. Each capital and many of the large provincial cities have excellent arts venues where you can enjoy everything from international stars to local theatre companies. And all the states have at least one festival, often several, devoted to the performing arts, featuring both Australian and international talent.

During the summer months many leading stars also perform outdoors. The Leeuwin Estate, a winery in Western Australia, was one of the first to introduce outdoor performances and has attracted such stars as Dame Kiri Te Kanawa, Shirley Bassey and Tom Jones. Many vineyards have followed suit, providing a night of great wine and entertainment.

The Black Grace Dance Company's New Works, Canberra Theatre Centre

TASTE FOR MUSIC
A number of world-recognized performing arts companies are based in Sydney, but all state capitals have their own symphony orchestras and theatre groups, and many states have youth orchestras and other specialist music groups. It's not essential to travel to a city for a night of entertainment. The leading companies frequently tour around the country, performing everywhere from the grandest theatres to parks. Less formal are the free concerts in local parks during the summer months. These cater for all musical tastes from jazz to Latin-American, but they are

also popular with Australia's top performance companies.
Opera Australia presents more than 260 performances a year, from traditional to contemporary. It performs at the Sydney Opera House for eight months of the year and resides at the Victorian Arts Centre, Melbourne.

THEATRE LIGHTS
Mel Gibson, Cate Blanchett, Geoffrey Rush and Judy Davis are just some of the cast of actors who began their careers in Australian theatre. The Sydney Theatre Company is a major force in Australian drama, operating from its home venue, The Wharf, on Sydney's harbour, and there's also the Drama Theatre and the Playhouse of the Sydney Opera House.
Expect style and passion at the Victorian Arts Centre, the usual home of the Melbourne Theatre Company. Performances range from classic and contemporary Australian to international plays.
Many of the world's hit musicals, such as *The Lion King*, are staged in Australia.

DANCE
The Australian Ballet is the largest ballet company in the country, employing more than 60 dancers and giving about 200 performances each year. Based in Melbourne, the company performs regionally, nationally and internationally. Western Australia is represented by the West Australian Ballet; the company is based in Perth at His Majesty's Theatre, and tours extensively. Queensland Ballet is based at the

historic Thomas Dixon Centre in Brisbane's West End.
The Sydney-based Bangarra Dance Theatre blends traditional Aboriginal and Torres Strait Islander history and culture with international contemporary dance influences; its home is The Wharf, on Sydney's harbour. The Tjapukai Dance Theatre, based near Cairns, also showcases Aboriginal dance.

MAKING AN ENTRANCE
Daily newspapers are the best way to find out about upcoming performances, or visit the website of the local state tourist authority.

Tune in with the Melbourne Symphony Orchestra

Australia's two major ticket booking agencies can provide information on events and take bookings: Ticketek, tel 132849, www.ticketek.com.au; Ticketmaster, tel 136100, www.ticketmaster.com.au.
Tickets to opera, ballet and big-time shows are sometimes hard to obtain, so book as early as possible. Performance starting times at more formal events are taken literally—latecomers are not admitted until there's a suitable break in the performance. Dress code varies with the audience: While some attend performances in suits, others are far more relaxed.

NIGHTLIFE

OK, it's a cliché, but many young Australians do work hard and party hard. As a result, every major city and many country towns have plenty of fun for all tastes and budgets after dark. Many hotels, clubs and restaurants also offer live music, especially on weekends.

PARTY HARD
Like many countries, Australia has embraced the lifestyle of nightclubs and discos, and many of the older establishments are still going strong. And just like everywhere else, the most popular venues are the ones with the longest wait.

Dance parties are also popular in the major cities, many of them all-night events, with various Australian DJs plus visiting international names.

Clubbing after dark down under— remember to take your party clothes

ON STAGE
Australians have a long tradition of going to their local hotel or pub to listen to up-and-coming bands. Some of Australia's best-known international performers started on the local hotel and pub scene. The tradition is still just as strong, but it's not all rock, grunge and techno— there's ample jazz, blues and acoustic, too. Attending pub venues is also a great way to meet the locals, and many hotels provide good food, allowing partygoers to make a night of it.

Although many restaurants offer live music, the style is generally more sedate and not

quite as loud as it can be in the pub.

Venues, acts and attractions are listed in guides published in metropolitan daily newspapers, usually on Thursday or Friday.

BAR ICE
There are, of course, those who want to enjoy a night without being blasted out by loud music. Stylish bars, clubs and lounges are common in all state capital cities, where the emphasis is on providing great drinks and a friendly environment. Such bars and clubs are particularly popular on week nights with businessmen and women; on weekends the dress is less formal.

Growing in popularity are bars attached to boutique breweries, where a range of local beers are on tap, together with traditional drinks.

GAY LIFE
The large gay, lesbian, bisexual and transgender community in Australia ensures plenty of bars and clubs catering specifically for these groups. Sydney and Melbourne have the largest number, and many clubs are found within specific suburbs. In other cities the venues are more scattered.

In Sydney the heart of all things gay can be found on Oxford Street, taking in the suburbs of Darlinghurst, Surry Hills and Paddington. The inner west suburbs of Newtown, Erskineville and Leichhardt also have a burgeoning pub/bar scene with a strong gay and lesbian background.

Sydney's downtown and Darling Harbour precincts also have an enormous range of

gay and straight chic bars and nightclubs.

Among Melbourne's gay and lesbian precincts are the northern suburbs of Fitzroy and Collingwood, and south of the city in Prahran, South Yarra and St. Kilda.

A GOOD BET
The entertainment of choice of many night-owls are the country's many casinos. Catholic in taste, they offer everything from gambling to live shows to movies.

Casinos can be found in Hobart, Perth, Launceston, Alice Springs, Darwin, Surfers Paradise, Adelaide, Canberra,

Place your chips on a lucky number at the casino

Melbourne, Townsville, Cairns and Brisbane.

Dress regulations usually apply at clubs and casinos. People wearing blue jeans, sandshoes (sneakers), thongs (flip-flops) or singlets (sleeveless T-shirts) will not be admitted. The smarter the establishment the more strict the dress code. A few of the more popular nightspots have 'minders' who have absolute discretion over who is admitted.

If you are thinking of drinking and driving, the advice is, don't—the legal alcohol level is 0.05 per cent in most states, and the police strictly enforce this law.

SPECTATOR SPORTS

If there's one thing Australians love, it's cheering their chosen teams or sports stars. Over the years they have had plenty to shout about.

IS IT FOOTBALL?

Talk to many sports lovers from Melbourne, Adelaide and Perth and they'll tell you that there's only really one winter sport—Australian Rules football. In truth, there is also nothing quite like attending Melbourne Cricket Ground when 90,000 fans are all screaming for their teams. While it obviously helps to understand the rules, the game is spectacular enough to ensure an enjoyable afternoon even if you don't.

England bat against Australia at the Sydney Cricket Ground

Australian Rules is played in New South Wales and Queensland, but most sports lovers in these states are fans of rugby league (rugby union is much less popular). On most weekends between April and September rugby union, rugby league and Australian Rules football matches are

Rugby league—a Brisbane Bronco runs for a winning try

SPECTATOR SPORTS

played around the country. To see one of these matches, often all you need do is turn up at the venue to be sure of a ticket, although when top teams are playing at some of the smaller stadiums it's a good idea to book ahead, as some matches sell out. Tickets for these and other sports can be booked on the telephone or via the web.

THE BEAUTIFUL GAME

While support for soccer isn't as strong in Australia as elsewhere in the world, there are many fans out there, especially during World Cup time or at international friendly games. Western Australian soccer matches attract the biggest crowds, in no small part due to the many British-born residents of Perth.

A HORSE, A HORSE …

In autumn and spring, sport attention turns to horse-racing. Races are held all around the country. The most famous is probably the Melbourne Cup, part of the Spring Racing Carnival that features some of Australia's top racehorses. Many of the same horses try again in Sydney's Golden Slipper and Sydney Cup in March.

SUMMER SPORT

Cricket, tennis and golf take over the sporting calendar in summer. Australia's best cricketers play in the local state competition (although many of the national team now play in fewer state matches) and at international level. There is rarely a problem getting a seat to watch state cricket, but given the popularity of the national team, it's wise to book ahead if you want to attend an international game.

The main tennis season starts around December, and finishes in late January with the staging of the Australian Open in Melbourne. One of the best times to attend the Open is in the first week. A ground pass takes you to the outside courts where you can see champions in action playing lesser-known opponents or practising.

Many of the world's top golfers head to Australia during the summer to take part in major tournaments.

DRIVE TIME

Melbourne also hosts another major event on the sporting

Horse and rider ready to start in the Birdsville Races, Queensland

calendar, the Formula One Grand Prix, held around Albert Park Lake, usually in March. Racing enthusiasts argue that the first two days of the race are the best time to attend as competitors are more relaxed and the crowds aren't as large.

Phillip Island, 140km (87 miles) southeast of Melbourne, also stages a Grand Prix, but for motorcyles. The race is held in October, the same time as the Indy 300 international motor race is staged on Queensland's Gold Coast. General admission tickets for both Victorian events can be purchased at the venue. Grandstand tickets need to be pre-purchased.

PARTICIPATORY SPORTS

The Australian love affair with sport goes way beyond just watching it. With more than 120 national and thousands of local, regional and state sporting organizations, it's estimated that 6.5 million people in Australia are registered sport participants. Not bad from a population of only 19 million. For visitors, there's no reason not to join in and continue your exercise regime while on holiday.

ON YOUR TOES
For many Australians, a morning or afternoon run or walk is the most popular form of exercise. Every capital city has special walking/cycling tracks that take in the most scenic attractions. The tracks around Melbourne, Perth and Sydney's Botanic Gardens, Canberra's Lake Burley Griffin, Brisbane's river and Darwin's harbour

Championship swimming at the Sydney Aquatic Centre

provide spectacular routes for a daily jog.

The same tracks are equally popular with cyclists, especially on weekends; bicycle rental establishments are available near the most popular cycling routes.

Generally it's safe to walk and run during the day, but after dark you should be careful, more so if you head off the beaten track or are in unlit or badly lit areas.

WET STUFF
Given that Australia has about 36,735km (22,775 miles) of coastline, it's no surprise that swimming is a popular

recreational sport. Although some beaches are perfect for swimming all year round, care must be taken at others. You must not swim off the northern Australian coastal beaches from around November to April because of the presence of potentially deadly box jellyfish. In the very far north, saltwater crocodiles can also be a (possibly fatal) problem.

The more energetic culture of surfing is alive and well all around Australia, and keen surfers will find plenty of challenges. Novice surfers can enrol at a 'learn to surf school' where you will be taught all the skills to impress your friends. Shops near the most popular surfing spots rent surfboards and all the gear you might need.

If you plan to swim at one of Australia's many surf beaches you must swim between the warning flags and heed the advice of the surf lifesavers as these waters can be very dangerous.

For those who prefer the safety of a local swimming pool there are plenty of options. Most councils in the major cities and many country towns maintain public swimming pools. Some offer indoor and outdoor pools, while some pools close during the winter. One of the most famous pools is the Sydney Aquatic Centre, which hosted the 2000 Olympics swimming competition. The price of a swim depends on the facilities and location. Local councils or the *Yellow Pages (www.yellowpages.com.au)* are good sources of information.

INDOORS AND OUTDOORS
Local councils and the *Yellow Pages* have listings and information on the many gyms dotted around the country. Most gyms have casual entry and many have a range of classes, such as aerobics. Some have squash courts, and there are also many 'stand alone' squash courts that are open to the public.

Some tennis clubs are open to members only, but two of Australia's most famous tennis stadiums—Melbourne Park, home of the Australian Open, and the Sydney Olympic Tennis Centre—are open to the public all year round.

Kangeroos avoid the green fees at Anglesea Golf Club, Victoria

SWING TIME
Australians have a passion for golf. Hundreds of courses are dotted all around Australia, and just about every town seems to have a course or is near one. In the past the best courses were private, but more new courses are opening that are top-notch and welcome the public. Many of these courses also offer accommodation. Naturally, the more popular the course, the more it costs to play.

Ausgolf *(www.ausgolf.com.au)* lists more than 1,500 courses around Australia, along with the cost of playing a round.

ACTIVITIES

Outback plains, mountains, rainforests, wild rivers and the world's largest coral reef—Australia *is* adventure. But you don't need to go far off the beaten track for a challenge: Zip across Sydney Harbour in a high-speed jetboat, ski down one of Australia's challenging ski slopes, or ride a Harley Davidson motorbike down the Great Ocean Road.

Adventure

THE HEIGHTS

If you have a head for heights, hot-air balloon flights are available in many parts of Australia. Or there is skydiving and bungee-jumping. And if you are into hang-gliding, then head for Queensland's Sunshine Coast and Mount Tamborine, New South Wales's Taree, Western Australia's Albany and Victoria's

Get a grip—the Willyabrup crag near Margaret River, Western Australia

Ararat. Australia also has around 100 gliding clubs, and joy flights can be taken with experienced pilots.

A HARD PLACE

There is no shortage of places to go abseiling and rock climbing or horse-riding and bush-walking. If you want the wilderness experience without the work, then a 4WD drive adventure is perhaps the best option—you can either rent a vehicle or join one of a number of tours.

OFFSHORE

White-water rafters have lots of choices, but many head to

the Tully River in Queensland and the Franklin in Tasmania.

If you prefer a more leisurely pace there's kayaking. A quiet paddle down the Northern Territory's Katherine Gorge is memorable, as is kayaking alongside dolphins in New South Wales' Byron Bay.

Many visitors combine a trip to Australia with the chance to learn to dive. The deep-sea diving off the New South Wales, Queensland and Western Australian coasts is truly spectacular.

Or swim with the whale sharks in Western Australia—they come to Exmouth at the end of summer.

Pampering

BEING PAMPERED

At one time it could be argued that Australians were slow to recognize the benefits of looking after their minds and bodies with a little pampering. Given the number of health resorts, day spas and luxury escapes now open in Australia, they have clearly caught up with the rest of the world.

Getting that essential facial or relaxing massage is easier than ever, especially in Sydney, Melbourne and Brisbane. Many of Australia's five-star hotels in the state capital cities and major tourist areas have spa treatments.

Increasingly popular are day spas run either by cosmetic or skin product manufacturers, or specialized spa operators such as Aveda, Jurlique, Angsana and Spa Chakra.

Health retreats are often situated in tranquil, idyllic surroundings—immersed in

rainforests or beside beaches where the environment is conducive to rest and relaxation.

If you take your health and relaxation seriously, Camp Eden is worth considering. Located in the lush hinterland behind the Gold Coast, it is one of Australia's leading holistic health retreats.

The Daintree Eco Lodge provides elegant luxury and effective treatments in the heart of the Wet Tropics of Queensland World Heritage Area, the world's oldest living rainforest.

Or combine pampering with sightseeing at Lilianfels in New South Wales' Blue Mountains, near Sydney.

Explore the Great Barrier Reef, Queensland

Children

Great zoos and wildlife parks, fun museums, numerous outdoor activities and child-friendly accommodation makes Australia a great place for families.

Australian operators are aware of the importance of families and go out of their way to cater for them, with family passes and plenty of activities for youngsters.

TALK TO THE ANIMALS

Seeing Australia's cuddly koalas and patting a kangaroo remain two of the most popular activities with children.

Over the years Australian zoos and wildlife parks have made great efforts to allow visitors to get as close as possible to the animals and now many offer walk-through enclosures.

The wildlife parks are a good way to see local wildlife—the parks near Alice Springs and Darwin are world famous. At Monkey Mia in Western Australia, children can get close-up to friendly dolphins. In southeastern Queensland, Currumbin Sanctuary on the Gold Coast is home to hundreds of rainbow lorikeets, and at Fleays Wildlife Park kangaroos and emus roam. Families also flock to Victoria's Phillip Island to watch fairy penguins walk each night from the

Making friends with a wallaby in Melbourne, Victoria

water to their sandy burrows. Too young to go deep-sea diving? Then try the Sydney Aquarium at Darling Harbour— you'll feel like you're really underwater.

ALL ABOARD

Families on holiday in Victoria often combine a trip to Phillip Island with a ride on the Puffing Billy steam train in the Dandenongs (see pages 93 and 95). Many of the other states also have rides on restored trains, including the Goolwa to Port Elliot steam train in South Australia and the Hotham Valley Tourist Railway in Western Australia. The Blue

Mountains in New South Wales has one of the world's steepest railways, the Zig Zag (see page 77).

MUSEUMS ARE US

The days of going to a museum and looking at exhibitions behind glass cases are gone: Hands-on learning is the go in all the major museums in Australia. Sydney's Darling Harbour (see page 62) is a child's delight due to such attractions as the Powerhouse Museum and the Australian National Maritime Museum. Questacon, the National Science and Technology Centre in Canberra (see pages 72–73), where learning is combined with lots of activities, is also highly entertaining.

Away from the coast, horse-riding, bushwalking and other sporting activities keep even the most energetic challenged. Many families choose to stay at the growing number of hotels with children's clubs, which provide activities and day care for children of all ages. Naturally, Australia's beaches are great places for kids to be fully entertained.

A great experience is to stay on a farm. Many farms all over Australia welcome families, and some even put on activities especially for children.

THEME PARKS

Queensland's Gold Coast has the reputation as Australia's theme park capital, though many other states can also fulfil a fun day out.

Victoria's Sovereign Hill recreates the dusty life in the 1850s, when gold was king. Built on a former goldmining site in Ballarat (see page 92), children can now pan for gold and keep their finds. You could be as lucky as Richard Jeffrey. The Cornish miner's discovery of the Welcome Nugget is recreated at the Red Hill Mine, using life-size holograms; at 69kg (152lb) it remains the

second-largest gold nugget in the world.

Wonderland Sydney, 42km (26 miles) west of central Sydney, is set in 60ha (148 acres) of landscaped grounds (see page 71). Admission includes the Australian Wildlife Park, home to 600 animals. Themed areas within the park include Old Botany Bay, Transylvania, Goldrush, the Beach and the Outback Woolshed. Stage shows are scheduled each day and thrilling rides are among the park's great draws.

Rides are a great attraction at Queensland's Gold Coast theme parks: Sea World, Warner Bros. Movieworld, Dreamworld and Wet'n'Wild

A hair-raising ride at Movie World, on Queensland's Gold Coast

(see page 115). In addition Sea World is also known for its dolphin and sea-lion shows. At Warner Bros. Movie World you can see real movies being made, watch stunt shows and experience virtual reality. At Dreamworld there are rare Bengal tigers on Tiger Island, the Thunder River Rapids Ride (you'll get wet), movies on a massive IMAX screen, a steam train ride, koalas, and the rather messy Slime Bowl.

Fans of IMAX theatres should go to Darling Harbour in Sydney or Carlton Gardens in Melbourne, which has the world's largest 3D screen (*www.imax.com.au*).

FESTIVALS AND EVENTS

The larger states vie for the title of 'event capital of Australia', so it's not surprising that the Australian calendar is filled year-round with a huge array of festivals and events. There's everything from a horse-race that stops the nation to the more usual artistic and musical festivals. Australia's multiculturalism is evident through various festivals—every Chinatown around the country comes alive during Chinese New Year, and other groups celebrate important days with equal gusto.

To start the year, fireworks displays and celebrations are held around the country on New Year's Eve; most people agree that the Sydney fore-shore is one of the best places to be. Regular major capital city events in January include the Sydney Festival, which covers street theatre, art shows, amusement parks, poetry

New Year's Eve fireworks at Sydney Harbour

readings, international drama and a free concert series. Hobart's similar festival celebrates its art and culture and Tasmania's great food. The performing arts and culture of Western Australia are highlighted at the Perth International Arts Festival.

Adelaide, hosts one of the country's most extensive arts events. Held biennially in even-numbered years in late February and early March, the Adelaide Festival involves hundreds of Australian and international performers. The Adelaide Fringe Festival runs parallel to the main event, beginning a week earlier with

performances in venues across the city, ranging from the crazy to the bizarre to the seriously intellectual.

One of Sydney's largest festivals, the Sydney Gay and Lesbian Mardi Gras, is held in March. This has prime place in the world's gay calendar, and a highlight is the fun-filled, provocative parade along Oxford Street.

March in Melbourne brings the Australian Grand Prix, the Melbourne International Comedy Festival, the Wine and Food Festival, and Moomba, known for its fireworks, music and river pageants.

Meantime in Canberra, Taste—Celebrating Food, Wine and the Arts—is staged. The festival highlights Canberra's and the surrounding region's food producers, chefs and artistic performers. The Hot Air Balloon Fiesta—the biggest in the southern hemisphere—is also held in Canberra in March. Around 50 balloons of all shapes and sizes fill the sky.

Early April is the time for the Melbourne International Flower and Garden Show (www.melbflowershow.com.au). Held at the Royal Exhibition Building and Carlton Gardens, it's a must for keen gardeners. Wine lovers head to the Barossa Vintage Festival at Barossa in South Australia.

In June it is the turn of Brisbane's gay and lesbian community to host their festival, while in Sydney cinema-goers can watch the glamour of the Sydney Film Festival. If you miss this, Melbourne has a film festival in July and August.

Spring is the signal for one of Canberra's most popular events, Floriade (www.floriade australia.com). From mid-September to October visitors come from all over the world to admire the amazing displays of bulbs and annuals.

In October and November Melbourne puts on its party face to celebrate the Spring Racing Carnival and the horse-race that brings the entire nation to a standstill, the Melbourne Cup. The Melbourne Festival, and the Australian Motorcycle Grand Prix at the Phillip Island Grand Prix Circuit, make October a busy month in Victoria.

The Hahn Premium Race Week at the Whitsunday Islands, Queensland

One of the world's classic blue-water yacht races starts on Boxing Day in Sydney in front of a vast crowd and culminates in a lively New Year's Eve party in Hobart, Tasmania.

What these premier events are to the major cities, agricultural shows are to many of the country towns. As well as providing family fun, displays of crafts, produce and livestock, and demonstrations of horse riding, sheep shearing and wood chopping give an insight to rural Australia.

In each state capital city the country comes to the city at least once a year in the form of Royal Agricultural shows.

NEW SOUTH WALES AND ACT

New South Wales, and Sydney in particular, is known for staging some great events, including the 2000 Sydney Olympics, the annual Gay and Lesbian Mardi Gras and New Year's Eve celebrations. Every month there seems to be some type of celebration or special event. But the good news is that even if your visit doesn't coincide with one of these activities, you'll still find plenty to do.

Tropfest, a free, outdoor film festival held in Sydney at the end of February

Sydney Harbour has become a popular destination with adventure-seekers thanks to the Harbour Bridge climb, jet-boating and sailing. Then there are Sydney's many beaches, popular all year round, especially Bondi and Manly.

Sydney Opera House is one of Australia's best-known landmarks, and it's a great place to experience a concert, watch a play or see dance companies.

For nightlife, Sydney has an active hotel/pub scene, often with live music. There is also a good mixture of dance clubs and gay clubs.

Shopping is a popular event with Sydneysiders. The Queen Victoria Building (known as QVB), the Strand Arcade and Sydney Central have a range of boutiques and one-off stores. Oxford Street, running through Darlinghurst and Paddington, is where to find the collections of Australian designers. Double Bay is where Sydney's high society shops. Bargains can be found at the many markets, in Surry Hills and at the Direct Factory Outlet near Homebush.

Homebush was the venue for the 2000 Olympics. At Sydney Olympic Park you can re-create some of the Games' great sporting feats in the tennis and aquatic centres.

Although not in New South Wales, Canberra is included in this section because of its proximity to Sydney. The National Gallery, the Australian Institute of Sport and Quest-acon are among the attractions.

The paths around Lake Burley Griffin are ideal for walkers and cyclists, while Canberra's national parks are a bush-walker's delight.

The rest of New South Wales is great for adventure. The Blue Mountains for walking and abseiling, and the coast for surfing, scuba-diving, snorkelling and windsurfing.

At Coffs Harbour you can explore the water and the World Heritage rainforests in Dorrigo National Park. Book a 4WD tour for easy exploration of these areas.

In winter, skiers head to the Snowy Mountains. During the summer they belong to white-water rafters, fishermen and horse riders.

Country towns have markets and art and craft shops. For unusual items try the artist studios of Broken Hill.

Shopping

BROKEN HILL

RED SANDS GALLERY
355 Wolfram Street, Broken Hill, NSW 2880
Tel 08 8088 7734
www.outbackgalleries.com.au

The gallery, in an old homestead, features the works of local artists who are inspired by the landscape. Also furniture, ceramics and gifts.
🔵 Tue–Sat 10–4

CANBERRA

NATIONAL GALLERY OF AUSTRALIA SHOP
Parkes Place, Canberra, ACT 2601
Tel 02 6240 6420
www.ngashop.com.au
The in-house shop sells good-quality prints, books and post-cards relating to the gallery's collections.
🔵 Daily 10–5 🔵

QUESTACON SHOP
King Edward Terrace, Canberra, ACT 2601
Tel 02 6270 2800
www.questacon.edu.au

The gift shop at Questacon, the science and technology museum, sells educational and fun toys for children of all ages; there are also books and CD-ROMs.

🕐 Daily 9–5 🚗 34 🚇

COFFS HARBOUR

COLORADO
Shop 38, Park Beach Plaza, 253 Pacific Highway, Coffs Harbour, NSW 2450
Tel 02 6650 9631
www.colorado.com.au
This branch of the Colorado chain, in the Park Beach Plaza, sells tough and functional leisure and outdoor clothing, boots and accessories. It's a good place to buy gear for exploring the rainforest national parks in the area.
🕐 Mon–Fri 9–5.30, Sat 9–4, Sun 10–2

HUNTER VALLEY

CAPERCAILLIE WINE COMPANY AND GALLERY
Londons Road, Lovedale, Hunter Valley, NSW 2904
Tel 02 4990 2904
www.capercailliewine.com.au
The Capercaillie Wine Company is one of the newest and smallest wineries in the Hunter Valley. Buy wines and browse the gallery, which has fine glass, ceramics, silks, timbers and original paintings.
🕐 Mon–Sat 9–5, Sun 10–5

SYDNEY

ABORIGINAL AND TRIBAL ART CENTRE
Sydney Opera House, NSW 2000
Tel 02 9247 4344
www.atac.citysearch.com.au
The gallery sells artworks from Aboriginal groups and regions. There's also a range of didgeridoos, boomerangs, pottery, bush jewellery, books and CDs.
🕐 Daily 10–5 🚗 Explorer bus (stop 1) 🚇 Circular Quay (CityRail)

COOGI KNITWEAR AT SYDNEYSCOPE
Shop 24, Gallery Level, Queen Victoria Building, George Street, NSW 2000
Tel 02 9264 8240
www.sydneyscopeartwear.com

Coogi knitwear is famous in Australia for bright colours and attention-grabbing designs, many of which have a distinctive Australian theme. Sydneyscope, in the Queen Victoria Building, has more than 1,500 Coogie designs.
🕐 Mon–Sat 10–6 (also Thu 6–9pm), Sun 11–5

DFS GALLERIA
155 George Street, The Rocks, NSW 2000
Tel 02 9258 7655
www.dfsgalleria.com.au
DFS Galleria is one of the largest department stores in Australia selling duty- and GST-free goods. It has four floors of Australian and international goods, including wines, opals, clothing, jewellery, perfumes, cosmetics, cameras and electronic equipment. Brands include Tiffany and Co and Burberry of London.

🕐 Daily 11–8 🚇 Circular Quay (CityRail)

DONE ART AND DESIGN
123 George Street, The Rocks, NSW 2000
Tel 02 9251 6099
www.done.com.au

One of the most popular tourist shops in The Rocks, Done Art and Design sells clothes, swimwear, homewares and souvenirs—all with designer and artist Ken Done's trademark colourful designs.
🕐 Daily 10–6 🚇 Circular Quay (CityRail)

FLAME OPALS
119 George Street, The Rocks, NSW 2000
Tel 02 9247 3446
www.flameopals.com.au
By buying their opals direct from the miners and manufacturing their own jewellery, Flame Opals offer competitive prices and a wide selection of stones. Buy them unset or as jewellery.
🕐 Mon–Fri 9–6.30, Sat 10–5, Sun 11.30–5 🚇 Circular Quay (CityRail)

GOODWOOD SADDLERY
237–239 Broadway, NSW 2000
Tel 02 9660 6788
www.goodwoods.com.au
Australian bushmen's gear such as Akubra hats, Driza-Bone coats and R. M. Williams boots can be found at this saddlery southwest of the city centre.
🕐 Mon–Fri 9.30–5.45, Sat 9–4.45, Sun 10–3.45 🚇 Central Station then 10 min walk

GOWINGS
Cnr Market and George streets, NSW 2000
Tel 02 9287 6394
www.gowings.com.au

This family-owned department store has been clothing the men of Sydney since 1868. The head office store, opposite the

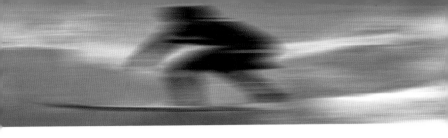

Queen Victoria Building, sells everything from suits and shirts to underwear and gifts—all at very reasonable prices. There are two other stores, at 319 George Street, Sydney, and 82 Oxford Street, Darlinghurst.
🅒 Mon–Fri 8.30–6 (also Thu 6–9), Sat 9–6, Sun 10–5 🚇 City Centre (Monorail)

JINTA DESERT ART
120 Clarence Street, NSW 2000
Tel 02 9290 3639
www.jintaart.com.au
This gallery sells works from many of Australia's leading Aboriginal artists from the Central Desert region, including Clifford Possum Japaltjarri and Emily Kame Kngwarreye, whose works are on display in some of the major art galleries. If you buy a painting you'll get a book that contains the traditional story (Dreaming) behind the painting.

🅒 Mon–Sat 10–6.30; Sun by appointment only

LUGGAGELAND
397 George Street, NSW 2000
Tel 02 9299 6699
www.luggageland.com.au
Luggageland, with its range of backpacks and day packs, is popular with visitors who discover that they have more souvenirs than luggage space.
🅒 Mon–Fri 9–5.30 (also Thu 5.30–8), Sat 9–5, Sun 10.30–5

NATIONAL MARITIME MUSEUM
2 Murray Street, Darling Harbour, NSW 2000
Tel 02 9298 3777
www.anmm.gov.au/store.htm

The museum shop has maritime books, gifts and souvenirs. Unusual gifts include compass cufflinks, lighthouse-shape egg cups, and clocks in the form of a submarine.

🅒 Daily 9.30–5 🚇 Harbourside (Monorail) 🚌

PADDY'S MARKET AT HAYMARKET
Cnr Thomas and Hay streets, Haymarket, NSW 2000
Tel 02 9325 6200
www.paddys.com.au
Tourists and locals rub shoulders at the largest and most traditional market in Sydney, within walking distance of Darling Harbour. More than 800 stalls sell everything from souvenirs to sheepskins, clothes to cosmetics and sporting goods to CDs. There's also a Paddy's Market at Flemington in western Sydney.
🅒 Fri–Sun 9–4.30, Thu 10–6 🚇 Haymarket (Monorail) 🚌

R. M. WILLIAMS
71 George Street, The Rocks, NSW 2000
Tel 02 9247 0204
www.rmwilliams.com.au
This famous bushman outfitter sells shirts, hats, moleskins, drills, jeans, oilskins and boots. There's another branch at 389 George Street near the Queen Victoria Building.
🅒 Mon–Sat 10–6, Sun 10–5 🚇 Circular Quay (CityRail)

SPRING ROW GIFT SHOP—THE ROCKS
115 George Street, The Rocks, NSW 2000
Tel 02 9 247 1851

Spring Row was the original name for George Street. This outlet, near the Museum of Contemporary Art at The Rocks, showcases crafts made from wood and glass, as well as ceramics, jewellery and Aboriginal art. Everything is hand made by Australian artists. Quality gifts also sold.
🅒 Mon–Sat 9–7, Sat 10–6, Sun 11–6 🚇 Circular Quay (CityRail)

STRAND HATTERS
Strand Arcade, 412 George Street, NSW 2000
02 9231 6884
www.strandhatters.com.au
This hat shop specializes in Australia's Akubra hats; more than 60 styles are available. Other brands include Barmah, and Monte Christie panamas. The staff will help fit, shape and steam your hat.

🅒 Mon–Fri 8.30–6 (also Thu 6–9pm), Sat 9–4.30, Sun 11–4 🚌 304 🚇 Town Hall (CityRail)

SURF, DIVE AND SKI
462 George Street, NSW 2000
Tel 02 9267 3408
www.sds.com.au
This long-established outlet sells everything to do with Australian surf culture, including boards, flippers, wetsuits, casual wear and sunglasses.
🅒 Mon–Thu 8.30–5.30 (also Thu 5.30–9pm), Fri 8.30–6, Sat 9–6

SYDNEY AIRPORT
International Terminal, Sydney Airport, Mascot
www.sydneyairport.com
There are now more than 120

stores at Sydney Airport's international terminal, including Gianni Versace, Oroton, Angus & Coote, Fish Records, and Ken Done Art and Design. All goods are available duty- and GST-free.

◎ Daily 6am–10pm 🍴 💻

VICTORIA'S BASEMENT
Cnr George and Market streets, NSW 2000
Tel 02 9261 2674
www.qvb.com.au
The majestic Queen Victoria Building has some pricey boutiques, but the goods in this outlet, tucked away in the basement, represent good value for money.

◎ Mon–Sat 9–6 (also Thu 6–9pm), Sun 11–5 🚇 Town Hall (CityRail)

WEEKEND MARKET AT FOX STUDIOS
Lang Road, Moore Park, NSW 1363
Tel 02 9383 4333
www.foxstudios.com.au
Fox Studios, in east Sydney, has a professional film studio as well as a number of cinemas, retail outlets, restaurants and shops.

The Weekend Market has stalls selling movie memorabilia, collectables, clothing, gifts, houseware, toys, art and crafts. There is also a Farmers' Market here Saturday and Wednesday.

◎ Sat–Sun 10–5; Farmers' Market: Wed 10–5, Sat 10–4 🍴 🚌 373 from Circular Quay 💻

WOOLLAHRA ANTIQUE CENTRE
160 Oxford Street, Woollahra, NSW 2025
02 9327 8840
www.antiquetoart.com.au/gallery/dealers/woollah/dealer.htm
Woollahra is home to many of Sydney's leading antiques dealers. More than 50 dealers are housed on three levels in the Woollahra Antique Centre, where they sell everything from furniture and glassware to porcelain, light fittings, jewellery and watches.

◎ Daily 10–6 💻 🚗 4km (2.5 miles) southeast of Sydney

Performance

CANBERRA

CANBERRA THEATRE CENTRE
London Circuit, Canberra, ACT 2601
Tel 02 6275 2700
www.canberratheatre.org.au

The Centre presents performing arts groups and entertainers from Australia and abroad.
🚇

THE STREET THEATRE
Cnr Childers Street and University Avenue, Canberra City, ACT 2601
Tel 02 6247 1519
www.thestreet.org.au
This is Canberra's prime location to see local artists performing in experimental theatre, music and dance.
💻 🚇

KATOOMBA

THE EDGE
225 Great Western Highway, Katoomba, NSW 2780
Tel 02 4782 8900
www.edgecinema.com.au
The Edge is a 40-minute documentary about the rugged attractions of the Blue Mountains, shown to dramatic effect on a 6-storey screen.
◎ 10.30–5.30 🚇 Katoomba 🚇

SYDNEY

CAPITOL THEATRE
13 Campbell Street, Haymarket, NSW 2000
Tel 02 9266 4800
This lavish theatre, dating from the 1920s, stages large-scale musicals and some classical music concerts.
🚇 Haymarket (Monorail) 🚇

CITY RECITAL HALL
Angel Place, NSW 2000
Tel 02 8256 2222
www.cityrecitalhall.com
Just off Martin Place, this is a 1,200-seat venue for chamber orchestras and soloists.

🚇 Martin Place (CityRail), Wynyard 🚇

DENDY MARTIN PLACE
19 Martin Place, NSW 2000
Tel 02 9233 8166
www.dendy.com.au
Watch the latest art-house movies at this central cinema complex.
◎ 11–9 🚇 Martin Place (CityRail), Wynyard 💻 🚇

DENDY OPERA QUAYS
2 East Circular Quay, NSW 2000
Tel 02 9247 3800
www.dendy.com.au
Art-house films in comfortable surroundings.
◎ Mon–Sat 10–9.30 🚇 Circular Quay (CityRail) 💻 Fully licensed

ENMORE THEATRE
130 Enmore Road, Newtown, NSW 2042
Tel 02 9550 2990
www.enmoretheatre.com.au
The 1,600-seat Enmore, a few kilometres from central Sydney, hosts rock acts such as the Dixie Chicks.
🚇 Newtown 💻

ENSEMBLE THEATRE
78 McDougall Street, Kirribilli, NSW 2061
Tel 02 9929 0644
www.ensemble.com.au
The Ensemble is a small theatre just over the Harbour Bridge. Mainstream productions by well-known playwrights.

North Shore ◨ Milsons Point
◨ Kirribilli Wharf from Circular Quay
◨ A$19–55 ◨

LA PREMIERE AT HOYTS FOX STUDIOS

Bent Street, Fox Studios, Moore Park, NSW 1363
Tel 02 9332 1300
www.hoyts.com.au
Five of the cinemas here have La Premiere areas, with private two-seat sofas, where you can have a glass or two of wine while watching a movie.
◨ Moore Park, from Central Station
◨ Daily 12.15–9.45 ◨

LG IMAX THEATRE

31 Wheat Road, off Southern Promenade, Darling Harbour, NSW 2000
Tel 02 9281 3300
www.imax.com.au

The IMAX cinema presents eye-popping movies (some in 3-D) on an eight-storey screen.
◨ Daily 10–10 ◨ Darling Park (Monorail), Convention (Light Rail), Town Hall (CityRail) ◨

LYRIC THEATRE

80 Pyrmont Street, Pyrmont, NSW 2009
Tel 02 9266 4800 (Ticketek, for bookings)
www.starcity.com.au
Part of Star City Casino, the Lyric stages interntional musical productions such as *Mamma Mia*.
◨ Explorer bus (stop 18) ◨ Star City (Light Rail) ◨ ◨

MOONLIGHT CINEMA

Centennial Park (Woollahra gate), Oxford Street, NSW 2000
Tel 02 99224871
www.moonlight.com.au

Outdoor movies in the park on summer evenings.
◨ Dec–Feb, 8.30pm; tickets at gate from 7pm ◨ 3.5km (2 miles) southeast of Sydney

THE SHOWROOM

80 Pirrama Road, Pyrmont, NSW 2009
Tel 02 9266 4800 (Ticketek, for bookings)
www.starcity.com.au
Part of Star City Casino, this 900-seat theatre hosts mostly musical performances. International stars Michael Crawford, kd lang and Tony Bennett have played here.
◨ Explorer bus (stop 18) ◨ Star City (Light Rail) ◨ ◨ Snackbar ◨

THE SYDNEY ENTERTAINMENT CENTRE

35 Harbour Street, Darling Harbour, NSW 2000
Tel 02 9320 4200
www.sydentcent.com.au
Sydney's largest indoor venue is the place to see the big-name rock acts and large-scale productions.
◨ Mon–Fri 9–5, Sat 10–1 ◨ Explorer bus (stop 17) ◨ Haymarket (Monorail, Light Rail) ◨ ◨

SYDNEY OPERA HOUSE

See page 68.

WHARF THEATRE

Pier 4, 5 Hickson Road, Walsh Bay, NSW 2000
Tel 02 9250 1777
www.sydneytheatre.com.au
This converted cargo-ship wharf houses two theatres where plays by the Sydney Theatre Company are staged.
◨ Free shuttle bus from Circular Quay
◨ Circular Quay (CityRail) ◨ ◨

TARONGA'S TOWER TWILIGHT SERIES

Taronga Zoo, Bradleys Head Road, Mosman, NSW 2088
Tel 02 9266 4800 (Ticketek, for bookings)
www.zoo.nsw.gov.au
Family-orientated concerts are held outdoors at Taronga Zoo in late summer.
◨ Performances Fri–Sun most evenings, Feb–Mar ◨ Taronga Wharf ◨

YIRIBANA ABORIGINAL AND TORRES STRAIT ISLANDER GALLERY

Yiribana Gallery, Art Gallery of NSW, The Domain, NSW 2000
Tel 02 9225 1744
www.artgallery.nsw.gov.au
See live performances and traditional art by indigenous performers and artists.
◨ Performances Tue–Sat at noon
◨ Museum (CityRail) ◨ Free ◨

WOLLONGONG

THE YALLAH WOOLSHED

Princes Highway, Yallah, NSW 2530
Tel 02 4262 2655
www.yallahwoolshed.com
Many of Australia's best-known country performers play here.
◨ Call for show details ◨ Wollongong (CityRail)

Nightlife

CANBERRA

ALL BAR NUN
Macpherson Street, O'Connor, ACT 2602
NSW 02 6257 9191
www.allbarnun.com.au
Popular with everyone from students to executives, All Bar Nun has one of the biggest ranges of international and domestic beers in Canberra.
🕐 Sun–Wed noon–11, Thu–Sat noon–late

BOBBY MCGEES
Rydges Lakeside Canberra, London Circuit, Canberra City, ACT 2601
Tel 02 6257 7999
www.rydges.com.au
Bobby McGees is a laid-back lounge, nightclub and bar.
🕐 Thu–Sat and Mon times vary
🎤 Non-members pay a cover charge some nights

CASINO CANBERRA
21 Binara Street, Canberra City, ACT 2608
Tel 02 6257 7074
www.casinocanberra.com.au
This is a European-style 'boutique' casino that also features entertainment areas.
🕐 Daily noon–6am

CENTRAL COAST

ETTALONG BEACH MEMORIAL CLUB
211 Memorial Avenue, Ettalong, NSW 2257
Tel 02 4341 1166
www.ettalongbeachclub.com.au
This club has bars, restaurants and Lizotte's, a dinner theatre.
🕐 Open daily 24 hours

SYDNEY

ANNANDALE HOTEL
Cnr Parramatta Road and Nelson Street, Annandale, NSW 2038
Tel 02 9550 1078
www.annandalehotel.com
This pub, a few kilometres from Sydney, has a reputation for featuring up-and-coming rock bands, as well as big-name acts.
🕐 11am–midnight 🚌 Annandale bus stop opposite 🎤 There are cover charges to hear the bands

ARQ
16 Flinders Street, Darlinghurst, NSW 2010
Tel 02 9380 8700
www.arqsydney.com.au
This multilevel clubbing venue has impressive lighting effects, with DJs, live acts and shows. Sunday is gay night.
🕐 Thu–Sun 9pm–late; closed Mon–Wed
🚌 Explorer bus to Darlinghurst
🎤 Cover charge at weekend

THE BAR AT SIR STAMFORD
Sir Stamford Hotel, 93 Macquarie Street, Circular Quay, NSW 2000
Tel 02 8274 5447
The lavish décor of this established nightspot has an Edwardian theme.
🕐 Mon–Sat noon–late, Sun noon–10
🚆 Circular Quay (CityRail)

CARGO BAR AND LOUNGE
62 The Promenade, King Street Wharf, NSW 2000
Tel 02 9262 1777
www.cargobar.com.au
A lively place for a drink or dance; the upstairs lounge here has a more relaxed atmosphere. Great views over Darling Harbour.
🕐 Mon–Thu 11am–1am, Fri–Sat 11am–4am, Sun 11am–midnight 🚌 Bus, train or ferry to King Street Wharf

COHI BAR
Shop 359, Harbourside, Darling Harbour, NSW 2000
Tel 02 9281 4440
www.cohibar.com.au
On two levels, Cohi Bar serves up harbour views, cocktails and, on weekends, urban funk and harmonic jazz.
🕐 Daily 10am–late 🚆 Harbourside (Monorail)

ESTABLISHMENT
252 George Street, NSW 2000
Tel 02 9240 3000
www.merivale.com
Establishment, the main bar in a boutique hotel near Circular Quay, attracts a sophisticated crowd who love the restored 19th-century interior.
🕐 Mon–Fri 11am–late, Sat 6pm–late
🚆 Circular Quay (CityRail)

HARBOUR VIEW
18 Lower Fort Street, The Rocks, NSW 2000
Tel 02 9252 4111
www.harbourview.com.au
One of Sydney's favourite heritage pubs; true to its name, it has great harbour views.
🕐 Daily 11–11

HEMMESPHERE
Level 4, 252 George Street, NSW 2000
Tel 02 9240 3040
www.merivale.com
Large leather club chairs define this stylish cocktail bar.
🕐 Tue–Fri 6–late (also Thu–Fri for lunch)

HOME
101 Cockle Bay Wharf, Cockle Bay, NSW 2000
Tel 02 9266 0600
www.cocklebaywharf.com.au
This nightclub has a lounge area and a huge dance floor.
🕐 Fri–Sat 10pm–7am, Sun 6–midnight
🚆 Darling Park (Monorail)

HUGO'S LOUNGE
33 Bayswater Road, Potts Point, NSW 2011
Tel 02 9357 4411
www.hugos.com.au

The long, sleek, black bar is the feature of Hugo's Lounge.
🕐 Tue–Sun 6–late 🚌 325, 327

LIZARD LOUNGE/THE EXCHANGE
34 Oxford Street, Darlinghurst, NSW 2010
Tel 02 9331 1936
This is one of the most popular gay venues in Sydney, with some of the best DJs in town.
🕐 Daily 10pm–6am 🚇 Museum

LONGRAIN
85 Commonwealth Street, Surry Hills, NSW 2010
Tel 02 9280 2888
www.longrain.com.au
Inner-city Surry Hills is home to several stylish bars. This is one of the best, located in an old warehouse.

🕐 Lunch: Mon–Fri noon–2.30; dinner: Mon–Sat 6–late 🚇 Central Station

LORD NELSON BREWERY HOTEL
Cnr Kent and Argyle streets, The Rocks, NSW 2000
tel 02 9251 4044
www.lordnelson.com.au
Built in 1841, the Lord Nelson is the oldest pub in Sydney. Sample the pub's own beers, produced in its micro-brewery.
🕐 Mon–Sat 11–11, Sun noon–10
🚇 Wynyard (CityRail)

THE NEWPORT ARMS HOTEL
Kalinya Street, Newport, NSW 2105
Tel 02 9997 4900
www.newportarms.com.au
This family-oriented pub in a Northern Beaches suburb stages live music and an out-door screen showing sport. There are also views over Pittwater.

🕐 Sat 10am–midnight, otherwise daily but closes earlier (around 10pm)
🚌 From Wynard Station (CityRail): L87, L88, L89 or L90

ORBIT LOUNGE BAR
Australia Square, 264 George Street, NSW 2000
Tel 02 9247 9777
www.summitrestaurant.com.au

This chic bar, 47 floors up in the Australia Square building, has sensational panoramic views over Sydney.
🕐 Mon–Fri noon–late, Sat 5pm–late

PLANET BOLLYWOOD
24 Bay Street, Double Bay, NSW 2028
Tel 02 9362 5222
A charming lounge bar and restaurant in an east Sydney suburb.
🕐 Tue–Sun 10–2 and 5pm–late
🚇 Edgecliff (CityRail)

QUAY
Customs House, cnr Loftus and Alfred streets, Circular Quay, NSW 2000
Tel 02 9251 3305
www.quaybarcafe.com.au
Lively bar in the historic Customs House opposite the ferry wharves at Circular Quay.

🕐 Daily 10am–late 🚇 Circular Quay (CityRail)

SOHO BAR AND LOUNGE
171 Victoria Street, Potts Point, NSW 2011
Tel 02 9358 6511
www.sohobar.com.au
In an art-deco hotel, the bar features Yu nightclub, where you can party all night.
🕐 Mon–Thu 10am–3am, Fri–Sun 10am–6am

STAR CITY CASINO
80 Pyrmont Street, Pyrmont, NSW 2009
Tel 02 9777 900
www.starcity.com.au
Sydney's casino has six bars, seven restaurants, two theatres, 1,500 poker machines and 200 gaming tables.
🕐 Open daily 24 hours 🚌 Explorer bus (stop 18) 🚆 Star City (Light Rail)

WINE BANC
53 Martin Place, NSW 2000
Tel 02 9233 5399
Wine Banc is a below-ground sleek and stylish wine bar with an impressive interior.
🕐 Mon–Thu noon–midnight, Fri noon–late (live jazz), Sat 6pm–late
🚇 Martin Place (CityRail)

WOLLONGONG
BEACH BAR
Novotel North Beach Hotel, 2–14 Cliff Road, North Wollongong, NSW 2500
Tel 02 4226 3555
The Beach Bar of the hotel has views over the Pacific and live music.
🕐 Wed–Thu 3pm–late, Fri–Sun 2pm–midnight 🚇 North Wollongong (CityRail)

Sports and Activities

ADAMINABY

REYNELLA KOSCIUSZKO RIDES
Reynella, Adaminaby, NSW 2630
Tel 02 6454 2386
www.reynellarides.com.au
Experienced guides lead you and your mount through the stunning mountain scenery of Kosciuzko National Park. Trout-fishing tours are also arranged.
Alpine Horse Rides operate Oct–May From A$866 for 3-day/4-night ride and from A$1,318 for 5-day/6-night ride

COFFS HARBOUR

WOW RAFTING
1448 Coramba Road, Coramba, NSW 2450
Tel 02 6654 4066
www.wowrafting.com.au
Take on the Nymboida River, one of the country's best whitewater rivers.
Daily 8.30–7.30, depending on rainfall 1-day A$153, 2-day A$325

KATOOMBA

BLUE MOUNTAINS ADVENTURE
84A Bathurst Road, Katoomba, NSW 2780
Tel 02 4782 1271
www.bmac.com.au
Climbing, mountain-biking and bushwalking for all skills.
Katoomba Abseiling A$119–A$255; rock-climbing A$155 (1 day); canyoning A$145, A$370 (3 days); mountain-biking A$95 (half day), A$155 (1 day)

SYDNEY

BRIDGECLIMB
5 Cumberland Street, The Rocks 2000
02 8274 7777
www.bridgeclimb.com.au

A guide leads a small group on an exhilarating and informative climb to the top of the Sydney Harbour Bridge. Climbers must be over 12 and physically fit.
Daily. Closed Dec 30–31 Circular Quay (CityRail) From A$145

HARBOUR JET
Shop 113A Harbourside, Darling Harbour, NSW 2000
Tel 02 9212 3555
www.harbourjet.com

Zoom around Sydney Harbour on a jet boat. You'll see the sights and experience head-spinning manoeuvres.
Tours depart at various times 443 or 888 from Circular Quay Rocket ferry from Circular Quay Adult from A$60, child from A$40 for 35-minute Jet Blast tour

MANLY SURF SCHOOL
North Steyne Surf Club, North Steyne, Manly, NSW 2095
Tel 02 9977 6977
www.manlysurfschool.com
Learn to surf at Manly Beach. Wetsuits and surfboards are provided.
Manly Wharf (regular ferries from Circular Quay) Daily 11–1 A$50 (2 hours), A$80 (1 day), A$250 (10 days), private lessons A$80 (per hour)

SYDNEY AQUATIC CENTRE
Olympic Boulevard, Sydney Olympic Park, Homebush, NSW 2127
Tel 02 9752 3666
www.sydneyaquaticcentre.com.au
Two 50m swimming pools, water slides, spray jets and other fun water activities.
From Lidcombe and Strathfield Olympic Park Homebush (by

Rivercat) Mon–Fri 5am–8.45pm, Sat–Sun 6am–7.45pm Adult A$5.80, child A$4.60, family A$18.50

SYDNEY CRICKET GROUND (SCG)
Driver Avenue, Moore Park, NSW 2021
Tel 02 9339 0999
www.sydneycricketground.com.au
One-day international and Test cricket matches; Australian Rules football takes over in winter. See page 65.

Moore Park Cricket: adult from A$46, child from A$21. Australian Rules: adult from A$19.50

SYDNEY INTERNATIONAL TENNIS CENTRE
Rod Laver Drive, Sydney Olympic Park, Homebush, NSW 2127
Tel 02 8746 0777 (02 8746 0444 for court hire)
www.sydneytennis.com.au
Play on one of 16 courts at this world-class tennis venue, or watch the professionals at state, national and international tournaments.
From Lidcombe and Strathfield Olympic Park Courts: Mon–Fri 6.30am–10.30pm, Sat–Sun 7.30–7; booking essential A$15 an hour 8–6, A$18 an hour 6–10pm

SYDNEY BY SAIL

National Maritime Museum, 2 Murray Street, Darling Harbour, NSW 2000
Tel 02 9280 1110
www.sydneybysail.com

Get afloat on Sydney Harbour with learn-to-sail courses, charters and overnight trips.

🅾 Office, daily 8.30–6 🚌 Explorer bus (stop 19) 🚡 Harbourside (monorail) 🚢 Pyrmont Wharf 🎫 3-hour harbour cruises from A$120, learn-to-sail courses from A$450, social racing from A$45

Children

COFFS HARBOUR

THE BIG BANANA

Pacific Highway, Coffs Harbour, NSW 2450
Tel 02 6652 4355
www.bigbanana.com

A massive concrete banana is the symbol of this theme park. There's a railway, ice rink, snow slope and toboggan rides.

🅾 Daily 9–4.30 🎫 Free; fee for activities 🅿

JAMBEROO

JAMBEROO RECREATION PARK

Jamberoo Road, Jamberoo, NSW 2533
Tel 02 4236 0114
www.jamberoo.net

Enjoy waterslides, bobsleds, racing cars, speed boats, a chairlift, train ride and mini-golf.

🅾 Sat–Sun, school and public holidays 10–5 🎫 Adult A$26, child A$23 (under 4s free) 🍴 🅿

SYDNEY

LOLLIPOPS PLAYLAND

Fox Studios, Driver Avenue, Moore Park, NSW 1363
Tel 02 9331 0811
www.lollipopsplayland.com.au

A multistorey funhouse with giant mazes, tunnels, cargo nets, ball pits and more.

🅾 Mon–Fri 9.30–7 (also Fri 7–8pm), Sat 9–8, Sun 9–7 🚌 Moore Park 🎫 Child (1–2) A$7.90, (2–9) A$10.90, adult A$4 🅿

SYDNEY AQUARIUM
See page 62.

WONDERLAND SYDNEY
See page 71.

Festivals and Events

JANUARY

The Sydney Festival is the main performing arts festival, strong on outdoor events such as Symphony in the Park (*www.sydneyfestival.com.au*).

MARCH

Sydney's Mardi Gras celebrates all things gay and lesbian with parades of outrageous floats. (*www.mardigras.org.au*).

Canberra Balloon Fiesta is the southern hemisphere's biggest gathering of hot-air balloons (*www.canberraballoonfiesta.com.au*).

APRIL

Agriculture is the theme at the Royal Easter Show at Sydney's Homebush Showground (*www.eastershow.com.au*).

MAY

Local and international authors take part in the Sydney Writers' Festival (*www.swf.org.au*).

Mercedes Australian Fashion Week, in Sydney, shows off the spring/summer collection of Australia's leading designers (*www.mafw.com.au*).

JUNE

The Sydney Film Festival shows all kinds of films from Australia and overseas (*www.sydneyfilmfestival.org*).

AUGUST

Thousands take part in the Sun-Herald City to Surf, a 14km (8.5-mile) fun run that starts in the city and finishes at Bondi (*www.smh.com.au/marketing/citytosurf*).

SEPTEMBER

The Mudgee Wine Celebration at Mudgee in the Central Ranges includes public tastings, arts and markets (*www.mudgeewine.com.au*).

The Australian Jockey Club stages its Spring Racing Carnival (*www.ajc.org.au*).

Opera in the Vineyards is the Hunter Valley's annual feast of wine, food, music and song at the Wyndham Estate winery, a 2-hour drive north of Sydney (*www.wyndhamestate.com.au*).

Floriade is a Canberra flower festival (*www.floriadeaustralia.com*).

OCTOBER

Jazz in the Vines is a jazz festival in late October at Tyrrells Wines in the Hunter Valley (*www.jazzinthevines.com.au*).

DECEMBER

On Boxing Day, thousands line Sydney Harbour for the start of the Sydney to Hobart Yacht Race (*www.cyca.com.au*).

Spectacular fireworks against a harbour backdrop set Sydney's New Year's Eve festivities apart (*www.newyearseve.com.au*).

WHAT TO DO

VICTORIA

If you're interested in shopping and sporting activities, then head to Melbourne and the state of Victoria. Melbourne is regarded by many as the shopping capital of Australia—Australians come from other states to shop.

Melbourne's Moomba Waterfest, a free, family festival held every March

Melbourne has distinct shopping areas: Bridge Road and Swan Street in Richmond are famous for discount shops. Chapel Street in Prahran is where young fashion designers hang out. Toorak Road in South Yarra and Toorak, High Street in Armadale and Collins Street in the city are the places to find leading Australian and international designers, while Southbank has shops selling everything from souvenirs to high fashion. There are also huge suburban shopping malls, including Chadstone (400 stores). The Queen Victoria Market is a must for all shoppers, no matter what budget.

Away from Melbourne, provincial cities have department stores and malls selling major brands of clothing, electronic goods, footwear and jewellery. You'll find locally made crafts in many towns at weekend markets.

Melbourne's sporting activities are also varied. In 2006 it will host the Commonweath Games. Melbourne Cricket Ground is the first stop for anyone interested in the Games. It's also the place for Australian Rules football in winter and cricket in summer.

Other major sporting events include the Melbourne Cup horse-race, the Australian Open tennis championship and the Australian Grand Prix. Many of the top sports venues are open to the public. You can play tennis at Melbourne Park and swim in a pool used for international events. Take a walk or run along the Yarra River and around the Botanic Gardens and you may see some of Australia's top athletes—it's a training area. Although water activities are limited because of Melbourne's cooler weather, you can still swim with the dolphins in Port Phillip Bay, and swim at the many beaches near the city.

Victoria has three major ski resorts, Mt. Buller, Falls Creek and Mt. Hotham. The season runs from June to September.

Victoria's mountain areas are popular with horse-riders. Rock-climbers go to Mt. Arapiles, while the many national parks are ideal for bushwalking.

Arts and culture are also well represented. The Victorian Arts Centre in Melbourne is the home of major productions.

Melbourne has many nightclubs, and Prahran and St. Kilda have pubs and clubs.

Shopping

DAYLESFORD

SWEET DECADENCE
57A Vincent Street, Daylesford, VIC 3460
Tel 03 5348 3202
The past winner of several tourism awards, Sweet Decadence is renowned for its handmade chocolates, cakes and novelty goods. The shop is in the middle of the pretty town of Daylesford, northeast of Ballarat. On request, staff will show visitors how the chocolates are made (weekdays only).
🕐 Daily 9.30–5 ▢

GEELONG

THE NATIONAL WOOL MUSEUM
26 Moorabool Street, Geelong, VIC 3220
Tel 03 5227 0701
www.geelongaustralia.com.au
Located in an 1872 woolstore, the museum is devoted to Australia's wool industry. The shop has a range of handmade woollen clothing such as sweaters, coats, hats and scarves. There are also pottery, glassware and souvenirs.
🕐 Daily 9.30–5 ▢ The Black Sheep Café

MELBOURNE

ACORN ANTIQUES
885–889 High Street, Armadale, VIC 3143
Tel 03 9500 0522
www.acornantiques.com.au
One of Melbourne's largest antiques showrooms, Acorn has been dealing in English and French antique furniture and decorative items for more than 20 years. The shop specializes in furniture from the 1840s to the early 20th century. Nearby are a number of other well-stocked antiques showrooms.
🕐 Mon–Sat 10–5, Sun 12–5 🚋 Tram 6

ALICE'S BOOKSHOP
629 Rathdowne Street, Carlton North, VIC 3054
Tel 03 9347 4656
www.alices.com.au

This antiquarian and second-hand bookstore has 20,000 books in four ground-level rooms. The emphasis is on the arts, literature, humanities, travel, and ancient and medieval history. Alice's also provides a free search service for out-of-print books. The shop is in Carlton North, a short tram ride from the city.
🕐 Daily 10.30–5 🚋 Trams 1, 22, 96

AUSKI

9 Hardware Lane, Melbourne, VIC 3000
Tel 03 9670 1412
www.auski.com.au

This is the place to go if you're thinking about a trip to the Victorian ski resorts. Auski hires and sells a full range of equipment, including children's and adults' clothing and skis, snowboards, walking boots, toboggans, helmets and car tyre chains. The shop is in the heart of Melbourne.
🕐 Mon–Fri 9.30–6, Sat 9.30–4, Sun (winter only) 11–4 🚋 Trams along Bourke Street

COUNTRY ROAD WAREHOUSE STORE

261 Bridge Road, Richmond, VIC 3121
Tel 03 9427 7077
www.countryroad.com.au
Country Road is one of Australia's most popular clothing and homeware brands. The Bridge Road branch sells samples, discontinued lines and previous season's men's and women's clothes, together with homeware items—all at heavily discounted prices. Bridge Road, Richmond, is Melbourne's main

area for discount outlets, so there are many other bargain-hunting possibilities nearby.
🕐 Mon–Sat 9.30–5.30 (also Thu 5.30–6pm and Fri 5.30–7pm), Sun 11–5 🚋 Tram 75 (East Burwood) or 48 (North Balwyn) from Flinders Street

DAN MURPHY'S

273 Chapel Street, Prahran, VIC 3181
Tel 03 9497 3388
www.danmurphys.com.au
Dan Murphy's is an enormous discount liquor store, with a wide range of Australian and international wines, beers and spirits. The store stocks everything from cheap wines to rare, collectable vintages. A great place to buy some of the best Australian wines.
🕐 Mon–Sat 9–8 (also Thu–Fri 8–9pm), Sun 10–6 🚋 Trams 78, 66 and 67 🚆 Prahran on Sandringham train from Flinders Street

DAVID JONES

310 Bourke Street, Melbourne, VIC 3000
Tel 03 9643 2222
www.davidjones.com.au
This is the main Melbourne city branch of the Australia-wide David Jones department store. It stocks most major Australian and international brands, and is a little more sophisticated than its competitor Myer, located across Bourke Street Mall. There is an excellent food hall.
🕐 Daily 10–6 (also Thu 6–7pm and Fri 6–9pm) 🚋 Trams along Bourke Street ♿

HENRY BUCK'S

320 Collins Street, Melbourne, VIC 3000
Tel 03 9670 9951
www.henrybucks.com.au
This menswear store has been in business for more than 110 years, mainly serving the needs of middle-aged men. It sells the company's own brands as well as imported labels, and offers a full tailoring service. It is in the heart of Melbourne city.
🕐 Mon–Fri 9–5.30 (also Fri 5.30–7pm), Sat 9–5 🚋 Trams to Collins Street

MELBOURNE MUSEUM SHOP

Carlton Gardens, Rathdowne Street, Carlton, VIC 3053
Tel 03 8341 7620
This two-level museum shop is a good place to buy reasonably priced and genuine Aboriginal items such as didgeridoos, boomerangs, shields, spears and pottery—all made in Victoria. The shop also sells general souvenirs, children's toys and books.
🕐 Daily 10.30–5 🚋 Tram 86 or 96 to Museum and Royal Exhibition Building stop, or City Circle Tram to Carlton Gardens ♿

MYER

314 Bourke Street, Melbourne, VIC 3000
Tel 03 9661 1111
www.myer.com.au

Myer is a department store that began life in Melbourne in 1911, and became part of an Australia-wide retail group in the 1980s. At Christmas, young children queue with their parents to see the Bourke Street Mall store's Yuletide window displays.
🕐 Mon–Sat 9–6 (also Thu 6–7pm and Fri 6–9pm), Sun 10–6 🚋 Trams along Bourke Street ♿

NATIONAL TRUST GIFT SHOP

Toorak Shop 13, The Village Walk, 493 Toorak Road, Toorak, VIC 3142
Tel 03 9827 9385
www.nattrust.com.au
A good selection of Australian-made products are at this shop, a fundraising venture of the National Trust, a non-profit, independent organization that works towards conserving and

protecting Australia's heritage. Many of the items are made by the volunteers who operate the shop, which is in one of Melbourne's most popular shopping precincts.

🕐 Mon–Fri 9.30–5, Sat 10–1 🚋 Tram 8

QUEEN VICTORIA MARKET
513 Elizabeth Street, Melbourne, VIC 3000
Tel 03 9320 5822
www.qvm.com.au

The Queen Victoria Market is the largest open-air market in the southern hemisphere, spread over 7ha (17 acres). About 1,000 traders sell everything from fruit and vegetables and local and imported gourmet foods, meat, fish and poultry, to hardware, clothing and authentic Australian objects and souvenirs.

🕐 Tue and Thu 6–2, Fri 6–6, Sat 6–3, Sun 9–4 🚋 Any tram heading north along Elizabeth and William streets 🚻

ST. KILDA ESPLANADE ARTS AND CRAFTS MARKET
Upper Esplanade, St. Kilda, VIC 3182
Tel 03 9209 6397

A row of colourful market umbrellas lining St. Kilda's Esplanade marks the site of the oldest art and crafts market in Melbourne. Browse for a bargain among more than 150 stalls, which mainly show handmade furniture, jewellery and accessories, metalwork, leatherwork, musical instruments, clocks, homewares and candles.

🕐 Sun 10–5 🚋 Tram 12 or 112, bus 606

WHAT TO DO

SHEPHERDS FLAT
LAVANDULA
350 Hepburn–Newstead road, Shepherds Flat, VIC 3461
Tel 03 5476 4393
www.lavandula.com.au

Near Hepburn Springs and Daylesford in central Victoria, Lavandula is a lavender farm that also includes gardens, a restaurant and farmyard animals. The shop carries a large range of home-grown lavender products, country-style goods, art and crafts, dried herbs and flowers.

🕐 Daily 10.30–5.30, Oct–May; Sat–Sun only, Jun–Sep 🍴 La Trattoria is fully licensed and serves Swiss Italian cuisine and lavender scones

TORQUAY
THE ROXY SHOP
Shop 3, Surf City Plaza, Torquay, VIC 3228
Tel 03 5261 4768
www.roxy.com

Torquay is the home of surfing in Victoria, and this surf shop sells Roxy brand clothes, swimwear, bodyboards and surfboards.

🕐 Daily 9–5.30

Performance

MELBOURNE
THE ASTOR
1 Chapel Street, St. Kilda, VIC 3182
Tel 03 9510 1414

One of Melbourne's first cinemas, the Astor opened in 1935. It now shows classic movies.

🕐 Mon–Fri 6.30–11.30, Sat 3–11.30, Sun 1–11.30 🚋 Tram or bus to Chapel Street, Prahran 🍴 Snack bar 🚻

THE COMEDY CLUB
1st floor, 180 Lygon Street, Carlton, VIC 3053
Tel 03 9348 1622, 03 9650 1977
www.thecomedyclub.com.au

This club played a major role in creating Melbourne's reputation as Australia's comedy capital. The line-up changes regularly and includes local and international stars.

🕐 Fri–Sat from 8.30pm (doors open 7pm) 🚌 Bus to Lygon Street or tram up Swanston Street, then a short walk 🍴 🚻

GASWORKS ARTS PARK
21 Graham Street, Albert Park, VIC 3206
Tel 03 8606 4206
www.gasworks.org.au

Gasworks is run by an independent community arts group and includes a 240-seat theatre and a gallery.

🚋 3km (2 miles) south of Melbourne

HER MAJESTY'S THEATRE
219 Exhibition Street, Melbourne, VIC 3000
Tel 03 8643 3300
www.hermajestystheatre.com.au

Opened in 1886, 'The Maj' remains a popular venue for ballet, opera and musicals.

🚋 Tram from Bourke Street to Exhibition Street, then a short walk 🚻

THE MALTHOUSE
113 Sturt Street, South Melbourne, VIC 3205
Tel 03 9685 5111

The Malthouse stages plays at the 499-seat Merlyn Theatre and the more intimate 196-seat Beckett Theatre.

🚋 Tram or bus to South Melbourne

PRINCESS THEATRE
163 Spring Street, Melbourne, VIC 3000
Tel 03 9299 9800
www.marrinertheatres.com.au
This beautiful Victorian theatre stages large-scale musicals and plays.
🚋 Tram along Bourke Street
🚉 Parliament 🔧

SIDNEY MYER MUSIC BOWL
Kings Domain, Linlithgow Avenue, Melbourne, VIC 3000
Tel 03 9281 8000
www.vicartscentre.com.au

This amphitheatre is tucked into the gardens of Kings Domain. It has state-of-the-art sound and lighting, and is used for free concerts in summer.
🚋 Tram along St. Kilda Road

VICTORIAN ARTS CENTRE
100 St. Kilda Road, Melbourne, VIC 3000
Tel 03 9281 8000
www.vicartscentre.com.au
The Arts Centre presents musicals, plays and concerts in a range of venues, including the 2,000-seat State Theatre and the 2,600-seat Melbourne Concert Hall.
🚋 Tram along St. Kilda Road 🔧

Nightlife

BENNETTS LANE JAZZ CLUB
25 Bennetts Lane (off Little Lonsdale Street), Melbourne, VIC 3000
Tel 03 9663 2856
Live local and international jazz acts perform at Bennetts Lane club every night.
🕐 Mon–Fri 9–midnight, Sat–Sun 8–midnight 🎫 Ticket prices vary

BOND
24 Bond Street (off Flinders Lane), Melbourne, VIC 3000
Tel 03 9629 9844
Futuristic décor with curves and lush fabrics at this chic bar.
🕐 Wed–Thu 4pm–1am, Fri 4pm–5am, Sat 8pm–5am

CROWN CASINO
8 Whiteman Street, Southbank, VIC 3006
Tel 03 9292 8888
www.crowncasino.com.au
Besides gambling, there are bars and clubs such as Fidel's Cigar Bar and Baccarat Bar.
🕐 Daily 24 hours

THE ESPLANADE HOTEL
11 The Esplanade, St. Kilda, VIC 3182
Tel 03 9534 0211
www.theesplanadehotel.com.au

A Melbourne icon, 'The Espy' is best known for its live bands. There's a great view over St. Kilda beach.
🕐 Daily until 1am 🚋 Tram to St. Kilda Beach 🎫 Cover charge for some bands

GIN PALACE
190 Little Collins Street (off Russell Place), Melbourne, VIC 3000
Tel 03 9654 0533
This plush basement bar specializes in martinis.
🕐 Daily 4pm–3am

HEAT DISCOTHEQUE AND COCKTAIL BAR
Level 3, Crown, Southbank, VIC 3006
Tel 03 9699 2222
www.heatdisco.com.au
A glitzy spot by the Yarra River with DJs and live bands.
🕐 Daily 9pm–late 🎫 Mon–Thu A$10, Fri–Sun A$12

THE LAUNDRY
50 Johnston Street, Fitzroy, VIC 3065
Tel 03 9419 7111
www.laundry.melb.net

DJs and bands play dance music at this informal venue. Dirty Laundry (Tuesday) is popular with the gay community.
🕐 3pm–3am most nights 🚋 Tram 96 (East Brunswick) or 112 (West Preston) 🎫 Small cover charge some nights

THE MARKET
143 Commercial Road, South Yarra, VIC 3141
Tel 03 9826 0933
www.markethotel.com.au
Popular with gay clubbers, the Market has live shows and the latest DJs.
🕐 Thu–Fri and Sun 9pm–late, Sat 10pm–10am 🚋 Tram 72 🎫 Non-members nightly A$3 before midnight, A$5–12 after midnight

MELBOURNE SUPPER CLUB
161 Spring Street, Melbourne, VIC 3000
Tel 03 9654 6300
A sophisticated place overlooking Parliament House.
🕐 Tue–Fri 5pm–4am (also Fri 4–6am), Sat 8pm–6am, Sun–Mon 8pm–4am
🚋 Trams along Bourke Street
🚉 Parliament

METRO NIGHTCLUB
20 Bourke Street, Melbourne, VIC 3000
Tel 03 9663 4288
www.metronightclub.com
With seven bars, the Metro is one of the largest nightclubs in the southern hemisphere. Live bands Thursday and Saturday.
🕐 Thu 9–late, Fri–Sat 10–late 🚋 Trams along Bourke Street 🎫 A$8 Thu, A$10 Fri–Sat

Sports and Activities

WATSON'S MOUNTAIN COUNTRY TRAIL RIDES
Three Chain Road, Mansfield, VIC 3724
Tel 03 5777 3552
www.watsontrailrides.com.au
Saddle up and explore the hills of the high country around Mansfield. Guided rides from 1 hour to a full day.
From A$30 per person for 1 hour

MELBOURNE

BALLOON SUNRISE
Stephenson Street parking area (behind Depot Hotel), Richmond, VIC 3122
Tel 03 9427 7596
www.balloonsunrise.com.au
Watch the sun rise over central Melbourne from a hot-air balloon. Breakfast is served after the hour-long flight.
Depart at dawn; meeting time confirmed the day before Richmond Adult from A$265, child A$175

FLEMINGTON RACECOURSE
Epsom Road, Flemington, VIC 3031
Tel 03 9371 7171
www.vrc.net.au
Home of the Melbourne Cup, Australia's premier horse race.
2 hours prior to first race Flemington Racecourse Adult from A$7, depending on event Northwest of the city

MELBOURNE CRICKET GROUND (MCG)
Jolimont Terrace, Jolimont, VIC 3002
Tel 03 9657 8879
www.mcg.org.au
Cricket (in summer) and Australian Rules football (in winter) are the major draws at Australia's biggest sports stadium. See page 85.
Trams 75 and 48 Jolimont, Richmond

MELBOURNE PARK
Batman Avenue, Melbourne, VIC 3000
Tel 03 9286 1244
www.melbournepark.com.au
Play on the courts used during the Australian Open. The com-

plex includes three show courts, 19 outdoor and four indoor courts.

Tennis: Mon–Fri 7am–11pm, Sat–Sun 9–6 Tram 70 Jolimont, Richmond Court hire from A$18 per hour

MELBOURNE SPORTS AND AQUATIC CENTRE
Aughtie Drive, Albert Park, VIC 3206
Tel 03 9926 1545
www.msac.com.au
This large sports venue has Olympic-sized pools, a wave pool, water slide, diving boards, and halls for everything from basketball to badminton, squash and yoga.
Swimming complex: Mon–Fri 5.30am–8pm, Sat–Sun 7am–8pm Tram 12 Wright Street on light rail 96 Swimming: adult from A$5.50, child from A$4.10. Squash: from A$19 per hour. Basketball court: from A$29

STRIKE ON CHAPEL
325 Chapel Street, Prahran, VIC 3181
Tel 03 9573 9573
www.strikeonchapel.com
This 10-pin bowling alley has public and private lanes, and also a bar, lounge, pool tables, games and karaoke.
Daily 10am–3am Trams 78, 79 Prahran From A$12 per game

NAGAMBIE

SKYDIVE NAGAMBIE
1232 Kettels Road, Nagambie, VIC 3608
Tel 03 5794 1466
www.skydivenagambie.com.au
Experience the thrill of skydiving in a solo or tandem jump. Just a 1-hour drive north of Melbourne.
Daily by appointment From A$295

THE DUNES GOLF LINKS
Browns Road, Rye, VIC 3941
Tel 03 5985 1334
www.thedunes.com.au
One of the best public 18-hole courses in Victoria.
Daily dawn–dusk 9 holes: adult from A$25, juniors from A$18

SORRENTO

POLPERRO DOLPHIN SWIMS
Sorrento Pier, Esplanade, Sorrento, VIC 3943
Tel 03 5988 8437
www.polperro.com.au
Watch or swim with bottlenose dolphins and seals in Port Phillip Bay.
Daily trips 8.30am and 1.30pm, Oct–Apr Dolphin watch: adult A$40, child A$27.50. Dolphin swim: A$95

TORQUAY

WESTCOAST SURF SCHOOL
Voss's Car Park, Torquay, VIC 3228
Tel 03 5261 2241
www.westcoastsurfschool.com
Surfing tuition for all ages and abilities at Torquay, one of the country's best surfing locations.
Daily classes 10–12 in summer school holidays and Easter, or on demand Adult from A$40, child (under 16) from A$30

Children

BALLARAT
SOVEREIGN HILL
See page 92.

MELBOURNE
MELBOURNE AQUARIUM
See page 85.

MELBOURNE ZOO
See page 88.

PUFFING BILLY
Old Monbulk Road, Belgrave, VIC 3160
Tel 03 9754 6800
www.puffingbilly.com.au
Take a ride on a steam train through 25km (15 miles) of rural scenery, including forests and fern gullies. There is also a lunch special and a night (wine and dine) special.
🕐 Daily 9–5 🚂 From A$7.50 (for a child, one-way, on a single section) to A$77 (for family, return, entire distance); extra for specials—booking essential 🚉 Belgrave

SCIENCEWORKS MUSEUM
See page 90.

PHILLIP ISLAND
PHILLIP ISLAND PENGUIN PARADE
Summerland Beach, Phillip Island, VIC 3922
Tel 03 5956 8300
www.phillipisland.net.au
Watch penguins emerge from the water at sunset and waddle across the beach to their burrows in the sand dunes. See page 95.
🕐 Daily from dusk 🐧 Penguin parade and visitor centre: adult A$15, child (under 4s free) A$7.50, family A$37.50

Festivals and Events

JANUARY
The world's hottest tennis players are at the Australian Open at Melbourne Park (*www.aus open.org*).
FEBRUARY
Melbourne's Chinese community celebrates the Chinese New Year Festival in Little Bourke Street.
MARCH
The Foster's Australian Grand Prix takes place on a street circuit at Albert Park, Melbourne. (*www.grandprix.com.au*).
Port Fairy Folk Festival is the premier folk music event in Australia (*www.portfairyfolk festival.com*).
The Superbike World Championships at Phillip

Island Circuit is an international event, with many high-profile riders (*www.phillip islandcircuit.com.au*).
The Melbourne International Comedy Festival stages more than 180 different shows and 2,000 performances (*www.comedyfestival.com.au*).
APRIL
The Melbourne International Flower and Garden Show at the Royal Exhibition Building and Carlton Gardens has more than 300 exhibitors and 10,000 cut flowers (*www. meldflowershow.com.au*).
Each year the world's top-ranked surf riders carve up the waves at Bells Beach in the Rip Curl Pro and SunSmart Classic (*www.surfvic.org.au*).

JULY–AUGUST
The Melbourne International Film Festival presents work from film-makers worldwide (*www.melbournefilmfestival. com.au*).
SEPTEMBER
The Royal Melbourne Show at Ascot Vale has animals and events, produce, art and crafts, and entertainment (*www.roy alshow. com.au*).
AFL Grand Final fever reaches its pitch at the MCG.
SEPTEMBER–OCTOBER
The Melbourne Fringe Festival celebrates the best arts fringe performers (*www.melbourne fringe.com.au*).

OCTOBER
The Melbourne Festival has an outstanding reputation for its attractions at various venues (*www.melbournefesti val.com.au*).

NOVEMBER
The Melbourne Cup horse race is an extremely popular sporting and social event. It is run on the first Tuesday in November—a public holiday in Victoria (*www.vrc.net.au*).

WHAT TO DO

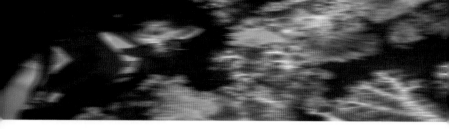

QUEENSLAND

Of all the states, Queensland—and the Gold Coast in particular—is one of the best places for families, thanks to its theme parks. It's also one of the best areas in Australia for anyone wanting to encounter water on their vacation. While other states also have great aquatic opportunities, Queensland has the infrastructure to make diving, snorkelling and sailing easily accessible.

Fun afloat at the Wet'n'Wild Water World theme park on the Gold Coast

Even though the Gold Coast may be a little over-developed, there's no doubt it is great for families. As well as theme parks there are 17 other themed attractions from wildlife parks to tropical plantations. It's also great for surfers, with 70km (45 miles) of coastline, including 35 beaches and Australia's largest expanse of calm waters.

The Gold Coast includes Queensland's largest shopping malls—Pacific Fair and Robina Town Centre—and more than 20 markets.

Brisbane has good shops, with most variety in Queens Street Mall. Paddington is famous for antiques, books and crafts, while Fortitude Valley is the place for contemporary art, as well as live music venues, clubs and pubs.

Take a trip to the 15ha (40-acre) South Bank Parklands where there's a palm-fringed swimming lagoon, shops, museums and markets. Some of Queensland's best-known animal parks are also easily accessible from Brisbane.

Noosa, on the Sunshine Coast, has a number of good quality boutiques and good markets close by. Morning walkers in Noosa National Park are often rewarded with close experiences with koalas. And whales can be watched from Hervey Bay.

At the Great Barrier Reef you can take air and boat tours to the reef and the many islands off the coast, along with windsurfing and water-skiing, paraflying and scuba-diving.

A great way to explore the Whitsunday Islands is to rent a sailboat; there are more than 70 islands to explore.

Reef and open-sea fishing are other pursuits, and Cairns has a game-fishing centre.

Cairns and Port Douglas are the best-known bases from where to explore the Great Barrier Reef. There are great markets here too. If you want to get away from the water, Daintree rainforest is accessible from Cairns, while horse-riding and biking are other popular activities.

Shopping

AUSTRALIAN WOOLSHED
148 Samford Road, Ferny Hills, QLD 4055
Tel 07 3872 1100
www.auswoolshed.com.au
The Woolshed's retail outlet, the Supply Store, stocks Australian-grown and -made products, including woollen clothing, sheepskin products and toys. The shop is in a northwest Brisbane suburb.
Mon–Sun 8.30–4 Ferny Grove

CRAFT VILLAGE MARKET
Stanley Street Plaza, South Bank Parklands, Brisbane, QLD 4101
Tel 07 3867 2051
www.ezeonline.com.au/southbank/southbank.asp
This open-air market features more than 130 stalls selling local produce and crafts—hats, jewellery, clothing, pottery, woodcraft and homewares—all home made. The South Bank Parklands are great for a stroll before or after shopping.
Fri 5–10pm, Sat 11–5, Sun 9–5
South Bank

PADDINGTON ANTIQUE CENTRE
167 LaTrobe Terrace, Paddington, QLD 4064
Tel 07 3369 8088
www.uqconnect.new/~zzpac/index.html
Occupying a former theatre built in 1929, Paddington Antique Centre has around 60 dealers. There are other antiques shops nearby.
Daily 10–5 Paddington (stop 11)

QUEENSLAND ABORIGINAL CREATIONS
Shop 1, cnr Little Stanley and Tribune streets, Southbank, Brisbane, QLD 4000
Tel 07 3224 5730
This shop, in the Queensland Department of Aboriginal and Torres Strait Islander Policy and Development, has a comprehensive selection of authentic Aboriginal objects and crafts. Items for sale include

boomerangs, didgeridoos, paintings, children's story books and clothing. You'll can learn about Aboriginal history.
⊙ Tue–Fri 10–5.30 (also Fri 5.30–8pm), Sat 10–5, Sun 10–4; closed Mon
▣ South Bank ▣ South Brisbane

QUILPIE OPALS
68 Queen Street, Brisbane, QLD 4000
Tel 07 3221 5789
www.quilpieopals.com.au
One of Queensland's best-known opal retailers, Quilpie Opals offers a lifetime guarantee on the workmanship of its jewellery and a certificate of authenticity for each item you buy. The shop in the heart of Brisbane sells many varieties of opal and settings. Stones can be bought individually or in jewellery pieces. You can also design your own jewellery.
⊙ Mon–Sat 9–6, Sun 10–2 ▣ Queen Street ▣ Queen Street Mall

BUNDABERG
SCHMEIDER'S COOPERAGE
3–7 Alexandra Street, East Bundaberg, QLD 4670
Tel 07 4151 8233
www.schmeider.bizland.com

Schmeider's Cooperage houses one of the largest selections of woodwork in Australia. Spinners, weavers, glassblowers, jewellers, potters and leatherworkers also display and sell their products here. You can walk through the woodwork workshop or watch glassblowing at the leisure centre.
⊙ Mon–Fri 9–5, Sat–Sun 9–3
▣ Bundaberg ▣

CAIRNS
CAIRNS NIGHT MARKETS
71–75 The Esplanade, Cairns, QLD 4870
Tel 07 4051 7666
www.nightmarkets.com.au
Cairns has several markets, but the Night Markets off the Esplanade are one of the most popular. They sell a wide range of manufactured and hand-made items, including clothing, toys, gifts, jewellery, opals and paintings.
⊙ Daily 5–11

GEO PICKERS CAMPING AND CANVAS
Shop 270 Mulgrave Road, Westcourt, QLD 4870
Tel 07 4051 1944
This shop sells and rents camping goods and specialist equipment, including tents, cooking utensils, clothing, mosquito hats and repellants—ideal for anyone off to explore north Queensland.
⊙ Mon–Fri 8.30–5, Sat 8.30–1

PRO-DIVE CAIRNS
Cnr Shield and Abbot streets, Cairns, QLD 4870
Tel 07 4031 6681
www.prodive-cairns.com.au
Pro-Dive, in the heart of Cairns, offers tuition for beginners and advice and dive trips for the experienced. The shop sells wetsuits, stinger bodysuits, snorkelling equipment, dive gear and souvenirs such as videos and T-shirts.
⊙ Daily 8.30am–9pm

TJAPUKAI ART GALLERY AND REGIONAL STORE
Kamerunga Road, Smithfield, QLD 4878
Tel 07 4042 9900
www.tjapukai.com.au
Part of the Tjapukai Aboriginal Cultural Park, one of Cairns' most popular tourist attractions, the store sells Aboriginal artworks and materials from Far North Queensland. Items include paintings, pottery, clapsticks, handcrafted emu eggs, didgeridoos and boomerangs.
⊙ Shop: daily 8.30–5.30. Park: daily 9–5 ▣

EUMUNDI
EUMUNDI MARKETS
Main Street, Eumundi, QLD 4562
Every Saturday morning the main street of the small town of Eumundi, in the Sunshine Coast hinterland, comes alive with more than 300 stalls selling everything from freshly grown produce to homemade crafts. Markets are also held on Wednesday and Sunday, but Saturday's is the main market. It pays to get there early as the markets become crowded as the morning goes on.
⊙ Sat 6.30–12.30

GOLD COAST
ART AND CRAFT MARKETS
Broadbeach, Coolangatta and Burleigh beaches
Tel 07 5533 8202
www.artandcraft.com.au

More than 200 outdoor stalls display a wide variety of locally handmade products, ideal for souvenirs and gifts. The markets are set up on the beachfront on the first and third Sunday of the month at Broadbeach, the second Sunday at Coolangatta and the last Sunday at Burleigh.
⊙ 8–2.30

BILLABONG SHOWROOM
1 Billabong Place, West Burleigh, QLD 4219
Tel 07 5589 9880.
www.billabong.com.au
Billabong is one of Australia's top brands of surfwear, now known worldwide. At this showroom you can buy all the equipment you may need for a

SHOPPING 197

beachside vacation, including bikinis and boardshorts. The staff are keen surfers and can offer advice.

🕐 Mon–Sat 9–5.30, Sun 10.30–4

DAVID JONES WAREHOUSE
Cnr Gold Coast Highway and Oxley Drive, Biggera Waters, QLD 4216
Tel 07 5561 5555
www.davidjones.com.au
This discount outlet of the David Jones department store is within the Harbour Town Outlet Shopping Centre on the Gold Coast Highway, which houses around 40 discount stores. David Jones sells ladies' fashions, menswear, shoes, accessories, childrenswear and homewares at prices lower than at their other stores.

🕐 Mon–Sat 9–5.30 (also Thu 5.30–7pm), Sun 10–5

KURANDA
KURANDA MARKETS
7 Therwine Street, Kuranda, QLD 4872
Tel 07 4093 7639
A tropical North Queensland institution, these breezy, relaxed markets near Cairns have handmade goods and artworks. Items can be packed ready for transport overseas.

🕐 Wed–Fri and Sun 9–3 🚆 Kuranda

PORT DOUGLAS
ANZAC PARK MARKET
Anzac Park, Wharf Street, Port Douglas, QLD 4871
The emphasis at this popular market is on handmade goods, including jewellery, clothing, crafts, pottery and painting. There are several food stalls.

🕐 Sun 6.30–4

Performance

BRISBANE
BRISBANE ARTS THEATRE
210 Petrie Terrace, Brisbane, QLD 4000
Tel 07 3369 2344 (Wed–Fri 1.30–5, Sat 11.30–3.30)
www.brisbane247.com/artstheatre
The 'Arts' is a venue popular with locals and visitors, who come for comedy, theatre and musicals.

🚆 Roma Street 🅿

BRISBANE ENTERTAINMENT CENTRE
Melaleuca Drive, Boondall, QLD 4034
Tel 07 3265 8111
www.brisent.com.au
International stars draw the crowds to this venue, 16km (10 miles) north from the city itself.

🚆 Boondall (Brisbane city council buses) 🚆 Boondall 🍴 🛍

QUEENSLAND PERFORMING ARTS CENTRE
Cnr Grey and Melbourne streets, South Bank, QLD 4101
Tel 07 3840 7444
www.qpat.com.au
Theatre, dance, opera, musicals, plays and classical music are performed at this modern arts venue.

🚆 South Bank 🚆 South Bank 🍴 🛍 🎭

CAIRNS
CAIRNS CIVIC THEATRE
Cnr Florence and Sheridan streets, Cairns, QLD 4870
Tel 07 4031 9955
Cairns' main venue for drama, musicals and visiting drama groups.

GOLD COAST
GOLD COAST ARTS CENTRE
135 Bundall Road, Surfers Paradise, QLD 4217
Tel 07 5581 6500
www.gcac.com.au
Here you will find two cinemas, a theatre and comedy club.

🕐 Restaurant, café and 500-seat cabaret-style venue: daily 9am–11pm
🍴 🛍

Nightlife

BRISBANE
THE BEAT NIGHTCLUB
677 Ann Street, Fortitude Valley, QLD 4006
Tel 07 3852 2661
A long-standing nightclub with three beer gardens. Upstairs is a gay venue.

🕐 Daily 8pm–5am 🚆 Fortitude Valley
💲 A$6 Sun–Thu, A$8 Fri–Sat, cover charge after 10.30pm

EMPIRE HOTEL NIGHTCLUB
339 Brunswick Street, Fortitude Valley, VIC 4006
Tel 07 3852 1216
A smart cocktail bar and nightclub with local and international DJs.

🕐 Cocktail bar: Mon–Sat 5pm–5am, Sun 5pm–3am. Nightclub: Mon–Thu 10pm–5am, Fri–Sat 9pm–5am, Sun 9pm–3am 🚆 Fortitude Valley
💲 Nightclub entrance fee A$10 after 10

HOTEL WICKHAM
308 Wickham Street, Fortitude Valley, QLD 4006
Tel 07 3852 1301

This gay and lesbian pub has a gaming room, drag shows and DJs every night.

🕐 Gaming room: from 9am. Hotel: Sun–Mon noon–midnight, Tue–Thu noon–2am, Fri–Sat noon–5am
🚆 Fortitude Valley

JAZZ CLUB
1 Annie Street, Kangaroo Point, QLD 4169
Tel 07 339 12006
Local and international jazz musicians play in a venue that overlooks the Brisbane River.

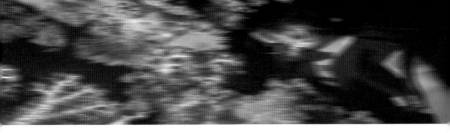

⏰ Sat 8–11.30pm, Sun 1.30–4.30pm
🚢 Ferry from Eagle Street ⚡ Members A$7, guests A$12

MARY STREET NIGHTCLUB AND BUZZARDS BAR
138 Mary Street, Brisbane, QLD 4000
Tel 07 3221 1511
DJs present music four nights a week.
⏰ Wed–Sat 9pm–5am ⚡ A$7

STADIUM NIGHTCLUB
183 Given Terrace, Paddington, QLD 4064
Tel 07 3369 6200
Music from the Top 40.
⏰ Thu–Sat 7pm–5am 🚏 Paddington

TREASURY CASINO
Queen Street Mall, Brisbane, QLD 4000
Tel 07 3306 8888
www.conrad.com.au
Brisbane's casino has bars, live entertainment and restaurants.
⏰ Daily 24 hours 🚏 Queen Street
🚏 Queen Street Mall

THE ZOO
711 Ann Street, Fortitude Valley, QLD 4006
Tel 07 3854 1381
Local and international cabaret, comedy acts and bands.
⏰ Wed–Sat 8pm–2am, occasionally Sun 8pm–midnight 🚏 Fortitude Valley
⚡ Normally A$12; depends on the act

CAIRNS

REEF CASINO
35–41 Wharf Street, Cairns 4870
07 4030 8888
www.reefcasino.com.au
A full range of gaming tables, bars and clubs.
⏰ Mon–Thu 10am–4am, continuously Fri 10am–Mon 4am

TROPOS
Cnr Lake and Spence streets, Cairns, QLD 4870
Tel 07 4031 2530
www.troposnightclub.com
DJs play the latest dance music at this popular nightclub.
⏰ Daily 8pm–3am (also Fri–Sat 3–5am)
⚡ A$6

THE WOOLSHED
City Place, Cairns, QLD 4870
Tel 07 4031 6304
A raucous backpackers' haunt with Top 40 hits and classics.
⏰ Sun–Thu 6pm–3am, Fri–Sat 6pm–5am ⚡ A$6 after 10

GOLD COAST

JUPITERS CASINO
Broadbeach Island, Gold Coast, QLD 4218
Tel 07 5592 8100
www.conrad.com.au
The casino has bars, live entertainment and restaurants.
⏰ Daily 24 hours 🚏 Broadbeach Island

MELBA'S ON THE PARK
46 Cavill Avenue, Surfers Paradise, QLD 4217
Tel 07 5592 6922
Top 40 music at one of the largest bars on the Gold Coast.
⏰ Daily 7pm–5am ⚡ Varies

SUNSHINE COAST

ROLLING ROCK NIGHTCLUB/ NEW YORK BAR
Bay Village, Hastings Street, Noosa Heads, QLD 4567
Tel 07 5447 2255
www.rollingrock.com.au

Dance to DJs and live bands, or relax in the cocktail bar.
⏰ Sun–Thu 9pm–late, Fri–Sat 8pm–late

Sports and Activities

AIRLIE BEACH

PROSAIL
Waterson Road, Airlie Beach, QLD 4802
Tel 07 4946 5433
www.prosail.com.au

Let an experienced crew take you on a three-day cruise on a schooner among the sun-drenched Whitsunday Islands.
⏰ Departs Thu and Sun ⚡ A$575 per person for 2 nights

BRISBANE

SUNCORP STADIUM
Milton, Brisbane, QLD 4000
Tel 07 3858 9111 (Brisbane Broncos), 07 3404 6726 (Ticketek)
www.broncos.com.au

Watch Brisbane's rugby league team, the Broncos, at their home ground.
⏰ Check with Broncos 🚏 Milton
⚡ Adult from A$19.50, child from A$8

CAIRNS

A. J. HACKETT BUNGY TOWER
MacGregor Road, Smithfield, QLD 4870
Tel 07 4057 7188
www.ajhackett.com.au

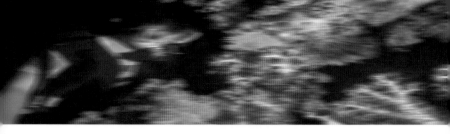

Bungee jump from a 50m (164ft) tower amid rainforest 15km (9.5 miles) north of Cairns; minimum age is 10.

🕐 Daily 10–5 🚌 Pick-up service at 9.15, noon and 3 (call to book) 💲 From A$109

ANGSANA RESORT SPA
1 Veivers Road, Palm Cove, QLD 4879
Tel 07 4055 3000
www.angsana.com

The spa, facing the beach at Palm Cove just north of Cairns, has individual treatments and pampering packages.

🕐 Daily 9am–10pm 🚌 Bus from central Palm Cove passes entrance 💲 Facials from A$95, massages from A$110 🍴 🛍

PARADISE PALMS GOLF COURSE
Paradise Palms Drive, Clifton Beach, QLD 4879
Tel 07 4059 1166
www.paradisepalms.com.au

A demanding 18-hole course.

🕐 Tee times 6.30–3.40 💲 A$120, including motorized cart and clubhouse facilities 🍴 🛍 23km (14.5 miles) north from Cairns

REEF MAGIC CRUISES
Shop 13, Hides Corner, Shields Street, Cairns, QLD 4870
Tel 07 4031 1588
www.reefmagiccruises.com

Board the catamaran *Reef Magic* to the outer Barrier Reef for five hours for snorkelling or scuba-diving. Basic scuba lessons are provided.

🕐 Tours depart daily at 9am 💲 Adult from A$109, child A$69, family A$320

R'N'R WHITE-WATER RAFTING
107 Draper Street, Cairns, QLD 4870
Tel 07 4051 7777
www.raft.com.au

Brave the rapids of the Tully River on half- or full-day trips. Rafters must be 13 or over.

🕐 Tully River tours daily 💲 Half-day from A$83, full-day from A$135, from Mission Beach or Cairns (A$10 extra)

FRASER ISLAND
THE FRASER ISLAND COMPANY
Tel 07 4125 3933
www.fraserislandco.com.au

Join your guide aboard a 4WD bus to explore Fraser Island. See page 109.

🕐 Depart daily at 8.25am 💲 Adult A$99, child A$55

GOLD COAST
PALM MEADOWS
Palm Meadows Drive, Carrara, QLD 4211
Tel 07 5594 2450
www.palmmeadows.com.au

An 18-hole tournament golf course designed by the Australian golfer Greg Norman.

🕐 Tee times 7–9, 11.30–1.30 💲 A$110 per player, A$65 pe junior playing with adult, including motorized cart 🍴 🛍

WALKIN' ON WATER SURF SCHOOL
Greenmount Beach, near Coolangatta
Tel 07 5534 1886
www.walkinonwater.com

Board-riding basics from the surf experts at Greenmount, one of the Gold Coast's best beaches.

🕐 Daily from about 6am (summer) 🚌 Surfside Bus Lines, alight at Twin Towns Services Club 💲 From A$40 for a 2-hour group lesson, A$65 personal lesson, equipment included

HERVEY BAY
HERVEY BAY WHALE WATCH
Lot 7, Urangan Street, Hervey Bay, QLD 4655

Tel 07 4128 9611
www.whalewatchingaustralia.com

Half-day cruises on a catamaran to see humpback whales.

🕐 Departs daily at 8am and 1pm, late Jul–early Nov 💲 Adult A$70, child A$45, family A$195

PORT DOUGLAS
QUICKSILVER CONNECTIONS
Marina Mirage, Port Douglas, QLD 4871
Tel 07 4087 2100
www.quicksilver-cruises.com

A catamaran whisks you to the outer Barrier Reef for diving or snorkelling. You can also view the reef from an underwater observatory.

🕐 Depart 10am, return 4.30pm (hotel pick-up from Cairns to Mossman) 💲 Adult from A$174, child A$87

SUNSHINE COAST
SUNCOAST SAFARIS
PO Box 162, Noosa Heads, QLD 4567
Tel 07 5474 0800
www.suncoastsafaris.com.au

Six-seater land cruisers take visitors on day tours to Fraser Island. See page 109.

🕐 Depart daily 6.30am, return by 4.30 💲 A$154 per seat

THE SUN SPA
Warran Road, Coolum Beach, QLD 4573
tel 07 5446 1234
www.coolum.regency.hyatt.com

The Sun Spa, part of the Hyatt Regency resort at Coolum, has more than 100 treatments, including massages.

🕐 Daily 6.30am–7pm 💲 From A$80 for a 1-hour massage 🍴 🛍

Children

BEERWAH
AUSTRALIA ZOO
Glasshouse Mountains Tourist Route, Beerwah, QLD 4519
tel 07 5494 1134
www.crocodilehunter.com

Australia Zoo is home to Steve Irwin, TV's Crocodile Hunter, and hundreds of native and exotic animals, including koalas, wallabies, snakes, alligators and crocodiles.

🕐 Daily 8.30–4 🚌 Buses available 🚌 Beerwah; free pick-up can be

arranged Adult A$23, child A$14, family A$65

BRISBANE

LONE PINE KOALA SANCTUARY
Jesmond Road, Fig Tree Pocket, Brisbane, QLD 4069
Tel 07 3378 1366
www.koala.net
See page 103.
Daily 8.30–5 430 half-hourly from Myer Centre, Queen Street Mall, Brisbane Mirimar Cruises from city Adult A$15, child A$10, family A$38

GOLD COAST

DREAMWORLD
Dreamworld Parkway, Coomera, QLD 4209
Tel 07 5588 1111
www.dreamworld.com.au
See page 115.
Daily 10–5 Brisbane–Gold Coast buses stop here. Shuttle services from major Surfers Paradise hotels Coomera then bus Adult A$56, child A$36

SEA WORLD
Sea World Drive, The Spit, Main Beach, QLD 4217
Tel 07 5588 2222
www.seaworld.com.au
See page 115.
Daily 9.30–5; rides 10–5 The Spit Adult A$56, child A$36

WARNER BROS. MOVIE WORLD
Oxenford, Gold Coast, QLD 4210
Tel 07 5573 3999
www.movieworld.com.au
See page 115.
Daily 9.30–5.30. Rides 10–5 Surfside Bus Lines shuttle, tel 131230 Helensvale then bus Adult A$56, child A$36. Superpass (entry to Movie World, Wet'n'Wild and Sea World, with a return visit to the park of your choice): adult A$147, child A$94

WET'N'WILD WATER WORLD
Pacific Motorway, Oxenford, QLD 4210
Tel 07 5573 2255
www.wetnwild.com.au
See page 115.
Daily 10–5, Nov–Feb (also 5–9pm Dec 27–Jan 26); 10–4.30, Mar–Apr and Sep–Oct; 10–4, May–Aug Helensvale then bus Adult A$35, child A$22

Festivals and Events

MARCH
For two weeks from early March, the world's best surfers compete at Burleigh Heads on the Gold Coast in the Quick-silver Pro and Roxy Pro.

The Gold Coast Festival showcases drama, film, comedy, music and cabaret over three weeks (www.gcac.com.au/goldcoastfestival).

APRIL–JULY
Australia's top horses compete in the Queensland Winter Racing Carnival (www.queenslandracing.com.au).

JULY
The Gold Coast Marathon on the first Sunday in July attracts competitors from all over the world for a full or half-marathon or 10km (6-mile) run, as well as walking and wheelchair races (www.goldcoastmarathon.com.au).

At the Cairns Show at Cairns Showgrounds you'll see animals, equestrian events, horticulture, live entertainment and sideshows (www.cairnsshow.com).

The Queensland Biennial Festival of Music presents fine performers from Australia and around the world. The festival lasts for two weeks and takes place in odd-numbered years. Performances are held in various towns and cities (www.qbfm.com.au).

AUGUST
The Royal Queensland Show is the state's main agricultural show, and is held annually at the RNA Exhibition Grounds, Bowen Hills, Brisbane. Events over the 10 days fulfil a 'country comes to the city' theme, include animal judging, exhibits, demonstrations, arena events and sideshows.

Riverfestival, on Brisbane's South Bank in late August, celebrates the Brisbane River, and includes fireworks, food and music (www.riverfestival.com.au).

Yachtsmen and women from all over the world compete in the Hahn Premium Race Week in the Whitsunday Islands (www.hiyc.org.au).

The Mount Isa Rodeo is the biggest event on Australia's rodeo calendar (www.isarodeo.com.au).

SEPTEMBER
Horses race on a dirt track at the Birdsville Races, an outback institution held on the first Saturday in September (www.birdsvilleraces.com).

The Noosa Jazz Festival at Noosa Heads features more than 100 Australian and international jazz performers (www.noosajazz.com.au).

The Brisbane Festival is a month-long international festival of dance, drama, music and the visual arts. Expect to see world premieres and world-class performers (www.brisbanefestival.com.au).

OCTOBER
In the Indy 300, the world's leading Indy car drivers race around a street circuit on the Gold Coast in late October (www.indy.com.au).

NORTHERN TERRITORY

In the Northern Territory, the active visitor is king. Apart from seeing the various national parks, you can try any of a range of adventures, including a scenic flight in a hot-air balloon over the MacDonnell Ranges, a camel ride in Alice Springs, a deep-sea fishing trip off Darwin or an overnight canoe tour of Katherine Gorge. Or you could just spend a couple of hours on a balmy evening in Darwin's outdoor cinema watching a movie while sitting in a deckchair.

A photo opportunity in Alice Springs Desert Park

Most festivals, both in Darwin and Alice Springs, are held in the winter and spring when temperatures and humidity levels are at their most pleasant. If you're in Alice Springs in September, don't miss the Henley-on-Todd Regatta, a joyful celebration of the waterlessness of this desert town's river. Alice also hosts the Camel Cup, a camel-racing carnival, in July.

Darwin is known for its outdoor markets, which sell everything from food and clothing to art and crafts. Many of the city's 50 or so different cultures use these markets to showcase their food and culture.

For many people, shopping in air-conditioned comfort will come as a welcome break from the heat and humidity of outside. The main tourist areas—Darwin, Uluru (Ayers Rock) and Alice Springs—have numerous stores selling souvenirs such as crocodile and kangaroo leather goods, and rugged Australian bushmen's clothing, from Akubra hats to R. M. Williams boots.

The strength of Aboriginal culture in the Northern Territory has resulted in reputable galleries and shops that sell good-quality Aboriginal art and handmade items, including didgeridoos.

In some shops you can watch the artists at work. A number of galleries, including two at the Uluru cultural centre, are run by Aboriginal communities, and they guarantee the authenticity of their works.

Shopping

ALICE SPRINGS

ALICE SPRINGS SOUVENIRS
64 Todd Mall, Alice Springs, NT 0870
Tel 08 8953 0222
Australian brand clothing such as R. M. Williams and Akubra, as well as Aboriginal art and crafts, boomerangs, didgeridoos and souvenirs. Purchases can be shipped overseas.
🕐 Daily 9–8

GONDWANA FINE ART GALLERY
43 Todd Mall, Alice Springs, NT 0870
Tel 08 8953 1577
www.gallerygondwana.com.au

Contemporary works of non-Aboriginal and Aboriginal artists, the latter including those from Central Australia, Cape York, the Tiwi Islands and Arnhem Land. Purchases can be shipped overseas.
🕐 Mon–Sat 9.30–1.30, 2.30–6

LEAPING LIZARD GALLERY
1/72 Todd Street, Alice Springs, NT 0870
Tel 08 8952 5552
Australian-made fine art and crafts, and goods made in Alice Springs, ranging from wood, glass and pottery to jewellery and children's clothes.
🕐 Mon–Fri 9–5.30, Sat 9–1.30 (also Sun 9–1.30, Apr–Dec)

DARWIN

MICK'S WHIPS
555 Parkin Road, Darwin River, NT 0837
Tel 08 8988 6400
www.mickswhips.com.au
Mick's Whips, an hour by road from Darwin, makes kangaroo

and crocodile leather goods such as belts, boots, hats, whips and wallets. The range of goods is also available at the Mindil Beach markets (see the whip-cracking demonstrations).

🕐 Daily from 8am, but phone first

MINDIL BEACH SUNSET MARKETS

Mindil Beach, off Gilruth Avenue, Darwin, NT 0800

Tel 08 8981 3454

www.octa4.net.au/mindil

A Darwin must-do. The bustling markets display the wares of more than 200 local craftspeople. There are also food stalls. The Thursday night markets are bigger than the Sunday markets.

🕐 Thu 5–10pm, Sun 4–9pm, May–Oct

HUMPTY DOO

THE DIDGERIDOO HUT

10 Arnhem Highway, Humpty Doo, NT 0836

Tel 08 89884457

Visitors to the Didgeridoo Hut, on a 10ha (25-acre) emu farm, can see Aboriginal artists at work and discuss their culture with them.

🕐 Daily 8–7 🚗 35km (22 miles) south-east from Darwin

ULURU (AYERS ROCK)

MARUKU ARTS

Uluru-Kata Tjuta Cultural Centre, Uluru-Kata Tjuta National Park, NT 0872

Tel 08 8956 2558/2153

www.maruku.com.au

Aboriginal artists from the Top End and Central Desert area display their works here: wooden tools and weapons, animal carvings, and paintings and jewellery. Maruku artists demonstrate their methods.

🕐 Daily 8–5.30, Oct–Mar; 8.30–5.30, rest of year

WALKATJARA ART

Uluru-Kata Tjuta Cultural Centre, Uluru-Kata Tjuta National Park, NT 0872

Tel 08 8956 2537

www.desart.com.au

This gallery is owned and operated by artists from the local Mutijulu Aboriginal community who sell ceramic vases and

plates, paintings, and T-shirts featuring local designs.

🕐 Daily 8.30–5.30

Performance

ALICE SPRINGS

THE SOUNDS OF STARLIGHT THEATRE

40 Todd Mall, Alice Springs, NT 0870

Tel 08 8953 0826

www.soundsofstarlight.com

The Sounds of Starlight show combines live music and lighting effects to evoke Central Australia's unique landscape.

🕐 Thu–Sat and Tue from 8pm (doors open 7.30) 🎟 Adult A$18, family A$60

DARWIN

DARWIN ENTERTAINMENT CENTRE

93 Mitchell Street, Darwin, NT 0800

Tel 08 8980 3366

www.darwinentcent.net.au

Darwin's main performing arts venue hosts plays, musicals and concerts.

DECKCHAIR CINEMA

Wharf Precinct, Darwin, NT 0800

Tel 08 8981 0700

www.deckchaircinema.com

Watch a movie from a deck-chair at this outdoor cinema. Bring a picnic dinner; alcohol is available on site.

🕐 Wed–Mon, Apr–Nov 🎟 Adult A$12, child A$6

Nightlife

ALICE SPRINGS

BOJANGLES SALOON

80 Todd Street, Alice Springs, NT 0870

Tel 08 8952 2873

www.boslivesaloon.com.au

Old photos, pioneers' belongings and motorbikes decorate

the interior of this lively bar. DJs provide music.

🕐 Daily 11.30am–2 or 3am

LIMERICK INN/LASSETERS HOTEL CASINO

93 Barrett Drive, Alice Springs, NT 0870

Tel 08 8950 7777

www.lassetershotelcasino.com

The Irish theme pub in the casino has live music.

🕐 Wed–Sat 10am–late, Sun 5–8

DARWIN

DISCOVERY AND LOST ARK

89 Mitchell Street, Darwin, NT 0800

Tel 08 8942 3300

www.discoverynightclub.com

Discovery is the largest dance club in the Northern Territory. Lost Ark is smaller, with open-air seating and live music.

🕐 Discovery: 9.30pm–4am, 2 nights a week in wet season, 3 nights in dry. Lost Ark: Sun–Thu 4pm–4am, Fri–Sat 4pm–2am 🎟 Discovery: A$8 Fri, A$10 Sat

MGM GRAND DARWIN CASINO

Gilruth Avenue, Darwin, NT 0800

Tel 08 8943 8888

www.mgmgrand.com.au

Darwin's casino also has restaurants and bars.

🕐 Gaming machines daily 24 hours; bars close Mon–Fri 3am, Sat–Sun at 4am

Sports and Activities

ALICE SPRINGS GOLF CLUB
Cromwell Drive, Alice Springs, NT 0870
Tel 08 8952 1921
www.alicespringsgolfcourse.com.au
Great views of the MacDonnell
Ranges are a bonus for golfers
at this 18-hole course.
🕒 6.30am–7.30pm 💲 From A$13 for 9
holes, A$20 for 18

FRONTIER CAMEL TOURS
Ross River Highway, Alice Springs,
NT 0870
Tel 08 8953 0444
www.cameltours.com.au
Guided camel treks along the
dry bed of the Todd River; all
tours include a meal.
🕒 Breakfast rides start at 6.30am, short
camel rides 10–noon, all year (also
1–2.30pm, Apr–Oct) 💲 Adult from
A$10, child from A$6 🍴

OUTBACK BALLOONING
Kennett Court, Alice Springs, NT 0870
Tel 08 8952 8723
www.outbackballooning.com.au

The 30-minute breakfast flights
over bushland are a great way
to see emus and kangaroos.
🕒 All year 💲 Adult from A$220, child
A$180 for 30-minute flight (includes
transfers and champagne breakfast)

OUTBACK QUAD ADVENTURES
Undoolya Station, 17km east of Alice
Tel 08 8953 0697
www.outbackquadadventures.com.au
Bounce around Undoolya cattle
station on a quad bike. No
experience necessary.
🕒 All year 💲 From A$169 per person
for 2 hours (includes transfers from Alice)

CULLEN BAY CHARTERS
Cullen Bay Marina, Darwin Harbour,
NT 0800
Tel 08 8981 3049
www.fishdarwin.com
www.divedarwin.com
Fishing and scuba-diving tours.
🕒 All year 💲 From A$110 per person for
half-day fishing, A$160 for half-day dive

DARWIN TURF CLUB
Dickwood Drive, Fannie Bay, NT 0820
Tel 08 8941 1566
www.darwincup.com.au
About 40 race meetings a year:
The highlight is the Darwin Cup
Carnival (Jul–Aug).
🕒 See race schedule 💲 From A$6 on
non-major race days; child under 18 free
when accompanied by an adult 🍴 🚻

NITMILUK TOURS
Nitmiluk Visitor Centre, Nitmiluk
(Katherine Gorge) National Park,
Katherine, NT 0850
Tel 08 8972 1253
A canoe is the best way to see
Katherine Gorge. Half-, full-day
or overnight tours.
🕒 Canoe hire 9–5, Apr–Nov 💲 Single
canoe: half day from A$31, full day A$47.
Double canoe: half day A$47, full day A$65

**PROFESSIONAL HELICOPTER
SERVICES**
Tourist Information Centre, Ayers Rock
Resort, NT 0872
Tel 08 8956 2003
www.phs.com.au
Fly above Uluru, Kata Tjuta or
Kings Canyon in a helicopter.
💲 From A$100 for 12- to 15-minute
flight around Uluru; from A$195 for 30-
minute flight over Uluru and Kata Tjuta

Festivals and Events

JULY
The Alice Springs Show, at
Blatherskite Park Showground,
is a traditional agricultural and
horticultural show which also
includes sideshows and arts
and crafts displays.
  Watch camel races at the
Camel Cup Carnival at Alice
Springs in mid-July (www.
camelcup.com.au).
  The Royal Darwin Show, at
Darwin Showgrounds in late
July, is an agricultural show
with displays of arts, crafts,
commerce and industry, cattle
and small livestock, an animal
nursery, sideshows and food
stalls.

AUGUST
The Darwin Cup Carnival
begins in late July and reaches
its climax in August with the
Darwin Cup horserace at
Fannie Bay Racecourse, Darwin
(www.darwincup.com.au).

The Festival of Darwin, held
in the city in mid- to late
August, celebrates the visual
and performing arts (www.dar
winfestival.org.au).
  The Darwin Fringe Festival
showcases less mainstream
drama, dance, poetry and
music (www.darwinfringe.
octa4.net.au).

SEPTEMBER
The Henley-on-Todd Regatta at
Alice Springs is a boat race
with a difference: Crews use
foot power to propel bottom-
less 'boats' along the dry bed
of the Todd River (www.hen
leyontodd.com.au).

WHAT TO DO

SOUTH AUSTRALIA

South Australia is known for its wines of distinction. Find your preferred vintage by touring the state's many wineries—the Barossa Valley alone has more than 50 wineries offering tastings and cellar door sales. Alternatively, Adelaide is well supplied with good wine outlets. The towns of the Adelaide Hills and Barossa Valley are also known for their antiques and arts and crafts shops.

South Australia produces most of the world's opals, so it's no surprise to find several opal dealers in Adelaide and Coober Pedy, the outback town where the opals are mined. Adelaide's opal jewellers lie in close proximity to each other, making it easy to compare prices.

Grant Burge Wines, near Tanunda in the Barossa Valley

The main focus of shopping in Adelaide is Rundle Mall, a pedestrians-only zone in which a dozen or so arcades house a total of more than 500 retail outlets. Look in adjoining Rundle Street for cutting-edge fashion and jewellery, as well as for stores stocked with outdoor gear. Hindley Street offers a mix of fashion boutiques, bookshops, travel goods stores, and pubs, restaurants and nightclubs.

A little farther from the heart of the city is North Adelaide. Here, Melbourne Street is known for its fashion outlets, and Magill Road and Grote Street for antiques shops.

For those who prefer cultural activities, Adelaide truly is the festival city. The world-class Adelaide Festival in February or March presents a heady brew of music, dance, art and literature every even-numbered year. Accompanying the mainstream programme is the Fringe Festival, a pot-pourri of often challenging alternative performances. WOMADelaide (World of Music and Dance), held annually in February or March, is a leading world music festival, in which dance and art also feature.

South Australia's predictable sunny weather draws the active and adventurous to its beaches and parks. Learn to surf, visit a sea-lion colony or watch an Australian Rules game. When the sun sets Adelaide's clubs and pubs will satisfy the night-owls.

Shopping

ADELAIDE

ADELAIDE CENTRAL MARKET
Grote Street, Adelaide, SA 5000
Tel 08 8203 7494
www.adelaide.sa.gov.au/centralmarket/
The people of Adelaide have been shopping for fruit and vegetables at the Central Market for more than 150 years. Cheeses and preserved meats are also available. Surrounding the produce market are arcades with specialist stores that sell a variety of goods, including souvenirs, books and craftworks. The market has a lively, bustling atmosphere, especially on Saturday mornings.
🕐 Tue 7–5.30, Thu 9–5.30, Fri 7am–9pm and Sat 7–3 🚌 City Loop. Close to Central Bus Station 🚌

JAMFACTORY CONTEMPORARY CRAFT AND DESIGN
19 Morphett Street, Adelaide, SA 5000
tel 08 8410 0727
www.jamfactory.com.au
A retail shop, part of the JamFactory Contemporary Craft and Design complex, sells high-quality work from the JamFactory studios dealing in ceramics, hot glass, metal design and contemporary furniture. You can also buy leather goods. Packaging and shipping assistance to your home country is provided.

🕐 Mon–Fri 9–5.30, Sat–Sun 1–5
🚌 City Loop to cnr Morphett and Grote Streets. Central Bus Station nearby.

WHAT TO DO

MISS GLADYS SYM CHOON
235A Rundle Street, Adelaide, SA 5000
Tel 08 8223 1500
www.missgladyssymchoon.com.au
An Adelaide institution, this shop sells men's and women's clothing and footwear. The shop stocks both its own in-house designed funky and hip labels, which it sells around Australia and exports to New Zealand, and the collections of some of Australia's best-known young fashion designers.
🕐 Mon–Sat 10–6 (also Fri 6–10pm), Sun 12–5 🚌 City Loop to cnr Rundle Street and East Terrace

NATIONAL ABORIGINAL CULTURAL INSTITUTE–TANDANYA
253 Grenfell Street, Adelaide, SA 5000
Tel 08 8224 3200
www.tandanya.on.net
The Institute displays contemporary and traditional Aboriginal artworks. Some of the works are for sale in the gift shop, which also has a range of authentic crafts. There is a resident artist (daily 1–4). Entry to the shop is free but there is a fee to enter the Institute; see page 141.
🕐 Daily 10–5 🚌 City Loop to Hindmarsh Square 👤 Adult A$4, child A$3; includes daily noon performance

NATIONAL WINE CENTRE
Cnr Botanic and Hackney roads, Adelaide, SA 5000
Tel 08 8222 9222
www.wineaustralia.com.au
The National Wine Centre of Australia adjoins the Botanical Gardens. The Centre's store sells Australian wines and wine-related merchandise, such as glassware, books and corkscrews.
🕐 Daily 10–5 🚌 City Loop to cnr North and East terraces then 500m walk. Buses from Adelaide station 🚌

OLYMPIC OPAL GEM MINE
5 Rundle Mall, Adelaide, SA 5000
Tel 08 8211 7440
www.olympic-opal.com.au
A re-created opal mine with walk-through tunnels gives an idea of what opals look like in nature. Besides opal jewellery, you can buy pearl jewellery, hand-blown glass, pottery and Aboriginal art and crafts.
🕐 Mon–Fri 9.30–6 (also Fri 6–9pm), Sat 9.30–5.30, Sun 11–5 🚌 City Loop to intersection of North Terrace and King William Street then short walk

THE OPAL MINE
30 Gawler Place, Adelaide, SA 5000
Tel 08 8223 4023
www.opalmine.com.au
Established in 1936, the Opal Mine sells black, boulder and light opals and South Sea pearls as both jewellery and loose gems. You receive a certificate of authenticity for goods worth more than A$100.
🕐 Mon–Fri 9–5.30 (also Fri 5.30–7pm), Sat 10–5 🚌 City Loop to intersection of North Terrace and Gawler Place

R. M. WILLIAMS FACTORY SECONDS OUTLET
121 Frost Road, Salisbury, SA 5108
Tel 08 8259 1000
www.rmwilliams.com.au
This suburban factory outlet sells discontinued, seconds, faulty and end-of-season clothing, footwear and other goods made by R. M. Williams, one of Australia's best-known outback clothing manufacturers. Savings of between 30 to 80 per cent can be made, but remember to double-check items for faults before purchasing.
🕐 Mon–Fri 9–5.30, Sat 9–12 🚌 Chidda 🚗 20km (12.5 miles) north of Adelaide

ADELAIDE HILLS

THE TOY FACTORY
Birdwood Road, Gumeracha, SA 4233
Tel 08 8389 1085
www.thetoyfactory.com.au
The Toy Factory makes and sells wooden toys, games (such as jigsaws) and children's furniture, including tables, chairs and CD racks. The outlet also features a 3ha (7-acre) bush park with kangaroos, wallabies and waterbirds. The Factory is a 45-minute drive from Adelaide.

🕐 Daily 9–5 🚗 39km (24 miles) northeast of Adelaide via A10 and B10

COOBER PEDY

THE OPAL CUTTER
Lot 880, Post Office Hill Road, Coober Pedy, SA 5723
Tel 08 86723086
www.opalcutter.com.au
Located underground in the opal-mining outback town of Coober Pedy (see page 143), the shop sells opals in rough and finished state. A range of handcrafted jewellery is also available, and goods come with a certificate of authenticity. This is a good place to find out how opals are mined and about life generally in Coober Pedy.
🕐 Mon–Sat 8.45–6, Sun 10–5 🚗 540km (356 miles) northwest from Port Augusta via Stuart Highway (A87)

BAROSSA VALLEY

THE BAROSSA SMALL WINEMAKERS CENTRE
Basedow Road, Tanunda, SA 5352
Tel 08 8563 3888
www.chateautanunda.com/wine/smallwine.php
The Winemakers Centre is a showcase for the Barossa Valley's small-scale wineries. The Centre is in the cellar-door sales area at historic Chateau Tanunda, just a short walk from the town of Tanunda. More than 50 wines from 20 small wineries are for sale, mostly handmade vintages produced in very small quantities.
🕐 Daily 10–5 🚗 See drive tour from Adelaide to the Barossa Valley, pages 236–237

WHAT TO DO

KANGAROO ISLAND

KANGAROO ISLAND GALLERY

1 Murray Street, Kingscote, SA 5223
Tel 08 8553 2868

The gallery shows the work of Kangaroo Island's artists and craftspeople. Items for sale include paintings, pottery, handknits, patchwork, jewellery, handmade paper, stained glass and photographs. This is a good place to buy that special Australian gift.

🕐 Daily 10–5

Performance

ADELAIDE

ADELAIDE ENTERTAINMENT CENTRE

Port Road, Hindmarsh, SA 5007
Tel 08 8208 2222
www.adelent.sa.gov.au

The Centre hosts large-scale events, such as pop concerts by star names.

🚆 Bowden from Adelaide station
🚌 🚊

ADELAIDE FESTIVAL CENTRE

King William Road, Adelaide, SA 5000
Tel 08 8216 8600
www.afct.org.au

The Festival Centre is Adelaide's main venue for drama, dance, classical music and opera.

🚌 City Loop to intersection of North Terrace and King William Road
🚆 Adelaide 🚌 🚊

THEBARTON THEATRE

Henley Beach Road, Torrensville, SA 5031
Tel 08 8443 5255

A venue for local and international musicians, and there are children's shows too.

🚌 Torrensville 🚆 2km (1.5 miles) east from West Terrace, Adelaide

Nightlife

ADELAIDE

HEAVEN NIGHTCLUB

7 West Terrace, Adelaide, SA 5000
Tel 08 8216 5216
www.heaven.com.au

Retro, trance, R & B and contemporary rock are among the musical flavours you can savour in Heaven. The website lists upcoming performances and costs.

🕐 Wed 8pm–5am, Thu 9pm–5am, Sat 9pm–6am 🚌 Central Bus Station in Grote Street 🚆 See website

MARS BAR

120 Gouger Street, Adelaide, SA 5000
tel 08 8231 9639

Everyone, gay or straight, is welcome at this gay and lesbian venue. Dance shows on Friday and Saturday nights.

🕐 Nightly 10.30pm–5am 🚌 Central Bus Station in Grote Street, or taxi (approx A$5) from city 🚆 Mon–Thu free, Fri–Sat A$8 which includes show

MINKE BAR AND SKYLAB NIGHTCLUB

17–19 Crippen Place, Adelaide, SA 5000
Tel 08 8211 8088
www.minkebar.com

Drink at Minke Bar, and dance to house, hip hop and funk at Skylab Nightclub. Visiting bands and DJs.

🕐 Minke Bar: Thu–Sun 10pm–5am; Skylab: Fri–Sat 10pm–5am 🚆 Skylab

A$8 (for club and bar); Minke Bar A$6 on Fri; up to A$25, depending on acts

THE PLANET HOTEL

77 Pirie Street, Adelaide, SA 5000
Tel 08 8359 2797
www.planetweb.com.au

Planet's DJs play the latest house music and hold regular theme nights saluting dance hits of past decades.

🕐 Wed, Fri and Sat 8pm–4am 🚆 A$5 Wed and Fri after 9, A$10 Sat after 10

THE RHINO ROOM

13 Frome Street, Adelaide, SA 5000
Tel 08 8227 1611

From comedy to live bands and from hip hop to electronica—each night a different theme.

🕐 Wed–Thu 8pm–1am, Fri–Sat 9pm–3am 🚌 City Loop 🚆 A$5–6 depending on acts

SKYCITY ADELAIDE

North Terrace, Adelaide, SA 5000
Tel 08 8218 4100
www.skycityadelaide.com.au

The former railway station now houses Adelaide's casino, which has the usual gambling attractions plus bars, restaurants, cafés and live entertainment.

🕐 Daily 10am–4am (also Fri–Sat 4–6am) 🚌 City Loop 🚆 Adelaide

SUGAR

Level 1, 274 Rundle Street, Adelaide, SA 5000
Tel 08 8223 6160

This classy club in the heart of town has a gallery, café, pool hall, DJ-record store, and DJs every night in the dance club.

🕐 Daily 2pm–3am (also Thu–Sun 3–4am) 🚆 A$6 Sat–Sun after 10

Sports and Activities

ADELAIDE

AAMI STADIUM

West Lakes Boulevard City, West Lakes, SA 5021
Tel 08 84406666

This is South Australia's main Australian Rules football ground. Visiting sides take on one of the local teams, Port Adelaide or Adelaide.

🕐 Season Apr–Sep 🚆 From A$20.40 🚆 10km (6 miles) northwest of Adelaide

ADELAIDE AQUATIC CENTRE

Jeffcott Road, North Adelaide, SA 5006
Tel 08 8344 4411
www.adelaideaquaticcentre.com.au

Enjoy swimming pools, a diving pool, gymnasium, sauna, and spa and steam rooms.

🕐 Daily 5am–10pm, in summer; Mon–Sat 5am–10pm, Sun 7am–8pm, rest of year 🚌 231, 233, 235 and 237 🚆 Adult A$5.25, child A$3.95, family from A$13.15

ROLLING ON MOUNTAIN BIKE TOURS

P.O. Box 19, Hove, SA 5048

Tel 08 8358 2401

http://members.ozemail.com.au/~rolling on

Rent a bike to explore Adelaide, one of Australia's most cycle-friendly cities.

🚲 From A$22 for 5 hours, plus A$8 delivery to your hotel

SWIM WITH THE DOLPHINS

Holdfast Shores Marina, Glenelg, SA 5045

Tel 04 1281 1838

www.dolphinboat.com.au

Watch or swim with dolphins on a boat trip from Glenelg.

🕐 Cruises depart Tue, Thu, Sat and Sun 8am 🚋 Trams to Glenelg 🐬 Watching: adult A$48, child A$38; swimming: adult A$98, child (over 8) A$88

THE VINE GOLF CLUB OF REYNELLA

Cnr Reynell Road and Mark Street, Happy Valley, SA 5159

Tel 08 8381 3300

This 18-hole course is one of South Australia's best.

🕐 Dawn–dusk; closed to the public Tue morning, Wed, Sat, and Sun before 11 ⛳ A$33 for 18 holes 🚌 18km (11 miles) south from Adelaide

FLEURIEU PENINSULA

DIVE THE EX-HMAS *HOBART*

Yankalilla Bay, Fleurieu Peninsula

Tel 08 8303 2033 (Visitor and Travel Centre, 18 King William Street, Adelaide)

www.dive-southaustralia.com

Qualified scuba-divers can join an underwater tour to explore the wreck of this warship.

🚌 75km (47 miles) south of Adelaide

KANGAROO ISLAND

SEAL BAY CONSERVATION PARK

Kangaroo Island

Tel 08 8559 4207

www.environment.sa.gov.au/parks

The park is home to 600 sea-lions, which you can see on a boardwalk tour. For a closer view join the 45-minute ranger-guided tour of the beach.

🕐 Seal Bay Conservation Park: daily 9–5. Guided tours of Seal Bay beach at regular intervals 9–4.15. During South Australian summer school holidays park open until 7.45 and the last tour is at 7pm 🐾 Boardwalk tours: adult A$9, child A$6.50, family A$24. Beach tours: adult A$12.50, child A$9.50, family A$34 🚌 Cape Jervis ferry to Kangaroo Island is 106km (66 miles) south of Adelaide; Seal Bay is on the south of the island

MOUNT LOFTY

CLELAND WILDLIFE PARK

Summit Road, Mount Lofty, SA 5152

Tel 08 8339 2444

www.environment.sa.gov.au/parks

Get close to native animals, including koalas.

🕐 Daily 9.30–5 🚌 163F park and ride bus from the city and link with 823 service (4 services a day) 🐨 Adult A$12, child A$8, family A$31 🍴

VICTOR HARBOR

RED SUN SAFARIS

4 Pildappa Avenue, Parkholme, SA 5043

Tel 08 8276 3620

www.redsunsafaris.com.au

Learn to surf at Victor Harbor.

🏄 From A$65 including transfer from Adelaide and Glenelg

Festivals and Events

FEBRUARY–MARCH

WOMADelaide is a major world music, art and dance festival in Adelaide's Botanic Park over three days each year (*www.womadelaide.com.au*).

The Adelaide Festival of the Arts, held in even-numbered years, includes music, theatre, dance, visual art, free outdoor events, locally made films, food and music, an architecture programme, Adelaide Writers' Week, masterclasses

and late-night venues (*www. adelaidefestival.org.au*).

The Adelaide Fringe Festival is held at the same time as the Adelaide Festival (above). It stages what's new across all forms of the independent arts (*www.adelaidefringe.com.au*).

MARCH–APRIL

The Clipsal 500, South Australia's V8 Supercar event, is held on a circuit that winds through Adelaide's streets (*www.clipsal500.com.au*).

NOVEMBER

The Mitsubishi Adelaide International Horse Trials is an annual event that attracts top Australian and international riders. Spectators enjoy four days of dressage, show jumping and cross-country competitions (*www.adelaidehorse trials.com.au*).

The Credit Union Christmas Pageant has been an Adelaide tradition since 1933. Join the thousands who line the route to watch a parade of 55 festive and fairytale floats, 12 marching bands and costumed characters (*www.cupageant. com.au*).

WHAT TO DO

WESTERN AUSTRALIA

Size, weather and location combine to make Western Australia a perfect destination for visitors looking for an active holiday.

Covering about a third of the continent, Western Australia offers everything from great surf around Margaret River to the coral Ningaloo Reef—which many argue is more spectacular than the Great Barrier Reef.

The coastal waters offer the chance to swim with whale sharks, manta rays and dolphins, and to go scuba-diving, while for the less energetic there are plenty of whale- and dolphin-watching cruises.

Shark Bay World Heritage Area includes the Monkey Mia dolphin beach

For those who prefer to stay on land there's the 1,000km (620-mile) Bibbulmun Track that runs from the Perth Hills to Albany, while adventure operators do business in many areas and offer everything from abseiling to caving.

Not that you need travel too far to be active, surrounded as you will be by water and parklands, and there are plenty of outdoor opportunities in Perth. Residents can be found on the bicycle and jogging tracks along the Swan River, while there are a number of excellent golf courses within a half-hour drive from the city.

Although the shopping in Perth isn't as good as in Sydney and Melbourne, Perth and Fremantle both have some great markets, particularly Fremantle Markets.

Western Australia is also a good place in which to buy pearls. While you may not find a bargain (pearls seem to be expensive wherever you go), the fact that many pearls are produced in this state means that the people you're dealing with at least have a great deal of expertise.

Aboriginal products are another good buy in Western Australia. Local Aboriginal communities are involved in the running of many of the shops and offer everything from fine art pieces to souvenirs with a difference.

Perth and Fremantle are great places to party and you'll find no shortage of bars and nightclubs, many of which are located in the Northbridge, Leederville and Fremantle areas.

Shopping

BROOME

PASPALEY PEARLS
2 Short Street, Broome, WA 6725
Tel 08 9192 2203
www.paspaleypearls.com
At Paspaley Pearls, one of the largest pearl outlets in Broome, you can buy loose pearls and designer jewellery and learn about pearls and the pearling industry. The shop is in the heart of Chinatown.
🕐 Mon–Fri 9.30–5, Sat 9.30–2, Sun 9.30–1

FREMANTLE

FREMANTLE MARKETS
Cnr South Terrace and Henderson Street, Fremantle, WA 6160
Tel 08 9335 2515
www.fremantlemarkets.com.au

Established in 1897, these markets have more than 170 stalls selling everything from food to crafts. Sheepskin and leather-goods, dried flowers, opals, shells and pottery are popular.
🕐 Sun–Mon 10–5, Fri 9–9, Sat 9–5
🚉 Fremantle 🚌

KALLIS AUSTRALIA PEARLS
Cnr Marine Terrace and Collie Street, Fremantle, WA 6160
Tel 08 9239 9330
www.artisansofthesea.com.au
Kallis is the largest pearl farm in Western Australia, and this shop sells loose pearls and a range of jewellery. Individual pieces can also be designed.
🕐 Mon–Fri 9.30–5, Sat–Sun 11–4
🚉 Fremantle

WHAT TO DO

MARGARET RIVER

THE CHOCOLATE COMPANY
Cnr Harman's Mill Road and Harman's
South Road, Willyabrup, WA 6280
Tel 08 9755 6555
www.chocolatefactory.com.au

Watch chocolates being made,
then buy from a large range,
from slabs of the stuff to handmade truffles. There's another
outlet in the Swan Valley.
⊙ Daily 9.30–5 🖵

**MARGARET RIVER REGIONAL
WINE CENTRE**
9 Bussell Highway, Cowaramup,
WA 6284
Tel 08 9755 5501
www.mrwines.com
Wines from most of the region's
winemakers are on sale here, a
good option for those with little
time to visit individual wineries.
Daily wine tastings.
⊙ Mon–Sat 10–7, Sun 12–6

PERTH

**CRAFTWEST CENTRE FOR
CONTEMPORARY CRAFT**
357–365 Murray Street, Perth, WA 6000
Tel 08 9226 2161
www.craftwest.com.au
Craftwest is the peak professional organization for contemporary craft and design in
Western Australia. At its retail
outlet you can buy handmade
ceramics, glass, jewellery, textiles, woodwork and, cards.
⊙ Mon–Fri 9–5.30 (also Fri 5.30–9pm),
Sat 9–5 🚌 Red CAT 🚇 Perth

CREATIVE NATIVE
32 King Street, Perth, WA 6000
Tel 08 9322 3398
www.creativenative.com.au

This gallery houses the largest
range of Aboriginal art and
crafts in Western Australia—
paintings, boomerangs, didgeridoos and rugs. Authentification
certificates are provided.

⊙ Mon–Fri 9–5.30, Sat 9–5, Sun 12–5
🚌 Red CAT 🚇 Perth

PERTH MINT
310 Hay Street, East Perth, WA 6004
Tel 08 9421 7222
www.perthmint.com.au

The Mint's shop sells coins,
medallions and bars, as well as
jewellery made specifically for
the mint using coins, natural
nuggets, Australian diamonds,
pearls and opals.
⊙ Mon–Fri 9–4, Sat–Sun 9–1 🚌 Red
CAT 🚇 Perth

SWAN VALLEY

HOUGHTON WINES
Dale Road, Middle Swan, WA 6056
Tel 08 9274 9540
www.houghton_wine.com.au
Wine, wine-related products,
and locally produced food and
crafts are on sale. There's also
an art gallery.
⊙ Daily 10–5 🖵

Performance

BROOME

SUN PICTURES GARDENS
27 Carnarvon Street, Broome, WA 6725
Tel 08 9192 3738
One of the oldest operating
outdoor movie theatres; see
page 155.
⊙ Movies start after dusk 🖵 🛗

PERTH

**BURSWOOD INTERNATIONAL
RESORT CASINO**
Great Eastern Highway, Burswood,
WA 6100
Tel 08 9362 7777
www.burswood.com.au
Perth's casino has nine restau-
rants, six bars and a theatre.
⊙ 24 hours 🚇 Burswood 🍴 🖵 🛗

HIS MAJESTY'S THEATRE
825 Hay Street, Perth, WA 6000
Tel 08 9265 0900
www.hismajestystheatre.com.au
This Edwardian theatre is
home to the West Australian
Opera and the West Australian
Ballet.
🚌 Red CAT 🚇 Perth 🖵 🛗

PERTH CONCERT HALL
5 St. George's Terrace, Perth, WA 6000
Tel 08 9231 9900 (tickets: 08 9484 1133)
www.perthconcerthall.com.au

Perth's main venue for classical music.
🚌 Blue CAT 🚇 Perth 🖵 🛗

THE PLAYHOUSE
3 Pier Street, Perth, WA 6000
Tel 08 9325 3344 (tickets: 08 9484 1133)
www.playhousetheatre.com.au
Several theatre companies are
based here and it is also used

by touring drama and dance groups.

🚌 Red CAT 🚉 Perth 🎭 🏛️

REGAL THEATRE
474 Hay Street, Subiaco, WA 6008
Tel 08 9388 2066 (tickets: 08 9484 1133)
www.regaltheatre.com.au
Stages everything from comedy acts and film festivals to musicals and rock bands.
🚉 Subiaco

SUNSET EVENTS
Western Power Parkland, May Drive, Kings Park, Perth, WA 6000
Tel 08 9385 5400
www.sunsetevents.com.au

The outdoor cinema in Kings Park operates during the summer months.
🎬 Tue–Sun dusk, Nov–Mar 🚌 Blue Cat 🚉 City West then 1km (0.6 mile) walk

Nightlife

FREMANTLE
THE CLINK
14–16 South Terrace, Fremantle, WA 6160
Tel 08 9336 1919
DJs plays the latest music Friday and Saturday nights, while Sunday is retro.
🎵 Thu 11pm–3am, Fri–Sat 9pm–5am, Sun 8–midnight 💷 A$10 Fri–Sat, A$3 Sun

METROPOLIS
58 South Terrace, Fremantle, WA 6160
Tel 08 9336 1609
www.metropolisfremantle.com.au
A choice of bars and dance floors at Fremantle's biggest and most popular club.
🎵 Fri–Sat 9pm–6am, Sun 9pm–1am 💷 A$5 Fri–Sat, A$8 after midnight Sat

PERTH
CONNECTIONS NIGHTCLUB
81 James Street, Northbridge, WA 6003
Tel 08 9328 1870
A gay and lesbian club with the latest dance music.
🎵 Wed 10pm–5am, Fri–Sat 10pm–6am, Sun 9pm–1am 🚉 Perth 💷 A$10 Fri, A$12 Sat, A$5 Sun

THE DEEN
84 Aberdeen Street, Northbridge, WA 6003
Tel 08 9227 9361
Live bands, DJs and six bars.
🎵 Fri–Sat and Mon 5pm–2am 🚉 Perth

HIP-E-CLUB
663 Newcastle Street, Leederville, WA 6007
Tel 08 9227 8899
Music from the 1970s, 80s and 90s; Top 40 on Wednesdays.
🎵 Tue 8pm–5am, Wed 9.30pm–5am, Fri 9pm–5am, Sat 8pm–5am, Sun 8pm–midnight 🚉 Leederville 💷 A$5 after 10 Tue, 11.30 Wed and 11 Fri

LLAMA BAR
1/464 Hay Street, Subiaco, WA 6008
Tel 08 9388 0222
www.llamabar.com
A chic place with live music on Wednesdays.
🎵 Thu–Sat 5pm–3am, Tue–Wed 5pm–midnight 🚉 Subiaco

NEW OFFICE NIGHTCLUB
133 Aberdeen Street, Northbridge, WA 6003
Tel 08 9228 0077
www.officenightclub.com.au
Live music and DJs, light shows and silhouette dancers.
🎵 Thu–Sat 10pm–late, Wed 8–late 🚉 Perth 💷 A$5 Wed, A$8 after 10 Thu–Sat

ONYZ LOUNGE BAR
72 Outram Street, West Perth, WA 6005
Tel 08 9321 8661
Club music into the early hours at this popular after-work club.
🎵 Thu–Fri 4pm–late, Sat 7pm–1am 🚉 City West

RISE
139 James Street, Northbridge, WA 6003
Tel 08 9328 7447
www.rise.net.au

One of Perth's most popular dance clubs.
🎵 Wed–Thu 9pm–4am, Fri–Sat 9pm–6am, Sun 9pm–1am 🚉 Perth 💷 A$5 before midnight, then A$10

UNIVERSAL BAR
221 William Street, Northbridge, WA 6003
Tel 08 9227 6771
An open, friendly bar known for its cocktails. Music ranges from funk to traditional blues.
🎵 Mon–Fri 4pm–late, Sat 4pm–2am 🚉 Perth

Sports and Activities

BROOME
RED SUN CAMELS
Cable Beach
Tel 08 9193 7423
www.redsuncamels.com.au
Sunset camel rides on Broome's Cable Beach.
🎵 Daily; sunset tours depart 90 minutes before dusk, which ranges from 4 to 5.30 depending on time of year 🚌 Bus to Cable Beach arrives at quarter to the hour 💷 Adult A$35, child 6–16 A$20, under 6 A$10

BUNBURY
DOLPHIN DISCOVERY CENTRE
Koombana Drive, Bunbury, WA 6230
Tel 08 9791 3088
www.dolphindiscovery.com.au
Observe dolphins off the coast from December to April, or swim with them along with the Centre's marine biologist.
🎵 Daily 8–5, Oct–May; 10–3, Jun–Aug 🚌 Bus from Bunbury 💷 Centre entry: adult A$2, child A$1. Dolphin watch: adult A$27, child A$20. Swim tour: A$99 per person 📷

WHAT TO DO

CORAL BAY

SNORKEL WITH MANTA RAYS
Robinson Street, Coral Bay, WA 6701
Tel 08 9942 5955
www.users.bigpond.com/coralbay/
Half-day tours snorkelling on
the Ningaloo Reef and swim-
ming with manta rays.
🕐 Daily 9–1 💲 Adult A$110, child A$80

MARGARET RIVER

JOSH PALMATEER SURF ACADEMY
Groups meet at the Margaret River
mouth parking area
Tel 08 9757 3850
Learn to surf at Western
Australia's most popular surf-
ing destination.
🕐 Daily 11–1 (closed winter) 💲 From
A$40 for a group lesson 🚗 Off Caves
Road, 9km (5.5 miles) east of Margaret
River

PERTH

ABORIGINAL HERITAGE TOUR
Pier 3, Barrack Square, Perth, WA 6000
Tel 08 9325 3341
www.captaincookcruises.com.au

A combination of a cruise on
the Swan River and a bushwalk
led by an Aboriginal guide.
🕐 Departs 11am and returns 2pm
🚌 Blue CAT 🚆 Perth 💲 Adult from
A$35, child A$20

ABOUT BIKE HIRE
Rear of Causeway parking area, Riverside
Drive, Perth, WA 6000
Tel 08 9221 2665
www.aboutbikehire.com.au
Rent a bicycle to pedal beside
the Swan River or off-road;
tours of the Munda Biddi Track.
🕐 Mon–Sat 10–5, Sun 9–5 🚌 Red CAT
💲 Adult from A$5, child A$4, for a half
hour

SUBIACO OVAL

Roberts Road, Subiaco, WA 6008
Tel 08 9381 2187
http://afl.com.au/?pg=tickets&spg=
stadiumsubiaco
Home to two Australian Rules
football teams, the West Coast
Eagles and Fremantle.
🕐 Matches Fri–Sun, Apr–Sep
🚆 Transperth park and ride service
🚉 Leederville and Subiaco 💲 Adult
from A$20.08, child A$4.62

SWAN VALLEY

THE VINES RESORT
Verdelho Drvive, The Vines, WA 6069
Tel 08 9297 0777
www.vines.com.au

The resort has two 18-hole
courses where many world
golf championships have been
played.
🕐 Dawn–dusk 💲 From A$35 for 9
holes, A$60 for 18 holes 🍴 🖥 🔧

Festivals and Events

JANUARY–FEBRUARY
The Perth International Arts
Festival attracts leading artists
and performers in music, film,
drama, dance, opera, song,
jazz and the visual arts
(*www.perthfestival.com.au*).
FEBRUARY
The Johnnie Walker Classic
Golf Tournament, in Perth, is
Australia's richest golf tourna-
ment, with a minimum of
A$2.5 million in prize money.
FEBRUARY/MARCH
The Leeuwin Estate Concert, at
the Leeuwin Estate Winery,
attracts top performers
(*www.leeuwinestate.com.au*).

APRIL
The Salomon Masters@
Margaret River is part of the
6-star world surfing qualifying
series. Other events include
surfing and skating demonstrations, jet-ski surfing, and a concert with international bands
(*www.salomonmasters. com*).
JULY–NOVEMBER
See one of the world's great
natural wildflower displays at
various locations. The season
starts in July in the Pilbara
(northern) region and heads
south until November.
SEPTEMBER
Rally-car teams from more
than a dozen nations take part
in Telstra Rally Australia, the
penultimate round of the FIA
World Rally Championship
(*www.rallyaustralia.com.au*).

The historic town of York
hosts the York Jazz Festival.
The Perth Royal Show showcases agricultural, horticultural,
viticultural, rural, technological
and mineral resources
(*www.perthroyalshow.com.au*).
The Kings Park Wildflower
Festival, in Perth, is an extensive native plant display and
wildflower exhibition
(*www.bgpa.wa.gov.au*).
OCTOBER
Spring in the Valley celebrates
the produce of the Swan
Valley, with displays of fine
wine, food, art and music
(*www.emrc.org.au*).
DECEMBER–JANUARY
World-class tennis players
compete in national teams in
the Hopman Cup in Perth
(*www.hopmancup.com.au*).

TASMANIA

Ruggedly beautiful landscapes are the draw on Tasmania, where you can go cycling, bushwalking and camping. Scenic flights give a fantastic overview. Although the island is not going to satisfy the shopping urges of those used to the razzle-dazzle of big cities like Sydney and Brisbane, there are some great markets, and lively, friendly pubs in which to be entertained.

Cruising on the Gordon River near Strahan

In Australian terms, Tasmania is probably ahead of the pack when it comes to quality souvenirs. The best souvenirs are its arts and crafts, made with materials unique to the island and with a distinctive sense of identity. Look for beautiful woodcraft in particular, using the precious endemic Huon and celery-top pine, black-wood and sassafrass. Turned Huon pine bowls are quite the mascots of Tasmanian tourism, and there is enough excellent jewellery, fleece-lined clothing and paintings to explore between adventures.

High-quality landscape painting and photography, both traditional and contemporary, have been inspired by the natural beauty and pristine wilderness and can be found all across the island.

Large chain stores and shopping complexes are thin on the ground, but in their place are a good number of traditional general stores and village markets. The weekly large-scale market at Salamanca Place, at the heart of the waterfront in Hobart, is as good a place as any to see a huge diversity of local craft. Haggling isn't customary but discounts could be negotiated after a friendly chat.

Boutique food and wine are other advantages of Tasmania's isolated marketplace. The clean air and water helps in the production of premium beer, cheese, stone fruits, berries, beef and wine. Roadside bargains abound.

When you're tired of shopping you can play a round of golf, watch a cricket match or go salmon or trout fishing.

If you're planning to immerse yourself in the true wilderness areas of Tasmania, you'll need to be well equipped. There are specific shops in Hobart, Launceston and Devonport that stock all of what you need for the season and destination. The staff are good sources of information and advice.

Shopping

CRADLE MOUNTAIN

THE WILDERNESS GALLERY
Doherty Cradle Mountain Hotel, Cradle Mountain Road, Cradle Mountain, TAS 7306
Tel 03 6492 1404
www.dohertyhotels.com.au

Tasmania's wild landscapes and unique plant and animal life have inspired many photographers. This gallery features the work of the best of them, and a shop sells cards and prints.
🕐 Daily 10–6 🎫 A$10

DELORAINE

ASHGROVE CHEESE
6173 Bass Highway, Elizabeth Town, TAS 7304
Tel 03 6368 1100
A short drive west of Deloraine is this farmhouse shop run by the Bennett family, who make English-style cheeses. Taste Cheddars, Cheshire, Gloucester and Wensleydale; Tasmanian native bush peppers flavour some varieties.
🕐 Daily 7.30–6 (7.30–5 in winter)

DEVONPORT

BACKPACKERS BARN
10–12 Edward Street, Devonport, TAS 7310
Tel 03 6424 3628
www.tasweb.com.au/backpack/visitus.htm
Close to the Bass Strait Ferry Terminal, this is an excellent starting point for Tasmanian adventures. The barn sells camping equipment and out-

WHAT TO DO

doors clothing, and the staff can make bookings for many adventure trips, including bushwalking and scenic flights.
⊙ Mon–Fri 9–6 (5 in winter), Sat 9–2 (noon in winter)

IMPRESSIONS AND BLUE GUM GALLERY
11 Best Street, Devonport, TAS 7310
Tel 03 6424 1287
This large store in Devonport is a hunting ground for the keen souvenir collector. There are numerous lines, from the cheap-and-cheerful such as stuffed-toy Tasmanian devils, to high-quality books, photographs, paintings, woodcraft, pottery and fine foods.
⊙ Daily 9–6

HOBART

KMART
1 Risdon Road, New Town, TAS 7008
Tel 03 6228 0141
www.kmart.com.au
The largest branch of a discount chain that has other stores in Devonport, Launceston and Burnie. This is a value-for-money place for most things you might need in the way of stationery, camping gear, cosmetics, toys, sports gear, footwear and photography.
⊙ Mon–Sat 8.30–6 (also Thu–Fri 6–9pm), Sun 10–5 ◉ Glenorchy

SALAMANCA MARKET
Salamanca Place, Hobart, TAS 7000
Tel 03 6238 2843
Spend an entertaining few hours or a whole day browsing among the stalls of this open-air market, which fills three waterfront blocks. Many of Tasmania's best artisans display their wares and there's plenty of good food and music.
⊙ Sat 8.30–3 ◉ Salamanca Place, Metro bus

TASMANIAN MAP CENTRE
96 Elizabeth Street, Hobart, TAS 7000
Tel 03 6231 9043
www.map-centre.com.au
This one-stop shop two blocks north of Hobart Mall has an extensive selection of maps and guide books for Tasmania and other destinations, and other guides for camping, walking and off-road driving.
⊙ Mon–Fri 9.30–5.30, Sat 10.30–2.30

WURSTHAUS KITCHEN
1 Montpelier Retreat (adjoins Salamanca Place), Hobart, TAS 7000
Tel 03 6224 0644
www.wursthaus.com.au
Undoubtedly Hobart's premier purveyors of gourmet deli products, Wursthaus Kitchen has a wide range of sausages, meats, olives, cheeses, wines and other treats.
⊙ Mon–Fri 8–6, Sat 8–5, Sun 10–4
◉ Salamanca Place, Metro bus

LAUNCESTON

DESIGN CENTRE OF TASMANIA
Cnr Tamar and Brisbane streets, Launceston, WA 7250
Tel 03 6331 5506
www.twdc.org.au
The Design Centre displays the work of some of Tasmania's best craftworkers and designers. Its Tasmanian Wood Design Collection is a world-class assemblage of contemporary woodwork that uses timber native to Tasmania. Pieces range from elegant items of furniture to delicate smaller items.
⊙ Daily 9.30–5.30 ◉ Adult A$2.20, child A$1.10, family A$5.50

MOUNTAIN DESIGNS
2/41 York Street, Launceston, TAS 7250
Tel 03 6334 0988
www.mountaindesigns.com.au
Mountain Designs stocks waterproof and thermal clothing, and climbing, camping, mountaineering and paddling equipment. Friendly staff give expert assistance.
⊙ Mon–Fri 8.30–6, Sat 9–4, Sun 11–3

Performance

DEVONPORT

CMAX CINEMAS
5–7 Best Street, Devonport, TAS 7310
Tel 03 6420 2111
A modern movie-theatre complex with first-release films.
⊙ Daily ◉ Adult A$12, child A$8

HOBART

DERWENT ENTERTAINMENT CENTRE
Brooker Highway, Hobart, TAS 7000
Tel 03 6273 0233
Star names perform at Tasmania's biggest live venue, a modern auditorium seating up to 6,000 people.
⊙ Dependent on shows ◉ Metro bus
◉ Most concerts A$40–70 ◉ ◉

FEDERATION CONCERT HALL
Adjacent to Grand Chancellor Hotel, Hobart, TAS 7000
Tel 03 6235 4535
www.tso.com.au
The Tasmanian Symphony Orchestra performs at this modern concert hall on Hobart's waterfront.
⊙ Check website for dates ◉ Adult A$40–80

PEACOCK THEATRE
Salamanca Arts Centre, 77 Salamanca Place, Hobart, TAS 7000
Tel 03 6234 8414
Part of the Salamanca Arts Centre, the theatre stages innovative dance, drama, debates and recitals.
◉ Salamanca, Metro bus ◉ A$15–30 ◉

STATE CINEMA
375 Elizabeth Street, North Hobart, TAS 7000
Tel 03 6234 6318
Tasmania's oldest (1913) cinema has an intimate atmosphere and shows quality films.
⊙ Daily, usually 2–3 sessions; matinées most days ◉ North Hobart, Metro bus

THEATRE ROYAL
29 Campbell Street, Hobart, TAS 7000
Tel 03 6233 2299
Completed in 1837, this architectural gem is Australia's oldest working theatre (with a resident ghost).
🕐 Box office: Mon–Fri 9–5, Sat 9–1
🚌 Metro bus 💲 A$30–80

LAUNCESTON
EARL ARTS CENTRE
10 Earl Street, Launceston, TAS 7250
Tel 03 6334 5579
A small venue staging experimental productions, recitals and touring shows.
💲 A$10–25

PRINCESS THEATRE
57 Brisbane Street, Launceston, TAS 7250
Tel 03 6323 3666
www.theatrenorth.com.au
This 19th-century theatre hosts an intermittent schedule of theatre and dance.
🕐 Box office: Mon–Fri 9–5.30, Sat 9.30–1 💲 A$20–100

STRAHAN
STRAHAN VISITOR CENTRE
The Esplanade, Strahan, TAS 7468
Tel 03 6471 7622
Every night sees an amusing performance of *The Ship that Never Was*, with plenty of audience participation.
🕐 Daily 5.30pm 💲 Adult A$12, child A$2

Nightlife

BURNIE
BEACH HOTEL
1 Wilson Street, Burnie, TAS 7320
Tel 03 6431 2333
This lively, friendly pub, within a stone's throw of the beach, has occasional live music.
🕐 Sun–Wed till late, Thu–Sat till 2am
💲 Free

DEVONPORT
BRIDGE HOTEL, FORTH
Main Road, Forth, TAS 7310
Tel 03 6428 2239
Bands play here regularly at the Bridge Hotel, a short drive west of Devonport.
🕐 Daily, Thu–Sat till 12pm or 2am
💲 Free most nights

WAREHOUSE NITECLUB
18–22 King Street, Devonport, TAS 7310
Tel 03 6424 7851
This popular place is an Aussie beer-barn style of nightclub. Touring bands sometimes play here.
🕐 Wed–Thu, 8pm–12pm, Fri–Sat 11pm–5am 💲 A$5

HOBART
NEW SYDNEY HOTEL
87 Bathurst Street, Hobart, TAS 7000
Tel 03 6234 4516
An Irish theme pub with 10 beers on tap, including Guinness, plus live performances most nights.
🕐 Mon–Sat 12–12, Sun 4–9pm
🚌 Redline coach 💲 Free most nights

REGINES
Wrest Point Casino, Hobart, TAS 7000
Tel 03 6211 1750
A sophisticated club at the Wrest Point Hotel. Dress up.
🕐 Mon, Wed–Sat 10pm–4am 🚌 Wrest Point, Metro bus 💲 Free Wed–Thu and Mon, A$4 Fri, A$5 Sat

THE REPUBLIC BAR
299 Elizabeth Street, Hobart, TAS 7000
Tel 03 6234 6954
Hobart's best pub-music venue hosting live blues, roots and jazz.
🕐 Daily till 2am 🚌 North Hobart
💲 Variable; pub free before bands start

SYRUP
39 Salamanca Place, Hobart, TAS 7000
Tel 03 6224 8249
Syrup is Hobart's best dance club, with a pulsating atmosphere and high-profile visiting DJs. Dance till dawn.
🕐 Wed–Sat 8pm–3 or 5am 💲 Free Wed–Thu, A$7 Fri–Sat

LAUNCESTON
LAUNCESTON COUNTRY CLUB CASINO
Country Club Avenue, Prospect, near Launceston, TAS 7250
Tel 03 6335 5741
This is one of the very few late-night options in Launceston. It's a 10-minute taxi ride from the city centre.
🕐 Nightly 10pm–4am 💲 Free

THE LOUNGE
63 St. John Street, Launceston, TAS 7250
Tel 03 6334 6622
The Lounge is Launceston's most stylish nightclub, with a dance club basement.
🕐 Wed–Thu 8pm–3am, Fri–Sat 5pm–5am 💲 A$5 Fri–Sat

ROSEVEARS WATERFRONT TAVERN
215 Rosevears Drive, West Tamar, TAS 7250
Tel 03 6394 4074
This charming old pub stands among vineyards and overlooks a quiet part of the Tamar River north of Launceston.
🕐 Daily till 11pm

Sports and Activities

HOBART
BELLERIVE OVAL
Derwent Street, Bellerive, TAS 7018
Tel 03 6211 4000
www.tascricket.com.au

This attractive ground by the Derwent River hosts the main inter-state cricket competition (the Pura Cup), as well as an international one-day game in January.
🕐 Tasmania play 4- and 1-day inter-state matches Nov–Mar 🚌 Metro bus
💲 Adult A$6 per day, Pura Cup matches; adult A$10, 1-day games

FISH WILD TASMANIA
115A King Street, Sandy Bay, TAS 7005
Tel 04 1834 8223 or 03 6223 8917
www.fishwildtasmania.com
Fish Wild's guided trips include sea-fishing along the southern coastline for salmon and

bream, and fly-fishing for trout in highland lakes.

⏰ Fishing all year; closed seasons for different fisheries (trout closed from end Apr–beg Aug) 🚇 Sandy Bay 🚗 From A$370 for 1 day

NORTH HOBART OVAL
Cnr Argyle and Ryde streets, North Hobart, TAS 7000
03 6234 9177
www.devilsfc.com
Watch an Australian Rules football match featuring the Tassie Devils.

⏰ 8 games each year Sat–Sun, Apr–Oct 🚌 Metro bus 🎟 Adult A$9, child A$5

TASAIR
Cambridge Airport
Tel 03 6248 5088
www.tasair.com.au
Take a scenic flight over wilderness and coastal areas, including remote Bathurst Harbour in the southwest.

⏰ All year, weather permitting 🛫 Cambridge Airport 🚗 Bathurst Harbour return A$300; 2.5-hour scenic flights over southern Tasmania A$176 🚌 14.5km (9 miles) east from Hobart

LAUNCESTON
AQUARIUS ROMAN BATHS
127–133 George Street, Launceston, TAS 7250
Tel 03 6331 2255
These baths follow the layout of a Roman bath, in which bathers enter a number of hot rooms in turn, and then warm and hot baths before a cold plunge. Massages, a beauty clinic, café, solarium and gymnasium complete the complex.

⏰ Daily 9–9 🎟 Baths from A$20; massage from A$38 🚗

COUNTRY CLUB GOLF COURSE
Country Club Avenue, Prospect, TAS 7250
Tel 03 6335 5740
A ritzy country club with a demanding 18-hole course.

⏰ Daily 7.30am–9pm, summer; 8–6, winter 🎟 18 holes A$22, 9 holes A$15

TASMANIAN EXPEDITIONS
23 Earl Street, Launceston, TAS 7250
Tel 03 6334 3477
www.tas-ex.com
Choose from about 20 adventure itineraries—paddling, cycling and walking. Tours are 3 to 13 days, or go on a half- or full-day climb.

⏰ Longer trips Oct–Apr; 3-day walking trips (Cradle Mountain, Freycinet National Park) all year 🎟 13-day walk, cycle, paddle: A$2,250 (costs and equipment). 3-day walks: A$540 all-inclusive. Half-day climb A$85

PORT ARTHUR
TASMAN GOLF CLUB
Point Puer Road, Port Arthur, TAS 7182
Tel 03 6250 2444
There's a trust system for green fees and a famous 8th hole over cliffs dropping to the sea at this 9-hole course.

⏰ Course: daily. Clubhouse/bar: Sun, Tue 🎟 Green fees A$12 per day

Festivals and Events

DECEMBER–JANUARY
The Hobart Summer Festival is the biggest festival in Tasmania. The highlight is the Taste of Tasmania, a food and wine festival that coincides with the arrival of the yachts in the Sydney to Hobart ocean classic.

Fans of folk and world music descend on the small coastal town of Cygnet, 50km (31 miles) south of Hobart for the The Cygnet Folk Festival. Local, interstate and international musicians from a wide range of cultures attend (www.cygnet folkfest.southcom.com.au).

FEBRUARY
Launceston stages its biggest event, Festivale, over three days in mid-February. City Park is filled with food and wine stalls, drama and music.

Hundreds of wooden boats drop anchor in Hobart's Constitution Dock and Sullivans Cove for the biennial Wooden Boat Festival. There are also boat-building exhibitions, model-boat displays, street drama and food stalls. The festival takes place in odd-numbered years (www.awood boatfest.com).

Near the end of February, cyclists from around the world take part in the National Penny Farthing Championships, the highlight of the Evandale Village Fair. The streets of historic Evandale also have stalls, street entertainment, music and dancing.

APRIL
Ten Days on the Island is a major arts festival, staged in odd-numbered years, that showcases the best visual and performance art from island cultures around the globe. Venues are across the state (www.tendaysonthe island.org).

The fastest touring, sports and GT cars in the world race in stages across the state for the five days of Targa Tasmania (www.targa.org.au).

MAY
Agfest, staged near Launceston over three days, is a huge agricultural trade show and fair (www.agfest.com.au).

OCTOBER–NOVEMBER
The Tasmanian Craft Fair at Deloraine is Australia's largest. It takes place over four days (www.tascraftfair.com.au).

WHAT TO DO

This chapter describes eight driving tours and seven walks that explore some of the best parts of Australia. Their locations are marked on the locator map on page 218.

Out and About

Out and About in Australia

The following walks and tours each give a taste of what to explore in Australia, whether urban, forest or outback. For cities there is the bush and harbour of Sydney, heritage and gardens of Melbourne, Brisbane and Adelaide, and the local feel of Hobart. Coastal routes go along the Great Ocean Road, the Sunshine Coast and to the Margaret River, or you can head inland to the canyons of the Blue Mountains, the craters of the Atherton Tableland, or the vineyards of the Barossa Valley. Then there are the wilder landscapes of the Northern Territory and Tasmania.

WALK 1

MOSMAN BAY WHARF TO CREMORNE WHARF

This easy walk along the shoreline of Mosman Bay takes in magnificent views of the city and harbour. Suburban houses blend with bushland and yacht anchorages, and signs along the route explain the history of the original Aboriginal inhabitants.

THE WALK

Distance: 2.25km (1.5 miles)

Allow: 35–45 minutes

Start: Mosman Bay Wharf

End: Cremorne Wharf

How to get there: Ferries from Circular Quay (see map page 61, B2) to Mosman Bay, Mon–Sat every 30 min, Sun hourly

On the crossing to Mosman Bay you pass by Fort Denison, built in the 1840s to protect Sydney from sea attack. From the wharf, head past the café and turn left to walk along the foreshore of the bottom end of Mosman Bay. Across the water is a marina and Mosman Rowing Club.

❶ About 100m (330ft) from the wharf, on the land side, is a sculpture of HMS *Sirius*, the principal naval escort ship of the First Fleet, which arrived in Port Jackson (Sydney Harbour) on 26 January 1788; a year later it was repaired in the bay. Across the road is Mosman's oldest building, The Barn, built as a whaling storehouse in 1831 when Mosman was the hub of a busy (and foul-smelling) whaling industry. It now has some of Sydney's most expensive real estate.

Walk towards the tall palms of Reid Park and follow the foreshore path as it curves around the head of the bay. Walk through the car park of Mosman Rowing Club.

❷ Smartly dressed visitors can sign in at the club for a drink and have lunch or dinner in the restaurant, or enjoy bistro-style snacks or barbecue meals on the verandah overlooking the yachts in the marina.

Climb the steps just past the rowing club entrance. Walk along the path, with harbour views to your left, and over a timber bridge. You enter a dense grove of trees where the path splits: Take the left-hand path up a short flight of steps and past some houses.

❸ You are now on the eastern side of Cremorne Point. Some of the larger houses on the

Right: Life in a Sydney suburb—a view over the marina of Mosman Bay
Bottom right: Lunch at Mosman Rowing Club

Point are examples of the local arts and crafts style (known as Federation), dating from the early 20th century. These and other traditional buildings have made the Point a Heritage Conservation Area.

A path leads down to the Sydney Amateur Sailing clubhouse; another turn-off leads to Old Cremorne Wharf. The path soon passes the Lex and Ruby Graham Gardens.

❹ This tangle of tropical foliage is a community garden established in 1957 by the Grahams, a local couple, and developed over nearly 30 years. Palms and tree ferns mix with the colours of exotic and native shrubs. Tracks through the gardens lead down to the water.

On from the gardens, a row of impressive old apartments is on your right. The main harbour comes into view ahead. Take the path to the left into a small park, pass the playground and continue through bushland, from where there are great views of the city. Continue 200m (660ft) along the path to the southerly Robertsons Point.

❺ The harbour opens up before you. If you wish, scramble down to a small white lighthouse on the shoreline. The peninsula was once occupied by the Cammeraygal people, who knew it as Wul-Warra-Jeung. Colonial settlement came only slowly after 1830.

Walk back to the playground. A path to your left leads to steps that go steeply down to the road below. Directly ahead is Cremorne Wharf where you can wait for a city-bound ferry.
  Uphill from the wharf there is a picnic area that has a public swimming pool on the harbour's edge. Both picnic ground and pool have magnificent views over Shell Cove to the city.

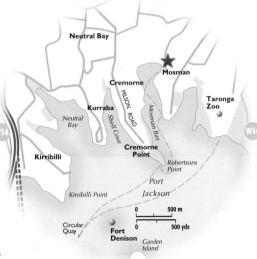

W14

WHEN TO GO
All year round.

WHERE TO EAT
Mosman Rowing Club restaurant (*Tue–Sun 12–3, Wed–Sun 6–9; breakfast Sun 8.30–10.30. Also bistro and barbecue meals daily 12–3.30, 6–9*).

PUBLIC TOILETS
Park above Cremorne Point Wharf and at Mosman Wharf.

BLUE MOUNTAINS ROUND TRIP

This circular drive explores the two sides of the Blue Mountains: The wild world of canyons, cliffs and forests, which can be sampled from lookouts and bush tracks; and the civilized world of welcoming towns, villages and gardens.

THE TOUR

Distance: Approximately 310km (192 miles)

Allow: 1 day or stay overnight

Start: Central Sydney

End: Central Sydney

Follow the Metroad 4 and 5 signs from the heart of the city to reach Parramatta Road (Metroad 4), which connects with the Western Motorway (M4) near Strathfield.

After about 20km (12.5 miles) the M4 ends, becoming the Great Western Highway (National Route 32), which begins a gradual climb into the mountains, passing a string of small towns. Beyond Springwood, turn right to visit the Norman Lindsay Gallery and Museum.

❶ The artist and writer Norman Lindsay (1879–1969) was infamous in the 1920s and 30s for his Bohemian lifestyle and paintings of voluptuous nudes. His rambling home is now a gallery and museum of his works and life (*daily 10–4*).

Return to the highway, turn right and head to the town of Wentworth Falls. Past the traffic lights, turn left on to Falls Road and follow signs to the Wentworth Falls picnic area.

❷ Lookouts near the picnic area give vistas of the forested Jamison Valley and the impressive Wentworth Falls. Tracks that fan out from the lookouts include strenuous descents into the valley, as well as medium to easy walks along the cliff top.

Rejoin the highway and drive west for 6km (3.5 miles) before turning

off to the left to reach Leura (see page 75).

❸ Leura is a small town with a picturesque main commercial street, The Mall. You can explore The Mall's cafés, tearooms, restaurants, galleries and gift shops, as well as the nearby residential streets with their attractive old weatherboard houses and well-tended gardens.

From the main street, turn on to Cliff Drive, which soon leads to Echo Point. This is the most popular viewpoint in the mountains, a clifftop perch overlooking the Jamison Valley. From the viewing platform near visitor information there is a vista of cliffs, eucalyptus forest and the Three Sisters, a dramatic rock formation.

From Echo Point you can detour to the busy main street of Katoomba, 'capital' of the Blue Mountains, where there are art, craft and antiques shops, and a good range of cafés and restaurants.

Otherwise continue on Cliff Drive for a short distance to Scenic World. This is the home of the Scenic Skyway, Scenic Railway and Sceniscender, which take you either high above or deep into the valley. (see page 76). There is also a recommended walk from here—see page 222.

From Scenic World, continue along Cliff Drive and then follow Narrow Neck Road, which brings

you to the highway west of Katoomba.

❹ The grand Hydro Majestic Hotel dominates the village of Medlow Bath. Originally constructed in 1904 as a spa for well-off Sydneysiders, it was rebuilt as a tourist hotel in the 1920s. Now restored, it is a good spot for refreshments, or even an overnight stay. The dining room overlooks the Megalong Valley.

Continue along the highway for about 7km (4 miles) to the town of Blackheath (see page 76). Turn right on to the main street and follow signs to Govett's Leap Lookout.

❺ From the lookout there are superb views of the deep, forested Grose Valley and its sandstone cliffs. Local legend has it that a bushranger named Govett galloped over the cliff to escape pursuing mounted police, so giving his name to this place.

From Blackheath, continue west on the highway for 5km (3 miles) to Mount Victoria, which consists of not much more than an old pub, tearooms and a few antiques shops. Turn off the highway and follow signs to the hamlet of Bell, 10km (6 miles) along the Darling Causeway. Once you reach Bell's Line of Road (State Route 40), turn right to Bilpin and Kurrajong. This scenic route back to Sydney has far less traffic than the Great Western Highway. About 8km (5 miles) east of Bell, turn left to the village of Mount Wilson.

Mount Tomah Botanic Garden

OUT AND ABOUT

The Three Sisters, near Echo Point

The spectacular Govetts Leap, above the Grose Valley

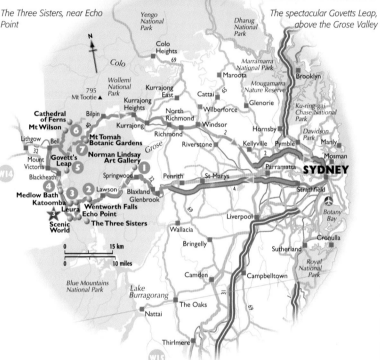

❻ Sydney's well-to-do founded Mount Wilson in the late 19th century as a cool retreat from the city's hot and humid summers. They built grand homes with large gardens planted with English trees and shrubs.

Many of these gardens are open to the public. One area with many large tree ferns is known as the Cathedral of Ferns.

Back on Bell's Line of Road, about 15km (9 miles) from the Mount Wilson turn-off, the next stop is Mount Tomah Botanic Garden.

❼ Mount Tomah Botanic Garden is the cool-climate branch of the Royal Botanic Gardens, Sydney (see page 65). Paths wind through impressive plantings of native and exotic species. The Australian plants include the rare Wollemi pine, which was discovered only in 1994.

Drive east on the Bell's Line of Road through the small rural settlements of Bilpin and Kurrajong Heights—with their orchards and roadside fruit stalls—and on to North Richmond, Richmond and Windsor.

From here, the fastest route back to Sydney is Metroad 2 (Windsor Road and Old Windsor Road), which becomes the M2 Motorway closer to the city. This route and its continuation (Metroad 1) take you over the Sydney Harbour Bridge and back to the city itself.

WHEN TO GO

All year round. Traffic is heaviest on weekends when Sydney people go on day trips to the mountain towns.

WHERE TO EAT

There are plenty of cafés and restaurants throughout the Blue Mountains, particularly in Leura, Katoomba and Blackheath.

Passing through Katoomba, the Paragon Restaurant (*Sun–Fri 8–5, Sat 8–8*) and Zuppa (*7.30am–11pm*), both on Katoomba Street, provide breakfasts and a good choice of snacks and meals in a casual setting.

Other suggestions are the spectacular Hydro Majestic Hotel at Medlow Bath and the Mount Tomah Botanic Garden.

PRINCE HENRY CLIFF WALK
AND THE THREE SISTERS

This scenic Katoomba walk follows a cliffside path along the northern edge of the Jamison Valley, within the Blue Mountains National Park. Lookouts give superb views of the valley's dense forest and sandstone outcrops.

THE WALK

Note: Although not long or difficult, the route is classified as moderate because it includes several sets of steps, some of which are fairly steep.

Distance:	Approximately 3km (2 miles)
Allow:	1.5 hours
Start:	Scenic World, Katoomba; see map page 221
End:	Echo Point, Katoomba
How to get there:	Train from Sydney Central to Katoomba; bus or taxi from station to Scenic World

At Scenic World, face the Three Sisters fountain, walk diagonally across the yard to your left and down a path until you come to the Prince Henry Cliff Walk sign.

Follow this path to a junction, turn left and walk past ferns, heath and bushland before crossing a small bridge. Walk up the steps to enter a park, part of Katoomba Falls Reserve. Follow the sign for Echo Point and walk down some more steps. The main track leads to the left, but head up the steps to the lookout.

❶ This lookout has a commanding view of the Jamison Valley, 300m (984ft) below. Orphan Rock, an outlier of the sandstone escarpment, is straight ahead and Katoomba Falls is to your left.

Go back to the main track, which heads away from the Jamison Valley. You soon reach a pool and Katoomba Cascades.

❷ This area of parkland surrounds the fast-flowing Katoomba Falls Creek, which downstream from here tumbles down the cliff to become Katoomba Falls. The cool, shady gully, surrounded by ferns and rocks, is a good spot for a break.

Cross the creek using the stepping stones, walk up some

fairly steep steps, and turn right to reach the grassy Katoomba Falls Park. Follow the signpost to Echo Point, walking through forest and heathland and under the Scenic Skyway cable car. You soon reach Cliff View Lookout with more views of the Jamison Valley.

Turn left and continue on the gravel track, fringed by heath on the right and weathered sandstone rocks on the left. The path then heads downhill to Wollumai Lookout.

❸ This is where you get your first view of the Three Sisters, three sandstone pillars that are all that remain of an eroded cliffline. An Aboriginal legend claims that the rocks are the daughters of a man who turned them to stone to protect them from the attentions of a bunyip (monster), but was unable to change them back again.

Follow the track down to Allambie Lookout, then into a eucalypt forest and past a rock overhang before heading up steps and a steep metal staircase to the Lady Darly Lookout for another good view.

Keep following the sign to Echo Point, through more forest and heath before emerging near the top of a cliff. Continue on the track, which brings you to the Echo Point car parking area and on to the fenced lookout at Echo Point itself.

❹ The view from here is one of the highlights of the Blue Mountains. It takes in a huge sweep of the Jamison Valley. The natural monoliths Mount Solitary and the Ruined Castle rise like islands in a sea of trees. The Three Sisters are close by.

Turn left at the lookout and follow the track under a stone

arch. You can turn right for a short detour (which later rejoins the main track) to see more valley views from Spooners Lookout, or keep going along a forested hillside. The main track then leads down some steps and through another archway to a lookout directly behind the Three Sisters.

❺ From here there are good views to the left, along the escarpment edge. You should be able to make out Sublime Point, just south of Leura.

Return to Echo Point by the same track. Here you will find a Blue Mountains Visitor Information Office (*daily 9–5*), toilets and the Three Sisters Pavilion, containing shops, eating places and the Blue Mountains World Heritage Exhibition. A number of other walking tracks start from Echo Point; most include very steep sections.

You can return to Scenic World by taxi, on foot along Cliff Drive (20–30 minutes), or by the Trolley Tours tourist bus service, which stops at Echo Point (*daily 11–5; all-day pass A$12*). To return to Katoomba, take a taxi or shuttle bus, or walk through town (about 30 minutes).

WHEN TO GO

All year round. The path is very popular at weekends, so try to go on a weekday.

WHERE TO EAT

Early in the walk, Katoomba Falls Kiosk serves snacks and drinks, and there are food and drink outlets in the Three Sisters Pavilion at Echo Point. Public toilets are at Scenic World and Echo Point.

PLACES TO VISIT

Scenic World, see pages 76, 220.
Blue Mountains, see pages 74–77.

OUT AND ABOUT

The legendary Three Sisters tower above the Jamison Valley

ALONG THE GREAT OCEAN ROAD

Hugging the rugged coastline of southwest Victoria for most of its 250km (155-mile) route, the Great Ocean Road is one of the world's most spectacular coastal roads; it was completed in 1932. The route takes in wild surf and beautiful beaches, massive cliffs and impressive rock formations, spectacular rainforests and abundant wildlife, and busy resort towns and sleepy holiday hamlets.

The famous surf town of Torquay—the GOR starts here

changing views of coastal scenery (to the left) and bush and farmland (to the right). Continue to Kennett River.

❸ At this holiday hamlet, walk or drive to the Grey River picnic ground to try to spot koalas in the trees. If none can be found, take a short detour by turning right up the hill on Grey Road, and drive for about 4km (2.5 miles) until surrounded by bushland—there are usually dozens of koalas snuggled in the branches of the eucalypts here.

Return to the Great Ocean Road and head west to Apollo Bay.

❹ Apollo Bay nestles in the foothills of the Otway Ranges, which descend to a sweeping arc of golden beaches. There is plenty to see and do here (see

OUT AND ABOUT

THE TOUR
Distance: 300km (186 miles) from Torquay to Warrnambool, plus drive to and from Melbourne
Allow: 2 days
Start: Melbourne
End: Melbourne

Drive from Melbourne to Geelong, 75km (46.5 miles) down the Princes Highway (Geelong Freeway), crossing the Westgate Bridge and heading around the western edge of Port Phillip Bay.

In Geelong (see page 94), follow the Great Ocean Road signs through the town, and then go 21km (13 miles) on the Surf Coast Road to Torquay. The Great Ocean Road—route B100—begins in this resort town (see page 97). The road then heads inland before winding down to the coast and Anglesea.

❶ Anglesea is a small holiday town at the mouth of the Anglesea River. Sample the coastal views at the memorial lookout. Just west of Anglesea, the fairways of the local golf course support hundreds of kangaroos and wallabies. You can clearly see them from Golf Links Road.

The Great Ocean Road sweeps west for 9km (6 miles) to Aireys Inlet, where the Split Point Lighthouse has wonderful views of the Bass Strait and the Otway Ranges.

Drive 5km (3 miles) west through Fairhaven to Eastern View, a stretch of road marked by long sandy beaches and hills dotted with holiday homes. The road starts to climb, and about 2km (1 mile) past Eastern View there is a signed turn-off to Cinema Point, one of the road's highest vantage points. The road then winds its way back to sea level to enter Lorne.

❷ This flourishing holiday town, between Loutit Bay and the cool Otway forests, has mild weather, lovely beaches and a touch of café culture. There are beautiful waterfalls and cool fern gullies to explore in nearby Angahook-Lorne State Park.

From Lorne, the road twists along a cliff edge, by turns giving

page 98), and the town is a good place for an overnight stay. For coastal panoramas, try Marriners Lookout (in Marriners Lookout Road) and Crows Nest (in Tuxion Road).

After Apollo Bay, the road climbs into the cool-climate rainforest of Otway National Park, whose attractions can be sampled at Maits Rest, 17km (10.5 miles) from Apollo Bay. About 20km (12 miles) from Apollo Bay, turn left on to a road that leads to Cape Otway.

5 Cape Otway, reaching into the wild Southern Ocean, is marked by Australia's oldest surviving lighthouse, which can be visited (see page 98). The ocean views are sensational, especially from the cliff walk.

Back on the Great Ocean Road, it is 33km (20 miles) to the town of Lavers Hill, the highest point on the road, and another 7km (4 miles) to Melba Gully State Park.

6 The park protects a very beautiful area of cool-climate rainforest. The short Madsen Track wanders past tree ferns, waterfalls, mosses and fungi above a canopy of tall myrtle beech, messmate and black-wood trees.

The road enters the coastal heathlands of Port Campbell National Park, fringed by cliffs that rise up to 70m (230ft) high. Soon the weathered stacks of the Twelve Apostles come into view; pull in to the parking area.

7 These rock pillars—the wave-eroded remains of the old cliffline—stand like sculpted chess pieces in the sea (see page 98). They are among a range of stunning natural features along this part of the coast, created over time by the waves.

One such feature is Loch Ard Gorge, a short distance to the west. In 1878, the sailing ship *Loch Ard* was wrecked here. The Twelve Apostles Interpretative Centre puts the nature and history of the coast into perspective.

Head west for about 11km (7 miles) to Port Campbell.

8 Port Campbell is a pretty village located beside a sheltered beach. The short Port Campbell Discovery Walk leads west from the town, giving excellent views of the cliffs to the east.

About 25km (15.5 miles) west of Port Campbell, the main road dog-legs to the right. Go straight

ahead on to a side road that leads to the Bay of Islands Coastal Park.

9 Along the coast here are dozens of little islands and rock stacks that seemingly float offshore from the cliffs. Besides stunning vistas, there are some easily accessible and safe swimming beaches.

Rejoin the Great Ocean Road, and head west to Warrnambool, the official end of the road. The return to Melbourne inland by the Princes Highway (National Route A1; about 3–4 hours) passes the volcanic Lake Corangamite, the largest saltwater lake in Victoria.

WHEN TO GO

All year round. November to March is the best time for swimming, but try to avoid the crowded Christmas holiday period.

WHERE TO EAT

Apollo Bay: Chris's Beacon Point Restaurant, 280 Skenes Creek Road.

Lorne: Marine Café, 6A Mountjoy Parade; Mermaids Café, 22 Great Ocean Road; Kosta's Taverna, 48 Mountjoy Parade.

Port Campbell: 20Ate Café and wine bar, 28 Lord Street.

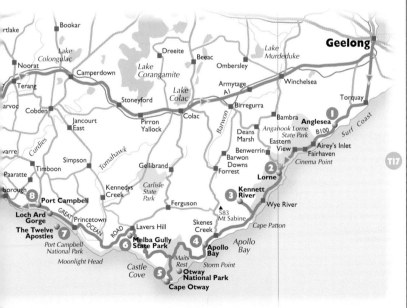

OUT AND ABOUT

MELBOURNE'S GOLDEN MILE

The gently undulating Golden Mile Heritage Trail, marked by 2,700 circular brass discs, follows part of the street grid pegged out by the official town surveyor, Robert Hoddle, soon after Melbourne was founded in 1835.

Distance: 4km (2.5 miles)

Allow: 2–3 hours

Start: Immigration Museum, cnr William and Flinders streets; see map page 83, B2

End: Royal Exhibition Building/ Melbourne Museum, Victoria Street, Carlton

How to get there: City Circle tram connects the start and end

Starting by the edge of the Yarra River on the steps of the Immigration Museum on Flinders Street, the trail's brass markers are embedded in the footpath about every 20m (65ft).

❶ The imposing Customs House (now the Immigration Museum, see page 84) was built on bustling Queen's Wharf by gold rush immigrant J. J. Clark in 1873. Hundreds of thousands of hopeful gold diggers disembarked here from England, Ireland, China and California.

From the museum, turn right up William Street and left at Flinders Lane. John Batman, Melbourne's founder, supposedly came ashore here in 1835 from Tasmania and declared it was 'the place for a village'. The sturdy bluestone buildings along Flinders Lane used to be dockside warehouses. Turn right into King Street up the hill, then right into the grand boulevard of Collins Street.

❷ Just next to the Rialto Towers, with the sky-high Melbourne Observation Deck (see page 85), is the magnificent former Rialto Hotel (now Le Meridien) and the nearby Olderfleet offices, two of Melbourne's best examples of 19th-century neo-Gothic architecture.

Detour left up William Street, past the grey stucco façade of the grand Australian Club, and right into Little Collins Street, the

heart of the legal profession (often referred to as 'Chancery Lane' after the London legal precinct). Two old legal chambers, Normanby Chambers (1883) and Stalbridge Chambers (1891), still stand. Turn right on to quiet Bank Place, containing the much-loved Mitre Tavern, a favourite meeting place for Melbourne lawyers and sporting men since the 1860s. Return left into Collins Street.

❸ The block between Queen and Elizabeth streets, a blend of old and new architecture, has always been Melbourne's business district. Victorian exuberance survives in the ornate banking chamber of the 1887 ANZ Gothic Bank (iron columns and gilded decoration), the adjoining Great Hall or Cathedral Room of the first Stock Exchange of Melbourne, and the 1891 domed banking chamber of the former Commercial Bank of Australia, hidden behind the modern

granite façade of 333 Collins Street. The ANZ Banking Museum at 380 Collins Street tells the city's financial history.

Continue along Collins Street across the Elizabeth Street intersection to the historic shopping heart of the city, traditionally known as the 'Block'. 'Doing the Block' was a favourite pastime in the late 1800s; the area's covered shopping arcades were modelled on those of London and Milan. Turn left into the hidden entrance to the grand Block Arcade, with its mosaic floor and 1907 ceiling murals.

Turn right at Little Collins Street, glimpsing the glass-vaulted Royal Arcade, and return to Collins Street via Howey Place and Capitol Arcade.

❹ Between the Town Hall on your left and the end of Collins Street at the Spring Street intersection are three blocks of fine churches, theatres and shops. Despite its raucous beginnings, Melbourne had an intellectual and religious side, and the area around the Russell Street intersection— often known as Holy Hill—was favoured by the Baptists, the Independents (St. Michael's Uniting Church, 1886), and the Scots (Scots Church, 1873).

Beyond the churches is the haughty, haute couture end of Collins Street. The Melbourne Club, on the left as you approach Spring Street, was founded by young squatters (sheep farmers) in 1839 and is still regarded as a bastion of the powerful and conservative Melbourne establishment.

The Spring Street intersection is dominated by the monumental Old Treasury (see Gold Treasury Museum, page 84).

Turn left up Spring Street to the classical 19th-century Parliament

The Tribute Gardens of the Immigration Museum

House, home to Australia's first Commonwealth Parliament from 1901 to 1927 (tours when the state Parliament is not sitting; tel 03 9651 8568). The Windsor Hotel across the street is the only remaining example of Melbourne's once plentiful grand Victorian hotels. Continue past the majestic 1886 Princess Theatre and turn left down Little Bourke Street.

❺ Colourful Chinatown developed around the boarding houses and stores established by the first immigrants from southern China in 1851, catering for their countrymen on their way to the goldfields (see page 84). The area in and around Little Bourke and Lonsdale streets was notorious for its brothels and barroom prostitutes.

Turn right at Punch Lane to Lonsdale Street. Number 32–34 is the site of the brothel where, it is rumoured, the gold-plated Mace of the Legislative Assembly, which mysteriously disappeared in 1891, was left by drunken parliamentarians. Turn left down Lonsdale Street to Exhibition Street, then right to Carlton Gardens across Victoria Street, leaving the grid of central Melbourne.

❻ Pass through the peaceful, shady Carlton Gardens to the glorious 1880 Royal Exhibition Building (see page 89). Saplings planted in 1880 now

tower above the golden dome. Carlton Gardens were part of a belt of parkland around the city, created by Victoria's first governor, Charles LaTrobe, in the early 1850s. Across Nicholson Street from the Exhibition Building is the bluestone Regency-style Royal Terrace (1853–58).

The walk ends in the plaza between the Royal Exhibition Building and the modern Melbourne Museum.

WHEN TO GO
All year round.

GUIDED TOURS
There is an excellent A$4 guide booklet to accompany the walk, available from many tourist outlets and sights.

Above: Journey's end—the Royal Exhibition Building
Left: The Spring Street vestibule of Parliament House

Tours of the Golden Mile leave Melbourne Visitor Information Centre at Federation Square:
☎ Bookings 1300 130 152, 03 9650 3663 🕐 Daily 1pm
💲 Adult A$20, child A$10; participants receive a free copy of the guide booklet

WHERE TO EAT
The heart of Melbourne has many opportunities for coffee, lunch or other refreshments. Three places are particularly in keeping with the Golden Mile theme:

The Mitre Tavern at 5 Bank Place nestles among skyscrapers. This little yellow pub is ideal for a glass of beer or Australian wine.

Hopetoun Tea Rooms, at the entrance to the Block Arcade, 282 Collins Street, is a survivor of the days when women used to wear hats and gloves to take tea when coming to the city.

Nearer the end of the trail, revive yourself at the elegant Windsor Hotel, 103–111 Spring Street, with a grand afternoon tea complete with scones, cakes and chocolate wonders.

PUBLIC TOILETS
Most major public buildings along the route have public toilets, all with disabled access.

OUT AND ABOUT

OLD BRISBANE
AND THE BOTANIC GARDENS

The walk explores the historic core of Brisbane, now hemmed in by the modern city. Fine colonial buildings reflect the city's origins as a penal settlement and its later development as capital of the colony of Queensland.

THE WALK

Distance: 3km (2 miles)

Allow: Half a day

Start: Anzac Square; see map page 102, B1

End: City Hall

How to get there: Anzac Square is opposite Central Station

Walk to Anzac Square, between Ann and Adelaide streets, and make your way to the square's focus, the Shrine of Remembrance.

❶ The sandstone Shrine of Remembrance was erected in 1930 as a memorial to Australian soldiers who died during World War I. A classical Doric colonnade surrounds an eternal flame. Distinctively shaped bottle trees, manicured lawns, and gardens and memorial sculptures add to the charm of the square.

Cross Adelaide Street and walk through Post Office Square to the General Post Office in Queen Street. Pass through the arcade beside the post office to

Right: City Botanic Gardens
Below: The Shrine of Remembrance in Anzac Square

Elizabeth Street and cross the street to the St. Stephen's Church complex, dominated by St. Stephen's Cathedral.

❷ Designed in the neo-Gothic style, the cathedral was begun in 1863 and completed in 1874. Constructed of porphyry stone, the main façade has twin spires and stained-glass windows.

Return to Elizabeth Street and go right, turn right again on to Eagle

Street and make your way to the riverside walkway at the Eagle Street Pier. Walk south to the Edward Street gates of the City Botanic Gardens.

❸ This is Brisbane's loveliest park, a gently undulating landscape spread with plantings of native and exotic species (see page 102).

The gardens front the Brisbane River, and you can walk down through the park to the foreshore. Look also for the avenue of bunya pines and the shady palm forest. The City Gardens Café on Alice Street is a good place for a break.

Follow the sign from the café southwest across Alice Street to the Old Government House.

❹ Old Government House is a grand neoclassical building built in 1862 as the colonial governor's residence, a role it served until 1910. The house is now occupied by the Queensland University of Technology.

Walk a short distance back along Alice Street to the heart of the city and Parliament House.

❺ The main part of the French Renaissance-style Parliament House was built in 1868 (see page 104). Note how the building's verandahs provide the interior with some shade from the sun.

Nearby, in George Street, is the ornate Victorian exterior of the Queensland Club. Nearly opposite is The Mansions, a striking group of 1890s terrace houses in red brick and pale limestone, now housing shops and restaurants.

Walk along George Street and go left through Queens Gardens to William Street. Cross the street to the Commissariat Stores.

OUT AND ABOUT

A building for money: The former Treasury is now the Casino

6 Convict workers constructed the Commissariat Stores in 1829 *(Tue–Sat 10–4)*. Originally only two storeys high, the third storey was added in 1913.

The Commissariat Stores was a government warehouse, storing goods brought from ships anchored in the nearby river. It now houses the museum and library of the Royal Historical Society of Queensland.

Return through the gardens to George Street and go left across the intersection with Queen Street to the former Treasury Building.

7 Now refurbished as the Treasury Casino, this grand Italianate-style structure was completed in 1889. As with Parliament House, its verandahs act as a cooling space to internal rooms. The interior retains many original features.

Opposite the Treasury Casino, walk down Queen Street Mall and cross the Albert Street intersection to the Regent Theatre.

8 The exuberant exterior of the Regent Theatre, which dates from 1928, has been described as Spanish Perpendicular–Gothic Rococo

in style. The Queen Street entrance leads past a booking hall, café and foyer to a monumental stairway. Originally designed to host live entertainment and films, the theatre is now exclusively a cinema.

Retrace your steps to Queen Street Mall, then turn right on to Albert Street to Brisbane City Hall.

9 Facing King George Square and bounded by Adelaide and Ann streets, City Hall is an impressive neoclassical structure dating from 1930 *(Mon–Fri 8–5, Sat–Sun 10–5, tours Mon–Fri 10, 1; tel 07 3403 8888)*. Sculptures dot the square. To the left of the entry foyer is Brisbane City Gallery, which hosts exhibitions of art and crafts *(daily 10–5)*. There are panoramic views of the city from the bell tower *(Mon–Fri 10–3, Sat 10–2.30)*.

WHEN TO GO
All year round.

WHERE TO EAT
There are numerous good refreshment outlets along the route.

Popular and well-known is Jimmy's on the Mall in Queen Street Mall, selling light meals and drinks around the clock.

City Gardens Café in Alice Street serves breakfast, lunch and afternoon tea. Or you can stock up for a picnic lunch in the Botanic Gardens.

PLACES TO VISIT
Customs House, Queen Street, see page 103.

A tall prospect–the bell tower of City Hall

OUT AND ABOUT

THE SUNSHINE COAST AND ITS HINTERLAND

The drive heads into the hills behind the Sunshine Coast, just north of Brisbane, and ends at the coastal resort of Noosa Heads. It offers a mix of mountain and coastal scenery, long sandy beaches, pretty mountain towns, broad sugar cane fields and pristine national parks.

THE TOUR

Distance: 290km (180 miles)	
Allow: 1–2 days	
Start: Brisbane	
End: Brisbane	

This trip can be accomplished in a day if you are selective with the places you visit. Otherwise an overnight stop around Noosa Heads will allow you to enjoy more of the sights and have an easier time.

From Brisbane take the Bruce Highway (Metroad 3, National Highway 1) north, and after 57km (35 miles) turn left on to the Glass House Mountains Tourist Drive. Drive through the town of Glass House Mountains and follow the signs to Australia Zoo.

❶ Australia Zoo, run by TV's 'crocodile hunter', Steve Irwin, has hundreds of native and other animals on display, including kangaroos, koalas, snakes and crocodiles (see page 121).

Continue for 3km (2 miles) to the town of Landsborough and turn left on to the Blackall Range Road to Maleny. After 12km (7 miles) turn left into Mary Cairncross Scenic Reserve.

❷ From the visitor centre a short track threads for 1.7km (1 mile) through subtropical rainforest. You may see brush turkeys or hear the distinctive calls of catbirds and whipbirds.

From the car park, which has a telescope, there are fine views south of the peaks of the Glass House Mountains. These are the eroded remains of a series of volcanoes that were

formed millions of years ago. Mount Coonowrin, rising to 377m (1,236ft), is the most dramatic.

Drive on for 5km (3 miles) to Maleny.

❸ This old dairy town has reinvented itself as a day-trip escape from the summer heat of the coast. Craft shops and art galleries jostle with cafés and restaurants, and the district has many good guesthouses.

Head 5km (3 miles) back on the road to Landsborough and take a left turn for the 12km (7-mile) mountain ridge drive to the town of Montville (see page 121). Continue north for 4km (2.5 miles) and turn left on to the access road to Kondalilla National Park.

Sandy beaches and the South Pacific Ocean at Noosa Heads

❹ Kondalilla National Park, running down the western slopes of the Blackall Range, encloses a remnant of the region's once-extensive rainforests, much of which were cleared for agriculture in the late 19th and early 20th centuries. The easy Kondalilla Falls 2.7km (1.7-mile) circuit walk passes through rainforest and crosses a creek suitable for swimming.

Drive north for 4km (2.5 miles) to the village of Mapleton.

❺ This attractive village has excellent views over the coastal plain to the Pacific Ocean. About 4km (2.5 miles) west of here is the turn-off to the small Mapleton Falls National Park, where there are picnic tables, barbecues and shelter sheds. The Wompoo Circuit walking track winds for 1.3km (0.8 miles) through rainforest.

From Mapleton, take the road to Nambour and after 14km (9 miles) turn on to the Bruce Highway to Yandina, 8km (5 miles) north. In Yandina follow signs to the Buderim Ginger Factory.

❻ The region's rich volcanic soils, high rainfall and warm climate are ideal for growing a range of tropical crops, including ginger. Visit Yandina's ginger processing plant for its large selection of ginger products (see page 121).

Travel north on the Bruce Highway for 16km (10 miles) to Eumundi.

❼ Eumundi was once the heart of dairy and timber industries. Nowadays its economy relies largely on tourists, who come mainly for the markets that are held on Wednesday and Saturday (see page 118).

Take the Eumundi–Noosa Road to Noosa Heads, a distance of about 25km (15.5 miles). You pass through agricultural districts before reaching the Noosa River and its tributaries and then the town itself.

❽ Noosa, surrounded by Noosa National Park, is the busy and stylish heart of the Sunshine Coast and marks its northern end (see page 118).

Take the coast road from Noosa south to Coolum Beach, a distance of 22km (14 miles), via the coastal villages of Sunshine Beach, Marcus Beach and Perigian Beach, which are worth stopping at for their beautiful beaches.

At Coolum Beach, take the road west to Yandina for 15km (9 miles), past fields of sugar cane, to rejoin the Bruce Highway for the return drive of 107km (66 miles) to Brisbane.

WHEN TO GO
April to October have fine, sunny days and cool nights. December and January are hottest and most crowded, while February tends to be rainy.

WHERE TO EAT
Montville: Monkey Business Café, 184 Main Street, is a popular, family-run café (*daily 9–9*).

Yandina: Buderim Ginger Factory, Factory Road, has good coffee and excellent ginger scones, as well as lunch snacks (*daily 9–5*).

Noosa Heads: Sails Beach Cafe & Bar, 75 Hastings Street, has great coffee, nice sweet things and ocean views (*daily 9–9*).

Coolum Beach: Tides Café, 1750 David Low Way, serves delicious coffee, snacks and meals all day.

PLACES TO VISIT
Brisbane, see pages 102–105.

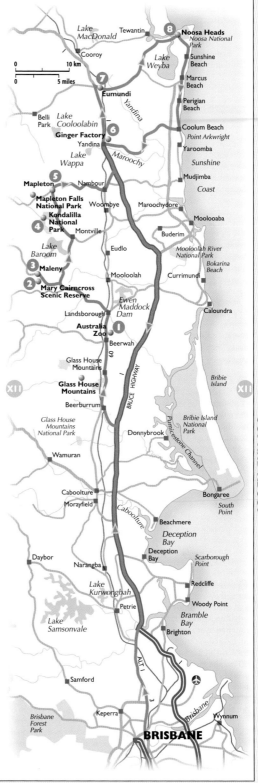

THROUGH THE ATHERTON TABLELAND

Explore the heart of the southern Atherton Tableland, its lush rainforests, crater lakes, farmlands and pretty country towns, all set between the Bellenden Ker/Bartle Frere Mountain Ranges and the Great Dividing Range.

THE TOUR

Distance: 325km (202 miles)	
Allow: 2 days	
Start: Cairns	
End: Cairns	

Drive south from Cairns along the Bruce Highway (National Highway 1) for 24km (15 miles) to Gordonvale. Look for the Atherton Tableland sign and turn right on to the Gillies Highway, which winds up the range (the hairpin bends can be slippery when wet). There are a couple of stopping points with views down the range.

After 31km (19 miles) turn right from the highway for the signposted Cathedral Fig, a 6km (4-mile) drive along a narrow road, 1.5km (1 mile) of which is unsealed.

❶ A 100m (330ft) walk from the car park leads through rainforest to the 500-year-old Cathedral Fig tree, within the Wet Tropics of Queensland World Heritage Site. As high as a 12-storey building and with a girth of 43m (141ft), the tree shelters birds, reptiles, tree kangaroos, sugar gliders and possums.

Backtrack to the Gillies Highway, and turn right on to it. After about 4km (2.5 miles), turn left into the Lake Barrine car park of the Crater Lakes National Park.

❷ Lake Barrine is a crater lake formed by the volcanic activity that moulded much of the Atherton region. It is surrounded by tropical rainforest. An easy 5km (3-mile) walking track circles the lake, or take a 40-minute guided boat trip. A pair of 100-year-old kauri pines stand 50m (160ft) high at the start of the walk. There are tearooms by the lake.

Continue on the highway southwest and after about 10km (6 miles) turn right to the town of Yungaburra.

❸ Yungaburra was once the hub of a thriving timber-felling area, and retains many early 20th-century buildings, some of which now house craft shops. One of north Queensland's best country markets is held on the fourth Saturday of each month.

A track leads from the town to the Curtain Fig tree, a tall strangler fig that has grown a spectacular curtain of aerial roots.

Yungaburra is a good place to break the drive and stay overnight. On day two, head south for 17km (11 miles) through mainly dairy country to the town of Malanda.

❹ Malanda is still very much an agricultural town, producing milk for most of north Queensland. Among its buildings is the Lake Eacham Hotel; built in 1911, it is said to be the largest timber building in Australia. The Malanda Gourmet Food Factory, in James Street, has a museum and interpretive display on the local food and dairy industry (daily 9.30–4.30).

Just outside the town, on the road to Atherton, is Malanda Falls Environmental Park, where the falls drop into the town's swimming pool. Nearby is a rainforest walking track. The Malanda Falls Visitor Centre explains the Tableland's volcanic origins.

Travel the scenic rural road for 24km (15 miles) south to Millaa Millaa. Just east of the town, take Scenic Route 9 through lush pastures to Millaa Millaa Falls.

❺ The Millaa Millaa Falls drops gracefully on to rocks, forming a beautiful curtain of water as it does so. You can stay and swim in a rock pool here, or drive a few kilometres farther east to visit Zillie Falls and, farther still, Ellinjaa Falls.

Back on the main road, drive southeast for 6km (4 miles) and look for the sign on the left for the turn-off to Mungalli Creek Dairy, 3km (2 miles) from the highway.

❻ Mungalli Creek Dairy has north Queensland's only boutique farmhouse cheese shop (daily 10–4). Taste the cheese and yogurt products made on the premises, or buy something to eat or drink at the dairy's tea room.

Rejoin the main road, now the Palmerston Highway, and drive 17km (11 miles) southeast to the small parking area just off the highway that indicates the start of the Wallicher and Tchupala Falls walks.

❼ Choose the track to Tchupala Falls, the more scenic of the two walks. You pass through a short section of rainforest to reach a lookout with a view over the falls. A gentle ribbon of water at dry times of the year, Tchupala Falls becomes a torrent in the wet season. Mosses and ferns thrive in the damp conditions. Climbing a series of steep steps brings views of the basalt gorge and Henrietta Creek.

Continue east on the Palmerston Highway in the direction of Innisfail. After 31km (19 miles) pass the turn-off for Innisfail and keep driving north along what is now the Bruce Highway. After 17km (10.5 miles) turn left to Josephine Falls, 8km (5 miles) from the highway.

❽ Park the car and walk 800m (2,625ft) through rainforest to the base of the falls, which is fed by rains falling on Mount Bartle Frere, Queensland's highest mountain, which rises above you.

Rejoin the Bruce Highway and drive north for 16km (10 miles).

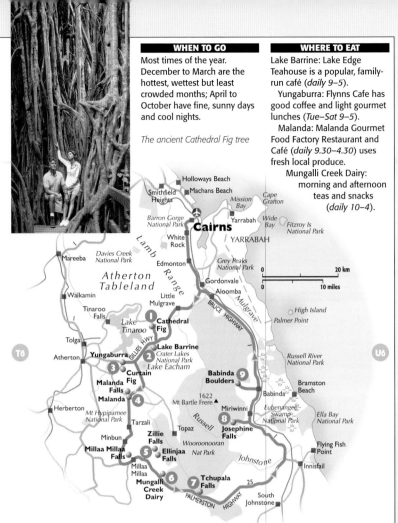

WHEN TO GO

Most times of the year. December to March are the hottest, wettest but least crowded months; April to October have fine, sunny days and cool nights.

The ancient Cathedral Fig tree

WHERE TO EAT

Lake Barrine: Lake Edge Teahouse is a popular, family-run café (*daily 9–5*).

Yungaburra: Flynns Cafe has good coffee and light gourmet lunches (*Tue–Sat 9–5*).

Malanda: Malanda Gourmet Food Factory Restaurant and Café (*daily 9.30–4.30*) uses fresh local produce.

Mungalli Creek Dairy: morning and afternoon teas and snacks (*daily 10–4*).

Holloways Beach
Smithfield Heights
Machans Beach
Mission Bay
Cape Grafton
Barron Gorge National Park
Yarrabah
Wide Bay
Fitzroy Is National Park
Cairns
White Rock
YARRABAH
Lamb Range
Mareeba
Davies Creek National Park
Edmonton
Grey Peaks National Park
0   20 km
0   10 miles
Atherton Tableland
Walkamin
Gordonvale
Aloomba
High Island
Palmer Point
Tinaroo Falls
Little Mulgrave
1 **Cathedral Fig**
Lake Tinaroo
Tolga
Russell River National Park
T6
Atherton
Yungaburra
2 **Lake Barrine**
Crater Lakes National Park
Lake Eacham
Babinda Boulders
9
U6
Curtain Fig
3
Malanda Falls
Malanda
4
Babinda
Bramston Beach
Herberton
Mt Hypipamee National Park
1622 Mt Bartle Frere ▲
Miriwinni
Eubenangee Swamp National Park
Ella Bay National Park
Tarzali
Russell
Topaz
Josephine Falls
8
Minbun
Zillie Falls
Wooroonooran
Nat Park
Flying Fish Point
Millaa Millaa Falls
5
Ellinjaa Falls
Johnstone
Innisfail
Millaa Millaa
Mungalli Creek Dairy
6
7 **Tchupala Falls**
25
South Johnstone
PALMERSTON HIGHWAY
GILLIES HWY
BRUCE HIGHWAY
Mulgrave

Some 7km (4 miles) after the town of Babinda, turn off to Babinda Boulders.

9 Babinda Boulders is a popular swimming and picnic spot with shaded picnic tables and toilets. The boulder-strewn watercourse has some good pools for summer swimming. Caution: It is dangerous to swim here after heavy rain. On the Wonga Track Rainforest Circuit, you cross the creek on a suspension bridge and do an easy 850m (2,790ft) round trip through lush vegetation; signs give information about various rainforest plants.

Go back to the highway, and head north for Cairns, which is about 60km (37 miles) away through arable land flanked by often mist-covered mountains.

Above: The fine cheeses of Mungalli Creek Dairy
Left: Millaa Millaa Falls

PLACES TO VISIT

Atherton Tableland and Kuranda, see page 108.
Cairns, see page 106.
Hinchinbrook Island, see page 116.
Mission Beach and Dunk Island, see page 117.
Undara National Park, see page 123.

OUT AND ABOUT

ADELAIDE: FROM NORTH TERRACE TO THE CENTRAL MARKET

Adelaide's compact central area is easy to explore on foot. The walk takes in the string of grand public buildings along North Terrace, the city's most attractive boulevard, the retail district of Rundle Mall, and the beautiful Botanic Gardens.

THE WALK

Distance: 5–6km (3–4 miles)

Allow: Half a day

Start: Adelaide Festival Centre; see map page 137, B2

End: Victoria Square or Central Market

How to get there: Adelaide Station is near Festival Centre, on North Terrace

Note: The final stop, Central Market, is open on Tuesday, Thursday, Friday and Saturday. On non-market days finish at Victoria Square.

At the Adelaide Festival Centre in King William Road (see page 137), face away from the park and the River Torrens and take the walkway to North Terrace. When you reach the Adelaide Casino at SkyCity, turn left and stay on the north side of North Terrace.

Walk past Parliament House. As you cross King William Road, Government House (the governor's residence) is just visible on your left behind its garden wall. Continue along North Terrace until you come to the State Library of South Australia.

❶ Three of the state's main cultural institutions line up side by side, making an impressive row of grand Victorian architecture. First is the State Library of South Australia, then the Art Gallery of South Australia, and finally the South Australian Museum (see page 141).

Diagonally opposite, near the Botanic Hotel, is Ayers House.

❷ Ayers House, built in 1846 of local bluestone, is a single-storey mansion that was once the home of Sir Henry Ayers, one of South Australia's early premiers (*Tue–Fri 10–4, Sat–Sun 1–4*). Owned by the National Trust, it houses a restaurant and museum of Adelaide.

From Ayers House, cross over North Terrace again to the Royal Adelaide Hospital, then continue on the original eastward direction until you reach the main gate of the Botanic Garden.

❸ It's worth taking some time to explore these beautifully landscaped gardens (see page 137). One option is to walk straight ahead from the main gate and bear left at an intersection to visit the Palm House, a striking 1875 glasshouse that contains a collection of plants from Madagascar.

You can then stroll to the middle of the gardens, past the Main Lake (where there is a restaurant and kiosk) to the Bicentennial Conservatory, with its rainforest plants. Nearby is the International Rose Garden.

Make your way through the gardens to the National Wine Centre of Australia, which faces Botanic Road.

❹ The Centre has the largest selection of Australian wines in the world. You can taste and

City skyline across the Torrens River at sunset

buy wines, and also learn about the winemaking process.

Walk back to the main gate of the Botanic Garden and on to North Terrace again. Almost diagonally opposite is East Terrace, with Rundle Park on the left and a hotel on the right. Walk south along East Terrace for one block with the park on your left and turn right on to Rundle Street with the park behind you.

❺ This is the East End of Rundle Street, one of Adelaide's main wining and dining precincts. Many of the cafés and restaurants that line the street have alfresco dining areas that make the most of Adelaide's sunny weather. This is a lively and popular place until well after dark.

Continue along Rundle Street for 400m (1,315ft) to King William Street through the pedestrian precinct of Rundle Mall.

❻ Rundle Mall is the retail hub of Adelaide. There are shopping complexes and department stores, including the Myer Centre and Adelaide Central Plaza, and flower stalls, restaurants, buskers and boutiques. Among the shopping arcades running off the mall is the ornate Adelaide Arcade, a good example of high Victoriana.

OUT AND ABOUT

Walk up the mall to where it finishes at King William Street. Turn left on to King William Street and walk three blocks past Grenfell, Pirie and Flinders streets to Victoria Square.

7 Adelaide's founder, Colonel William Light, planned this square as the city's official centre. In the middle, a fountain celebrates the rivers that supply Adelaide's water, and a statue commemorates the British queen after whom the square was named. Facing Victoria Square are the Glenelg tram terminus, the Supreme Court, the Cathedral of St. Francis Xavier and the Hilton Hotel.

If it is a Tuesday, Thursday, Friday or Saturday, continue to Central Market by crossing over to the Hilton Hotel and walking west for a block along Grote Street.

8 Flowers, fruit, vegetables, small goods, cheeses, meats and seafood are among the produce for sale at the vibrant Central Market (see page 139). Refresh yourself at one of the cafés and food stalls.

To return to the start point at the Adelaide Festival Centre, walk back to Victoria Square and north along King William Street, passing the Town Hall on your right. Continue for about 0.6km (0.3 mile) until you reach North Terrace and cross into King William Road. The Festival Centre is on your left.

Top: View to the northern side of North Terrace
Above: The Victorian Palm House in the Botanic Garden
Left: Victoria Square fountain

WHEN TO GO
All year round.

WHERE TO EAT
En route, Ayers House, the Botanic Garden and the National Wine Centre all have restaurants.
 Alfresco's on Rundle Street is a popular restaurant.
 On market days you can get food and refreshments at the Central Market.

PLACES TO VISIT
Migration Museum, see page 140.
Tandanya, see page 141.

THE BAROSSA VALLEY
FROM WILLIAMSTOWN TO SPRINGTON

The Barossa Valley is Australia's best-known wine region. There are many other attractions apart from wine, however—historic towns, a unique German influence, good food and unspoiled rural scenery.

THE TOUR

Distance: 50–90km (30–55 miles)	
Allow: 1 day	
Start: Adelaide	
End: Adelaide	

From central Adelaide proceed east along North Terrace with the Botanic Garden on your left. Cross Dequetteville Terrace and continue to Payneham Road. Branch left along Lower North East Road and after 1km (0.6 mile) take Gorge Road on the right.

Continue on Gorge Road through Athelstone and alongside the River Torrens (B31) to Chain of Ponds. Turn right on to the B10. After Gumeracha, go north on Forreston Road and join the B34 to Williamstown. From here, drive north a short distance on the B31, then turn left on to Yettie Road to the Barossa Reservoir and Whispering Wall.

❶ The retaining wall of the Barossa Reservoir is known as the Whispering Wall because of its peculiar acoustic properties. The curve of the wall is such that a person standing at one end can hear a whisper spoken at the other end, 140m (460ft) away.

Off Williamstown Road are the Barossa Goldfields, scene of a gold rush in the 1860s. Walking tracks lead past the old workings.

Return to the B31 and head north to Lyndoch.

❷ Lyndoch bills itself as the gateway to the Barossa Valley because of the numerous wineries in the immediate area. The largest is Chateau Yaldara, 5km (3 miles) northwest of Lyndoch.

An alternative bouquet is the Lyndoch Lavender Farm, 7km (4 miles) southeast of town off the B31. Stroll through 2.5ha (6 acres) of lavender, or sample some of the herb products (*Sep–Feb daily 10–4.30; Mar–Aug Mon, Fri 10–4.30*).

From Lyndoch take the Barossa Valley Way (B19) to Tanunda. Nearing Tanunda, turn right on to Bethany Road to Bethany.

❸ Bethany was the first German settlement in the valley in 1842. The layout of the village—long strips of farmland stretching out behind the cottages—is in the traditional Hufendorf style brought here by the settlers. Historic buildings include the 1851 Herberge Christi Church, and the Landhaus, a mud-and-stone house built in the 1840s and now a restaurant. The picnic area on Bethany Creek was originally the village common.

Bethany Wines, on Bethany Road, is a long-established and picturesque family-owned winery. A few kilometres southeast of the winery, on Mengler Hill Road, is Mengler Hill Lookout, which has a magnificent view of the Barossa and its sea of vineyards.

From Bethany, go back to the Barossa Valley Way for the short drive to Tanunda.

❹ Tanunda, on the banks of the North Para River, preserves much of its German heritage, including three Lutheran churches and the town's marketplace, the Ziegenmarkt (Goat Market). Shops sell German breads, sausages and pastries.

The main wineries in the area are Chateau Tanunda, Richmond Grove, Peter Lehmann Wines, Rockford Wines, Kaiser Stuhl and Basedow. For more information visit the Barossa Wine and Visitor Centre in Murray Street (*Mon–Fri 9–5, Sat–Sun 1–4*).

From Tanunda continue on the Barossa Valley Way to Nuriootpa, at the northern end of the valley.

❺ Nuriootpa is the commercial heart of the Barossa. Winery production facilities straddle the railway line. Along the banks of the North Para River are public parks, a swimming pool and shaded picnic spots. The Penfolds Winery is located at the northern end of town on Tanunda Road.

Go back 1km (0.6 mile) along the Barossa Valley Way then turn left to Angaston (B10), about 7km (4.5 miles) from the turn-off.

The best of the Barossa, in the main street of Angaston

❻ Angaston is an attractive rural settlement among the rolling Barossa Ranges. Walk down the tree-lined main street to savour art and craft shops, galleries, tearooms and restaurants. Schulz Butchers sell excellent German mettwursts. The Angas Park Fruit Company, also in the main street, sells locally grown and processed dried fruit, as well as nuts.

Wineries nearby are Saltram, Yalumba and Henschke Cellars. Some 5km (3 miles) southeast of town on the Eden Valley Road is Collingrove Homestead, a country house dating from the 1850s. It is open to the public (*Oct–Jun Mon–Fri 1–4.30, Sat–Sun 11–4.30*), and has a restaurant and accommodation.

From Angaston, head south along the B10 through the Eden Valley with its gum-studded pastures and rocky hilltops. Springton is about 20km (12 miles) south of Angaston.

7 The town's main drawcard is the Herbig Family Tree. This huge, old, hollow gum tree was once home to a German pioneer, Johann Herbig, his wife and two children, for five years from 1855.

Continue on the B10 via Mount Pleasant and Birdwood to Chain of Ponds, where you fork left on to the B31 for the return drive to Adelaide.

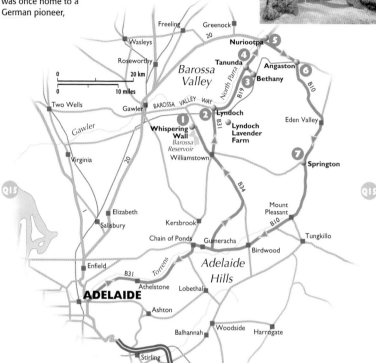

Above right: The Herbig Family Tree, Springton
Right: Learning to pick grapes at the Barossa Vintage Festival, Tanunda

WHEN TO GO
All year round, though summers are hot. In autumn (March to May) the vine leaves turn beautiful shades of red and gold.

WHERE TO EAT
Angaston: The Vintners, Nuriootpa to Angaston road, (see page 272).

PLACES TO VISIT
Adelaide, see pages 137–141.
Adelaide Hills and Hahndorf, see page 141.
Barossa Valley, see page 142.
Murray River, see page 145.
Yorke Peninsula, see page 145.

DARWIN TO LITCHFIELD NATIONAL PARK

The wide open spaces of the Top End encompass a diversity of attractions, including a crocodile farm, a wildlife park, two nature reserves and—the drive's highlight—a superb national park.

THE TOUR

Distance: 280km (174 miles)
Allow: Full day
Start: Darwin
End: Darwin

From central Darwin take the Stuart Highway (National Highway 1) out of the city. After about 25km (15.5 miles), turn left for the 10km (6-mile) drive to Howard Springs Nature Park.

❶ Howard Springs Nature Park contains about 1,000ha (2,470 acres) of monsoon rainforest and eucalypt woodland. Its main attractions are a spring-fed swimming pool and shaded picnic and barbecue areas nearby. Fish, including barramundi—the Top End's best eating fish—can often be seen from the weir, and wallabies are attracted to the picnic areas.

The park can be crowded on weekends during the dry season when Darwin people flock to the park to cool off.

Return to the Stuart Highway and continue south to Darwin Crocodile Farm, located on the Stuart Highway.

❷ Nearly 10,000 saltwater and freshwater crocodiles, ranging in size from hatchlings to monsters 5m (16ft) long, are held captive at this farm (*daily 9–4*). The inmates are housed in natural-looking billabongs (ponds) and display pens, which have wide pathways to allow good viewing.

Many visitors time their arrival to see one of the daily feeding displays (noon and 2pm), when the farm's handlers hand-feed the larger crocodiles.

The reptiles are raised for their meat and skin and, not surprisingly, crocodile meat features prominently on the menu at the farm's restaurant. The gift shop sells goods made from crocodile skin, such as belts, wallets and key rings.

Continue south for 10km (6 miles) and take the Berry Springs turn to the right. After about another 10km, turn right into Berry Springs Nature Park.

❸ Berry Springs Nature Park is set around the spring-fed pools of Berry Creek. A short walking circuit, starting from the picnic area, takes you through typical Top End vegetation of monsoon rainforest (featuring palms and ferns) and dry eucalypt woodland. An interpretative display provides information about the park's flora, fauna and history.

It is a short drive to the adjoining Territory Wildlife Park (see page 131), an open-air zoo set in 400ha (988 acres) of bushland. The park is an excellent introduction to the wildlife of the Northern Territory, both native and feral, in natural settings. The larger animals include water buffalo, banteng (a type of Asian ox), pigs, deer, wallabies and emus.

Other attractions include a walk-through aviary, an aquarium, the Monsoon Forest Walk and a lagoon teeming with water birds. A free shuttle 'train' links major exhibits.

Return to the Stuart Highway and continue south for 39km (24 miles) then turn right to Batchelor, 14km (9 miles) west of the highway.

❹ Stretch your legs at Batchelor, a town built in the 1950s to house workers on the nearby Rum Jungle uranium mine (now abandoned). Wallabies are often seen grazing on the residents' lawns. The 3m (10ft) high castle in the main street is a replica of one near the builder's home in Germany.

Drive on for another 21km (13 miles) through flat country dotted with termite mounds to Litchfield National Park.

❺ The prime attractions at this 146sq-km (57sq-mile) national park are the four main waterfalls, each with a refreshing swimming hole (see page 130). There are also walking tracks, superb views of the surrounding wild country, strange-looking termite mounds, and arresting sandstone rock formations.

Most of the major sights are close to the sealed road that runs through the park. The magnetic termite mounds are 17km (10.5 miles) from the park entrance; Florence Falls and Buley Rockhole 23km (14 miles); the Lost City 28km (17 miles), down a 4WD track; Tolmer Falls 40km (25 miles); Tjaynera (Sandy Creek) Falls 45km (28 miles), down a 4WD track; and Wangi Falls 52km (32 miles).

A large picnic area and kiosk are located at Wangi Falls, the park's most popular spot. Swimming holes are often closed after heavy rain because of dangerous currents.

Return to Darwin via Batchelor and the Stuart Highway.

The Lost City in Litchfield National Park—the weathered sandstone outcrops look like sculptures

OUT AND ABOUT

Wangi Falls in Litchfield National Park

A refreshing dip in Berry Springs Nature Park

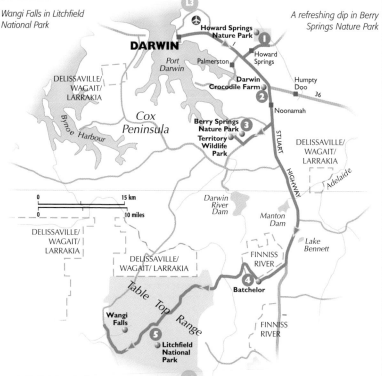

Don't snap—feeding time at Darwin Crocodile Farm

WHEN TO GO

Most times of the year. December to March are the hottest and wettest—but least crowded—months; April to October, the dry months, is high tourist season.

WHERE TO EAT

Darwin Crocodile Farm: The café serves light meals including crocodile delicacies such as Croc Burgers and Crocodile Drumsticks.

Territory Wildlife Park: Light refreshments and full meals from a self-service buffet (*daily 8.30–4*).

PLACES TO VISIT

Darwin, see page 125.

UBIRR ROCK ART SITE

At the northern border of Kakadu National Park, Ubirr Rock has some of the oldest rock art in the world. The short walk stops at three 'galleries' and a vantage point for a Kakadu panorama.

THE WALK

Distance: 1km (0.6 miles)

Allow: 2 hours

Start: Ubirr car parking area

End: Ubirr car parking area

How to get there: Ubirr Rock is 36km (22 miles) north of Jabiru, in Kakadu National Park, and 283km (176 miles) east of Darwin

There are three main galleries of Aboriginal rock art: the Main Gallery, the Namarrgarn Sisters and the Rainbow Serpent. At the start of the track, take the right branch and walk for 300m (985ft) past the Mabuyu Gallery to the Main Art Gallery.

The rangers ask that you follow signs, keep to defined walking paths and do not touch the painted rock surfaces. The Main Gallery and Rainbow Serpent Gallery have wheelchair access.

❶ Aboriginal people have occupied northern Australia for at least 23,000 years, and probably for much longer. The rock shelters and overhangs of Ubirr, like the Main Gallery, were lived in until recent times, and the Aboriginals took advantage of the abundant food supplies in the East Alligator area.

Rock art here, as elsewhere at Ubirr, is mainly in the X-ray style. This shows the internal organs of animals and humans as well as the figure's outward appearance. The Ubirr images date from between 300 and 1,500 years ago, and some have been repainted over the years.

Aboriginals caught game such as catfish, mullet and long-necked turtles in nearby watercourses, and depicted these and other foods on the rocks before you. More recent paintings show Europeans who came to hunt water buffalo in the 1880s—one white man is shown with a pipe in his mouth and hands on hips.

High up on the ceiling of the overhang are red and yellow sorcery images said by Aboriginals to have been painted by beings called Mimi spirits. Near the Main Gallery is a red-ochre painting of a thylacine (Tasmanian tiger), a species that became extinct on the Australian mainland about 2,000 to 3,000 years ago.

Take the path up the rock face past the Crosshatching Gallery to the Namarrgarn Sisters site.

❷ In this gallery the Namarrgarn Sisters are depicted pulling string apart. In an Aboriginal myth the Namarrgarn Sisters throw down pieces of string from their home in the stars, attach the string to humans' internal organs, and bring sickness to those people when they make their way down the string.

Walk up the 250m (820ft) track along the rock face to Nadab Lookout.

❸ The lookout gives amazing vistas over Cahills Plain (Nardab), the Cannon Hill outliers (Garrkanj and Nawurrkbil) to the north, and the East Alligator River and floodplain. Visit late afternoon for beautiful sunsets over the wetlands. The river, outlined by a fringe of trees to the northeast, marks the boundary between Kakadu and the Aboriginal-owned Arnhem Land.

Until recent years water buffalo, introduced from Asia, grazed on the plains, doing terrible damage to the landscape. Since their removal in the late 1980s the natural vegetation is returning. In the evenings short-eared rock wallabies frequent the rocks around the art sites; some may be spotted resting during the day.

Retrace your steps and take the return section of the circular path, and detour on to the boardwalk that runs past the Rainbow Serpent art site.

❹ This gallery has a painting of a Rainbow Serpent on a cliff wall above a site that has traces of many generations. In traditional Aboriginal beliefs the Rainbow Serpent is the ancestor that created people and the world in which they live.

Stories about the Rainbow Serpent vary from place to place, but to Kakadu Aboriginals the Serpent is a powerful female, ever present, and usually resting in quiet waterways unless disturbed. They believe that when the Serpent passed through Ubirr she painted her image on the rock as a reminder of her presence.

Follow the trail back to the car park.

OUT AND ABOUT

WHEN TO GO

April to October. Ubirr is open Apr–Nov daily 8.30–dusk; Dec–Mar 2–dusk. Entry free.

There are ranger talks at the Main Gallery May to September at 9.30, noon and 4; the Namarrgarn Sisters at 10.30 and 5.30; and the Rainbow Serpent at 11.30 and 4.

The roads to Ubirr are sealed, but can be inundated during the wet season. If in doubt, check local road conditions at Bowali Visitor Centre, Jabiru (*daily 8–5; tel 08 8938 1120*), or call 1800 246 199.

WHERE TO EAT

The closest refreshment stop is Border Store Manbiyarra, 3km (2 miles) south of Ubirr, where snacks, lunch, and morning and afternoon teas are served (*daily 8.30–5.30*).

PLACES TO VISIT

Kakadu National Park, see pages 128–129.

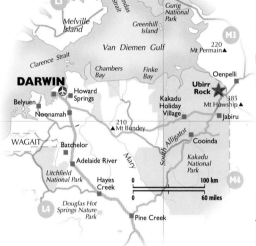

Opposite: The landscape of Ubirr Rock
Above: On top of Ubirr Rock
Below: Ancient Aboriginal rock art in the Main Gallery

OUT AND ABOUT

MARGARET RIVER ROUND TRIP

The coastal drive from Perth to Margaret River encounters rolling hills, dramatic forests, fantastic beaches, and wonderful food and wine. As a day-trip, you should leave Perth as early as possible; for a more relaxing experience, stay overnight at Margaret River.

THE TOUR

Distance:	654km (406 miles)
Allow:	1–2 days
Start:	Perth
End:	Perth

From Perth take the Old Coast Road (National Route 1) to Bunbury then the Bussell Highway (State Route 10) to Busselton. While the towns along the way are worth exploring—including Mandurah, Bunbury and Busselton—these should only be considered if you have more than a day. Otherwise you'll be rushed when you get to Margaret River. From Busselton take Caves Road along the coast to Dunsborough.

Note: It's worthwhile finding information on the region's wineries before leaving Perth.

❶ Dunsborough is a small resort on the western shores of Geographe Bay. There are good beaches and from June to December opportunities for whale-watching. About 13km (8 miles) farther west (no-through road) is the northern section of Leeuwin–Naturaliste National Park, which preserves fine coastal scenery.

From Dunsborough, travel on Caves Road south for about 8km (5 miles) to Yallingup.

❷ It's worth stopping here to look at the pounding surf that breaks on Yallingup beach. The size of the waves makes this a popular destination for surfers.

Continue south on Caves Road for about 15km (9 miles) through vineyards to the intersection with Hammons South Road.

❸ Many of the Margaret River region's wineries are located along or just off the stretch of road between Yallingup and Gracetown, in an area known as the Wilyabrup Valley.

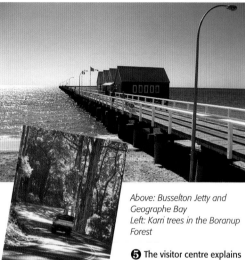

Above: Busselton Jetty and Geographe Bay
Left: Karri trees in the Boranup Forest

Choose a winery or two and drop by for tasting and cellar-door sales.

One of the larger wineries is Vasse Felix, on Caves Road near Hammons South Road. The Old Winery Gallery here has regular art exhibitions, showing works by Australian artists including Arthur Boyd, Sidney Nolan and Lloyd Rees.

Just past the Margaret River turn-off (on the left) is the road to Prevelly Park. Turn right here and take Rivermouth Road, which leads to the mouth of the Margaret River and the Indian Ocean.

❹ This is one of the most popular spots in the area for surfing. The Margaret River Masters international surfing competition is held here in April each year. It's usually very windy on the beach, but the views are great.

Return to Caves Road and continue south to CaveWorks.

❺ The visitor centre explains the caves that riddle the limestone bedrock of this area (see page 158). There are some 350 caves, but only about a dozen are open to the public. Among them is Lake Cave, which can be entered on a tour from CaveWorks. Its main feature is an underground lake, above which hangs a limestone formation that looks like an upturned table.

Just north of CaveWorks is Mammoth Cave, known for its size and the bones of extinct animals. It also features a self-guiding system allowing you to explore the cave at your own pace (*daily 9–4*).

About 4km (2.5 miles) south of CaveWorks, turn right on to Boranup Drive, which leads into Boranup Forest.

❻ Tall pale-barked karri trees, reaching 60m (197ft) or more, dominate the forest's slopes and valleys. A gravel road, suitable for two-wheel-drive vehicles, winds through the forest past picnic spots. Near the end of the drive, not far before it rejoins Caves Road, is Boranup Lookout,

OUT AND ABOUT

which has views over the forest to the west coast and Hamelin Bay.

Rejoin Caves Road and continue south to Bushby Road. Turn left and join the Bussell Highway for the northward journey to Margaret River.

❼ Margaret River township (see page 158) is the heart of the region and is a good location to spend the night. The Margaret River Wine Tourism Showroom, within the Margaret River Visitors Centre on the main street, has information about local wineries.

Drive north on the Bussell Highway in the direction of Busselton to the small settlement of Cowaramup.

❽ A visit to the Margaret River Regional Wine Centre provides another chance to learn about the region's wineries. There are also several art and craft galleries, and the Candy Cow, renowned for its fudge and honeycomb.

Just north of town, at the junction with Harmons Mill Road, is Fonti Farm, where you can taste and purchase the cheeses, ice cream and yogurt of the Margaret River Dairy Company (daily 9.30–5).

A short distance down Harmons Mill Road is the Margaret River Chocolate Factory, which sells premium chocolates and has a café (daily 9–5).

Continue north on the Bussell Highway to Busselton and Perth.

WHEN TO GO
All year round.

WHERE TO EAT
Wilyabrup Valley: winery restaurants and cafés between Yallingup and Gracetown.
   Margaret River: VAT 107, 107 Bussell Highway (daily 9am–late).

PLACES TO VISIT
Augusta, see page 155.
Bunbury, see page 156.
Margaret River, see pages 158–159.

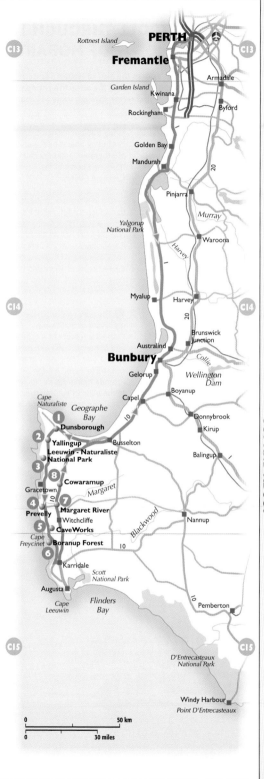

OUT AND ABOUT

A STROLL THROUGH THE HEART OF HOBART

Take in the best of Hobart's historic waterfront, pass through the heart of the attractive residential area of Battery Point, and return through lively Salamanca Place.

THE WALK

Distance: 3.5km (2 miles)	
Allow: 1 hour	
Start : Seaward corner of Victoria Dock and Hunter Street	
End: Seaward corner of Victoria Dock and Hunter Street	

Leave the harbour warehouses and the fishing fleet crammed against the dock and head to the city (see page 162). Turn at Mures Fish Centre, passing the moored fish punts, cross Davey Street, and go through a car parking area to reach Macquarie Street and the Tasmanian Museum and Art Gallery.

❶ The museum and art gallery incorporate the 1808 Commissariat Store, Hobart's oldest building. The collections relate to the island's history, including convicts and Tasmanian Aboriginals, and there is a good selection of colonial art.

Cross Argyle Street to the Tasmanian Maritime Museum in the Carnegie Building.

❷ The maritime museum tells the story of the island's sea-faring tradition using objects (including boat models) and photographs. Touring exhibitions are shown in the Carnegie Gallery.

Return to Macquarie Street and turn left up the hill, past the tall General Post Office on the right and the Town Hall on the left, to Franklin Square, which fronts the first Government House. Face the harbour and walk down to Davey Street and turn right to walk along it to St. David's Park.

❸ The park was originally the graveyard of St. David's Cathedral (corner of Macquarie and Murray streets) and on the lowest side some early graves can still be seen. A large band rotunda marks the mid-point of the park. In autumn the old deciduous trees glow with russet colours.

Emerge at the highest corner of the park, on Harrington Street. Turn left, cross the first intersection, then turn left on to Hampden Road. Follow it to Battery Point, past 19th-century mansions, and cottages to No. 103, the Narryna Folk Museum.

❹ The museum occupies one of the area's oldest buildings, built in 1836. Its original fittings include rare colonial Huon pine furniture (see page 162).

Continue down Hampden Road and turn left into Arthur Circus.

❺ This well preserved circle of one- and two-bedroom cottages is built around a village green. St. George's Anglican Church completes the early colonial picture.

Back on Hampden Road, walk a short distance and turn right into Colville Street. Walk for about 100m (330ft) to a pub called the Shipwrights Arms.

❻ The name of the pub reflects the maritime occupations of the original inhabitants—sailors, boat builders, labourers, sea captains. The Shipwrights Arms is decorated inside with maritime images and historical snippets.
The surrounding mariners' cottages made up the hub of the early seafaring community in Hobart.

Small craft and warehouses line Victoria Dock

OUT AND ABOUT

Go back to Hampden Road. Follow it for another 200m (660ft) as it changes to the long, sweeping curve of Castray Esplanade around Princes Park.

❼ Stop for a while to take in the harbour views. The park was originally the site of a gun battery that protected the harbour; the suburb was named after the battery. The 1818 signalling station has survived.

Continue on Castray Esplanade, with Sullivans Cove on your right, to Salamanca Place.

❽ Salamanca Place is dominated by early colonial warehouses and buildings redolent of the harbour's maritime and commercial origins. They now house art galleries, bookshops, gift shops, cafés, pubs and restaurants. Salamanca Market is held here on Saturdays.

Princes Wharf, alongside the cove, is the main venue for the Taste of Tasmania Festival around New Year's Day.

Follow the curve of the wharf back to the start at Victoria Dock. Pass the sandstone Parliament House and the modern Brooke Street Pier to the Derwent Ferry departure wharves.

❾ Two ships here give a sense of early Hobart's bustling waterfront. Pride of place belongs to the restored *May Queen*, one of only five wooden boats of its age (1820s) in the world still afloat.

Another sailing treasure, the *Lady Nelson*, a colonial square rigger, is moored at nearby Elizabeth Street Pier. The *Lady Nelson* is available for charter and regularly sails the Derwent in the warmer months.

From Elizabeth Street Pier you can return Victoria Dock.

The Saturday Salamanca market is a Hobart institution—more than 300 stallholders sell everything from fresh local produce and art and crafts to delicious hot coffee and mouth-watering snacks

WHEN TO GO
All year round.

WHERE TO EAT
Jackman McRoss Bakery, 57–59 Hampden Road, Battery Point (*Mon–Fri from 6am, Sat–Sun 5am*).

PUBLIC TOILETS
Both museums; Franklin Square; St. Davids Park.

The colonial row houses of Battery Point recall early Hobart

OUT AND ABOUT

FROM HOBART TO STRAHAN BY THE LYELL HIGHWAY

This east–west drive across Tasmania samples a cross-section of the island's landscapes, from farmland to wild mountains. Journey's end is beautiful Strahan, gateway to the remote West Coast.

THE TOUR

Distance: 350km (218 miles)	
Allow: 2 days	
Start: Hobart	
End: Strahan	

From Hobart, drive northwest on the Brooker Highway (National Highway 1). At Granton, the Lyell Highway (A10) takes over from the Brooker and leads through rural scenery along the Derwent River to New Norfolk.

1 New Norfolk is the major town of the Derwent Valley, and a former hub for hop-growing (see page 167). The Bush Inn is a good place to stop for refreshments, and there are walks along the riverside.

Continue on the Lyell Highway to the town of Hamilton, passing poppy fields, old hop-drying oast houses, scattered farms and one-pub hamlets like Gretna Green.

2 Stroll around the wide streets of Hamilton to admire the historic sandstone buildings. The town grew rapidly in the early 1800s, but stagnated from the middle of the 19th century. The lack of subsequent development preserved many of the town's early buildings.

Soon after Hamilton, the highway climbs to higher, wilder country. Native vegetation takes over from farmland until eventually all signs of agriculture vanish. Drive to Derwent Bridge, passing through the buttongrass plains that characterize Tasmania's southwest highlands.

3 Approaching the hamlet of Derwent Bridge, you can see some of the numerous peaks of the central highlands and the southwest. Mount Olympus rises to the north-west and marks the western

corner of Lake St. Clair. A 5km (3-mile) side road going north from the middle of the settlement leads to the lake, at the southeastern end of Cradle Mountain-Lake St. Clair National Park (see page 163). Cynthia Bay is well worth a visit, as are the nearby café and interpretation office.

Derwent Bridge is a good area for an overnight stop. Before leaving, top up the fuel tank, as it's is the last filling station for the next 83km (51 miles).

Return to the highway and drive west into the mountains. After about 15km (9.5 miles) the dramatic peak of Mount King William I rises south of the road to 1,324m (4,342ft). There are several stopping points for lookouts and nature trails along this part of the highway, the first one being King William Saddle.

4 The lookout gives excellent views of this mountainous country, much of which is encompassed by Cradle Mountain-Lake St. Clair National Park to the north, and Franklin-Gordon Wild Rivers National Park to the south.

The saddle marks a change in vegetation: The distinctive west coast temperate rainforest—notable for king billy pines and pandani—takes over from the eucalypts and buttongrass of the east.

A short drive away is the Surprise Valley Lookout, which has wonderful views of the U-shape glacial valley and Frenchmans Cap to the southwest.

Continue west, descending steeply by the Mount Arrowsmith pass. Pull in where the highway crosses the Franklin River.

5 The Franklin River Nature Trail starts here, and leads for an easy 1km (0.6 mile) into temperate rainforest.

After the walk, drive a few kilometres west along the highway to Donaghy's Hill, where a moderate 40-minute return climb takes you to Donaghy's Hill Lookout. There are magnificent views from here southwest to Frenchmans Cap, which at 1,443m (4,733ft) is the most inspiring peak of the region.

Drive on for several kilometres, descending the Victoria Pass. Cross the Nelson River Bridge, and turn into the parking area for Nelson Falls.

6 Nelson Falls is a level 20-minute walk through jungle-like temperate rainforest. Colourful fungi and a tangle of creeping vines and ferns predominate. The falls are spectacular after good rains.

On from here, the Bradshaw Bridge takes the Lyell Highway across Lake Burbury, with mountains and high ridges rising

Nelson Falls, just a short walk from the Lyell Highway on the way to Queenstown

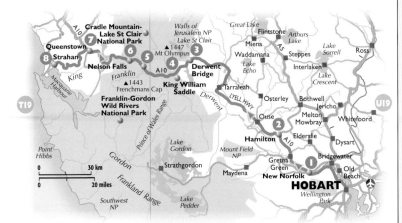

from its shores. A few kilometres farther are the small towns of Gormanston and Linda and then Queenstown just beyond.

7 Gormanston and Linda are fascinating run-down mountain towns that evoke the heyday of the mining boom during the late 19th century. The period Royal Hotel by the side of the highway at Linda is undergoing restoration. This is strange-looking country—mountainous, but with the worked-over appearance of a vast quarry.

A winding descent along the highway brings you to Queenstown. After so much wilderness, Queenstown comes as a shocking yet fascinating contrast, as more than 100 years of mining have stripped the vegetation and soil on hills around the town to bare rock.

Queenstown itself has a number of Victorian buildings, including a former hotel that now houses the Galley Museum, telling the town's story in photographs. Steam trains of the West Coast Wilderness Railway run from here to Strahan on a rugged and scenic route.

The last stage is a winding 40-minute drive to Strahan.

8 The town and port have much to offer the visitor, including museums, restaurants, bushwalks and cruises on Macquarie Harbour (see page 167).

Above: The scars of more than a century of mining at Queenstown
Below: Strahan's harbour

WHEN TO GO
All year round. October to April are the ideal, warmer months; other times are beautiful, if cool to cold.

WHERE TO EAT
Derwent Bridge: Lake St. Clair Visitor Centre; Derwent Bridge Hotel; Derwent Bridge Roadhouse (fuel stop).

PUBLIC TOILETS
At Derwent Bridge or Lake St. Clair. There's a basic composting toilet at the Franklin River Nature Trail (stop No. 5), between Derwent Bridge and Queenstown.

**Bus travel is a comfortable way to sightsee in a friendly atmosphere.
Most Australian buses are equipped with reclining seats, individual reading lights,
anti-glare windows and on-board video entertainment, plus air-conditioning and restrooms.
Bus drivers are often good sources of local knowledge.**

Approximate adult one-way fares for bus travel on popular daily express routes:

Route	Hours	Fare
Adelaide–Alice Springs	19	A$168
Adelaide–Brisbane	33	A$204
Adelaide–Perth	34	A$238
Alice Springs–Uluru	6	A$74
Alice Springs–Darwin	19	A$184
Brisbane–Cairns	28	A$182
Cairns–Darwin	41	A$372
Canberra–Melbourne	9.5	A$59
Hobart–Launceston	2.5	A$22
Melbourne–Brisbane	25	A$164
Melbourne–Adelaide	10	A$56
Perth–Darwin	56	A$522
Sydney–Adelaide	22	A$121
Sydney–Brisbane	15	A$89
Sydney–Canberra	4.5	A$36
Sydney–Melbourne	14	A$62

McCAFFERTY'S EXPRESS COACHES

Luxury buses travel to more than 900 destinations every day, throughout Australia. McCafferty's have offices in all the major cities and many smaller towns, including Alice Springs, Cairns, Mount Isa, Rockhampton, Townsville and Surfers Paradise.
☎ 13 20 30 (within Australia)
www.mccaffertys.com.au

Sample Journey
Perth–Adelaide, 2,070km (1,051 miles)
Time: 39.5 hours
Fare: Adult A$251

GREYHOUND PIONEER

Greyhound operates throughout Australia, covering all major cities and many other destinations, including Cairns and the Great Barrier Reef, the Red Centre (Uluru, Coober Pedy, Broken Hill), Kakadu (seasonal), Kalgoorlie, Broome, Monkey Mia, Kalbarri and Exmouth.
☎ 13 20 30 (within Australia), 07 4690 9888
www.greyhound.com.au

Sample Journey
Adelaide–Alice Springs, 1,570km (976 miles)

Time: 20 hours (includes 15 stops at bus stations, roadhouses and fuel stations)
Fare: Adult A$177

Bus Passes

McCafferty's and Greyhound Pioneer bus passes are interchangeable between the two operators. Validity ranges from one month to a year.

Aussie Explorer Pass Choose as many passes as you need from 17 pre-selected routes (travelling in one direction).

Aussie Kilometre Pass As the name suggests, you purchase a set amount of kilometres, up to 20,000km (12,400 miles); sample price, A$312 for 20,000km (travel in any direction).

MURRAYS AUSTRALIA

Murrays claims to be Australia's largest luxury bus company. It operates non-stop express services up and down the east coast from Melbourne to Cairns via Canberra, Sydney, the Gold Coast and Brisbane.
☎ 13 22 51 (within Australia)
www.murrays.com.au

Sample Journey
Sydney–Canberra, 284km (177 miles)
Time: 3.5 hours.
Fare: Adult A$35

COUNTRYLINK

Countrylink (see page 42) is the long-distance passenger rail and bus operator from New South Wales to Victoria and Queensland.
☎ 13 22 32 (within Australia)
www.countrylink.nsw.gov.au
or visit a Countrylink Travel Centre

Bus Pass
East Coast Discovery Pass Economy travel between Melbourne and Cairns.

TASMANIAN BUS COMPANIES

There are no passenger trains in Tasmania. Buses are the best option after car rentals for getting around.

The two main companies are Tigerline and 'Tasmania's own' Redline. All bus services use luxury buses (no first- or second-class tickets).

Redline
☎ 03 6233 9466,
1300 360 000
www.tasredline.com.au
● Major routes only—Hobart, Launceston, Devonport, Burnie; Devonport to Cradle Mountain tour 26 December to mid-April.
● Air-conditioning, videos, reclining seats, seatbelts and a restroom with drinking fountain.
● No catering on buses.
● No smoking.

Tigerline
☎ 03 6272 6611,
1300 653 633
www.tigerline.com.au
● Services to west and east coasts.
● Air conditioning, reclining seats and video on some buses.
● No catering on buses.
● No smoking.

Bus Passes
Redline Tassie Pass 10 days unlimited travel to all Redline destinations for A$160.
Tigerline Explorer Pass 10 days unlimited travel for A$160.

FLY-BUS TOURS

You can see more of Australia by combining a bus tour with an air link. Tours with Greyhound and McCafferty's express buses are combined with Qantas flights; there are several planned itineraries or—within reason—you can design your own. Flights must be purchased at least three days before departure.

Sample journey
Perth–Alice Springs by air
Alice Springs–Sydney by bus
Fare: $812

The operator **Experience Trips Australia** also arranges itineraries.
☎ 02 9221 4711,
1300 301 359
www.experiencetrips.com.au

OUT AND ABOUT

This chapter lists places to eat alphabetically in each of Australia's states. Places to eat in each capital city are listed first, followed by others listed alphabetically by town. Note that some establishments offer both food and accommodation.

Eating

EATING OUT IN AUSTRALIA

For about 150 years since its discovery by Captain Cook in 1770 Australia did not have its own cuisine. Even now many Aussies cannot describe the cooking style of their country, where the traditions of early English, Cornish, Welsh, Scots and Irish settlers have fused with the tastes of later immigrants and international styles.

BOUNTIFUL AUSTRALIA

No visitor to Australia need go hungry. Inexpensive meals are available at pubs in almost every town, while major cities have everything—Spanish tapas bars, restaurants with every national food, brasseries, bistros, cafés and hotels. Even motels serve continental or filling English/American breakfasts. You can find food at roadside filling stations, museums, universities and wineries, while American-influenced burger, chicken and pizza outlets abound.

Most metropolitan city shopping complexes and major markets have food halls offering inexpensive dishes from around the world. Or try Australian bakeries, whose breads now range from foccacia to French-inspired Vietnamese. Pies, quiches and sweet treats can be enjoyed at alfresco tables outside some bakeries and they are certainly a good source for picnics and barbecues.

HOME-GROWN

Australia is rich in meat, seafood, fish, vegetables and fruit, including tropical varieties such as mangoes, bananas, rambutan, custard apples, papayas and avocado. There are macadamia nuts in tropical Queensland and cold-climate produce in the apple isle, Tasmania. Citrus fruits—oranges, mandarins, lemons and limes—grow from South Australia's Riverland on the Murray River to Queensland.

ABORIGINAL FOOD

You can experience the food of Australia's Aboriginals—traditional hunters and gatherers—at places such as Adelaide's Tandanya (see page 141). On any tour to discover Aboriginal culture, you are inevitably introduced to bush tucker, sustenance for thousands of years. Kangaroo, the world's healthiest meat, may be on the menu or

the long-legged bird, the emu. More likely you'll be shown how to eat berries and leaves in the bush and how to get early morning water from dew-fresh leaves—survival stuff for the stranded.

TRADITIONS

Until the 1960s the typical Australian evening meal followed the British tradition: meat (usually roasted or stewed) and two or three vegetables. Dining out was uncommon for everyone except commercial travellers (travelling salesmen), who stayed and dined at country pubs. Lunch was a sandwich, a meat pie with tomato sauce, or a pasty.

The pasty (or pastie, an envelope of pastry filled with meat and vegetables) is still revered among the Yorke Peninsula Copper Triangle towns of South Australia, where it was imported by miners from Cornwall. These pioneers—and their cuisine—are commemorated at Kernewek Lowender, the world's biggest Cornish festival, held in odd-numbered years.

Meat pies, too, are still very popular takeout meals. You may be lucky enough to find shops selling gourmet varieties. One of these, Fredo Pies, at Frederickton on the New South Wales north coast, sells some 100 varieties, including emu and crocodile. South Australia went one step further and created the pie floater (a meat pie in pea soup or gravy). Pie floaters are sold from pie carts outside Adelaide's general post office, the railway station and casino, and in suburban Norwood.

CHEFS OF THE WORLD

Ship travellers to the old country—Britain—found French flavours in London and Paris. On their return French restaurants emerged slowly, but initially catering only for the wealthy. Cantonese cooks—assiduous vegetable gardeners—arrived

NEW SOUTH WALES & ACT

Sydney's restaurants, brasseries, bistros, bars, hotels and coffee shops serve all types of food. But it's Australia's most expensive dine-out city, from $A40 to $A90 for, respectively, a two-course lunch and dinner at quality places—often more. Then add beverages. The *Sydney Morning Herald Good Food Guide* has excellent suggestions with prices. Look for Sydney rock oysters, small but tasty. Hit suburban pubs for great steak with veg or salad counter lunches and dinners from about $A7.

Canberra, Australia's capital, host to international diplomats, has similar eating options to Sydney though prices are slightly less. There are many foreign restaurants, and outlets for the grain-fed beef, lamb and south-coast seafood of New South Wales. Major dining areas are the CBD , Dickson and cosmopolitan Manuka. Wine bars offer lunches that are the equal of their wines.

VICTORIA

Melbourne—in competition with Sydney—has hundreds of cafés, restaurants, bistros, brasseries and delis. Take your pick by the Yarra River—a mid-market two-course meal is from $A30 to $A50. In suburban Richmond you can opt for Greek and Vietnamese, in Carlton go Mediterranean. The *Age Good Food Guide* has recommendations with prices.

Australia's smallest mainland state is dairy-rich. From regional Gippsland a gourmet-deli trail loops east along the Princes Freeway for 145km (90 miles), well-signed from the Baw Baw turnoff. Finish at Yarragon with tea rooms and produce stores. In the central north of the state, one-time Ned Kelly territory, Milawa Gourmet Country merges with one of Australia's oldest wine-growing areas, around Rutherglen, where wineries serve modern-Australian lunches. Victoria is a fish state too: A huge fishing fleet sails out of Lakes Entrance on the southeast coast.

QUEENSLAND

Almost the size of western Europe, Queensland has everything from hinterland beef (Rockhampton is Australia's beef capital) to scallops and mud crabs. Try the mud crabs in ravioli or just break them apart as locals do. The nation's sugar industry is based here too, so don't be surprised when chefs caramelize fish and vegetables. Prices are just above South Australia's—so among the least expensive.

NORTHERN TERRITORY

There are various menus on the long route from Darwin to Alice Springs—expect crocodile and camel meat particularly, barramundi (a tender fish), water buffalo, magpie geese and bush tucker; kangaroo or emu are gourmet tucker. Alice Springs restaurants vary from Irish late-night premises with Indian influences to an inexpensive—from $A15—dinner at a Turkish café. In the

dry season at Darwin's Mindil Beach Thursday markets, food stalls display inexpensive treats from Brazilian to Balinese, and Laotian to Portuguese, with almost all national dishes in among them.

SOUTH AUSTRALIA

South Australia is the festival state. Most festivals focus on food, from German to Greek, via Italian, Spanish and Polish. The January Tunarama Festival at Port Lincoln on the Eyre Peninsula not surprisingly features tuna. The Peninsula also yields Australia's biggest oysters and famed King George whiting.

Per capita, South Australia has more eateries than any state and is probably the nation's cheapest. And it produces Australia's finest wines, recognised internationally. The most famous are from the Barossa Valley, which often accompany a cuisine known as Barossan, based on German traditions and refined with fresh produce. Many wineries have restaurants, as do the wine-growing areas of McLaren Vale, Clare Valley, citrus-rich Riverland, Coonawarra (revered for its reds) and cool-climate wineries in the Adelaide Hills. The last area also produces great olives and berry fruits.

Kangaroo Island's own wine industry is catching up, and there is a food culture here based on corn-fed chicken, seafood, including marron (freshwater lobster), and fine cheeses, including brie and camembert.

WESTERN AUSTRALIA

The state occupies a third of the continent, its southern corner punctuated by orchards and farms. Wonderful wine comes from the Margaret River region, but beer is the beverage of choice in outback regions, often accompanying sensational seafood and steaks transported inland. Seafood lovers can look forward to blue manna crabs, prawns and salmon, as well as local lamb, goat's cheese, White Rocks veal and marron.

Perth suburb Northbridge has a large migrant population and one of the nation's greatest concentrations of restaurants. For alfresco dining head to the port of Fremantle. In these areas, consider $A38 to $A52 for two courses.

TASMANIA

Tasmania, 200km (124 miles) from Melbourne across the Bass Strait, has clung to British food traditions and is known as the gourmet isle. Devonshire tea rooms are everywhere, serving fresh scones, jam and cream, adopted from Devon, England. Local seafood, from oysters to Tasman Peninsula salmon, is among the highlights around Hobart's harbour, where fish punts, pubs, restaurants, cafés and sushi bars serve at less than Melbourne prices. For Thai, Indonesian, Indian, Lebanese and Italian foods, walk to North Hobart. Mutton-bird pâté is unique to the island. Tasmania also produces good wines though they are fairly expensive. King Island, offshore to the north, is famed for its cheeses.

EATING

MAJOR RESTAURANT CHAINS

	Price per meal (A$)	Alcohol	Child Menu	Takeout	Phone Number	Website
RESTAURANTS, FAST FOOD AND CAFÉS						
Ali Baba Lebanese	5–10			✔	02 6292 1178	www.alibaba.net.au
BB's Espresso	5			✔	07 5591 3242	www.rfg.com.au
Billy Baxter's	5	✔			03 9796 4489	www.petsparadise.com.au
Chicken Treat	5			✔	08 9272 7799	www.chickentreat.com.au
Coffee Club	5			✔	07 3010 3000	www.coffeeclub.com.au
Dôme	5			✔	08 9386 3099	www.domecoffees.com.au
Domino's Pizza	10–12			✔	13 18 88	www.dominos.com.au
Eagle Boys Dial-A-Pizza	10			✔	07 3254 1799	www.eagleboys.com.au
Fancy Fillings	6				02 9363 9055	–
Fasta Pasta	10	✔	✔		–	www.fastapasta.com.au
Hogs Breath Café	10–25	✔	✔		–	www.hogsbreath.com.au
Hungry Jacks	3–5		✔	✔	03 9831 7100	www.hungryjacks.com.au
Jamaica Blue	3–5			✔	03 9827 8388	www.jamaicablue.com
KFC	5		✔	✔	–	www.KFC.com.au
La Porchetta Pizza	10	✔	✔	✔	–	www.laporchetta.com.au
Lonestar Steakhouse	16–25	✔	✔	✔	–	www.lonestarsteakhouse.com.au
McDonald's	3–5		✔	✔	02 9875 6666	www.mcdonalds.com.au
Montezuma's	12–15	✔	✔	✔	–	www.montezumas.com.au
Mr Bird's MYO	10			✔	08 9474 5955	www.mrbirdsmyo.com
Muffin Break	6			✔	–	www.muffinbreak.com.au
Nando's	15		✔	✔	–	www.nandos.com.au
Pizza Haven	12–15			✔	131 241	www.pizzahaven.com.au
Pizza Hut	12–15	✔	✔	✔	–	www.pizzahut.com.au
Pure & Natural	10			✔	03 9820 3133	www.purenat.com
Red Rooster	8–10		✔	✔	1800 632 145	www.redrooster.com.au
Sizzler	15	✔	✔		–	www.sizzler.com.au
Taco Bill Mexican	16	✔	✔		–	www.tacobill.com.au
Tim's Surf 'n' Turf	15	✔	✔		–	www.cairns.net.au/~tims

during the gold rushes of the 1800s. They opened small establishments where the adventurous tried 'chow food'—fried rice and chicken chow mein. Meanwhile German pioneers established vineyards, especially in the Barossa Valley, South Australia, from the 1840s.

After World War II large-scale migration brought more Europeans, particularly Italians and Greeks. Their presence revolutionized Australian cooking. Mediterranean aromas wafted from their kitchens and gradually Anglo-Saxon Australians entered new Italian restaurants.

Asian food, now the trendiest, has also impacted enormously on Australia. Japanese food arrived in the early 1960s, followed by Thai and Vietnamese in the 70s and 80s respectively.

Australia is no longer content with steak, eggs and chips, though damper (bread baked in fire ashes), and hearty camp stews and barbecues are still traditional on 4WD bush or outback tours. Now you can dine in every capital city on any cuisine. Fusion food, also called modern Australian, combines East and West and is the popular choice in many fine restaurants.

IN THE RESTAURANT

TIPPING

A service charge, from 10 to 15 per cent, is included at all upscale eateries in Australia. In other restaurants you can reward good service with a 10 per cent tip, but it is not compulsory.

SMOKING

Most states have passed laws banning smoking from restaurants and other enclosed places. Some establishments may have outside smoking areas—check when booking if you want to smoke.

DRESS CODE

Although Australians may dress up for formal occasions, for socializing and dining they dress casually. It's polite, however, to wear reasonable footwear to restaurants.

Outlets	State	Description
40	NSW, ACT, VIC	Lebanese kebabs
18	QLD	Coffee, light meals
16	NSW, QLD, SA	Coffee, light meals
58	WA	Chicken burger, light meals
88	All except TAS	Coffee
21	VIC, QLD, WA	Coffee
248	All except VIC	Pizza
139	All except SA, TAS	Pizza
14	NSW, VIC, QLD, WA	Gourmet takeout sandwiches
30	VIC, QLD, NT, SA, WA	Italian-style fresh pasta
40	All except VIC	Steak meals
180+	All	Burgers
90	NSW, VIC, QLD, WA	Coffee
400+	NSW, ACT, VIC, QLD	Chicken meals
50	All except NT	Pizza restaurant
20	NSW, QLD, WA	Texan-style steak meals
725+	All	Burgers
21	NSW, VIC, QLD, SA	Mexican restaurant
28	VIC, QLD, WA	Buffet make your own
140	All	Bakery café, light meals, coffee
65	NSW, VIC, QLD, WA	Portuguese-style meals
170+	All	Pizza
330	All	Pizza
39	All except TAS	Café, healthy light meals
290+	All except SA, TAS	Burgers and chicken meals
28	NSW, ACT, QLD, WA	Steak, seafood, pasta
22	VIC	Mexican restaurant
8	NSW, QLD, NT	Steak, seafood, pasta

MENU READER

Abalone: seafood mollusc

Anzac biscuits: biscuits made with flour, oats, coconut and golden syrup

Balmain bug: crayfish, named after a Sydney suburb

Barbie: barbecue

Barramundi: or barra, a large freshwater fish found in the northern and western states

Bunya Bunya nuts: similar to macadamia nuts

BYO: Some restaurarnts allow you to 'bring your own' wine, but usually charge $A3–5 per person or bottle

Capsicum: pepper

Damper: fire-baked bread in a camp oven

Egg plant: aubergine

Flake: shark, as served in fish and chip take-aways

Kakadu plums: native plums, used in pies or as a preserve

Lamington: sponge cake with a chocolate and coconut topping

Lemon myrtle: tree whose lemon-scented leaves are used in cooking

Lilly-pilly: berries of a native tree eaten as bush tucker

Marron: freshwater crayfish native to Western Australia

Middy: medium-size glass of beer, usually 0.285 litre (0.5 pint) but can be larger

Moreton Bay bug: crayfish again, found in Queensland and the north

Pie floater: meat pie in pea soup or gravy

Quandong: small native fruit often served in pies or tarts or as a preserve

Yabby: freshwater crayfish

Schooner: large glass of beer, usually 0.425 litre (0.75 pint)

Stubby: small bottle of beer

Tinnie: can of beer

Witchetty grub: a grub or larva eaten by Aboriginals

Zucchini: courgette

Unless stated otherwise, the prices are for a two-course lunch (L) for two people and a three-course dinner (D) for two people. The wine price is for a bottle of house wine.

SYDNEY

AQUA DINING
North Sydney Olympic Pool, cnr Paul and Northcliff streets, Milsons Point, Sydney, NSW 2061
Tel 02 9964 9998
www.aquadining.com.au
Superbly set above the North Sydney Olympic Pool, the stylish dining room has stunning views of Sydney Harbour.

The modern Australian cuisine features dishes such as freshly shucked Pacific oysters with a caviar and verjuice dressing, and grilled wild barramundi fillet with basil gnocchi, asparagus and a champagne caviar sauce. The wine list is extensive. Booking advised.

⑤ ⓘ Sun–Fri noon–2.30, 6.30–10, Sat 12–2, 6–10 🍴 L A$130, D A$170, Wine A$39 🚇 Milsons Point then 5-minute walk ⛴ Circular Quay to Milsons Point

BLACKBIRD CAFÉ
Balcony Level, Cockle Bay Wharf, Darling Park, Sydney, NSW 2000
Tel 02 9283 7385
www.blackbirdcafé.com.au
To the west of the city, this is a large, buzzing, all-day diner-style café; light, airy and modern with comfortable couches, bar stools and conventional table seating. The outdoor dining area offers great views over Darling Harbour.

The eclectic fare includes breakfasts, pastas, pizzas, salads and some Asian options, plus cakes, beer, wine and cocktails. Limited wine list.

⑤ ⓘ Daily 8am–1am 🍴 L A$30–A$40, D A$40–A$50, Wine A$20 🚉 Town Hall 🚝 Monorail Darling Park

BONDI TRATT
34 Campbell Parade, Bondi Beach, Sydney, NSW 2026
Tel 02 9365 4303
Lively café above Bondi Beach, with a superb view of the action from the outdoor tables.

Breakfasts are popular, with bacon and eggs, but also poached fruits, pancakes and muesli creations. There's also a good range of pizzas, pastas,

daily fish specials and kangaroo dishes. The wine list is reasonable; BYO corkage is A$3 per person.

⑤ ⓘ Daily 7am–10.30pm 🍴 L A$50, D A$70, Wine A$18 🚍 378 from Central Station, 380, 382 and L82 from Circular Quay and city 🚌 Bondi Junction then buses 380, 382 or L82 🚇 8km (5 miles) east from the city

CAPTAIN COOK CRUISES
Depart Jetty 6, Circular Quay, Sydney, NSW 2000
Tel 02 9206 6666
www.captaincook.com.au

What could be better than a cruise around Sydney Harbour enjoying good food, with entertainment in the evenings?

The food is modern Australian, with an emphasis on seafood: examples are smoked salmon with a herb salad, and skinned ocean trout fillet with minted cucumbers, salsa, light mayonnaise, crushed potatoes and wilted Chinese greens. Vegetarian options and children's portions are available, as are reduced fat and low salt dishes. The range of Australian wines is extensive. Booking essential.

⑤ ⓘ 12.30 departure for lunch cruise, 5 for sunset, 7 for dinner 🍴 L A$110 (buffet), A$118 (à la carte), D A$150 (A$198 including live entertainment), Wine A$15.50 🚉 Circular Quay 🚍 Any bus to Circular Quay

CASA ASTURIANA
77 Liverpool Street, Sydney, NSW 2000
Tel 02 9264 1010
Authentic Spanish meals are served in this informal Little Spain establishment, a convenient stop between Darling Harbour and Hyde Park near the southern end of George Street. Expect good tapas, sherry and seafood paella, and a choice of Spanish wines.

⑤ ⓘ Mon–Sat 12–3, 5.30–11, Sun 12–10 🍴 L, D A$50, Wine A$19 🚉 Town Hall 🚝 Monorail World Square

CHINTA RIA—TEMPLE OF LOVE
The Roof Terrace, Cockle Bay Wharf, Darling Park, Sydney, NSW 2000
Tel 02 9264 3211
www.cocklebaywharf.com
Colourful, circular Asian restaurant with dramatic décor—the focus is a huge Buddha statue—and a lively atmosphere enlivened by blues, jazz and soul music. The outdoor eating area looks over Darling Harbour.

The cuisine is Malaysian with Chinese and Indian influences and features laksas, satays, noodle dishes, curries and tofu dishes. The wine list is fairly limited and corkage for BYO is A$5.50 per bottle. Lunch booking advised.

⑤ ⓘ Mon–Sat noon–2.30, 6–11, Sun noon–10 🍴 Entrées A$6–A$9, large dishes A$13.80–A$28.80, desserts A$6.50, Wine A$23.50 🚉 Town Hall 🚝 Metro Monorail from City Centre to Darling Park

DOYLE'S ON THE BEACH
11 Marine Parade, Watsons Bay, Sydney, NSW 2030
Tel 02 9337 2007
www.doyles.com.au
On the waterfront at the charming harbour village of Watsons Bay, Doyle's is an 1880s timber and brick building with superb views up the harbour towards the city.

The seafood menu is usually served with french fries, rice or mashed potatoes; salads or roast vegetables are available for an additional cost. Try the Balmain bugs with avocado and macadamia nuts in a honey vinaigrette. The extensive wine list includes a good range of wines by the glass. Booking advisable.

⑤ ⓘ Mon–Sat noon–3, 6–9.30, Sun 11.30–3 and 6–9 🍴 L A$110, D A$140, Wine A$30 🚍 324, 325 from city ⛴ Circular Quay to Watsons Bay lunchtimes; water taxis evenings 🚇 10km (6 miles) from the city

EDNA'S TABLE

204 Clarence Street, Sydney, NSW 2000
Tel 02 9267 3933

The key ingredients at this simple, modern, but stylish dining room west of the Sydney Tower are Australian bush foods—the house special is chargrilled kangaroo. Other native options include crocodile, macadamia nuts or lemon myrtle. There is an equally good vegetarian menu and a select list of Australian wines.

🚫 🕐 Mon–Fri 12–3, Tue–Sat 6–10
🍴 L A$92, D A$123, Wine A$27
🚉 Town Hall 🚊 Metro Monorail Darling Park

GOLDEN CENTURY

393 Sussex Street, Sydney, NSW 2000
Tel 02 9212 3901

A large, bustling and very popular seafood restaurant in Sydney's Chinatown—the Cantonese menu attracts even local residents. Crabs and lobsters are offered fresh from the tank and steamed fish is among the house specials. BYO wine or choose a take away.

🚫 🕐 Daily 12–5, Sun–Thu 5–11, Fri–Sat 5–12 🍴 L, D from A$34
🚉 Town Hall 🚊 Metro Monorail Garden Plaza

GRAND TAVERNA

Sir John Young Hotel, cnr George and Liverpool streets, Sydney, NSW 2000
Tel 02 9267 3608

This Spanish bistro is in the back room of an ordinary looking pub in the small 'Spanish Quarter' to the south of the city. The environment is lively and tables are mostly large and communal.

Authentic Spanish fare is served, including mixed tapas and paella, and a good range of seafood, including barbecued octopus or mussels. The most famous dish here is the delicious and colourful paella. Lunch booking advised.

🚫 🕐 Daily noon–3, 5.30–11 (Sun 5.30–9.30) 🍴 L A$50, D A$70, Wine A$15 🚉 Town Hall 🚊 Any bus to Central Station (Railway Square)

GUILLAUME AT BENNELONG

Sydney Opera House, Bennelong Point, Sydney, NSW 2000
Tel 02 9241 1999
www.guillaumeatbennelong.com.au
One of Sydney's finest dining venues, this elegant restaurant

has superb views of The Rocks and harbour. Guillaume Brahimi is one of Australia's most respected chefs and he serves modern Australian cuisine with French influences.

Guillaume's signature dish is an entrée of basil-infused tuna. Other tempting items are confit of Atlantic salmon on braised endive with red wine sauce, and chocolate soufflé with almond milk ice-cream. Booking essential.

🕐 Thu–Fri noon–3, Mon–Sat 5.30–late
🍴 L A$130, D A$170, Wine A$38. Pretheatre menu 5.30–7: A$110 for two courses, A$130 for three courses
🚉 Circular Quay 🚊 Any bus to Circular Quay

THE MALAYA

39 Lime Street, King Street Wharf, Sydney, NSW 2000
Tel 02 9279 1170
www.themalaya.com.au

A Sydney institution, the Malaya is on the first floor of the waterfront King Street Wharf complex, with excellent views across Darling Harbour. The décor is stylish with an open kitchen and full-length windows.

The food is primarily Malaysian, but with Chinese, Indonesian and other Asian influences. The restaurant is particularly famous for its laksas; other signature dishes include beef rendang and satays. The wine list is fairly limited. Booking essential.

🚫 🕐 Daily noon–3, 6–late
🍴 L, D A$65, Wine A$27 🚊 Wynyard Station 🚊 Metro Monorail Darling Park

MARIGOLD CITYMARK

Levels 4 & 5, 683 George Street, Haymarket, Sydney, NSW 2000
Tel 02 9281 3388
www.citysearch.com.au

A large restaurant on two levels, with elegant, oriental décor. Most mealtimes are noisy but it's all part of the experience. Classic Chinese fare is available, the speciality being yum cha lunches offering over 100 varieties of dim sum.

The à la carte menu includes mud crab in chilli sauce, deep fried spicy salt and pepper prawns, steamed scallops in their shell with black bean sauce, Peking duck, and hotpot of duck with chestnuts. Booking advised.

🚫 🕐 Daily 10–3, 5.30–midnight
🍴 Entrées A$5–A$15, mains A$18–A$30, yum cha lunch A$15–A$20 per person, Wine A$29 🚉 Central Station or Town Hall 🚊 Metro Monorail to Powerhouse Museum

OPERA BAR

Lower Concourse, Sydney Opera House, Bennelong Point, Sydney, NSW 2000
Tel 02 9247 1666
www.operabar.com.au

A long bar-café in a superb location with great views of the harbour and bridge. Live entertainment, including jazz and soul bands, is on Saturday and Sunday afternoons.

While specials change, examples of the modern Australian bistro menu are duck and mushroom risotto with peas and chives, poached chicken salad with coriander, mint and lime, or roast capsicum and tomato soup with parmesan toast. A good range of Australian wines is available by the glass.

🚫 🕐 Daily 11am–1am 🍴 Dishes A$9–A$26, desserts A$10, Wine A$30
🚉 Circular Quay 🚊 Any bus to Circular Quay

ROCKPOOL

107 George Street, The Rocks, Sydney, NSW 2000
Tel 02 9252 1888
www.rockpool.com

One of the country's best restaurants, the interior is large and stylish. The owner, Neil Perry, is a celebrity chef.

Innovative modern Australian cuisine features gourmet produce such as Barossa and Kangaroo Island chicken and a large range of seafood such as snapper, red emperor and seared tuna studded with anchovy and roast garlic with bone marrow and red wine sauce. The extensive wine list has an excellent range of both Australian and imported wines.

Booking advised (essential at weekends).

🚫 ⏰ Tue–Sat 6–11pm 🍴 D A$200, Tasting Menu A$300, Wine A$36 🚇 Circular Quay 🚌 Any bus to Circular Quay

SAILORS THAI CANTEEN
106 George Street, The Rocks, Sydney, NSW 2000
Tel 02 9251 2466

A lively, canteen-style café in the historic Sailors Home, its modern minimalist décor features an enormous stainless steel communal table.

The innovative Thai food includes stir-fried marinated beef with ginger, black fungus and Asian celery, rice noodles with pork and Asian broccoli, curry of grilled fish, Pad Thai noodles, and desserts such as pomegranate and smoked coconut sorbets. There is a small wine list.

🚫 ⏰ Mon–Fri 12–2, Mon–Sat 6–late 🍴 Dishes A$15.50–A$26, Wine A$25 🚇 Circular Quay 🚌 Any bus to Circular Quay

SEAN'S PANORAMA
270 Campbell Parade, Bondi Beach, Sydney, NSW 2026
Tel 02 9365 4924
The ocean view across Bondi Beach accompanies a changing, modern Australian menu. This charming, small restaurant has a limited wine list or BYO (corkage A$8).

🚫 ⏰ Sat–Sun 12–3, Wed–Sat 6.30–9.30 🍴 L, D A$68 🚇 Bondi Junction 🚗 7km (4.5 miles) southeast from the city

SHIMBASHI SOBA ON THE SEA
Shop 6, Woolloomooloo Wharf, Woolloomooloo, Sydney, NSW 2011
Tel 02 9357 7763
Woolloomooloo Wharf is a beautifully renovated shipping wharf jutting out into Woolloomooloo Bay. Yoshinori Shibazaki is one of only a few dozen soba chefs in the world, so a visit here is a real treat.

The best dishes are the 'combination meals' that feature either soba or udon noodles with salad, pickles, miso soup, rice and either chicken teriyaki or beef sukiyaki. The wine list is limited and corkage for BYO is A$8 per bottle. Booking advised.

🚫 ⏰ Daily noon–10 🍴 Dishes A$17–A$24, desserts A$7, Wine A$26 🚇 Kings Cross then 15-minute walk 🚌 312 from central Sydney or Kings Cross

SLOANES CAFÉ
312 Oxford Street, Paddington, Sydney, NSW 2021
Tel 02 9331 6717
Friendly, lively café near the Paddington Markets with quite a small interior but a pleasant courtyard at the back.

All-day breakfasts are available as well as focaccias, pastas, soups, salads, a mezze plate and more substantial meat and chicken dishes. The coffee is excellent, there is a good range of cakes and desserts, and the café is known for its fresh fruit juices and whips. Corkage for BYO is A$2 per person.

🚫 🍴 Mon–Wed 6.30–6, Thu–Sat 6.30–10.30, Sun 7–6 🍴 L A$35 🚌 378, 380, 382, L82 from the city 🚗 3km (2 miles) east from central Sydney, near Paddington Markets

SUMMIT RESTAURANT
Level 47, Australia Square, 264 George Street, Sydney, NSW 2000
Tel 02 9247 9777
www.summitrestaurant.com.au
High on the 47th floor of the Australia Square building, this claims to be the world's largest revolving restaurant, with superb views out to the Blue Mountains.

The innovative modern Australian cuisine features local seafood, lamb, chicken and vegetarian dishes. A buffet lunch and dinner are available

on Sundays. There is an extensive wine list. Booking advised.

🚫 ⏰ Sun–Fri noon–3, Mon–Sun 6–9.30. Orbit Bar daily 5–late 🍴 L A$95, D A$140, Wine A$30; Sunday buffet A$118; bar snacks A$6.50–A$15 🚇 Wynyard Station 🚌 Any bus to Circular Quay (alight at Wynyard Station)

SYDNEY FISH MARKET
Bank Street, Pyrmont, Sydney, NSW 2009
Tel 02 9660 1611
www.sydneyfishmarket.com.au
The Sydney Fish Market is one of the world's best seafood markets. There are many places to eat within the complex, including Christie's Seafoods, Claudio's Quality Seafoods, Fish Market Sushi Bar, Nicholas Seafoods and the Fish Market Café.

Seafood of all types can be enjoyed, including fish and chips, sushi and sashimi, freshly shucked oysters, chilli mud crab, and grilled or fried fish. Pizzas, breakfasts and coffee are also available at a couple of the cafés. All accept BYO.

🚫 ⏰ Daily 7–4 🍴 From A$5 for single sushi to A$50 seafood platter 🚊 Metro Light Rail from Central Station or Darling Harbour to Fish Market

TETSUYA'S
529 Kent Street, Sydney, NSW 2000
Tel 02 9267 2900
The fusion of Japanese, French and modern Australian cuisines comes at a price, but then this is innovative, perfectly cooked food. Among the many courses are the finest veal, salmon and Tasmanian ocean trout. Booking advised.

🚫 ⏰ Fri–Sat 12–2.30, Tue–Sat 6.30–9.30 🍴 Degustation Menu $170 per person 🚇 Wynyard 🚊 Metro Monorail Darling Park

EATING

BOATHOUSE BY THE LAKE

Grevillea Park, Menindee Drive, Russell, Canberra, ACT 2600

Tel 02 6273 5500

A modern Australian menu and local Riesling complement the stunning view over Lake Burley Griffin to Capital Hill. It's a detour from the city but the outside dining area is perfect for a relaxing lunch.

◐ ◯ Mon–Fri 12–2, Mon–Sat 6–10 🍴 L, D A$84, Wine A$24 🚌 3km (2 miles) southeast of the city

THE CHAIRMAN AND YIP

108 Bunda Street, Civic, Canberra, ACT 2601

Tel 02 6248 7109

Canberra's favourite Asian restaurant, northeast of City Hill, is essentially Cantonese but Thai, Japanese and other influences make up the fusion menu. Stir-fried tiger prawns, duck, or salmon with wasabi and spinach sauce are among the perennials that provide excellent value. There is a good Australian wine list or BYO (corkage A$6).

◐ ◯ Mon–Fri 12–3, Mon–Sat 5.30–11 🍴 L, D A$56, Wine A$26 🚌 Any bus to Civic

FIRST FLOOR

Green Square, Jardine Street, Kingston, Canberra, ACT 2604

Tel 02 6260 6311

In one of Canberra's liveliest dining and nightlife areas, First Floor is a large, popular, buzzing (noisy) restaurant with floor-to-ceiling windows.

The cuisine is modern Australian with international influences. Typical dishes may be South Coast oysters, Thai red curry of shredded beef fillet, pumpkin, Chinese broccoli and Hokkien noodles or fresh prawn and scallop risotto. There are several vegetarian options. The wine list is extensive. Booking advised.

◐ ◯ Mon–Fri noon–2, 6–10.30, Sat 6–10.30 🍴 L A$80, D A$90, Wine A$20 🚌 38, 39, 80 🚌 4.5km (3 miles) southeast from the city

GUS' CAFÉ

Shop 8, Garema Place, Bunda Street, Civic, ACT 2601

Tel 02 6248 8118

www.canberra.citysearch.com.au

A central city café with two large covered outdoor areas.

Breakfasts include a huge plate of bacon, eggs, sausages, tomato, onion and mushrooms on focaccia bread, while main meals include pasta, nachos, salads, sirloin steaks, stroganoff and fish dishes. There are several vegetarian options. The wine list is moderate—corkage for BYO is A$3 per bottle. Worth a stop for the excellent coffee.

◐ Outside tables only ◯ Sun–Thu 7.30am–11pm, Fri–Sat 7.30am–midnight 🍴 Breakfast A$7–A$14, L A$30, D A$45, Wine A$20 🚌 Any bus to Civic

OTTOMAN CUISINE

Cnr Broughton and Blackall streets, Barton, Canberra, ACT 2600

Tel 02 6273 6111

www.canberra.citysearch.com.au

The best Turkish restaurant in Australia is in a beautiful art-deco building. The elegant oblong room has large windows and creates a rather formal atmosphere, but with impeccable service.

Chef/owner Serif Kaya prepares innovative food, such as Narli karides (king prawns pan-sautéed with a savoury pomegranate sauce), Dana kulbasti (tender slices of veal with mild spices, served on eggplant and baby spinach with tangy lemon sauce) and Baklava pastries. The wine list is extensive and corkage is A$8 for BYO. Booking essential.

◯ Tue–Fri noon–2.30, 6–10.30, Sat 6–10.30 🍴 L A$90, D A$120, Wine A$18 🚌 34, 35, 36 🚌 4km (2.5 miles) southeast from the city, near Capital Hill

SAMMY'S KITCHEN

Garema Centre, Bunda Street, Civic, Canberra, ACT 2601

Tel 02 6247 1464

A noisy, busy and crowded city Asian restaurant that serves good-value food in a no-frills environment.

The cuisine is Chinese and Malaysian, with a large choice of hot fresh dishes. Entrées and soups include garlic king prawns, satay sticks, spring rolls and hot and sour soup. There is a good range of laksas, rice dishes and noodle dishes, featuring Singapore, Hokkein and rice noodles, as well as curries, stir-fries and hot pots. The wine list is limited, but corkage for BYO is A$3 per bottle. Booking advised for dinner.

◯ Tue–Thu 11.30–2.30, 5–10.30, Fri–Sat 11.30–2.30, 5–11.30, Sun 11.30–2.30, 5–10 ◐ L A$40, D A$50, Wine A$12.50 🚌 Any bus to Civic

SILO BAKERY

36 Giles Street, Kingston, Canberra, ACT 2604

Tel 02 6260 6060

Silo is a small bakery/café in Kingston. It has a minimalist look, with grey walls, black floors, a wood and marble counter, and outdoor and indoor seating areas.

Popular are breakfasts, snacks such as sandwiches, cakes and coffee, as well as lunches. Silo is also a bakery and cheese shop, selling wonderful pastries, coffee, sourdough bread and a good range of cheeses. A wide range of wines is available. Lunch booking essential.

◐ Outside tables only ◯ Tue–Sat 7–4 🍴 Breakfast A$11.50, L A$45, Wine from A$24 🚌 38, 39, 80 🚌 4.5km (3 miles) southeast from the city, near Parliamentary Triangle

THE TRYST

The Lawns, Bougainville Street, Manuka, Canberra, ACT 2603

Tel 02 6239 4422

A trendy brasserie in the lively Manuka dining precinct, with colourful vibrant décor. There is an open kitchen and an outdoor seating area. The innovative cooking is modern Australian with Mediterranean and Asian influences.

Some sample dishes are prawns sautéed with garlic, chilli, ginger, shiitake mushrooms and julienne snow peas, and oven baked lamb served on lentils and green beans with capsicum relish. There is an extensive wine list and corkage for BYO is A$3 per person. Booking advised.

◐ Outside tables only ◯ Mon–Sat 10–10 (lunch 12–2.30, dinner from 6), Sun 10–6 (closed for dinner) 🍴 L A$80, D A$100, Wine A$18 🚌 35, 36, 39 🚌 5km (3 miles) southeast from the city, near Parliamentary Triangle

EATING

ARMIDALE

JITTERBUG MOOD

115 Rusden Street, Armidale, NSW 2350
Tel 02 6772 3022

A 5-minute walk from the national bus terminal, this restaurant is a real find. It has a small redbrick frontage with a pleasant upstairs seating area.

Starters include goat's cheese ravioli, with mains such as Scotch fillet steak or Mediterranean chargrilled vegetable pie. Puddings are a real treat, with delights like Polish coffee and walnut cake. There is an extensive list of Australian wines, and a good range of beers; also BYO (wine only). Booking advised.

Ⓢ Ⓖ Tue–Sat 6.30–10 Ⓦ D A$40, Wine A$18

BATEMANS BAY

JAMESON'S ON THE PIER

Old Punt Road, Batemans Bay, NSW 2536
Tel 02 4472 6405

With a wonderful waterside setting by the bridge and its own launch, Jameson's sets the right tone for its superb seafood menu. The renovated restaurant is light and airy with linen tablecloths and a choice of indoor or shaded outdoor seating.

Cooking is modern Australian with dishes such as tempura king prawns and chargrilled tuna steaks, and there are some good vegetarian options. Friendly service. There is a good selection of Australian wines and some options from New Zealand. Booking advised for evenings and busy summer lunchtimes.

Ⓢ Outside tables only Ⓖ Tue–Sun 12–2.30, Tue–Sat dinner from 6 Ⓦ L A$20, D A$50, Wine A$30

BELLINGEN

THE OLD BUTTER FACTORY CAFÉ

1 Doepel Lane, Bellingen, NSW 2454
Tel 02 6655 2150

On the main road northwest from the Pacific Highway, this relaxed café is part of a complex housing shops as well as an alternative-therapy centre.

The 19th-century buttery was originally the hub of the dairy industry in the Bellinger Valley and it has been converted into a charming café serving breakfasts, light lunches and afternoon teas. Seating is in a cool, light and airy room with large windows, or out on the verandah beneath palms.

Ⓖ 9–5.30 Ⓦ Meals from A$7

Ⓑ Kings Brothers (1300 555 611) run daily to Bellingen from Nambucca Heads and Urunga Ⓒ On State Route 78 from the Pacific Highway to Dorrigo

BLACKHEATH

VULCAN'S

33 Govetts Leap Road, Blackheath, NSW 2785
Tel 02 4787 6899

Just off the Western Highway close to the Blue Mountains National Park, Vulcan's attracts more than just passing tourists. Diners return for the slow-cooked country flavours served with proficiency and style. Book ahead. Wine is BYO only, A$2.50 corkage per person.

Ⓢ Ⓖ Fri–Sun 9am–11.30pm

Ⓦ L A$68, D A$90

BOWRAL

HORDERNS

Horderns Road, Bowral, NSW 2576
Tel 02 4861 1522
www.milton-park.com.au

Milton Park Hotel stands in a country estate in the Southern Highlands, about a 1-hour drive southwest from Sydney.

Horderns restaurant in the hotel uses the best local ingredients in a modern Australian menu touched by French provincial finesse. Main courses include salmon, venison and duck, and the wine list is predominantly Australian with a selection of fine reds.

Ⓢ Designated areas Ⓖ Daily 12–2.30, 7–9 Ⓦ L A$86, D A$137, Wine A$28

THAT NOODLE PLACE

279 Bong Bong Street, Bowral, NSW 2576
Tel 02 4861 6930

This stylish café on the main shopping street is attached to the excellent That Noodle Shop.

The superb food is Asian fusion with plenty of vegetarian options. Starters include Vietnamese Banghoi steamed rice balls or Malaysian spring rolls, and there are superb noodle broths, including Japanese miso and soba, Thai seafood curry, and stir-fried Hokkien noodles. There is a limited list of beers and wines and a small BYO corkage fee.

Ⓖ Fri–Sun 12–2.30, Tue–Sun 6–9 Ⓦ L A$25, D A$30, Wine A$18

COFFS HARBOUR

MANGROVE JACK'S CAFÉ

Coffs Promenade, 321 Harbour Drive, Coffs Harbour, NSW 2450
Tel 02 6652 5517

A fashionable café between the CBD and the harbour, on a sweeping bend of Coffs Creek, it serves breakfasts, lunches and evening meals. Seating is mostly outdoors on sheltered dark-wood decks overlooking Coffs Creek.

Breakfast may include pancakes, omelettes, fruit salads and sausages; lunch may be pumpkin risotto, BBQ eye-fillet steak or burgers; while evening meals (booking advised) have a modern Australian bent, and include oysters and catch of the day on prawn and potato hash.

Ⓖ Daily 7.30–4, Mon–Sat 6pm–late (Fri–Sat winter) Ⓦ L A$15, D A$50, Wine $20

TIDE & PILOT BRASSERIE

1 Marina Drive, Coffs Harbour, NSW 2450
Tel 02 6651 6888

tide & pilot

Right on the marina, with beach views, there are two separate eating areas. The lower deck, with views of the marina, is informal for breakfast and lunches, with the most popular fare being fresh fish and chips. Upstairs (booking advised) has a relaxed, intimate atmosphere with views over the bay as well as the marina, with options such as seafood risotto and a wide selection of dishes, including lobster, at the seafood bar. Steaks, lamb and similar dishes are available for those less keen on seafood.

Both decks offer outdoor and indoor seating. The wine list has a good selection of Australian wines, including several 'champagnes'.

Ⓢ Outside tables only Ⓖ 7am–late; closed some Sun evenings: call to check Ⓦ L A$50, D A$100, Wine A$18

GLEN INNES

HERITAGE CAFÉ

215 Grey Street, Glen Innes, NSW 2370
Tel 02 6732 6123

EATING

A tiny sugar-pink confection in the heart of Glen Innes, the interior is all subtle dark wood and wrought iron seating, and there is a shady courtyard. Food is modern Australian with Spanish/Italian touches.

During the day, pancakes, sandwiches, burgers, snacks and a bewildering array of coffees are on offer. In the evenings, things step up a notch, with Mexican delights or dishes with a Celtic touch. BYO only. Booking advised for evenings.

⬤ Outside tables only ⬤ Mon–Fri 8.30–4.30, Sat 8.30–2, Thu–Sat 6–9, second Sun of month (market day) 8.30–2 ⬤ Breakfast A$10, L A$15, D A$35 ⬤ The block south from Main Street just beyond Bi-Lo

KATOOMBA

DARLEY'S AT LILIANFELS

Lilianfels Avenue, Echo Point, Katoomba, NSW 2780
Tel 02 4780 1200

This renowned restaurant is in Lilianfels House, a country hotel dating from the 1880s. The comfortable dining room has panelling and fireplaces.

The Australian country cuisine has French influences and relies on quality regional produce. Likewise, the comprehensive wine list is devoted to native vintages.

⬤ ⬤ Daily 6–9 ⬤ D A$156, Wine $35

PARAGON RESTAURANT

65 Katoomba Street, Katoomba, NSW 2780
Tel 02 4782 2928

This 1930s Australian milk-bar has an art-deco interior that is worth seeing as much as the natural attractions in the Blue Mountains. Echo Point and the Three Sisters rock formation are 2km (1.5 miles) farther south along Katoomba Street.

Stop for a late breakfast or Devonshire teas. Light meals include soup, pasta, and home-made bread and pies.

⬤ ⬤ Tue–Sun 10–5 ⬤ Dishes from A$15, Wine A$22

THE SWISS COTTAGE

132 Lurline Street, Katoomba, NSW 2780
Tel 02 4782 2281

A 10-minute walk from the town on the way to Echo Point, this is a traditional, elegant Australian homestead and

has deep verandahs, a landscaped garden and generous parking.

The menu includes stuffed mushrooms and octopus salad to start, King Island Scotch fillet and saucisson vaudois to follow, with desserts such as death by chocolate or fresh strawberries and kirsch ice-cream. There is an extensive selection of Australian wines or BYO. Booking advised.

⬤ Outside tables only ⬤ Wed–Sun from 11, Thu–Sat from 6, Sun 12–2.30, 6–9 ⬤ L A$30, D A$50, Wine A$18 ⬤ Station at far end of Katoomba High Street, a good walk away

ZUPPA

36 Katoomba Street, Katoomba, NSW 2780
Tel 02 4782 9247

At the end of the town's main street, this trendy café is a Katoomba institution. It has a dark-wood, art-deco interior and pavement seating. Generous breakfasts and main meals are available daily. It is a relaxed, friendly place with free papers and a piano for guest use.

Choose from pancakes, maple syrup and strawberries; muesli, yogurt and fruit; or a full fry-up before 11.30am or an all-day breakfast; and grilled barramundi fillet or cannelloni crêpes with ricotta and spinach for lunch or an evening meal. There are plenty of vegetarian options.

⬤ Outside tables only
⬤ 7.30am–11pm ⬤ Breakfast A$5–A$10, main meals A$15

MOUNT TOMAH

MOUNT TOMAH BOTANIC GARDEN RESTAURANT

Bells Line of Road via Bilpin, Mount Tomah, NSW 2758
Tel 02 4567 2060

Spectacularly set in the heart of the Blue Mountains, this simple but stylish restaurant provides excellent fresh dishes at both indoor and outdoor tables.

Lunches include pumpkin and sweet-potato soup, spinach and bacon salad or roasted king prawns to start, with mains including galantine of spatchcock filled with veal and bacon. Vegetarian options include goat's cheese tart, and there is a children's menu. Good wheelchair access. BYO.

⬤ Outside tables only ⬤ Daily 12–2.30 (also Sat 6–9 in summer) ⬤ L A$50, D A$80

NEWCASTLE

VIEW FACTORY BRASSERIE

Cnr Scott and Telford streets, Newcastle, NSW 2300
Tel 02 4929 45801

Close to Newcastle beach, this red-brick building conceals a quiet, club-like atmosphere with dark-wood floors, potted palms, leather sofas and contemporary Australian art.

The food is modern-fusion. Pan-fried barramundi fillet rubs shoulders with Thai fishcakes or the more traditional bangers and mash. Vegetarian options are available and there is a good list of Hunter Valley wines or BYO.

⬤ In lounge area ⬤ Tue–Sun 11am–late ⬤ L A$20, D A$30, Wine A$17.50 ⬤ Newcastle then 2-minute walk

POKOLBIN

CHEZ POK

Peppers Guesthouse, Ekerts Road, Pokolbin, NSW 2320
Tel 02 4998 7596, 02 9302 4333
www.peppers.com.au

Beautifully set in its own fragrant gardens, Chez Pok is decorated in French-provincial style. The menu has French, Asian and Italian influences.

For lunch, try calve's liver or vegetarian wontons followed by chargrilled beef medallions or pan-fried reef fish. For dinner, home-baked bread accompanies smoked quail, turnip or fig terrine entrées, with pan-fried skate wings or slow-roasted white rabbit to follow. There is a good but pricey selection of local wines. Booking advised.

⬤ Outside tables only ⬤ Daily 7.30–10, 12–2, 7–9 ⬤ L A$35, D A$80, Wine A$40. Sat five-course Hunter Gourmet dinner A$77 per person

ESCA BIMBADGEN

Bimbadgen Estate, Lot 21 McDonalds Road, Pokolbin, NSW 2320
Tel 02 4998 4666
www.bimbadgen.com.au

This smart restaurant attached to the Bimbadgen Estate winery in the heart of the Lower Hunter Valley has superb views across the estate's vineyards.

Esca serves generous portions of modern Australian fare. Entrées include dishes such as grilled quail or gruyere soufflé and mains of pan-roasted spatchcock, chargrilled ocean trout or loin of lamb. There is a great selection of local wines. Booking essential.

🚭 🕙 Daily 12–2.30 🍴 L A$40, Wine A$25 🚗 7km (4.5 miles) west from Cessnock

ROBERTS
Halls Road, Pokolbin, NSW 2320
Tel 02 4998 7330

This beautiful heritage home in the heart of the Hunter Valley has dark-wood floors and elegant, linen-covered tables.

The sophisticated menu includes handmade pastas, farmhouse cheeses and home-made breads, crisp fried brains, oysters, and mains such as venison steaks, rack of lamb, milk-fed veal and exotic fungi. Vegetarians are not well catered for. The wine list emphasises local wines, but there is a good selection of wines from other regions of the country. Booking advised.

🚭 🕙 Daily 12–2.30, 7–9.30 🍴 Lunch weekday special A$29 per person, D A$60, Wine A$30

PORT MACQUARIE
SIGNATURES STEAK AND SEAFOOD
2/72 Clarence Street, Port Macquarie, NSW 2444
Tel 02 6584 6144

Close to Town Wharf, this trendy brasserie, with polished tile floors, rattan chairs and chrome tables, is very popular.

On the menu are local oysters, the catch of the day, and regulars such as barramundi fillet and local T bone steaks. Vegetarians can choose from several imaginative dishes. There is a good selection of Australian Hunter Valley wines.

🚬 Separate smoking area 🕙 12–2.30, 6–9 🍴 L A$25, D A$45, Wine A$17 🚌 Countrylink bus from Wauchope stops nearby

TAMWORTH
INLAND CAFÉ
407 Peel Street, Tamworth, NSW 2340
Tel 02 6761 2882

Modern, chic café, with benches along one side and a curving bar along the other. Picture windows open out on to the street, where there is shaded outdoor seating.

The menu includes a wide choice of cakes, coffees and pastries, plus good lunchtime meals that change seasonally, such as Thai-style chicken and Hokkien noodles or light beer battered barramundi fish fillets, as well as soups and sandwiches. There are limited vegetarian options.

🚭 Outside tables only 🕙 Mon–Wed 7.30am–6pm, Thu 7.30am–10pm, Sun 8.30am–4pm 🍴 L A$30, D A$40

ULLADULLA
CAFÉ ALFRESCO
Wason Street, Ulladulla, NSW 2539
Tel 02 4454 1443

Overlooking the harbour, this modern bistro is a great lunch spot with plenty of outdoor seating in a shady location.

Service is friendly and they provide imaginative home-made soups, hot salads, sandwiches, cooked breakfasts and pasta dishes, with some good vegetarian options.

Evening meals are also served, with steaks very popular. BYO wine in the evenings.

🚭 Outside tables only 🕙 Daily 12–2.30, 6–9. Closed Mon, Sun dinner in winter 🍴 Breakfast/L A$6–A$12, D A$30

ELIZAN'S
39 Burrill Street, Ulladulla, NSW 2539
Tel 02 4455 1796
www.guesthouse.com.au

Part of the Ulladulla Guesthouse, Elizan's provides fine French dining with a modern Australian style. Resident chef Luke Asplin also uses a tropical South Pacific approach. Original artwork decorates the walls and you can eat outdoors on the verandah in fine weather.

Try the tender Milton beef or peppered kangaroo steaks. The wine list contains local wines as well as other Australian and some French choices. Booking advised.

🚭 Outside tables only 🕙 Daily breakfast 8.30–10, Mon, Thu–Sat dinner from 6.30 🍴 D A$50, Wine A$25

BEAR BRASS
Shop 3A, River Level, Southgate Complex, Southbank, VIC 3006
Tel 03 9682 3799
www.bearbrass.com.au

Bear Brass has both alfresco and indoor dining, with views over the Yarra River to the city. An international menu includes snacks such as Turkish bread and dips, and meals of spiced chorizo sausages or grilled Sagan Aki with dried prosciutto, through to porter-house steak or red duck curry with coconut rice.

🚭 Outside only 🕙 Daily 8am–10pm 🍴 L, D A$30, Wine A$22 🚋 Tram down Swanston Street to Princes Bridge, then boardwalk to Southgate 🚉 Flinders Street

BEDI'S
118 Park Street, South Melbourne, VIC 3205
Tel 03 9690 8233

Bedi's is a small, busy and inexpensive restaurant in the suburb of South Melbourne, which is characterized by its leafy plane trees, little parks and advertising agencies.

The restaurant, regarded as one of Melbourne's best authentic Indian, serves a wide range of curries and North Indian food in casual, no-fuss surroundings; its chicken butter cream is described as a particular speciality. BYO. Booking advised.

🚭 🕙 Mon–Fri 12–2, 6.30–10, Sat 6.30–10 🍴 L A$40, D A$55, Wine A$25 🚋 Tram 1 or 12 south along Kings Way from central Melbourne to Park Street

CAFÉ DI STASIO
31 Fitzroy Street, St. Kilda, Melbourne, VIC 3182
Tel 03 9525 3999

One of the city's leaders in style and class, the menu in this top-notch Italian restaurant includes saltimbocca, carpaccio and, of course, a range of pasta.

This is no chianti and gingham Italian bistro, but instead a delight for diners looking for first-class Italian food served in elegant, but always cheerful, surroundings. The excellent wine list has more than 400 wines. Booking advised, especially at weekends.

🚭 🕙 Daily 12–3, 6–11 🍴 L A$50, D A$125, Wine A$24

EATING

CAFFEINE AT REVAULT BAR
344 Swanston Street, RMIT University, Melbourne, VIC 3000
Tel 03 1854 1683
A low-price, cheerful, colourful and funky café-bar in the basement of a heritage building. Try gourmet foccacias, pizza and sushi rolls, and cakes, along with fast, good coffee and a choice of teas.
🚫 🍴 Mon–Fri 7am–late
🍷 Breakfast/L A$13, Wine A$18
🚊 Tram from Swanston Street to RMIT University

CECCONI'S
Ground level, Crown Entertainment Complex, Southgate, Melbourne, VIC 3006
Tel 03 9686 8648
www.cecconis.com
Forming part of the Crown Casino Complex, a visit here is an event in itself. In winter, watch the gas fireballs exploding in the air outside.
This classy restaurant has everything you would expect to find—pasta, risotto, ossobuco, rabbit and many other Italian classics. Don't miss the tiramisu for dessert. The wine list is long but expensive, however. Booking advised.
🚫 🍴 Sun–Fri 12–3, daily 6–late
🍷 L A$100, D A$125, Wine A$40
🚊 Tram along Spencer Street to the Crown Entertainment Complex (south bank of the Yarra River)

FRANCE SOIR
11 Toorak Road, South Yarra, Melbourne, VIC 3141
Tel 03 9866 8569
www.france-soir.com.au
France Soir is in the elegant inner city suburb of South Yarra, a classy yet buzzing place for either dinner or lunch.
The menu is classic French bistro, offering everything from onion soup to escargots, to steak frites and boeuf bourguignon. Booking essential.
🚫 🍴 Daily 12–3, 6–12 🍷 L A$80, D A$100, Wine A$27 🚊 Tram 8 from Flinders Street Station in the city to Toorak 🚉 From Flinders Street to South Yarra

GROSSI FLORENTINO
80 Bourke Street, Melbourne 3000
Tel 03 9662 1811
www.grossiflorentino.com.au
The grandest of Melbourne's formal restaurants, the Grossi

Florentino, with its dining-room murals and chandeliers, is where the famous and wealthy regularly relax. The restaurant is renowned for its exemplary Tuscan food. Favourites include suckling lamb and their signature chocolate soufflé.
Downstairs is a stylish bistro, The Florentino Grill, and the adjacent cellar wine bar serves inexpensive pasta. Booking is essential for Florentino's Mural Room, the Wynn Room and the Grill. The Cellar Bar at ground level is ideal for a quick pasta meal.
🚫 🍴 Florentino's: Mon–Fri 12–3, 6–11, Sat 6–11 🍷 Florentino's: L A$140, D A$170, set menu (6 courses plus coffee) A$110 per person, Wine A$35
🍴 The Grill: Mon–Sat noon–3, 6–11
🍷 The Grill: L A$100, D A$120
🍴 Cellar Bar: Mon–Sat 7am–12pm
🍷 Cellar Bar: LA$20
🚊 Any tram up Bourke Street, including the 96 light-rail tram from St. Kilda, or free City Circle tram to Parliament House 🚉 Parliament

HOPETOUN TEA ROOMS
Shops 1 & 2 Block Arcade, 282 Collins Street, Melbourne, VIC 3000
Tel 03 9650 2777
The Victorian tea rooms in the fashionable Block Arcade have refreshed shoppers for more than a century. Afternoon teas are the perennial favourites with savoury sandwiches and delicious cakes. More substantial light meals include pasta and pizzas.
🚫 🍴 Mon–Thu 9–5, Fri 9–6, Sat 10–3:30 🍷 Light meals A$5–A$11
🚊 Tram up Bourke Street
🚉 Flagstaff

JACQUES REYMOND RESTAURANT
78 Williams Road, Prahran, Melbourne, VIC 3181
Tel 03 9525 2178
www.jacquesreymond.com.au
Jacques Reymond's excellent international flavours are achieved by a combination of the best ingredients and classic French techniques. Try the dégustation menu if you cannot decide on the à la carte dishes. There are equally good vegetarian options and the wine selection matches the quality of the food.
🚫 🍴 Thu–Fri 12–2, Tue–Fri 6.30–10, Sat 7–10 🍷 L A$76, D A$180, W A$44
🚉 Prahran then 1.5km (1-mile) walk

JIMMY WATSON'S WINE BAR & RESTAURANT
333 Lygon Street, Carlton, Melbourne, VIC 3053
Tel 03 9347 3985

Jimmy Watson's has been a part of Carlton for more than 60 years and is the place to go for excellent Victorian, Australian and imported wines (and share opened bottles).
You can just sit and enjoy a glass of wine, eat a casual lunch, or enjoy a dinner of modern European fare. Jimmy Watson's is also the home of the Jimmy Watson Memorial Trophy, one of Australia's most famous wine prizes.
🚫 🍴 Mon 10.30–6, Tue–Sat 10.30–late 🍷 L A$80, D A$90, Wine A$16 🚌 200 or 201 from Russell Street along Lygon Street 🚊 Tram along Swanston Street from the city to Melbourne University

JOE'S GARAGE
366 Brunswick Street, Fitzroy, Melbourne, VIC 3065
Tel 03 9419 9944
Like just about everything else in Brunswick Street, Joe's Garage is bright, loud and hip. The menu, like the atmosphere, is casual and covers everything from breakfast through to late night snacks. The crowds are often huge, teeming with young people and students. Quick, noisy but enjoyable. Evening bookings accepted.
🚫 🍴 Daily 7.30am–1am 🍷 L A$45, D A$60, Wine A$19, BYO corkage A$2.50 per person 🚊 Light-rail tram 109 up Collins Street and along Brunswick Street; get off after Johnson Street stop

KRI KRI MEZETHOPOLEION
39–41 Little Bourke Street, Melbourne, VIC 3000
Tel 03 9639 3444
Diners at Kri Kri have the chance to share small dishes, rather than the groaning plates of meats often found in

EATING

Melbourne's other Greek restaurants. This is a casual but interesting little restaurant, well worth a visit.

Dishes include dolmades, white beans in tomatoes, eggplant baked with fetta and olives, and saganaki, along with meatballs, spicy sausages and a selection of seafood. Booking advised.

Ⓢ Ⓞ Tue–Fri 12–3, Mon–Wed 5–10, Thu–Sat 5–11 Ⓦ L A$44, D A$66, Wine A$13.50 Ⓣ Any tram up Bourke Street to Exhibition Street

LEMONGRASS

176 Lygon Street, Carlton, Melbourne, VIC 3053

Tel 03 9662 2244

This Thai restaurant is, somewhat improbably, on Lygon Street in Carlton, which is generally known as Little Italy. The food may not be the cheapest Thai around, but this is a top restaurant whose menu is based on ancient Siam recipes.

Along with the standard red and green curries, there are some more unusual dishes, such as poo ja (stuffed blue swimmer crab) and a green papaya salad. Booking advised.

Ⓢ Ⓞ Mon–Fri 12–2.30, 5.30–11, Sun 5.30–10.30 Ⓦ L A$70, D A$90, Wine A$24. Buffet–all you can eat–lunch A$22 per person Ⓣ 200 or 201 from Russell Street, City, along Lygon Street. Tram along Swanston Street from the city to Melbourne University, stop at Queensberry Street or Grattan Street

THE NUDEL BAR

76 Bourke Street, Melbourne, VIC 3000

Tel 03 9662 9100

This busy, lively eatery is at the fashionable end of Bourke Street. At street level there is casual, counter seating while upstairs there are tables. Noodle dishes, pasta and soups are briskly served. The wine list is limited but changes often.

Ⓢ Ⓞ Mon–Sat 11am–10.30pm, Sun 11–2 Ⓦ Dishes from A$15, W A$20 Ⓣ Any tram up Bourke Street

THE OXFORD SCHOLAR HOTEL

427 Swanston Street, Melbourne, VIC 3000

Tel 03 9663 1619

This stately 1887 Aussie pub in central Melbourne has 14 beers on tap, a beer garden, pool tables, juke box and large

TV screens for sports fans. Popular with business workers, students and visitors, it serves quality meals alfresco or indoors. Specials include fish or risotto dishes, and homemade hamburgers and pies.

Ⓞ Outdoors only Ⓞ Mon–Fri 10am–late Ⓦ L, D $30, Wine $14.50 Ⓣ Tram up Swanston Street to Latrobe Street 🚉 Central Station (Swanston Street exit)

RICHMOND HILL CAFÉ & LARDER

48–50 Bridge Road, Richmond, Melbourne, VIC 3121

Tel 03 9421 2808

www.rhcl.com.au

Bridge Road, in the suburb of Richmond, is a busy shopping area well known for its clothes stores. Weary shop browsers can refuel at this casual, welcoming café and cheese shop.

Light meals are available throughout the day, or end an outing with dinner after 6pm. The Mediterranean-style food is excellent though the wine list is limited. Don't forget to try the cheeses from small, quality Australian dairies. There is a choice of indoor and outdoor seating.

Ⓢ Ⓞ Mon 9–5, Tue–Fri 9am–late, Sat 8.30am–late, Sun 8.30–5 Ⓦ Dishes A$7–A$16, D A$122, Wine glass A$9 🚉 West Richmond 🚗 2km (1.5 miles) east from the city

THE STOKEHOUSE

30 Jacka Boulevard, St. Kilda, Melbourne, VIC 3182

Tel 03 9525 5555

www.stokehouse.com.au

Housed in a 1920s two-storey timber building overlooking St. Kilda beach, and with sweeping views over Port Phillip Bay, The Stokehouse is home to two restaurants. Downstairs is a casual drop-in café and bistro, while upstairs is a more classy and expensive dining room, which is a favourite in showbiz circles.

During the summer months dining on the open-air balcony as the sun sets is a simply stunning experience. Booking advised, especially for upstairs.

Ⓢ Ⓞ Dining room: daily noon–3, 6–10.30 Ⓞ Café: Mon–Sat 12–12, Sun 10am–1am Ⓦ L A$100, D A$130, Wine A$30 Ⓣ St. Kilda light-rail tram 96 down Bourke Street from the city to the Esplanade near the pier and Acland Street

THY THY 1

Level 1, 142 Victoria Street, Richmond, Melbourne, VIC 3121

Tel 03 9429 1104

Victoria Street, Richmond, is the hub of Melbourne's Vietnamese community and Thy Thy 1 is one of its most popular restaurants.

A mixed clientele dine at the paper-covered tables, from students to the well-heeled, as well as the Vietnamese locals. They are all here for the fresh, yet budget-cheap food. Busy, noisy, quick and fun. BYO.

Ⓢ Ⓞ Daily 8am–10pm Ⓦ L A$40, D A$50 Ⓣ 42 Mont Albert tram from Collins Street

TIAMO

303–305 Lygon Street, Carlton, Melbourne, VIC 3053

Tel 03 9347 5759

Tiamo means 'I Love You' in Italian and that's how many Melburnians feel about this busy little restaurant that personifies the real Carlton, away from its tourist strip. Mix with students, Italian families, academics and the inner-city types who live in the area.

The menu is traditional Italian, quickly served and cheaply priced. BYO.

Ⓢ Ⓞ Mon–Sat 7am–11pm, Sun 8am–10pm Ⓦ L A$35, D A$50, Wine A$16 Ⓣ 200 or 201 from Russell Street, City, along Lygon Street Ⓣ Tram along Swanston Street from the city to Melbourne University

TIDES SEAFOOD GRILL & OYSTER BAR

Pier 35 Marina, 263–329 Lorimer Street, Port Melbourne, VIC 3207

Tel 03 9645 6433

www.rivers.net.au

Tides overlooks the Yarra River at Fisherman's Bend, Port Melbourne, so diners can watch the sea traffic–from laden tankers to pleasure craft–as it moves in and out of Port Phillip Bay. Owners of small boats can moor at the door and stroll in for oysters, a drink or a seafood feast on its outside deck.

It will come as no surprise to learn that the menu is focused on contemporary seafood meals. Booking advised.

Ⓢ Ⓞ Mon–Sat 12–3.30, 6–10.30, Sun 12–3.30 Ⓦ L A$80, D A$110, Wine A$25 🚢 Williamstown ferry from Southgate in the city stops at Pier 35 on request

EATING

TOOFEY'S SEAFOOD RESTAURANT

162 Elgin Street (cnr of Drummond Street), Carlton, Melbourne, 3053
Tel 03 9347 9838
www.toofeys.com.au
Toofey's is reckoned to have the best seafood in Melbourne. The restaurant waits to see what is available at the fish markets each day before printing its menu. Diners may choose a Spring Bay scallop tortelli, a red mullet soup, deep-fried whiting or a flathead meunière. Booking essential.
Ⓢ Ⓘ Tue–Fri 12–2.30, 6–10.30, Sat 6–10.30 🍴 L A$88, D A$120, Wine A$29 🚌 200 or 201 from Russell Street along Lygon Street and Elgin Street 🚊 Tram along Swanston Street from the city to Melbourne University and Lygon Street

VLADO'S CHARCOAL GRILL

61 Bridge Road, Richmond, Melbourne, VIC 3121
Tel 03 9428 5833
One of Melbourne's favourite restaurants, Vlado's is a temple for meat lovers. The set four-course meal can include a mixed grill meat platter, various sizes of steak, finishing off with a filling dessert.
The décor may seem dated and dingy, but with all that food to enjoy, you shouldn't notice.
Ⓢ Ⓘ Mon–Fri 12–3.30, 6–11, Sat 6–11 🍴 Set menu A$120 (four meat courses and coffee), Wine A$20 🚊 Tram down Flinders Street and along Bridge Road

WALTER'S WINE BAR

Upper level 3, Shop 1, Southgate, Southbank, Melbourne, VIC 3006
Tel 03 9690 9211
www.walterswinebar.com.au
Walter's not only has stunning views of the Yarra River and the Melbourne skyline, it has one of the city's best wine cellars. It is in the Southgate complex next to the Victorian Arts Centre, making a perfect place to drop in for a drink or snack before or after a show. It's a favourite haunt of actors and one of the most likely places to get a late evening meal in Melbourne.
Ⓢ Ⓘ Daily noon–late 🍴 L A$80, D A$125, Wine A$35 🚊 Any tram down Swanston Street to the Victorian Arts Centre stop 🚉 Flinders Street then walk across bridge to Southgate

BALLARAT

THE BOATSHED RESTAURANT

Wendouree Parade, Ballarat, VIC 3350
Tel 03 5333 5533
www.ballarat.com/boatshed
This casual restaurant is right on the edge of Lake Wendouree. Stop for coffee, breakfast, lunch, afternoon tea or a sunset dinner.
The international menu includes oysters, pasta, risottos and fish and chips (french fries). Extensive choice of local and Australian wines.
Ⓢ Ⓘ Daily 7 am–late 🍴 Dishes A$12–A$20; D A$84, Wine A$25

L'ESPRESSO

417 Sturt Street, Ballarat, VIC 3350
Tel 03 5333 1789
www.ballarat.com/lespresso
This Italian-style café is in the heart of Victoria's historic gold town. Home-made lunch favourites include an assortment of pastas, risottos and desserts, all made with the best ingredients. Extensive list of Australian wines.
Ⓢ Ⓘ Daily 7.30–6 🍴 Dishes from A$12, Wine A$28

BEECHWORTH

THE BANK RESTAURANT

86 Ford Street, Beechworth, VIC 3747
Tel 03 5728 2223
www.thebankrestaurant.com
The wealth generated by the gold rush in the 1850s can be seen in the old Bank of Australasia building in which this restaurant is housed. It has retained its grandeur, with 6m (18ft) ceilings and classic furnishings. The original gold vault now holds a treasure of wines.
Alfresco dining in the tree-lined, brick-paved courtyard is a feature in warmer weather, and accommodation is also available.
Ⓢ Ⓘ Wed–Sun 6–late, Sun 12–3 🍴 D A$80, Wine A$21

BENDIGO

RISTORANTE BAZZANI

2–4 Howard Place, Bendigo, VIC 3550
Tel 03 5441 3777
www.bazzani.com.au
Bazzani's is in a row house in the heart of Bendigo, a town affectionately known as the 'Paris end of Pall Mall'.
The array of delights include stunning fresh food, gourmet treats, casual light lunches and quality regional wines, including wine from the Bazzani family label, Warrenmang. Lunch, dinner, morning/afternoon tea or snacks are also available outdoors in the Piazza courtyard that overlooks Rosalind Park.
Ⓢ Ⓘ Tue–Sat 12am–late 🍴 L A$60, D A$90, Wine from A$22

DAYLESFORD

LAKE HOUSE

King Street, Daylesford, VIC 3460
Tel 03 5348 3329
www.lakehouse.com.au
The Lake House cascades down the side of a hill overlooking Lake Daylesford in the goldfields hill country of central Victoria, and is one of Victoria's premier country hotels.
All the food is prepared on the premises and has a French influence. A glass of wine at sunset with the kookaburra chorus is a delightful way to end a day exploring the Daylesford region, especially if it included bathing in the famous mineral waters at Hepburn Springs. Booking essential.
Ⓢ Ⓘ Daily breakfast 8–11, 12–3, 7–late 🍴 L A$90, D A$120, Wine A$27. Sat grand dinner A$164

HEALESVILLE

HEALESVILLE HOTEL

256 Maroondah Highway, Healesville, VIC 3777
Tel 03 5962 4002
www.healesvillehotel.com.au
Local pubs are few and far between in the Yarra Valley, and only the Healesville Hotel, with its solid façade and high-ceiling dining room, has made an effort to replace its counter teas with modern Australian food.
There are light meals in the front bar, and the restaurant in the middle of this restored country hotel serves pasta from Healesville, local beef fillet or fresh salmon.
Ⓢ Ⓘ Daily12–3, 6–9; bar meals 12–9 🍴 L A$55, D A$65, bar meals A$5–A$17, Wine A$25

MILAWA

THE EPICUREAN CENTRE

Brown Brothers Vineyard, Bobinawarrah Road, Milawa, VIC 3678
Tel 03 5720 5540
www.brown-brothers.com.au

The Brown Brothers winery is the heart and soul of the country village of Milawa.

The menu is strong on the best locally sourced ingredients, changing seasonally to reflect the availability of the produce. Each à la carte dish is carefully matched with a glass of Brown Brothers wine, and the Centre showcases the winery's new releases.

🚫 ⓘ Daily 11–3 🍴 Lunch A$60
🚗 Northeast Victoria, 64km (40 miles) south from Rutherglen

MILDURA
STEFANO'S
Seventh Street, Mildura, VIC 3500
Tel 03 5023 0511
www.milduragrandhotel.com
Stefano's is a renowned restaurant housed in the bowels of Mildura's Grand Hotel. A set price, five-course meal is served in the white-washed cellars, using only seasonal local Sunraysia produce to make old regional and family Italian-inspired recipes.

Dining Room One, upstairs, has a more standard menu and is slightly cheaper, while the adjacent family restaurant is the Pizza Caffe, serving hearty wood-fired pizzas in a fun and noisy environment. Booking essential.

🚫 ⓘ Stefano's: Mon–Sat 7–late
🍴 Stefano's 5-course dinner A$150
ⓘ Dining Room One: Tue–Sun 12–3, dinner from 6.30 🍴 Dining Room One: L A$70, D A$90, Wine A$27 ⓘ Pizza Caffe: daily 11–late 🚗 In the far northwest of Victoria, 400km (248 miles) east from Adelaide, 295km (183 miles) south from Broken Hill

PAYNESVILLE
CAFÉ ESPAS
Raymond Island Foreshore, Paynesville, VIC 3880
Tel 03 5156 7275
www.espas.com.au
Café Espas is close to the Gippsland Lakes, a short walk from the ferry. Its intimate

dining room also serves as a gallery for co-owner/painter Brendan Sim-Jeuken's work.

Enjoy coffee, cakes, lunch and dinner indoors or on the verandah, and watch the yachts, and black swans, dolphins and pelicans that live in the area. Local seafood is a feature.

🚫 ⓘ Fri–Sat 10am–late, Sun lunch 10–4 🍴 L A$50, D A$65, Wine A$18
🚗 290km (180 miles) east from Melbourne via Bairnsdale

PHILLIP ISLAND
BOYLE'S RESTAURANT AT THE CASTLE
7–9 Steel Street, Cowes, Phillip Island, VIC 3922
Tel 03 5952 1228
www.thecastle.com.au
The restaurant, part of a small guesthouse close to the beach, uses the best of the local produce, especially seafood. Seasonal lobster (order in advance) is a house special and the desserts are excellent. The vegetarian dishes are equally good and the wine list is extensive. Reservations only.

🚫 ⓘ Thu–Sun 6.30–9, Jan; Fri–Sat 6.30–9, Feb–Dec 🍴 D A$130, Wine A$27

THE JETTY RESTAURANT
11–13 The Esplanade, Cowes, Phillip Island, VIC 3922
Tel 03 5952 2060
This renowned restaurant, opposite Cowes jetty, is a good place to top off a tour of the island or round off a visit to the Penguin Parade (see page 95). Like elsewhere on the island, seafood is prominent, especially lobster. Booking advised.

🚫 ⓘ Daily 5–9 (also Sun 12–2)
🍴 L A$60, D A$76, Wine A$18

PORTARLINGTON
PORT PIER CAFÉ
6 Piers Street, Portarlington, VIC 3223
Tel 03 5259 1080
Port Pier Café is at the jetty in Portarlington, which is on the

Bellarine Peninsula. The outlook is complete with fishing boats and mussel farms.

The café serves great Spanish tapas, paella and, of course, mussel dishes. BYO. Parents can sit outdoors and admire the view, while the kids play on the beach.

🚫 ⓘ Thu–Mon, 11am–late
🍴 L A$50, D A$75, Wine A$16
🚗 27km (17 miles) east from Geelong

QUEENSCLIFF
THE VUE
46 Hesse Street, Queenscliff, VIC 3225
Tel 03 5258 1544
www.vuegrand.com.au
The imposing 1881 Vue Grand Hotel, with beautiful Victorian brickwork, has a grand dining room where you can enjoy excellent French-style food accompanied by Bellarine Peninsula wines.

Chandeliers, linen tablecloths and old-style glamour make this a restaurant for a special occasion.

🚫 ⓘ Daily noon–2.30, 6.30–9
🍴 L A$75, D A$100, Wine A$26

RED HILL
MAX'S AT RED HILL ESTATE
Red Hill Estate Winery, 53 Red Hill–Shoreham, Red Hill South, VIC 3937
Tel 03 5931 0177
www.redhillestate.com.au/restaurant
Max's at Red Hill nestles in the property's vineyard with stunning views across Westernport to Phillip Island.

The menu is a spectrum of international and Asian influences, using the best of the local produce, such as Flinders mussels poached in a Red Hill Estate Chardonnay cream sauce.

Each meal is matched with suggested glasses of Red Hill Estate wines, bottles of which can be bought from the cellar door. Booking advised.

🚫 ⓘ Daily 12–3, Fri–Sat 6–late (also Thu Nov–Easter) 🍴 L A$80, D A$105, Wine A$20

EATING

SORRENTO

THE BATHS

3278 Point Nepean, Sorrento, VIC 3943
Tel 03 5984 1500

The Baths are housed in a classic seafront pavilion on the front beach.

The menu, which covers breakfast through to dinner, has Asian and Mediterranean café standards, but the portions are generous and the wines well priced. The fish and chips outlet at the back of the pavilion is a great option on a fine summer evening, when you just want to sit on the beach. Booking advised.

🚱 🅿 Daily 9am–late 🍷 L A$60, D A$75, Wine A$22 🚍 39km (24 miles) southwest from Mornington, on the western tip of the Mornington Peninsula

THE CASTLE AT DELGANY

Peppers Delgany Portsea, Point Nepean Road, Portsea, Phillip Island, VIC 3944
Tel 03 5984 4000
www.peppers.com.au

Part of the Peppers chain, the hotel's battlements justify the name. The restaurant within serves a fine combination of modern European, Asian and Australian cuisines, accompanied by locally produced wines. Choose an outdoor table for breakfast or lunch, overlooking the gardens.

🚱 🅿 Daily 12–3, 7–9.30 (degustation menu Saturday dinner) 🍷 L A$80, D A$104, Wine from A$5 per glass

YERING

YERING STATION RESTAURANT

38 Melba Highway, Yering, VIC 3775
Tel 03 9730 1107
www.yering.com

Yering Station's wine bar and restaurant is in an elegant sandstone and glass building overlooking the vineyards of Yering Station and the Yarra Ranges. You can eat inside by the full-length windows, or outside on the terrace.

The menu changes seasonally, with many of the fresh ingredients, such as trout, berries and cheeses, sourced locally and cooked in a modern Australian style with Asian and French touches. Yering Station wines are available.

🚱 🅿 Mon–Fri 12–3, Sat–Sun 12–4, wine bar daily 10–6 🍷 L A$70, Wine A$18 🚍 3km (2 miles) south from Yarra Glen in the Yarra Valley

ANISE

697 Brunswick Street, New Farm, Brisbane, QLD 4005
Tel 07 3358 1558

Reputed to be Australia's best wine bar, this tiny shopfront, with its designer décor, is run by wine buff Tony Harper. It seats only 20 people, so it's often crowded.

Regional French food is served, such as stuffed pig's trotters with cider, goose liver paté and roast duck. Vegetarian options are also available. There is, of course, a superb range of wines from Australia and Europe. Booking advised.

🚱 🅿 Mon–Fri 12am–1am (closed lunch Mon–Tue), Sat–Sun 8am–1am 🍷 L A$60, D A$76, Wine A$28 🚍 190, 193, 191 from Adelaide Street stand 16

CHA CHA CHAR WINE BAR AND GRILL

Shop 5, Eagle Street Pier, Eagle Street, Brisbane, QLD 4000
Tel 07 3211 9944
www.chachacharrestaurant.01.com.au

The large glass walls in this plantation-style restaurant provide splendid river views. The restaurant's aim is to source the best meat products and present them as both innovative and traditional dishes using a variety of cooking techniques.

Typical dishes include quail barbecued with green pea noodles, eye filet with truffle potato whip, or kangaroo and golden shallot tart with fried cabbage and parsley oil. The wine list is comprehensive. Booking advised.

🚱 On balcony 🅿 Mon–Fri 12–2.30, Mon–Sun 6–9 🍷 L A$100, D A$116, Wine A$30 🚢 Inner city ferry to Eagle Street Pier

CIRCA

483 Adelaide Street, Brisbane, QLD 4000
Tel 07 3832 4722
www.circarestaurant.com.au

One of Brisbane's best restaurants, the dining room has stylish floor-to-ceiling glass walls and there is a modern bar area. The enclosed verandah looks out to the river.

The food shows modern Australian style with French influences: steamed zucchini flowers, with tomato broth and

puy lentils; roast chicken basted with foie gras in puff pastry; or barramundi served with a blend of parsnips, leeks and aioli. Excellent vintage wines are on offer. Booking advised.

🚱 🅿 Tue–Fri 12–2.30, Mon–Sat 6–9 🍷 L A$80, D A$104, Wine A$27 🚍 City Loop

CITY GARDENS CAFÉ

City Gardens Alice Street, Botanical Gardens, Brisbane, QLD 4000
Tel 07 3229 1554

Experience heritage charm by dining in this Federation-style (1903) cottage, set amid subtropical vegetation in the lovely City Botanic Gardens. There is an open-sided terrace for warm weather and, inside, a fireplace warms winter nights.

Hearty breakfasts are served as well as modern-style lunches such as warm salad of Moroccan spiced lamb, Devonshire teas and a variety of light refreshments. A fair range of Australian wines is available. Booking advised.

🚱 🅿 Daily 8–5 🍷 L A$70, Wine A$17 🚍 City Loop

CUSTOMS HOUSE BRASSERIE

399 Queen Street, Brisbane, QLD 4000
Tel 07 3365 8921

In the Customs House complex on a prime riverside location, the restaurant has a modern interior with contemporary art on the walls, and a terrace with shade umbrellas.

The modern Australian cuisine includes dishes such as

EATING

smoked trout and avocado on pressed tomato with orange dill dressing, or Thai-style green duck curry with potato, eggplant and basil leaves served with jasmine rice. There is a comprehensive Australian wine list. Booking advised.

🚫 ⏰ Mon–Sat 12–2.30, Tue–Sat 6–9, Sun brunch 10–3 🍷 L A$80, D A$100, Wine A$25

E'CCO BISTRO
100 Boundary Street, Brisbane, QLD 4000
Tel 07 3831 8344
www.eccobistro.com
The minimalist design and clean, bright interior provide the atmosphere, but it is the high standard of cooking that has made this one of Brisbane's best restaurants.

Chef Philip Johnson produces simple, uncomplicated food from fresh seasonal ingredients. Examples are grilled whiting with fennel, watercress, celery leaves and roasted garlic mayo; and seared Atlantic salmon with a salad of green pawpaw, coriander, chilli, lime and cashews. The comprehensive Australian wine list includes liqueurs. Booking advised.

🚫 ⏰ Mon–Fri 12–2.30, 6–9, Sat 6–9 🍷 L A$80, D A$104, Wine A$30

GREEN PAPAYA
898 Stanley Street East, East Brisbane, QLD 4019
Tel 07 3217 3599
www.greenpapaya.com.au
So popular is this venue, one of Australia's best Vietnamese restaurants, that the owner runs cooking classes featuring her signature dishes.

The traditional north Vietnamese cuisine relies on fresh ingredients. Delicious examples are grilled prawns marinated in chilli, garlic and lemon myrtle, served with herbed mayonnaise sauce; crabmeat omelette; and black rice pudding with palm sugar and coconut. There is a reasonable selection of Australian wines plus cocktails and liqueurs. Booking advised.

🚫 ⏰ Fri 12–2.30, Tue–Sat 6–9 🍷 L A$80, D A$104, Wine A$22 🚌 184, 185, 210 from Ann Street

IL CENTRO
Eagle Street Pier, Eagle Street, Brisbane, QLD 4000
Tel 07 3221 6090
www.il-centro.com.au
Enjoy top food overlooking the Brisbane River, just north of the City Botanic Gardens. The dining room is contemporary with an open kitchen where modern Australian food is prepared with an Italian twist.

Dishes include grilled Moreton Bay bugs, chargrilled herb and chilli marinated octopus, herb crumbed marinated Koorana Farm crocodile, veal scallopine with fettuccine carbonara, and kangaroo strip loin with red wine risotto cake. There is a comprehensive Australian wine list including liqueurs. Booking advised.

🚫 ⏰ Sun–Fri 12–2.30, daily 6–9 🍷 L A$80, D A$100, Wine A$28 🚢 CityCat to Eagle Street Pier

JIMMY'S ON THE MALL
Queen Street Mall, Brisbane, QLD 4000
Tel 07 3229 9999
The fast, efficient service here, available all day, makes Jimmy's an ideal place for a light meal or a coffee break from city shopping.

The menu changes regularly, but among the tasty, reasonably priced dishes are freshly shucked Tasmanian oysters, king prawns and Moreton Bay bugs with lemon dill and Riesling saffron cream, and wok-tossed vegetables. There is an extensive Australian wine list with wines available by the glass.

🚫 ⏰ Daily, 24 hours 🍷 L A$70, D A$90, Wine A$25

MONDO ORGANICS
166 Hardgrave Road, West End, Brisbane, QLD 4101
Tel 07 3844 1132
www.mondo-organics.com.au
In the heart of alternative West End, this was Australia's first organic restaurant. It also includes an organic produce outlet. The interior has a Japanese-style design.

Dishes cover vegetarian, vegan, wheat-free and dairy-free options. The menu includes seared squid with greens, eastern salsa and grilled lime; roasted pumpkin with mixed endive and cashews and red wine dressing; and smoked tofu with besan battered spinach, beans, chilli and almonds. Booking advised.

🚫 Restricted ⏰ Tue–Sat 12–2.30, 6–9 (also Sat breakfast), Sun 12–2.30 🍷 L A$92, D A$110, Wine A$24 🚌 190, 194 from Adelaide Street stand 47

SIGGI'S AT STAMFORD PLAZA
Stamford Plaza Brisbane, cnr Edward and Margaret streets, Brisbane, QLD 4000
Tel 07 3221 1999
The Stamford Plaza hotel is in the restored Port Office overlooking the Brisbane River, and Siggi's is a good place to celebrate a special occasion. The service is attentive and the menu is international.

Dishes include red claw crayfish and gazpacho with a salad of sand crab and fresh fish, and roast turkey tenderloin on pearl barley risotto with zucchini flowers and golden shallots. There is a comprehensive list of Australian wines. Booking advised.

🚫 Restricted; cigars on sale ⏰ Tue–Sat dinner 🍷 D A$150, Wine A$35 🚌 City Loop

SUMMIT RESTAURANT
Sir Samuel Griffith Drive, Mount Coot-tha Lookout, Brisbane, QLD 4066
Tel 07 3369 9922
www.brisbanelookout.com

Close to the Botanic Gardens and next to Mount Coot-tha Lookout, west of the city, this is a great place for Sunday brunch. The renovated building has panoramic views of Brisbane and its surroundings.

The regularly changing menu often includes chargrilled fillet of Queensland beef served with baked sweet potato, cinnamon cream and pesto field mushrooms. The wine list contains some Queensland vintages. Booking advised.

🚫 ⏰ Daily 12–2.30, 6–9, Sun brunch from 8am 🍷 L A$70, D A$115, Wine A$27 🚌 471 from Adelaide Street stand 45 🚗 8km (5 miles) west from Brisbane via Milton Road (State Route 32)

EATING

BALLANDEAN
THE VINEYARD CAFÉ
New England Highway, Ballandean, QLD 4382
Tel 07 4684 1270
www.vineyard-cottages.com.au

In the Granite Belt, south of Stanthorpe, this converted country church is part of the Vineyard Cottages complex. The décor is simple and the service friendly.

Dishes include warm salad of New England smoked trout with crispy leeks and egg, caper and parsley dressing, and fresh New England rainbow trout poached in a fragrant coconut milk. The select wine list represents local vineyards. Booking advised.

Ⓢ Ⓒ Sat–Sun 12–2.30, Fri–Sat 6–9
Ⓤ L A$30, D A$55, Wine A$28

BURLEIGH HEADS
MERMAIDS CAFÉ AND BAR
Burleigh Beach Pavilion, 43 Goodwin Terrace, Burleigh Heads, QLD 4220
Tel 07 5520 1177

Right by one of Australia's finest surfing beaches, this is the best place on the southern Gold Coast for an informal meal at any time of day. It has great sea views, and entertainment on Sunday afternoons.

The modern Australian menu includes a variety of breakfast pancakes (a house special), baked sea perch with coconut served in pernod cream sauce, and to finish, tequila sunset—raspberry mint and tequila granita sorbet with saffron peach. Booking advised on Friday, Saturday and Sunday breakfast.

Ⓢ Outside tables only Ⓒ Mon–Thu 12–9pm, Fri–Sun 7am–9pm Ⓤ L A$70, D A$90, Wine A$26

CAIRNS
METROPOLIS
1/15 Spence Street, Cairns, QLD 4870
Tel 07 4041 0277
www.metropolis.cairns.net.au
A popular restaurant with a large dining area and music on Fridays and Saturdays.

A variety of interesting dishes includes fried calamari with plum and berry sauce; Saganaki pan-fried Greek cheese with lemon; chilli mussels cooked in salsa with chilli, wine and fresh herbs; and lamb rack marinated with herbs and chargrilled with vegetables and potatoes. There is also a good wine list and a cocktail bar. Booking advised.

Ⓢ Smoking areas and cigar lounge
Ⓒ Daily breakfast, 12–2.30, 6–1am
Ⓤ L A$80, D A$100, Wine A$25

PERROTTA'S AT THE GALLERY
Cairns Regional Art Gallery, cnr Shields and Abbott Streets, Cairns, QLD 4870
Tel 07 4031 5899
There is always a crowd here, so arrive early. It is a great place for coffee, with an excellent selection of light meals and snacks.

Example dishes are pan-fried coral trout with white beans, radicchio, oven-dried tomatoes and pinenut-anchovy dressing, and a number of vegetarian alternatives. The regularly changing wine list includes wines from small producers. Dinner booking advised.

Ⓒ Daily 8am–late Ⓤ L A$78, D A$98, Wine A$24

RED OCHRE GRILL
43 Shields Street, Cairns, QLD 4870
Tel 07 4051 0100
www.redochregrill.com.au
This place is a must. It pioneered Australian bush tucker cuisine, using native fruits, game, meat and seafood. There are Aboriginal paintings and Peter Jarver photographic prints.

Among the unusual dishes are Mirrawinni ostrich fillet with yam croquettes, Vietnamese pickles and lemon aspen sambal (relish); prawns; calamari and scallops with lemon myrtle fettuccini; and kangaroo sirloin with quandong chilli glaze with sweet potato hot cake. There is a good Australian wine list and various local beers. Booking advised.

Ⓢ Restricted Ⓒ Mon–Sat 12–2.30, 6–9, Sun 6–9 Ⓤ L A$70, D A$100, Wine A$26.50

MAIN BEACH
FELLINI
Waterfront Level 1, Marina Mirage, Seaworld Drive, Main Beach, QLD 4217
Tel 07 5531 0300
www.fellini.com.au
For a big night out Gold Coast style, this elegant modern Italian restaurant has great views over the marina.

Delicious dishes include ravioli filled with roasted duck and vegetables cooked with a light duck and tomato reduction finished with grated parmesan; and grilled Moreton Bay bugs topped with fire-roasted capsicum, fresh garlic, parsley, zested lime and extra virgin olive oil. There is a comprehensive international wine list. Booking advised.

Ⓢ Ⓒ Daily 12–3. 6.30–late
Ⓤ L A$100, D A$130, Wine A$21

MISSION BEACH
SCOTTY'S BAR AND GRILL
167 Reid Road, Mission Beach, QLD 4850
Tel 07 4068 8870
www.scottysbeachhouse.com.au
Scotty's quality home-style food comes at reasonable prices and is excellent value for money. Informality rules and nearly all tastes are catered for.

Among the dishes are New Zealand oysters; coral trout grilled with stir-fry vegetables and Anita's tropical sauce; and grilled kangaroo steak with chilli quandong sauce, mashed potatoes and vegetables. Vegetarian options and meals for children are available.

EATING

Ⓢ Ⓒ Daily 5–9, Sun 12–9 Ⓦ L A$30,
D A$35, Wine A$14.50

NOOSA HEADS

RICKY RICARDO'S RIVER BAR AND RESTAURANT

Quamby Place, Noosa Heads,
QLD 4567
Tel 07 5447 2455
www.rickyricardos.com

One of Noosa's top restaurants, Ricky Ricardo's has a stunning location facing the Noosa River. The inside is modern but simple, or there is seating outside.

The seasonally changing menu has Mediterranean influences, including tapas. Especially tasty are sand crab and roast garlic tart with salad of white asparagus and curly endive, and tomato and pine nut risotto with crispy fried zucchini flowers. There is a comprehensive Australian wine list. Booking advised.

Ⓢ Ⓒ Daily 12–late Ⓦ L A$90,
D A$110, Wine A$28 Ⓔ Noosa River ferry stops outside

PORT DOUGLAS

MANGO JAM

24 Macrossan Street, Port Douglas,
QLD 4871
Tel 07 4099 4611

A popular no-frills restaurant with modern décor. The verandah tables are shaded by canopies and palm trees.

Mango Jam serves modern Australian cuisine and wood-fired pizzas. Alternative dishes include chicken and mushroom fettucini with pesto, vegetables in a fresh tomato concasse with spaghetti, or fettucine with salami, chilli, black olives, garlic and onion in a Napoli sauce. The wine list is Australian.

Ⓢ Ⓒ Daily Ⓦ L A$50, D A$75, Wine A$22

SALSA BAR & GRILL

26 Wharf Street, Port Douglas,
QLD 4871

Tel 07 4099 4922
www.salsa-port-douglas.com.au

At the trendy end of Port Douglas, the restaurant's plantation-style décor has an ocean backdrop.

The food shows influences of the Pacific Rim, southwestern America and California. Dishes include sand crab pannacotta with smoked salmon, mustard fruit empanada with goat's cheese and mango and macadamia parfait. The wine list includes good Australian and New Zealand vintages. Booking advised.

Ⓢ Restricted Ⓦ L A$60, D A$140, Wine A$20

YANDINA

SPIRIT HOUSE

4 Ninderry Road, Yandina, QLD 4561
Tel 07 5446 8994
www.spirithouse.com.au

Set in Asian-inspired gardens complete with stream and duck pond, the restaurant prepares Thai-West fusion dishes.

Enjoy Chiang Mai larb of chicken with mint, lime and chilli, vegetarian flat rice noodles, or cauliflower and tofu with Shanghai noodles and cucumber relish. There is a good Australian wine list. Booking essential.

Ⓢ Ⓒ Daily 12–2.30, Wed–Sat 6–9 Ⓦ L A$98, D A$116, Wine A$24 Ⓔ 10km (6 miles) south from Eumundi

YUNGABURRA

EDEN HOUSE

20 Gillies Highway, Yungaburra,
QLD 4872
Tel 07 4095 3355
www.edenhouse.com.au

Part of the Eden House Garden Cottages in the Atherton Tableland town of Yungaburra, the restaurant is in a Queensland heritage home.

The international menu has dishes such as fillet of barramundi coated with macadamia nuts and topped with avocado and a lemon chive hollandaise, and duck braised in a citrus and star anise stock with caramelized vegetables and a mandarin glaze. There is a good list of Australian wines. Booking advised.

Ⓢ Ⓒ Daily 6–9; lunch on Yungaburra Market Day (4th Sat of month) Ⓦ L A$40, D A$80, Wine A$20 Ⓔ 13km (8 miles) east from Atherton, 70km (44 miles) southwest from Cairns

CORNUCOPIA MUSEUM CAFÉ

Conacher Street, Bullocky Point, Fannie Bay, NT 0820
Tel 08 8981 1002

Part of the Museum and Art Gallery complex, this modern café has great views of Darwin Harbour and the pandanus fringed foreshore.

The cuisine is modern Australian. They serve a great brunch including eggs Benedict as well as Thai smoked chicken salad, Greek salad with marinated octopus, and vegetarian curry. There is a small range of Australian wines. Booking advised for Fridays and Saturdays.

Ⓢ Ⓒ Daily 9–5 (no meals after 3.30) Ⓦ L A$78, Wine A$25

CRUSTACEANS ON THE WHARF

Darwin Wharf Precinct, Darwin,
NT 0800
Tel 08 8981 8658

This large, open restaurant is on Darwin's restored wharf and has fine harbour views. Its seafood specials include chilli crab with tomato and coriander and Taste of the Orient seafood platter.

Also available is crocodile served with a chilli mango or native pepper, or barbecued kangaroo with vegetables and a native rosella sauce. Children's meals are available by request, but vegetarians are not well catered for. Booking advised.

Ⓢ Ⓒ Dinner Mon–Sat 6.30–late Ⓦ D A$90, Wine A$20

DRAGON COURT

MGM Grand Casino, Gilruth Avenue, Darwin, NT 0800
Tel 08 8943 8888
www.mgmgrand.com.au

Smart Chinese restaurant in the MGM Grand Casino. Booking advised.

Ⓢ Ⓒ Wed–Sun dinner Ⓦ D A$100, Wine A$30 Ⓔ 4 from the city

HANUMAN

28 Mitchell Street, Darwin, NT 0800
Tel 08 8941 3500

One of Darwin's best restaurants, Hanuman's has a sleek, minimalist design. The formally dressed staff provide exceptional service.

Nonya and Thai dishes are on the menu, and there is a

EATING

Tandoori oven. Sample dishes include Hanuman oysters with basil leaves, barramundi baked in banana leaves, and pepper prawns with curry leaves. There are good vegetarian options and an excellent wine list. Booking essential.

Ⓢ Ⓒ Mon–Fri 12–2.30, 6.30–8 Ⓛ L A$70 (set special A$22 per head), D A$90, Wine A$28

PEE WEES AT THE POINT
Alec Fong Lim Drive, East Point, NT 0820
Tel 08 8981 6868
www.peewees.com.au
North of the city, this relaxed, modern restaurant is bordered on three sides by natural vine forest and has stunning harbour views. Go at sunset.

The cuisine is Australian Creole with dishes such as smoked salmon salad garnished with cherry tomatoes, Lebanese cucumber, Spanish onion, black olives and baby capers, or grilled antipasto. Booking advised.

Ⓢ Ⓒ Daily 6–8 Ⓛ D A$90, Wine A$27 🚗 4km (2.5 miles) north from central Darwin

THE WATERHOLE
All Seasons Premier Darwin Central, cnr Knuckey and Smith streets, Darwin, NT 0800
Tel 08 8981 9120

Regarded as the best hotel dining in Darwin, the restaurant has a relaxed atmosphere and efficient service.

The food is modern Australian with Asian and European influences. Try the Shanghai prawns wrapped in warm noodles; wild barramundi on jasmine rice and bok choy, served with a kaffir lime leaf butter sauce: or grilled loin of kangaroo on sweet potato mash, with blueberry and port wine juice. There is an extensive wine list. Booking advised.

Ⓢ Ⓒ Daily 6–9 Ⓛ D A$100, Wine A$22

ALICE SPRINGS

BLUEGRASS RESTAURANT
Cnr Stott Terrace and Todd Street, Alice Springs, NT 0870
Tel 08 8955 5188
The original meeting hall in Alice Springs has been renovated by Kay Hellyer and chef husband Phil as a restaurant with courtyard dining.

The changing blackboard menus have enticed guests from around the world: vegetarian dishes, Indian curries, pasta, rib-eye steaks and pork. Of particular note is the seafood antipasto platter with bug tails, barramundi, prawns, smoked salmon, oysters, pickled squid, taramasalata and Turkish bread. Also popular is red-wine glazed kangaroo.

Ⓒ Wed–Mon 6–late. Closed Dec 25–Jan 14 Ⓛ D A$90, Wine A$23

HANUMAN RESTAURANT
82 Barrett Street, Alice Springs, NT 0870
Tel 08 8953 7188
Objects from northern Thailand and authentic dishes prepared with fresh seafood, vegetables and herbs make this a memorable dining spot. Host Jimmy Shu's signature dish is grilled Hanuman oysters, with the flavours of fresh lemongrass sauce and basil.

Chicken, beef and pork are prepared in Thai style (not necessarily hot). Notable side dishes include grilled eggplant salad with prawns, chicken and onions. The six-course lunch for A$16 per person is a bargain. The wine list has over 60 choices. Booking advised.

Ⓒ Mon–Fri 12–3.30, Mon–Sat 6–10.30 Ⓛ L A$64, D A$70, Wine A$24

MALATHI AND SEAN'S IRISH BAR AND RESTAURANT
51 Bath Street, Alice Springs, NT 0870
Tel 08 8952 1858
www.seansirishbar.com
Unwind at Alice's only beer garden for Sunday jam sessions, karaoke on Thursdays, live entertainment on Friday and Saturday, and great food at one of NT's zaniest places. If Irish Sean and his Malaysian-Indian wife Malathi had their way, every day would be St. Patrick's, 17 March, when feasting and entertainment reach their zenith.

Malathi's Indian, Malay, Thai and Indonesian restaurant dishes contrast with Sean's Irish fare, including his evergreen, Champ—mashed potatoes with butter, scallions and sausages.

Ⓒ Irish food daily 3.30pm–2am. Other cuisines Wed–Sat 6.30–9.30 Ⓛ D A$40, Wine A$19.50

OSCARS CAFÉ AND RESTAURANT
Shop 1, Cinema Complex, 86 Todd Mall, Alice Springs, NT 0870
Tel 08 8953 0930
Apart from meals, this popular café is a good stop just for an early or late coffee. The Mediterranean dishes derive their flavours from Portuguese and Spanish influences, and fresh fish, including barramundi, is regularly flown in.

Ⓒ Daily 9–late Ⓛ L A$50, D A$80, Wine A$20

SULTAN'S KEBABS
Shop 4/52 Hartley Street, Alice Springs, NT 0870
Tel 08 8953 3322
One could be in the Middle East on Friday and Saturday nights when the belly-dancers arrive. Joining them, some diners get so excited they even dance on their tables at this typically Turkish restaurant. Sunday to Thursday, traditional international recorded music is played by hosts Denise and Emenver Calisir to make foreign guests feel at home.

Dips come with hot Turkish bread. Most mains, including seven different kebabs, are with rice and salad. A huge platter awaits vegetarians.

Ⓒ Mon–Sat 11–late, Sun 5–late Ⓛ L A$38, D A$50, Wine A$16

AYERS ROCK RESORT

KUNIYA RESTAURANT
Sails in the Desert Hotel, Ayers Rock Resort, NT 872
Tel: 08 8957 7888
www.voyages.com.au
The décor of this elegant restaurant, which overlooks the hotel swimming pool, is based on an Aboriginal story about the mythical woman python, Kuniya.

The menu successfully blends traditional and contemporary ingredients, such as the roast kumera and mudcrab pancake on a bed of spinach with horseradish aioli,

EATING

followed by the cylindrical chocolate mousse decorated with a toffee tier, as well as indigenous flavours like kangaroo and lemon myrtle. There is an extensive range of fine Australian wines.

🕐 Daily from 7–9.30 💲 D A$120, Wine A$35

AYERS ROCK RESORT
SOUNDS OF SILENCE/YULARA
Nr Ayers Rock Resort, NT 0872
Tel 08 8957 7888
www.voyages.com.au

This is not a restaurant in the usual sense of the word. From the Ayers Rock Resort in the Yulara complex, a coach takes you to a desert dune area in the Uluru-Kata Tjuta National Park from where you can see both Uluru (Ayers Rock) and Kata Tjuta (the Olgas).

Champagne is served accompanied by the stirring sounds of the didgeridoo. As the sun sets you can see both Uluru and Kata Tjuta changing colour in the distance. Hors d'oeuvres are served in a private dining area as the sun goes down over the horizon.

Dinner consists of an Australian barbecue buffet prepared by the resort's chefs using indigenous meats—camel steaks, kangaroo steaks or chargrilled emu. There's often some crocodile and maybe some Northern Territory buffalo. Barramundi is served for fish lovers and there are vegetarian options. You only take what suits from the buffet, but there is something for everyone. Bush salads, Australian wines and refreshing desserts accompany the barbecue.

As darkness sets in, the expansive night sky of the Australian outback shines with thousands of stars. You are treated to an entertaining journey through the southern skies

by the resident astronomer, who guides you through the constellations, and picks out various stars and planets that are significant to Aboriginal people. There's an opportunity to study the stars in greater detail through a powerful telescope.

For a taste of what to expect, visit the website and try the interactive Guide to the Stars. The duration of the Sounds of Silence dinner is about 4 hours. As this is an outdoor setting, smoking is permitted. Although it's not essential to book in advance the dinners are very popular and numbers are limited. The price may seem expensive, but the whole experience with food, wine and entertainment is well worth it.

🕐 Every night, unless prevented by extreme weather 💲 All inclusive A$115 per person

BERRY SPRINGS
TERRITORY WILDLIFE PARK
Cox Peninsula Road, Berry Springs, NT 0837
Tel 08 8988 6574
www.territorywildlifepark.com.au

For refreshment during a visit to the splendid wildlife park, try the self-service, bistro-style park café.

Dishes include beef curries, roast beef and vegetables, salads, hot french fries, rice pies and Black Forest cake. Children's meals are also provided and there are some vegetarian dishes. There is wine by the glass and beer.

🕐 Daily 8.30–4 💲 L A$28, Wine A$5 per glass 🚌 Darwin Day Tours (tel 08 8924 1111)

JIM JIM
THE MIMI RESTAURANT AND BARRA BISTRO
Gagudju Lodge Cooinda, Kakadu Highway, Jim Jim, NT 0886
Tel 08 8979 0145
www.gagudjulodgecooinda.com.au

A 3-hour drive east from Darwin near the popular Yellow Water recreation area in Kakadu National Park, the restaurant has wood panelling and modern furnishings.

The food is Australian bush cuisine with local delicacies such as kangaroo, barramundi, emu and crocodile served with tangy fruits and aromatic herbs. The Barra Bistro is a

large open-sided dining area with fixed bench seating. The wine list includes top Australian producers.

🕐 🕐 6–9.30, 11.30–2.30, 6.30–9. Dining limited Dec 1–Mar 19
💲 L A$75, D A$95, Wine A$18
🚗 296km (184 miles) east from Darwin via the Arnhem Highway, 49km (30 miles) southwest from Jabiru, near Yellow Water recreation area in Kakadu National Park

KATHERINE
KIRBY'S
Cnr Giles Street and Katherine Terrace, Katherine, NT 0851
Tel 08 8972 1622

This modern hotel restaurant has a mix of modern and traditional cuisines, including Northern Territory specialist dishes such as buffalo fillet, along with Thai dishes.

Other possibilities are baked avocado seafood, ham and mushroom duxelles, as well as scallops with a fresh and chunky tomato-and-basil concassé wrapped in zucchini and lightly poached. Vegetarian dishes are also available, as is a children's menu. The Australian wine list is reasonably priced.

🚭 🕐 Mon–Fri 12–2, 6.30–9, Sat 6.30–9 💲 L A$50, D A$80, Wine A$18

PINE CREEK
THE PAVILION RESTAURANT
Stuart Highway, Pine Creek, NT 0847
Tel 08 8976 1232

This cosy restaurant is in a wild-horse sanctuary, Bonrook Resort, close to the junction of the Stuart and Kakadu highways. It has country-style décor and good service.

The modern Australian cuisine uses fresh local produce and game meats, including barramundi with lemon-basil butter sauce, prawns and wild rice; pork with outback spices and rosella chutney; and wattleseed and banana cheesecake. There is a good Australian wine list.

🚭 🕐 Apr–Nov 12–2.30, 6–9
💲 L A$80, D A$110, Wine A$29
🚗 220km (137 miles) south from Darwin, 90km (56 miles) north from Katherine, 7km (4.5 miles) south from Pine Creek

EATING

CENTRAL MARKET FOOD COURTS AND CAFÉS

Gouger Street, Adelaide, SA 5000
Tel 08 8203 7203
www.adelaide.sa.gov.au/centralmarket

For Adelaide's cheapest, most varied food, mainly great Asian and some Mediterranean, head for its buzziest, colourful central market to breakfast, lunch and people-watch at more than 50 food stalls and restaurants.

At Market Plaza and the International Food Plaza it's mainly Chinese, Thai, Malay and Vietnamese specials, such as noodles, sushi, curries, vegetarian, purist vegan food and drinks. Enjoy a filling breakfast at Kelly's Kitchen, 38 Gouger Street (*daily 7–3; tel 08 8231 2049*).

Ⓢ Ⓒ Mon–Thu 7–5, Fri 9–9, Sat 9–4; Sun 11–2 for yum cha. Closed public holidays Ⓥ Stall meal A$16, Wine from A$3 per glass

CHIANTI CLASSICO

160 Hutt Street, Adelaide, SA 5000
Tel 08 8232 7955
A place to be seen, this historic stone building in Adelaide's funky east end houses a smart Italian restaurant.

Breakfast may be fruit salad, bacon and eggs or ricotta hot cakes, while lunch specials include northern Italian dishes such as pappardelle al'Anatra, home-made egg pasta, roast duck, capsicums, spinach and toasted pinenuts with entrées from antipasto to beer-battered zucchini flowers filled with ricotta and pinenuts. Wines include exclusive Italian reds.

Ⓢ Ⓒ Daily 7.30–10.30, 12–3, 6–10.30 Ⓥ L A$70, D A$90, Wine A$27

CHLOE'S RESTAURANT

36 College Road, Kent Town, Adelaide, SA 5067
Tel 08 8362 2574

Possessing the largest wine list in Australia, Chloe's is in a Victorian mansion with three intimate dining areas, replete with antiques and period paintings. The modern Australian and French menu changes seasonally.

Host Nick Papazahariakis's exciting cuisine also includes dishes with Mediterranean and Asian influences, such as boned quail in crisp pastry with shiitake mushroom farce, yogurt and coriander sauce. A Greek he may be, but you won't find moussaka on his menu. Wheelchair accessible.

Ⓢ Ⓒ Mon–Sat 12–3, 6.30–9 Ⓥ L A$90, D A$130, Wine A$26 Ⓑ 2km (1.5 miles) northeast from central Adelaide

CIBO

8–10 O'Connell Street, North Adelaide, SA 5006
Tel 08 8267 2444
The relaxed Cibo has something for everyone. For a breakfast or short stop take an excellent coffee, pastry or gelato in the courtyard.

Lunch or dinner dishes include antipasto, oven pizzas, risotto or pasta, matched by wines from around the world. There is a Cibo espresso bar at 218 Rundle Street.

Ⓢ Ⓒ Daily 9–11.45, 12–3, 6–9.30 Ⓥ L A$160, D A$220, Wine A$30

THE GRANGE RESTAURANT

Hilton Adelaide, Victoria Square, Adelaide, SA 5000
Tel: 08 8217 2000
www.hilton.com
This prestigious fusion restaurant has achieved renown due to the creative mastery of consultant chef Cheong Liew. Top service too.

The Chinese influence is evident in dishes such the chicken baked in salt crust. Evening attire.

Ⓢ Ⓒ Tue–Sat 7–12 Ⓥ D Tue–Fri A$170, Sat A$220, Wine A$40

JARMER'S

297 Kensington Road, Kensington Park, Adelaide, SA 5068
Tel 08 8332 2080
www.jarmers.net.au
Austrian-born owner-chef Peter Jarmer is president of prestigious La Chaine des Rotisseurs. His elegant, pastel-hued restaurant is renowned for superb soufflés, pralines

and main-course sauces in true European-French style.

Among his seasonally changing menu, Peter's signature dish is galette of sea scallops with braised leeks and carrot beurre blanc. Wheelchair accessible.

Ⓢ Ⓒ Tue, Fri 12–2.30, Tue–Sat from 6 Ⓥ L A$80, D A$108, Wine A$22 Ⓑ 7km (4.5 miles) east from central Adelaide

KY CHOW

82 Gouger Street, Adelaide, SA 5000
Tel 08 8221 5411
This ordinary Cantonese restaurant is always packed because the food is sensational and extremely cheap.

An exceptional combination is the acclaimed roast duck in bay berry sauce along with a steamed barramundi, Chinese greens and steamed rice. Booking advised.

Ⓢ Ⓒ Mon–Sat 12–2.30, 5.30–11, Sun 5.30–11 Ⓥ Two courses A$30, three courses A$40, Wine A$22

THE SUMMIT

Summit Road, Mount Lofty, Adelaide, SA 5152
Tel 08 8339 2600
Enjoy wonderful views over Adelaide with modern Australian dishes made with fresh ingredients plus great wines from the region.

Ⓢ Ⓒ Mon–Tue 9–5, Wed–Sun 9–late Ⓥ L A$90, D A$120, Wine A$22.50 Ⓑ 19km (12 miles) southeast from Adelaide via Princes Highway (A1/M1)

WINDY POINT RESTAURANTS

Belair Road, Belair, Adelaide, SA 5052
Tel 08 8278 8255
www.windypointrestaurant.com.au
Perched on a viewpoint overlooking the city, there are two restaurants here. Both have floor-to-ceiling windows, so no worries about the wind.

The contemporary restaurant serves Australian cuisine influenced particularly by Japan and Malaysia. The more casual Café Mediterranean specializes in Greek, Italian, Spanish and Turkish dishes.

Ⓢ Ⓒ Restaurant: Mon–Sat 6–late; last orders 9.30 Ⓥ D A$80, Wine A$25 Ⓒ Café Mediterranean: Fri–Sun 12–2.30, Tue–Sun 6–9.30 Ⓥ L A$56, D A$70, Wine A$25 Ⓑ 9km (5.5 miles) south from Adelaide via Pulteney Street, which becomes Unley Road then Belair Road, uphill to Windy Point at left

EATING

ADELAIDE HILLS

BRIDGEWATER MILL

Mount Barker Road, Bridgewater,
Adelaide Hills, SA 5155
Tel 08 8339 3422
www.bridgewatermill.com.au

On the road east to Mount
Barker, Bridgewater Mill with
its 19th-century functioning
water wheel is the showcase
for winemaker Brian Croser's
Petaluma wines. The winery's
restaurant is one of South
Australia's finest. Chef Tu Thai
is a Francophile with an intu-
ition for blending the flavour
and textures of Asia and
Europe.

Particularly special are his
Kangaroo Island marron with
crustacean mousseline and
truffle cream, or the seared yel-
lowfin tuna with roasted beet-
root and wasabi mayonnaise.
Ⓢ Ⓦ Thu–Mon 12–2.30. Wine tastings daily 10–5 🍴 L A$106, Wine
A$21.50 🚗 23km (14.5 miles) south-
east from Adelaide along Princes
Highway and Eastern Freeway (A1/M1)
to Bridgewater exit

BAROSSA VALLEY

BARR-VINUM

Franklin House, 6–8 Washington Street,
Angaston, SA 3553
Tel 08 8564 3688
This European-style bistro, in
a charming cottage with a traditional verandah, serves
regional dishes using good
local produce.

Run by the local McLean
Farm winery, the restaurant
also showcases Barossa, classic Australian and international
wines, which can be tasted by
the glass.
Ⓢ Ⓦ Tue–Sun 10am–11pm
🍴 L, D A$111, Wine A$28

THE VINTNERS

Nuriootpa–Angaston road, Angaston,
SA 5353
Tel 08 8564 2488
www.vintners.com.au

Vines drape the outside of this
excellent and popular restaurant. Dishes focus on local
Barossa produce bought fresh
from local growers. Combining
Australian with Asian and
Mediterranean influences, the
cuisine is called Barossan.

The menu changes season-
ally, but if it's on, go for wild
duckling roasted and served
with savoury cabbage and
pickled cherries. The wine list
well represents this acclaimed
wine-producing region.
Booking essential.
Ⓢ Ⓦ Wed–Sun 12–2.30, 6–late,
Mon–Sat 6–late 🍴 L A$76, D A$96,
Wine A$22 🚗 5km (3 miles) east from
Nuriootpa on road to Angaston, near
junction with Stockwell Road

CEDUNA

THE BIGHT RESTAURANT

35 Eyre Highway, Ceduna, SA 5890
Tel 08 8625 2208
The unpretentious façade of
Highway One Motel and
Roadhouse hides a mecca for
seafood lovers. In this spacious, airy restaurant, with
signed prints of the
Mediterranean, hosts Sonia
Coleman and Greg Limbert
present a select menu high-
lighting Eyre Peninsula's
seafood.

Oysters and garlic are sensational as are the generous
seafood baskets, local tuna
and King George whiting, all
freshly caught. The menu also
includes creative kangaroo,
steak, lamb and chicken
dishes.
Ⓢ Ⓦ Mon–Sat from 6, last orders
8.30. Closed most public holidays
🍴 D A$72, Wine A$14.00 🚗 1km
(0.6 mile) west from Ceduna

CLARE

CLARE COUNTRY CLUB

White Hut Road, Clare, SA 5453
Tel 08 8842 1060
www.countryclubs.com.au
The Clare Country Club is a
modern, colonial-style hotel
overlooking Clare golf course
and Inchiquin Lake. Pool, spa,
sauna, tennis court and a gym
are available at the hotel.

The cuisine of the in-house à
la carte restaurant is Australian
with Asian and European influences—pumpkin soup, crusty
breads, pesto pasta, steak,
kangaroo, seafood and sun-
dried tomatoes, and chicken.
The wine list exclusively

promotes the Clare Valley vineyards. Book for dinner.
Ⓢ Ⓦ Daily 7–9, 11–2, 6.30–9.30
🍴 L A$25, D A$35, Wine A$15. Hotel
from A$138 🚗 Just north from Clare

THORN PARK COUNTRY HOUSE

College Road, Sevenhill, SA 5453
Tel 08 8843 4304
www.thornpark.com.au
This luxurious gourmet retreat
in 60 pastoral acres rightly
belongs under Staying. But
tired travellers may want to
combine fine dining with
excellent accommodation.
Hosts David Hay and Michael
Speers serve breakfast and
dinner from their large kitchen
where they also conduct cook-
ery courses. Extensive list of
Clare Valley wines.

The colonial homestead in
local stone and Mintaro slate,
with gracious rooms and lush
gardens, is full of antiques and
works of art.
Ⓢ Ⓦ All year 🍴 A$320 (B & B)
🛏 6 🚗 Between Sevenhill and Clare

COOBER PEDY

UMBERTO'S RESTAURANT

Hutchison Street, Coober Pedy, SA 5723
Tel 1800 088 521
www.desertcave.com.au
The amazing opal-mining town
of Coober Pedy has a luxury
hotel, The Desert Cave Hotel,
which is partly underground.
Umberto's, however, is above
ground level. Spacious and
cool, it provides silver-service
Italian, Asian and Australian
variations on outback produce.

Some unusual dishes are
chargrilled kangaroo with stout
and aniseed glaze served with
wild mushrooms, polenta and
chive mash, or barramundi
steak, wrapped in potato and
served on roast leek and onion
tart with chive and chilli tartare
sauce. A delicious dessert is
Umberto's Gemstone, made
with fresh brie glazed with toffee and with water crackers
and balsamic strawberries.
Ⓢ Ⓦ Daily 7–late, last orders 10.30
Ⓦ D A$90, Wine A$20

COONAWARRA

CHARDONNAY LODGE

Riddoch Highway, Coonawarra,
SA 5263
Tel 08 8736 3309
www.chardonnaylodge.com.au
This country lodge/motel is on
the doorstep of Australia's

EATING

most-famed region for red-wine production. The cuisine in its quality restaurant is local, with Mediterranean influences, and about 100 fine Coonawarra wines are available. A coffee shop is open all day.

🚫 🕐 All year. Restaurant daily 12–2.30, 6–8.30 🍽 L A$28, D A$92, Wine A$22. Rooms from A$145; includes continental breakfast 🛏 38 ⌨ 🚫 🅿 8km (5 miles) north from Penola

EYRE PENINSULA
DERHAM'S FORESHORE MOTOR INN
Watson Terrace, Whyalla, SA 5600
Tel 08 8645 8877
www.derhamsforeshore.com.au
Derham dynamo Barbara and husband Tom run a stylish motel/restaurant-bar right on Whyalla's beachfront. With its pool, this extraordinary motel caters for special events and is close to major attractions.

Seafood from the Eyre Peninsula features strongly, including salmon, kingfish and locally bred Murray cod. You can also have oysters, served in 15 different ways.

🚫 🕐 Daily 12–2, 6.30 till late 🍽 L A$30, D A$60, Wine $17.50. Rooms from A$120, excluding breakfast 🛏 40; 1 self-catering apartment ⌨ 🅿 From Highway 1 through town to the foreshore

FLINDERS RANGES
PRAIRIE HOTEL, PARACHILNA
Cnr High Street and West Terrace, Parachilna, SA 5730
Tel 08 8648 4894
www.prairiehotel.com.au

Feast on kangaroo burgers, wallaby and emu pâté at this laid-back, colonial homestead, and discover Jane and Ross Farghers' prairie hospitality. South Australian wines are selected from the Barossa and Clare valleys, Coonawarra and the Adelaide Hills.

Stay in original heritage

rooms, including two executive spa rooms, or in separate cabins, units and backpacker dorms a short distance away from the main house. Meet laconic locals in the bar, and enjoy the innovative cuisine served all day. The cast and crew of the 2002 film *The Rabbit-Proof Fence* stayed here.

🚫 🕐 Daily. Food served 8am–9pm; restaurant menu served 12–3, 6–9 🍽 L A$60, D A$80, Wine A$18. Hotel A$145–327; backpackers A$30 single 🛏 12; 100 backpackers in separate units ⌨ 🅿 194km (121 miles) northeast from Port Augusta, on the B83 road

KANGAROO ISLAND
THE OLD POST OFFICE RESTAURANT
Penneshaw, Kangaroo Island, SA 5222
Tel 08 8553 1063
Good dining choices on Kangaroo Island are limited but the Penneshaw restaurant is worth a trip away from the main town of Kingscote.

Seafood specials mark out the seasonally changing menu. Booking advised.

🚫 🕐 Tue–Sat 5.30–9, Aug–Jun 🍽 D A$90, Wine A$27.50

OZONE SEAFRONT HOTEL
The Foreshore, Kingscote, Kangaroo Island, SA 5223
Tel 08 8553 2011
www.ozonehotel.com

The two-storey Ozone is a welcoming Aussie pub, dating from 1920, overlooking Nepean Bay. There is a pool and sauna-spa for guests.

The busy, airy bistro has a wide range of starters and mains, based on fresh island produce and fish, with Asian dishes and gluten-free and vegetarian menus. Wines are mainly from Kangaroo Island. Order dinner in advance.

🚫 🕐 Daily 7–9, 11–3, 5–8.30 (dinner to order) 🍽 L A$25, D A$30, Wine A$25. Rooms from A$104 🛏 37

RIVERLAND
BANROCK STATION WINE AND WETLAND CENTRE
Holmes Road, Kingston-on-Murray, SA 5331
Tel 08 8583 0299
www.banrockstation.com.au

At Australia's biggest wine eco-tourism venue, lunch is served at the cellar door or on a large deck. The vista includes the start of a 7km (4.5-mile) boardwalk trail winding through trees and bush, which has been rejuvenated for wildlife conservation.

The food is light, innovative and inexpensive. Lamb river-mint curry pie, pumpkin peanut lemon myrtle pasty or kangaroo pepperleaf sausage roll with bush tomato chutney are among the unusual dishes available. Grazing, tasting plates (such as smoked kangaroo prosciutto with pepperleaf mustard and parmesan) are also served.

🚫 🕐 Daily 12–2, grazing and teas 10–4, wine-tasting 10–5 🍽 L A$30, Wine A$7.50 plus A$3 corkage 🅿 220km (137 miles) northeast from Adelaide on the Sturt Highway, 32km (20 miles) east from Waikerie near Kingston-on-Murray

BELL'S CAFÉ

Jetty 2, Eastern Pavilion, Barrack Street
Jetty, Perth, WA 6000
Tel 08 9421 5886
Enjoy a coffee and a cake
watching the boats depart
from Barracks Jetty for
Fremantle and Rottnest Island.
The lower part of the two-
storey restaurant is a café and
the upper level is used for
functions. On a nice day it's
pleasant to eat outside.

The menu is modern classic
with a range of daily specials
on offer, such as chicken man-
dalay and oysters. Children's
and vegetarian meals are available. Booking advised for eating outside.

Ⓢ Ⓒ Sun–Thu 8–5, Fri–Sat 8am–late
Ⓦ L A$59, D A$73, Wine A$21 Ⓑ Blue
CAT stop 19 (Barrack Square)

C RESTAURANT LOUNGE

Level 33, 44 St. Georges Terrace, Perth,
WA 6000
Tel 08 9220 8333
www.crestaurant.com.au
This revolving restaurant high
above St. George's Terrace has
great views of the Swan River,
Kings Park, Rottnest Island and
the Darling Ranges. The plush
lounge is perfect for pre-dinner
cocktails.

The modern Australian cuisine includes seafood, pasta,
steak, California rolls and
Australian specials such as
marron and kangaroo.
Vegetarian items are available
and children's meals can be
provided on request. The wine
list is extensive with top
Australian wines.

Ⓢ Ⓒ Daily 12–2.30, 6–9 (no Sat
lunch) Ⓦ L A$60, D A$100, Wine A$25

CLANCY'S FISH PUB

51 Cantonment Street, Fremantle,
WA 6160
Tel 08 9335 1351
www.clancysfishpub.com.au
The building's colourful inte-
rior, large open fireplace and
good food have ensured
Clancy's popularity for years.

The menu includes seafood
chowder, classic fish and chips,
fresh shucked oysters, octopus,
and cajun calamari served with
chips and sweet chilli sauce.
Seafood and vegetarian
options are available. A range
of Australian and international
bottled and draught beers is

available, including a selection
of beers from small Western
Australian breweries. A number of Australian wines are
also available.

Ⓢ Outside tables only Ⓒ Mon–Sat all
day, Sun 12–10pm Ⓦ L A$50, D A$70,
Wine A$17.50 Ⓑ CAT bus stops nearby

FRASER'S RESTAURANT

Fraser Avenue, Kings Park, West Perth,
WA 6005
Tel 08 9481 7100
www.frasersrestaurant.com.au
At the top of Kings Park,
Fraser's is renowned for its fan-
tastic views over the Swan
River and the Perth skyline.
Featuring indoor and terrace
dining, the design of the
restaurant is contemporary
with plenty of natural light.

The cuisine is modern
Australian with an emphasis
on seafood, such as wok-fried
baby octopus with chilli, ginger
paste and bean sprouts, or
assorted seafood with tiger
prawns in a curry. The wine list
runs to over ten pages.
Booking essential.

Ⓢ Ⓒ Daily 7.30am–late Ⓦ L A$90,
D A$115, Wine A$23 Ⓑ From central
Perth to Kings Park or Blue CAT stop 20
(Mount Hospital)

INDIANA TEA HOUSE

99 Marine Parade, Cottesloe, Perth,
WA 6011
Tel 08 9385 5005
www.indiana.com.au

Come here to watch the sun
setting on Cottesloe Beach.
Built on the site of the original
19th-century Indiana Tea

House, the building recalls the
Raj days of palms and cane.

The restaurant is renowned
for its Moreton Bay bug salad
(Moreton Bay bugs are unique
to Australia and taste like lobster). There are fine wines
from the Margaret River region.
Booking advised.

Ⓢ Ⓒ Daily 12–4, 6–9 Ⓦ L A$90,
D A$120, Wine A$22 Ⓑ 72 from central Perth Ⓡ Cottesloe then 10-minute
walk

KAILIS' FISH MARKET CAFÉ

Fishing Boat Harbour, 46 Mews,
Fremantle, WA 6160
Tel 08 9335 7755
www.kailis.com
On a warm sunny day there is
no better way to enjoy seafood
than to sit outside this café on
Fremantle's waterfront watching the action in the harbour.

The area comprises a fresh
seafood market, a restaurant
providing cooked seafood, and
a café selling sandwiches,
freshly baked cakes and ice
creams. Alcoholic beverages
are also available but only
when a meal is ordered. Wines
are mostly Australian, by the
glass or bottle.

Ⓢ Ⓒ Daily 8am–late Ⓦ Fish and
chips A$13, seafood delight A$23
Ⓑ CAT bus stops nearby

LITTLE CREATURES BREWING

40 Mews Road, Fremantle, WA 6160
Tel 08 9430 5555
www.littlecreatures.com.au
In its time this restaurant and
brewery near Fremantle
Harbour has been a crocodile
farm and yacht yard. The old
viewing gallery now looks
down on the brewery. The dining area has communal tables
and leather booths, while the
open kitchen is a feature.

Its wood-fired oven produces
crisp Italian-style pizza, and
specials include prosciutto-
wrapped tiger prawns and
hand-cut frites. Beer is the
great attraction here so the
wine list is limited.

Ⓢ Ⓒ Mon–Sat 10am–midnight,
Sun 10–10 Ⓦ L A$60, D A$75, Wine
A$20 Ⓡ Fremantle

MISS MAUD

Cnr Pier and Murray streets, Perth,
WA 6000
Tel 08 9325 3900
www.missmaud.com.au
The people of Perth have been
feasting on Miss Maud's smor-

EATING

gasbords for over 30 years. The restaurant is part of the Miss Maud Swedish Hotel.

Breakfast smorgasbords include bacon, sausages, eggs, grilled tomatoes, mushrooms, pancakes, Swedish muesli, muffins, pastries, fresh fruit juices, coffee and tea.

Lunch and dinner smorgasbords include king prawns, freshly cooked yabbies, a roast meats carvery, home-made bread, salads, soup, cakes, pastries, coffee and tea. The dinner smorgasbord also has fresh oysters.

Ⓢ Ⓓ Daily 6.45-10, 12–2.30, 5.30–9.30 🍴 Breakfast smorgasbord A$18.95, L A$26.95, D A$33.95, Wine A$17 (surcharges Sun and public holidays)

THE OLD SWAN BREWERY RESTAURANT
173 Mounts Bay Road, Perth, WA 6000
Tel 08 9211 8999
www.oldswanbrewery.com.au
This historic building beside the Swan River has great views from every seat. The restaurant has a microbrewery with interactive displays and a café.

The menu includes emu and buffalo, as well as the more usual fish, beef and chicken. The café-restaurant has an extensive wine list. Booking advised for restaurant.
Ⓢ Ⓓ Daily 7am–11pm 🍴 L A$50, D A$70, Wine A$23 🚌 71 and 72

THE RED HERRING
26 Riverside Road, East Fremantle, WA 6158

Tel 08 9339 1611
www.redherring.com.au
Seafood lovers looking for a special night out will enjoy this restaurant on the edge of the Swan River. It has its own jetty.

The modern Australian menu changes regularly to take advantage of the seafood available, but crayfish and fresh oysters are frequent specials. Children's and vegetarian dishes are provided. Popular, so booking advised.
Ⓢ Ⓓ Daily lunch/dinner 12 till late, Sat–Sun and public holidays breakfast 7–11 🍴 L A$95, D A$114, Wine A$20.50

ROUNDHOUSE RESTAURANT & TEA ROOMS
9 Fleet Street, Fremantle, WA 6160
Tel 08 9431 7555
www.roundhouserestaurant.com.au
The Roundhouse is Western Australia's oldest building. Next door in one of the old Pilot Cottages is this popular restaurant. There are formal dining rooms, a more relaxed sitting room, a courtyard and a balcony with views over Fremantle.

Open for breakfast, lunch, Devonshire cream teas and dinner, the cuisine combines English and Australian food with a good selection of seafood and Western Australian meat. BYO, A$3 corkage per bottle.
Ⓢ Ⓓ Sun–Thu 8.30–5.30, Fri–Sat 8.30am–10.30pm 🍴 L A$46, D A$68 🚌 Fremantle then CAT bus

SAIL AND ANCHOR
64 South Terrace, Fremantle, WA 6160
Tel 08 9335 8433
www.sailandanchor.com.au
The balcony of this old-fashioned Aussie pub has great views over Fremantle. The Anchor was one of Australia's first pub breweries and its beer is internationally renowned. Pub and casual meals, such as soup, tapas, salads, fish and potatoes, garlic prawns and pizzas, are served in a courtyard.

Eight beers are brewed here and there is a good selection of Western Australian wines. Booking advised for restaurant.
Ⓢ Some areas of the pub
Ⓓ Mon–Thu 11am–12pm, Fri– Sat 11am–1am, Sun 10–10 🍴 L A$45, D A$50, Wine A$16 🚌 Several buses stop nearby

BROOME

TIDES GARDEN RESTAURANT AND CHARTERS RESTAURANT
47 Carnarvon Street, Broome, WA 6725
Tel 08 9192 1303
www.mangrovehotel.com.au
Both restaurants are part of the Mangrove Hotel, overlooking Roebuck Bay. This is one of the best places to watch Broome's famous Staircase to the Moon, when the lunar light falling across the mudflats creates the illusion of rising stairs. The Charters is the indoor restaurant, while the Tides is a similar size outdoors.

The menu is modern with different dishes each night; seafood is a house special. Vegetarian and children's meals are also available, while vegan meals are served on request. The wine list is extensive. Booking advised.
Ⓢ Ⓓ Charters: daily breakfast 6.30–10, dinner 6–9, Apr–Dec. Tides:daily 12–3, 6–10 🍴 L A$50, D A$70, Wine A$15 🚌 Bus from Broome stops outside the Mangrove

CAVERSHAM

SANDALFORD CAVERSHAM ESTATE RESTAURANT
3210 West Swan, Caversham, WA 6055
Tel 618 9374 9300
www.sandalford.com
The vine-covered pergola in this attractive winery restaurant has views over the vineyard and a garden courtyard. The exposed limestone and wood interior has an open fire.

The modern Australian menu changes regularly but its most popular dish, locally caught marron (freshwater crayfish), is always available. There's a children's menu as well as vegetarian options. Sandalford wines are sold and guests can also join a winery tour.
Ⓢ Ⓓ Daily 12–3, Fri–Sat 6–late 🍴 L A$128, D A$180, Wine A$19.95 🚌 Perth central to Midland then 52 bus to Sandalford. The bus only runs every 90 minutes (tel 13 62 13)

DWELLINGUP

MILLHOUSE CAFÉ AND CHOCOLATE CO
Lot 47 McLarty Street, Dwellingup, WA 6213
Tel 08 9538 1122
South from Perth in the foothills of the Darling Range, the Millhouse Café and

EATING

Chocolate Co is renowned for its hand-made chocolates. The style of the restaurant is equally attractive, built of locally milled she-oak timber.

The menu ranges from focaccias and wood-fired pizzas to West Australian barramundi with potato cakes and a fresh crisp summer salsa. Children's meals are available and include fish and chips.

🛇 ⊙ Fri–Sat 9–late, Sun 8–5, Thu 9–4 🍴 L A$25, D A$40 🚗 96km (60 miles) south from Perth

KALBARRI

BLACK ROCK CAFÉ
80 Grey Street, Kalbarri, WA 6536
Tel 08 9937 1062

The Black Rock Café is a great place to sit back and relax after a day touring Kalbarri National Park (see page 156). Modern Australian food is served with a range of special dishes according to the season, but usually featuring seafood. The café overlooks the mouth of the Murchison River and the Indian Ocean.

Meals for children, vegans and vegetarians are also available. Margaret River produced Pallandri wines are an additional attraction. Booking advised.

🛇 ⊙ Daily 7am–late 🍴 L A$36, D A$70, Wine A$15.95

KALGOORLIE

DANIEL SHEA'S
45 Egan Street, Kalgoorlie, WA 6430
Tel 08 9021 4544

Part of the Mercure Hotel Plaza in the shopping area of Kalgoorlie, Daniel Shea's is named for the friend and partner of the founder of Kalgoorlie, Paddy Hannan.

It provides modern Australian cuisine with a range of daily specials and an extensive wine list. Children's and vegetarian meals are available on request. Booking advised.

🛇 Bar only ⊙ Daily 6.30–10 🍴 D A$70, Wine A$29.50

MARGARET RIVER

1885 RESTAURANT
Grange Motel, 18 Farrelly Street, Margaret River, WA 6285
Tel 08 9757 3177
www.grangeonfarrelly.com.au

The Grange is a small modern motel in the heart of Margaret River, near the Bussell Highway. The dining room is a former homestead built at Karridale in 1885. It was moved to Margaret River in the 1950s and used as a convent school before conversion to a restaurant.

Fresh local fish, venison and cheeses are served in the plantation-style interior, along with an excellent selection of Margaret River wines.

🛇 ⊙ Mon–Sat 6.30–9 🍴 D non-residents call for prices. Rooms from A$130 ❶ 29 ⊠

LEEUWIN ESTATE WINERY RESTAURANT
Stevens Road, Margaret River, WA 6285
Tel 08 9759 0000
www.leeuwinestate.com.au

The Leeuwin Estate produced its first commercial vintage in 1979 and has since become an internationally renowned winery. Other attractions are an art gallery and sell-out concerts.

The restaurant is popular with both foreign and local visitors to the vineyard. Regional produce is served inside or on the verandah, and includes lamb, venison and seafood; marron is a house special. Wines, of course, come from the estate. For lighter refreshments, come for the morning and afternoon teas. Booking advised.

🛇 Outside only ⊙ Daily 10–4.30 (L 12–2.30, Sat D 6.30–8.30) 🍴 L A$77, D A$116, Wine A$17.95 🚗 Go 6km (3.5 miles) south from Margaret River on the Bussell Highway, then turn right on to Gnaraway Road

VAT 107
107 Bussell Highway, Margaret River, WA 6285
Tel 08 9758 8877
www.vat107.com.au

With its polished floorboards and marble bars, VAT 107 is often described as a city restaurant in a country location. The menu changes regularly to take advantage of fresh produce, including venison and marron.

Popular standards include seafood laksa, Szechuan duck and lamb, and there is homemade sourdough bread. Children's and vegetarian meals are available. The wine list includes Western Australian wines. Booking advised.

⊙ Daily 9am–late 🍴 L A$90, D A$120, Wine A$25

JACKMAN MCROSS
57–59 Hampden, Battery Point, Hobart, TAS 7004
Tel 03 6223 3186

This prominent café on Battery Point, close to St. George's Church, is an exceptional bakehouse with some of the friendliest service in Hobart.

For light meals expect fresh bread and a delectable choice of pastries, pizzas, pies and rich sweets. A breakfast of strong coffee and a half-size buttermilk fruit loaf is a rich, satisfying treat and good value for money.

🛇 ⊙ Mon–Fri 7.30–6, Sat–Sun 7–5. Closed public holidays 🍴 A$10 per person 🛇 No Visa

KELLEYS SEAFOOD RESTAURANT
5 Knopwood Street, Battery Point, Hobart, TAS 7004
Tel 03 6224 7225
www.kelleys.com.au

Guests are greeted by one of the Kelley brothers, who are dedicated surfers, fishermen and seafood specialists. Their renowned restaurant is intimate and easy-going.

Try Accidental Occy made from southern octopus, tenderized and grilled, with sweet and sour cucumber, orange and ginger glaze. There is an extensive wine list. Booking essential.

🛇 ⊙ Mon–Fri 12–3, 6–late, Sat–Sun 6–late 🍴 L A$60, D A$80, Wine A$20

MIT ZITRONE
333 Elizabeth Street, North Hobart, TAS 7000
Tel 03 6334 3220

In the heart of the North Hobart dining and entertainment precinct, 'Mit Zit' is one of the city's most innovative restaurants.

Chef Chris Jackman's creativity has produced poached leg of veal with celeriac, sautéed apples and baked semolina gnocchi. Don't miss the sublime cakes. BYO. Booking advised.

🛇 ⊙ Tue–Sun 11am–late 🍴 L A$30, D A$75 🚌 Metro buses from Elizabeth Street 🚗 1.5km (1 mile) north from Hobart Mall

RETRO CAFÉ
33 Salamanca Place, Hobart, TAS 7000
Tel 03 6223 3073

EATING

All roads in Hobart lead to the waterfront and Salamanca and the Retro is the hub. It is decorated with 1950s records, posters, Americana and local paintings.

This is a good place to watch life on the waterfront, including artists, lawyers and politicians, and enjoy Hobart's best coffee. There is a simple but good-tasting breakfast and light meals for lunch.

🅢 Outside tables only 🅘 Mon–Sat 8–6, Sun 8.30–6 🅛 L A$20

TASTE OF ASIA
358 Elizabeth Street, North Hobart, WA 7000
Tel 03 6236 9191

Offering some of the best value in Hobart, the Taste of Asia is extremely popular, particularly for take outs, so it is best to get in early or after the 6.30–7.30pm rush.

The food is dependably good Malaysian, Thai, Indian, Burmese and Chinese, with little extras such as an assortment of side dishes for curries. Sushi is also available. BYO.

🅢 🅘 Mon–Fri 12–9, Sat 4–9 🅛 L A$12, D A$20 🅟 Any Metro bus heading north on Elizabeth Street; Metro buses to North Hobart 🅡 1.5km (1 mile) north from Hobart Mall

TAVERN 42 DEGREES SOUTH (KNOWN AS T42)
Elizabeth Street Pier, Hobart, TAS 7000
Tel 03 6224 7742

This glamorous, fashionable bar and restaurant—known as T42—is inside Elizabeth Pier, one of the old warehouses jutting from the waterfront.

The modern Australian food changes seasonally and there is a superb range of reasonably priced wines. The bar is very busy in the evening with an emphasis on dance music. Booking advised.

🅢 Area 🅘 Mon–Fri 7.30am–late, Sat–Sun 8.30am–late (8.30–3 brunch) 🅛 L A$52, D A$72, Wine A$23

COLES BAY
EDGE OF THE BAY
2308 Main Road, Coles Bay, TAS 7215
Tel 03 6257 0102
www.edgeofthebay.com.au

With a wonderful setting on Coles Bay looking across to the Hazards Mountains, this innovative restaurant is run by four friends who share an intimate and friendly atmosphere.

The imaginative, modern cuisine includes game and wallaby in winter and fresh local seafood in summer. Vegan and vegetarian meals are available. The wine list focuses on Tasmanian and Australian wines with a list of cellar specials. Booking essential.

🅢 🅘 Daily from 6.30 🅛 D A$80, Wine A$22 🅡 On the main road into Coles Bay

EAGLEHAWK
EAGLEHAWK CAFÉ
5131 Arthur Highway, Eaglehawk, TAS 7179
Tel 03 6250 3331

Just over the sandy isthmus that connects the Tasman Peninsula to the Tasmanian mainland is this lively, friendly eatery. French-born Annick Thomas is both a fine chef and a culture vulture. Plenty of local artwork is shown here as well as good browsing magazines and a choice of areas in which to eat.

The food is modern Australian with hints of provincial France and Asia. Friday cocktails are served around the house piano.

🅢 Outside tables only 🅘 Summer Mon–Sat 10.30am–late, low season Thu–Sun from 5 🅛 L A$36, D A$64, Wine A$14 🅡 Descend steep hill into Eaglehawk Neck, turn right towards Port Arthur and café is 150m on the left

ELIZABETH TOWN
CHRISTMAS HILLS RASPBERRY FARM CAFÉ
9 Christmas Hills Road, Bass Highway, Elizabeth Town, TAS 7304
Tel 03 6362 2186
www.raspberryfarmcafe.com

Just off the road from Deloraine to Devonport is this country farm where you can observe the raspberry pickers in the summer or watch water birds. Eat by the fire or on an all-weather deck, or even picnic on the grass.

The country-style menu makes innovative use of raspberries and the sweets menu is very popular. Vegan, vegetarian and children's meals are available. The wine list favours Tasmanian vineyards.

🅢 Outside tables only 🅘 Daily 7–5 🅛 L A$40, Wine A$13 🅡 15km (9.5 miles) northwest from Deloraine on Highway 1 to Devonport

GOWRIE PARK
WEINDORFERS
Wellington Street, Gowrie Park, TAS 7306
Tel 03 6491 1385

Hearty home cooking with a Swedish influence makes this restaurant, within sight of Mount Roland, an excellent lunch stop.

There is a strong emphasis on local farm produce aided by a good range of local wines as well as Tasmanian beers. Vegan, vegetarian and children's meals are available. Booking advised.

There is more for the family: a good collection of antique vehicles and farm equipment, as well as pet rabbits and a grassy area for kids.

🅢 🅘 Daily 10–late, Oct–May (Sat–Sun only Jun–Jul) 🅛 L A$28, D A$50, Wine A$16 🅡 15km (9.5 miles) southwest from Sheffield on the C136 to Cradle Mountain

LATROBE
HOUSE OF ANVERS
Bass Highway, Latrobe, TAS 7307
Tel 03 6426 2958

Refreshments to die for are at this Belgian chocolate factory in a large old homestead. There is an indoor and outdoor café and you can watch the chocolate-making process. Igor Van Gerwen, the proprietor, swears that Tasmanian butter is the richest he has tasted. That and 64 per cent cacao content make for very rich chocolate. Try the French-

Belgian style breakfast consisting of chocolate croissant or brioche. Truffles are another house special.

🚫 Outside tables only 🕐 Daily 7–5 🍴 L A$40 🚗 10km (6 miles) southeast from Devonport on Highway 1 to Launceston, 5km (3 miles) from Latrobe, on the right side of the road

LAUNCESTON

FEE AND ME
190 Charles Street, Launceston, TAS 7250
Tel 03 6331 3195
www.feeandme.com

Stately Morton House (1835) was once a school for respectable ladies and is now an impressive, formal restaurant, one of the best in Tasmania.

The cuisine draws on many cultures. A seasonal special is local asparagus with lemon verbena, hollandaise and puff pastry. The menu ranges from light to increasingly rich dishes served as a series of small courses rather than mains-size dishes. The wine list is superb. Booking advised.

🚫 🕐 Mon–Sat from 7 🍴 D A$54–A$69, Wine A$30

FLUID
25–26 Seaport Boulevard, Launceston, TAS 7250
Tel 03 6334 3220
One of Launceston's newest restaurants and part of the waterfront redevelopment by the Tamar River. The modern interior has sculpted leather artworks by one of Tasmania's most acclaimed artists, Gary Greenwood.

Chef Fergus Carmichael combines modern and traditional cuisines with such seafood specials as Eastern crab salad with Chinese mushrooms, cashew nuts, soba noodles and wasabi. The wine list is extensive.

🚫 Outside tables only 🕐 Daily 10.30am–late 🍴 L A$40, D A$90, Wine

A$17 🚗 Go north from central Launceston on Wellington or Charles Street, turn off just before Charles Street Bridge

THE GORGE RESTAURANT
Cataract Gorge Cliff Grounds, Launceston, TAS 7250
Tel 03 6331 3330
Originally set up as a tea room in 1892, this restaurant has a most romantic setting in the Cataract Gorge and Cliff grounds. At night the cries of free-ranging peacocks echo through one of Launceston's oldest gardens. View Cataract Gorge cliffs by moonlight or wander around the gently lit paths and rotunda.

The meals are traditional and sumptuous, with meat and seafood dishes complemented by a strong wine list. It's popular for weddings so booking is essential.

🕐 Tue–Sat 12–2.30, 6.30–9, Sun 12–2.30. Kiosk daily 9–5 for Devonshire teas 🍴 L A$50, D A$80, Wine A$20 🚗 Cross Kings Bridge and drive to top of Trevallyn

HARI'S CURRY
150–152 York Street, Launceston, TAS 7250
Tel 03 6331 6466
Possibly Launceston's best value eating, though dining facilities are modest and there are almost unceasing Bollywood classics playing on the TV. Hari Singh and his family belong to the tiny Indian community in Launceston and produce authentic northern Indian favourites.

Tandoori is a house special and there is a great range of naan and batura breads. Vegetable curry is available, but no vegan dishes. BYO.

🚫 🕐 Daily 5–10 🍴 D A$45

NOVAROS RESTAURANT

28 Brisbane Street, Launceston, TAS 7250
Tel 03 6334 5589

This warm, classic Italian restaurant in a terrace near City Park is very popular. The wine list contains many Italian labels and a few Tasmanian wineries. Booking advised.

🚫 🕐 Daily 6.30–late 🍴 D A$80, Wine A$18

STILLWATER AT RITCHIE'S MILL
Paterson Street, Launceston, TAS 7250
Tel 03 6331 4153
By day this is an informal café, but in the evening it becomes one of Australia's best creative restaurants. Set inside a picturesque 19th-century flour mill on the banks of the River Tamar, it has good views of the yacht basin. The mill gallery sells gifts.

Freestyle modern Australian food can be served as a series of small courses instead of one main course. Local seafood and game are specials. The wine list has over 400 choices with a Tasmanian bias. Booking advised.

🚫 🕐 Daily 8.30am–late 🍴 L A$50, D A$120, Wine A$29

STRAHAN

FRANKLIN MANOR
The Esplanade, Strahan, TAS 7468
Tel 03 6471 7311
www.franklinmanor.com.au

Established gardens, big rhododendrons and timber verandahs mark this luxurious restaurant, close by the harbour and near Regatta Point.

Chef Meyjitte Boughenout produces food that is modern French and Australian using local seafood. Specials are crayfish, abundant on the west coast, scallops and oysters. Four- and eight-course dinners with matching wines to each dish are also available. The extensive wine list is extremely good. Booking advised.

🚫 🕐 Daily from 6.30 🍴 D A$130, Wine A$28 🚗 150m from town centre, around harbour to Regatta Point

EATING

This chapter lists places to stay alphabetically in each of Australia's states. Places to stay in each capital city are listed first, followed by others listed alphabetically by town. Note that some establishments offer both food and accommodation.

Staying

STAYING IN AUSTRALIA

Camping off-road in the barren outback may be the cheapest and most basic option but Australia is not the world's end for accommodation.

WHAT IS AVAILABLE?

Australia has accommodation options to suit every budget, from camping grounds to exclusive resorts. It is usually easy to find

somewhere to stay on arrival in a destination, but if you book ahead you might be able to negotiate a special deal. Tourist offices can help you find a bed for the night, and most places are listed on the internet.

PITCH HERE

Caravan and camp grounds are everywhere—look for shaded sites that provide relief from the sun. Caravan pitches go from about A$20 and tent pitches from A$11. Often, basic supplies can be bought. Many parks rent on-site caravans from A$35, or cabins with cooking facilities from A$40. Check if bed linen can be hired. Remember that distances between towns can be vast, so never venture into the outback without sufficient water, fuel and provisions. Always allow for the risk that your vehicle could break down in hot, isolated areas.

BACKPACK

Backpacker hostels are widespread, often former old hotels, some brightly painted with big signs. Look for backpacker handbills at airports, train stations and bus terminals or local tourist offices. Average nightly cost is about A$15. At these prices expect shared dormitories, rooms and bathrooms.

MOTELS

Some country pubs offer accommodation but often they have given way to motels. Expect to pay about A$60 for a double/twin per night with bathroom and tea/coffee facilities. All have fans or air-conditioning and heating, and many have swimming pools. Breakfast, delivered to your door, from continental to full English, is extra. Some motels have excellent dining rooms. Children are accommodated, sometimes at no extra cost, depending on their age. Away from cities, many fully-booked establishments will even telephone rivals to find available rooms or direct you elsewhere.

HOTELS

The usual range of hotels is available in the populated parts of the country and prices can range from A$150 to over A$1,000 per night for a double room. Luxury hotels abound in the capital cities and popular resorts, including Hilton, Hyatt,

Marriott, Oberoi, Sheraton and Stamford. See the chart on page 283 for a guide to the major accommodation chains in Australia.

Queensland dominates in resort hotels, mainly on islands—there are 74 in the Whitsundays alone. Resorts are set on several hectares, usually by a beach. Accommodation is motel style, often smart, with pool, and most hotels have a spa and walking areas. Some offer sports, from snorkelling and diving to tennis and golf.

SERVICED APARTMENTS

You can book serviced apartments in most of the major cities for stays of a few nights to many months. Prices range considerably from about A$220 upwards.

B & B

Bed-and-breakfast establishments, first adopted from Britain by Tasmania, are prolific. Most are now smart, some charging as much as luxury hotels. If you are looking for an inexpensive option then it might be best to book a motel, as B & B prices usually range from A$125 per double for a modest B & B to more than A$450 per double.

B & Bs may be restored pioneer cottages, churches or fine country houses. In country areas there are farm-stays, where you can reside in-house with the family or in separate premises.

TIPPING

Australians are not great tippers. Only in luxury hotels is a tip expected, by the boy who carries luggage to and from your room. A A$2 coin will suffice but some may anticipate a A$5 note. In-house hairdressers do not expect tips.

MINIBARS

Hotel minibars are expensive, usually double the high street retail prices.

TELEPHONE CALLS

Telephone charges from modest motel to top hotel are expensive, from 50 to 100 per cent more from your room. If you ring from a phone booth, it's 40 cents unlimited time for local calls, escalating to time rates for intrastate, interstate and international calls. Buy phonecards from post offices or use coins.

STAYING

ACCOMMODATION CHAINS

Chain	Regional Coverage	Number of Places	Contact Number and Website
Accor Hotels	Booking website for many major chains, including Ibis, Mercure, Novotel, Sofitel	49	AUS 1300 656 565 www.accorhotels.com
Best Western	International chain with a nationwide network of independent owners and operators	300	AUS 131 779 UK 0800 39 31 30 www.bestwestern.com.au
Big 4 Holiday Parks	Nationwide accommodation ranges from camping pitches to cabins on parks with good facilities	160	AUS 1800 632 444 AUS 03 9813 2055 www.big4.com.au
Big Country Motels	Mid-price motel chain in Victoria	25	www.wilmap.com.au bigcountrymotels
Budget Motel Chain International	No frills motel chain providing clean and comfortable rooms nationwide	300	AUS 1800 811 223 www.budget-motel.com.au
Country Haven	Reasonable price motel chain extending across the eastern states	75	Call individual hotels listed on www.countryhaven.com.au
Crowne Plaza	Mid-price international hotel chain with expected facilities; main cities nationwide except Tasmania	11	AUS 1300 363 300 UK 0800 40 50 60 www.ichotelsgroup.com
Flag Choice Hotels	Nationwide hotel-motel group with a good standard in rooms and facilities	330	AUS 03 9243-2400 UK 0800 444 444 www.flagchoice.com.au
Formule 1	Budget motel chain in New South Wales, Melbourne and Brisbane	17	AUS 02 8586 2888 www.formule1.com.au
Golden Chain	Nationwide mid-price motel chain; all properties are individually owned	250	AUS 02 6687 2144 www.goldenchain.com.au
Hilton	Expensive international hotel chain with good facilities; Sydney and major cities	7	AUS 02 9287 0707 UK 08705 909090 www.hilton.com
Holiday Inn	Mid-price international hotel chain; main cities nationwide except Tasmania	13	AUS 1300 363 300 UK 0800 40 50 60 www.ichotelsgroup.com
Hyatt	Expensive international hotel chain with properties in most states	8	AUS 131 234 UK 0845 888 1226 www.hyatt.com
Ibis	Inexpensive international group with hotels in most major cities	13	AUS 1300 88 44 00 www.ichotelsgroup.com
Intercontinental	Expensive international group; hotels in Sydney and Perth	2	AUS 1800 221 335 UK 0800 0289 387 www.ichotelsgroup.com
Medina	Australian group of exclusive apartments in most capital cities	20	AUS 1300 300 232 www.medinaapartments.com.au
Metro Hospitality Group	Australian chain of mid-price hotels and apartments in most capital cities	10	AUS 1800 00 4321 www.metrohospitalitygroup.com
Oakford Australia	Apartment hotels and town houses in Sydney, Canberra, Melbourne, Brisbane and Hobart	13	Sydney 1800 657 392 1800 627 902 Melbourne 1800 818 237 Brisbane 1800 642 188 Hobart 1800 620 462 www.users.onaustralia.com.au/oakadm
QUEST	Australia's largest provider of served apartments; mid-price to expensive in cities and major towns	80	AUS 1800 334 033 AUS 03 9645 7566 www.questapartments.com.au
Radisson	Mid-price to expensive international hotel group in major cities	5	AUS 1800 333 333 UK 0800 374411 www.radisson.com
Rydges	Australian owned group of expensive hotels in major towns	22	AUS 02 9261 3199 www.rydges.com
Sheraton	Expensive resort-style international hotel group in major cities and Queensland	13	AUS 07 3231 2040 www.sheraton.com
Top Tourist Parks	Inexpensive camping sites and cabins in parks; nationwide except Tasmania	170	Call individual hotels listed on www.toptouristparks.com.au

STAYING

AARONS HOTEL

37 Ultimo Road, Haymarket, Sydney, NSW 2000
Tel 02 9281 5555
www.aaronshotel.com.au
A clean hotel representing good value in a city location by Darling Harbour. The bedrooms are a good size and there are family rooms that accommodate up to six. The more expensive Courtyard Rooms have their own small private courtyard.

The fifth-floor restaurant, Café Nine, serves breakfast (continental and cooked), lunch, dinner and snacks from 6.30am–late.
All year A$130 (standard room)–A$160 (courtyard room); includes breakfast 93 At the southern end of the city next to Chinatown and Central Station, just south from Darling Harbour

DE VERE HOTEL

44–46 Macleay Street, Potts Point, Sydney NSW 2011
Tel 02 9358 1211
www.deverehotel.com.au
A friendly, good-value hotel in the trendy bayside suburb of Potts Point, just past the Kings Cross area, with a wide choice of cafés and restaurants nearby. It is pleasantly decorated in contemporary style with adequate and comfortable bedrooms.

The bedrooms all include a private bathroom with bath and shower, tea/coffee-making facilities, fridge and hairdryer, and some have a small balcony. Self-contained studio apartments are also available. A full buffet breakfast is served in the breakfast room.
All year A$125.90–A$237.30 including breakfast 100
1.5km (1 mile) east from city centre, near Kings Cross

FOUR POINTS SHERATON

161 Sussex Street, Darling Harbour, Sydney, NSW 2000
Tel 02 9299 4000
www.fourpoints.com
Most of the 631 rooms including 45 suites have balconies and views across Darling Harbour or over the city. Some rooms have been specially designed for visitors with mobility problems Decorated in a nautical theme, the hotel is convenient for shopping and nightlife as well as tourist attractions such as the aquarium and the Powerhouse Museum. It also has all the other facilities you'd expect in a major international hotel, including a choice of dining rooms. There is also an historic pub dating from the 1850s.
All year A$205 (city views)–A$255 (harbour views); includes breakfast 631 On the west side of the city, not far from the aquarium

HOTEL IBIS DARLING HARBOUR

70 Murray Street, Pyrmont, NSW 2000
Tel 02 9563 0888
www.accorhotels.com.au
This large, modern hotel is a good-value option in the rather expensive Darling Harbour area.

Many rooms overlook the harbour and the city skyline. All are clean and light, with colour TV and videos, tea/coffee-making facilities, fridge, radio, hairdryer, iron and STD/ISD phone. The hotel restaurant, bistro, serves breakfast and dinner.
All year A$145–A$160; breakfast A$15 extra or ask for 'dollar breakfast' special 256 Metro Monorail to Harbourside or Convention stops at Darling Harbour 1km (0.5 mile) from city centre on the west side of Darling Harbour

METRO APARTMENTS SYDNEY

132–136 Sussex Street, Sydney, NSW 2000
27–29 King Street, Sydney, NSW 2000
Tel 02 9290 9200
www.metrohospitalitygroup.com
Enjoy the excellent views of Darling Harbour from these apartments, which are in two adjacent buildings on the west side of the city. They include fully serviced one-bedroom suites and apartments.

The King Street property has 15 apartments as well as a rooftop pool and barbecue facilities. The Sussex Street property has 35 apartments with large windows. All sleep up to four people. They have a balcony, fully equipped kitchen, living and dining area, shower and bath.
All year A$170–A$207 excluding breakfast 50 King Street only Wynyard, Darling Park Metro Monorail On west side of the city,

one block from Darling Harbour and King Street Wharf

THE RUSSELL

143A George Street, The Rocks, Sydney, NSW 2000
Tel 02 9241 3543
www.therussell.com.au
This delightful Victorian building has been renovated to provide boutique-style accommodation. The sitting room and its bar, furnished in period style, opens on to a balcony over George Street. There is also a rooftop garden.

The bedrooms are all furnished in Victorian style; most have private bathrooms. There are fresh flowers, tea/coffee-making facilities, bathrobes, toiletries and gourmet chocolates. Boulders Restaurant serves breakfast, lunch (Mon–Fri) and dinner.
All year A$140–A$255 (A$320 for suite or apartment) including breakfast 29

THE WESTIN SYDNEY

1 Martin Place, Sydney, NSW 2000
Tel 02 8223 1111
www.starwood.com
www.westin.com.au

This deluxe hotel occupies two buildings—a modern 31-storey tower, and the beautifully restored Sydney GPO building, dating from 1887. The hotel is famous for its 'Heavenly' beds and glass-walled bathrooms.

Facilities include a 24-hour business centre, health club, boutiques, the Lobby Bar and Lobby Lounge, the Mosaic Restaurant and a basement-level food court.

The bedrooms are spacious and include minibar, fridge, desk, safe, tea/coffee-making facilities, iron and bathrobes.
All year A$495–A$1,000+ (suite). 'Best available' rates start from A$295, excluding breakfast 415 Indoor heated pool

STAYING

CANBERRA

THE BRASSEY OF CANBERRA
Belmore Gardens and Macquarie Street,
Barton, ACT 2600
Tel 02 6273 3766
www.brassey.net.au
This colonial-style brick building dates from 1927 and is set
in the leafy suburb of Barton
surrounded by attractive lawns
and gardens.

Some rooms have period furnishings; the standard rooms
are more contemporary. All
have minibars, tea/coffee-mak-
ing facilities, irons, hair dryers
and internet connections.

The Belmore Restaurant provides a hot buffet breakfast,
lunch (Friday only) and dinner.
The hotel also has a Garden
Bar decorated in 1920s style.
All year A$132–A$159 including
breakfast 81 6km (4 miles)
southwest of city, 1km (0.5 mile) from
Parliamentary Triangle

CROWNE PLAZA
1 Binara Street, Canberra City,
ACT 2601
Tel 02 6247 8999
www.sixcontinentshotels.com
Reliable, modern, city centre
hotel close to the main shopping mall, restaurants and
National Convention Centre.
Some rooms overlook Glebe
Park. There is a restaurant,
cocktail lounge and an atrium
lounge and bar. The restaurant, Brindabella, serves modern Australian lunches and
dinners daily, and the Atrium
Lounge serves tea, coffee,
drinks and cocktails. All the
bedrooms have internet
access, colour TV with movies,
and minibars. Suites, intercon-
necting rooms and non-smok-
ing rooms are available.
All year A$156–A$175 excluding
breakfast 295 Outdoor heated
pool

FORREST INN AND APARTMENTS
30 National Circuit, Forrest, ACT 2603
Tel 02 6295 3433
www.forrestinn.com.au
Set in parkland, the Forrest Inn
has a good range of moder-
ately priced accommodation in
two separate two-storey complexes. All rooms are furnished
in modern motel-style and the
apartments overlook a garden
and barbecue area.

The apartments (one- and
two-bedroom, accommodating
up to five people) include a
full kitchen, spacious dining
area and lounge.
All year A$120 (motel
room)–A$142 (2-bedroom apartment)
excluding breakfast 76 motel units,
26 apartments 35, 36, 39
4km (2.5 miles) south of city, immediately south of Capital Hill

HYATT HOTEL
Commonwealth Avenue, Yarralumla,
ACT 2600
Tel 02 6270 1234
www.canberra.park.hyatt.com
The place to stay in Canberra.
The building dates from the
1920s and has been restored
to its original opulent art-deco
style. It is surrounded by extensive gardens, parkland and
several embassies.

The luxurious bedrooms
have marble bathrooms, full
business facilities, minibar,
hairdryer, iron and ironing
board. There are also a number of suites. The Promenade
Café is a stylish dining room
for breakfast, lunch and dinner.
The Tea Lounge serves traditional afternoon tea.

All year A$210–A$500 excluding
breakfast 249 Indoor pool
Spa, sauna, gymnasium
31, 32 3km (2 miles) south of
city, near Parliamentary Triangle

CENTRAL TILBA

MOUNT DROMADERY HOTEL
Bate Street, Central Tilba, NSW 2546
Tel 02 4473 7223
A traditional pub in a superb
setting with adequate accom-
modation.
All year A$60 Signs off
Princes Highway

COFFS HARBOUR

THE DUNES APARTMENTS
28 Fitzgerald Street, Coffs Harbour Jetty,
NSW 2450
Tel 02 6652 4522, 1800 023 851
www.dunes.com.au

Beyond an unprepossessing
approach, the Dunes has fully
equipped one-, two- and
three-bedroom apartments. All
have balconies, some overlooking the pool.

The apartments are spacious,
clean and light, and the
kitchens include a microwave
oven. Each apartment also has
its own washing machine.
There is a tennis court and a
children's play area.
All year A$128–A$185
Heated outdoor pool, spa and
sauna From the Pacific Highway
turn along Ocean Street to the coast,
left on to Ocean Parade then left on to
Fitzgerald Street

EDEN

THE CROWN AND ANCHOR INN
239 Imlay Street, Eden, NSW 2551
Tel 02 6496 1017
www.crownandanchoreden.com.au

A beautiful conversion of an
1840s inn, this bed-and-breakfast has open fires, antiques,
and ocean views from every
room. All bedrooms have
private bathrooms and there is
a relaxing guest lounge. Guests
are greeted with a complementary glass of champagne.

The inn is close to good
restaurants, and whale-
watching is available locally
in October and November.
All year A$150–A$170 including
breakfast

JERVIS BAY

JERVIS BAY GUESTHOUSE
1 Beach Street, Huskisson, NSW 2540
Tel 02 4441 7658
www.jervisbayguesthouse.com.au
Overlooking the beautiful
white sand beaches of Jervis
Bay, this stylish guesthouse
has the charm of a traditional
timber house but with modern
amenities.

With just four rooms, one
with its own spa and each with
a verandah, this is a quiet spot

STAYING

for a relaxing break. There are traditional stone floors downstairs and wooden upstairs, and fine furniture throughout—this truly feels like home.

⊙ All year 🛏 A$160–A$220 including breakfast 🔄

KATOOMBA
BLUE MOUNTAINS YHA
207 Katoomba Street, Katoomba, NSW 2780
Tel 02 4782 1416
www.yha.com.au

This pleasant hostel in the middle of town has retained many original art-deco features. The dance floor of the former ballroom is now a lounge area and games room, and to one side there is a spacious eating and cooking area.

The largest dorm rooms hold eight people, and there are plenty of double and twin rooms, many with private bathrooms.

⊙ All year 🛏 A$19–A$70/100 (double/family room with private bathroom)

THE CARRINGTON
Katoomba Street, Katoomba, NSW 2780
Tel 02 4782 1111
www.thecarrington.com.au
Several generations of British royalty have favoured this grand hotel, built in the 1880s. The hotel offers all today's mod cons and is only minutes from the Three Sisters rock formation and local shops.
⊙ A$139 (traditional room)–A$465 (Carrington Suite)

LILIANFELS
Lilianfels Avenue, Echo Point, Katoomba, NSW 2780
Tel 02 4780 1200
www.orient-express.com
This luxurious hotel started life in 1889 as the palatial summer retreat of a New South Wales politician. Set in an English-style garden, it looks over the rugged cliffs and wild forests of the Jamison Valley. Guests can laze on the shady verandah, or work out in the gym or swimming pool.

The rooms have been individually decorated with lush fabrics, silk drapes and marble bathrooms and the windows open to the mountain air. The hotel's restaurant, Darley's at Lilianfels (see page 259), is renowned for French cuisine.
⊙ All year 🛏 A$410–A$735 🏊 Indoor heated pool 🔄 🚗 90-minute drive from Sydney, just next to Three Sisters rock formation

POKOLBIN
PEPPERS GUESTHOUSE
Ekerts Road, Pokolbin, Hunter Valley, NSW 2320
Tel 02 4993 8986
www.peppers.com.au
In the heart of the Hunter Valley, Peppers Guesthouse provides luxury accommodation and fine dining at Chez Pok (see page 259).

The colonial-style rooms in this traditional building have modern amenities, as do the four rooms in the separate, self-contained homestead. The lush garden and the reception area, with its polished floors, Turkish rugs and fresh flowers, help make for a relaxing stay.

⊙ All year 🛏 A$277–A$347; Homestead A$924. Meals extra ⓘ 47 🏊 Heated pool, spa and sauna, massages 🔄 🚗 At Cessnock, turn left at first T-junction, then first right; after 6km (4 miles), turn left on to Broke Road. Ekerts Road is 5km (3 miles) along Broke Road on left

PORT MACQUARIE
SUNDOWNER BREAKWALL TOURIST PARK
1 Munster Street, Port Macquarie, NSW 2444
Tel 02 6583 2755
www.sundowner.net.au
Accommodation at this large tourist park at the mouth of the Hastings River ranges from luxury riverside cottages (sleeping up to five people) to fixed-site trailer houses and powered camping pitches.

The leafy setting is quiet, with native palms lining the avenues, and there are superb views across the river and to the Great Dividing Range beyond.
⊙ All year 🚐 Cabins/cottages A$72–A$100 (A$100–A$250 Christmas and Easter); powered sites A$24 (A$35 Easter, Christmas); tent pitches A$22 (A$32 Easter, Christmas) 🏊 Outdoor heated pool 🔄 More expensive accommodation only 🚌 All buses, including Countrylink from Wauchope, stop at tourist information centre two streets west along Clarence Street 🚗 Signs from Pacific Highway to tourist information centre; Munster Street is first right off Clarence Street

ULLADULLA
ULLADULLA GUESTHOUSE
39 Burrill Street, Ulladulla, NSW 2539
Tel 02 4455 1796
www.guesthouse.com.au

This friendly and relaxing guesthouse has the luxury of a smart hotel. The verandah overlooks the palm-fringed outdoor pool and there is a guest lounge.

All rooms have private bathrooms, with marble baths and private spas in the more expensive rooms.
⊙ All year 🛏 A$178–A$238 excluding breakfast 🏊 Heated outdoor saltwater pool and indoor spa 🔄 🚗 Turn off Princes Highway at South Street, Ulladulla Guesthouse is on right at next junction

STAYING

THE COMO

630 Chapel Street, South Yarra, VIC 3141
Tel 03 9825 2222, 1800 033 400
www.mirvachotels.com.au
In the heart of a vibrant, trendy district, the Como delivers personal service in luxurious surroundings and is a favourite of media celebrities. There are one- and two-bedroom suites, penthouses, and spacious studios.

Facilities include a gymnasium, covered swimming pool and rooftop sun deck. The So Bar at the Como is a popular meeting place, while the Brasserie serves breakfast using fresh seasonal food in stylish surroundings.
🅰 All year 🛏 A$249–A$1,300 including breakfast 🛏 105 ⬛ Indoor heated pool 🔲 ♿ 🚊 Any tram down Toorak Road to South Yarra 🚉 South Yarra then tram 🚊 Along Alexandra Avenue on south side of Yarra River, right at Chapel Street

GEORGIAN COURT

21–25 George Street, East Melbourne, VIC 3002
Tel 03 9419 6353
www.georgiancourt.com.au
An inexpensive bed-and-breakfast in one of Melbourne's most historic and elegant suburbs, the 100-year-old Georgian Court lies within walking distance of the main tourist attractions and shops. There are single, double, triple and family rooms: Note that some rooms share bathrooms.
🅰 All year 🛏 A$99–A$135 including breakfast 🛏 12 ♿ 🚌 Bus 246 down Hoddle Street

THE HILTON ON THE PARK

192 Wellington Parade, East Melbourne, VIC 3002
Tel 03 9419 2000
www.melbourne.hilton.com

One of Melbourne's favourite hotels, the Hilton on the Park is opposite the Melbourne Cricket Ground and beside the lovely Fitzroy Gardens.

All the large bedrooms have private bathrooms and most have stunning views across the city. There is an excellent restaurant, a fully equipped day spa and treatment rooms, wedding chapel, Aussie-style pub and gaming room.
🅰 All year 🛏 A$220–A$395 including breakfast 🛏 404 ⬛ Outdoor heated pool ♿ 🚊 Trams 48 or 75 along Flinders Street 🚉 Jolimont

MAGNOLIA COURT BOUTIQUE HOTEL

101 Powlett Street, East Melbourne, VIC 3002
Tel 03 9419 4222
www.magnolia-court.com.au
Situated in a leafy, tranquil area, this family-run boutique hotel is constructed from three distinct buildings.

Magnolia Court has its own breakfast café where guests can begin the day with a full cooked breakfast. You can choose to sit inside or outside on a warm sunny morning. There are a range of rooms from a luxury self-contained apartment to compact units.
🅰 All year 🛏 A$160–A$275 including breakfast 🛏 27 ♿ 🚊 Trams 48 or 75 along Wellington Parade 🚉 Jolimont

THE MANSION HOTEL AT WERRIBEE PARK

K Road, Werribee, VIC 3030
Tel 03 9731 4000
www.mansionhotel.com.au
An alternative to staying in the city, this is a peaceful hotel in the beautiful Werribee Park. A former Catholic seminary, it has been converted to the height of luxury.

The hotel has contemporary guest rooms and suites with their own bathrooms. Facilities include a fitness centre and spa, beauty treatments, gymnasium, tennis courts, and a library and snooker room. Joseph's Restaurant looks across the expansive gardens.
🅰 All year 🛏 A$172–A$420 excluding breakfast 🛏 92 ⬛ Indoor pool 🔲 🚗 30km (19 miles) southwest from city on Geelong Road over Westgate Bridge to Werribee Park

ROBINSONS IN THE CITY

405 Spencer Street, Melbourne, VIC 3003
Tel 03 9329 2552
www.robinsonsinthecity.com.au
The city's first bakery, dating from the 1850s, has been restored to form the only B & B accommodation in central Melbourne. It is on the north-west fringe, close to the Flagstaff Gardens, the new restaurant precinct and Queen Victoria Market.

All the rooms have bathrooms. The home-cooked breakfast is a special treat.
🅰 All year; reception 5.30am–late 🛏 A$185–A$225 including breakfast 🛏 6 ♿ Most rooms 🚊 City Circle tram to cnr Latrobe and Spencer streets

THE SEBEL MELBOURNE

394 Collins Street, Melbourne, VIC 3000
Tel 03 9211 6600, 1800 500 778
www.mirvachotels.com.au
A favourite in a central location, the Sebel occupies the former 1875 Bank of Australasia building, which has been magnificently and painstakingly restored.

The hotel has spacious studios and self-contained suites, the latter with living and dining areas, business desks, kitchenette and laundry. The loft suites have spa baths. For stylish dining, or just a coffee and cake, try the Treasury Restaurant, although there are plenty of good places to eat within walking distance.
🅰 All year 🛏 A$185–A$550 including breakfast 🛏 115 ♿ 🚊 Any tram along Collins Street

THE WINDSOR

103 Spring Street, Melbourne, VIC 3000
Tel 03 9633 6002, 1800 033 100
www.thewindsor.com.au
Built in 1883, this is one of Melbourne's most elegant hotels and one of the Oberoi chain of hotels. Dubbed the 'Grand Duchess of Spring Street', it combines Victorian opulence with modern comforts and facilities.

The rooms and suites are renowned for their grandiose proportions, open fireplaces, marble bathrooms and historic connections.

The restaurant and cocktail bar, One Eleven Spring Street, is famous for its traditional afternoon teas. Particularly splendid is the Grand Ballroom where special functions are held.
🅰 All year 🛏 A$500–A$2,400 including breakfast; cheaper packages available 🛏 180 ♿ 🚊 City Circle tram

BALLARAT

CRAIG'S ROYAL HOTEL

10 Lydiard Street South, Ballarat,
VIC 3350
Tel 03 5331 1377, 1800 648 051
www.craigsroyal.com
Built in the 1850s during
Victoria's gold rush, this charming hotel has spacious lounges
with leather couches and open
fires in winter, and several
restaurants and bars. Some of
the grander rooms in the north
tower have their own bal-
conies with views over the city.

The accommodation ranges
from traditional rooms with
shared bathroom facilities to
deluxe spa suites with private
bathrooms. The hotel is close
to the main shops, theatre and
art gallery.

🕐 All year 🏨 A$130–A$350 including
breakfast ⓘ 44 🔣 🔣 Ballarat

METUNG

MCMILLANS OF METUNG

155–167 Metung Road, Metung,
VIC 3904
Tel 03 5156 2283
www.mcmillansofmetung.com.au
McMillans of Metung has a
great location on the shores of
Bancroft Bay and is renowned
for its friendly service.

Eleven holiday cottages stand
within 3ha (8 acres) of lakeside lawn, gardens and bushland. All come with linen,
crockery, cutlery and towels,
along with dishwashers and
microwaves, television and
video facilities, a barbecue and
covered parking.

Other facilities include two
swimming pools, a tennis
court, a golf-driving range, and
gymnasium and sauna. You
can take a dolphin-spotting
boat trip around the bay.

🕐 All year 🏨 From A$198 excluding
breakfast 🏊 Outdoor pools 🔣 🔣
🚗 10km (6 miles) off the Princes
Highway between Bairnsdale and Lakes
Entrance

MILDURA

MILDURA GRAND HOTEL

Seventh Street, Mildura, VIC 3502
Tel 03 5023 0511, 1800 034 228
www.milduragrandhotel.com
In the heart of Mildura on the
Murray River, the Grand Hotel
has rooms to suit all budgets
and tastes. They range from
presidential suites overlooking
the garden with its magnificent
roses and palm trees, to older,
renovated, rooms at the rear
of the hotel (all with private
bathrooms).

The Don Carrazza family run
the renowned Stefano's
restaurant as well as the hotel.
There is also a gymnasium, a
spa and a sauna.

🕐 All year 🏨 A$110–A$462 including
breakfast ⓘ 102 🔣 🔣

MOUNT BUFFALO

MOUNT BUFFALO CHALET

Mount Buffalo Road, Mount Buffalo
National Park, VIC 3740
Tel 03 5755 1500, 1800 037 1500
www.mtbuffalo.com
This is one of Australia's most
spectacular locations, high up
overlooking the cliffs of Mount
Buffalo National Park. The
emphasis here is on the outdoors, the views and the
wildlife.

The dining room has a country hotel atmosphere and
guests can retire to one of
three lounges after dinner.
Four types of room are available, most with private
bathrooms. The Tower and
Heritage rooms have wonderful views over the surrounding
national park.

🕐 All year 🏨 A$105–A$300; includes
breakfast ⓘ 100 🏊 Outdoor unheated
pool 🔣 Dining room only 🚗 26km
(16 miles) from the Great Alpine Road
at Porepunkah

PORTSEA

PEPPERS DELGANY PORTSEA

Point Nepean Road, Portsea, VIC 3944
Tel 03 5984 4000
www.peppers.com.au

Named after a small village in
County Wicklow, Eire, the deluxe Delgany was built as a
private estate in the 1920s. The
sandstone building, in the style
of a European castle, sits on a
hill in 5ha (12 acres) of carefully tended gardens.

Rooms are spacious and elegant and some have open fires
and spa baths. For leisure,
there is a tennis court, croquet
lawn, swimming pool and
excellent gym with an on-site
health spa.

The hotel is right next door
to the Portsea Golf Club and a
short drive from championship
courses.

🕐 All year 🏨 A$278–A$434 ⓘ 32
🔣 🔣

QUEENSCLIFFE

QUEENSCLIFF HOTEL

16 Gellibrand Street, Queenscliff,
VIC 3225
Tel 03 5258 1066
www.queenscliffhotel.com.au/store
Built in 1887 for wealthy
Victorian society, the hotel has
retained its period feel. There
are several sitting rooms, three
dining areas and a bar.

The pretty bedrooms are
small but most rooms look
over the parkland facing on to
Port Phillip Bay. The conservatory dining area has a formal
style, while the Courtyard
Restaurant is more casual.

🕐 All year 🏨 A$190–A$290 including
breakfast ⓘ 17 🔣 Regular buses from
Geelong 🚗 31km (19 miles) southeast
from Geelong on the Bellarine Highway

YARRA VALLEY

CHATEAU YERING HISTORIC HOUSE HOTEL

Melba Highway, Yering, Yarra Valley,
VIC 3770
Tel 03 9237 3333, 1800 237 333
www.chateau-yering.com.au
This luxurious small hotel in
the Yarra Valley marks the site
of the area's first vineyard. The
sprawling homestead was built
in 1854 and is decorated with
antique furniture, works of art
and fine fabrics. Its beautiful
gardens border the Yarra River.

The suites are luxurious and
Eleonore's Restaurant is one of
the best in the state. For casual
eating there is the Sweetwater
Café.

🕐 All year 🏨 A$445–A$839 including
breakfast ⓘ 20 🏊 Outdoor unheated
pool 🔣 🚗 5km (3 miles) south from
Yarra Glen on Melba Highway (B300)

STAYING

AIRLIE BEACH

CORAL SEA RESORT

25 Oceanview Avenue, Airlie Beach, QLD 4802
Tel 07 4946 6458
www.coralsearesort.com

This is the only waterfront resort on the Whitsunday coast, a short walk from Airlie Beach. The accommodation comprises suites, two-bedroom apartments, family units and one-, two- and three-bedroom luxury penthouses.

The suites are decorated in nautical colours with boating prints and yachting memorabilia, and have a spa bath. There are two restaurants, and beauty treatments are available. Guests can enjoy water sports from a private jetty.

🅖 All year 🅦 A$185–A$520 excluding breakfast 🅦 Apartments A$220–A$490 🅘 77 🅰 Outdoor pool 🅢 🅑 26km (16 miles) northeast from Proserpine off Bruce Highway

ATHERTON TABLELAND

ROSE GUMS WILDERNESS RETREAT

Land Road, Butchers Creek, QLD 4872
Tel 07 4096 8360
www.rosegums.com.au

These luxury chalets are in a wildlife sanctuary on the coastal mountain ranges of the Atherton Tableland. The nearby Wooroonooran National Park is a World Heritage Site that includes the 1,662m (5,451ft) Mount Bartle Frere.

The chalets are set within 93ha (230 acres) of tropical forest. Each is fully self-contained, with a kitchen and verandah. Sizes range from studios for couples to family chalets sleeping up to six. They all have a large spa bath and wood-burning fireplace.

There is no restaurant, but a complementary breakfast hamper is supplied.

🅖 Seasonal closing 🅦 A$180 (family chalets: extra adults A$30, children A$15) 🅑 82km (50 miles) southwest from Cairns, 15km (9 miles) east from Malanda, 18km (11 miles) southeast from Yungaburra

BRISBANE

THE CHIFLEY ON GEORGE

103 George Street, Brisbane, QLD 4000
Tel 07 3221 6044
www.chifleyhotels.com

Only a short distance from the South Bank Parklands, the Queensland Cultural precinct and the Casino, the Chifley on George is also convenient for the city centre.

The rooms include deluxe and executive suites and spa rooms. All are equipped with minibar, fridge and tea/coffee-making facilities, and have air-conditioning and heating.

Mediterranean-influenced food is served in the Brasserie.

🅖 All year 🅦 A$129–A$185 excluding breakfast 🅘 99 🅰 Outdoor pool 🅢 🅑 Brisbane Loop

METRO INN TOWER MILL BRISBANE

239 Wickham Terrace, Brisbane, QLD 4000
Tel 07 3832 1421
www.metroinns.com.au

The 10-storey high Brisbane stands opposite the city's oldest building, the convict-built Tower Mill, next to the Brisbane Private Hospital, and close to Queen Street Mall.

Each room has a balcony and panoramic view. The rooms are well equipped and have traditional décor and air-conditioning. The rooftop restaurant and bar overlook the city.

🅖 Seasonal closing 🅦 A$90–A$145 excluding breakfast 🅘 80 🅢 🅑 Roma Street, Central

RENDEZVOUS HOTEL

255 Ann Street, Brisbane, QLD 4000
Tel 07 3001 9888
www.rendezvoushotels.com

Close to the Queen Street Mall shopping and entertainment precinct, the Rendezvous occupies a former government building and overlooks the formal gardens of Anzac Square.

Rooms and one- or two-bedroom apartments are available, the latter with living/dining areas and kitchens. Many of the rooms are panelled and decorated in period style.

There is no restaurant but there are plenty of nearby places to eat. The hotel elevator gives direct access to a shopping arcade with a large selection of stores.

🅖 All year 🅦 A$150–A$250 excluding breakfast 🅘 138 🅢 🅑 Opposite Central Station

RYDGES SOUTH BANK

Cnr Grey and Glenelg streets, South Bank, Brisbane, QLD 4101
Tel 07 3255 0822
www.rydges.com.au

The hotel is in the heart of the South Bank Parklands, within easy reach of the Queensland Performing Arts Centre, Queensland Museum and Queensland Art Gallery.

The rooms in the 15-storey building have air-conditioning, desks, minibar and tea/coffee-making facilities.

The Café Bar, Parklands Bar & Grill Restaurant, and the Crown Lager Bar provide refreshments and meals. There is also a gymnasium with a sauna and spa.

🅖 All year 🅦 A$152–A$185 excluding breakfast 🅘 305 🅦 🅢 🅑 Buses to Exhibition Centre or South Brisbane bus station 🅑 South Brisbane

CAIRNS

CAIRNS RESORT BY OUTRIGGER

53–57 The Esplanade, Cairns, QLD 4870
Tel 07 4046 4141
www.outrigger.com

The Esplanade address is in the heart of Cairns and this luxury hotel has fine city and ocean views. The one- and two-bedroom units include a fully equipped kitchen and tea/coffee-making facilities, and are furnished in modern and traditional styles to high standards.

Among the sport facilities are a pool, fitness room, sauna, whirlpool spa and health club. There is also a shopping and restaurant complex.

ⓖ All year 🏨 A$170–A$350 excluding breakfast ① 123 ▦ Outdoor pool 🌊 🚌 500m from bus terminal 🚉 1km (0.5 mile) from Cairns station

LILYBANK B & B
75 Kamerunga Road, Stratford, Cairns, QLD 4870
Tel 07 4055 1123
www.lilybank.com.au
Once the homestead of the area's first tropical fruit plantation, Lilybank is a 10-minute drive north of the city This traditional Queenslander house has shady verandahs all around. Every room has a private bathroom and there is a refreshing saltwater pool.

ⓖ All year 🏨 A$88–A$110 including breakfast ① 5 ▦ Outdoor pool 🌊 🚌 10 mins from Cairns

CAPE TRIBULATION
CAPE TRIB BEACH HOUSE
Rykers Road, Cape Tribulation, QLD 4873
Tel 07 4098 0030
www.capetribbeach.com.au
Idyllically remote, this resort is on the edge of the Wet Tropics World Heritage Site. The beach is unbelievably beautiful as the rainforest comes down to the water's edge. But be prepared for wet weather, especially from December to April.

The resort consists of a variety of wooden cabins with verandahs—either bunkhouses or rooms (some with private bathrooms). The rooms are simply furnished, with fans or air-conditioning, but no TV, phone or radio. There is a separate shared kitchen, or try the beachfront bar and bistro.

ⓖ All year 🏨 A$30–A$100 excluding breakfast ▦ Outdoor pool 🌊 Most rooms 🚗 Follow Captain Cook Highway north from Cairns for about 100km (62 miles), through Mossman, and cross Daintree River by cable ferry. Cape Trib Beach House is 38km (24 miles) north

GREAT KEPPEL ISLAND
GREAT KEPPEL RESORT
Great Keppel Island, QLD 4700
Tel 07 4125 2343
www.greatkeppel.com.au
This is an action-packed holiday option for under-35s on a 1,454ha (3,591-acre) island. Free activities across 17 magnificent sandy beaches are included in your stay: You can try anything from archery to windsurfing. There are four grades of accommodation to suit the budget, and plenty of bars, cafés, restaurants and clubs.

ⓖ All year 🏨 From A$252 for 2-night package ▦ Outdoor pool 🌊 🚗 An easy day's drive from Brisbane, then a boat trip from Yeppoon

HERVEY BAY
KINGFISHER BAY
Kingfisher Bay Resort & Village, PMB 1, Urangan, Hervey Bay, QLD 4655
Tel 07 4120 3333, 1800 072 555
The resort overlooks the sea, lakes and bushland. The self-contained villas have either two or three bedrooms, and some have spa baths. The well-equipped rooms have bush or lagoon views.

There are three restaurants, four bars, a licensed jetty hut and a coffee shop and café. The restaurants showcase Australian seafood and native meats. Bush tucker and Australian wine tastings are weekly features.

Beauty treatments and a range of shops are also available.

ⓖ All year 🏨 Rooms A$270 excluding breakfast 🏨 Villa A$825 (3 nights) ① 152 rooms, 109 villas ▦ 4 outdoor pools (1 heated) 🌊

NOOSA HEADS
FRENCH QUARTER
62 Hastings Street, Noosa Heads, QLD 4567
Tel 07 5430 7100
www.frenchquarter.com.au
A luxury resort across the road from Noosa's Main Beach. The complex has a French provincial style with a mixture of terracotta roof tiles, stucco walls and shutters.

Most of the suites overlook the central lagoon-style pools and spa and all have a spa bath. They are self-contained with cooking and laundry facilities. Lorenza's, the resort's restaurant and bar, combines

popular fare with modern Italian cuisine.

ⓖ All year 🏨 A$456–A$538 ① 119 ▦ Outdoor pool 🌊

PORT DOUGLAS
RYDGES REEF RESORT
Port Douglas Road, Port Douglas, QLD 4871
Tel 07 4099 5577
www.portdouglas.rydges.com
This expansive resort is surrounded by luxuriant gardens. The first-rate accommodation ranges from hotel rooms and suites to self-contained villas. All rooms have a balcony or courtyard and many have views of the Great Dividing Range. The activity centre includes a gymnasium, pool, floodlit tennis courts, and pitch and putt golf.

Palms Restaurant and the Garden Room serve breakfast and dinner, and the Terrace-house Restaurant overlooks a secluded pool. Cascades has a pizza bar, and guests have access to the Rydges Treetop Resort restaurants close by.

ⓖ All year 🏨 Rooms A$150–A$185 excluding breakfast. Villas (3-bed) A$250 ① 282 rooms, 180 villas ▦ 5 outdoor pools 🏐 🌊 🚌 Shuttle bus to Port Douglas. Airport pick-up transfer available: adult A$23, child A$12.50 🚗 73km (45 miles) northwest from Cairns

SURFERS PARADISE
COURTYARD SURFERS PARADISE RESORT
Cnr Gold Coast Highway and Hanlan Street, Paradise Centre, Surfers Paradise, QLD 4217
Tel 07 5579 3499
www.marriott.com
Right in the heart of Surfers Paradise, this large, bright resort includes rooms with private balconies and ocean or mountain views, suites, and a penthouse with outdoor spa.

The site is packed with shops and entertainment, and there are four local restaurants—Hard Rock Café, Melba's, Rez Two Fifty Two and The Verandah. Among the sports facilities are a gymnasium, spa and tennis court.

ⓖ All year 🏨 A$169–A$350 excluding breakfast ① 404 ▦ Outdoor pool 🏐 🌊 🚗 25km (15 miles) north from Coolangatta Airport along Gold Coast Highway to Cavill Avenue, Surfers Paradise; turn right on to southbound Gold Coast Highway to Hanlan Street

STAYING

ALICE SPRINGS

ORANGEWOOD

9 McMinn Street, Alice Springs, NT 0870
Tel 08 8952 4114
www.orangewood-BNB.au.com

Few older homes with high-quality B & B accommodation exist in Alice Springs, but 1940s Orangewood has three double rooms (with private bathrooms) in the main house and one in the cottage in the citrus grove to the rear, where there is also a pool.

Hosts Lynne and Ross Peterkin prepare full breakfasts, in rooms filled with antiques in the main house. There are tea/coffee-making facilities.

🌐 All year 🏷 A$187 including breakfast 🛏 4 🏊 Outdoor pool 🚗 From Todd Mall, cross Todd River at Wills Terrace Causeway, turn left into Sturt Terrace and take second right

DARWIN

CARLTON HOTEL DARWIN

The Esplanade, Darwin, NT 0801
Tel 08 8980 0800
www.carltonhotels.com.au

This elegant, modern hotel overlooks Darwin Harbour and is a short walk from the shopping and business districts. It has a 24m (78ft) swimming pool, a spa bath and waterfall, and a sun terrace with a pool bar.

The spacious rooms have modern furniture and include a minibar and interactive television.

The Esplanade Coffee Shop prepares superb cakes and pastries, while the Carlton Lounge serves afternoon teas and cocktails.

🌐 All year 🏷 A$198–A$236 🛏 197 🏊 Outdoor pool 🎬 🚗

RYDGES PLAZA DARWIN

32 Mitchell Street, Darwin, NT 0801
Tel 08 8982 0000
www.rydges.com

Right in the heart of Darwin's business and shopping district, this towering hotel looks across Darwin Harbour. Lobby shops include a hairdresser, travel agent and tour desk.

The spacious rooms have private bathrooms, TV with in-house movies, tea/coffee-making facilities, minibar, hairdryer, and air-conditioning. There is a spa, and the outdoor pool has a tropical setting.

🌐 All year 🏷 A$165–A$234 excluding breakfast 🛏 233 🏊 Outdoor pool 🚗

JABIRU

GAGADJU CROCODILE INN

1 Flinders Street, Jabiru, NT 0886
Tel 08 89792800
www.sixcontinentshotels.com
This unique hotel, in the heart of Kakadu National Park, is built in the form of a crocodile. It is a good base for exploring the rugged beauty of the vast park.

The simply furnished rooms include fridge, hairdryer, in-room movies, minibar, phone, radio and TV. Most overlook the central courtyard with its billabong and shaded swimming pool.

The Escarpment Restaurant is open all day. Light meals are also available from the Gingas Tavern public bar.

🌐 All year 🏷 A$169–A$271 excluding breakfast 🛏 110 🏊 Outdoor pool 🚗 Greyhound Shuttle Bus from Darwin 🚗 8km (5 miles) south from Jabiru Airport, 270km (167 miles) east from Darwin Airport

KATHERINE

MERCURE INN KATHERINE

Mercure Inn Katherine, Stuart Highway, Katherine, NT 0850
Tel 08 8972 1744
Set among lawns and tropical palms, this motel-style inn has tennis courts and a large, partly shaded pool.

The rooms include TV with movies, phone and radio. The large self-catering family units

contain a kitchenette.

🌐 All year 🏷 A$130–A$148 excluding breakfast 🏊 Outdoor pool 🚗 4km (2.5 miles) south from Katherine on Stuart Highway

YULARA

YULARA RESORT

Yulara Drive, Yulara, NT 0872
Tel 08 8957 7888
www.voyages.com.au
Yulara is just outside Uluru-Kata Tjuta National Park (Ayers Rock and The Olgas) and is the only base for exploring these attractions. There is a range of accommodation.

Longitude 131° is a collection of 15 elevated tents. Each has a wall of glass allowing uninterrupted views of sunrise on the rock (from A$1,495 for two nights including all meals).

Sails in the Desert Hotel is luxurious with superb restaurants (from A$445).

The stylish, top-quality Desert Gardens Hotel is set amid native shrubs and gum trees (A$426–A$494 in high season, Jul–Nov).

Outback Pioneer Hotel and Lodge has comfortable, affordable hotel rooms with private bathrooms, budget cabins and air-conditioned dormitories (from A$383).

Emu Walk Apartments shelter in gardens of native trees in the middle of the resort and consist of light, spacious one- and two-bedroom apartments (from A$426).

The Lost Camel has self-contained guest rooms around lush courtyards and a swimming pool (from A$383).

Ayers Rock Resort Campground has tent sites, powered sites, air-conditioned cabins, coach sites, a pool, showers, toilets and laundry facilities (from A$12.60 per person).

🌐 All year 🚗 🚗 🚗 20km (12 miles) from Uluru, 53km (33 miles) from Kata Tjuta

ADELAIDE

NORTH ADELAIDE HERITAGE GROUP

109 Glen Osmond Road, Eastwood, SA 5063
Tel 08 8272 1355
www.adelaide.heritage.com

Wake up in Adelaide's original fire station, wander around a manor or the residence of a Federation founder, or stare up at the ceiling of a heritage-listed chapel. Antiques dealer Rodney Twiss and his wife Regina, an interior designer, have renovated 22 self-contained properties within 2km (1.2 miles) of Adelaide city.
🅒 All year 🅦 A$546 excluding breakfast 🄸 22 premises 🄴 Locations revealed when booking confirmed

RAMADA PLAZA PIER HOTEL & SUITES

16 Holdfast Promenade, Glenelg, SA 5045
Tel 08 8350 6688
www.ramadainternational.com
A strip of palm-lined sand separates this suburban beach resort from the sea. Else relax in the gym, sauna, spa or indoor heated pool.
There are three restaurants and a café serving Thai, Malay, Mediterranean and contemporary Australian cuisines.
🅒 All year 🅦 From A$185 including breakfast 🏊 Indoor pool 🄰 🄲 🄰 Tram from Victoria Square to Jetty Road 🄴 From the southwest end of West Terrace follow Anzac Highway to Holdfast Promenade

THORNGROVE MANOR

2 Glenside Lane, Stirling, SA 5152
Tel 08 8339 6748
www.slh.com/australia/adelaide/hotel_oveaus
A flamboyant escape in the Adelaide Hills, Thorngrove Manor is a Victorian gothic revival building with baroque turrets and fantasy towers. The garden is equally historic.

The suites have their own spa baths, dining areas and, from the terraces, unspoiled tree-top views. Antiques and plush soft furnishings make this a romantic escape.
🅒 All year 🅦 A$175–A$395 including breakfast 🄸 6 🄴 A 15-minute drive from Adelaide

BAROSSA VALLEY

THE WORKMAN'S COTTAGE, SEPPELTSFIELD

Box 608, Tanunda, SA 5352
Tel 08 8562 8444
www.workmanscottage.com
This excellent B & B in Australia's premier wine region is part of an 1853 worker's cottage at the Seppelt's estate, close to the winery. Settle into the brass-bedded retreat with private bathroom, antiques, sauna and a cottage garden.
A breakfast of fruits, fresh and grilled with cheese, local meats and muffins is delivered to the entrance.
🅒 All year 🅦 A$170 🄸 1 🄴 On the Sturt Highway leading to the Barossa Valley, turn at the Seppeltsfield Marananga exit sign. The cottage is 1km (0.5 mile) along this road

FLINDERS RANGES

WILPENA POUND RESORT

Wilpena Pound Resort, via PO Hawker, SA 5434
Tel 08 8648 0004.
www.wilpenapound.com.au

A great location at the foot of the spectacular Wilpena Pound. This is a complex of modern motel with pool, self-contained units, shady 101ha

(250-acre) caravan and camping park, and backpacker accommodation. Captain Starlight's Restaurant and Poddy Dodger's bar provide food and drink. Other facilities include a shop, vehicle fuel, an ATM and an Internet kiosk.
The resort organizes scenic flights, 4WD and regional coach tours, gourmet picnics, and economical holiday packages.
🅒 All year 🅦 Motel from A$125; self-contained unit A$185; tent/caravan pitch A$22 plus A$6.50 parking fee 🄸 60 motel and self-contained units, 400 tent and caravan pitches

KANGAROO ISLAND

CAPE FORBIN RETREAT

RSD 404 Newland Mail Service, Kingscote, Kangaroo Island, SA 5223
Tel 08 8559 3219
www.capeforbinretreat.com.au
A self-contained hideaway for a romantic couple or up to six people, in a wilderness protection area above the northwest cape. The sun sets over a deserted beach encircled by cliffs. To find the Retreat, your hosts provide a map to guide you through isolated bush and farmland. The kitchen and relaxation areas are spacious and the furniture is a mixture of modern and period pieces.
🅒 All year 🅦 A$220 (plus A$25 for each extra person 🄸 1 (sleeps up to 6) 🄴 60km (37 miles) northwest from Parndana

LYNDOCH

BELLE COTTAGES

Box 481, Lyndoch, SA 5351
Tel 08 8524 4825
www.bellescapes.com
Christabelle Cottage is a former ironstone church built in 1849, retaining many original features. Modern comforts include a mezzanine bedroom and a sunny atrium. It is one of five self-catering Lyndoch heritage properties, ranging from an 1850s schoolhouse and 1860s cottage to the 1930s Bluebelle, Daisybelle and Rosebelle cottages. All have modern conveniences, spas, period furniture, log fires and gardens. A warm welcome includes complementary sparkling wine and port.
🅒 All year 🅦 A$190–A$220 including breakfast 🄸 5 self-catering properties 🄲 🄴 58km (36 miles) northeast from Adelaide along Main North Road, through Gawler to Lyndoch Highway. Hosts take guests to the secret address

STAYING

BROOME

CABLE BEACH CLUB RESORT

Cable Beach Road, Cable Beach,
WA 6726
Tel 08 9192 0400
www.cablebeachclub.com

For many years this has been *the* place to stay in Broome. It is still very popular due to the Cable Beach location with its many facilities.

There are studio rooms with views of the garden, pool or ocean. The more luxurious bungalows are suitable for families or groups of adults. For dining there is Lord Macs Buffet, the Boardwalk Café, the more formal Club Restaurant, the Sunset Bar and bars by the pools.

🎦 All year 🛎 Garden suites A$199–A$290 🛏 263 🏊 2 outdoor pools 🆗 🚗 6km (4 miles) north from Broome

FREMANTLE

ESPLANADE HOTEL

Cnr Marine Terrace and Essex Street,
Fremantle, WA 6160
Tel 08 94324000
www.esplanadehotelfremantle.com.au

This attractive heritage building is a short walk from the city centre and close to the Indian Ocean and swimming beaches. Some of the rooms have balconies overlooking parkland or the Marine Harbour, and some have spas, but all are well equipped.

There are two restaurants, two outdoor pools, three outdoor spas, a sauna and a health club.

🎦 All year 🛎 A$270–A$499 🛏 259 🏊 2 outdoor heated pools 🆗 🚗 Fremantle CAT from station

KALBARRI

BEST WESTERN KALBARRI PALM RESORT

Porter Street, Kalbarri, WA 6536
Tel 08 9937 2333
www.bestwestern.com.au/kalbarri

Kalbarri Palm Resort, only 150m (500ft) from Kalbarri's small main shopping area and 200m (660ft) from the beach, lies within 2ha (5 acres) of landscaped gardens. The accommodation ranges from standard motel suites, deluxe suites and family apartments to executive suites.

The resort has barbecue facilities, a children's playground, two outdoor pools, a tennis court, spa, a bowling green and an indoor cricket pitch. A guest laundry and irons are also available.

🎦 All year 🛎 A$80–A$110 🛏 78 🏊 2 outdoor heated pools 🆗 🚗 Transfers available from bus station to resort

MARGARET RIVER

MARGARET RIVER HOLIDAY SUITES

Cnr Wilmott Avenue and Town View Terrace, Margaret River, WA 6285
Tel 08 9758 7088
www.holidaysuites.com.au

Just off the main street, Margaret River Holiday Suites has accommodation for a range of budgets.

Five standards of room are available. The older part of the hotel has double and twin rooms, or triple rooms with a mini-kitchen. Twenty new deluxe rooms include spa suites and studio apartments. Some of the rooms look out over the formal garden with its fountain.

🎦 All year 🛎 A$99–A$129 excluding breakfast 🆗

PERTH

BURSWOOD INTERNATIONAL RESORT CASINO

Great Eastern Highway, Burswood, WA 6100
Tel 08 9362 7777
www.burswood.com.au

With fantastic views across the Swan River to the city, this is one of Perth's most popular tourist attractions.

Surrounded by parkland, Burswood comprises a hotel, a 24-hour casino, nine restaurants, six bars, a 2,300-seat theatre and a 20,000-seat indoor stadium.

Leisure facilities include a health and fitness centre, spa and beauty treatments, and an 18-hole golf course. All rooms are well equipped.

🎦 All year 🛎 A$225 including breakfast 🛏 413 🏊 Indoor and outdoor pool 🆗 🚗 Burswood Resort 🚗 3km (2 miles) east from Perth centre via the Causeway or Graham Farmer Freeway

CITY WATERS LODGE

118 Terrace Road, Perth, WA 6000
Tel 08 9325 1566
www.citywaters.com.au

For the price-conscious traveller, this collection of self-catering studios is an easy stroll to the city and Barrack Street Jetty.

All of the one- or two-bedroom units have kitchens and bathrooms but the resident on-site managers can provide a continental breakfast.

🎦 All year 🛎 A$79–A$118 🛏 72 🆗 🚗 Transfers available to and from airport

EMERALD HOTEL

24 Mount Street, Perth, WA 6000
Tel 08 9382 1246
www.emeraldhotel.com.au

In a quiet cul-de-sac just a short walk from Perth's shopping malls and King's Park, the Emerald is a good option for comfortable and reasonably priced accommodation.

The hotel has a mixture of standard and deluxe rooms. Rooms with extra cooking facilities, and baths as well as showers, are available on request. There are leisure facilities and a health club.

🎦 All year 🛎 A$72.50–A$156 🛏 101 🆗 🚗 CAT stop near the hotel 🚗 Turn off west end of St. George's Terrace

PARMELIA HILTON PERTH

14 Mill Street, Perth, WA 6000
Tel 08 9215 2000

In the heart of the city, the Parmelia overlooks the Swan River. It has a good restaurant and wine bar and there's an impressive selection of premium wines and champagnes by the glass. There is a gym, a pool, and bicycles for hire.

🎦 All year 🛎 From A$148 🛏 273 🆗 🏊 Outdoor pool

CRADLE MOUNTAIN

CRADLE MOUNTAIN LODGE

Cradle Mountain Road, TAS 7306
Tel 03 6492 1303
www.poresorts.com.au

This luxurious retreat looks out across Tasmania's famed World Heritage wilderness area. Guests stay in warm wood cabins, which have been carefully designed to blend in with the surrounding environment. Each has a log fire with plenty of wood and kindling available.

The Lodge itself has a formal restaurant with a wine cellar, or guests can have a more casual meal in the Tavern Bar.

All year A$230–A$500 including breakfast 93 82km (51 miles) southwest from Devonport via B14 to Sheffield then C136 and C132 roads

DERWENT BRIDGE

DERWENT BRIDGE CHALETS

Lyell Highway, east end of Derwent Bridge, TAS 7410
Tel 03 6289 1000
www.troutwalks.com.au

Highland chalets cluster at the edge of tall snow-gum forest, close to Lake St. Clair and the Upper Derwent River.

Each self-catering chalet is laid out with attention to practical requirements, and you can relax on a verandah while watching the early mist rise through the trees. Continental breakfast is delivered every morning with coffee and newspaper. There is a laundry but no TV (reception is poor).

All year A$125–A$200 including breakfast 8 170km (105 miles) from Hobart via the Lyell Highway; turn at Derwent Bridge 500m (1,650ft) before Lake St. Clair turn

HAWLEY BEACH

LAROOMA COTTAGES

Larooma Road, Hawley Beach, TAS 7307
Tel 03 6428 6754
www.laroomacottages.com.au

Larooma is a historic farm with a sensational outlook across Port Sorell to the coast and headlands of Narawntapu National Park. You can walk to a nearby penguin rookery.

The self-contained one-, two- and four-bedroom waterfront cottages are in one of Tasmania's most pleasant and mildest coastal settings. Each cottage has modern conveniences, while two have open fires and spas. Continental breakfast on request.

All year A$135 excluding breakfast 3 22km (14 miles) east from Devonport via the Bass Highway and B74 to Hawley Beach

HOBART

HOTEL GRAND CHANCELLOR

1 Davey Street, Hobart, TAS 7000
Tel 03 6235 4535
www.hgchobart.com.au

There are panoramic views of Constitution Dock and historic waterfront warehouses from this modern hotel, housed in one of Hobart's tallest buildings.

Meehan's Restaurant and Cocktail Bar serves excellent local seafood, and there are other dining options.

All year A$160–A$195 excluding breakfast 234 Indoor pool

MOINA

LEMONTHYME LODGE

Dolcoath Road, off Cradle Mount Link Road, Moina, TAS 7306
Tel 03 6492 1112
www.lemonthyme.com.au

This luxury lodge stands in temperate rainforest near Cradle Mountain, with scattered rustic cabins looking over the trees to the distant mountains. There is an abundance of wildlife, nearby waterfalls, and six bush walks starting from the lodge.

Rooms have a bath or spa, while the luxury suites have a spa looking over the balcony. There is a good restaurant in the main lodge building.

All year A$99–A$299, some options including breakfast 65km (40 miles) southwest from Devonport via Wilmot or Sheffield

PORT ARTHUR

PORT ARTHUR LODGE

Arthur Highway, Port Arthur, TAS 7182
Tel 03 6250 2262
www.portarthurlodge.com

Set in natural bushland, this is the ideal place for bushwalking, fishing or photography. Eighteen waterfront cabins have wide decks with views of the wilderness.

The Lodge is a leisurely stroll along a shoreline forest trail to Port Arthur Historic Site.

All year A$149–A$189 excluding breakfast 18

RICHMOND

MILLHOUSE ON THE BRIDGE

2 Wellington Street, Richmond, TAS 7025
Tel 03 6260 2428
www.millhouse.com.au

This is possibly the most romantic setting of any cottage stay in Tasmania. The former mill is beside Australia's oldest convict-built bridge, constructed in about 1853, with 2ha (5 acres) of river frontage and a view to Australia's oldest Catholic church.

The house is filled with antiques. There is also one self-contained cottage, separate from the house. Cooked breakfast is provided and other meals are available on request.

All year A$140–A$180 including breakfast 5 100m (330ft) from town centre, over Richmond Bridge on right

STRAHAN

RENISON COTTAGES

32–38 Harvey Street, Strahan, TAS 7468
Tel 03 6471 7390
www.renisoncottages.com.au

Three historic mining town cottages have been relocated here and renovated to sleep two to five people. They are in a quiet, bush setting close to the town, with cottage gardens full of native plants.

All cottages are self-contained, with log fires, and there is a separate laundry building.

All year A$173–A$190 including breakfast 3 Half way along Harvey Street, 300m (1,000ft) from town centre

STAYING

Planning

WEATHER

WEATHER DOWN UNDER
Australia is in the southern hemisphere, so its seasons are the opposite to those in Europe and North America. Summer is from December to March, and winter, which in most places is mild rather than cold, lasts from June to September.

Northern Australia has a tropical climate while southern Australia is temperate. In the tropical regions high humidity is confined to relatively few areas. The country as a whole does not suffer extremes of cold, most snow falling in the ski fields in the southeast and in Tasmania. Overall the climate is well suited to outdoor activities for most of the year.

New South Wales, ACT
The climate of New South Wales is temperate, with warm or hot summers and mild for the rest of the year. It is seldom cold, especially by the coast, and extreme weather is rare. Rainfall is generally moderate.

The Canberra region, in the south, is sunny for most of the year. Summer is hot and dry, autumn mild, and winter is cold with occasional snow.

Victoria
Victoria has four distinct seasons: sunny, but changeable, hot summers; a colourful autumn

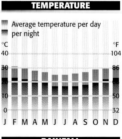

Broadbrimmed hats protect you from the rain as well as the sun

South Australia
One of the driest regions of Australia, the state enjoys mild winters and hot to very hot summers. Some rain falls in the summer, but frost has never been recorded in Adelaide.

Northern Territory
The northern part of the Territory (Top End) is a tropical region, with two seasons. The wet (summer) season can have heavy rainstorms, especially around the coast, with some flooding, while the dry (winter) season is hot. The southern part of the state, however, is desert, with little rain. Days are hot and sunny—over 40°C (104°F) in the summer—but the nights are cold.

Western Australia
Accounting for around one-third of the total landmass of the country, Western Australia has a number of climatic zones. The north suffers heavy rains in the wet (summer) season; the interior is drier and hotter; and the southwest has a more temperate climate, with occasional snow on the Stirling Range.

Tasmania
The island has a temperate climate. At sea level, summers

with moderate temperatures; cold winters with snow in the Great Dividing Range ski fields; and fresh, bright spring days.

Queensland
Tropical Queensland has very hot sun, even during the winter, and high humidity on the coast; rain is rare during this period. Monsoonal rains fall in summer (Dec–Feb), particularly in the north, and these can be accompanied by very high winds; this period is the cyclone season in north Queensland.

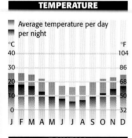

Sydney
TEMPERATURE

■ Average temperature per day
■ per night

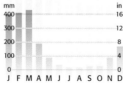

Cairns
TEMPERATURE

■ Average temperature per day
■ per night

Alice Springs
TEMPERATURE

■ Average temperature per day
■ per night

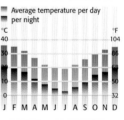

RAINFALL

Average rainfall

RAINFALL

Average rainfall

RAINFALL

Average rainfall

The Henley-on-Todd regatta is contested on the dry river bed

are mild, and winters generally cool to mild. Mountainous areas have cold winters, and snow may fall even in summer.

EXTREME WEATHER

● The tropical north experiences intense storms called tropical cyclones between about December and February. Damage by cyclones can be very severe. Less destructive are tornadoes, which occur in southwest Australia along the coastal strip from Perth to Cape Leeuwin.
● Snow falls mainly in the southeast of Australia on the Snowy Mountains and northern tablelands of New South Wales, Victoria and, rarely, in parts of Queensland. Tasmania also has snow in the summer on areas over 1,400m (4,500ft).
● The Australian sun can be dangerous, causing skin damage and eventually skin cancer. Temperatures, particularly in the desert areas, can reach 40°C (104°F) or more. In high summer, burning can happen in about 10 minutes; indeed, sunburn can occur even in overcast conditions.
● El Nino is a warm ocean current that produces changes in climate patterns through the Pacific. In Australia it creates an increased probability of drier and more cloudy conditions, particularly in the east.

WEATHER INFORMATION

Newspapers, radio and television all carry forecasts. Several websites provide information, as

Skiing at Perisher Blue in the Snowy Mountains

Perth

TEMPERATURE

■ Average temperature per day
■ per night

°C		°F
40		104
30		86
20		68
10		50
0		32
	J F M A M J J A S O N D	

RAINFALL

Average rainfall

mm		in
400		16
300		12
200		8
100		4
0		0
	J F M A M J J A S O N D	

TIME DIFFERENCES				
	GMT 12am	WST	CST	EST
Western Standard Time	8pm	0	+1.30	+2
Central Standard Time	9.30pm	+1.30	0	+0.30
Eastern Standard Time	10pm	+2	+0.30	0
San Francisco	4am	+16	+17.30	+18
Chicago	6am	+14	+15.30	+16
New York	7am	+13	+14.30	+15
London	12am	+8	+9.30	+10
Paris	1pm	+7	+8.30	+9
Johannesburg	2pm	+6	+7.30	+8
Tokyo	9pm	-1	-0.30	+1
Berlin	1pm	+7	+8.30	+10

well as background about climate and weather trends in general.
- www.bom.gov.au—the national Bureau of Meteorology has information down to local level and specialized forecasts.
- www.weatherchannel.com—this American site has great detail on Australian weather, including useful 10-day forecasts.
- www.meto.gov.uk—this British site has comprehensive information about the Australian climate and 5-day forecasts.
- www.wunderground.com—hundreds of Australian towns are on this site, with daily forecasts.

TIME ZONES
Australia is covered by 3 time zones:

Eastern Standard Time
New South Wales
Queensland
Tasmania
Victoria

Central Standard Time
Northern Territory
South Australia

Western Standard Time
Western Australia

SUMMER DAYLIGHT SAVING		
	Hour forward	**Hour back**
NSW	Oct last Sun	Mar last Sun
ACT	Oct last Sun	Mar last Sun
Vic	Oct last Sun	Mar last Sun
Qld	no change	no change
NT	no change	no change
SA	Oct last Sun	Mar last Sun
WA	no change	no change
Tas	Oct first Sun	Mar last Sun

Most states observe daylight saving in the summer, advancing clocks by one hour at the start and putting them back one hour at the end.

DOCUMENTATION

PASSPORTS AND TOURIST VISAS

All visitors to Australia must carry a valid passport and visa. Ensure next of kin details are written in the back of your passport. Tourist visas are free of charge and for many countries are now available in an electronic format—an ETA (Electronic Travel Authority). These can be obtained from travel agents or via the web from www.immi.gov.au and they generally last for three months within the year after the visa is issued. They should be applied for at least two months before travelling; they cannot be arranged at Australian airports.

If you want to stay for more than three months then apply for a longer term visa from the local Australian Embassy or High Commission. If your visit to Australia is unexpectedly extended you must apply for a further visa at an Australian visa office before your ETA expires.

WORKING VISAS

Applicants must be aged 18 to 30, single or married without dependent children. You have to show that any work is to support yourself while on holiday. You must also have a return ticket, or sufficient funds for a return fare and the first part of your stay, and show that you intend to leave Australia at the end of the authorized stay. The maximum stay is 12 months from the date of initial entry to Australia, whether or not you spend the whole period in Australia. In addition you cannot work any

longer than three months with one employer. A charge applies to the visa application.

For more information see www.immi.gov.au.

If you intend to earn a salary in Australia you will need a tax file number. In order to get this you must open an account with an Australian bank. To open a bank account you need your passport, plus additional identification such as a driving licence.

DRIVING LICENCE

If you plan to drive a car in Australia you will need to take your driving licence. An International Driving Permit (IDP) is not essential but in some states it can be useful; apply via your motoring organization.

CUSTOMS REGULATIONS

Australia has laws on the importation of illegal drugs, firearms, weapons, ammunition, protected wildlife and products

DUTY-FREE GOODS
You can bring the following into Australia:
A$400 of goods (including gifts) excluding tobacco or alcohol (A$200 for travellers under 18)
1.125 litres alcohol
250 cigarettes, or 250 grams of cigars or tobacco
Personal items and also goods owned for at least a year

made from them, and some medicinal products, including performance enhancing drugs. You must declare if you are carrying medication: It is wise to take a letter or a prescription from your doctor describing the medication and your medical condition. Food items, particularly fruit and meat, cannot be taken into the country and will be confiscated on arrival. Some particular foodstuffs, including fruit and honey, cannot be taken across some state borders.

TOURIST REFUND SCHEME (TRS)

It is possible to claim a refund of the Goods and Services Tax (GST) and Wine Equalisation Tax (WET) paid on goods bought in Australia. The refund only applies to goods carried as hand luggage or worn when you leave the country. The refund is paid on goods costing A$300 or more, bought from the same store, no more than 30 days before you leave. You may buy goods from several stores, provided each store's tax invoice totals at least A$300 (GST inclusive).

When leaving Australia through an international airport, look for the TRS booth in the departures area after you have passed through passport control. The booths are also at cruise liner terminals. You must produce the relevant goods (to prove you are taking them out of the country), the tax invoice from the retailer, and your passport and international boarding pass. You will then be paid the refund.

PLANNING

Before you leave, ensure that someone at home has your detailed itinerary. It may also be useful to establish an email account that you can access through the Internet anywhere. And re-confirm your flights just in case they are oversubscribed. Make a list of the following before you leave:

● Passport number and date issued.
● Serial numbers of tickets.
● Credit card numbers and emergency number.
● Serial number of travel insurance policy and emergency contact number.
● Driving licence number.
● Serial numbers of traveller's cheques.
● Serial numbers of valuables.
● Copies of prescriptions for spectacles/contact lenses.

Give one copy to someone you can reach in an emergency, and keep one yourself separate from your luggage. In addition, it is worth taking a photocopy of your passport, travel insurance, tickets and other important documents.

WHAT TO WEAR

Most people in Australia dress casually, wearing lighter clothing in the summer months of December, January and February, and heavier clothing in the winter months of June, July and August. In the more northern latitudes most days are warm. Australians may dress up to go to the opera, or for formal occasions, but the best guide is to wear whatever feels comfortable, although most establishments require reasonable footwear. Remember that it gets very cold at night in the desert areas.

The selection of clothes depends on the type of holiday you are planning. In any event, take a good sun hat with a deep brim and sunglasses. Sunscreen is a must. If you will be walking take good boots, a torch and a compass. It may also be useful to take a strong day bag.

CLOTHING SIZES

See www.bsi-global.com for BS EN 13402-3; final European standard expected 2004.

Australia	UK	USA	
90	36	36	SUITS
96	38	38	
102	40	40	
108	42	42	
114	44	44	
120	46	46	
7	6	8	SHOES
8	7	8.5	
9	8	9.5	
10	9	10.5	
11	10	11.5	
12	11	12	
37	14.5	14.5	SHIRTS
38	15	15	
39/40	15.5	15.5	
41	16	16	
42	16.5	16.5	
43	17	17	
8	8	6	DRESSES
10	10	8	
12	12	10	
14	14	12	
16	16	14	
18	18	16	
20	20	18	
6	4.5	6	SHOES
6.5	5	6.5	
7	5.5	7	
7.5	6	7.5	
8	6.5	8	
8.5	7	8.5	
9	7.5	9	

CONVERSION CHART

From	To	Multiply by
Inches	Centimetres	2.54
Centimetres	Inches	0.3937
Feet	Metres	0.3048
Metres	Feet	3.2810
Yards	Metres	0.9144
Metres	Yards	1.0940
Miles	Kilometres	1.6090
Kilometres	Miles	0.6214
Acres	Hectares	0.4047
Hectares	Acres	2.4710
Gallons	Litres	4.5460
Litres	Gallons	0.2200
Ounces	Grams	28.35
Grams	Ounces	0.0353
Pounds	Grams	453.6
Grams	Pounds	0.0022
Pounds	Kilograms	0.4536
Kilograms	Pounds	2.205
Tons	Tonnes	1.0160
Tonnes	Tons	0.9842

CLOTHING SIZES

NB: British clothes sizes will start to be shown in metric units from 2004.

METRIC CONVERSIONS

Australia uses the metric system, and the basic conversions are as in the table above.

ELECTRICAL DEVICES

Australian electricity is generally 240V as in Britain, though the three flat-pin plug sockets are of a different form. North America uses 110V, so it will be necessary to use a voltage plug adapter, or a separate power cord with an Australian plug.

Be careful if you are taking a DVD player. A DVD made for one zone is not necessarily compatible with a DVD player in any other zone. The USA is zone 1, Australia is zone 4, and Europe is a different zone.

TRAVEL INSURANCE

Travel insurance is important and you should look for a policy that covers all the activities you expect to enjoy in Australia.

You should also look for good medical cover as not all aspects of medical care are covered by Reciprocal Health Agreements (see pages 298–299).

Most Australians dress casually but a visit to the races can be an occasion to dress formally

PLANNING

HEALTH

USEFUL WEBSITES

www.fco.gov.uk
The British Foreign and Commonwealth Office site includes health advice for visitors to Australia.

www.who.int
The World Health Organisation provides comprehensive health advice for all nationalities.

www.cdc.gov
Health advice for visitors from the US.

www.masta.org
Information on travel clinics in Britain and their locations.

MEDICAL ADVICE

You should see your doctor 4 to 6 weeks before you go to ensure you have any necessary vaccinations. Alternatively you could visit a specialist Travel Clinic. These clinics provide professional advice about all travel health recommendations. It is a good idea to know your blood group before you travel, as this will save time in case of an emergency.

For your own safety, it is recommended that your polio and tetanus inoculations are up to date; if they are more than 10 years old, get a booster injection. Hepatitis A and typhoid inoculations are not absolutely necessary, but it is wise to have them, particularly if you are also visiting Asian countries. Yellow Fever vaccination certificates are required only if you have visited a country where it is endemic before arriving in Australia.

AVOIDING JET LAG

- On the flight, drink sufficient fluid to prevent dehydration.
- If you want to sleep during the flight, only do so if it coincides with night time at your destination.
- When you arrive, try to be active in bright light between noon and 6pm and relax between 4am and 10am local time. On the second day get out between 10am and 4pm and relax between 2am and 8am. On the third day get out between 8am and 2pm and relax between midnight and 7am.

HEALTHY FLYING

- Long-haul flights can have consequences for your health. The most widely publicized concern is Deep Vein Thrombosis (DVT). DVT is the forming of a blood clot in the body's deep veins, particularly in the legs. The clot can move around the bloodstream and could be fatal.
- Those most at risk include the elderly, pregnant women and those using the contraceptive pill, smokers and the overweight. If you are at increased risk of DVT, see your doctor before departing. Flying increases the likelihood of DVT because passengers are often seated in a cramped position for long periods of time and may become dehydrated.
- Other health hazards for flyers are airborne diseases and bugs spread by the plane's air-conditioning system. These are largely unavoidable, but if you have a serious medical condition seek advice from a doctor before you go.

To minimize risk:
- drink water (not alcohol)
- don't stay immobile for hours at a time
- stretch and exercise your legs periodically (see diagrams below)
- wear elastic flight socks that support veins and reduce the chances of a clot forming
- a small dose of aspirin may be recommended; this thins the blood before the flight.

EXERCISES

1 ANKLE ROTATIONS   **2 CALF STRETCHES**   **3 KNEE LIFTS**

Lift feet off the floor. Draw a circle with the toes, moving one foot clockwise and the other counterclockwise

Start with heel on the floor and point foot upward as high as you can. Then lift heels high keeping balls of feet on the floor

Lift leg with knee bent while contracting your thigh muscle. Then straighten leg pressing foot flat to the floor

HEALTH CARE IN AUSTRALIA

Australia's health-care system is called Medicare and includes both public and private hospitals. The costs of health care are comparable with other developed countries. You should obtain adequate health insurance to cover the costs of any unexpected treatment during a visit to Australia.

Australia has Reciprocal Health Agreements with eight countries, but the benefits vary.

These agreements do not cover overseas students studying in Australia, who need to take out Overseas Student Health Cover. See www.health.gov.au/private-health/providers/oscover.htm.

The Reciprocal Health Agreements do not cover dental treatment, private medical care, ambulance cover, treatment that is not immediately necessary, medical evacuation to your home country, or funeral expenses; additional health

PLANNING

RECIPROCAL HEALTH AGREEMENTS

Country	Public Hospital	Out of Hospital	MediSubsidized Medicine
Britain	yes	yes	yes
Finland	yes	yes	yes
Ireland	yes	yes	yes
Italy	6 months only	6 months only	6 months only
Malta	6 months only	6 months only	6 months only
Netherlands	yes	yes	yes
New Zealand	yes	no	yes
Sweden	yes	yes	yes

insurance should account for these risks.

If you require treatment, state that you wish to be treated as a Medicare public patient under a Reciprocal Health Agreement. Any Medicare office (tel 13 20 11 within Australia) will confirm what documentation is required.

PHARMACIES

Pharmacies (chemists) are widely distributed. The main chains are Amcal Chemists and Chemmart. They sell a similar range of over-the-counter medicines as British or American pharmacies, and they also dispense prescription medicines.

Local hotels and telephone directories usually have lists of chemists open outside normal trading hours.

SURGERIES

Surgeries are common in populated areas. If your accommodation cannot recommend one, ask at the local pharmacy or check a phone book.

In suburban areas surgeries are often found in shopping malls.

Most surgeries will expect payment at the time of treatment: keep the receipt for claiming insurance or, if you are eligible, Medicare.

DENTAL SURGERIES

Dentists are plentiful and the standard of treatment is high— as are the bills. In an emergency go to the casualty wing of a local hospital, or locate a dentist from the phone book. Medical insurance is essential.

EMERGENCY—CALL 000

You are likely to be billed for using an ambulance. Again, this should be refunded by your insurance company.

HEALTH RISKS IN AUSTRALIA

Road Accidents

Vehicle accidents form the greatest risk overall, in Australia as in other countries. Accidents on holiday are often more complicated to deal with, so it is important to follow the obvious safety rules, such as wearing a seat belt, keeping to the speed limit, wearing a crash helmet on a scooter or motorbike, and not drinking and driving.

Sun Protection

Take care in the sun when visiting any part of Australia— sunburn or even sunstroke can ruin your holiday. Follow the advice of the Slip, Slop, Slap campaign:
● Slip on a shirt.
● Slop on some sunscreen.
● Slap on a hat.
Sunscreen creams are inexpensive in Australia. It is advisable to use high-factor sunscreen on all exposed skin (SPF 30+)—at least factor 15 for adults and total blockout for children. In hot sun you should also wear loose clothing, avoid vigorous exercise, and drink plenty of water. If walking in the heat, try to drink at least 1 litre (1.76 pints) of water per hour. Wear good-quality

sunglasses in strong sunshine to protect your eyes.

Diarrhoea

The most common travel illness is diarrhoea, caught from contaminated food or water. Food and water in populated areas should be safe—check with locals about water quality in outback areas. There are several good antibiotics available to take with you, and it is also important to ensure that you drink plenty of fluids with the treatment.

Mosquito-borne Diseases

Malaria is very rare in Australia, but international travel increases the risks of it spreading. There are other mosquito-borne diseases to beware of, such as Ross River fever and Murray River encephalitis. The main risk, however, is dengue fever, which can be caught in northern Queensland and the Torres Strait Islands. It is an unpleasant, flu-like illness that can last at least a week. The mosquitoes that carry this virus bite during the day. Protection involves avoiding swampy, stagnant water; watching for insects around dusk; using insect repellent; and wearing long-sleeved shirts and long trousers in areas where dengue fever is a risk.

Poisonous Creatures

Australia is home to a good number of poisonous snakes and other venomous creatures. Treat all snakes with caution. Generally, snakes will not attack you unless you threaten them. They are rarely seen in populated areas. The best advice is to look where you are walking; walk noisily so they can feel you coming; step on to fallen tree trunks rather than stepping over them; wear long trousers and shoes when walking through grass or bush; and do not put your hands into dark crevices. Carry a crepe bandage and a mobile phone, so that if you or a companion is bitten, you can use the bandage to slow the spread of the venom while help is summoned.

Sydney funnel web spiders found on the New

A wide-brimmed hat keeps the sun off and makes you feel cooler: in extreme heat try wetting your hat with water

South Wales coastline also have a poisonous bite, and it is important to get rapid treatment with anti-venom.

Some other poisonous creatures live in the sea. Round much of the coast of Australia jellyfish can give a very painful sting. In the tropics, you will see signs warning of the box jellyfish for several months of the year. Take heed of the signs as this species has tentacles many metres long and the sting can be fatal. There are also some brightly coloured sea snakes that are not usually aggressive, but which have a deadly venom.

Dangerous Animals
Sharks swim off the coasts of Australia but they rarely attack swimmers. Where there is particular risk, warning notices are posted on the beaches. In northern areas, saltwater crocodiles are also dangerous and occasionally attack people. They move very quickly, so make sure you know where they are likely to be found. The crocodiles frequent marine estuaries, rivers and lagoons, and are most dangerous during the breeding season (September to April). There may be warning notices, but it is always wise to keep away from places where they may lurk, including beach areas.

FLYING DOCTOR
The Royal Flying Doctor Service is a charitable service that provides medical emergency and primary health care services, together with communication and

Never disregard a warning sign

education assistance, to people who live, work and travel in regional and remote Australia. They have 12 base stations, which it is possible to visit, and they offer practical advice to those planning a trip to the outback. In particular they advise taking a high frequency radio compatible with the Flying Doctor service; see www.rfds.org.au.

MONEY

CHANGING MONEY
It is easy to change money in Australia. Banks and exchange bureaus often charge a commission, but the rates will be better than in airports, hotels and the smaller money exchange shops. It is sensible to make sure you have some Australian currency before arriving.

Traveller's cheques may seem unnecessary in the age of credit cards, but their benefit is that they can be refunded if they are lost or stolen (provided you have kept a note of the serial numbers). Exchange rates for traveller's cheques can be better than for foreign cash, and it may be even more cost effective to take them in Australian denominations. Note that identification—usually your passport—may be required when exchanging traveller's cheques or cash.

CREDIT CARDS
MasterCard and Visa are the most useful cards in Australia, followed by Bankcard (issued by

LOST/STOLEN CREDIT CARDS

American Express
1300 132 639
www.americanexpress.com

Diners Club
1800 360 060
www.dinersclub.com

Mastercard
1800 120 113
www.mastercard.com

Visa
1800 450 346
www.visa.com

banks in Australia), American Express and Diners Club. Should you lose your card, contact the issuer listed in the table above.

CASH MACHINES
If the bank issuing your credit or debit card is part of the Plus, Cirrus or Visa networks, there will be plenty of ATMs (Automatic Teller Machines) for withdrawing money. But always check with your bank to confirm you can use your card in Australia: It may be necessary to change your PIN or even have a new card issued.

EFTPOS
Most Australian shops, hotels, restaurants and petrol stations use EFTPOS (Electronic Funds Transfer at Point of Sale) at their cash tills, which accept Australian credit or debit cards. These cards can also be used to withdraw cash. If you intend to stay in Australia for a length of time it would be worthwhile opening an Australian bank account, which is necessary to access EFTPOS. In remote country areas, however, EFTPOS is less common.

TIPPING
In general, Australians do not tip excessively. In an expensive restaurant 10 per cent is acceptable, but a tip is not expected in pubs, bars or cafés. In taxis it is usual to round up the

PLANNING

The Australian unit of currency is the dollar; 100 cents equal one dollar.

Notes are in denominations of A$100, A$50, A$20, A$10 and A$5. Coins are A$2, A$1, 50¢, 20¢, 10¢ and 5¢ denominations. Note that because there are no 1- or 2-cent coins, shops round amounts up or down when they give you change.

fare, and hotel porters might expect A$1–A$2 per bag.

No offence will be taken if you do not tip, and only tip if you have been given good service.

DISCOUNT CARDS
Student cards allow reduced price admission to museums and other attractions, and often provide discounts on transport.

Most useful is the International Student Exchange card (ISE; www.isecard.com), but other options are the International Student, Youth and Identity cards that can be used by students and teachers in full-time education and by anyone under 26.

The Hostelling International Membership Card (www.hostel-booking.com) is a good option for backpackers and travellers on a budget, and there are other cards available from hostels.

Particularly useful is the VIP Card (www.backpackers.com.au) that not only provides hundreds of discounts, but also functions as a rechargeable phonecard.

The Tourist Australia Travel Card (www.touristaustralia.com.au) provides discounts in exchange for a year's membership.

Pensioners may be able to obtain discounts by showing their card from home, but most of these discounts are limited to Australian citizens.

If travelling by car you can buy a pass to all the charging national parks in a state, which may give a considerable saving on paying the full price each time. You must buy a pass for each state, so you need to plan your itinerary in order to calculate the best value. See the national park websites on page 308.

BANKS
● Most banks open Mon–Fri 9.30–4, until 4.30 Fri. Some banks open Sat morning.
● There are around 50 banks in Australia, of which 14 are domestically owned.

The major banks are given in the table below.

10 EVERYDAY ITEMS AND HOW MUCH THEY COST	
Takeaway sandwich	A$3.00
Bottle of water (1 litre)	A$2.50
Cup of tea or coffee	A$2.40
Glass of beer (1 litre)	A$2.50
Glass of wine	A$4.50
Daily newspaper	A$1.20
Camera film (36)	A$5.00
Cigarettes (20 pack)	A$8.00
Petrol/gas (1 litre)	A$0.95
Can of Coke	A$2.00

EXCHANGE RATES	
At time of publication	
US $10	A$15.18
Canada $10	A$10.99
UK £10	A$24.36
New Zealand $10	A$8.92
Euro €10	A$17.21
See www.xe.net for the latest rates.	

BANKS		
Name	**Telephone**	**Website**
Commonwealth Bank	Tel 13 22 21	www.commbank.com.au
National Bank	Tel 13 22 65	www.national.com.au
ANZ Bank	Tel 13 13 14	www.anz.com
Westpac Bank	Tel 13 20 32	www.westpac.com.au

PLANNING

COMMUNICATION

TELEPHONES

Calls to Australia
● The code for calling Australia is 61. However, the dial code depends on the country you are calling from. So, to call Australia from these countries, dial:

Canada	011-61
New Zealand	00-61
United Kingdom	00-61
USA	011-61

This is followed by the state code omitting the 0, then the subscriber number.

Calls in Australia
● There are two main telephone operators in Australia, Telstra (www.telstra.com) and Optus (www.optus.com.au). For calls within Australia it is best to use a local phonecard, available from post offices and newsagents. The minimum charge for a local call is 40 cents. Phonecards are also available for international calls.

MOBILE PHONES
● Australia uses the same Global System for Mobile (GSM) as the rest of the world (except for North America and Japan) at 900MHz and 1800MHz. However, some American GSM phones designed for 1900MHz can also handle standard GSM. CDMA (Code Division Multiple Access) phones are more likely to be compatible from one country to another; but check in advance. Even if your phone is compatible, check the recharger to make sure that it too will work in Australia.
● Coverage is good in most urban areas but can be poor or non-existent in remote areas. If you plan to travel away from the major population centres or off the main highways, you should check the network coverage maps provided by Telstra: See www.telstra.com. The Telstra website also has information about the various types of mobile phone.
● A mobile phone is an expensive means to phone home.

E-MAIL
● E-mail is an excellent way to contact people at home and other travellers abroad. A number of Internet e-mail accounts (such as www.hotmail.com) can be

You can also find telephone numbers using the White Pages and Yellow Pages websites (www.whitepages.com.au; www.yellowpages.com.au).

Public telephones are still widely available in populated areas

accessed from any terminal. These accounts can get clogged up with junk mail. If you sign up with an Australian ISP provider, make sure that calls are charged at the local rate.
● www.netcafeguide.com has a large listing of Internet cafés. The helpful www.yellowpages.com.au is another good search tool. Minimum café charges vary from A$2 to A$12 depending where you are.
● Public libraries provide free Internet links but these are often intended for research, although some libraries have computers

for accessing e-mails. Many hostels have Internet links.
● WiFi HotSpots also provide access to Internet e-mail accounts and the Internet itself. The HotSpots are often located in cafés, hotels, transportation terminals and stores. You use your own WiFi enabled laptop or PDA (personal digital assistant)—most recent equipment is enabled—via a WiFi provider. For worldwide HotSpots and providers see www.wifi411.com or the websites of the major telecomms companies.
● If you are taking a laptop with you there are a number of things to check. You should use a global PC card modem, or buy a local PC card modem in Australia. RJ-45 and Telstra EX1-160 four-pin telephone plugs are used. An Australian plug adapter and an AC adapter will also be needed. Remember that laptops are easily stolen, so take care.

MAIL
● Post offices open Mon–Fri 9–5; some also open Sat 9–12.
● Stamps can be bought from post offices or post office agencies in newsagents, or from Australia Post shops.
● Major post offices will hold mail for visitors by arrangement, but it will be necessary to provide identification before it can be collected.

POSTAGE RATES OUTSIDE AUSTRALIA:		
Postcards and greetings cards		A$1
Air mail letters under 50 grams	from:	A$1.65
Parcels up to 250 grams	air mail:	A$8
	sea mail:	A$5.50

See Australia Post www.auspost.com.au.

FINDING HELP

Mounted police are usually only found in city centres

LOST PROPERTY
● Leave photocopies of your travel documentation and tickets with relatives at home. This will help if replacements are needed. You can also take another set of photocopies with you.
● Rather than take risks, leave valuable belongings in a secure place, such as a hotel safe.
● For items lost in transit, contact the transportation operator.
● Contact the local police station for items lost in Australia.
● The website noticeboard www.internetlostandfound.com.au is a useful way to advertise lost goods or search for found items. In small towns, stores and supermarkets usually have a community noticeboard where signs can be posted for free.

MONEY PROBLEMS
Relatives and friends can send you extra money in an emergency. Western Union Money Transfer can quickly supply funds across a global network to the nearest bank; www.westernunion.com.

CONSULATES
In an emergency the consul can help in a number of ways, but not necessarily financial. Work permits *cannot* be arranged through the consul.
● Accidents—relatives and friends can be contacted, and advice given on procedures for repatriation if necessary.
● Financial—although they will advise on how to transfer funds, they will not pay your outstanding bills. In emergencies they may give a limited loan for repatriation.
● Legal—legal advice *cannot* be provided, but they can supply a list of local lawyers.
● Medical—a list of local doctors can be supplied, but they cannot help to get improved medical care, or pay medical bills.
● Passports—they can issue emergency passports.

THE LAW
Always avoid trouble as the police can be very strict, especially for drugs offences. Various states, especially Victoria, are increasingly strict about speeding and drink-driving. Stick to the limits. If you are stopped or arrested, the following advice may be useful.
● Fines for minor offences are paid by post or to the clerk of the court. You will not be asked to pay the police officer, and do not offer to do so under any circumstance.
● If you are arrested, give your name and address, but otherwise say nothing before contacting your consul or a lawyer.
● Remain calm and polite—do not become abusive.
● Your rights will be explained to you by the police. It is your right to contact your consul.
● You will be allowed to make one telephone call; contact a relative or friend who can organize assistance.
● You can be held for a reasonable time (usually 4 hours) before you must be charged or released.

CONSULATES AND EMBASSIES			
Country	**Website**	**Address**	**Telephone**
Canada	www.dfait-maeci.qc.ca/australia	Level 5, 111 Harrington Street, Sydney NSW 2000	02 9364 3000
		123 Camberwell Road, Hawthorn East VIC 3123	03 9811 9999
		267 St. George's Terrace, Perth WA	08 9322 7930
New Zealand	www.nzembassy.com/australia	Commonwealth Avenue, Canberra ACT 2600	02 6270 4211
		Level 10, 55 Hunter Street, Sydney NSW 2000	02 8256 2000
South Africa	www.rsa.emb.gov.au	State Circle, Yarralumla, ACT 2601	02 6273 2424
United Kingdom	www.uk.emb.gov.au	39 Brindabella Circuit, Canberra Airport ACT 2601	02 9520 2105
		1 Macquarrie Place, Sydney NSW 2000	02 9247 7521
		90 Collins Street, Melbourne VIC 3000	03 9652 1600
		77 St. George's Terrace, Perth WA 6000	08 9224 4700
USA	www.usembassy-australia.gov	Moonah Place, Yarralumla, ACT 2601	02 6214 5600
		19–29 Martin Place, Sydney NSW 2000	02 9373 9200
		553 St. Kilda Road, Melbourne VIC 3000	03 9526 5900
		16 St. George's Terrace, Perth WA 6000	08 9231 9400

PLANNING

COMFORT AND SAFETY

Feeling comfortable and secure on holiday is more often a matter of taking sensible precautions.

● Keep money and other valuables secure from pickpockets, or alternatively locked in a safe.

● The most serious danger on holiday is traffic accidents, although focus on road safety has cut Australia's road toll over the years. Take as much or more care than you do at home; don't drink and drive; and keep in mind the road conditions in Australia. Roads in the outback are often just tracks, so you will often need to use a 4-wheel drive if you plan to travel there. Try not to drive outside of populated areas at night, dawn or dusk as many animals are attracted to headlamps—and hitting a kangaroo, wombat or other large animal can seriously damage your vehicle. Road trains are another hazard—keep well out of their way, and allow at least 1km (0.6 mile) to overtake them.

● Australia is home to a number of poisonous and dangerous creatures. So long as you are aware of the risks (see pages 299–300) and you don't touch or threaten them, you should not be harmed.

LOOKING AFTER CHILDREN

Australia has plenty of attractions for children to enjoy, but perhaps most of all they will relish the open-air life. There are many family-oriented hotels, motels, camping parks and restaurants that provide special arrangements and meals. Baby-changing facilities are available in some public toilets. There are concessions for children on buses, trains and at most tourist attractions.

All the advice about living in a hot climate applies especially to children. In particular, protect them from the sun.

● Remember Slip, Slop, Slap: Slip on a shirt, Slop on some sunscreen and Slap on a hat.

● Ensure children drink plenty of water, and keep them within view when near the sea, rivers, lakes and swimming pools.

● Teach your children to be careful about spiders, jellyfish, snakes, bees and wasps, ants, cane toads and dingoes. Apart from remote areas in general, dangerous creatures lurk around rock pools or ponds.

● Kangaroos will defend if cornered, but may be attracted to food at barbecue or picnic areas, and occasionally become nosey.

● Any toys left outside overnight must be thoroughly checked in the morning for spiders or other dangerous creatures.

BEACH SAFETY

One of the great attractions of Australia is the sunny weather, but treat the sun with respect, particularly on the beach.

● Wear sunscreen, sun hat, shirt and sunglasses.

● Swim or surf only at places patrolled by lifeguards, or check with locals first.

● Swim only between the yellow and red flags.

● Don't swim after a meal or under the influence of alcohol or drugs.

● If you get into trouble, don't struggle against the current—raise an arm and wait for help or swim parallel to the beach for a distance. If you are unsure whether sea conditions are safe, then ask a lifeguard.

OUTBACK SAFETY

It is undeniably an exciting holiday adventure to explore the Australian outback. But all trips must be planned carefully.

● Wear appropriate clothing and walking shoes; take some warm clothes as it can get cold at night.

● Take a hat, sunscreen and insect repellent.

● Take plenty of water—1 litre (1.75 pints) per hour if walking—stored in small containers rather than one large one.

● Do not pack too much on your vehicle's roof rack.

● Pack a first-aid kit.

● Carry a high-frequency radio compatible with the Flying Doctor Service. Mobile phones and CB radios will often not work in remote areas.

● Plan your route carefully and tell others where you are going.

● If you break down, you must stay with the car—it is far easier for rescuers to see a car than a person. Never try to walk out of a remote area. Set up some type of shelter and remain in the shade as motionless as possible.

PUBLIC TOILETS

Public toilets are common in Australian cities and are clearly marked. Remote areas are also well served with toilet facilities, but do check for wildlife. The website www.toiletmap.gov.au has a list and map of 13,000 public toilets, with access details for people with disabilities.

WOMEN ON HOLIDAY

Generally, Australia is a safe place for female travellers. It is always worthwhile, however, taking standard precautions.

● Avoid walking alone late at night in dark streets in either cities or rural areas.

● Be careful if staying or drinking by yourself in pubs.

● Do not hitch-hike alone.

● If you are going out late, arrange a lift or taxi home. Australia only has reputable, clearly marked, licensed taxis.

● If you are driving alone, carry a mobile (cell) phone. Lock the car doors when stationary, particularly at night. And do not pick up hitch-hikers.

● Sit near the driver or conductor on buses, and avoid empty carriages on trains.

Children are at particular risk from the sun as their skin is more sensitive

TOURIST INFORMATION

There are tourist information centres in most towns and resorts. The main state offices and those for the larger and more popular places are given here.

Australian Capital Territory
Canberra Visitors Information Centre
✉ 330 Northbourne Avenue, Canberra ACT 2601
☎ 02 6205 0044
www.canberratourism.com.au
🕑 Mon–Sat 9–5

New South Wales
Tourism New South Wales
✉ GPO Box 7050, Sydney NSW 2001
☎ 02 9931 1111
www.tourism.nsw.gov.au

New South Wales Travel Centre
✉ International Terminal, Sydney Airport NSW 2020
☎ 02 9667 6050

Sydney Visitors Centre
✉ 106 George Street, The Rocks, Sydney NSW 2000
☎ 1300 361 967
www.sydneyvisitorcentre.com

Blue Mountains Heritage Centre
✉ Govetts Leap Road, Blackheath NSW 2785
☎ 02 4787 8877

Byron Bay Visitor Centre
✉ The Old Station Master's Cottage, 80 Jonson Street, Byron Bay NSW 2481
☎ 02 6680 9279

Port Macquarie Visitor Information Centre
✉ Clarence Street, Port Macquarie NSW 2444
☎ 02 6581 8000
www.portmacquarieinfo.com.au

Victoria
Information Victoria
✉ 356 Collins Street, Melbourne VIC 3000
☎ 1300 366 356
www.vic.gov.au

Tourism Victoria
✉ Melbourne Town Hall, Swanston Street, Melbourne VIC 3000
☎ 13 28 42
www.visitvictoria.com

Melbourne Visitors Centre
✉ Federation Square, Melbourne VIC 3000
☎ 03 9658 9658
www.melbourne.vic.gov.au

Great Ocean Road
✉ M1 north of Geelong
☎ 1800 620 888
www.greatoceanrd.org.au

Queensland
Tourism Queensland
✉ GPO Box 328, Brisbane QLD 4000
☎ 07 3535 3535
www.tq.com.au

Queen Street Mall Visitors Information Centre
✉ Queen Street, Brisbane QLD 4000
☎ 07 3006 6290
www.brisbanetourism.com au

Cairns–Visitor Information
✉ 5 The Esplanade, Cairns QLD 4870
☎ 07 4051 3588
www.tnq.org.au

Northern Territory
NT Tourism Commission
✉ 43 Mitchell Street, Darwin NT 0801
☎ 08 8999 3900
www.nttc.com.au

NT Tourism Commission
✉ 67 North Stuart Highway, Alice Springs NT 0871
☎ 08 8951 8555
www.nttc.com.au

Tourism Top End
✉ Knuckey Street, Darwin NT 0800
☎ 08 8981 4300

Central Australian Tourism Industry Association
✉ Gregory Terrace, Alice Springs NT 0870
☎ 08 8952 5199
www.catia.asn.au

Uluṟu-Kata Tjuṯa National Park Cultural Centre (Ayers Rock)
✉ Main road to Uluru NT 0872
☎ 08 8956 3138

South Australia
South Australian Tourism Commission
✉ 18 King William Street, Adelaide SA 5000
☎ 1300 655 276

South Australian Visitor and Travel Centre
✉ 18 King William Street, Adelaide SA 5000
☎ 1300 655 276
www.southaustralia.com

Kangaroo Island Visitor Information Centre
✉ PO Box 336VG, Penneshaw, Kangaroo Island SA 5222
☎ 08 8553 1185
www.tourkangarooisland.com.au

Western Australia
Western Australian Tourist Commission
✉ Level 6, 16 St. George's Terrace, Perth WA 6000
☎ 08 9220 1700
www.wa.gov.au

Western Australian Visitor Centre
✉ Albert Facey House, Forrest Place, Perth WA 6848
☎ 1300 361 351
www.westernaustralia.net

Albany Visitors Information Centre
✉ Old Railway Station, Princess Royal Drive, Albany WA 6332
☎ 08 9841 1088

Kalbarri Visitors Information Centre
✉ Grey Street, Kalbarri WA 6536
☎ 1800 639 468
www.kalbarriwa.info

Broome Visitors Information Centre
✉ Broome Highway, Broome WA 6725
☎ 08 9192 2222

Tasmania
Tourism Tasmania
✉ Level 2, 22 Elizabeth Street, Hobart TAS 7000
☎ 1800 806 846
www.discovertasmania.com

Tasmania Online
www.tas.gov.au

Information Officers in Surfers Paradise help visitors get the most from their holiday

PLANNING

The Pinnacles are limestone pillars in Nambung National Park

NATIONAL PARKS

New South Wales National Parks and Wildlife Service
☎ 02 9585 6444
www.npws.nsw.gov.au

Visitor Information Centre
✉ 110 George Street, The Rocks, Sydney NSW 2000
☎ 02 9247 5033

Parks Victoria
☎ 03 9637 8325
www.parkweb.vic.gov.au

Queensland Parks and Wildlife Service
☎ 07 3227 7111
www.epa.qld.gov.au

Northern Territory Parks and Wildlife Commission
☎ 08 8999 5511
www.nt.gov.au/paw

South Australian Department for Environment and Heritage
☎ 08 8204 1910
www.denr.sa.gov.au

Western Australian Department of Conservation and Land Management
☎ 08 9442 0300
www.calm.wa.gov.au

Tasmania Parks and Wildlife Service
☎ 03 6233 6191
www.dpiwe.tas.gov.au

NATIONAL TRUST

The Australian National Trust cares for some 300 historic properties.

Australian Council of National Trusts
✉ 14–71 Constitution Avenue, Campbell ACT 2601
PO Box 1002, Civic Square, Canberra ACT 2612
☎ 02 6247 6766
www.nationaltrust.org.au

ACT
☎ 02 6273 4744
www.act.nationaltrust.org.au

New South Wales
☎ 02 9258 0123
www.nsw.nationaltrust.org.au

Victoria
☎ 03 9654 4711
www.nattrust.com.au

Queensland
☎ 07 3229 1788
www.nationaltrustqld.org

Northern Territory
☎ 08 8981 2848
www.northernexposure.com.au/trust

South Australia
☎ 08 8212 1133
www.nationaltrustsa.org.au

Western Australia
☎ 08 9321 6088
www.ntwa.com.au

Tasmania
☎ 03 6344 6233
www.tased.edu.au/tasonline/nattrust

AUSTRALIAN TOURIST COMMISSION
The offices of the official Australian Tourist Commission are a useful stop for research and free information before you travel. Ask for a copy of the latest Travellers' Guide brochure.

UK
Gemini House, 10–18 Putney Hill, London SW15 6AA, tel 020 8780 2229

USA
2049 Century Park East, Suite 1920, Los Angeles CA 90067, tel 310 229 4870

Australia
Level 4, 80 William Street, Woolloomooloo, Sydney NSW 2011, tel 02 9360 1111
www.australia.com
www.aussie.net.au

NATIONAL PARKS
Contact the relevant state or territory authority for information on national parks or reserves within that state (see table). The federal government administers six national parks, including Kakadu and Uluṟu-Kata Tjuṯa.

NATIONAL TRUST
Members of the British National Trust have reciprocal membership of the Australian National Trust (see table).

PLACES OF WORSHIP
Local churches, mosques, temples and synagogues are listed in phone books, or see www.yellowpages.com.au, or contact the nearest tourist office.

St. Andrew's is the Catholic Cathedral in central Melbourne

PLANNING

Anglican Church
The General Secretary
PO Box Q190, QVB Post Office,
Sydney, NSW 2001
Tel 02 9265 1525
www.anglican.org.au
The dioceses and parishes of the
Anglican Church of Australia are
listed in the website.

Buddhism
www.buddhanet.net/
aus_buds.htm.
Australian organizations are listed
in the website.

Catholic Church
The Australian Catholic Bishops
Conference
PO Box 368, Canberra, ACT 2601

Tel 02 6201 9845
www.catholic.org.au
Contacts for dioceses are in the
website.

Hinduism
Hindu Council of Australia
17 The Crescent, Homebush,
NSW 2140
www.hinducouncil.com.au
The Hindu Council's website has
a list of temples.

Islam
Australian Federation of Islamic
Councils (AFIC)
932 Bourke Street, Sydney,
NSW 2000
Tel 02 9319 6733
Search for mosques, prayer

times and Islamic organizations
at www.islamicfinder.org.

Judaism
The Great Synagogue, Sydney
166 Castlereagh Street, Sydney,
NSW 2000; tel 02 9267 2477;
www.greatsynagogue.org.au
Search for synagogues at
www.synagogues.com, or
www.join.org.au.

Uniting Church
PO Box A2266, Sydney South,
NSW 1235; tel 02 8267 4204
www.nca.org.au
In Australia, the Congregational,
Methodist and Presbyterian
traditions combined to form the
Uniting Church in 1977.

OPENING HOURS

PUBLIC HOLIDAYS

Australia has 10 national public holidays. In addition, each state has some public holidays of its own, and some grant additional public holidays for major events.

January	1	New Year's Day
	26	Australia Day
March	1st Monday	Labour Day (WA)
	2nd Monday	Eight Hour Day (Tas)
		Labour Day (Vic)
	3rd Monday	Canberra Day (ACT)
March/April	Easter	(Good Friday to Easter Monday)
April	25	Anzac Day
May	1st Monday	May Day (NT)
		Labour Day (QLD)
	3rd Monday	Adelaide Cup Day (SA)
June	1st Monday	Foundation Day (WA)
	2nd Monday	Queen's Birthday (not WA)
August	1st Monday	Picnic Day (NT)
September	Last Monday	Queen's Birthday (WA)
October	1st Monday	Labour Day (NSW, ACT, SA)
November	1st Tuesday	Melbourne Cup Day (Melbourne)
December	25	Christmas Day
	26	Boxing Day

SCHOOL HOLIDAYS

Most Australian schools run on a four-term academic year, with the school year starting in February.

January	Much of the month in most states
March/April	Easter (one or two weeks)
June/July	Two weeks
December	Two weeks
	From mid-December

OPENING TIMES

There are no standard opening times across Australia. Places in large cities tend to have longer opening hours, and the smaller and more remote places are more limited. The times below give a general guide.

Business Hours	Mon–Fri 8.30–5
Banks	Mon–Thu 9–4, Friday 9–4.30
	Some banks Sat 9–12
Post Offices	Mon–Fri 9–5, (some) Sat 9–12
Stores	Mon–Fri 8.30–5, Sat 9–1
City stores late night	Thu or Fri until 9
	City stores may open all day Sat–Sun
Bigger supermarkets in large cities	Daily 24 hours
Tourist Information	Major cities daily 9–5. Smaller places may shut earlier and open fewer hours Sat–Sun

Melbourne Cup: Place your bets

There are thousands of sites on the Internet with information about Australia, but, as elsewhere in the world, not all are reliable. The select list below includes the addresses of organizations that are of main value to visitors, and these often have links to related websites.

Backpackers
● www.backpackertours.com.au; details of tours and discount card.
● www.backpackeurope.com; one of the best backpacker sites.
● www.bugaustralia.com; concise, practical information.
● www.backpackers.com.au; useful hostel search.
● www.netcafeguide.com; comprehensive listing of Internet cafés.

Banks
● www.anz.com
● www.commbank.com.au
● www.national.com.au
● www.westpac.com.au

Communication
● www.auspost.com.au; includes the cost of sending items by post.
● www.telstra.com; the national telecommunications organization with information about mobile (cell) phones and landlines.
● www.whitepages.com.au; online directory enquiries.
● www.yellowpages.com.au; indispensable for directory enquiries on products and services.

There are all sorts of maps, brochures and books available to help your plan your trip

Documentation and Visas
● www.australia.org.uk; Australian Tourist Commission in the UK with advice on all aspects of travel to Australia, including help with visas.
● www.eta.immi.gov.au; apply here for an electronic visa.
● www.fco.gov.uk; Britain's Foreign and Colonial Office, with advice on visas, consulates, and how to get help abroad.
● www.immi.gov.au; Department of Immigration and Multicultural and Indigenous Affairs, with application forms.
● www.travel.state.gov; US Department of State Bureau of Consular Affairs.

Embassies and Consulates
● Canada www.dfait-maeci.qc.ca/australia
● Germany www.germanembassy.org.au
● South Africa www.rsa.emb.gov.au
● UK www.uk.emb.gov.au
● USA www.usembassy-australia.gov
● For details of other embassies and consulates see www.embassyworld.com.

Tourist Information
● www.abs.gov.au;

Melbourne Ambassadors will help you get more from your visit

facts and figures from the Australian Bureau of Statistics.
● www.access-able.com; an American site with good information for disabled travellers.
● www.airportsaustralia.com; compendium of travel resources with distances from the nearest airport or city.
● www.atn.com.au; hotels and tourist attractions by state.
● www.ausemade.com.au; online travel booking.
● www.babs.com.au; bed and breakfast in Australia.
● www.bibbulmuntrack.org.au; WA's great long-distance trail.
● www.calm.wa.gov.au; Western Australian Department of Conservation and Land Management.
● www.citysearch.com.au; listings for all major cities and tourist areas.
● www.coastalwatch.com.au; surfing conditions, information and events.
● www.customs.gov.au; what you can and cannot take.
● www.ea.gov.au; Department of the Environment and Heritage.
● www.jasons.com.au; travel information compiled by Jasons Australia Travel Channel.
● www.lets-travel-australia.com.au; directory of travel resources and itineraries.
● www.nationaltrust.org.au; the main site for the National Trust of Australia, with links to the National Trusts for each state.

PLANNING

- www.toiletmap.gov.au; valuable information covering all Australia.
- www.tourinfocentre.com.au; for budget travellers.
- www.touristaustralia.com.au; useful travel links.
- www.traveldownunder.com.au; online travel booking.
- www.travelmate.com.au; online travel booking.
- www.virtualtourist.com; personal opinions on attractions.

Health

- www.who.int; comprehensive health advice for all countries from the World Health Organisation.
- www.cdc.gov; health advice for American travellers.
- www.doh.gov.uk/traveladvice; helpful travel information from Britain's Department of Health.
- www.fco.gov.uk; includes health advice for travellers abroad.
- www.health.gov.au; details of health cover for overseas students studying in Australia.
- www.masta.org; British clinics providing travel medicine.

- www.rfds.org.au; Australia's Royal Flying Doctor Service.
- www.tmb.ie; the Tropical Medicine Bureau in Ireland.

Media

- www.abc.net.au; ABC radio and television channels.
- www.couriermail.news.com.au; Queensland's *Courier-Mail.*
- www.dailytelegraph.news.com.au; *Daily* and *Sunday Telegraph.*
- www.i7.aol.com.au; Television Network 7.
- www.news.com.au/nt; *Northern Territory News.*
- www.ninemsn.com.au; Television Network 9.
- www.sbs.com.au; Special Broadcasting Service radio and television channels.
- www.ten.com; Television Network 10.
- www.theaustralian.news.com.au; *The Australian* newspaper.
- www.smh.com.au; *Sydney Morning Herald.*
- www.theadvertiser.news.com.au; South Australia's *Adelaide Advertiser.*

- www.theage.com.au; Victoria's *The Age.*
- www.themercury.news.com; Tasmania's *Hobart Mercury.*
- www.thewest.com.au; *The West Australian.*

Motoring Organizations
See page 44.

Weather

- www.bom.gov.au; the national Bureau of Meteorology, with comprehensive weather information and forecasts.
- www.met-office.gov.uk; this British site has information about the Australian climate and 5-day forecasts.
- www.weatherchannel.com; an American site with great detail on Australian weather, including useful 10-day forecasts.
- www.wunderground.com; has the present conditions and forecasts for hundreds of towns.

Working Holidays

- www.travelalternatives.org; advice, including work visas, for those planning to work their way round Australia.

MEDIA

NEWSPAPERS AND MAGAZINES			
Newspapers			
National	The Australian		www.theaustralian.news.com.au
	The Weekend Australian		
	Australian Financial Review		www.afr.com
Australian Capital Territory	Canberra City News		www.citynews.com.au
	Canberra Times		www.canberra.yourguide.com.au
New South Wales	Daily Telegraph		www.dailytelegraph.news.com.au
	Sydney Morning Herald	Friday entertainment listings	www.smh.com.au
Victoria	The Age	Friday entertainment listings	www.theage.com.au
	Herald Sun	Thursday entertainment listings	www.heraldsun.news.com.au
Queensland	Courier-Mail		www.couriermail.news.com.au
Northern Territory	Northern Territory News		www.news.com.au/nt
	The Guide	Free, monthly	
	Alice Springs News	Every Wednesday	www.alicespringsnews.com.au
	Centralian Advocate	Twice-weekly in Alice Springs	
South Australia	The Advertiser	Thursday entertainment listings	www.theadvertiser.news.com.au
Western Australia	West Australian		www.thewest.com.au
	Sunday Times		www.sundaytimes.news.com.au
Tasmania	The Mercury	Thursday entertainment listings	www.themercury.news.com
	Tasmanian Travelways	Free paper with accommodations	
Magazines			
National	Australian Geographic	Illustrated nature and wildlife	www.ausgeo.com.au
	Australian Gourmet Traveller	Popular food and travel	www.gourmet.ninemsn.com.au
	The Bulletin	News and current affairs	www.bulletin.ninemsn.com.au
	Business Review Weekly	Authoritative business news	www.brw.com.au
	Outdoor Australia	Illustrated outdoor adventure	www.outdooraustralia.com
	Wild	Wilderness adventure	www.wild.com.au

City newsstands sell all the usual wares from papers to postcards

of cable or satellite pay-to-view channels (see table below). Not all channels are available in all regions.

All channels broadcast commercials, except for the Australian Broadcasting Commission (ABC TV).

RADIO
The national stations are run by the Australian Broadcasting Commission, ABC (www.abc.net.au). The main frequencies are shown in the table below, but these vary in the regions; check the local press for details. In addition there are dozens of commercial radio stations broadcasting across Australia.

Special Broadcasting Service (SBS) Radio www.sbs.com.au broadcasts multicultural programmes in 68 languages. There is a different language programme every hour 6am–midnight, covering home and international news, culture, music and sport.

SBS Radio
Sydney   97.7 FM, 1107 AM
Melbourne 93.1 FM, 1224 AM

NEWSPAPERS
Most Australian newspapers are state-oriented; there are a few nationals, the main one being *The Australian.* Most of the major papers have websites (see panel on page 309). These can give you a feel for the local area and usually carry listings of what's on. You can buy some international newspapers at larger newsagents across Australia but these are likely to be a day or two out of date because of the distance and time difference.

MAGAZINES
As in most countries, there are hundreds of magazines in Australia catering for all interests. Many well-known international titles have editions in Australia, but there are also widely read Australian magazines (see panel on page 309) which are also exported widely in the Asia-Pacific region.

TELEVISION
There are five terrestial TV networks and a growing number

TELEVISION		
ABC	Publicly funded: news, current affairs and cultural programmes	www.abc.net.au
7 Network	Largest commercial channel: news, current affairs and entertainment	www.i7.aol.com.au
9 Network	News, entertainment and sport	www.ninemsn.com.au
10 Network	Repeats and bought-in programmes	www.ten.com
SBS	Publicly funded, multicultural channel: good news programmes	www.sbs.com.au
Pay to view		
Optus	Covering Sydney, Melbourne, Brisbane and Adelaide	www.optus.com.au
Foxtel	Covering Sydney, Melbourne, Brisbane, the Gold Coast, Adelaide and Perth	www.foxtel.com.au
Austar	Darwin	www.austar.com.au
Imparja	Channel for Aboriginal viewers	www.imparja.com.au

ABC RADIO								
	Canberra	Sydney	Melbourne	Brisbane	Darwin	Adelaide	Perth	Hobart
NewsRadio	1440 AM	630 AM	1026 AM	936 AM	102.5 FM	972 AM	585 AM	729 AM
	Continuous news							
Radio National	846 AM	576 AM	621 AM	792 AM	657 AM	729 AM	810 AM	585 AM
	Social, cultural and political issues							
Triple J	101.5 FM	105.7 FM	107.5 FM	107.7 FM	103.3 FM	105.5 FM	99.3 FM	92.9 FM
	New music for young Australians							
Classic FM	102.3 FM	92.9 FM	105.9 FM	106.1 FM	107.3 FM	103.9 FM	97.7 FM	93.9 FM
	Classical, jazz and contemporary music							
Local Radio	For local frequency see www.abc.net.au/radio/localradio							
	News, local issues, sport, talkback							
Radio Australia	For local frequency see www.abc.net.au/ra							
	Asia-Pacific audience							
DiG Radio	www.abc.net.au/dig							
	New and popular music on the Internet							

BOOKS AND FILMS

BOOKS

Understanding Australia's history and culture enhances any visit to the country. It has a rich literary tradition, but it does not take itself too seriously. These books are enjoyable to read and will help to inform any holiday there.

Literature

Bill Bryson, *Downunder* (2000)—the entertaining story of his walk across Australia, trying to discover why Australians are so laid back.

Peter Carey, *Oscar and Lucinda* (1988)—partly set on an ocean liner sailing to Australia.

Peter Carey, *True History of the Kelly Gang* (2000)—novel in the form of Ned Kelly's diary.

Sean Condon, *Sean and David's Long Drive* (1996)—non-driver Condon and his mate set off on a tour around the country, stumbling across numerous hazards.

Albert Facey, *A Fortunate Life* (1981)—the award-winning autobiography of an ordinary man as a manual worker, soldier and family man.

Kate Grenville, *Lilian's Story* (1985)—an unusual woman's struggle for independence.

Robert Hughes, *The Fatal Shore* (1986)—an epic description of the transportation of men, women and children from Georgian Britain into a horrific penal system.

Thomas Keneally, *The Chant of Jimmie Blacksmith* (1972)—the tragic consequences when a 19th-century white girl marries an Aboriginal, by the author of Schindler's Ark.

D. H. Lawrence, *Kangaroo* (1923)—classic story of early settlers' conflicts.

David Malouf, *Remembering Babylon* (1993)—lyrical story about the hostility between early British settlers and Aboriginal people.

Jan Morris, *Sydney* (1992)—evocative portrait of the city.

Banjo Paterson, *The Man from Snowy River* (1895)—High Country bushman's poem by the writer of *Waltzing Matilda*.

Nevil Shute, *A Town Like Alice* (1950)—book and memorable film about English girl meeting Australian soldier in Alice Springs.

Patrick White, *Voss* (1957)—an explorer meets an orphan in 19th-century Australia.

Tim Winton, *Cloudstreet* (1991)—gives a graphic picture of life in Western Australia.

Tim Winton, *Dirt Music* (2002)—a remote love story set in the north of Western Australia. Winner of the Miles Franklin Award, 2000.

Aborigal Culture and Issues

Bruce Chatwin, *The Songlines* (1987).

James Cowan, *Aborigine Dreaming* (2002).

Josephine Flood, *Archaeology of the Dreamtime* (1983).

Matthew Kneale, *English Passengers* (2000).

Ann McGrath (ed.), *Contested Ground* (1995).

Christobel Mattingley and Ken Hampton (ed.), *Survival in Our Land* (1988).

Henry Reynolds, *The Other Side of the Frontier* (1982).

Reference:

Ivan Holliday: *A Field Guide to Australian Trees* (3rd edition, 2002, New Holland).

The Mammals of Australia (rev. edition, 2002, New Holland).

Penguin Good Australia Wine Guide (2003, Penguin Books Australia).

Ken Simpson and Nicolas Day: *Field Guides to Birds of Australia* (6th edition,1999, Viking Australia).

Traveller's Atlas of Australia (2003, Explore Australia).

Children's books

Graeme Base's picture books.

May Gibbs, *Snugglepot and Cuddlepie* (1918).

Paul Jennings—any of his stories.

Norman Lindsay, *The Magic Pudding* (1918).

Juli Vivar and Mem Fox, *Possum Magic* (1983).

FILMS

The Australian film industry is internationally regarded as in the first rank of creative and technical excellence. Actors, such as Nicole Kidman, work on the world stage and receive the highest awards. To understand the nature and character of the country there are a number of popular films that repay watching.

Babe (1995)—animated feature about a pig who thinks he's a sheepdog; based on a children's story by Dick King-Smith.

Crocodile Dundee (1986)—hugely entertaining film, made in the Top End desert.

Dead Calm (1989)—the thriller that launched Nicole Kidman's career.

Death in Brunswick (1990)—a black comedy about a witness to a gangland killing.

The Dish (2000)—Sam Neill stars in the story of Australia's contribution to landing a man on the moon.

Evil Angels (A Cry in the Dark) (1988)—story of the mother who claimed a dingo stole her baby, starring Meryl Streep.

Gallipoli (1981)—an early Mel Gibson film about the horrors of the infamous World War I battle in Turkey.

Mad Max I, II and III (1979, 1981, 1985)—George Miller's post-apocalyptic adventures brought Mel Gibson international stardom.

Muriel's Wedding (1995)—comedy starring Toni Collette (Muriel) who moves from small-town Australia to start a new life in Sydney.

Picnic at Hanging Rock (1975)—a schoolgirls' picnic goes badly wrong when some of them disappear in the bush.

Priscilla, Queen of the Desert (1994)—comedy starring Terence Stamp and Guy Pearce: drag queens drive a bus through the outback.

Rabbit Proof Fence (2002)—some Aboriginal girls walk thousands of miles to find their mother.

Shine (1996)—virtuoso Australian pianist struggles with mental illness.

Story of the Kelly Gang (1906)—the world's first full-length feature film (*Ned Kelly*, made in 1970, starred Mick Jagger). The 2003 release *Ned Kelly*, directed by Australian Gregor Jordan stars Heath Ledger.

Strictly Ballroom (1993)—Australian ballroom dancer's zest for life.

Walkabout (1971)—two children are left stranded in the outback and are led back to safety by an Aboriginal boy.

AUSTRALIAN COLLOQUIALISMS

Australia has some very colourful words, some of which are becoming known outside the country. Others, however, can cause much bafflement.

Adrians	drunk
arvo	afternoon
Aussie salute	flicking off flies
back of Burke	any remote place
barbie	barbecue
barrack	support a sports team
bathers	swimming costume
better than a poke in the eye with a blunt stick	better alternative
billabong	waterhole
Bluey	a nickname for a redhead
bonzer	excellent
Buckleys	no chance
have a burl	have a go
cark it	to die
cheapie	inexpensive or inferior item
chuck a uey	make a U-turn
chunder	to vomit
ciggie	cigarette
cobber	friend
crook	badly made or feeling sick
croweater	someone from South Australia
dag	an odd or amusing person
damper	a bread made from flour, salt and water
digger	an Australian soldier, particularly one who served in World War I
dingbat	an eccentric or peculiar person
dinkum	genuine, as in the term fair dinkum
dead horse	tomato sauce
doona	duvet or quilted eiderdown
drongo	stupid
drop-kick	a stupid person
dunny	a toilet
eau de cologne	telephone in rhyming slang
fang it	exert force so that someone will lend you something, take what's not yours, or go extremely fast
flake	fillet of shark
footie	football
furphy	rumour
galah	a small cockatoo, or a silly person
garbo	garbage collector
gone troppo	moved to tropical Australia, or crazy because of drink or the heat
greenie	an environmentalist
grog	alcohol—beer, wine or spirits
grouse	very good
gum boots	wellington boots
gum tree	eucalyptus tree
hard yacker	hard work
hoo-roo	good-bye
humbug	to ask for drinks or cigarettes from someone
illywhacker	a con man who would take advantage of the gullible
jarmies	pyjamas
Joe Blake	snake
jumbuck	sheep
kelpie	Australian sheep or cattle dog
king brown	Mulga snake, or a large bottle of beer
lairy	vulgar
larrikin	a mischievous young person
larry	a hoe for mixing cement
lemon	something shoddy or faulty
middy	a medium sized glass, usually of beer
milk bar	corner shop/ convenience store
nipper	young child
nong	idiot
ocker	boorish Australian workman
open slather	free-for-all
pokie	a slot machine
poddy-dodger	someone who steals unbranded calves
pom	an English person
pressie	present
not the full quid	someone not quite on the ball
rack off	go away
ridgy-didge	genuine
ripper	terrific
rug rat	a small child
sanger	sandwich
schoolies' week	boisterous end-of-year fun for school leavers
schooner	large glass (of beer)
seppo	American
shark biscuit	surfer with no experience
she'll be apples	everything is fine
skite	brag
slab	a box of 24 beer cans
snag	sausage
spine bashing	loafing about
spit the dummy	baulk at something
squatter	wealthy sheep farmer
station (cattle/ sheep)	ranch
stickybeak	a person who pries or interferes
stinker	a very hot day
strawbs	strawberries
stubby	small bottle, usually of beer
sundowner	a workman who arrives at a house in the evening and gets shelter for the night
surfie	a surfboard rider
tall poppies	high achievers
tinnie	a can of beer
togs	bathing suit or clothing in general
ute	a pick-up truck
vegies	vegetables
verbal diarrhoea	ceaseless flow of talk
walkabout	wandering, generally in relation to Aboriginal people
wax-head	surfer
wowser	prudish person
yahoo	a lout

PLANNING

KEY FIGURES IN AUSTRALIAN HISTORY

Henry Ayers (1821–97) Premier of South Australia

Joseph Banks (1743–1820) Botanist accompanying James Cook on *Endeavour* voyage of 1768

William Barak (1823–1903) Aboriginal elder and painter of the Yarra Yarra tribe of Victoria

Sir Edmond Barton (1849–1920) Australia's first Prime Minister, 1901–1903

George Bass (1771–1803) English surgeon and explorer who, with Matthew Flinders, discovered Bass Strait

Arthur Boyd (1862–1940) Australian watercolourist

John Job Crew Bradfield (1867–1943) Civil engineer and designer of the Sydney Harbour Bridge

Don Bradman (1908–2001) Cricketer, regarded as Australia's greatest batsman

Robert O'Hara Burke (1821–61) Irish-born explorer who died on the return trip from the first south–north crossing of Australia

Martin Cash (1808–77) Irish-born bushranger

Joseph Benedict Chifley (1885–1951) Prime minister 1945–49

Caroline Chisholm (1808–77) English-born philanthropist, best known for work with immigrant women

Captain James Cook (1728–79) Navigator and explorer who first mapped the east coast of Australia in 1770 in the *Endeavour*

Edith Dircksey Cowan (1961–32) First Australian woman Member of Parliament

William Dampier (1652–1715) English explorer who landed in northwestern Australia in 1688 and 1699

Sir William Dobell (1899–1970) Portrait painter and winner of Archibald Prize in 1943, 1948 and 1959

Sir George Russell Drysdale (1912–81) English-born landscape artist

Edward John Eyre (1815–1901) English-born explorer of southwestern and central Australia

Matthew Flinders (1774–1814) English explorer who was first to circum-navigate Van Diemen's Land

Emanuel Phillips Fox (1865–1915) Australian artist and one of the founders of Melbourne Art School

Vida Jane Mary Goldstein (1869–1949) Feminist and suggragist

Francis Howard Greenway (1777–1837) Convict architect, later pardoned and appointed Sydney's civil architect in 1816

Walter Burley Griffin (1876–1937) US architect who designed the city of Canberra

Sir Roy Burman Grounds (1905–81) Architect of Victorian Arts Centre and Australian Acadamy of Science in Canberra

Sir Hans Heysen (1877–1968) German-born landscape artist and nine-time winner of the Wynne Prize

Ned Kelly (1855–80) Bushranger and leader of the Kelly gang

Sir John Robert Kerr (1914–91) Governer-general who dismissed the Whitlam government in 1975

John Simpson Kirkpatrick (1882–1915) English-born Australian soldier at Gallipoli who rescued the wounded with a donkey

Emily Kame Kngwarraye (1910–96) Aboriginal artist

Peter Lalor (1827–89) Irish-born leader of the Eureka rebellion in 1854 and later elected to Victorian parliament

George Washington Thomas Lambert (1873–1930) Russian-born painter and war artist

William Light (1786–1839) Naval captain and surveyer who founded Adelaide

Lady Joan Lindsay (1896–1984) Artist and novelist, author of *Picnic at Hanging Rock* (1967)

Norman Lindsay (1879–1969) Influential literary figure and author of the children's book *The Magic Pudding* (1918)

Frederick McCubbin (1855–1917) Landscape painter and one of the founders of the Heidelberg School

Blessed Mary Mackillop (1842–1909) Catholic nun beatified in 1995

Lachlan Macquarie (1762–1824) Governer of New South Wales 1810–1821, responsible for many public works

Sir Douglas Mawson (1882–1958) Member of Shackleton's Antarctic expedition in 1907 and later leader of the Australian Antarctic expedition of 1911–14

Sir Robert Gordon Menzies (1894–1978) Australia's longest-serving Prime Minister 1939–41 and 1949–66

Albert Namatjira (1902–1959) Watercolourist who was the first Aboriginal artist to achieve international acclaim

Arthur Phillip (1738–1814) British naval officer and captain general of the First Fleet

Tom (Thomas William) Roberts (1856–1931) Landscape artist and co-founder of the Heidelberg School

Arthur Streeton (1867–1943) Autralian landscape painter and co-founder of the Heidelberg School

Sir Paul Edmund de Strzelecki (1797–1873) Polish-born explorer and scientist

John McDouall Stuart (1815–66) Scottish-born explorer of central Australia

Charles Sturt (1795–1869) Indian-born explorer of eastern Australia and Darling River area

Abel Janszoon Tasman (1603–59) Dutch navigator who 'discovered' Tasmania, and named it Van Diemen's Land

Truganini (1812–76) The last surviving Tasmanian Aboriginal woman

William Charles Wentworth (1792–1872) Explorer and politician

Brett Whiteley (1939–92) Prolific and outrageous Australian painter

(Edward) Gough Whitlam (1916–) Prime minister 1972–75

William John Wills (1834–61) English-born explorer of central Australia who perished on the 1860–61 expedition with Robert O'Hara Burke

GLOSSARY OF TERMS FOR US VISITORS

anticlockwise	counterclockwise
aubergine	eggplant
autumn	fall
big wheel	Ferris wheel
bill	check (at restaurant)
biscuit	cookie
bonnet	hood (car)
boot	trunk (car)
bottle shop	liquor store
bowls	lawn bowls
busker	street musician
caravan	trailer house
car park	parking lot
carriage	car (on a train)
casualty	emergency room (hospital department)
chemist	pharmacy
chips	french fries
coach	long-distance bus
corridor	hall
crèche	day care
directory enquiries	directory assistance
dual carriageway	two-lane highway
en suite	a bedroom with its own private bathroom; may also just refer to the bathroom
fireworks	firecrackers
full board	a hotel tariff that includes all meals
garage	filling station
GP	doctor
half board	hotel tariff that includes breakfast and either lunch or dinner
handbag	purse
high street	main street
hire	rent
jelly	Jello™
junction	intersection
layby	rest stop
level crossing	grade crossing
licensed	a café or restaurant that has a license to serve alcohol (beer and wine only unless it's 'fully' licensed)
lift	elevator
main line station	a train station as opposed to an underground or subway station (although it may be served by the underground/subway)
mobile phone	cell phone
motor home	RV
nappy	diaper
pavement	sidewalk
petrol	gas/fuel
phone box	phone booth
pudding	dessert
purse	change purse
return ticket	roundtrip ticket
rocket	arugula
roundabout	traffic circle or rotary
self-catering	accommodation including a kitchen
single ticket	one-way ticket
surgery	doctor's office
tailback, traffic jam	stalled line of traffic
takeaway	takeout
taxi rank	taxi stand
ten-pin bowling	bowling
T-junction	an intersection where one road meets another at right angles (making a T shape)
toilets	restrooms
torch	flashlight
trolley	cart
trousers	pants
way out	exit

GLOSSARY OF AUSTRALIAN WORDS

Anzac	an Australian or New Zealand soldier
BYO	Bring Your Own: A fom of licensing that allows you to take alcohol purchased elsewhere into a restaurant
corroboree	an Aboriginal gathering
dasyurid	carnivorous and insectivorous marsupial such as the Tasmanian Devil
eucalypt	a group of approximately 600 species of trees of the genus Eucalyptus
First Fleet	the ships bringing convict settlers in 1788
fossick	to hunt for gems
Gondwana	the southern-hemisphere supercontinent that began to split and drift apart 150 million years ago.
kookaburra	world's largest kingfisher, well-known for its laughing call
lorikeets	nectar-eating parrots
macropod	superfamily of herbivorous marsupials including kangaroos and wallabies
marsupial	mammals with pouches for developing the young such as the koala and kangaroo
monotreme	mammals that lay eggs such as the platypus and echidna
possum	a family of herbivorous arboreal marsupials
rosellas	brightly coloured parrots living in forested areas
Southern Cross	a constellation in the southern sky represented on the Australian flag
wattle	common name for 900 species of trees and shrubs in the genus Acacia

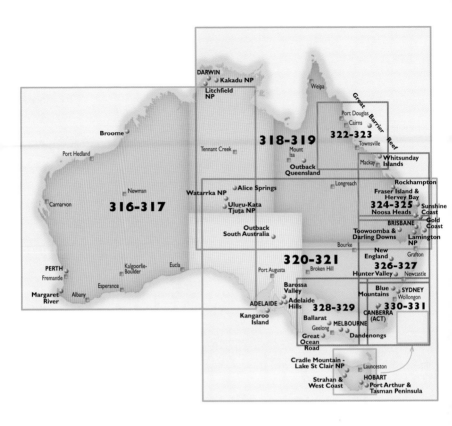

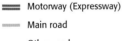

316-317

318-319

320-321

322-323

324-325

326-327

328-329

330-331

DARWIN
Kakadu NP
Litchfield NP
Weipa

Broome
Port Douglas
Cairns
Great Barrier Reef
Townsville
Port Hedland
Tennant Creek
Mount Isa
Mackay
Whitsunday Islands
Outback Queensland

Newman
Watarrka NP
Alice Springs
Longreach
Rockhampton
Fraser Island & Hervey Bay
Sunshine Coast

Carnarvon
Uluru-Kata Tjuta NP
Noosa Heads
Gold Coast
BRISBANE
Outback South Australia
Toowoomba & Darling Downs
Lamington NP

Bourke
New England
Grafton
PERTH
Kalgoorlie-Boulder
Eucla
Port Augusta
Broken Hill
Hunter Valley
Newcastle

Fremantle
Barossa Valley
Blue Mountains
SYDNEY
Wollongong

Margaret River
Esperance
Albany
ADELAIDE
Adelaide Hills
CANBERRA (ACT)

Kangaroo Island
Ballarat
MELBOURNE
Geelong
Dandenongs
Great Ocean Road

Cradle Mountain-Lake St Clair NP
Launceston
Strahan & West Coast
HOBART
Port Arthur & Tasman Peninsula

Motorway (Expressway)
Main road
Other road
Untarred road
Railway
State border
City / Town
National park
World Heritage Area
Restricted Aboriginal Land
Featured place of interest
Airport
1531 ▲ Height in metres

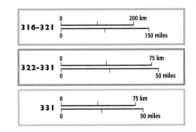

| 316-321 | 0 | 200 km |
| | 0 | 150 miles |

| 322-331 | 0 | 75 km |
| | 0 | 50 miles |

| 331 | 0 | 75 km |
| | 0 | 50 miles |

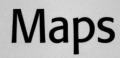

Maps

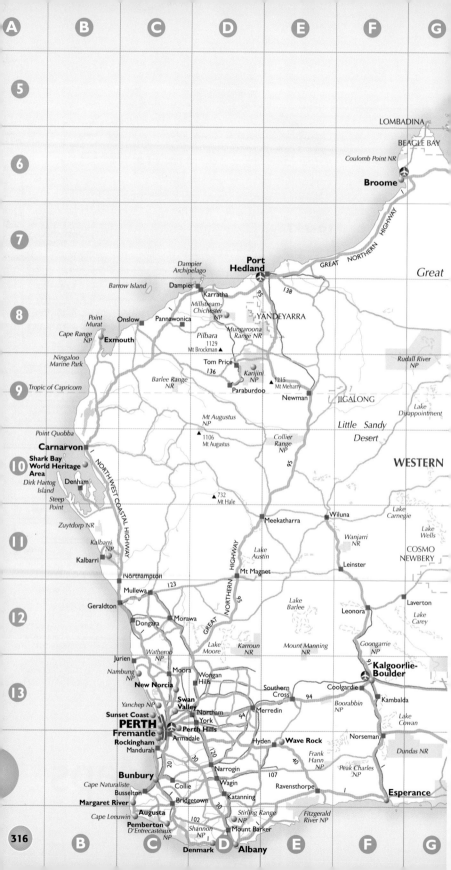

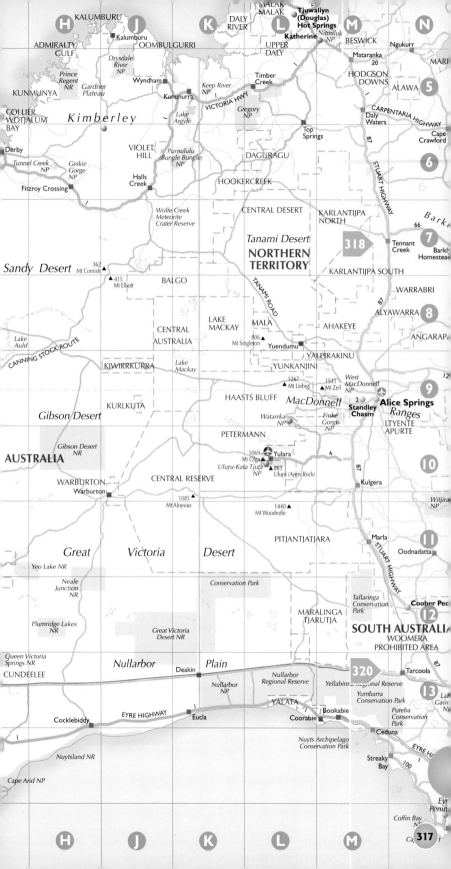

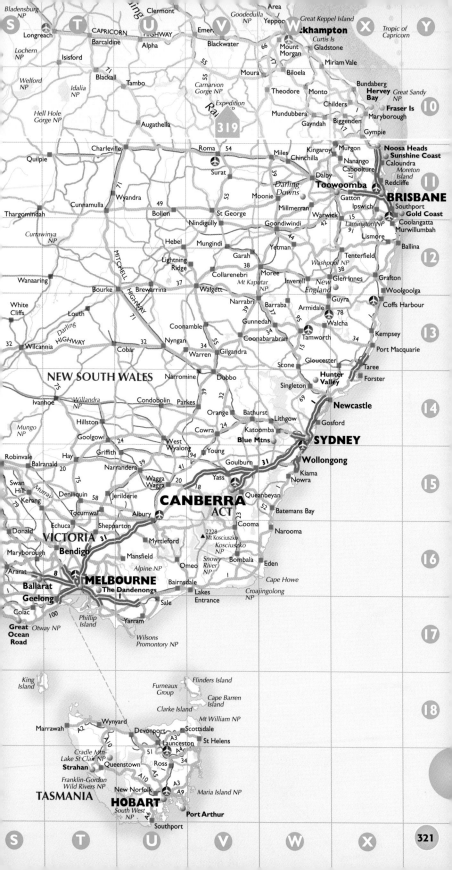

HOPE VALE

Kalinga

Lakefield NP

Hope Vale
Endeavour River NP
Cooktown
Mt Cook NP
▲ Black Mountain

Laura

Helenvale

823
Mt Lukin ▲

Lakeland

Daintree NP
Cape Tribulation

457
Mitre Peak ▲

Palmerville

Daintree

Daintree NP

Kennedy

Mossman
Port Douglas

81
Mt Carbine

44
Green Island NP

Scrutton

Gamboola

Staaten River NP

Great

Kuranda
Cairns

Hann Tableland

Mareeba
Gordonvale

Walsh

Chillagoe

Dimbulah

Atherton Tableland

Lynd

Atherton
Lake Tinaroo

Wooroonooran NP

Innisfail

Bulleringa NP

Ravenshoe

Mission Beach

Mt Garnet

Dunk Island

Forty Mile Scrub NP

Tully

Herbert

Rockingham Bay

Gilbert River

Mount Surprise

Undara Volcanic NP

Lumholtz NP

Cardwell

Georgetown

Burdekin

Dividing

Forsayth

Einasleigh

62

Ingham

The Lynd Junction

Greenvale

Star

Clara

Clarke

63

Norman

Burdekin

Q U E E N S L A N D

Great Basalt Wall NP

Charters Towers

Burleigh

White Mountains NP

Pentland

HIGHWAY

Porcupine Gorge NP

Richmond

78

Hughenden

FLINDERS

Torrens Creek

Maxwelton

Prairie

Stamford

Towerhill

Whitewood

Wokingham

Lake Buchanan

Yarrowmere

Corfield

Uanda

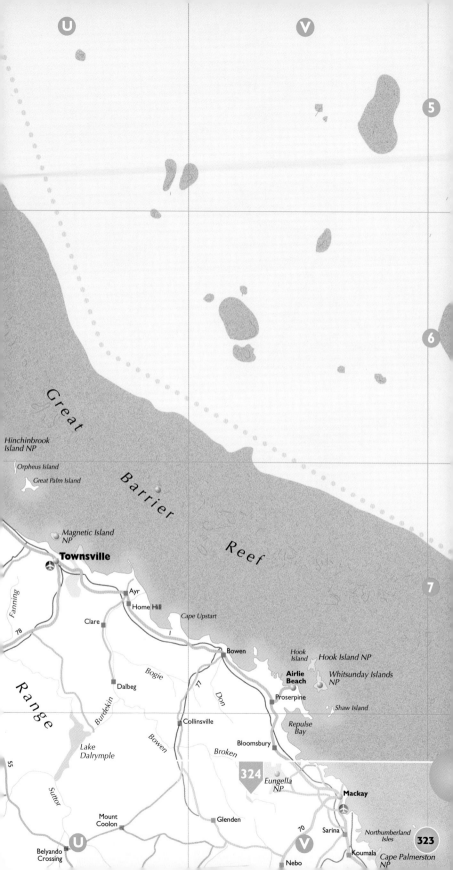

U

V

5

6

7

Great

Barrier

Reef

Hinchinbrook
Island NP

Orpheus Island
Great Palm Island

Magnetic Island
NP

Townsville

Fanning

78

Ayr
Home Hill

Clare

Cape Upstart

Bowen

Hook
Island

Hook Island NP

**Airlie
Beach**

Whitsunday Islands
NP

Proserpine

Shaw Island

Range

Bogie

Dalbeg

Burdekin

77

Don

Collinsville

Bowen

Repulse
Bay

Bloomsbury

Lake
Dalrymple

Broken

55

324

Eungella
NP

Mackay

Suttor

Mount
Coolon

Glenden

70

Sarina

Northumberland
Isles

323

Belyando
Crossing

U

V

Nebo

Koumala

Cape Palmerston
NP

Dalbeg

Bogie

Hook Island NP

Airlie Beach V

Whitsunday Islands NP

Proserpine

Shaw Island

Collinsville

Don

Repulse Bay

Bloomsbury

77

Burdekin

Lake Dalrymple

Bowen

Broken

Eungella NP

Mackay

Mount Coolon

Glenden

Sarina

Great

Koumala

Northumberland Isles

Percy Isles

Nebo

70

Cape Palmerston NP

Carmila

8

Diamond

Goonyella Mine

Moranbah

Isaac

Dipperu NP

Long Island

Mistake

55

St Lawrence

Torilla Peninsula

Dysart

May Downs

Ogmore

Military Training Area

Marlborough

Blair Athol

Clermont

Great

67

Fitzroy

Goodedulla NP

Capella

Mackenzie

Rockhampton

55

9

Rubyvale

Sapphire

66

Emerald

CAPRICORN HIGHWAY

Wycarbah

Westwood

Bogantungan

Anakie

Blackwater

Dingo

Duaringa

66

Mount Morgan

Willows

Lake Maraboon

Comet

Blackdown Tableland NP

Wowan

39

17

Springsure

Dividing

Baralaba

Dawson

Nogoa

55

Rolleston

60

Banana

Moura

Biloela

Q U E E N S L A N D

Warrego

Carnarvon Gorge NP

Lake Nuga Nuga

Palmgrove NP

Theodore

10

Sandy

Range

Expedition NP

Cracow

Dawson

Taroom

Injune

Wandoan

39

55

Mungallala

54

Mitchell

Roma

54 Yuleba

Miles

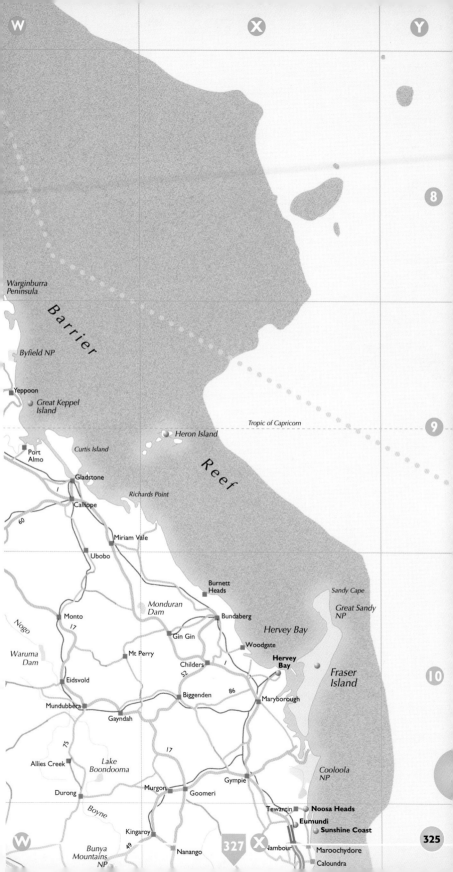

Warginburra
Peninsula

Barrier

Byfield NP

Yeppoon

Great Keppel
Island

Heron Island

Tropic of Capricorn

9

Port
Almo

Curtis Island

Gladstone

Reef

Richards Point

Calliope

60

Miriam Vale

Ubobo

Burnett
Heads

Sandy Cape

Monduran
Dam

Great Sandy
NP

Monto

17

Bundaberg

Nogo

Gin Gin

Hervey Bay

Woodgate

Waruma
Dam

Mt Perry

Childers

Hervey
Bay

52

1

Fraser
Island

Eidsvold

Biggenden

86

Maryborough

Mundubbera

Gayndah

75

Allies Creek

Lake
Boondooma

17

Cooloola
NP

Durong

Murgon

Gympie

Boyne

Goomeri

Tewantin

Noosa Heads

Eumundi

Kingaroy

49

Sunshine Coast

Nanango

Nambour

Maroochydore

Bunya
Mountains
NP

Caloundra

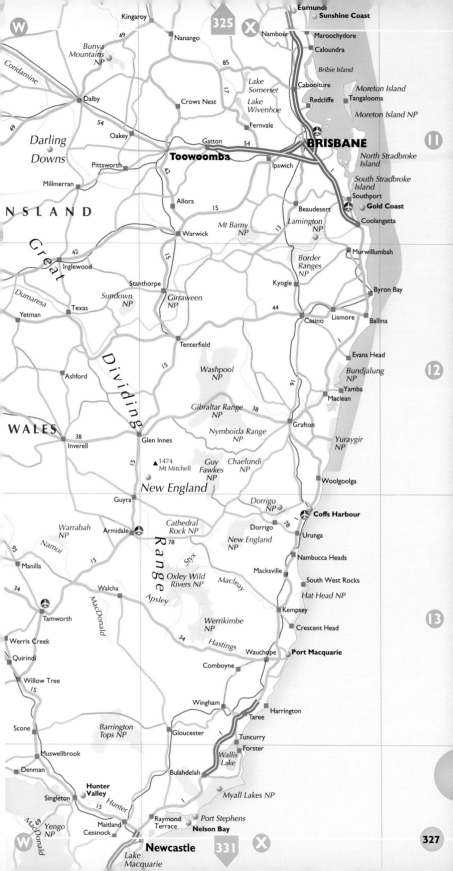

Eumundi
Sunshine Coast
Nambour
Maroochydore
Caloundra
Bribie Island
Caboolture
Redcliffe
Moreton Island
Tangalooma
Moreton Island NP

BRISBANE
Ipswich
North Stradbroke Island
South Stradbroke Island
Southport
Gold Coast
Coolangatta

Kingaroy
49
Nanango
85
Bunya Mountains NP
Dalby
Crows Nest
17
Lake Somerset
Lake Wivenhoe
Fernvale
Gatton
54

Condamine
54
Oakey
Darling Downs
Pittsworth
Toowoomba
42
Allora
15
Beaudesert
13
Lamington NP
Mt Barny NP
Millmerran

II

N S L A N D
Warwick
Murwillumbah
Great
42
Inglewood
Border Ranges NP
Kyogle
Byron Bay
Stanthorpe
Girraween NP
15
44
Dumaresa
Texas
Sundown NP
Casino
Lismore
Ballina
Yetman

Evans Head
Tenterfield
15
Washpool NP
91
Bundjalung NP
12
Ashford
Dividing
Yamba
Maclean
Gibraltar Range NP
38
W A L E S
38
Inverell
Nymboida Range NP
Grafton
Yuraygir NP
51
Glen Innes
▲1474
Mt Mitchell
Guy Fawkes NP
Chaelundi NP
Woolgoolga
New England
Guyra
Dorrigo NP
Armidale
Cathedral Rock NP
Coffs Harbour
95
Warrabah NP
78
Dorrigo
78
Urunga
Namoi
15
Styx
New England NP
Nambucca Heads
Manilla
Range
Oxley Wild Rivers NP
Macleay
Macksville
South West Rocks
34
Walcha
Apsley
Hat Head NP
Tamworth
MacDonald
Kempsey
Werrikimbe NP
13
Werris Creek
34
Hastings
Crescent Head
Quirindi
Wauchope
Port Macquarie
Comboyne
Willow Tree
15
Wingham
Harrington
Scone
Barrington Tops NP
Taree
Muswellbrook
Gloucester
Tuncurry
Forster
Denman
Wallis Lake
Bulahdelah
Hunter Valley
Myall Lakes NP
Singleton
Hunter
15
Maitland
Raymond Terrace
Port Stephens
Yengo NP
Cessnock
Nelson Bay
MacDonald

Lake Macquarie

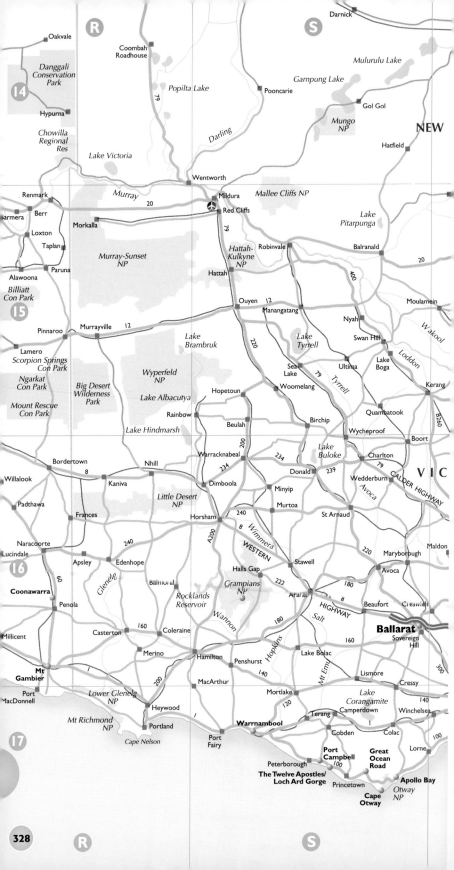

Oakvale

Coombah
Roadhouse

Darnick

Danggali
Conservation
Park

Mulurulu Lake

79

Popilta Lake

Garnpung Lake

Pooncarie

Gol Gol

14

Hypurna

Mungo
NP

Hatfield

NEW

Chowilla
Regional
Res

Darling

Lake Victoria

Wentworth

Renmark

Murray

20

Mildura

Mallee Cliffs NP

Red Cliffs

Lake
Pitarpunga

Berri

armera

Morkalla

79

Loxton

Taplan

Murray-Sunset
NP

Hattah-
Kulkyne
NP

Robinvale

Balranald

20

Paruna

Hattah

400

Alawoona

Ouyen

12

Manangatang

Nyah

Billiatt
Con Park

Murrayville

12

Swan Hill

Moulamein

Wakool

15

Pinnaroo

Lake
Brambruk

220

Lake
Tyrell

Ultima

Lake
Boga

Kerang

Lamero
Scorpion Springs
Con Park

Sea
Lake

79

Loddon

Ngarkat
Con Park

Wyperfeld
NP

Hopetoun

Woomelang

Tyrell

Quambatook

B260

Mount Rescue
Con Park

Big Desert
Wilderness
Park

Lake Albacutya

Rainbow

Beulah

Birchip

Wycheproof

Boort

16

Lake Hindmarsh

Nhill

Warracknabeal

200

Lake
Buloke

Charlton

79

V I C

Bordertown

8

Kaniva

Dimboola

234

Donald

239

Wedderburn

Avoca

CALDER HIGHWAY

Willalook

Minyip

Padthawa

Little Desert
NP

Horsham

240

Murtoa

St Arnaud

Frances

A200

8

Wimmera

WESTERN

220

Maryborough

Maldon

Naracoorte

240

Stawell

180

Avoca

Lucindale

60

Apsley

Edenhope

Halls Gap

Grampians
NP

222

Ararat

HIGHWAY

8

Beaufort

Creswick

Coonawarra

Glenelg

Balmoral

Rocklands
Reservoir

Salt

Ballarat

Penola

Casterton

160

Coleraine

Wannon

180

Lake Bolac

160

Sovereign
Hill

Millicent

Merino

Hamilton

Hopkins

Lismore

300

Mt
Gambier

1

Penshurst

140

Cressy

Port
MacDonnell

Lower Glenelg
NP

200

MacArthur

Mortlake

Mt Emu

Lake
Corangamite

140

Mt Richmond
NP

Heywood

120

Camperdown

Winchelsea

17

Portland

1

Terang

Cobden

Colac

100

Cape Nelson

Port
Fairy

Warrnambool

Port
Campbell

100

Great
Ocean
Road

Lorne

Peterborough

The Twelve Apostles/
Loch Ard Gorge

Princetown

Cape
Otway

Apollo Bay

Otway
NP

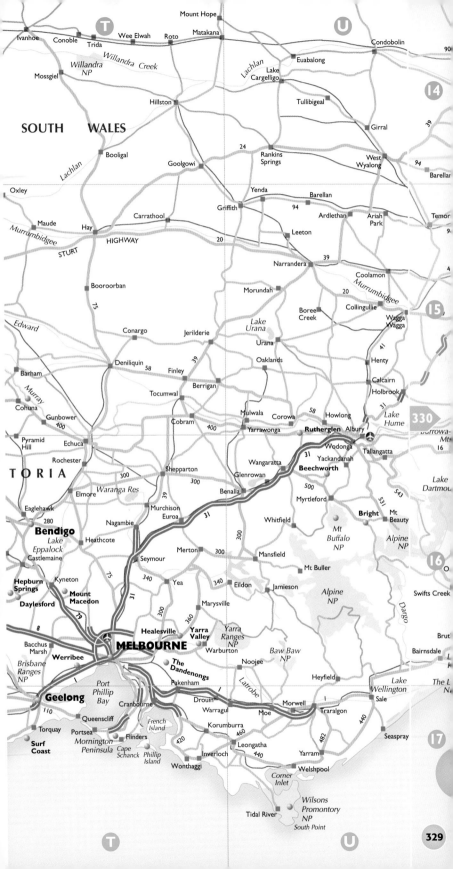

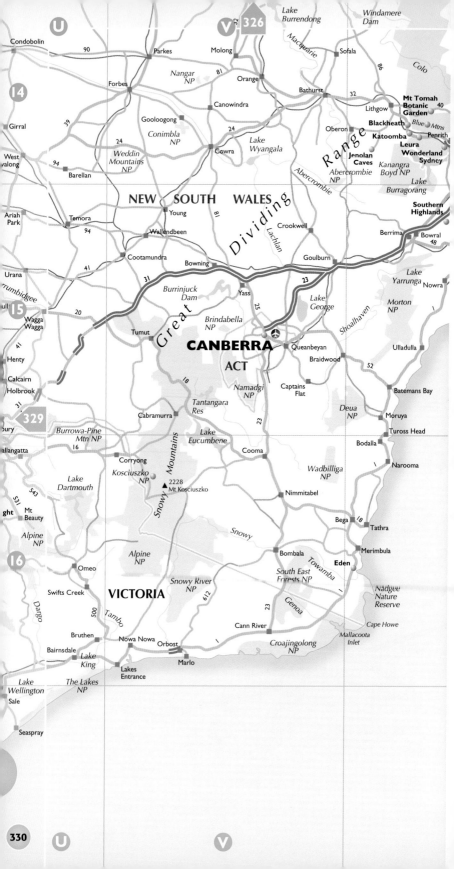

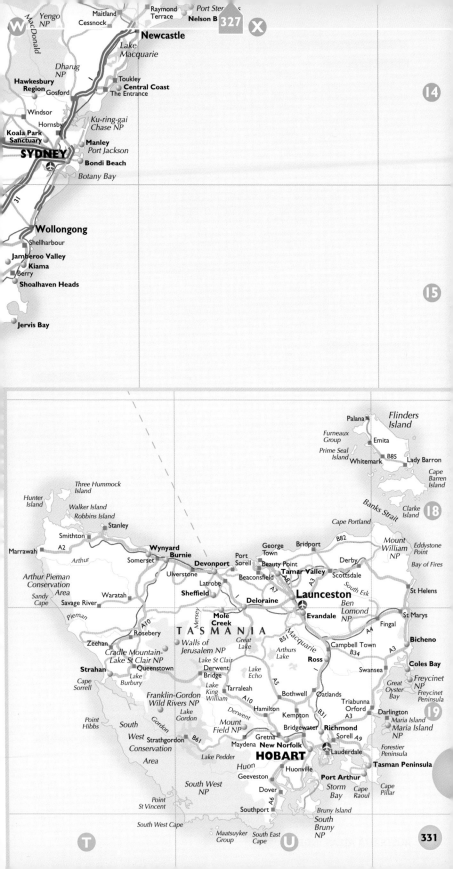

ACKNOWLEDGMENTS

Abbreviations for the credits are as follows:
AA = AA World Travel Library, **t** (top), **b** (bottom), **c** (centre), **l** (left), **r** (right)

UNDERSTANDING AUSTRALIA

4lcl AA/Bill Bachman; **4cl** AA/Steve Watkins; **4c** AA/Mike Langford; **4cr** AA/Bill Bachman; **4rcr** Tourism New South Wales; **5** AA/Paul Kenward; **6cl** AA/Adrian Baker; **6c** AA/Mike Langford; **6cr** AA/Bill Bachman; **7tl** AA/Steve Day **7tlc** AA/Steve Day; **7tc** AA/Adrian Baker; **7cl** AA/Bill Bachman; **7cr** AA/Bill Bachman; **7cbl** AA/Adrian Baker; **7bl** Tourism Queensland; **8tr** AA/Steve Watkins; **8trc** AA/Steve Watkins; **8cl** Kimberley Tourist Association; **8tcr** AA/Mike Langford; **8brc** AA/Mike Langford; **8/9** AA/Simon Richmond; **8b** AA/Mike Langford; **9tl** Sydney Fish Market; **9tc** AA/Mike Langford; **9b** Crown and Anchor Inn; **10tr** South Australian Tourist Commission; **10tlc** AA/Adrian Baker; **10cl** South Australian Tourist Commission; **10c** AA/Mike Langford; **10brc** Tourism Queensland; **10br** South Australian Tourist Commission

LIVING AUSTRALIA

11 South Australian Tourist Commission; **12/13bg** Tourism Queensland; **12tl** AA/Bill Bachman; **12tr** Tourism Queensland; **12c** AA/Steve Day; **12cr** South Australian Tourism Commission; **12b** AA/Adrian Baker; **13tl** AA/Adrian Baker; **13tl** AA/Adrian Baker; **13tc** AA/Steve Day; **13cl** AA/Simon Richmond; **13tr** Tourism Queensland; **13cr** South Australian Tourism Commission; **14/15bg** AA/Bill Bachman; **14tl** Northern Territory Tourist Commission; **14tc** AA/Bill Bachman; **14cl** Tourism New South Wales; **14tc** AA/Bill Bachman; **14cl** Tourism New South Wales; **14cr** AA/Bill Bachman; **14/15** AA/Steve Watkins; **14b** Northern Territory Tourist Commission; **15tl** Northern Territory Tourist Commission; **15tc** Auscape (Tim Acker); **15cr** Northern Territory Tourist Commission; **15c** Northern Territory Tourist Commission; **15bc** Empics Ltd; **16/17bg** AA/Mike Langford; **16tl** AA/Mike Langford; **16tc** South Australian Tourist Commission; **16tr** Northern Territory Tourist Commission; **16cl** South Australian Tourist Commission; **16cr** Henley on Todd Regatta (www.henleyontodd.com.au); **16b** Australian Sports Commission; **17tl** South Australian Tourist Commission; **17tr** Voyages Camel Cup (www.camelcup.com.au); **17tcr** AA/Simon Richmond; **17cl** Empics Ltd; **17cr** AA/Bill Bachman; **18/19bg** Sydney Dance Company/Tracey Carrodus & Josef Brown in Graeme Murphy's Salome. Photo by Jeff Busby; **18tl** Faber and Faber (Photo by Marion Ettinger); **18tc** Penguin Books Australia; **18tr** AA/Bill Bachman; **18c** Sydney Dance Company in Graeme Murphy's Ellipse. Photo by Branco Gaica; **18b** © Australia Zoo; **19t** Tourism Queensland; **19ct** Rex Features Ltd; **19cbl** Rex Features Ltd; **19cb** Rex Features Ltd; **19cbr** AA/Bill Bachman; **20/21bg** AA/Steve Watkins; **20tc** AA/Adrian Baker; **21tr** AA/Matthew Cawood; **20cl** AA/Simon Richmond; **20c** AA/Lee Karen Stow; **20b** AA/Steve Day; **21tl** AA/Matthew Cawood; **21tc** AA/Steve Day; **21tr** AA/Bill Bachman; **21cl** AA/Andy Belcher; **21cb** AA/Steve Watkins; **21cr** Northern Territory Tourist Commission; **21b** AA/Andy Belcher; **22bg** AA/Steve Watkins; **22tl** South Australian Tourist Commission; **22tc** AA/Steve Watkins; **22c** South Australian Tourist Commission; **22cr** Auscape (Jean-Paul Ferrero); **22cbl** AA/Andy Belcher; **22cbc** Tourism Queensland

THE STORY OF AUSTRALIA

23 AA; **24/25bg** AA/Steve Watkins; **24c** AA; **24bl** AA/Steve Watkins; **24/25** Australian Tourist Commission; **25cl** Tourism Queensland; **25c** AA/Steve Watkins; **25cr** AA; **25bl** AA/Matthew Cawood; **25br** AA; **26/27bg** AA; **26c** AA/Bill Bachman; **26cr** AA/Steve Day; **26bl** AA/Bill Bachman;

26/27 AA/Steve Day; **27cl** AA; **27c** AA; **27cr** AA; **27br** AA; **28/29bg** AA/Christine Osbourne; **28cr** AA; **28c** AA/Bill Bachman; **28b** AA/Adrian Baker; **28/29** AA/Christine Osbourne; **29cl** Archives of Tasmania; **29bc** AA/Bill Bachman; **29bl** AA; **30/31bg** Bridgeclimb; **30c** Northern Territory Tourist Commission; **30bl** National Archives of Australia; **30/31** AA/Steve Day; **31cl** AA; **31bl** AA/Bill Bachman; **31c** AA/Mike Langford; **31cr** Northern Territory Tourist Commission; **31b** National Archives of Australia; **32/33bg** Australian War Memorial; **32c** Hulton Archive/Getty Images; **32bl** Australian War Memorial; **32/33** Rex Features Ltd; **33cl** Warner Bros/Kobal Collection/Tomasetti, Lisa; **33cr** AA/Adrian Baker; **33bl** PA Photos; **33br** PA Photos; **34bg** AA/Adrian Baker; **34cl** AA/Bill Bachman; **34cr** Office of the Prime Minister of Australia; **34bl** AA/Adrian Baker; **34br** Rex Features Ltd

ON THE MOVE

35 AA/Steve Watkins; **36** Digital Vision; **37** Digital Vision; **38** Digital Vision; **39t** AA/Wyn Voysey; **39c** AA/Mike Langford; **40t** Digital Vision; **40b** AA/Mike Langford; **41t** Digital Vision; **41c** AA/Mike Langford; **42/43** South Australian Tourist Commission; **42c** AA/Mike Langford; **43c** Tourism Queensland; **44t** Digital Vision; **44b** AA/Andy Belcher; **45t** Digital Vision; **45tlcl** AA/Andy Belcher; **45tcl** AA/Mike Langford; **45tcr** AA/Andy Belcher; **45trcr** AA/Mike Langford; **45cl** AA/Mike Langford; **45c** AA/Mike Langford; **45cr** AA/Mike Langford; **46t** Digital Vision; **46c** AA/Steve Day; **47t** Digital Vision; **47b** AA/Andy Belcher; **48t** Digital Vision; **48ct** http://www.path.unimelb.edu.au/~bernardk/victoria/melb/hook_turn.html; **48c** http://www.path.unimelb.edu.au/~bernardk/victoria/melb/hook_turn.html; **48b** http://www.path.unimelb.edu.au/~bernardk/victoria/melb/hook_turn.html; **49t** Digital Vision; **49c** AA/Mike Langford; **50t** Digital Vision; **50c** AA/Bill Bachman; **50b** AA/Bill Bachman; **51t** Digital Vision; **51c** Sunbus; **52t** Digital Vision; **52c** AA/Mike Langford; **53t** Digital Vision; **53c** AA/Mike Langford; **53b** AA/Bill Bachman; **54t** AA/Wyn Voysey; **54b** AA/Andy Belcher; **55** Photodisc; **56** AA/Simon McBride

THE SIGHTS

58 AA/Mike Langford; **59 onward (background)** South Australian Tourism Commission; **59tl** AA/Steve Day; **59tc** AA/Steve Day; **59tr** AA/Mike Langford; **59b** AA/Mike Langford; **60tl** AA/Steve Day; **60tc** AA/Steve Day; **60b** Perth Zoo; **62t** AA/Steve Day; **62c** Tourism New South Wales; **63tl** AA/Steve Day; **63tc** Museum of Sydney; **63tr** Tourism New South Wales; **64t** AA/Mike Langford; **64c** AA/Paul Kenward; **65tl** AA/Mike Langford; **65tc** AA/Mike Langford; **65tr** Pictures Colour Library; **66** AA/Mike Langford; **67t** AA/Steve Day; **67cl** AA/Steve Day; **67cr** AA/Mike Langford; **68cl** AA/Steve Day; **68c** Australian Tourist Commission; **68cr** AA/Steve Day; **69t** Tourism New South Wales; **69c** AA/Mike Langford; **70t** AA/Steve Day; **70c** AA/Mike Langford; **71tl** AA/Paul Kenward; **71tc** AA/Steve Day; **71tr** Historic Houses Trust for New South Wales; **71b** AA/Steve Day; **72t** AA/Paul Kenward; **72c** George Serras, National Museum of Australia; **73cl** Tourism New South Wales; **73c** AA/Paul Kenward; **73cr** AA/Paul Kenward; **74/75** Blue Mountains Tourism; **74cl** Tourism New South Wales; **74c** Tourism New South Wales; **75r** Blue Mountains Tourism; **75c** AA/Simon Richmond; **76t** Tourism New South Wales; **76b** AA/Simon Richmond; **77cl** AA/Simon Richmond; **77c** Blue Mountains Tourism; **77cr** Tourism New South Wales; **78tl** Australian Reptile Park; **78tc** AA/Adrian Baker; **78tr** Tourism New South Wales; **79t** AA/Steve Day;

Abbreviations for the credits are as follows:
AA = AA World Travel Library, t (top), b (bottom), c (centre), l (left), r (right)

79 inset AA/Paul Kenward; 79tr Tourism New South Wales; 80tl Tourism New South Wales; 80tc Tourism New South Wales; 81tl Tourism New South Wales; 81tc Tourism New South Wales; 81tr AA/Paul Kenward; 83tl AA/Bill Bachman; 83tc AA/Bill Bachman; 84tl AA/Bill Bachman; 84tc AA/Bill Bachman; 84tr AA/Bill Bachman; 85tl AA/Bill Bachman; 85tc AA/Bill Bachman; 85tr AA/Bill Bachman; 86t AA/Bill Bachman; 86c AA/Bill Bachman; 87cr AA/Bill Bachman; 88cl AA/Bill Bachman; 88cr AA/Bill Bachman; 88b Old Melbourne Gaol; 89tl AA/Bill Bachman; 89tc AA/Bill Bachman; 89tr AA/Bill Bachman; 90tl AA/Bill Bachman; 90tc Luna Park; 90tr Luna Park; 90c AA/Bill Bachman; 91tl AA/Bill Bachman; 91tc AA/Bill Bachman; 91tr AA/Bill Bachman; 92tl AA/Bill Bachman; 92tc AA/Bill Bachman; 92c AA/Bill Bachman; 93t AA/Bill Bachman; 93c AA/Bill Bachman; 93b AA/Bill Bachman; 94tl AA/Bill Bachman; 94tc Auscape (Jean-Marc La Roque); 95tl AA/Bill Bachman; 95tc Phillip Island Nature Park; 95b AA/Bill Bachman; 96 Auscape (Jean-Marc La Roque) 97t AA/Bill Bachman; 97c Auscape (Jaime Plaza van Roon); 97cl AA/Simon Richmond; 97cr Australian Tourist Commission; 98l Auscape (Jean-Marc La Roque) 98c AA/Simon Richmond; 98cr Auscape (David Parer & Elizabeth Parer-Cook); 99 AA/Bill Bachman; 100tl AA/Bill Bachman; 100tr AA/Bill Bachman; 100b AA/Bill Bachman; 102tl AA/Andy Belcher; 102tc AA/Andy Belcher; 102tr AA/Andy Belcher; 103tl AA/Andy Belcher; 103tc AA/Andy Belcher; 103tr Tourism Queensland; 103b Lone Pine Koala Sanctuary; 104tl AA/Adrian Baker; 104tc AA/Andy Belcher; 105t South Bank Corporation; 105c Queensland Performing Arts Centre; 106t AA/Andy Belcher; 106cl Tourism Queensland; 106cr AA/Andy Belcher; 107 Tourism Queensland; 108tl AA/Lee Karen Stow; 108tc Tourism Queensland; 108tr Tourism Queensland; 108cl AA/Andy Belcher; 109tl AA/Andy Belcher; 109tc AA/Andy Belcher; 109cr AA/Andy Belcher; 110 main Tourism Queensland; 110cl Tourism Queensland; 110c Tourism Queensland; 111t Tourism Queensland; 111b Tourism Queensland; 112 Australian Tourist Commission; 113 main Tourism Queensland; 113t Tourism Queensland; 113c AA/Andy Belcher; 114c Tourism Queensland; 114b Tourism Queensland; 115t AA/Andy Belcher; 115c Conrad Jupiters–Gold Coast; 115b AA/Andy Belcher; 116t Tourism Queensland; 116b main AA/Andy Belcher; 116 inset AA/Andy Belcher; 117tl AA/Andy Belcher; 117tc AA/Andy Belcher; 117tr AA/Andy Belcher; 117b AA/Andy Belcher; 118t AA/Andy Belcher; 118c AA/Andy Belcher; 119t Tourism Queensland; 119c Tourism Queensland; 120t main Tourism Queensland; 120t inset AA/Andy Belcher; 120c AA/Andy Belcher; 121t Tourism Queensland; 121c Tourism Queensland; 121b AA/Paul Kenward; 122tl AA/Andy Belcher; 122tc SmartWine (Stanthorpe Wine Centre); 123tl AA/Lee Karen Stow; 123tc Tourism Queensland; 125t Northern Territory Tourist Commission; 125c Northern Territory Tourist Commission; 125b Mindil Beach Sunset Market Association; 126t Auscape (Michael Jensen); 126c Northern Territory Tourist Commission; 127tl AA/Steve Watkins; 127tc Northern Territory Tourist Commission; 127tr Northern Territory Tourist Commission; 128t AA/Steve Watkins; 128c Northern Territory Tourist Commission; 128cl AA/Steve Watkins; 129cl AA/Steve Watkins; 129c Northern Territory Tourist Commission; 129cr Northern Territory Tourist Commission; 130bl AA/Steve Watkins; 130tr Northern Territory Tourist Commission; 131tl Territory Wildlife Park (Photographer NTTC); 131tc AA/Steve Watkins; 131tr Northern Territory Tourist Commission; 131b Territory Wildlife Park (Photographer Ian Morris);

132/133 AA/Simon Richmond; 132 AA/Adrian Baker; 133c Northern Territory Tourist Commission; 133b Northern Territory Tourist Commission; 134 Northern Territory Tourist Commission; 135cl Northern Territory Tourist Commission; 135c Northern Territory Tourist Commission; 135cr Northern Territory Tourist Commission; 137tl South Australian Tourist Commission; 137tc Adelaide Festival Centre; 138b National Wine Centre; 138tr South Australian Tourist Commission; 139tl South Australian Tourist Commission; 139tc Investigator Science and Technology Centre; 139tr South Australian Tourist Commission; 140tl Historic Trust of South Australia; 140tc South Australian Tourist Commission; 140tr Adelaide Gaol; 140b Historic Trust of South Australia; 141tl Historic Trust of South Australia; 141tc Historic Trust of South Australia; 142t Grant Burges Wine; 142c Jacob's Creek Wines; 143tl AA/Adrian Baker; 143tc South Australian Tourist Commission; 144tl AA/Matthew Cawood; 144tc South Australian Department for Environment and Heritage; 144b South Australian Tourist Commission; 145tl South Australian Tourist Commission; 145tc City of Mount Gambier Council; 145tr AA/Adrian Baker; 146t South Australian Tourist Commission; 146c South Australian Tourist Commission; 148tl Photodisc; 148tr AA/Adrian Baker; 149tl AA/Mike Langford; 149tr Auscape (Daniel Zupanc); 150t AA/Mike Langford; 150c AA/Mike Langford; 151cl AA/Mike Langford; 151c AA/Adrian Baker; 151cr AA/Mike Langford; 151cb AA/Mike Langford; 152tl Perth Zoo; 152c Rottnest Island Authority; 152b Rottnest Island Authority; 153tl Scitech Discovery Centre; 153tc AA/Mike Langford; 153tr AA/Mike Langford; 153b AA/Mike Langford; 154b AA/Mike Langford; 154t Photo Index; 155tl AA/Steve Watkins; 155tc Kimberley Tourism Association; 155b Kimberley Tourism Association; 156tl Auscape (Jean-Marc La Roque); 156tr Auscape (Jean-Paul Ferrero); 157tl Auscape (Kathie Atkinson); 157tr Kimberley Tourism Association; 157b Claire Strange; 158t AA/Mike Langford; 158cl AA/Mike Langford; 158c AA/Mike Langford; 158cr AA/Mike Langford; 159t AA/Mike Langford; 159b AA/Mike Langford; 160tl Pemberton Visitors Centre; 160tc provided by the Gascoyne Tourism Association; 160tr Photo Index; 162b Spectrum Colour Library; 162t Photo Index; 163t Australian Tourist Commission; 163c AA/Simon Richmond; 164tl Australian Tourist Commission; 164tc Photo Index; 164tr Photo Index; 165tl Tasmania Parks and Wildlife Service (Joe Shemesh of Storm Front Productions); 165tc Eye Ubiquitous; 165tr Photo Index; 166tl Spectrum Colour Library; 166c Corbis; 167tl Rick Eaves; 167tl Federal Hotels and Resorts; 167c Federal Hotels and Resorts; 168tl Rick Eaves; 168tr Rick Eaves

WHAT TO DO

169 AA/Kirk Lee Alder; 170t AA/Ken Paterson; 170cl AA/Mike Langford; 170cr Weekend Markets at Fox Studios; 171t AA/Ken Paterson; 171cl Strand Hatters; 171cr AA/Adrian Baker; 172t AA/Ken Paterson; 172c AA/Mike Langford; 173t AA/Ken Paterson; 173c AA/Mike Langford; 174cl Black Grace Dance Company's New Works/Canberra Dance Company; 174cr AA/Bill Bachman; 175t Brand X Pictures; 175cl AA/Bill Bachman; 175cr Burswood International Resort Casino; 176t AA/Caroline Jones; 176cl AA/Mike Langford; 176cr Birdsville Race Club/Cameron Richardson; 176b Action Photographics/Brisbane Broncos; 177t AA/Caroline Jones; 177cr AA/Bill Bachman; 178t R'n'R Rafting; 178cl AA/Steve Watkins; 178cr AA/Andy Belcher; 179t R'n'R Rafting; 179cl AA/Christine Osbourne; 179cr AA/Andy Belcher; 180t AA/Mike Langford;

180cl AA/Mike Langford; 181t AA/Mike Langford; 181cl Image supplied courtesy of Tropfest; 181br Questacon; 182t AA/Mike Langford; 182b DFS Galleria; 182tl AA/Mike Langford; 183t AA/Mike Langford; 183c ANMM; 183bl Malcolm Jagamarra painting "Water Dreaming", Jinta Desert Art 1998; 183tl AA/Mike Langford; 183cr Strand Hatters; 184t AA/Mike Langford; 184tc Quantum Leap at The Playhouse–Out of Bounds/Canberra Theatre Centre; 185t AA/Mike Langford; 185tc Moonlight Projects; 185cr Tower Twilight at Taronga Summer Concert Series; 186t AA/Mike Langford; 186tr AA/Mike Langford; 187t AA/Mike Langford; 188t AA/Mike Langford; 188bl Blue Mountains Adventure Company; 188c Harbour Jet–Convention Centre Jetty, Darling Harbour; 188cr AA/Mike Langford; 189t AA/Mike Langford; 189c AA/Bill Bachman; 190/191 Westcoast Adventure; 190c AA/Bill Bachman; 191c Myer Grace Bros; 192/193 Westcoast Adventure; 192cr AA/Bill Bachman; 192cl AA/Bill Bachman; 193tl AA/Bill Bachman; 193tr AA/Bill Bachman; 194/195 Westcoast Adventure; 194tc AA/Bill Bachman; 194br Westcoast Adventure; 195tl AA/Bill Bachman; 195c Phillip Island Motor Sports Pty Ltd; 195cr AA/Bill Bachman; 195br Melbourne International Arts Festival–Photo Liu Chen-Hsiang; 196t Tourism Queensland; 196c AA/Andy Belcher; 197t Tourism Queensland; 197cr Foto Force/Gold Coast Art and Crafts Markets; 198t Tourism Queensland; 199t Tourism Queensland; 199br Action Photographics/Brisbane Broncos; 199cr Rolling Rock Club and Bar, Noosa Heads; 200t Tourism Queensland; 200br Walkin' on Water Surf School; 200c The Fraser Island Company–www.fraserislandco.com.au; 201t Tourism Queensland; 201tr Photos supplied courtesy of Riverfestival Brisbane; 201br Birdsville Race Club/Cameron Richardson; 202/203 Walkatjara Art; 202c Alice Springs Desert Park, Photographer Mike Gillam; 202ct Northern Territory Tourist Commission; 203ct Walkatjara Art; 203tr Northern Territory Tourist Commission; 204t Walkatjara Art; 204br Outback Ballooning; 204cr Northern Territory Tourist Commission; 205t AA/Matthew Cawood; 205c Grant Burges Wines; 205b JamFactory Contemporary Craft and Design, Adelaide; 206/207 AA/Matthew Cawood; 207c Brand X Pictures; 208bl Former HMAS Hobart, Fleurieu Peninsula, South Australia–Photography by Stuart Hutchison; 208br Credit Union Christmas Pageant; 209t AA/Jon Davison; 209c provided by the Gascoyne Tourism Association; 209b AA/Mike Langford; 210t AA/Jon Davison; 210c Perth Mint; 211t AA/Jon Davison; 212t AA/Jon Davison; 212cl Captain Cook Cruises; 212c Telstra Rally Australia/McKlein; 212c The Vines Resort; 213t AA; 213c Federal Hotels Resort; 213c The Wilderness Gallery; 214t AA; 215t AA; 215br Tasmanian Cricket Association; 216t AA; 216cb Tasmanian Expeditions

OUT AND ABOUT

217 South Australian Tourism Commission; 219t Tourism New South Wales; 219b AA/Mike Langford; 220b Blue Mountains Tourism; 221tl Blue Mountains Tourism; 221tr Tourism New South Wales; 223 main Blue Mountains Tourism; 223t Tourism New South Wales; 224 AA/Simon Richmond; 226t Bill Bachman; 226b AA/Bill Bachman; 227t AA/Bill Bachman; 227c AA/Bill Bachman; 228c AA/Andy Belcher; 228b Tourism Queensland; 229t Tourism Queensland; 229b Tourism Queensland; 230 AA/Andy Belcher; 223t Tourism Queensland; 223bc Tourism Queensland; 223br Tourism Queensland; 234t South Australian Tourism Commission; 235t South Australian Tourism Commission; 235c South Australian Tourism Commission; 235b South Australian

Tourism Commission; 236 South Australian Tourism Commission; 237t South Australian Tourism Commission; 237b South Australian Tourism Commission; 238 Northern Territory Tourist Commission; 239tl Northern Territory Tourist Commission; 239tr Northern Territory Tourist Commission; 239b Northern Territory Tourist Commission; 240 Northern Territory Tourist Commission; 241t Northern Territory Tourist Commission; 241b Northern Territory Tourist Commission; 242c AA/Mike Langford; 242b AA/Mike Langford; 244 World Pictures; 245t Spectrum Colour Library; 245bl Spectrum Colour Library; 246 Photo Index; 247c Eye Ubiquitous; 247b Federal Hotels Resort

TASTING

249 AA/Clive Sawyer; 250lcl South Australian Tourism Commission; 250cl Northern Territory Tourist Commission; 250cr Tourism Queensland; 250rcr Tourism Queensland; 254b Tourism New South Wales; 256tl Tourism New South Wales; 256cr Tourism New South Wales; 265tr Tourism Queensland; 266 Tourism Queensland; 267tl Tourism Queensland; 267bl Tourism Queensland; 268 Tourism Queensland; 270 Northern Territory Tourist Commission; 271 South Australian Tourism Commission; 272 South Australian Tourism Commission; 273t South Australian Tourism Commission; 273b South Australian Tourism Commission

STAYING

281 AA/Clive Sawyer; 282l Northern Territory Tourist Commission; 282r Tourism Queensland; 289tl Tourism Queensland; 289b Tourism Queensland; 291cr Yulara Resort; 291bl Northern Territory Tourist Commission; 295bc South Australian Tourism Commission

PLANNING

295 South Australian Tourism Commission; 296 Tourism Queensland; 297t Henley on Todd Regatta (www.henleyon-todd.com.au); 297b AA/Simon Richmond; 299 AA/Mike Langford; 300 AA; 301 AA/Paul Kenward; 302 AA/Steve Watkins; 304 AA/Mike Langford; 305 AA/Christine Osbourne; 306 AA/Steve Day; 307 AA/Andy Belcher; 308t AA/Adrian Baker; 308b AA/Steve Day; 309 Photographs supplied by the Victoria Racing Club; 310t AA/Paul Kenward; 310b AA/Bill Bachman; 312 AA/Bill Bachman

Project editor
Tony Chapman

Interior Design
David Austin, Alan Gooch, Carole Philp

Additional Design Work
Peter Davies, Jo Tapper

Picture research
Chris Butler, Vivien Little

Cover design
Tigist Getachew

Internal repro work
Susan Crowhurst, Ian Little, Michael Moody

Production
Lyn Kirby, Caroline Nyman

Mapping
Maps produced by the Cartography Department of AA Publishing

Main contributors
Judith Bamber, Jenny Burns, Michael Buttler, Rick Eaves, Jane Gregory, Kerry Kenihan, Anne
Matthews, Sue Neales, Ingrid Ohlsson, Rod Ritchie, Pamela Wright

Copy editor
Andrew Renshaw

ISBN 1-4000-1385-2

Published in the United States by Fodor's Travel Publications and simultaneously
in Canada by Random House of Canada Limited, Toronto.
Published in the United Kingdom by AA Publishing.

Fodor's is a registered trademark of Random House, Inc., and Fodor's See It
is a trademark of Random House, Inc.
Fodor's Travel Publications is a division of Fodor's LLC.

Color separation by Keenes
Printed and bound by Leo, China

Special Sales: Fodor's Travel Publications are available at special discounts for bulk purchases for
sales promotions or premiums. Special editions, including personalized covers, excerpts of existing
guides, and corporate imprints, can be created in large quantities for special needs. For more
information, contact your local bookseller or write to Special Marketing, Fodor's Travel Publications,
1745 Broadway, New York, NY 10019. Inquiries from Canada should be directed to your local
Canadian bookseller or sent to Random House of Canada, Ltd., Marketing Department,
2775 Matheson Blvd. East, Mississauga, Ontario L4W 4P7.

A01514
Mapping produced from map data © New Holland Publishing (South Africa) (Pty) Ltd. 2003
Relief map images supplied by Mountain High Maps ® Copyright © 1993 Digital Wisdom, Inc.
Weather chart statistics supplied by Weatherbase © Copyright 2003 Canty and Associates, LLC
RACV assistance with distance/time charts gratefully acknowledged

Important Note: Time inevitably brings changes, so always confirm prices, travel facts, and
other perishable information when it matters. Although Fodor's cannot accept responsibility
for errors, you can use this guide in the confidence that we have taken every care to ensure
its accuracy.

Fodor's Key to the Guides

AMERICA'S **GUIDEBOOK LEADER** PUBLISHES GUIDES FOR
EVERY KIND OF TRAVELER. CHECK OUT OUR MANY SERIES
AND FIND YOUR **PERFECT MATCH**.

FODOR'S GOLD GUIDES
America's favorite travel-guide series
offers the most detailed insider reviews
of hotels, restaurants, and attractions
in all price ranges, plus great background information, smart tips, and
useful maps.

COMPASS AMERICAN GUIDES
Stunning guides from top local
writers and photographers, with
gorgeous photos, literary excerpts,
and colorful anecdotes. A must-have
for culture mavens, history buffs, and
new residents.

FODOR'S CITYPACKS
Concise city coverage in a guide
plus a foldout map. The right choice for
urban travelers who want everything
under one cover.

FODOR'S WHERE TO WEEKEND
A fresh take on weekending, this series
identifies the best places to escape
outside the city and details loads of
rejuvenating activities as well as cool
places to stay, great restaurants, and
practical information.

FODOR'S AROUND THE CITY
WITH KIDS
Up to 68 great ideas for family
days, recommended by resident
parents. Perfect for exploring in your
own backyard or on the road.

FODOR'S TRAVEL
HISTORIC AMERICA
For travelers who want to experience
history firsthand, this series gives in-
depth coverage of historic sights, plus
nearby restaurants and hotels. Themes
include the Thirteen Colonies, the Old
West, and the Lewis and Clark Trail.

FODOR'S FLASHMAPS
Every resident's map guide, with 60
easy-to-follow maps of public transit,
parks, museums, zip codes, and more.

FODOR'S LANGUAGES
FOR TRAVELERS
Practice the local language before you
hit the road. Available in phrase books,
cassette sets, and CD sets.

THE COLLECTED TRAVELER
These collections of the best published
essays and articles on various European
destinations will give you a feel for the
culture, cuisine, and way of life.

FODOR'S HOW TO GUIDES
Get tips from the pros on planning the
perfect trip. Learn how to pack, fly
hassle-free, plan a honeymoon or cruise,
stay healthy on the road, and travel with
your baby.

KAREN BROWN'S GUIDES
Engaging guides—many with easy-to-
follow inn-to-inn itineraries—to the most
charming inns and B&Bs in the U.S.A.
and Europe.

BAEDEKER'S GUIDES
Comprehensive guides, trusted since
1829, packed with A–Z reviews and
star ratings.

OTHER GREAT TITLES
FROM FODOR'S
Baseball Vacations, The Complete
Guide to the National Parks, Family
Vacations, Golf Digest's Places to
Play, Great American Drives of the
East, Great American Drives of the
West, Great American Vacations,
Healthy Escapes, National Parks of
the West, Skiing USA.

Dear Traveler

From buying a plane ticket to booking a room and seeing the sights, a trip goes much more smoothly when you have a good travel guide. Dozens of writers, editors, designers, and cartographers have worked hard to make the book you hold in your hands a good one. Was it everything you expected? Were our descriptions accurate? Were our recommendations on target? And did you find our tips and practical advice helpful? Your ideas and experiences matter to us. If we have missed or misstated something, we'd love to hear about it. Fill out our survey at www.fodors.com/books/feedback/, or e-mail us at seeit@fodors.com. Or you can snail mail to the See It Editor at Fodor's, 1745 Broadway, New York, New York 10019. We'll look forward to hearing from you.

Karen Cure
Editorial Director